The treatment of

in the Ottoman Empire

Documents presented to Viscount Grey of Fallodon

Editor: Arnold Toynbee

Alpha Editions

This edition published in 2024

ISBN : 9789361478680

Design and Setting By
Alpha Editions
www.alphaedis.com
Email - info@alphaedis.com

As per information held with us this book is in Public Domain.
This book is a reproduction of an important historical work. Alpha Editions uses the best technology to reproduce historical work in the same manner it was first published to preserve its original nature. Any marks or number seen are left intentionally to preserve its true form.

PREFACE BY VISCOUNT BRYCE.

In the summer of 1915 accounts, few and scanty at first, but increasing in volume later, began to find their way out of Asiatic Turkey as to the events that were happening there. These accounts described what seemed to be an effort to exterminate a whole nation, without distinction of age or sex, whose misfortune it was to be the subjects of a Government devoid of scruples and of pity, and the policy they disclosed was one without precedent even in the blood-stained annals of the East. It then became the obvious duty of those who realised the gravity of these events to try to collect and put together all the data available for the purpose of presenting a full and authentic record of what had occurred. This has been done in the present volume. It contains all the evidence that could be obtained up till July 1916 as to the massacres and deportations of the Armenian and other Eastern Christians dwelling in Asia Minor, Armenia and that north-western corner of Persia which was invaded by the Turkish troops. It is presented primarily as a contribution to history, but partly also for the purpose of enabling the civilised nations of Europe to comprehend the problems which will arise at the end of this war, when it will become necessary to provide for the future government of what are now the Turkish dominions. The compilation has been made in the spirit proper to an historical enquiry, that is to say, nothing has been omitted which could throw light on the facts, whatever the political bearing of the accounts might be. In such an enquiry, no racial or religious sympathies, no prejudices, not even the natural horror raised by crimes, ought to distract the mind of the enquirer from the duty of trying to ascertain the real facts.

As will be seen from the analysis which follows, the evidence here collected comes from various sources.

A large, perhaps the largest, part has been drawn from neutral witnesses who were living in or passing through Asiatic Turkey while these events were happening, and had opportunities of observing them.

Another part comes from natives of the country, nearly all Christians, who succeeded, despite the stringency of the Turkish censorship, in getting letters into neutral countries, or who themselves escaped into Greece, or Russia, or Egypt and were there able to write down what they had seen.

A third but much smaller part comes from subjects of the now belligerent Powers (mostly Germans) who were in Turkey when these events were happening, and subsequently published in their own countries accounts based on their personal knowledge.

In presenting this evidence it has been necessary in very many cases to withhold the names of the witnesses, because to publish their names would be to expose such of them as are still within the Turkish dominions, or the relations and friends of these persons, to the ruthless vengeance of the gang who now rule those dominions in the name of the unfortunate Sultan. Even in the case of those neutral witnesses who are safe in their own countries, a similar precaution must be observed, because many of them, or their friends and associates, have property in Turkey which would at once, despite their neutral character, be seized by the Turkish Government. These difficulties, inevitable in the nature of the case, are of course only temporary. The names of the great majority of the witnesses are known to the editor of this book and to myself[1], and also to several other persons[2], and they can be made public as soon as it is certain that no harm will result to these witnesses or to their friends. That certainty evidently cannot be attained till the war is over and the rule of the savage gang already referred to has come to an end.

The question now arises—What is the value of this evidence? Though the names of many of the witnesses cannot be given, I may say that most of them, and nearly all of those who belong to neutral or belligerent countries, are persons entitled to confidence in respect of their character and standing, and are, moreover, persons who have no conceivable motive for inventing or perverting facts, because they are (with extremely few exceptions) either neutrals with no national or personal or pecuniary interests involved, or else German subjects. Were I free to mention names, the trustworthiness of these neutrals and Germans would at once be recognised.

Let us, however, look at the evidence itself.

(i) Nearly all of it comes from eye-witnesses, some of whom wrote it down themselves, while others gave it to persons who wrote it out at the time from the statements given to them orally. Nearly all of it, moreover, was written immediately after the events described, when the witnesses' recollection was still fresh and clear.

(ii) The main facts rest upon evidence coming from different and independent sources. When the same fact is stated by witnesses who had no communication with one another, and in many cases did not even speak the same language, the presumption in favour of its truth becomes strong.

Take, for instance, the evidence (Section VIII.) regarding the particularly terrible events at Trebizond. We have a statement from the Italian Consul-General (Doc. 73, from the Kavass of the local branch of the Ottoman Bank, a Montenegrin under Italian protection (Doc. 74, and from an Armenian girl whose family lived in the neighbourhood of the Italian Consulate, and who was brought out of Turkey by the Italian Consul-General as his maidservant. The testimony of these three witnesses exactly tallies, not only as to the public crimes committed in the city before they left it, but also as to their personal relations with one another (for they each mention the others explicitly in their several statements). Yet they were in no touch whatever with one another when their respective testimonies were given. The Consul-General gave his at Rome, in an interview with an Italian journalist; the Kavass gave his in an interview with an Armenian gentleman in Egypt; and the girl hers in Roumania to a compatriot resident in that country. The three statements had certainly never been collated till they came, by different channels, into the hands of the editor of this book. In addition to this, there is a statement from another foreign resident at Trebizond (Doc. 72, which reached us through America.

Or take the case of the convoys of exiles deported from the Vilayet of Erzeroum, and, in particular, from the towns of Erzeroum and Baibourt. We have a second-hand account of their fate in Doc. 2 a despatch from a well-informed source at Constantinople; we have a first-hand account, which completely bears out the former, from a lady who was herself deported in the third convoy of exiles (Doc. 59; we have the narrative of two Danish nurses in the service of the German Red Cross at Erzindjan, who witnessed the passage of the Baibourt exiles through that place (Doc. 62; and finally there are three witnesses from the town of H., several days' journey further along the exiles' route, who refer independently to the arrival of convoys from Erzeroum and the neighbourhood. One of these latter witnesses is a (third) Danish Red Cross nurse (Doc. 64, one a neutral resident at H. of different nationality, and one an Armenian inhabitant of the town.

These are two typical instances in which broad groups of events are independently and consistently recorded, but there are innumerable instances of the same kind in the case of particular occurrences. The hanging of the Armenian Bishop of Baibourt, for example, is mentioned, at second-hand, in Doc. 7 (written at Constantinople) and Doc. 12 (a selection of evidence published in Germany); but it is also witnessed to by the author of Doc. 59 an actual resident at Baibourt who was present there at the time of the murder. Again, the disappearance of the Bishop of Erzeroum on the road to exile is not only recorded in Doc. 11 a memorandum from a competent source at Bukarest, but is confirmed, in Docs. 57 and 76, by testimony obtained from eye-witnesses on the spot after the Russian occupation of Erzeroum had left them free to speak out.

(iii) Facts of the same, or of a very similar, nature occurring in different places, are deposed to by different and independent witnesses. As there is every reason to believe—and indeed it is hardly denied—that the massacres and deportations were carried out under general orders proceeding from Constantinople, the fact that persons who knew only what was happening in one locality record circumstances there broadly resembling those which occurred in another locality goes to show the general correctness of both sets of accounts.

Thus, the two Danish Red Cross nurses (Doc. 62 state that they twice witnessed the massacre, in cold blood, of gangs of unarmed Armenian soldiers employed on navvy work, along the road from Erzindjan to Sivas. In Doc. 7 (written at Constantinople) we find a statement that other gangs of unarmed Armenian soldiers were similarly murdered on the roads between Ourfa and Diyarbekir, and Diyarbekir and Harpout; and the massacre on this latter section of road is confirmed by a German lady resident, at the time, at Harpout (Doc. 23.

Again, there is frequent mention of roads being lined, or littered, with the corpses of Armenian exiles who had died of exhaustion or been murdered on the way. If these allusions were merely made in general terms, they might conceivably be explained away as amplifications of some isolated case, or even as rhetorical embellishments of the exiles' story without foundation in fact. But when we find such statements made with regard to particular stretches of road in widely different localities, and often by more than one witness with regard to a given stretch, we are led to infer that this wholesale mortality by the wayside was in very deed a frequent concomitant of the Deportations, and an inevitable consequence of the method on which the general scheme of Deportation was organised from headquarters. We hear in Doc. 7 for instance, of corpses on the road from Malatia to Sivas, on the testimony of a Moslem traveller; we hear of them on the road from Diyarbekir to Ourfa in Doc. 12 (a German cavalry captain), and on the road from Ourfa to Aleppo in Doc. 9 (an Armenian witness), in Doc. 135 (an interned Englishwoman), and also in Doc. 64 (a Danish Red Cross nurse). The latter gives the detail of the corpses being mangled by wild beasts, a detail also mentioned by the German authors of Docs. 12 and 23. Similar testimony from German officers regarding the road between Baghdad and Aleppo is reported independently in Docs. 108 and 121.

(iv) The volume of this concurrent evidence from different quarters is so large as to establish the main facts beyond all question. Errors of detail in some instances may be allowed for. Exaggeration may, in the case of native witnesses, who were more likely to be excited, be also, now and then, allowed for. But the general character of the events stands out, resting on foundations too broad to be shaken, and even details comparatively unimportant in themselves are often remarkably corroborated from different quarters. The fact that the Zeitounli exiles at Sultania were for some time prevented by the local Turkish authorities from receiving relief is attested in Doc. 4 (Constantinople) and Doc. 123 (the town of B. in Cilicia), as well as in Doc. 125 from Konia. The malicious trick by which the exiles from Shar were deflected from a good road to a bad, in order that they might be compelled to abandon their carts, is recorded independently in Docs. 12 and 126.

(v) In particular it is to be noted that many of the most shocking and horrible accounts are those for which there is the most abundant testimony from the most trustworthy neutral witnesses. None of the worst cruelties rest on native evidence alone. If all that class of evidence were entirely struck out, the general effect would be much the same, though some of the minor details would be wanting. One may, indeed, say that an examination of the neutral evidence tends to confirm the native evidence as a whole by showing that there is in it less of exaggeration than might have been expected.

Docs. 7 and 9, for instance, both of which are native reports at second-hand, refer in somewhat rhetorical terms to the corpses of murdered Armenians washed down by the waters of the Tigris and Euphrates. Yet their words are more than justified by many concrete and independent pieces of evidence. The description in Doc. 12 (German material) of how barge-loads of Armenians were drowned in the Tigris below Diyarbekir, renders more fully credible the accounts of how the Armenians of Trebizond were drowned wholesale in the Black Sea. Doc. 12 also contains the statement, from a German employee of the Baghdad Railway, that the Armenian exiles who reached Biredjik were drowned in batches every night in the Euphrates; and similar horrors are reported from almost every section of the Euphrates' course. Docs. 56, 57, 59 and 62 describe how the convoys of exiles from the Vilayet of Erzeroum were cast into the Kara Su (western branch of the Euphrates) at the gorge called Kamakh Boghaz, and were then either shot in the water or left to drown. The author of Doc. 5 was present at such a scene, though she was herself spared, and the information in Docs. 56 and 57 was obtained direct from a lady who was actually cast in, but managed to struggle to the bank and escape. The authors of Doc. 62 received their information from a gendarme who had been attached to a convoy and had himself participated in the massacre. Doc. 24 records the experiences of an Armenian woman deported from Moush, who was driven with her fellow-exiles into the Mourad Su (eastern branch of the Euphrates), but also managed to escape, though the rest were drowned. Doc. 66 describes corpses floating in the river in the neighbourhood of Kiakhta, and Doc. 137 the drowning of exiles in the tributaries of the Euphrates between Harpout and Aleppo. These are evidently instances of a regular practice, and when we find the exiles from Trebizond and Kerasond being disposed of in the same fashion in a comparatively distant part of the Turkish Empire, we are almost compelled to infer that the drowning of the exiles *en masse* was a definite part of the general scheme drawn out by the Young Turk leaders at Constantinople.

Perhaps the most terrible feature of all was the suffering of the women with child, who were made to march with the convoys and gave birth to their babies on the road. This is alluded to in Doc. 12 from a German source, at second-hand, but in Docs. 129 and 137 we have the testimony of neutral witnesses who actually succoured these victims, so far as the extremity of their plight and the brutality of their escort made succour possible. It should be mentioned that in Doc. 68 an Armenian exile testifies to the kindness of an individual Turkish gendarme to one of her fellow-victims who was in these straits.

(vi) The vast scale of these massacres and the pitiless cruelty with which the deportations were carried out may seem to some readers to throw doubt on the authenticity of the narratives. Can human beings (it may be asked) have perpetrated such crimes on innocent women and children? But a recollection of previous massacres will show that such crimes are part of the long settled and often repeated policy of Turkish rulers. In Chios, nearly a century ago, the Turks slaughtered almost the whole Greek population of the island. In European Turkey in 1876 many thousands of Bulgarians were killed on the suspicion of an intended rising, and the outrages committed on women were, on a smaller scale, as bad as those here recorded. In 1895 and 1896 more than a hundred thousand Armenian Christians were put to death by Abd-ul-Hamid, many thousands of whom died as martyrs to their Christian faith, by abjuring which they could have saved their lives. All these massacres are registered not only in the ordinary press records of current history but in the reports of British diplomatic and consular officials written at the time. They are as certain as anything else that has happened in our day. There is, therefore, no antecedent improbability to be overcome before the accounts here given can be accepted. All that happened in 1915 is in the regular line of Turkish policy. The only differences are in the scale of the present crimes, and in the fact that the lingering sufferings of deportations in which the deaths were as numerous as in the massacres, and fell with special severity upon the women, have in this latest instance been added.

The evidence is cumulative. Each part of it supports the rest because each part is independent of the others. The main facts are the same, and reveal the same plans and intentions at work. Even the varieties are instructive because they show those diversities of temper and feeling which appear in human nature everywhere.

The Turkish officials are usually heartless and callous. But here and there we see one of a finer temper, who refuses to carry out the orders given him and is sometimes dismissed for his refusal. The Moslem rabble is usually pitiless. It pillages the houses and robs the persons of the hapless exiles. But now and then there appear pious and compassionate Moslems who try to save the lives or alleviate the miseries of their Christian neighbours. We have a vivid picture of human life, where wickedness in high places deliberately lets loose the passions of racial or religious hatred, as well as the commoner passion of rapacity, yet cannot extinguish those better feelings which show as points of light in the gloom.

It is, however, for the reader to form his own judgment on these documents as he peruses them. They do not, and by the nature of the case cannot, constitute what is called judicial evidence, such as a Court of Justice obtains when it puts witnesses on oath and subjects them to cross-examination. But by far the larger part (almost all, indeed, of what is here published) does constitute historical evidence of the best kind, inasmuch as the statements come from those who saw the events they describe and recorded them in writing immediately afterwards. They corroborate one another, the narratives given by different observers showing a substantial agreement, which becomes conclusive when we find the salient facts repeated with no more variations in detail than the various opportunities of the independent observers made natural. The gravest facts are those for which the evidence is most complete, and it all tallies fatally with that which twenty years ago established the guilt of Abd-ul-Hamid for the deeds that have made his name infamous. In this case there are, moreover, what was wanting then, admissions which add weight to the testimony here presented, I mean the admissions of the Turkish Government and of their German apologists.[3] The attempts made to find excuses for wholesale slaughter and for the removal of a whole people from its homes leave no room for doubt as to the slaughter and the removal. The main facts are established by the confession of the criminals themselves. What the evidence here presented does is to show in detail how these things were effected, what cruelties accompanied them, and how inexcusable they were. The disproval of the palliations which the Turks have put forward is as complete as the proof of the atrocities themselves.

In order to test the soundness of my own conclusions as to the value of the evidence, I have submitted it to the judgment of three friends, men for whose opinion everyone who knows them will have the highest respect—a distinguished historian, Mr. H.A.L. Fisher (Vice-Chancellor of the University of Sheffield); a distinguished scholar, Mr. Gilbert Murray (Professor of Greek in the University of Oxford); and a distinguished American lawyer of long experience and high authority, Mr. Moorfield Storey, of Boston, Mass.—men accustomed in their respective walks of life to examine and appraise evidence; and I append the letters which convey their several views.

This preface is intended to deal only with the credibility of the evidence here presented, so I will refrain from comment on the facts. A single observation, or rather a single question, may, however, be permitted from one who has closely followed the history of the Turkish East for more than forty years. European travellers have often commended the honesty and the kindliness of the Turkish peasantry, and our soldiers have said that they are fair fighters.

Against them I have nothing to say, and will even add that I have known individual Turkish officials who impressed me as men of honesty and goodwill. But the record of the rulers of Turkey for the last two or three centuries, from the Sultan on his throne down to the district Mutessarif, is, taken as a whole, an almost unbroken record of corruption, of injustice, of an oppression which often rises into hideous cruelty. The Young Turks, when they deposed Abd-ul-Hamid, came forward as the apostles of freedom, promising equal rights and equal treatment to all Ottoman subjects. The facts here recorded show how that promise was kept. Can any one still continue to hope that the evils of such a government are curable? Or does the evidence contained in this volume furnish the most terrible and convincing proof that it can no longer be permitted to rule over subjects of a different faith?

BRYCE.

LETTER FROM MR. H.A.L. FISHER,
VICE-CHANCELLOR OF SHEFFIELD UNIVERSITY,
TO VISCOUNT BRYCE.

The University,

Sheffield,

August 2nd, 1916.

MY DEAR LORD BRYCE,

The evidence here collected with respect to the sufferings of the Armenian subjects of the Ottoman Empire during the present war will carry conviction wherever and whenever it is studied by honest enquirers. It bears upon the face of it all the marks of credibility. In the first place, the transactions were recorded soon after they took place and while the memory of them was still fresh and poignant. Then the greater part of the story rests upon the word of eye-witnesses, and the remainder upon the evidence of persons who had special opportunities for obtaining correct information. It is true that some of the witnesses are Armenians, whose testimony, if otherwise unconfirmed, might be regarded as liable to be over-coloured or distorted, but the Armenian evidence does not stand alone. It is corroborated by reports received from Americans, Danes, Swiss, Germans, Italians and other foreigners. Again, this foreign testimony comes for the most part from men and women whose calling alone entitles them to be heard with respect, that is to say, from witnesses who may fairly be expected to exceed the average level of character and intelligence and to view the transactions which they record with as much detachment as is compatible with human feeling. Indeed, the foreign witnesses who happened to be spectators of the deportation, dispersion, and massacre of the Armenian nation, do not strike me as being, in any one case, blind and indiscriminate haters of the Turk. They are prompt to notice facts which strike them as creditable to individual members of the Moslem community.

I am also impressed with the cumulative effect of the evidence. Whoever speaks, and from whatever quarter in the wide region covered by these reports the voice may proceed, the story is one and the same. There are no discrepancies or contradictions of importance, but, on the contrary, countless scattered pieces of mutual corroboration. There is no contrariety as to the broad fact that the Armenian population has been uprooted from its homes, dispersed, and, to a large though not exactly calculable extent, exterminated in consequence of general orders issued from Constantinople. It is clear that a catastrophe, conceived upon a scale quite unparalleled in modern history, has been contrived for the Armenian inhabitants of the Ottoman Empire. It is found that the original responsibility rests with the Ottoman Government at Constantinople, whose policy was actively seconded by the members of the Committee of Union and Progress in the Provinces. And in view of the fact that the representations of the Austrian Ambassador with the Porte were effectual in procuring a partial measure of exemption for the Armenian Catholics, we are led to surmise that the unspeakable horrors which this volume records might have been mitigated, if not wholly checked, had active and energetic remonstrances been from the first moment addressed to the Ottoman Government by the two Powers who had acquired a predominant influence in Constantinople. The evidence, on the contrary, tends to suggest that these two Powers were, in a general way, favourable to the policy of deportation.

Yours sincerely,

HERBERT FISHER.

LETTER FROM PROFESSOR GILBERT MURRAY, REGIUS PROFESSOR OF GREEK IN THE UNIVERSITY OF OXFORD, TO VISCOUNT BRYCE.

82, Woodstock Road,

Oxford,

June 27th, 1916.

DEAR LORD BRYCE,

I have spent some time studying the documents you are about to publish relative to the deportations and massacres of Armenians in the Turkish Empire during the spring and summer of 1915. I know, of course, how carefully a historian should scrutinize the evidence for events so startling in character, reported to have occurred in regions so far removed from the eyes of civilized Europe. I realize that in times of persecution passions run high, that oriental races tend to use hyperbolical language, and that the victims of oppression cannot be expected to speak with strict fairness of their oppressors. But the evidence of these letters and reports will bear any scrutiny and overpower any scepticism. Their genuineness is established beyond question, though obviously you are right in withholding certain of the names of persons and places. The statements of the Armenian refugees themselves are fully confirmed by residents of American, Scandinavian and even of German nationality; and the undesigned agreement between so many credible witnesses from widely separate districts puts all the main lines of the story beyond the possibility of doubt.

I remain,

Yours sincerely,

GILBERT MURRAY.

LETTER FROM MR. MOORFIELD STOREY, EX-PRESIDENT OF THE AMERICAN BAR ASSOCIATION, TO VISCOUNT BRYCE.

735, Exchange Building,

Boston, U.S.,

7th August, 1916.

MY DEAR SIR,

I have examined considerable portions of the volume which contains the statements regarding the treatment of the Armenians by the Turks, in order to determine the value of these statements as evidence.

I have no doubt that, while there may be inaccuracies of detail, these statements establish without any question the essential facts. It must be borne in mind that in such a case the evidence of eye-witnesses is not easily obtained; the victims, with few exceptions, are dead; the perpetrators will not confess; any casual spectators cannot be reached, and in most cases are either in sympathy with what was done or afraid to speak. There are no tribunals before which witnesses can be summoned and compelled to testify, and a rigid censorship is maintained by the authorities responsible for the crimes, which prevents the truth from coming out freely, and no investigation by impartial persons will be permitted.

Such statements as you print are the best evidence which, in the circumstances, it is possible to obtain. They come from persons holding positions which give weight to their words, and from other persons with no motive to falsify, and it is impossible that such a body of concurring evidence should have been manufactured. Moreover, it is confirmed by evidence from German sources which has with difficulty escaped the rigid censorship maintained by the German authorities—a censorship which is in itself a confession, since there is no reason why the Germans should not give full currency to such evidence unless the authorities felt themselves in some way responsible for what it discloses.

In my opinion, the evidence which you print is as reliable as that upon which rests our belief in many of the universally admitted facts of history, and I think it establishes beyond any reasonable doubt the deliberate purpose of the Turkish authorities practically to exterminate the Armenians, and their responsibility for the hideous atrocities which have been perpetrated upon that unhappy people.

Yours truly,

MOORFIELD STOREY.

LETTER, DATED ALEPPO, 8th OCTOBER, 1915, FROM FOUR MEMBERS OF THE GERMAN MISSIONS STAFF IN TURKEY TO THE IMPERIAL GERMAN MINISTRY OF FOREIGN AFFAIRS AT BERLIN.[4]

We think it our duty to draw the attention of the Ministry of Foreign Affairs to the fact that our school work will be deprived, for the future, of its moral basis and will lose all authority in the eyes of the natives, if it is really beyond the power of the German Government to mitigate the brutality of the treatment which the exiled women and children of the massacred Armenians are receiving.

In face of the scenes of horror which are being unfolded daily before our eyes in the neighbourhood of our school, our educational activity becomes a mockery of humanity. How can we make our pupils listen to the Tales of the Seven Dwarfs, how can we teach them conjugations and declensions, when, in the compounds next door to our school, death is carrying off their starving compatriots—when there are girls and women and children, practically naked, some lying on the ground, others stretched between the dead or the coffins made ready for them beforehand, and breathing their last breath!

Out of 2,000 to 3,000 peasant women from the Armenian Plateau who were brought here in good health, only forty or fifty skeletons are left. The prettier ones are the victims of their gaolers' lust; the plain ones succumb to blows, hunger and thirst (they lie by the water's edge, but are not allowed to quench their thirst). The Europeans are forbidden to distribute bread to the starving. Every day more than a hundred corpses are carried out of Aleppo.

All this happens under the eyes of high Turkish officials. There are forty or fifty emaciated phantoms crowded into the compound opposite our school. They are women out of their mind; they have forgotten how to eat; when one offers them bread, they throw it aside with indifference. They only groan and wait for death.

"See," say the natives: "Taâlim el Alman (the teaching of the Germans)."

The German scutcheon is in danger of being smirched for ever in the memory of the Near Eastern peoples. There are natives of Aleppo, more enlightened than the rest, who say: "The Germans do not want these horrors. Perhaps the German nation does not know about them. If it did, how could the German Press, which is attached to the truth, talk about the humanity of the treatment accorded to the Armenians who are guilty of High Treason? Perhaps, too, the German Government has its hands tied by some contract defining the powers of the [German and Turkish] States in regard to one another's affairs?"

No, when it is a question of giving over thousands of women and children to death by starvation, the words "Opportunism" and "definition of powers" lose their meaning. Every civilised human being is "empowered" in this case to interfere, and it is his bounden duty to do so. Our prestige in the East is the thing at stake. There are even Turks and Arabs who have remained human, and who shake their heads in sorrow when they see, in the exile convoys that pass through the town, how the brutal soldiers shower blows on women with child who can march no farther.

We may expect further and still more dreadful hecatombs after the order published by Djemal Pasha. (The engineers of the Baghdad Railway are forbidden, by this order, to photograph the Armenian convoys; any plates they have already used for this must be given up within twenty-four hours, under penalty of prosecution before the Council of War.) It is a proof that the responsible authorities fear the light, but have no intention of putting an end to scenes which are a disgrace to humanity.

We know that the Ministry of Foreign Affairs has already, from other sources, received detailed descriptions of what is happening here. But as no change has occurred in the system of the deportations, we feel ourselves under a double obligation to make this report, all the more because the fact of our living abroad enables us to see more clearly the immense danger by which the German name is threatened here.

MEMORANDUM BY THE EDITOR.

As far as their contents are concerned, the documents collected in this volume explain themselves, and if any reader wishes for an outline of the events they describe, as a guide to their detail, he will find it in the "Historical Summary" at the end of the book, especially in Section V. In this preliminary memorandum the Editor has simply to state the sources, character and value of the documents, and to explain the system on which they have been edited.

The sources of the documents are very varied. Some of them were communicated to the Editor directly by the writers themselves, or, in the case of private letters, by the persons to whom the letters were addressed. Several of those relating to the distribution of relief in Russian Caucasia have been placed in his hands by the courtesy of the British Foreign Office. Others, again, he owes to the courtesy of individuals, including Lord Bryce, who has superintended the work throughout, and given most generously of his time and thought towards making it as accurate and complete as possible; several members of the American Committee for Armenian and Syrian Relief[5]; the Rev. G.T. Scott, Assistant Secretary of the Board of Foreign Missions of the Presbyterian Church in the U.S.A.; M. Arshag Tchobanian; Dr. Herbert Adams Gibbons; Dr. William Walter Rockwell, of the Union Theological Seminary of New York; the Rev. Stephen Trowbridge, Secretary of the American Red Cross Committee at Cairo; the Rev. I.N. Camp, a missionary in the service of the American Board of Commissioners for Foreign Missions, at present stationed at Cairo; Aneurin Williams, Esq., M.P.; the Rev. Harold Buxton, Treasurer of the Armenian Refugees (Lord Mayor's) Fund; Mr. J.D. Bourchier, correspondent of the London *Times* newspaper in the Balkans; Mrs. D.S. Margoliouth, of Oxford; the Rev. F.N. Heazell, Organising Secretary of the Archbishop of Canterbury's Assyrian Mission; Mr. G.H. Paelian, an American citizen resident in London; Mr. A.S. Safrastian, of Tiflis; and Mr. H.N. Mosditchian, of London. Another source of material has been the Press. Despatches, letters and statements have been reprinted in this volume from the columns of English, American, Swiss, French, Russian, Italian and also German newspapers, and from Armenian journals published at Tiflis, London and New York. The editors of *Ararat*, *Gotchnag* and the *New Armenia* have shown the Editor of this volume every possible kindness, and have courteously presented him with free copies of their current issues.

The documents are all rendered here in English, but they reached the Editor's hands in various languages—not only English but French, Italian, German and Armenian. The translations from the French, German and Italian have been made by the Editor with the assistance of his wife. For the translation of documents from the Armenian he is indebted to Mr. Paelian, who has devoted a large part of his scanty leisure to doing the Editor this most valuable service. But for Mr. Paelian's promptness and good will, the work might have been considerably delayed.

The character of the documents varies with the writers. Some of the witnesses are native Armenian or Nestorian inhabitants of the Near East, who were either victims of the atrocities themselves or were intimately connected with others who played a direct part in the scenes described. A majority of the witnesses, however, are foreign residents in the Ottoman Empire or the Persian Province of Azerbaijan, and nearly all these, again, are citizens of neutral countries, either European or American—missionaries, teachers, doctors, Red Cross nurses or officials. A few witnesses (and these are the weightiest of all) are subjects of states allied to Turkey in the present war.

The value of the documents of course depends upon the witnesses' standing and character, and upon the opportunities they possessed of knowing the facts. The Editor is certain in his own mind that all the documents published here are genuine statements of the truth, and he presents them in this assurance. Errors will, doubtless, be here and there discovered, but he believes that any errors there may be have been made in good faith, and that they will prove to touch only points of detail, which do not affect the truth of the whole. At the same time he realises that, considered as legal evidence before a court, the documents differ considerably in probative value. From this legal point of view, they can be tabulated in several classes:—

(*a*) Evidence published by the editor of a German journal in Germany, and suppressed by the Imperial German Censorship (Doc. 12. This evidence is, of course, above any suspicion of prejudice against the Turks.

(*b*) Documents written by German eye-witnesses of the events they describe (Docs. 18, 23, 91, 145), or by neutral eye-witnesses resident in Turkey in the service of German missionary or philanthropic institutions, or of the German Red Cross (Docs. 62, 64, 117, 142). This evidence is equally above suspicion of partiality against the Turks or in favour of the Armenians.

(*c*) Documents written by other neutral eye-witnesses, principally American and Swiss, who have no connection, either public or private, with the Turco-German Alliance or with the Entente, and who are presumably without bias towards either party. Documents of such authorship constitute the bulk of the material in this volume, and practically all of them are written at first hand. There are no apparent grounds for not reposing full confidence in them.

(*d*) Documents written by Armenian or Nestorian natives of the regions concerned. This native evidence may be thought to have somewhat less cogency than the rest, as the witnesses have suffered personally from the horrors they describe, and are open to stronger influences of prejudice and emotion than foreign observers. Errors of detail are more likely to occur here, especially as regards estimates of numbers. The Editor wishes to repeat, however, that, after comparing the different statements of these native witnesses with one another, and with the documents in the three preceding classes, he is convinced of the substantial accuracy of all the evidence, of whatever class, that is presented in this volume.

The total body of evidence is large, as the considerable bulk of the volume shows, and this is the more satisfactory because the Ottoman Government has taken every possible precaution to prevent any knowledge of its proceedings from reaching the outer world. Private postal and telegraphic communications were suspended between Constantinople and the provinces, and between one province and another. There was a stringent censorship of outgoing mails, even the consuls of neutral countries were forbidden to telegraph in cypher, and travellers leaving Turkey were searched and divested of every scrap of paper, whether written upon or blank, in their possession. A quotation from a letter, written by the author of one of our documents[6] just after she had safely passed beyond the Ottoman frontier, will give some idea of the severity of this official embargo upon news of every sort:

"As I was coming out from under the hands of the censor, I was asked to write to you, telling you something of the real situation in our part of the world. In my opinion the censorship now is worse than it was in the olden days, for now they have such highly trained men. One of our censors had a five years' training in the New York Post Office. If our letters seem to tell you little, please remember that there are the strictest orders against the censor's passing anything on politics, war or even poverty. Any sentences that even touch on these subjects are either cut out or marked or blotted out with ink. A German lady even wrote to a friend of hers in Germany, telling her of poverty in BM. and asking her to send relief funds. She purposely mentioned no causes for this poverty, but only said there was such a condition. The only parts of the letter that reached her friend were the opening and closing sentences. The knife had claimed the rest. So, as Mrs. E. said: 'Please tell our friends in America that when we write about concerts and field meets and such things, that does not show that the country is safe or that work is as usual. We write about that simply because there is nothing else about which we are allowed to write.'"

Nearly all our evidence, therefore, comes from residents in Turkey who witnessed, like this lady, the events that occurred in some particular district or districts, and subsequently left Turkey for some other country, where they could record what they had seen without endangering their lives. Yet, even on neutral ground, these witnesses are not beyond the reach of Turkish resentment. Many of them are anxious to take up their work again in Turkey at the earliest opportunity, and nearly all of them still have interests in the country, or fellow-workers, or friends, who are so many gages in the Ottoman Government's hands. That Government is known to have agents in Europe, and possibly in America as well, whose business it is to inform against anyone who exposes its misdeeds; and the Young Turkish gang, by whom the Ottoman Government is controlled, have no shame and no scruple about wreaking vengeance by any and every means upon accusers whose indictments they are wholly unable to answer before the judgment seat of the civilised world. It is, therefore, absolutely essential to withhold in many cases the names of the witnesses themselves, and of people, or even of places, mentioned in their testimony. In fact, some of the documents have only been communicated to the Editor on this express condition—for instance, the document enclosed with the letter quoted a few lines above. "May I ask you, however," continues this very letter, "not to publish my name or that of any missionary from BM., not even the name of BM. itself or any of the places which I shall mention, as the censorship is so strict and terrible now that the mention of names brings us under suspicion at once. May I instance? Dr. E. and Dr. L. have been under such suspicion or ill-will that they have not been able to get a simple family letter through to members of their family in America for months, and the whole station of AC. is under sufficient suspicion to prevent most of the letters they write to you and Mr. N, from reaching their destination. The reason, we feel quite certain, is a report on Moslem work which was sent to you."

And the same considerations are urged even more emphatically by Miss A., the author of Doc. 137 who is our chief witness for the occurrences at AC. itself:—

For the sake of the people left in Turkey, and especially my orphan children, I hope nothing will be published as from me. If any word of it should get into Turkey, it might have very serious consequences for them.

"Although very few magazines or papers were allowed into the interior, yet occasionally we saw one. In the coast towns, pieces are being cut from the papers, and sold at high prices to Turks. I left my post just because I thought my presence there might make it hard for those under my charge; but if anything that I am supposed to have told gets back into Turkey, I fear the whole of my community may have to suffer. I do not think that those outside Turkey fully realise what danger there is, even in letters, to those left in the country. The local authorities seemed to be always on the watch for something to find as a cause of complaint against both missionaries and Armenians.

"The poor refugees that we saw in BF. as we passed through begged us to help them, but, when we got to BJ., the missionaries there said they had been forbidden to give aid. One woman had been taken to the Government Building because she had been found helping some poor families in her own district that she had been visiting for years. There were many sick at BF., and the pastor and others sent post-cards, begging us to send help quickly. One man asked me to lend him some money, saying I could get it back from his brother in America. It was the danger to him that made me hesitate. The money was finally sent, but one feared to think what it might be an excuse for. And so over all the country.

"All the time when people were in great need, the question was in one's mind: 'Will relief endanger their lives?' New rules were constantly being sprung upon us. A person would write a letter, but before it reached its destination it would be 'against the regulations.'

"All money in banks and all property belonging to the exiles was confiscated by the Government. The people who were deported from AC. did not know it, but when they had used up all that they had taken with them, they would write to us. It was in this way that we found out that they had neither money nor property left; but we were powerless to let them know what the difficulty was, so they would write again and again.

"All the time, we felt we were in a trap. The most courageous Armenians dared not come to see me, nor could I go to their homes. We had to meet at some public building if they wanted to see me about anything.

"No one living in freedom can understand what it feels like to be in Turkey these days."

In face of this, the reader will see for himself that the publication of names, under present circumstances, would often be a grave and perilous breach of trust, and the Editor has, therefore, (though only where absolutely necessary, and without making any change whatever affecting the substance of the documents), substituted arbitrary symbols for the names of persons and places in the text, in the manner shown in the preceding quotation. A complete key to these symbols has been prepared and communicated, in confidence, to the British Foreign Office, Lord Bryce, Dr. Barton, and the Rev. G.T. Scott; and this key will be published as soon as circumstances permit, or, in other words, as soon as the dangers which would threaten the persons referred to have ceased to exist.

The Ottoman Government and its allies, whose good name is almost as seriously compromised as the Ottoman name by the facts, may be expected to make what capital they can out of the precautions imposed by their own treatment of their Christian subjects, and to impugn the genuineness of the documents that have been edited in the way here described. That was the course they adopted in the case of the evidence relating to the conduct of the German Army in Belgium, which was published with the same, equally necessary, reservations. The Editor can best forestall such disingenuous criticism by stating clearly the principles on which this suppression of names has been made:

(*a*) Names of persons are not published in this volume unless they have already appeared publicly, in the same connection, in print, or unless the person in question is clearly beyond the reach of Turkish revenge.

(*b*) Names of places are published wherever possible. They are only withheld when they would be certain to reveal the identity of persons mentioned in connection with them.

(*c*) All names withheld are represented in the text by capital letters of the alphabet or combinations of capital letters. These letters are not the initials of the names in question, but were assigned in an arbitrary order, as the various documents happened to come into the Editor's hands.

(*d*) The name of a place is always represented by the same symbol throughout the volume, *e.g.*, "X." stands for the same place, whether it occurs in Section I. or Section XI.

(*e*) In the case of the names of people the same symbol only stands for the same person within a single section, *e.g.*, "Miss A." stands for the same person, in whatever document it occurs in Section XVII.; but in the documents of Section XI. "Miss A." represents someone different.

The Editor wishes to state, once more, that these documents in which names are represented by symbols are not a whit less valid, as evidence, than the documents in which no such substitutions have had to be made. If the reader desires confirmation of this, the Editor would refer him to the gentlemen mentioned above, who have been placed in possession of the confidential key.

There are other documents, however, where the names have, on similar grounds, been withheld from the Editor himself, either by the authors of the documents or by those through whose hands the Editor obtained them, or where the ultimate source of the testimony is for some reason obscure. The Editor has been careful to indicate these cases as conspicuously as possible. Where there is any name, either of a place or of a person, unknown to him in the text, he has represented it by a blank (———). Where the name of the author of the document is unknown to him, he has stated this in a footnote to the title by which the document is headed.[7]

The Editor is, of course, aware that these documents which he only possesses in a defective form cannot be presented as evidence in the strict sense by himself, and can plausibly be repudiated by the parties whose crimes they describe. He is the more content to admit this legal objection to them because they merely confirm what is established by the other evidence independently of them. They constitute no more than twenty-two out of the 150 documents in the whole collection, and, if they are passed over, the picture presented by the far larger mass of documents that cannot be impugned remains perfectly precise and complete. The Editor has chosen to publish them, in their natural order, with the rest, because he has no more doubt about their genuineness than about the genuineness of the others—and with good reason, for, out of the twenty-two documents in question, not less then eleven have been communicated to him by the American Committee for Armenian and Syrian Relief—citizens of high standing in a neutral country and gentlemen of unimpeachable good faith. He repeats, however, that these twenty-two documents are in no way essential to the presentation of the case as a whole.

The documents are arranged in groups, in a geographical order, which is adjusted as far as possible to the general chronological order in which the different regions were affected by the Ottoman Government's scheme. The first group or section contains documents that do not confine themselves to any one region, but give general descriptions of events occurring throughout the Ottoman Empire. These documents are for the most part earlier in date than those relating to particular districts, and are therefore placed at the beginning. The second section opens the geographical series with the documents relating to Van, the north-easternmost province of the Ottoman Empire in the direction of the Caucasus and Azerbaijan. The third section deals with Bitlis, the province adjoining Van on the west, which suffered next in order; the fourth with Azerbaijan, the Persian province on the eastern side of Van, which suffered during the Turkish offensive in the winter of 1914-5; the fifth with Russian Trans-Caucasia, where the refugees from Van and Azerbaijan sought refuge in August, 1915. The succeeding sections follow one another in geographical order from east to west, beginning with Erzeroum, the border province adjoining Van on the north-west along the Russo-Turkish frontier. Erzeroum constitutes the sixth section, Mamouret-ul-Aziz the seventh, Trebizond the eighth, Sivas the ninth, Kaisaria the tenth, the town of X. the eleventh, Angora the twelfth, Constantinople and the adjacent districts the thirteenth. From this point the sections run in reverse order from north-west to south-east, following the track of the Baghdad Railway. The fourteenth section deals with places along this route between (but excluding) Adapazar and Aleppo; the fifteenth deals with Cilicia, the region through which the Baghdad Railway passes half-way along its course, and this is the only case in which the chronological and geographical arrangements seriously conflict, for the Cilicians were the first to suffer—

they were already being deported twelve days before fighting broke out at Van. The sixteenth section is Jibal Mousa, a group of villages adjoining Cilicia on the south; the seventeenth the Armenian colonies at Ourfa and AC., two cities on the Mesopotamian fringe; the eighteenth Aleppo, upon which nearly all the convoys of exiles converged; and the nineteenth Damascus and Der-el-Zor, the two districts where the greater part of the survivors were finally deposited. A twentieth section has also been added for documents received while the volume was in the press.

Wherever a date is given without further indication, it may be assumed to be in "New Style." Where two alternative dates are given (*e.g.*, 26th September/9th October), the first is "Old Style" and the second "New." Dates are never given in "Old Style" alone. Where sums of money are given in Turkish or Persian units, the English equivalent is usually added in brackets. Sums given in dollars have always been translated into English pounds sterling.

The names of places have not been spelt on any consistent system, there being no recognised system in general use. The Editor has merely endeavoured to standardise the spelling of each particular name wherever it occurs.

An index of all places referred to by name in the documents that are in the Editor's possession, whether the name has been withheld in the text or not, has been compiled for him most accurately by Miss Margaret Toynbee, to whom he is grateful for this important addition to the usefulness of the book. This index is printed at the end of the volume. The map which accompanies it has been compiled by the Editor himself from various sources, chiefly from Kiepert's excellent sheets of Asia Minor, in the Map Room of the Royal Geographical Society, where he has received most kind and valuable assistance from the staff.

I. GENERAL DESCRIPTIONS.

The Ottoman Government did its utmost to prevent the news of what it was doing to the Armenians from leaking through to the outer world. A stringent censorship was established at all the frontiers, private communication was severed between Constantinople and the provinces, and the provinces themselves were isolated from one another. Nearly all our information has been obtained from witnesses who succeeded in making their way out of Turkey after the massacres and deportations had occurred, and who wrote down their experiences after reaching America or Europe. The evidence of these witnesses is first-hand, but it is mostly confined to the particular region in which each witness happened to reside, and it has therefore been grouped in this collection province by province, in geographical order. We possess, however, certain general accounts which reached Europe and America at an earlier date, for the most part, than the individual narratives, and they are printed here in advance of the rest—partly for the chronological reason, and partly because they give a broad survey of what happened, which may impress the general features upon the reader before he approaches the detailed testimony of the sections that follow.

In contrast to the bulk of our evidence, the majority of these preliminary documents give their information at second-hand; but practically every statement they make is more than borne out in detail by the first-hand witnesses, and this is particularly the case with the more startling and appalling of the facts they record.

The most interesting document in this section is No. 12, which was compiled from German sources, published in a German journal, and immediately suppressed by the German Censorship.

1. DESPATCH[8] FROM MR. HENRY WOOD, CORRESPONDENT OF THE AMERICAN "UNITED PRESS" AT CONSTANTINOPLE; PUBLISHED IN THE AMERICAN PRESS, 14th AUGUST, 1915.

So critical is the situation that Ambassador Morgenthau, who alone is fighting to prevent wholesale slaughter, has felt obliged to ask the co-operation of the Ambassadors of Turkey's two Allies. They have been successful to the extent of securing definite promises from the leading members of the Young Turk Government that no orders will be given for massacres. The critical moment for the Armenians, however, will come, it is feared, when the Turks may meet with serious reverses in the Dardanelles or when the Armenians themselves, who not only are in open revolt but are actually in possession of Van and several other important towns, may meet with fresh successes. It is this uprising of the Armenians who are seeking to establish an independent government that the Turks declare is alone responsible for the terrible measures now being taken against them[9]. In the meantime, the position of the Armenians and the system of deportation, dispersion, and extermination that is being carried out against them beggars all description.

Although the present renewal of the Armenian atrocities has been under way for three months, it is only just now that reports creeping into Constantinople from the remotest points of the interior show that absolutely no portion of the Armenian population has been spared. It now appears that the order for the present cruelties was issued in the early part of May, and was at once put into execution with all the extreme genius of the Turkish police system—the one department of government for which the Turks have ever shown the greatest aptitude, both in organisation and administration. At that time sealed orders were sent to the police of the entire Empire. These were to be opened on a specified date that would ensure the orders being in the hands of every department at the moment they were to be opened. Once opened, they provided for a simultaneous descent at practically the same moment on the Armenian population of the entire Empire.

At Broussa, in Asiatic Turkey, the city which it is expected the Turks will select for their capital in the event of Constantinople falling, I investigated personally the manner in which these orders were carried out[10]. From eye-witnesses in other towns from the interior I found that the execution of them was everywhere identical. At midnight, the police authorities swooped down on the homes of all Armenians whose names had been put on the proscribed list sent out from Constantinople. The men were at once placed under arrest, and then the houses were searched for papers which might implicate them either in the present revolutionary movement of the Armenians on the frontier or in plots against the Government which the Turks declare exist. In this search, carpets were torn from the floors, draperies stripped from the walls, and even the children turned out of their beds and cradles in order that the mattresses and coverings might be searched.

Following this search, the men were then carried away, and at once there began the carrying out of the system of deportation and dispersion which has been the cruellest feature of the present anti-Armenian wave. The younger men for the most part were at once drafted into the Army. On the authority of men whose names would be known in both America and Europe if I dared mention them, I am told that hundreds if not thousands of these were sent at once to the front ranks at the Dardanelles, where death in a very short space of time is almost a certainty. The older men were then deported into the interior, while the women and children, when not carried off in an opposite direction, were left to shift for themselves as best they could. The terrible feature of this deportation up to date is that it has been carried out on such a basis as to render it practically impossible in thousands of cases that these families can ever again be reunited. Not only wives and husbands, brothers and sisters, but even mothers and their little children have been dispersed in such a manner as to preclude practically all hope that they will ever see each other again.

In defence of these terrible measures which have been taken, the Turks at Constantinople declare that no one but the Armenians themselves is to blame. They state that when the present attack began on the Dardanelles, the Armenians were notified that if they took advantage of the moment when the Turks were concentrating every energy for the maintenance of the Empire, to rise in rebellion, they would be dealt with without quarter. This warning, however, the Armenians failed to heed. They not only rose in rebellion, occupying a number of important towns, including Van, but extended important help to the Russians in the latter's campaign in the Caucasus.[11]

While this is the Turkish side of the situation, there is also another side which I shall give on the authority of men who have passed practically their entire lives in Turkey and whose names, if I dared mention them, would be recognised in both Europe and America as competent authority. According to these men, the decision has gone out from the Young Turk party that the Armenian population of Turkey must be set back fifty years. This has been decided upon as necessary in order to ensure the supremacy of the Turkish race in the Ottoman Empire, which is one of the basic principles of the Young Turk party. The situation, I am told, is absolutely analogous to that which preceded the Armenian massacres under Abd-ul-Hamid. So far, however, the Young Turks have confined themselves to the new system of deportation, dispersion and separation of families.

---

1. Memorandum by the Editor, page xli.

2. Memorandum by the Editor, page xl.

3. For instance, the conversation of a German officer reported in Doc. 108 p. 420. For the general attitude of the Turks and German towards the treatment of the Armenians, see "Historical Summary," chapter V.

On the 11th January, 1916, Herr von Stumm, Chief of the Political Department of the German Foreign Office, gave the following answer in the Reichstag to a question from Dr. Liebknecht:

"It is known to the Imperial Chancellor that revolutionary demonstrations, organised by our enemies, have taken place in Armenia, and that they have caused the Turkish Government to expel the Armenian population of certain districts and to allot to them new dwelling-places. An exchange of views about the reaction of these measures upon the population is now taking place. Further information cannot be given."

4. A copy of this letter was communicated to the *Berner Tagwacht* by Dr. Forel, a Swiss gentleman, and reproduced in the *Journal de Génève*, 17th August, 1916. It was signed by four persons—Dr. Gräter (of Swiss nationality), Dr. Niepage (of German nationality), and two others whose names have been withheld by Dr. Forel.—EDITOR.

5.

AMERICAN COMMITTEE FOR ARMENIAN AND SYRIAN RELIEF.

70, Fifth Avenue, New York.

Including work of the Armenian Relief, the Persian War Relief, and the Syrian-Palestine Relief Committees.

James L. Barton.	Samuel T. Dutton.	Walter H. Mallory.
Chairman.	*Secretary.*	*Field Secretary.*

Charles R. Crane, *Treasurer.*

Arthur J. Brown.	John Moffat.
Edwin M. Bulkley.	John R. Mott.
John B. Calvert.	Frank Mason North.
John D. Crimmins.	Harry V. Osborne.
Cleveland H. Dodge.	George A. Plimpton.
Charles W. Eliot.	Rt. Rev. P. Rhinelander.
William T. Ellis.	Karl Davis Robinson.
James Cardinal Gibbons.	William W. Rockwell.
Rt. Rev. David H. Greer.	George T. Scott.
Norman Hapgood.	Isaac N. Seligman.
Maurice H. Harris.	William Sloane.
William I. Haven.	Edward Lincoln Smith.

Hamilton Holt.	James M. Speers.
Arthur Curtiss James.	Oscar M. Straus.
Frederick Lynch.	Stanley White.
Chas. S. MacFarland.	Talcott Williams.
H. Pereira Mendes.	Stephen S. Wise.

6. Doc. 121

7. In other words, wherever the title of a document is given without such a footnote, that means that the Editor is in possession of the author's name, even if the name is not published but represented by a symbol (*e.g.*, "Dr. L."), or by such periphrases as "A foreign resident," &c.

8. For full text see page 572.

9. See "Historical Summary," Chapter V.

10. Compare Doc. 101

11. For the real facts see Section II.

2. DESPATCH, DATED 11th JUNE, 1915, FROM AN ESPECIALLY WELL INFORMED NEUTRAL SOURCE AT CONSTANTINOPLE; COMMUNICATED BY THE AMERICAN COMMITTEE FOR ARMENIAN AND SYRIAN RELIEF.

A week before anything was done to Baibourt, the villages all round had been emptied of their Armenian inhabitants. The forced exodus from Baibourt took place on the 1st June[12]. All the villages, as well as three-fourths of the town, had already been evacuated. The third convoy included from 4,000 to 5,000 people. Within six or seven days from the start, all males down to below fifteen years of age had been murdered.

Persecutions, accompanied by horrible torture, have taken place in the Armenian village of Baghtchedjik or Bardizag (2,000 families), in Ovadjik (600 families), in Arslanbeg (600 families), in Döngöl (65 families), in Sabandja (1,000 families), in Ismid, etc. The inhabitants of Kurt-Belené (6,000 to 7,000 families) have been expelled.

In Arabkir the Armenian population has been converted to Islam, after 2,000 males had been killed.

12. See Doc. 59

3. EXTRACT FROM A LETTER[13], DATED ARABKIR, 2th JUNE/8th JULY, 1915, COMMUNICATED BY THE AMERICAN COMMITTEE FOR ARMENIAN AND SYRIAN RELIEF.

The Armenian population has been converted to Islam; it was a means of escaping from the forced migration. Orthodox Turks are given the wives of absent husbands or their daughters. We have been told that, according to an order from the Padishah, everybody must embrace Islam[14].

4. LETTER FROM AN AUTHORITATIVE SOURCE, DATED CONSTANTINOPLE, 15th/28th JUNE, 1915; PUBLISHED IN THE NEW YORK JOURNAL "GOTCHNAG," 28th AUGUST, 1915.

In America you have probably not yet heard of the terrible crisis through which the Armenians of Turkey are passing at this moment. The severe censorship to which all communications between Constantinople and the provinces are subjected, and the absolute embargo on travelling under which the Armenians have been placed, have resulted in depriving us, even in Constantinople, of all but the scantiest information regarding the whole provincial area. And yet what we know already is sufficient to give you some idea.

In every part of Turkey the Armenian population is in a more or less serious plight, in suspense between life and death. Apart from the distress produced by the illegal requisitions, the paralysis of industry, the ravages of the typhus, and the mobilisation of the men—first of those from 20 to 45, and then of those from 18 to 50 years of age—thousands of Armenians have been suffering during the last two months in prison or in exile.

At the beginning of the month of April, immediately after the events at Van, the Government issued an order requisitioning Armenian houses, schools, and episcopal residences, even in the most obscure corners of the provinces, and making the possession of arms, which were allowed until now, or of books and images, which were freely sold in public, a pretext for imprisonments and convictions. The effect of this order has been such that in the prisons of Kaisaria alone there are, at the present moment, more than 500 Armenians in custody, without reckoning those who, by a mere administrative act and without any charge being brought against them, have been deported into districts inhabited entirely by Mohammedans.

However, even this state of things is mild enough in comparison with the condition of affairs in Cilicia and the provinces bordering on the Caucasus. The Turkish Government is now putting into execution its plan of dispersing the Armenian population of the Armenian provinces, taking advantage of the preoccupation of all the European Powers, and of the indifference of

Germany and Austria. They began to execute this plan about four months ago, starting with Cilicia[15], where the entire Armenian population of Zeitoun, Dört Yöl and the neighbourhood, and a considerable part of the population of Marash and Hassan-Beyli, have been removed from their homes by brute force and without warning.

Some of the exiles, about 1,000 families, have been sent to the Sultania district of the Vilayet of Konia[16]. The majority, however, have been dispersed among the villages of the province of Zor, beyond Aleppo, and through the districts in the immediate neighbourhood of Aleppo itself—Moumbidj, Bab, Ma'ara, Idlib, etc. This compulsory emigration is still in progress. The same fate is in prospect for Adana, Mersina, Hadjin, Sis, etc. As can be seen from the despatches and letters which arrive from these districts, all these people are being deported without the possibility of taking anything with them, and this into districts with a climate to which they are absolutely unaccustomed. There, without shelter, naked and famished, they are abandoned to their fate, and have to subsist on the morsel of bread which the Government sees good to throw to them, a Government which is incapable of providing even its own troops with bread.

The least details of this compulsory emigration that reach us at Constantinople, reduce one to tears at their recital. Among those 1,000 families deported to Sultania there are less than fifty men. The majority made the journey on foot; the old people and the young children died by the wayside, and young women with child miscarried and were abandoned on the mountains. Even now that they have reached their place of exile, these deported Armenians pay a toll of about ten victims a day in deaths from sickness and famine. At Aleppo they need at present £35 (Turkish) a day to provide the exiles with bread. You can imagine what their situation must be in the deserts, where the native Arabs themselves are near starvation.

A sum of money has been sent from Constantinople to the Katholikos of Cilicia, who is at the present moment at Aleppo, witnessing the misery and agony of his flock. At Aleppo, at any rate, the authorities permit the distribution of relief to these unfortunate people; at Sultania, on the other hand, it has so far been impossible to bring any relief within their reach, because the Government refuses permission, in spite of the efforts of the American Embassy.

The same state of affairs now prevails at Erzeroum, Bitlis, Sairt, etc. According to absolutely trustworthy information which we have received, they have begun, during the last two or three weeks, to deport the Armenians of Erzeroum and the neighbourhood towards Derdjan; the rest have been given several days' grace. From Bitlis and Sairt we have just had despatches forwarded to us, imploring relief. From Moush we have no news, but the same state of affairs must certainly prevail there also[17]. At Khnyss[18] there has been a massacre, but we do not yet know how serious it was. In the neighbourhood of Sivas several villages, Govdoun among others, have been burnt....

---

13. Name of author withheld.

14. See Doc. 82, page 324.

15. See Section XV.

16. See Docs. 123 and 125.

17. See Section III.

18. See Doc. 53.

5. LETTER FROM THE SAME SOURCE, DATED CONSTANTINOPLE, 12/25th JULY, 1915; PUBLISHED IN THE NEW YORK JOURNAL "GOTCHNAG," 28th AUGUST, 1915.

Since my last letter, our nation's position has unhappily become more serious, inasmuch as it is now not merely the Armenians of Cilicia who have been deported, but the Armenians of all the native Armenian provinces. From Samsoun and Kaisaria on the one hand to Edessa on the other, about a million and a half people are at this moment on their way to the deserts of Mesopotamia, to be planted in the midst of Arab and Kurdish populations. These people cannot take with them anything but the barest necessities, because of the impossibility of transport and the insecurity of the roads; so that very few of them indeed will succeed in reaching the spot marked out for their exile, while, if immediate relief is not sent them, they will die of hunger....

6. LETTER FROM THE SAME SOURCE, DATED CONSTANTINOPLE, 13/26th JULY, 1915, AND ADDRESSED TO A DISTINGUISHED ARMENIAN RESIDENT BEYOND THE OTTOMAN FRONTIER.

Since the 25th May last, events have followed hard upon one another, and the misery of our nation is now at its zenith.

Apart from a few rumours about the situation of the Armenians at Erzeroum, we had heard of nothing, till recently, except the deportation of the inhabitants of several towns and villages in Cilicia. Now we know from an unimpeachable source that the Armenians of all the towns and all the villages of Cilicia have been deported *en masse* to the desert regions south of Aleppo.

From the 1st May onwards, the population of the city of Erzeroum, and shortly afterwards the population of the whole province, was collected at Samsoun and embarked on shipboard. The populations of Kaisaria, Diyarbekir, Ourfa, Trebizond, Sivas, Harpout and the district of Van have been deported to the deserts of Mesopotamia, from the southern outskirts of Aleppo as far as Mosul and Baghdad. "Armenia without the Armenians"—that is the Ottoman Government's project. The Moslems are already being allowed to take possession of the lands and houses abandoned by the Armenians.

The exiles are forbidden to take anything with them. For that matter, in the districts under military occupation there is nothing left to take, as the military authorities have exerted themselves to carry off, for their own use, everything that they could lay hands on.

The exiles will have to traverse on foot a distance that involves one or two months' marching and sometimes even more, before they reach the particular corner of the desert assigned to them for their habitation, and destined to become their tomb. We hear, in fact, that the course of their route and the stream of the Euphrates are littered with the corpses of exiles, while those who survive are doomed to certain death, since they will find in the desert neither house, nor work, nor food.

It is simply a scheme for exterminating the Armenian nation wholesale, without any fuss. It is just another form of massacre, and a more horrible form.

Remember that all the men between the ages of 20 and 45 are at the front. Those between 45 and 60 are working for the military transport service. As for those who had paid the statutory tax for exemption from military service, they have either been exiled or imprisoned on one pretext or another. The result is that there is no one left to deport but the old men, the women and the children. These poor creatures have to travel through regions which, even in times of peace, were reputed dangerous, and where there was a serious risk of being robbed. Now that the Turkish brigands, as well as the gendarmes and civil officials, enjoy the most absolute licence, the exiles will inevitably be robbed on the road, and their women and girls dishonoured and abducted.

We are hearing also from various places of conversions to Islam. It seems that the people have no other alternative for saving their lives.

The courts martial are working everywhere at full pressure.

You must have heard through the newspapers of the hanging of 20 Huntchakists at Constantinople. The verdict given against them is not based on any of the established laws of the Empire. The same day twelve Armenians were hanged at Kaisaria, on the charge of having obeyed instructions received from the secret conference held at Bukarest by the Huntchakists and Droshakists. Besides these hangings, 32 persons have been sentenced at Kaisaria to terms of hard labour, ranging from ten to fifteen years. Most of them are honest merchants who are in no sort of relation with the political parties. Twelve Armenians have also been hanged in Cilicia. Condemnations have become daily occurrences. The discovery of arms, books and pictures is enough to condemn an Armenian to several years' imprisonment.

Besides this many people have succumbed under the rod. Thirteen Armenians have been killed in this way at Diyarbekir, and six at Kaisaria. Thirteen others have been killed on their way to Shabin Kara-Hissar and Sivas. The priests of the village of Kourk with their companions have suffered the same fate on the road between Sou-Shehr and Sivas, although they had their hands pinioned and were defenceless.

I will spare you the recital of other outrages which have occurred sporadically all over the country, under the cloak of searches for arms and for revolutionary agents. Not a single house has been left unsearched, not even the episcopal residences, the churches or the schools. Hundreds of women, girls, and even quite young children are groaning in prison. Churches and convents have been pillaged, desecrated and destroyed. Even the Bishops are not spared. Mgr. Barkev Danielian (Bishop of Broussa), Mgr. Kevork Tourian (Bishop of Trebizond), Mgr. Khosrov Behrikian (Bishop of Kaisaria), Mgr. Vaghinadj Torikian (Bishop of Shabin Kara-Hissar), and Mgr. Kevork Nalbandian (Bishop of Tchar-Sandjak) have been arrested and handed over to the courts martial. Father Muggerditch, locum-tenens of the Bishop of Diyarbekir, has died of blows received in prison. We have no news of the other bishops, but I imagine that the greater part of them are in prison.

We are so cut off from the world that we might be in a fortress. We have no means of correspondence, neither post nor telegraph.

The villages in the neighbourhood of Van and Bitlis have been plundered, and their inhabitants put to the sword. At the beginning of this month, there was a pitiless massacre of all the inhabitants of Kara-Hissar with the exception of a few children who are said to have escaped by a miracle. Unhappily we learn the details of all these occurrences too late, and even then only with the utmost difficulty.

So you see that the Armenians in Turkey have only a few more days to live, and if the Armenians abroad do not succeed in enlisting the sympathy of the neutrals on our behalf, there will be extraordinarily few Armenians left a few months hence, out of the million and a half that there were in Turkey before the war. The annihilation of the Armenian nation will then be inevitable.

7. LETTER FROM THE SAME SOURCE, DATED CONSTANTINOPLE, 2/15th AUGUST, 1915, AND ADDRESSED TO THE SAME ARMENIAN RESIDENT BEYOND THE OTTOMAN FRONTIER.

Since I wrote my last letter (of which you have acknowledged the receipt), we have been able to obtain more precise information from the provinces of the interior. The information with which we present you herewith is derived from the following witnesses: an Armenian lady forcibly converted to Islam, and brought by an unforeseen chance to Constantinople; a girl from Zila, between nine and ten years old, who was abducted by a Turkish officer and has reached Constantinople; a Turkish traveller from Harpout; foreign travellers from Erzindjan, and so on. In fine, this information is derived either from eye-witnesses or from actual victims of the crimes.

It is now established that there is not an Armenian left in the provinces of Erzeroum, Trebizond, Sivas, Harpout, Bitlis and Diyarbekir. About a million of the Armenian inhabitants of these provinces have been deported from their homes and sent southwards into exile. These deportations have been carried out very systematically by the local authorities since the beginning of April last. First of all, in every village and every town, the population was disarmed by the gendarmerie, and by criminals released for this purpose from prison. On the pretext of disarming the Armenians, these criminals committed assassinations and inflicted hideous tortures. Next, they imprisoned the Armenians *en masse*, on the pretext that they had found in their possession arms, books, a political organisation, and so on—at a pinch, wealth or any kind of social standing was pretext enough. After that, they began the deportation. And first, on the pretext of sending them into exile, they evicted such men as had not been imprisoned, or such as had been set at liberty through lack of any charge against them; then they massacred them—not one of these escaped slaughter. Before they started, they were examined officially by the authorities, and any money or valuables in their possession were confiscated. They were usually shackled—either separately, or in gangs of five to ten. The remainder—old men, women, and children—were treated as waifs in the province of Harpout, and placed at the disposal of the Moslem population. The highest official, as well as the most simple peasant, chose out the woman or girl who caught his fancy, and took her to wife, converting her by force to Islam. As for the children, the Moslems took as many of them as they wanted, and then the remnant of the Armenians were marched away, famished and destitute of provisions, to fall victims to hunger, unless that were anticipated by the savagery of the brigand-bands. In the province of Diyarbekir there was an outright massacre, especially at Mardin, and the population was subjected to all the afore-mentioned atrocities.

In the provinces of Erzeroum, Bitlis, Sivas and Diyarbekir, the local authorities gave certain facilities to the Armenians condemned to deportation: five to ten days' grace, authorisation to effect a partial sale of their goods, and permission to hire a cart, in the case of some families. But after the first few days of their journey, the carters abandoned them on the road and returned home. These convoys were waylaid the day after the start, or sometimes several days after, by bands of brigands or by Moslem peasants who spoiled them of all they had. The brigands fraternised with the gendarmes and slaughtered the few grown men or youths who were included in the convoys. They carried off the women, girls and children, leaving only the old women, who were driven along by the gendarmes under blows of the lash and died of hunger by the roadside. An eye-witness reports to us that the women deported from the province of Erzeroum were abandoned, some days ago, on the plain of Harpout, where they have all died of hunger (50 or 60 a day).

The only step taken by the authorities was to send people to bury them, in order to safeguard the health of the Moslem population.

The little girl from Zila tells us that when the Armenians of Marsovan, Amasia and Tokat reached Sari-Kishila (between Kaisaria and Sivas), the children of both sexes were torn from their mothers before the very windows of the Government Building, and were locked up in certain other buildings, while the convoy was forced to continue its march. After that, they gave notice in the neighbouring villages that anyone might come and take his choice. She and her companion (Newart of Amasia) were carried off and brought to Constantinople by a Turkish officer. The convoys of women and children were placed on view in front of the Government Building at each town or village where they passed, to give the Moslems an opportunity of taking their choice.

The convoy which started from Baibourt was thinned out in this way, and the women and children who survived were thrown into the Euphrates on the outskirts of Erzindjan, at a place called Kamakh-Boghazi.[19] Mademoiselle Flora A. Wedel Yarlesberg, a Norwegian lady of good family who was a nurse in a German Red Cross hospital, and another nurse who was her colleague, were so revolted by these barbarities and by other experiences of equal horror, that they tendered their resignations, returned to Constantinople, and called personally at several Embassies to denounce these hideous crimes.

The same barbarities have been committed everywhere, and by this time travellers find nothing but thousands of Armenian corpses along all the roads in these provinces. A Moslem traveller on his way from Malatia to Sivas, a nine hours' journey, passed nothing but corpses of men and women. All the male Armenians of Malatia had been taken there and massacred; the women and children have all been converted to Islam. No Armenian can travel in these parts, for every Moslem, and especially the brigands and gendarmes, considers it his duty now to kill them at sight. Recently Messieurs Zohrab and Vartkes, two Armenian members of the Ottoman Parliament, who had been sent off to Diyarbekir to be tried by the Council of War, were killed, before they got there, at a short distance from Aleppo. In these provinces one can only travel *incognito* under a Moslem name. As for the women's fate, we have already spoken of it above, and it seems unnecessary to go into further particulars about their honour, when one sees the utter disregard there is for their life.

The Armenian soldiers, too, have suffered the same fate. They were also all disarmed and put to constructing roads.[20] We have certain knowledge that the Armenian soldiers of the province of Erzeroum, who were at work on the road from Erzeroum to Erzindjan, have all been massacred. The Armenian soldiers of the province of Diyarbekir have all been massacred on the Diyarbekir-Ourfa road, and the Diyarbekir-Harpout road. From Harpout alone, 1,800 young Armenians were enrolled and sent off to work at Diyarbekir; all were massacred in the neighbourhood of Arghana. We have no news from the other districts, but they have assuredly suffered the same fate there also.

In certain towns, the Armenians who had been consigned to oblivion in the prisons have been hanged in batches. During the past month alone, several dozen Armenians have been hanged in Kaisaria. In many places the Armenian inhabitants, to save their lives, have tried to become Mohammedans, but this time such overtures have not been readily accepted, as they were at the time of the other great massacres. At Sivas, the would-be converts to Islam were offered the following terms: they must hand over all children under twelve years of age to the Government, which would undertake to place them in orphanages; and they must consent, for their own part, to leave their homes and settle wherever the Government directed.

At Harpout, they would not accept the conversion of the men; in the case of the women, they made their conversion conditional in each instance upon the presence of a Moslem willing to take the convert in marriage. Many Armenian women preferred to throw themselves into the Euphrates with their infants, or committed suicide in their homes. The Euphrates and Tigris have become the sepulchre of thousands of Armenians.

All Armenians converted in the Black Sea towns—Trebizond, Samsoun, Kerasond, etc.—have been sent to the interior, and settled in towns inhabited exclusively by Moslems. The town of Shabin-Karahissar resisted the disarming and deportation, and was thereupon bombarded. The whole population of the town and the surrounding country, from the Bishop downwards, was pitilessly massacred.

In short, from Samsoun on the one hand to Seghert[21] and Diyarbekir on the other, there is now not a single Armenian left. The majority have been massacred, part have been carried off, and a very small part have been converted to Islam.

History has never recorded, never hinted at, such a hecatomb. We are driven to believe that under the reign of Sultan Abd-ul-Hamid we were exceedingly fortunate.

We have just learned the fate of some of the provincial bishops. Mgr. Anania Hazarabedian, Bishop of Baibourt, has been hanged without any confirmation of the sentence by the Central Government[22]. Mgr. Bosak Der-Khoremian. Bishop of Harpout, started on his road to exile in May, and had barely left the outskirts of the town when he was cruelly murdered. But we have still no news of the Bishops of Seghert, Bitlis, Moush, Keghi, Palou, Erzindjan, Kamakh, Tokat, Gurin, Samsoun and Trebizond, or for a month past of the Bishops of Sivas and Erzeroum. It is superfluous to speak of the martyred priests. When the people were deported, the churches were pillaged and turned into mosques, stables, or what not. Besides that, they have begun to sell at Constantinople the sacred objects and other properties of the Armenian churches, just as the Turks have begun to bring to Constantinople the children of the unhappy Armenian mothers.

It appears that the massacres have been less cruel in Cilicia, or at least we have no news yet of the worst. The population, which has been deported to the provinces of Aleppo and Der-el-Zor and to Damascus, will certainly perish of hunger. We have just heard that the Government has refused to leave in peace even the insignificant Armenian colonies at Aleppo and Ourfa, who might have assisted their unhappy brethren on their southward road; and the Katholikos of Cilicia, who still remains at Aleppo, is busy distributing the relief we are forwarding to him.

We thought at first that the Government's plan was to settle the Armenian question once and for all by clearing out the Armenians of the six Armenian provinces and removing the Armenian population of Cilicia, to forestall another danger in the future. Unhappily their plan was wider in scope and more thorough in intention. It consisted in the extermination of the whole Armenian population throughout the whole of Turkey. The result is that, in those seven provinces where the Government was pledged to introduce reforms, there is not one per cent. of the Armenian population left alive. So far, we do not know whether a single Armenian has reached Mosul or its neighbourhood. And this plan has now been put into execution even in the suburbs of Constantinople. The majority of the Armenians in the district of

Ismid and in the province of Broussa have been forcibly deported to Mesopotamia, leaving behind them their homes and their property. In detail, the population of Adapazar, Ismid, Gegvé, Armasha and the neighbourhood has been removed—in fact, the population of all the villages in the Ismid district (except Baghtchedjik, which has been granted several days' grace). The Principal of the Seminary at Armasha has also been removed with his colleagues in orders and his seminarists[23]. They have had to leave everything behind, and been able to take nothing with them on their journey. Six weeping mothers confided their little ones to the Armenians of Konia, in order to save their lives, but the local authorities tore them away from their Armenian guardians, and handed them over to Moslems.

So now it is Constantinople's turn. In any case, the population has fallen into a panic, and is waiting from one moment to another for the execution of its doom. The arrests are innumerable, and those arrested are immediately removed from the capital. The majority will assuredly perish. It is the retail merchants of provincial birth, but resident in Constantinople, who are so far being deported—among them Marouké, Ipranossian Garabed, Kherbekian of Erzeroum, Atamian Karekin, Krikorian Sempad of Bitlis, etc. We are making great efforts to save at any rate the Armenians of Constantinople from this horrible extermination of the race, in order that, hereafter, we may have at least one rallying point for the Armenian cause in Turkey.

Is there anything further to add to this report? The whole Armenian population of Turkey has been condemned to death, and this decree is being put into execution energetically in every corner of the Empire, under the eyes of the European Powers; while, so far, neither Germany nor Austria has succeeded in checking the action of their ally and removing the stain of these barbarities, which also attaches to them. All our efforts have been without result. Our hope is set upon the Armenians abroad.

19. See Docs. 59, 60, 61, 62. The witnesses at Erzindjan were not Norwegians but Danes—EDITOR.

20. See Docs. 23 and 62.

21. Sairt (?)

22. See Doc. 59.

23. See Doc. 99.

8. EXTRACTS FROM A LETTER, DATED ATHENS, 8th/21st JULY, 1915, FROM AN ARMENIAN FORMERLY RESIDENT IN

TURKEY TO A PROMINENT ARMENIAN IN WESTERN EUROPE.

Events have been taking place in Turkey of which I imagine that you have no first-hand or reliable information, on account of the strict censorship and scarcity of travellers.... And as I have been able to obtain reliable information, I have thought it my duty as an Armenian to submit it to your Excellency.

Mr. A., who was a missionary teacher at the town of B. in Cilicia for four years, and with whom I am acquainted personally (and I have good reason to believe in every word he says), arrived in this city only yesterday, coming from AE. in company with Miss B., the daughter of the Director of Mr. A.'s college, with whom I am also acquainted personally.

They just began to inform me by saying that the condition of the Armenians in Cilicia was awful. The town of Dört Yöl, after having been cleared of its Armenian population, has been peacefully occupied by Turkish families, and not by the military authorities. The whole of the Armenian inhabitants have been sent away—turned out of their homes—and are naturally suffering from hunger. The exposure is something that cannot be described. Before evacuation, some nine leading merchants were hanged, on the accusation that they were in communication with the British fleet and were spying for the Allied Forces[24].

Zeitoun has met the same fate. There is not a single Armenian left in Zeitoun, and all the houses are occupied by Turkish people. My friends could not understand what exactly had happened to the Zeitounlis, but the fact is that special care has been taken by the Turkish authorities that too many of them should not be left together. Attempts have been made to make them Mohammedans, and it is known that the authorities attempted to distribute one, two, or three families to each Turkish village in the district of Marash.

They have attempted to do the same thing to Hadjin, but, somehow or other, only half the inhabitants have left, whose homes have naturally been occupied by the Turks.

The Turks of Tarsus and Adana are showing the same disposition as they did before the massacres of 1909.

Missionaries from Beirout state that the same persecution is being carried out against Christian Syrians.

Dr. C., for many years a missionary in Smyrna, and latterly in AD., was exiled to Angora. He states that there were thirty Armenians exiled with him from AD. on the simple charge that they had either themselves been Huntchakists or had friends belonging to the said Party. Extortion of money, robbery and insults are usual, and conditions in general are worse than at any period in the time of Hamid. Dr. C. has been in Turkey for 35 years and knows Turkish.

At Kaisaria they hanged eight Armenians. About the same time they hanged twenty-six at Constantinople, and this immediately after the note of the Powers threatening to hold Turkish officials responsible for massacres of Armenians. Imprisonment and exile are common things, and the Reverend Missionary finished by saying that "I ought to be glad I was out of it."

Dr. C., coming from Constantinople, gave me the further information that massacres had been going on round Bitlis for some time. And then, from correspondents at Bitlis, his informants had had news that whole villages were embracing Mohammedanism in order to escape tortures, because the object of the massacres was not simply to kill, but to torture.

A resident at Mardin had telegraphed by code to Constantinople informing his correspondent there that the same conditions existed at Mardin as during 1895.

The American Ambassador at Constantinople, after asking the Turkish Government to stop the massacres, went to the German Ambassador. But Herr Wangenheim said he could not interfere in any way with Turkey's internal affairs!!!

All these informants do not hide their belief, based on what they have actually seen, that German policy is at the back of the movement for a clean Mohammedan "Turkey for the Turks."

I will give your Excellency another coincident piece of evidence. In May, 1914, I travelled with Dr. Niazim Bey, who is the spirit of the Union and Progress Party, when he was on the mission of establishing a boycott—nominally against the Greeks only, though it proved to be against the Armenians as well. The Doctor said that the work of the Turkish Government was very complicated, and he laid all the fault of it on the ancestors of the modern Turks, who, in spite of their being victorious and defying all Europe, nay all the world, had not been far-sighted enough to cleanse all the country they ruled of the Christian element, but had yielded to their chivalrous feelings and allowed the Christians to live. Had they done this bit of cleaning up at a time when nobody could protest, there would have been an easy task now for the heads of the Government in governing, and so on.

The Russian retreat has intoxicated the Turks. They think they have their chance now, and evidence shows that their almighty ally Germany encourages them in their effort at house cleaning. The note of the Allied

Powers is no deterrent, even if the Turkish officials were not sure of final victory, because they feel that, if they lose, Turkey is not the place to offer them a happy shelter, and, with the money they are making now, the officials responsible can hide themselves in a country where they cannot be found or cannot be extradited. And some of the bolder spirits, like Talaat and Enver, have openly said that they do not expect to live if defeated, even without the threat of the Allies to bring them to account.

The Armenians in Turkey have not been able to conceal their feelings, and when I myself was in Constantinople, prudent man though I am, I was unable to conceal my feelings myself, or at least so effectively as not to be perceived by the Turks.

As early as September last, the Turkish comic paper *Karagoz* had written one day that "If the Armenians were cheerful, there was certainly news of victory for the Allies; if not, it had been the reverse." But if, in spite of the Armenians concealing their feelings, the Turks had definitely adopted the policy—as no doubt they had—of exterminating the Christians in Turkey, then we have at least the satisfaction that we have hurt them with the display of what we felt.

I believe that the Germans did not want to exterminate the Armenians unless the latter proved of military danger in the present game; but I imagine the Armenians have incurred the Germans' displeasure in this regard.

That Germany, or the Germans in Turkey, are for the above reason encouraging the Turks in their attempt at extermination, is proved by the fact that wholesale massacres and deportations have been specific to regions of which the inhabitants might be of especial help to an invading army. For instance, Dört Yöl and Zeitoun would be of excellent help had the Allies made a landing at Payas. Bitlis is next door to Van; the Russian army is getting towards Bitlis, and naturally the Armenians of Bitlis would be of great value to them, as indeed the Armenians of Van have been already.

Take the case of Erzeroum, again a frontier town, which, besides individual hangings, has been the scene of wholesale massacres; while towns far away from the theatre of war, such as Angora, Broussa, Konia, Constantinople, etc., although not exempted from persecution, have still not been subjected to wholesale massacres and deportations.

24. See Doc. 123.

9. LETTER, DATED 3rd/16th AUGUST, 1915, CONVEYED BEYOND THE OTTOMAN FRONTIER BY AN ARMENIAN REFUGEE FROM CILICIA IN THE SOLE OF HER SHOE[25]

In haste and in secret I seize this opportunity of bringing to your ears the cry of agony which goes out from the survivors of the terrible crisis through which we are passing at this moment. They are exterminating our nation, mowing it down. Perhaps this will be the last cry from Armenia that you will hear; we have no longer any fear of death, we see it close at hand, this death of the whole people. We are waifs who cry for the lives of our brothers. These lines cannot describe our misery; it would need volumes of reports to do justice to that.

(1.) At the present moment there are at ―――― more than 10,000 deported widows and children (among the latter one sees no boys above eleven years of age). They had been on the road for from three to five months; they have been plundered several times over, and have marched along naked and starving; the Government gave them on one single occasion a morsel of bread—a few have had it twice. It is said that the number of these deported widows will reach 60,000; they are so exhausted that they cannot stand upright; the majority have great sores on their feet, through having had to march barefoot.

(2). An enquiry has proved that, out of 1,000 people who started, scarcely 400 reached ――――. Out of the 600 to be accounted for, 380 men and boys above eleven years of age, and 85 women, had been massacred or drowned, out of sight of the towns, by the gendarmes who conducted them; 120 young women and girls and 40 boys had been carried off, with the result that one does not see a single pretty face among the survivors.

(3.) Out of these survivors, 60 per cent. are sick; they are to be sent in the immediate future to ――――, where certain death awaits them; one cannot describe the ferocious treatment to which they are exposed; they had been on the road for from three to five months; they had been plundered two, three, five, seven times; their underclothes even had been ransacked; so far from being given anything to eat, they had even been prevented from drinking while they were passing a stream. Three-quarters of the young women and girls were abducted; the remainder were forced to lie with the gendarmes who conducted them. Thousands died under these outrages, and the survivors have stories to tell of refinements of outrage so disgusting that they pollute one's ears.

(4.) The massacres have been most violent in the eastern provinces, and the population has been deported wholesale towards the Hauran Desert, Gereg and Mosul, where the victims are doomed to a death from natural causes more infallible than massacre. When one remembers that these people were leading a comfortable European life, one is forced to conclude that they will never be able to survive in an alien and inhospitable climate, even if the knife and the bullet do not previously do their work.

My friends, I have not time to tell you more; one may say with truth that not a single Armenian is left in Armenia; soon there will be none left in Cilicia either. The Armenian, robbed of his life, his goods, his honour, conveys to you his last cry for help—help to save the lives of the survivors! Money to buy them bread! There is a rumour here that the Government will allow the women and the children under seventeen years of age to leave the country. How are they to do it? Where are they to go? What ship is to take them? Who will provide the funds? From moment to moment we are waiting for relief, to stave off the death of the Nation. Be quick, never mind how; send us money, we have no means of communication!

Send, through the agency of the American Government, *money, money, money*; the bearer of this letter deserves every reward; she will tell you all the details. Zohrab, Vartkes Daghavarian and their five companions have been murdered by the gendarmes at Sheitan-Deré, between Ourfa and Diyarbekir, where thousands of headless corpses make the passers-by shudder; the Euphrates bears down its stream thousands of corpses of men and women; photographs of this have been taken by Europeans. Fifteen thousand Zeitounlis have been deported to Der-el-Zor, where they are suffering the worst atrocities. Thousands of babies at the breast have been thrown into rivers or abandoned by the wayside by their mothers. The urgent need is *money*! Make that clear to the Armenian colony in America. *Money! Money!*

One thousand six hundred Armenians have had their throats cut in the prisons at Diyarbekir. The Arashnort was mutilated, drenched with alcohol, and burnt alive in the prison yard, in the middle of a carousing crowd of gendarmes, who even accompanied the scene with music. The massacres at Beniani, Adiaman and Selefka have been carried out diabolically; there is not a single man left above the age of thirteen years; the girls have been outraged mercilessly; we have seen their mutilated corpses tied together in batches of four, eight or ten, and cast into the Euphrates. The majority had been mutilated in an indescribable manner.

The above facts have been gathered from official sources and eye-witnesses.

The American Consul is able to arrange for the despatch of funds. We are unable to realise any of our property, either national or private, because it has all been confiscated by the Government. The Government has even confiscated the convents, the churches and the schools. Black famine reigns in this town; we have 15,000 deported Armenians here, who are being sent on in batches to Arabia. The whole of Armenia is being cleared out.

I sign this letter with my blood!

---

25. The author of the letter has been identified by an Armenian resident abroad who recognised his hand-writing.—EDITOR.

10. LETTER FROM MR. N., A FOREIGN RESIDENT AT CONSTANTINOPLE, DATED 27th AUGUST, 1915; COMMUNICATED BY THE AMERICAN COMMITTEE FOR ARMENIAN AND SYRIAN RELIEF.

The Armenians of Bardizag have generally speaking been deported. A promise secured by Mr. Morgenthau that Protestants should be exempted from deportation has kept the people at Nicomedia (Isnik) for nearly a week. They are camped in the open near the Railway Station, exposed to the weather and to the insults of the populace, apparently to be deported a few days later on. Whether we shall succeed in saving the Protestants remains to be seen. Deportation has taken place generally throughout all the region contiguous to Nicomedia, Adapazar, Konia, Marsovan, Sivas, Harpout, Diyarbekir and to some parts of the American Central Mission. Many people have already lost their lives, and others, as for instance those in this city, have lost hope as to their final security. I shall enclose a few letters which will give an idea of the situation throughout the land.

Prof. QQ.[26] has just arrived from X. He has been four weeks on the journey, having been delayed considerably at S. He states that the Armenians have left, having been deported from X. and the vicinity. Mr. Morgenthau endeavoured to save the Mission *entourage* at X. from deportation; the promises securing this, however, were not fulfilled. Even the hundred girls and young women held in the College Compound could not be saved from this dreadful fate. To the bold stand made by the Mission people, on behalf of their pupils and teachers, the Kaimakam himself opposed his personal authority, threatening to hang anyone who attempted to prevent the carrying out of his orders for the deportation of the people. These orders, here as elsewhere, seemed to respect neither age nor condition....

The movement against the Armenians has now well-nigh covered the entire country. Many prominent Armenians have lost their lives; hardly a family has escaped experiencing to some extent the severity of this blow. It looks as if the patronage from this community for the American schools has been quite cut off. Teachers and pupils alike have been sent into exile, or have suffered death or have been carried off to Turkish communities or harems. There is an ugly rumour that the turn of the Greeks will come next. Should Greece move, this will probably be realised....

26. Author of Docs. 56 and 57.

11. MEMORANDUM DATED 15/28th OCTOBER, 1915, FROM A WELL-INFORMED SOURCE AT BUKAREST, RELATING TO THE EXTERMINATION OF THE ARMENIANS IN TURKEY.

1. At *Vezir Köprü* (district of Marsovan) all Armenian women and girls from 7 to 40 years of age have been *sold at auction*. Women were also presented to the buyers without payment.

2. At *Kaisaria* more than 500 Armenian families were forced to embrace Islam. A father asked his son in Constantinople to follow his example, "in order to prevent worse consequences for his parents."

3. All Armenian judicial officials in the provinces have been discharged. All Turkish officials who have shown special zeal in the extermination of the Armenians have been promoted. Thus Zeki Bey, Kaimakam of *Develou* (Kaisaria), the man who directed in person the terrible tortures of the Armenian prisoners and was responsible for the death of most of them, has been made mektoubdji of the Vilayet of Constantinople.

4. The Young Turk Government has published, as an excuse or perhaps as a means of exciting greater hatred against the Armenians, a book entitled *The Armenian Separatist Movement*, which is as ridiculous as it is criminal. The reader finds in it not only copies of entirely fictitious publications, but actually pictures of enormous depots of arms and munitions purporting to be Armenian.

5. In *Konia*, and everywhere else, the wives of the Armenian soldiers who have not been deported have been taken as servants or concubines into Turkish families.

6. In *Marash* more than three hundred Armenians have been executed by Court Martial, besides the numerous victims murdered in the course of the deportations. At *Panderma* many important Armenians have been condemned to death by the Court Martial. The vicar Barkev Vartabed has been condemned to five years' penal servitude. The Archbishop of Erzeroum, His Grace Sempad, who, with the Vali's authorisation, was returning to Constantinople, was murdered at Erzindjan by the brigands in the service of the Union and Progress Committee. The bishops of Trebizond, Kaisaria, Moush, Bitlis, Sairt, and Erzindjan have all been murdered by order of the Young Turk Government. According to reports from travellers, all the Armenian population of Trebizond has been massacred without exception. Almost the whole male population in Sivas, Erzeroum, Harpout, Bitlis,

Baibourt, Khnyss, Diyarbekir, etc., has been exterminated. At Tchingiler, a small village in the district of Ismid, 300 men have been murdered because they did not obey the order to leave their houses. The people deported from Rodosto, Malgara and Tchorlu, who have been deprived of all their possessions in accordance with the new "temporary law" of the 13/26th September, have been separated from their families and sent on foot from Ismid to Konia on the arbitrary order of the notorious Ibrahim, dictator of the Ismid district. Thousands of poor Armenians expelled from Constantinople are made to march on foot from Ismid to Konia and still further, after they have delivered up everything they possess to the gendarmes, including their shoes. Those who can afford to travel by rail are also fleeced by the gendarmes, who not only demand the price of the ticket from Constantinople to their destinations, but extract the whole of their money by selling them food at exorbitant prices. They demand payment even for unlocking the door of the water-closet.

7. German travellers from Aleppo describe the misery of the deported Armenians as terrible. All along the route they saw corpses of Armenians who had died of hunger.

The Arab deputies from Bagdad and Syria report that the misery in the deserts of Hauran is indescribable:—

"The railway discharges into the mountains vast numbers of Armenians, who are abandoned there without bread or water. In the towns and villages, the Arabs try to bring them some relief; but generally the Armenians are abandoned at five or six hours' distance from their homes. We saw on the way numbers of women and old men and children dying of hunger, who did not know where to look for help."

Some Armenians are leading a life of misery among the Arabs, forty or forty-five hours' journey from Bagdad. Every day numbers of them die of hunger. The Government gives them no food. Moreover, fresh troops have been sent to Bagdad, and these will be a new scourge to the unfortunate exiles.

8. Three Special Commissions have been sent through the provinces to liquidate the abandoned goods and estates of the Armenians, in conformity with the new "temporary law" of the 13/26th September, 1915.

12. INFORMATION REGARDING EVENTS IN ARMENIA, PUBLISHED IN THE "SONNENAUFGANG" (ORGAN OF THE "GERMAN LEAGUE FOR THE PROMOTION OF CHRISTIAN CHARITABLE WORK IN THE EAST"), OCTOBER, 1915; AND IN THE "ALLGEMEINE MISSIONS-ZEITSCHRIFT," NOVEMBER, 1915.

This testimony is especially significant because it comes from a German source, and because the German Censor made a strenuous attempt to suppress it.

The same issue of the "Sonnenaufgang" contains the following editorial note:—

"In our preceding issue we published an account by one of our sisters (Schwester Möhring) of her experiences on a journey, but we have to abstain from giving to the public the new details that are reaching us in abundance. It costs us much to do so, as our friends will understand; but the political situation of our country demands it."

In the case of the "Allgemeine Missions-Zeitschrift," the Censor was not content with putting pressure on the editor. On the 10th November, he forbade the reproduction of the present article in the German press, and did his best to confiscate the whole current issue of the magazine. Copies of both publications, however, found their way across the frontier.

Both the incriminating articles are drawn from common sources, but the extracts they make from them do not entirely coincide, so that, by putting them together, a fuller version of these sources can be compiled.

In the text printed below, the unbracketed paragraphs are those which appear both in the "Sonnenaufgang" and in the "Allgemeine Missions-Zeitschrift"; while paragraphs included in angular brackets (<>) appear only in the "Sonnenaufgang," and those in square brackets ([ ]) only in the "Allgemeine Missions-Zeitschrift."

Between the 10th and the 30th May, 1,200 of the most prominent Armenians and other Christians, without distinction of confession, were arrested in the Vilayets of Diyarbekir and Mamouret-ul-Aziz.

<It is said that they were to be taken to Mosul, but nothing more has been heard of them.>

[On the 30th May, 674 of them were embarked on thirteen Tigris barges, under the pretext that they were to be taken to Mosul. The Vali's aide-de-camp, assisted by fifty gendarmes, was in charge of the convoy. Half the gendarmes started off on the barges, while the other half rode along the bank. A short time after the start the prisoners were stripped of all their money (about £6,000 Turkish) and then of their clothes; after that they were thrown into the river. The gendarmes on the bank were ordered to let none of them escape. The clothes of these victims were sold in the market of Diyarbekir.]

<About the same time 700 young Armenian men were conscribed, and were then set to build the Karabaghtché-Habashi road. There is no news of these 700 men either.

It is said that in Diyarbekir five or six priests were stripped naked one day, smeared with tar, and dragged through the streets.>

In the Vilayet of Aleppo they have evicted the inhabitants of Hadjin, Shar, Albustan, Göksoun, Tasholouk, Zeitoun, all the villages of Alabash, Geben, Shivilgi, Furnus and the surrounding villages, Fundadjak, Hassan-Beyli, Harni, Lappashli, Dört Yöl and others.

[They have marched them off in convoys into the desert on the pretext of settling them there. In the village of Tel-Armen (along the line of the Bagdad Railway, near Mosul) and in the neighbouring villages about 5,000 people were massacred, leaving only a few women and children. The people were thrown alive down wells or into the fire. They pretend that the Armenians are to be employed in colonising land situated at a distance of from twenty-four to thirty kilometres from the Bagdad Railway. But as it is only the women and children who are sent into exile, since all the men, with the exception of the very old, are at the war, this means nothing less than the wholesale murder of the families, since they have neither the labour nor the capital for clearing the country.]

A German met a Christian soldier of his acquaintance, who was on furlough from Jerusalem. The man was wandering up and down along the banks of the Euphrates searching for his wife and children, who were supposed to have been transferred to that neighbourhood. Such unfortunates are often to be met with in Aleppo, because they believe that there they will learn something more definite about the whereabouts of their relations. It has often happened that when a member of a family has been absent, he discovers on his return that all his family are gone—evicted from their homes.

[For a whole month corpses were observed floating down the River Euphrates nearly every day, often in batches of from two to six corpses bound together. The male corpses are in many cases hideously mutilated (sexual organs cut off, and so on), the female corpses are ripped open. The Turkish military authority in control of the Euphrates, the Kaimakam of Djerablous, refuses to allow the burial of these corpses, on the ground that he finds it impossible to establish whether they belong to Moslems or to Christians. He adds that no one has given him any orders on the subject. The corpses stranded on the bank are devoured by dogs and vultures. To this fact there are many German eye-witnesses. An employee of the Bagdad Railway has brought the information that the prisons at Biredjik are filled regularly every day and emptied every night—into the Euphrates. Between Diyarbekir and Ourfa a German cavalry captain saw innumerable corpses lying unburied all along the road.]

<The following telegram was sent to Aleppo from Arabkir:—"We have accepted the True Religion. Now we are all right." The inhabitants of a village near Anderoum went over to Islam and had to hold to it. At Hadjin six families wanted to become Mohammedans. They received the verdict: "Nothing under one hundred families will be accepted."

Aleppo and Ourfa are the assemblage-places for the convoys of exiles. There were about 5,000 of them in Aleppo during June and July, while during the whole period from April to July many more than 50,000 must have passed through the city. The girls were abducted almost without exception by the soldiers and their Arab hangers-on. One father, on the verge of despair, besought me to take with me at least his fifteen-year-old daughter, as he could no longer protect her from the persecutions inflicted upon her. The children left behind by the Armenians on their journey are past counting.

Women whose pains came upon them on the way had to continue their journey without respite. A woman bore twins in the neighbourhood of Aintab; next morning she had to go on again. She very soon had to leave the children under a bush, and a little while after she collapsed herself. Another, whose pains came upon her during the march, was compelled to go on at once and fell down dead almost immediately. There were several more incidents of the same kind between Marash and Aleppo[27].

The villagers of Shar were permitted to carry all their household effects with them. On the road they were suddenly told: "An order has come for us to leave the high road and travel across the mountains." Everything—waggons, oxen and belongings—had to be left behind on the road, and then they went on over the mountains on foot. This year the heat has been exceptionally severe, and many women and children naturally succumbed to it even in these early stages of their journey.

There are about 30,000 exiles of whom we have no news at all, as they have arrived neither at Aleppo nor at Ourfa.>

---

27. "We have just picked up fifteen babies. Three are already dead. They were terribly thin and ailing when we found them. Ah! If we could only write all that we see."—*Extract from a letter dated Marash, 4th June, 1915, published in "Sonnenaufgang," September, 1915.*

13. STATEMENT MADE BY A FOREIGN RESIDENT AT CONSTANTINOPLE TO A SWISS GENTLEMAN AT GENEVA; COMMUNICATED BY THE LATTER.

When I left Turkey early in March (1916), the Armenian situation was as follows:—

In general deportations had ceased, but local interference with Armenians continued. Quite often Armenians who had remained in the villages or cities between the Taurus Mountains and Constantinople have been sent from one locality to another within the province, or even to localities in other provinces.

Arrests of Armenians in the Capital continue with considerable frequency. Those arrested were usually sent to some interior province, often to be killed or to be left to die from ill-treatment or lack of food.

Extortion of money and supplies from Armenians, and discriminations against them in the distribution of bread and other food supplies, continue out of all proportion to these practices as applied to other Ottoman subjects.

The suffering of all Armenians, and especially of those in exile, is very great, and many are dying from lack of proper food and from disease. Anti-Armenian feeling among Moslems is increasing.

Early in January of this year, trustworthy reports from Aleppo gave 492,000 as the number of deported Armenians who were at that time in the regions of Mosul, Der-el-Zor, Aleppo and Damascus[28]. Most of these are women and children and old men, practically all of whom are in great need of food and other necessities of life. Without physicians and medicine, disease is reaping a rich harvest from these exiles.

The Turkish Minister of the Interior has stated that about 800,000 Armenians have been deported, and that about 300,000 of these people have been killed or have perished from other causes. Other estimates place the number of deported at 1,200,000, and the number who have perished from all causes at 500,000.

---

28. See Doc. 139, d.

14. CABLEGRAM, DATED 4th MAY, 1916, TRANSMITTED THROUGH THE STATE DEPARTMENT AT WASHINGTON TO THE AMERICAN COMMITTEE FOR ARMENIAN AND SYRIAN RELIEF, FROM THE COMMITTEE'S REPRESENTATIVES IN TURKEY.

Aleppo.

Relief work here supports 1,350 orphans, who are only a portion of the destitute children now in the city. It has also furnished food to families in nine destitute centres, including Hama, Rakka, Killis and Damascus. £1,500 (Turkish) monthly are being used at Aleppo for orphans; £600 (Turkish) are being used for the poor of Aleppo; £2,245 (Turkish) are being used in the destitute centres. This is considered to be a minimum allocation, and ten times the amount would not meet the full needs. The work is being overseen by the German and American Consuls. So insufficient are the funds that many exiles in the destitute places have only grass to eat, and they are dying of starvation by hundreds. £1,000 (Turkish) are required each week for the Aleppo centre.

Marash.

Ten thousand Armenians are threatened with deportation, and all are in a most needy condition. Attempted industrial assistance for Moslems and Christians was stopped by Government. Christians are not allowed to do any business, and the price of food is very high. Export from Agno to Marash has been forbidden, and many people are dying of starvation. £1,600 (Turkish) are needed here monthly.

Aintab.

Forty-five hundred Armenians remain here, two-thirds of whom are on relief lists. Four hundred refugee women and children in city and neighbourhood require £1,000 (Turkish) each month.

Tarsus.

This being a station on the route taken by the exiles from the region north of Tarsus, the roads are always full of people in miserable condition. According to Government estimates, 92,000 exiles have passed through Tarsus, while, according to other reports, the number is much larger. Typhus is very prevalent. The needs here require £500 (Turkish) a month.

Adana.

The situation here in general resembles that at Agno, with the special feature that many children need to be saved and fed. £500 (Turkish) monthly are needed.

Sivas.

In addition to the local Christian population remaining here, 25,000 destitute refugees, including women and children from coast cities, have been added. All need help. Monthly requirements amount to £600 (Turkish).

Konia.

Two thousand orphans. £1,500 (Turkish) monthly required for the needs of this city and neighbouring places.

Harpout.

This place asks for £400 (Turkish) monthly.

Marsovan and Kaisaria.

£500 (Turkish) monthly are needed.

Smyrna.

There has been much sickness here and there is a scarcity of food. £400 (Turkish) monthly are needed.

Broussa.

£200 (Turkish) monthly are being used here.

II.
VILAYET OF VAN.

The Vilayet of Van had a higher percentage of Armenians in its population than any other province of the Ottoman Empire; it was also the border province of the north-eastern frontier, towards Russian and Persian territory, and as such was the earliest to be exposed to invasion after the breakdown of the Turkish offensive against the Caucasus in the winter of 1914-1915.

The documents contained in this section give a detailed and perfectly self-consistent account, from five independent sources, of those events at Van which led to the first open breach between the Armenians in the Ottoman Empire and the Turks, and which gave the Government a pretext for extending the scheme of deportation already operative in Cilicia to the whole Armenian population under its jurisdiction.

The evidence makes it clear that there was no unprovoked insurrection of the Armenians at Van, as the Ottoman Government asserts in its official apologia. The Armenians only took up arms in self-defence, and the entire responsibility for the outbreak rests with Djevdet Bey, the local governor—whether he was acting on his own initiative or was simply carrying out instructions from Constantinople.

15. THE AMERICAN MISSION AT VAN: NARRATIVE PRINTED PRIVATELY IN THE UNITED STATES BY MISS GRACE HIGLEY KNAPP (1915).

The first part of this narrative, down to and including the sub-section headed "Deliverance," has been transcribed almost word for word by Miss Knapp from a letter she wrote at Van, on the 24th May, 1915, to Dr. Barton, and has, therefore, all the value of contemporary evidence.

The period of the (first) Russian occupation of Van is also covered by two further letters from Miss Knapp to Dr. Barton—a long one written piece-meal on the 14th, 20th and 22nd June, and a second dated 20th July. These contain much more detail than the three corresponding sub-sections of her narrative, but the detail is principally devoted to personal matters and to the care of the Moslem refugees. As neither subject was strictly relevant to the purpose of the present collection, it seemed better to reprint the narrative rather than the letters in the case of these sections also.

There is also a letter (published in the Eleventh Report of the Women's Armenian Relief Fund) from Miss Louie Bond to Mrs. Orpin, written on the 27th July, almost the eve of the evacuation; but this, too, is practically entirely devoted to personal matters.

For the period of the retreat there are no contemporary letters, but only an undated memorandum by Miss Knapp, which agrees word for word with the latter part of her present narrative, from the beginning of the section headed "Flight" to the end.

The Setting of the Drama and the Actors Therein.

Van was one of the most beautiful cities of Asiatic Turkey—a city of gardens and vineyards, situated on Lake Van in the centre of a plateau bordered by magnificent mountains. The walled city, containing the shops and most of the public buildings, was dominated by Castle Rock, a huge rock rising sheer from the plain, crowned with ancient battlements and fortifications, and bearing on its lakeward face famous cuneiform inscriptions. The Gardens, so-called because nearly every house had its garden or vineyard, extended over four miles eastward from the walled city and were about two miles in width.

The inhabitants numbered fifty thousand, three-fifths of whom were Armenians, two-fifths Turks. The Armenians were progressive and ambitious, and because of their numerical strength and the proximity of Russia the revolutionary party grew to be a force to be reckoned with. Three of its noted leaders were Vremyan, member of the Ottoman Parliament; Ishkhan, the one most skilled in military tactics; and Aram, of whom there will be much to say later. The Governor often consulted with these men and seemed to be on the most friendly terms with them.

The American Mission Compound was on the south-eastern border of the middle third of the Gardens, on a slight rise of ground that made its buildings somewhat conspicuous. These buildings were a church building, two large new school buildings, two small ones, a lace school, a hospital, dispensary and four missionary residences. South-east, and quite near, was a broad plain. Here was the largest Turkish barracks of the large garrison, between which and the American premises nothing intervened. North and nearer, but with streets and houses between, was another large barracks, and farther north, within rifle range, was Toprak-Kala Hill, surmounted by a small barracks dubbed by the Americans the "Pepper Box." Five minutes' walk to the east of us was the German Orphanage managed by Herr Spörri, his wife and daughter (of Swiss extraction) and three single ladies.

The American force in 1914-1915 consisted of the veteran missionary, Mrs. G.C. Raynolds (Dr. Raynolds had been in America a year and a half collecting funds for our Van college, and had been prevented from returning by the outbreak of war); Dr. Clarence D. Ussher, in charge of the hospital and medical work; Mrs. Ussher, in charge of a philanthropic lace industry; Mr. and Mrs. Ernest A. Yarrow, in charge of the Boys' School and general work; Miss Gertrude Rogers, principal of the Girls' School; Miss Caroline Silliman, in charge of the primary department, and two Armenian and one Turkish kindergarten; Miss Elizabeth Ussher, in charge of the musical department; Miss Louise Bond, the English superintendent of the hospital; and Miss

Grisel McLaren, our touring missionary. Dr. Ussher and Mr. Yarrow had each four children; I was a visitor from Bitlis.

Between the Devil and the Deep Sea.

During the mobilization of the fall and winter the Armenians had been ruthlessly plundered under the name of requisitioning; rich men were ruined and the poor stripped. Armenian soldiers in the Turkish army were neglected, half starved, set to digging trenches and doing the menial work; but, worst of all, they were deprived of their arms and thus left at the mercy of their fanatical, age-long enemies, their Moslem fellow-soldiers. Small wonder that those who could find a loophole of escape or could pay for exemption from military duty did so; many of those who could do neither simply would not give themselves up. We felt that a day of reckoning would soon come—a collision between these opposing forces or a holy war. But the revolutionists conducted themselves with remarkable restraint and prudence; controlled their hot-headed youth; patrolled the streets to prevent skirmishes; and bade the villagers endure in silence—better a village or two burned unavenged than that any attempt at reprisals should furnish an excuse for massacre.

For some time after Djevdet Bey, a brother-in-law of Enver Pasha, minister of war, became Governor General of Van Vilayet, he was absent from the city fighting at the border. When he returned in the early spring, everyone felt there would soon be "something doing." There was. He demanded from the Armenians 3,000 soldiers. So anxious were they to keep the peace that they promised to accede to this demand. But at this juncture trouble broke out between Armenians and Turks in the Shadakh region, and Djevdet Bey requested Ishkhan to go there as peace commissioner, accompanied by three other notable revolutionists. On their way there he had all four treacherously murdered. This was Friday, the 16th April. He then summoned Vremyan to him under the pretence of consulting with this leader, arrested him and sent him off to Constantinople.

The revolutionists now felt that they could not trust Djevdet Bey, the Vali, in any way and that therefore they could not give him the 3,000 men. They told him they would give 400 and pay by degrees the exemption tax for the rest. He would not accept the compromise. The Armenians begged Dr. Ussher and Mr. Yarrow to see Djevdet Bey and try to mollify him. The Vali was obdurate. He "must be obeyed." He would put down this "rebellion" at all costs. He would first punish Shadakh, then attend to Van, but if the rebels fired one shot meanwhile he would put to death every man, woman and child of the Christians.

The fact cannot be too strongly emphasized that there was no "rebellion." As already pointed out, the revolutionists meant to keep the peace if it lay in their power to do so. But for some time past a line of Turkish entrenchments had been secretly drawn round the Armenian quarter of the Gardens. The revolutionists, determined to sell their lives as dearly as possible, prepared a defensive line of entrenchments.

Djevdet Bey said he wished to send a guard of fifty soldiers to the American premises. This guard must be accepted or a written statement given him by the Americans to the effect that it had been offered and refused, so that he should be absolved from all responsibility for our safety. He wished for an immediate answer, but at last consented to wait till Sunday noon.

Our Armenian friends, most of them, agreed that the guard must be accepted. But the revolutionists declared that such a force in so central a location menaced the safety of the Armenian forces and that they would never permit it to reach our premises alive. We might have a guard of five. But Djevdet Bey would give us fifty or none. Truly we were between the devil and the deep sea, for, if both revolutionists and Vali kept their word, we should be the occasion for the outbreak of trouble, if the guard were sent; if it were not sent, we should have no official assurance of safety for the thousands who were already preparing to take refuge on our premises. We should be blamed for an unhappy outcome either way. On Monday, when Dr. Ussher saw the Vali again, he seemed to be wavering and asked if he should send the guard. Dr. Ussher left the decision with him, but added that the sending of such a force might precipitate trouble. It was never sent.

Meanwhile Djevdet Bey had asked Miss McLaren and Schwester Martha, who had been nursing in the Turkish military hospital all winter, to continue their work there, and they had consented.

War! "Ishim Yok, Keifim Tchok."

On Tuesday, the 20th April, at 6 a.m., some Turkish soldiers tried to seize one of a band of village women on their way to the city. She fled. Two Armenian soldiers came up and asked the Turks what they were doing. The Turkish soldiers fired on the Armenians, killing them. Thereupon the Turkish entrenchments opened fire. The siege had begun. There was a steady rifle firing all day, and from the walled city, now cut off from communication with the Gardens, was heard a continuous cannonading from Castle Rock upon the houses below. In the evening, houses were seen burning in every direction.

All the Armenians in the Gardens—nearly 30,000, as the Armenian population of the walled city is small—were now gathered into a district about a mile square, protected by eighty "teerks" (manned and barricaded houses) besides walls and trenches. The Armenian force consisted of 1,500 trained riflemen possessing only about 300 rifles. Their supply of ammunition was not great, so they were very sparing of it; used pistols only, when they could, and employed all sorts of devices to draw the fire of the enemy and waste their ammunition. They began to make bullets and cartridges, turning out 2,000 a day; also gunpowder, and after awhile they made three mortars for throwing bombs. The supply of material for the manufacture of these things was limited, and methods and implements were crude and primitive, but they were very happy and hopeful and exultant over their ability to keep the enemy at bay. Some of the rules for their men were: Keep clean; do not drink; tell the truth; do not curse the religion of the enemy. They sent a manifesto to the Turks to the effect that their quarrel was with one man and not with their Turkish neighbours. Valis might come and go, but the two races must continue to live together, and they hoped that after Djevdet went there might be peaceful and friendly relations between them. The Turks answered in the same spirit, saying that they were forced to fight. Indeed, a protest against this war was signed by many prominent Turks, but Djevdet would pay no attention to it.

The Armenians took and burned (the inmates, however, escaping) the barracks north of our premises, but apart from this they did not attempt the offensive to any extent—their numbers were too few. They were fighting for their homes, their very lives, and our sympathies could not but be wholly on their side, though we strove to keep our actions neutral. We allowed no armed men to enter the premises, and their leader, Aram, in order to help us to preserve the neutrality of our premises, forbade the bringing of wounded soldiers to our hospital, though Dr. Ussher treated them at their own temporary hospital. But Djevdet Bey wrote to Dr. Ussher on the 23rd that armed men had been seen entering our premises and that the rebels had prepared entrenchments near us. If, at the time of attack, one shot were fired from these entrenchments, he would be "regretfully compelled" to turn his cannon upon our premises and completely destroy them. We might know this for a surety. We answered that we were preserving the neutrality of our premises by every means in our power. By no law could we be held responsible for the actions of individuals or organisations outside our premises.

Our correspondence with the Vali was carried on through our official representative, Signor Sbordone, the Italian consular agent, and our postman was an old woman bearing a flag of truce. On her second journey she fell into a ditch and, rising without her white flag, was instantly shot dead by Turkish soldiers. Another was found, but she was wounded while sitting at the door of her shack on our premises. Then Aram said that he would permit no further correspondence until the Vali should answer a letter of Sbordone's, in which the latter had told Djevdet that he had no right to expect the Armenians to surrender now, since the campaign had taken on the character of a massacre.

Djevdet would permit no communication with Miss McLaren at the Turkish hospital, and would answer no question of ours concerning her welfare, though after two weeks he wrote to Herr Spörri that she and Schwester Martha were well and comfortable. Dr. Ussher had known the Vali as a boy and had always been on the most friendly terms with him, but in a letter to the Austrian banker who had taken refuge on the German premises, the Vali wrote that one of his officers had taken some Russian prisoners and cannon and that he would cause them to parade in front of "His Majesty Dr. Ussher's fortifications, so that he, who with the rebels was always awaiting the Russians, should see them and be content." This letter ended with the words: "Ishim yok, keifim tchok" ("I have no work and much fun.") While he was having no work and much fun, his soldiers and their wild allies, the Kurds, were sweeping the countryside, massacring men, women, and children and burning their homes. Babies were shot in their mothers' arms, small children were horribly mutilated, women were stripped and beaten. The villages were not prepared for attack; many made no resistance; others resisted until their ammunition gave out. On Sunday, the 25th, the first band of village refugees came to the city. At early dawn we heard them knocking, knocking, knocking at our gate. Dr. Ussher went out in dressing gown and slippers to hear their pitiful tale and send the wounded to the hospital, where he worked over them all day.

THE MISSION'S FIRST-AID TO THE INJURED.

Six thousand people from the Gardens had early removed to our premises with all their worldly possessions, filling church and school buildings and every room that could possibly be spared in the missionary residences. One woman said to Miss Silliman: "What would we do without this place? This is the third massacre during which I have taken refuge here." A large proportion of these people had to be fed, as they had been so poor that they had bought daily from the ovens what bread they had money for, and now that resource was cut off. Housing, sanitation, government, food, relation with the revolutionist forces, were problems that required great tact and executive ability. The Armenians were not able to cope with these problems unaided. They turned to the missionaries for help.

Mr. Yarrow has a splendid gift for organisation. He soon had everything in smoothly running order, with everyone hard at work at what he was best fitted to do. A regular city government for the whole city of thirty thousand inhabitants was organised with mayor, judges, and police—the town had never been so well policed before. Committees were formed to deal with every possible contingency. Grain was sold or contributed to the common fund by those who possessed it, most of whom manifested a generous and self-sacrificing spirit; one man gave all the wheat he possessed except a month's supply for his family. The use of a public oven was secured, bread tickets issued, a soup kitchen opened, and daily rations were given out to those on our premises and those outside who needed food. Miss Rogers and Miss Silliman secured a daily supply of milk, and made some of their schoolgirls boil it and distribute it to babies who needed it, until 190 were being thus fed. The Boy Scouts, whom thirteen year-old Neville Ussher had helped organize in the fall, now did yeoman's service in protecting the buildings against the dangers of fire, keeping the premises clean, carrying wounded on stretchers, reporting the sick, and, during the fourth week, distributing milk and eggs to babies and sick outside the premises.

Our hospital, which had a normal capacity of fifty beds, was made to accommodate one hundred and sixty-seven, beds being borrowed and placed on the floor in every available space. Such of the wounded as could walk or be brought to the hospital came regularly to have their wounds dressed. Many complicated operations were required to repair the mutilations inflicted by an unimaginable brutality and love of torture. Dr. Ussher, as the only physician and surgeon in the besieged city, had not only the care of the patients in his hospital, the treatment of the wounded refugees and of the wounded Armenian soldiers, but his dispensary and out-patients increased to an appalling number. Among the refugees exposure and privation brought in their train scores of cases of pneumonia and dysentery, and an epidemic of measles raged among the children. Miss Silliman took charge of a measles annex, Miss Rogers and Miss Ussher helped in the hospital, where Miss Bond and her Armenian nurses were worked to the limit of their strength, and after a while Mrs. Ussher, aided by Miss Rogers, opened an overflow hospital in an Armenian school-house, cleared of refugees for the purpose. Here it was a struggle to get beds, utensils, helpers, even food enough for the patients. Indeed all this extra medical and surgical work was hampered by insufficient medical and surgical supplies, for the annual shipment had been stalled at Alexandretta.

Dark Days.

At the end of two weeks the people in the walled city managed to send us word that they were holding their own and had taken some of the government buildings, though they were only a handful of fighters and were cannonaded day and night. About 16,000 cannon balls or shrapnel were fired upon them. The old-fashioned balls sunk into the three-feet thick walls of sun-dried brick without doing much harm. In time, of course, the walls would fall in, but they were the walls of upper stories. People took refuge in the lower stories, so only three persons lost their lives from this cause. Some of the "teerks" in the Gardens were also cannonaded without much damage being done. It seemed the enemy was reserving his heavier cannon and his shrapnel till the last. Three cannon balls fell on our premises the first week, one of them on a porch of the Usshers' house. Thirteen persons were wounded by bullets on the premises, one fatally. Our premises were so centrally located that the bullets of the Turks kept whizzing through, entered several rooms, broke the tiles on the roofs, and peppered the outside of the walls. We became so used to the pop-pop-pop of rifles and booming of cannon that we paid little attention to them in the daytime, but the fierce fusillades at night were rather nerve-racking.

A man escaping from Ardjish related the fate of that town, second in size and importance to Van in the vilayet. The kaimakam had called the men of all the guilds together on the 19th April, and, as he had always been friendly to the Armenians, they trusted him. When they had all gathered, he had them mown down by his soldiers.

Many of the village refugees had stopped short of the city at the little village of Shushantz, on a mountain side near the city. Here Aram bade them remain. On the 8th May we saw the place in flames, and Varak Monastery near by, with its priceless ancient manuscripts, also went up in smoke. These villagers now flocked into the city. Djevdet seemed to have altered his tactics. He had women and children driven in by hundreds to help starve the city out. Owing to the mobilisation of the previous fall, the supply of wheat in the Gardens had been very much less than usual to begin with, and now that 10,000 refugees were being given a daily ration, though a ration barely sufficient to sustain life, this supply was rapidly approaching its limit. The ammunition was also giving out. Djevdet could bring in plenty of men and ammunition from other cities. Unless help came from Russia, it was impossible for the city to hold out much longer against him, and the hope of such help seemed very faint. We had no communication with the outside world; a telegram we had prepared to send to our embassy before the siege never left the city; the revolutionists were constantly sending out appeals for help to the Russo-Armenian volunteers on the border, but no word or sign of their reaching their destination was received by us. At the very last, when the Turks should come to close quarters, we knew that all the population of the besieged city would crowd into our premises as a last hope. But, enraged as Djevdet was by this unexpected and prolonged resistance, was it to be hoped that he could be persuaded to spare the lives of one of these men, women and children? We believed not. He might offer the Americans personal safety if we would leave the premises, but this, of course, we would not do; we would share the fate of our people. And it seemed not at all improbable that he would not even offer us safety, believing, as he seemed to believe, that we were aiding and upholding the "rebels."

Those were dark days indeed. Our little American circle came together two evenings in the week to discuss the problems constantly arising. We would joke and laugh over some aspects of our situation, but as we listened to the volley firing only two blocks away, we knew that at any hour the heroic but weakening defence might be overpowered; knew that then hell would be let loose in the crowded city and our crowded compound; knew that we should witness unspeakable atrocities perpetrated on the persons of those we loved, and probably suffer them in our own persons. And we would sing:

"Peace, perfect peace; the future all unknown!

Jesus we know and He is on the throne,"

and pray to the God who was able to deliver us out of the very mouth of the lion.

On Saturday forenoon a rift seemed to appear in the clouds, for many ships were seen on the lake, sailing away from Van, and we heard that they contained Turkish women and children. We became a "city all gone up to the housetops," wondering and surmising. Once before such a flight had taken place, when the Russians had advanced as far as Sarai. They had retreated, however, and the Turkish families had returned.

That afternoon the sky darkened again. Cannon at the Big Barracks on the plain began to fire in our direction. At first we could not believe that the shots were aimed at our flag, but no doubt was permitted us on that point. Seven shells fell on the premises, one on the roof of Miss Rogers' and Miss Silliman's house, making a big hole in it; two others did the same thing on the boys'-school and girls'-school roofs. On Sunday morning the bombardment began again. Twenty-six shells fell on the premises before noon.

When the heavy firing began Dr. Ussher was visiting patients outside and Mrs. Ussher was also away from home at her overflow hospital, so I ran over from our own hospital to take their children to the safest part of the house, a narrow hall on the first-floor. There we listened to the shrieking of the shrapnel and awaited the bursting of each shell. A deafening explosion shook the house. I ran up to my room to find it so full of dust and smoke that I could not see a foot before me. A shell had come through the three-feet-thick outside wall, burst, scattering its contained bullets, and its cap had passed through a partition wall into the next room and broken a door opposite. A shell entered a room in Mrs. Raynold's house, killing a little Armenian girl. Ten more shells fell in the afternoon. Djevdet was fulfilling his threat of bombarding our premises, and this proved to us that we could hope for no mercy at his hands when he should take the city.[29]

DELIVERANCE.

In this darkest hour of all came deliverance. A lull followed the cannonading. Then at sunset a letter came from the occupants of the only Armenian house within the Turkish lines which had been spared (this because Djevdet had lived in it when a boy) which gave the information that the Turks had left the city. The barracks on the summit and at the foot of Toprak-Kala were found to contain so small a guard that it was easily overpowered, and these buildings were burned amidst the wildest excitement. So with all the Turkish "teerks," which were visited in turn. The Big Barracks was next seen to disgorge its garrison, a large company of horsemen who rode away over the hills, and that building, too, was burned after midnight. Large stores of wheat and ammunition were found. It all reminded one of the seventh chapter of II. Kings.

The whole city was awake, singing and rejoicing all night. In the morning its inhabitants could go whither they would unafraid. And now came the first check to our rejoicing. Miss McLaren was gone! She and Schwester Martha had been sent with the patients of the Turkish hospital four days before to Bitlis.

Mr. Yarrow went to the hospital. He found there twenty-five wounded soldiers too sick to travel, left there without food or water for five days. He found unburied dead. He stayed all day in the horrible place, that his presence might protect the terrified creatures until he could secure their removal to our hospital.

On Wednesday, the 19th May, the Russians and Russo-Armenian volunteers came into the city. It had been the knowledge of their approach that had caused the Turks to flee. Some hard fighting had to be done in the villages, however, before Djevdet and his reinforcements were driven out of the province. Troops poured into the city from Russia and Persia and passed on towards Bitlis.

Aram was made temporary governor of the province, and, for the first time for centuries, Armenians were given a chance to govern themselves. Business revived. People began to rebuild their burned houses and shops. We re-opened our mission schools, except the school in the walled city, the school-house there having been burned.

The Tables Turned.

Not all the Turks had fled from the city. Some old men and women and children had stayed behind, many of them in hiding. The Armenian soldiers, unlike Turks, were not making war on such. There was only one place where the captives could be safe from the rabble, however. In their dilemma the Armenians turned, as usual, to the American missionaries. And so it came to pass that hardly had the six thousand Armenian refugees left our premises when the care of a thousand Turkish refugees was thrust upon us, some of them from villages the Russo-Armenian volunteers were "cleaning out."

It was with the greatest difficulty that food could be procured for these people. The city had an army to feed now. Wheat—the stores left by the Turks—was obtainable, but no flour, and the use of a mill was not available for some time. The missionaries had no help in a task so distasteful to the Armenians except that of two or three of the teachers of the school in the walled city, who now had no other work. Mr. Yarrow was obliged to drop most of his other duties and spend practically all his time working for our protégés. Mrs. Yarrow, Miss Rogers and Miss Silliman administered medicines and tried to give every one of the poor creatures a bath. Mrs. Ussher had bedding made, and secured and personally dispensed milk to the children and sick, spending several hours daily among them.

The wild Cossacks considered the Turkish women legitimate prey, and though the Russian General gave us a small guard, there was seldom a night during the first two or three weeks in which Dr. Ussher and Mr. Yarrow did not have to drive off marauders who had climbed over the walls of the compound and eluded the guard.

The effect on its followers of the religion of Islam was never more strongly contrasted with Christianity. While the Armenian refugees had been mutually helpful and self-sacrificing, these Moslems showed themselves absolutely selfish, callous and indifferent to each other's suffering. Where the Armenians had been cheery and hopeful, and had clung to life with wonderful vitality, the Moslems, with no faith in God and no hope of a future life, bereft now of hope in this life, died like flies of the prevailing dysentery from lack of stamina and the will to live.

The situation became intolerable. The missionaries begged the Russian General to send these people out to villages, with a guard sufficient for safety and flocks to maintain them until they could begin to get their living from the soil. He was too much occupied with other matters to attend to us.

After six weeks of this, Countess Alexandra Tolstoi (daughter of the famous novelist) came to Van and took off our hands the care of our "guests," though they remained on our premises. She was a young woman, simple, sensible, and lovable. We gave her a surprise party on her birthday, carrying her the traditional cake with candles and crowning her with flowers, and she declared she had never had a birthday so delightfully celebrated in all her life. She worked hard for her charges. When her funds gave out and no more were forthcoming and her Russian helpers fell ill, she succeeded where we had failed and induced the General to send the Turks out into the country with provision for their safety and sustenance.

The Pestilence that Walketh in Darkness.

Our Turkish refugees cost us a fearful price.

The last day of June Mrs. Ussher took her children, who had whooping cough, out of the pestilential atmosphere of the city to Artamid, the summer home on Lake Van, nine miles away. Dr. Ussher went there for the week-end, desperately in need of a little rest. On Saturday night they both became very ill. Upon hearing of this I went down to take care of them. On Monday Mr. and Mrs. Yarrow also fell ill. Ten days yet remained till the time set for closing the hospital for the summer, but Miss Bond set her nurses to the task of sending the patients away and went over to nurse the Yarrows. This left me without help for five days. Then, for four days more, two Armenian nurses cared for the sick ones at night and an untrained man nurse helped me during the daytime. Miss Rogers had come down on Thursday, the day after commencement, for the cure of what she believed to be an attack of malaria. On Friday she too fell ill. Fortunately, there was at last a really good Russian physician in town, and he was most faithful in his attendance. The sickness proved to be typhus. Later we learned that at about the same time Miss Silliman, who had left for America on her furlough on the 15th June, accompanied by Neville Ussher, had been ill at Tiflis with what we now know was a mild form of the same disease. Dr. Ussher might have contracted it from his outside patients, but the others undoubtedly contracted it from the Turkish refugees.

Mrs. Yarrow was dangerously ill, but passed her crisis safely and first of all. Miss Bond then came to Artamid, though Mr. Yarrow was still very ill, feeling that the Usshers needed her more on account of their distance from the doctor. Miss Ussher took charge of the Yarrow children up in Van; Mrs. Raynolds managed the business affairs of the mission.

Mrs. Ussher had a very severe form of the disease, and her delicate frame, worn out with the overwork and terrible strain of the months past, could make no resistance. On the 14th July she entered into the life eternal.

We dared not let the sick ones suspect what had happened. Dr. Ussher was too ill at the time and for more than two weeks longer to be told of his terrible loss. For three months preceding his illness he had been the only physician in Van, and the strain of over-work and sleeplessness told severely now. After he had passed his typhus crisis, his life was in danger for a week longer from the pneumonia which had been a complication from the first. Then followed another not infrequent complication of typhus, an abscess in the parotid gland which caused long-continued weakness and suffering, at one time threatened life and reason, and has had serious consequences which may prove permanent. Mr. Yarrow was so ill that his life was quite despaired of. It was by a veritable miracle that he was restored to us.

FLIGHT.

Meanwhile the Russian army had been slowly advancing westward. It had not been uniformly successful as we had expected it to be. Indeed, the Russians seemed to fight sluggishly and unenthusiastically. The Russo-Armenian volunteers, who were always sent ahead of the main army, did the heavy fighting. By the last week of July the Russians had not yet taken Bitlis, only ninety miles distant from Van. Suddenly the Turkish army began to advance towards Van, and the Russian army to retreat.

On Friday, the 30th July, General Nicolaieff ordered all the Armenians of the Van province, also the Americans and other foreigners, to flee for their lives. By Saturday night the city was nearly emptied of Armenians and quite emptied of conveyances. Nearly all our teachers, nurses, employees had left. It was every man for himself and no one to help us secure carriages or horses for our own flight. We at Artamid, with a sick man to provide for, would have had great difficulty in getting up to the city in time, had not Mrs. Yarrow risen from her sick-bed to go to the General and beg him to send us ambulances. These reached us after midnight.

There was little question in our minds as to our own flight. Our experience during the siege had shown us that the fact of our being Americans would not protect us from the Turks. Had not our two men, Mr. Yarrow and Dr. Ussher, been absolutely helpless we might have debated the matter. As it was, we women could not assume the responsibility of staying and keeping them there, and even if we had stayed we could have found no means to live in a deserted city.

We were fifteen Americans and had ten Armenian dependents—women and children—to provide for. The head nurse of the hospital, Garabed, plucky and loyal little fellow that he was, had sent on his mother and wife and had remained behind to help us get out of the country. Dr. Ussher's man-cook, having been with us at Artamid when the panic began, had been unable to secure conveyance for his sick wife. We greatly needed his help on the journey, but this involved our providing for a third sick person. We had three horses, an American grocer's delivery cart, really not strong enough for heavy work on rough and mountainous roads, and a small cart that would seat three. Our two other carts were not usable.

We begged the General to give us ambulances. He absolutely refused—he had none to spare. But, he added, he was to be replaced in a day or two by General Trokin; we could appeal to him when he came; the danger was not immediate. Somewhat reassured and not knowing how we could manage without help from the Russians, we made no effort to leave that day. But the next day, Monday, we heard that the volunteers who were trying to keep the road open to Russia would not be able to do so much longer—there was no time to lose. We set to work.

One of our teachers who had not succeeded in getting away before Monday morning, kindly took a small bag of clothing on his ox-cart for each of us. We spread the quilts and blankets we should need on the way on the bottom of the delivery cart, intending to lay our three sick people on these. Garabed, who had never driven a team in his life, must drive two of our horses in this cart. Mrs. Raynolds would drive the third horse harnessed to the small cart, and take the babies and what food there was possibly room for; no provisions could be bought on the way. The rest of us must walk, though Mrs. Yarrow and Miss Rogers were newly risen from a sick bed and the children were all under twelve. We put loads on the cows we must take with us for the sake of the babies and the patients. But the cows were refractory; they kicked off the loads and ran wildly about the yard, tails up, heads down, whereupon the single horse broke loose and "also ran," smashing the small cart.

At this moment, the "psychological moment," two doctors of the Russian Red Cross rode into our yard. Seeing our plight they turned and rode out again. They returned a little later and on *their own responsibility* promised to take us with the Red Cross caravan. Thank the Lord!

We now put our loads on the delivery cart; put the wheels of the smashed cart on the body of a wheelless cart, and now that we might take a little more with us than food and bedding, packed in bags what we felt to be absolutely necessary. What we left behind we should never see again; we felt certain that the Russian soldiers before they left would loot our houses and perhaps burn them to forestall the Turks.

The Red Cross provided us with two ambulances with horses and drivers, and a stretcher carried between two horses for Dr. Ussher. He was usually taken into one of their sick tents when we camped at night; most of the rest of us slept on the ground in the open.

We left on Tuesday, the 3rd August. The Russians appeared to have received news that made them very uneasy, and, indeed, General Trokin himself left Van that very afternoon, as we learned later. The next day at sundown we heard the firing between the Kurds and the volunteers who were so gallantly trying to keep them at bay, to keep the road to Russia open as long as possible. It sounded startlingly near. We travelled till two a.m. that night in order to reach Bergri, where we should be, not safe, but beyond the line along which the Turks would try to intercept travellers. We were just in time. General Trokin's party, that had left Van only a few hours later than we, were unable to reach Bergri, and had to return and get out by the longer route through Persia. Had we with our slower rate of travel been obliged to do this, we might not have been able to get out at all.

The Arrow that Flieth by Day.

That afternoon—Thursday afternoon—we forded a wide and deep river, then entered a narrow valley, from the mountains commanding which Kurds suddenly began to fire down on the Red Cross caravan and the thousands of foot travellers. One man in an ambulance was killed, others wounded. The drivers of ambulances and litters whipped up their horses to a mad gallop. It was a race for life. The sight of those gasping, terror-stricken thousands was one never to be forgotten. The teacher who had taken our bags of clothing threw everything off his ox-cart in order to escape with his life. The Armenians on our long wagon threw off much of the luggage to lighten it, and thus we lost most of what we had brought with us.

Once out of the valley we were comparatively safe. We met a force of volunteers and Cossacks who entered the valley to engage with the Kurds. Mrs. Raynolds had been riding in the small cart. After the danger was over, while getting out of the cart, she fell and broke her leg below the knee. The Red Cross physicians set it at once, but she suffered greatly during the remainder of the journey over the rough roads, though lying at full length in one of our ambulances. She was quite helpless. Mr. Yarrow lay, too, in his ambulance, which he was unable to leave day or night during the journey, except when he was carried into a Red Cross tent on Sunday.

On Friday all but the four helpless ones and the babies walked over Mt. Taparez. On Saturday we again climbed on foot a high mountain, from sundown till three o'clock the next morning. The caravan rested on Sunday at a Red Cross camp near the top of Tchingli Mt. at the foot of Mt. Ararat. Here Dr. Ussher had two severe operations on his face without anæsthetics. On Monday at sunset we reached Igdir. Dr. Ussher was taken to a military hospital for officers, and the military sent him on to Tiflis on Thursday. We could not secure carriages until Wednesday morning to take us to the railway station at Etchmiadzin. We arrived in Tiflis the next morning.

Safe!—But Sorrowing.

Most of us had lost nearly everything but the clothes we stood in, and these we had worn day and night during the ten days' journey. Small wonder that the first hotel we went to had "no rooms." Mr. Smith, the American Consul, was most kind and did everything he could for us. He secured a room in a private hospital for Mrs. Raynolds and a bed in the city hospital for Dr. Ussher.

Dr. Ussher was again brought to death's door by very severe dysentery contracted on the road. He had become a nervous and physical wreck and in appearance the ghost of himself.

Dysentery was epidemic among the scores of thousands of refugees from Van Province who had crowded into Transcaucasia. The very air seemed poisoned; our children were all ill, and it seemed to us that they would not get well until we could leave Tiflis.

Mrs. Raynolds' broken bone refused to knit. She seemed also to be suffering from a collapse of her whole system. She would lie there patient, indifferent to what was going on about her, sunk in memories of the past, perhaps—who can say?

On the 24th August we were astounded at receiving a telegram from Dr. Raynolds. We had not heard of his leaving America and here he was at Petrograd! It seems he had started for Van as soon as he had heard of the Russian occupation, in company with Mr. Henry White, who was to teach in our college. At Petrograd he learned from the ambassador that the Van missionaries were in Tiflis, but of the reason therefor he had heard not a word, nor had he heard of his wife's condition.

Mrs. Raynolds brightened for a moment when told that her husband was on the way to her. Then the things of earth seemed to slip away from her; she might not tarry even for the dear one's coming. On Friday, the 27th August, her tired spirit found rest. Two days later Dr. Raynolds arrived to find wife gone, house gone, the work of his lifetime seemingly in ruins, the people he had loved exiles and destitute.

On Tuesday Mrs. Raynolds was laid to rest in the German Lutheran cemetery, and around her were gathered many of those whom she had lived to serve.

Then Dr. Raynolds and Mr. White decided that there was nothing left for them to do but return with us to America, and we left that week for Petrograd. There the American managers of what corresponds to our Y.M.C.A. were exceedingly kind and helpful. The city was so full of refugees from Poland that we had to sleep on tables in the Association halls the first night, but succeeded in securing rooms the next day. The children recovered, and Dr. Ussher's improvement in health from the time of our arrival in Petrograd was simply wonderful. Mr. Yarrow seemed now quite himself again, although in reality he had not fully regained his strength.

Travelling up by rail round the Gulf of Bothnia, we spent a few days in Stockholm and sailed from Christiania on the 24th September, on the Danish ship "Hellig Olav."

We had had absolutely no news from any station in Turkey since the middle of April, and from America only what information Dr. Raynolds had brought us. On our arrival in New York, on the 5th October, we heard of the massacre of the Armenians in Bitlis by Djevdet Bey as soon as he had reached there after having been driven from Van. We heard of Miss Ely's death there in July, and of my brother's death, on the 10th August, in Diyarbekir[30]; we heard that Miss McLaren was ill with typhus in Bitlis, and later that she was well; we learned of the massacre of Armenians all over Turkey and of their deportation. The Van refugees have been fortunate by comparison in that they could flee. Money for their relief has been sent to Transcaucasia; a few of them have succeeded in securing passports and getting to America.

---

29. *The shelling of the mission buildings is also described by Mr. Yarrow, in an interview published in the New York "Times" 6th October, 1915, the day after his arrival in America:—*

"For twenty-seven days 1,500 determined Armenians held Van against 5,000 Turks and Kurds, and for the last three days they were shelled with shrapnel from a howitzer brought up by a Turkish company headed by a German officer. I myself saw him directing the fire of the gun.

"Two days before the Russians came to Van, the Turks deliberately fired at the mission buildings. They stood out prominently and could not be mistaken, and also flew five American flags and one Red Cross flag as a protection. The firing was so accurate that the shots cut the signal halyards and brought the flags to the ground."

30. See Doc. 23, page 89.

16. VAN: LETTER DATED VAN, 7th JUNE, 1915, FROM MR. Y.K. RUSHDOUNI; PUBLISHED IN THE "MANCHESTER GUARDIAN," 2nd AUGUST, 1915.

The day after Germany's declaration of war on Russia, martial law was proclaimed in Van, and the Turkish Government set about the work of mobilisation. The Armenians responded to the call in a better mood than the Moslems, many of whom either ran away or did not present themselves for service. But from the very beginning the authorities adopted a harsh attitude towards the Armenians in the Vilayet. Under the pretence of requisitioning, they ruthlessly plundered and looted the Armenians. Business was brought to an absolute standstill, and the import and sale of wheat in the city was forbidden on the plea that it was needed to provision the armies—though ways and means were always found if the applicant was a Moslem. As for the Armenian soldiers in the Turkish army, they were neglected, half-starved, set to do all the menial work, and, worst of all, disarmed and left over to the mercies of their Moslem comrades, who managed to kill a few hundreds altogether in various parts. It became evident that the Government was bent on the systematic destruction of the Armenian population. A feeling of despondency seized hold of all.

When Turkey went into the war the distress of the people reached an even higher pitch, especially when the Government armed all the males of the Moslem population between the ages of 15 and 60 and gave up Christian villages to fire and sword at the slightest pretext. Pelou, the largest village of the Kavash district, was reduced to a heap of ruins. Twelve villages in the Gargar district, on the Persian frontier, Bashkala, and Sarai, with the Nestorian and Armenian villages round, were ruthlessly wiped out after the Russian retreat[31], and of their population only a few old crippled women were left as survivors. News of this sort was constantly being brought to the town by refugees from distant places like Boghaz-Kessen, Hazaren, Nordoz, &c. This pouring in of the refugees aggravated the problem of living in the city of Van.

On the other hand, the three leaders of the former Revolutionary Party called Dashnagists, who since the proclamation of the Constitution had been changed into a political party and had come to an understanding with the Young Turks, exhorted the people to endure in silence. Better, they said, that some villages be burned and destroyed unavenged than give the slightest pretext to the Moslems for a general massacre. One of the first villages to defend itself was Bairak, whose inhabitants succeeded in keeping the soldiers and Kurdish mob from entering the village. The Turkish Government sent a peace commission composed of Armenians and Turks to quiet down matters there, which was done. At the same time a message was sent to the Governor-General, Djevdet Bey, a brother-in-law of Enver Pasha, then on the border, to come to Van. Djevdet Bey, on his arrival, demanded 4,000[32] soldiers from the Armenians. The Armenians were so anxious to keep the peace that they promised to accede to this demand under an altered form approved by the Government. But at this juncture trouble broke out between Armenians and Turks in the Shadakh region. Some say that this was started at the instigation of Djevdet Bey. This Governor had requested Ishkan, one of the three Dashnagist leaders, to go there as peace commissioner, accompanied by three other notable Armenians. On their way there, however, on Friday, the 16th April, all four were treacherously murdered.

The Armenians now felt that they could not trust the Governor, and, instead of giving him the 4,000 men, they told him they would give 400 and pay the exemption tax for the rest, in instalments. In the meantime they asked the American missionaries, Dr. Ussher and Mr. Yarrow, and the Italian agent Signor Sbordone, to try to mollify the Governor. The attitude of the Governor was wavering. At times he would be moderate and swear that peace would be kept. At other times he was harsh and irreconcilable, declaring that he intended to put down "rebellion" at all costs. First he would punish Shadakh, then he would attend to Van; if the rebels fired one shot it would be a signal for him to attack, and neither Turks nor Armenians would be left in the Vilayet.[33]

Things continued in this suspense till the 20th[34] April, when some Turkish soldiers tried to seize some village women on their way to the city. The women fled. Two Armenians came up and asked the Turks what they were doing. The Turkish soldiers fired on the Armenians and killed them. This served as a signal. The booming of cannons and rattle of rifles began from every side, and it was realised that the Armenian quarter was besieged. In the evening houses in the Armenian quarter could be seen burning in every direction. The Governor-General had sworn that not a single house should be left in Van, except the one where his father had lived as Governor-General. Under the command of Armenag Yegarian, of the Ramgavar Party, the Armenians, nearly 30,000 in number now, began to man and barricade houses and open trenches. Eighty such barricaded positions, called in Armenian "teerks," were held by the Armenians, and the enclosed area of about two square miles was gradually connected in between by deep trenches. To assure regularity, a Provisional Government was set up, and a military court was appointed to deal with military affairs. Everyone capable of doing something, male or female, young or old, was set to work. Women and girls were busy cooking, mending, sewing, making bedding for homeless refugees and soldiers, and nursing wounded people and motherless children. About 1,300[35] young men were under arms day and night trying to hold the enemy at bay. Lads were employed as messengers between the "teerks." The rest of the men were used as workmen to dig trenches and build new walls and barricades, as the old ones crumbled before the cannon-fire. About 16,000 cannon-shots were fired at the handful of inhabitants in the old city under the Castle Rock.

After some days, refugees began to pour in from near and far.[36] The Government had not succeeded in besieging the eastern side of the Armenian quarter, and it was still possible to enter the city. On the 16th May no less than 12,000 bread-tickets were issued to refugees. At the same time, owing to privation and exposure, an epidemic of measles broke out among the children, and dysentery and pneumonia among the adults, and many who had escaped the sword of the Moslem fell victims to disease.

As the supply of ammunition was very meagre and the intention of the Armenians was to prolong their defence till help might come from Armenian volunteers, they were very sparing in its use. They used pistols when they could, and employed all kinds of devices to draw the fire of the enemy and waste his ammunition. At the same time they began to devise means of making bullets and cartridges, and manufacturing smokeless gunpowder and bombs, and succeeded in turning out daily 4,000[37] cartridges, and even in making three mortars for throwing bombs and bursting shells. In the meantime the Provisional Government issued strict orders for keeping the neutrality of foreign institutions and premises, forbidding armed men to pass through these parts or carry the wounded Armenian soldiers to the American Mission Hospital. A manifesto was also sent to the Turks to the effect that the quarrel was with one man, Djevdet Bey, not with their Turkish neighbours. Governors come and go, but the two races must continue to live together. Gradually, however, the Armenians succeeded in ousting the Turks from their positions. On the 17th May, after nearly four weeks' resistance, it became obvious that the enemy was putting forward his last efforts.

At sunset a daring dash put to flight the remaining Turkish soldiers in the two northern barracks on Toprak-Kalé Hill and below. These two barracks were at once burnt. About midnight another attack put the southern great barracks in Armenian hands, and these, too, were set on fire. Towards morning the news spread that the Turks and soldiers had left the city. It was understood that the Government, on hearing of the approach of the Russian army and the Armenian volunteers, had ordered a systematic retreat some days before, and the last regiment, with the Governor, had evacuated the town on the night of the 18th May. Immediately hungry and starved people rushed toward the Turkish quarters to satisfy their feelings of justice by plundering and burning. Shortly after, news came that the Russian army, with Armenian volunteers, was in sight. The joy of the people was boundless; tears of gladness and of emotion for what they had suffered during the past month, rolled down their cheeks as they made them welcome. The keys of the captured city and of the castle were immediately taken and laid at the feet of the Russian General, who gave orders to the Armenians to organise a Provisional Government for the affairs of the town.

---

31. The Russians had made a preliminary incursion over the border after the Turkish declaration of war.—*Editor.*

32. Miss Knapp gives the number as 3,000 (Doc. 15.

33. *Miss Knapp makes the following observation at this point:*—

"The fact cannot be too strongly emphasised that there was no 'rebellion.' As already pointed out, the Revolutionists meant to keep the peace if it lay in their power to do so. But for some time past a line of Turkish entrenchments had been secretly drawn round the Armenian quarter of the Gardens. The Revolutionists, determined to sell their lives as dearly as possible, prepared a defensive line of entrenchments."

34. At 6.0 a.m. (Miss Knapp).

35. "About 1,500 trained riflemen possessing only about 300 rifles." (Miss Knapp).

36. "A man escaping from Ardjish related the fate of that town, second in size and importance to Van in the Vilayet. The Kaimakam had called the men of all the guilds together on the 19th April, and as he had always been friendly to the Armenians they trusted him. When they had all gathered, he had them mown down by his soldiers. Many of the village refugees had stopped short of the city, at the little village of Shushantz, on the mountain side near the city. Here Aram bade them remain. On the 8th May, we saw the place in flames, and Varak Monastery near by, with its priceless ancient manuscripts, also went up in smoke. These villagers now flocked into the city." (Miss Knapp).

37. 2,000. (Miss Knapp).

17. VAN: NARRATIVE BY MR. Y.K. RUSHDOUNI, PUBLISHED SERIALLY IN THE ARMENIAN JOURNAL "GOTCHNAG," OF NEW YORK.

Van is a city built on a level plain, and has at the present time an area of about ten or twelve square miles.

The Old City is small (scarcely a single square mile in area); its centre is the market place and an ancient rock fortress. The real Van is the Aikesdan (the Vineyards), which rises slowly towards the East on an imposing scale. In Aikesdan each house, with few exceptions, has a vineyard and a garden. Its streets are broad and tree-lined. On each side of these trees run small rivulets, which are bordered by rows of willow and poplar trees. Van is in reality a beautiful, extensive and attractive garden. On its western side, about two or three miles distant, there stretches the beautiful blue lake of Van, surrounded by high, snow-clad mountains, the most prominent of which are Sipan, Nimroud, Kerkour and Azadk.

On the eastern side of Van rise the mountains of Varak, on the slopes of which stand the village of Shoushantz (named after Shoushanig, the daughter of Sennacherib), and also the famous monastery of Varak, with its seven altars, where Khrimean Hairik published his "Ardsouig Vaspouragani" ("The Eagle of Vaspouragan"). On the slopes of these mountains are also found the monasteries of Garmeror and St. Gregory, the chapel of St. Lousavorich (The Illuminator), and Gatnaghpur, Khachaghpur, Salnabad and Abaranchan, fountains of historical fame. There are also the Upper Varak villages—the historic summer resorts of Sultan Yailassi and Keshish Göl.

On the north side of Van there is the ancient and famous Toprak-Kalé (Earthern Fort). Again in the same direction are the villages of Shahbagh and Araless, behind which extends the district of Van-Dosb.

On the southern side of the city, beyond the hills of Artamid, one reaches the Valley of Haig; Vostan, the capital of Rushdounik; and the mountains of Ardosr, with the tomb of Yeghishé on their slopes.

The Armenian and the Turkish quarters in Van were divided, and, except for a few streets, were all at some distance from each other. These two elements in the population had no relations with each other except those of a commercial nature. The Market and the Old City were in the hands of the Armenians, but were surrounded by Turkish quarters. There were Armenian houses which were eight miles away from the market-place, and to go there and back it was necessary to pass through the Turkish quarters. The Armenians covered this distance on foot, horseback or spring-wagons—these being the only means of transportation.

The day after war had been declared by Germany against Russia, Turkey declared a "state of war" in Van, and called all the young men between 21 and 45 to the colours, without distinction of race or religion. For the needs of the Army the Government requisitioned all the goods and provisions in the Market. In some cases they made partial payments, but afterwards they gave promissory notes to all the owners, which were payable after the war. This was a heavy loss to the Armenians, as the whole Market was practically in their hands. They lost all their petroleum, sugar, raisins, soap, copper, European clothing and various other commodities, besides almost half their remaining goods.

Owing to the sudden declaration of war and the requisitioning of the Market, it was impossible for the Armenians to transfer their goods elsewhere or to hide them, especially as the Market was an hour-and-a-half's distance from the Armenian quarters of Aikesdan.

All the tradesmen, shopkeepers, farmers and men of all vocations immediately answered the call to arms. A crowd gathered in front of the Government Building in such a way that it was impossible to keep order. There were some people who waited for three days continuously, from morning till night, and were unable to get a chance to register their names. The Dashnakist party encouraged the Armenians to do their duty faithfully as citizens. Mr. Aram, one of their leaders, collected together 350 to 400 fine young men, and, to the accompaniment of Turkish music, songs and dances, led them to the Government Building to register. The Government officials were considerably surprised at this willingness on the part of the Armenians; they held them up as an example in upbraiding the Turks, and particularly the Kurds, who had answered the call very reluctantly.

The Government treated the Armenians very liberally, exempting all the Gregorian and Protestant teachers of 25 years of age, and allowing them to continue their schools, on the condition that they would all go to the Government Building and register, so that in case of necessity they might be called up as militia for the protection of the City.

During the first two weeks this impartial treatment by the Turkish Government filled the Armenians with gladness and trust, and the Armenian soldiers that had deserted returned and gave themselves up. The only thing which gave rise to anxiety was the financial crisis. Trade and farming had completely stopped. The merchants were robbed, and all the traders were in the hands of the Government. It was the time to prepare for the annual taking of stock, but there were no available means.

Under the pretence of supplying the needs of the Army, the Government confiscated all the provisions. This was the first symptom of injustice and partiality. The understanding was that every man would be entitled to buy a certain amount of food and wood after informing the Government of the number and needs of his family, and after obtaining permission from them, and that every month those families whose men were on active service would receive 30 piastres (5s.) per head.

At this time the Armenians' claims were very often ignored; and because the Government was aware that the Armenians would not, whatever happened, go hungry and without clothing or wood for fuel, it collected from all the Armenian quarters and villages, in the form of a heavy tax, a certain quantity of wheat, wood, sheep, fat, and clothing. In addition the majority of the Armenian and Syrian soldiers were left without arms and clothing, and very often without anything to eat, under the pretence that the clothing and the arms were not yet ready, and that they had no means of transporting food in so short a time. This caused the desertion of many from the Army, and some remained away altogether. Others borrowed money and asked the Government, through influential officials, to be allowed to pay exemption money, and it seems that the Government also was trying to find a means to come to an understanding with the Armenians. It therefore published a special notice announcing that all the non-Moslems above 26 years of age would be exempted from the Army by payment of a special fee. The Armenians sold everything to pay the Government, that they might profit by this occasion. The period of exemption was extended by the Government to the following spring.

It is worth mentioning here that, according to the Turkish officials, there were about the same number of deserters among the Turks and Kurds, but they never paid as much exemption money as the Armenians did.

The Government sided with the Germans even when they were neutral, whereas the Armenians—unfortunately—sympathised with the Allies. But even then no special injustice was done. The Government showed kindness to the Armenians, at least on the surface, while the Governor, Tahsin Pasha, had such close relations with the leaders of the Dashnakist party that people thought he was their special friend. Besides this, it was arranged that two Armenian Members of the Ottoman Parliament who were the representatives of Van, Messrs. Vahan Papazian and Vremyan, should stay with the people to keep them and the Government on good terms with one another.

After the entry of the Turks into the war, however, the situation assumed a different aspect. The Government began to adopt a cold and suspicious attitude towards the Armenians, who had performed their duty towards the Government to the best of their ability, and even after the abolition of the "Capitulations" had joined the Turks in their celebrations of the event. In spite of all this, the coolness between them was very marked, and this became especially apparent after it was found that the Armenians had supplied volunteers to the Russians, and that they were the very troops who had occupied Bayazid. It was then reported that all the Kurdish tribes had gone over to the side of the Russians and had caused great prejudice to the Turks. This terrified the Turks to such a degree that many rich women went to the American missionary ladies of Van to ask their protection, saying: "We are not afraid of the Russians as much as we are of the Kurds." But the unfortunate part was that, in Government circles, the dominant topic of conversation was the Armenian Volunteers.

It was before this that Tahsin Bey summoned the heads of the Dashnakists (the heads of the Hunchakists were already in prison) and pointed out to them that the Armenians had begun a volunteer movement, and that this movement would be dangerous to them; and afterwards in a special letter he suggested to them, and especially to Mr. Vremyan, that they should write to the heads of the Dashnakists of Bayazid and stop this movement. This letter was sent to Mr. Toros, the head of the Dashnakists of Ardjish, but Mr. Toros was killed by a Turkish gendarme. At the same time it was stated that the Turkish Government had made special overtures to the Dashnakists and proposed that they should form bands of chettis composed of Turks and Armenians and raid Caucasia, but I do not know how it happened that this was refused by the Armenians[38].

A short time after the Turks intervened in the war, all the Armenians in the Turkish Army were disarmed and employed as ordinary labourers. The arms of the Armenian gendarmes in the local districts were taken and given to the Turks, while the latter were left free on the understanding that they would be called up, though this never actually took place. This general disarming filled the Armenians with fear and suspicion. Those of the disarmed Armenians who found means of escape, deserted, and some whom I knew personally were sent back by the officials.

Turkey had not yet declared war, but she was mobilising her forces, when the members of the Armenian Reform Committee came to Van with M. Hoff, the Inspector-General. The Government did not carry out the plan, which was prepared and announced to the Armenians, for receiving the Inspector-General and his party with pomp and ceremony, but they sent them to the beautiful little village of Artamid on the southern side of the city, situated on the shore of Lake Van. After they had stayed there a few days they were sent back again, carrying with them the scheme of Armenian Reforms.

Shortly after Turkey had declared war, Tahsin Pasha was called to Erzeroum, and in his place Djevdet Bey, the brother-in-law of Enver Pasha, was selected as Governor for Van.

About the end of the autumn, when the Russian Army had annihilated the Turkish Army on the Persian border, had taken Bashkalé and Sarai, and was moving towards Van, there was a violent panic among the Turkish officers and general public. Many of the officers sold their property and transferred their families by boats to Bitlis. Other prominent families, like the Hamoud-oglou—who had done great harm to the Armenians—took the same course. Among the rank and file those that were afraid addressed themselves to the Armenians, who received them very kindly. The object of the Armenians was to teach some dangerous officers a good lesson, but they had no intention whatever of harming the innocent officers and the Turkish public.

I met many who said very plainly: "Here is a good opportunity for us to show our Turkish compatriots and neighbours that we Armenians never harboured any bad intentions towards them, but had always demanded simply a state of equality, which would be beneficial to all who wished to live a peaceful life."

At the time when the Turkish army was annihilated on the Persian border, and there was not even the militia in Van and less than 400 gendarmes between Van and Bitlis, it would have been very easy for the Armenians to occupy the greater part of the provinces of Van and Moush, if they had wanted to revolt and massacre the Turks (who were in fear of their lives) or do what the Turks had done in the past to the "Giaours" ("Infidels").

The Government knew this, and for this reason treated the Armenians very flatteringly. The Armenian people was thankful to be able to live without fear and to have friendly and sincere relations with their Turkish neighbours. The Dashnakist Party also, who had been in close touch with the Government, were content with this situation, and were satisfied now that the Government considered them of importance and asked their advice on the welfare of the "Vatan" (Fatherland).

Unfortunately this state of affairs was of short duration. Suddenly the Russian army retreated. The different fragments of the Turkish Army rallied again, and instead of pursuing the enemy, they exterminated the Armenian and Syrian population of Bashkalé, Sarai and all the surrounding villages. They had massacred all the male population, and in certain places—according to the reports of a Turkish commander who was a Russian subject—had thrown them into wells. The most beautiful of the women had been distributed among the Moslems, and some of them were even sent to Van; the old and weak women who remained were collected together and driven to various places like a herd of cattle. The Armenian Bishop of Van sent a Turco-Armenian delegation to the Government to ask its help for the sufferers, but the Government entirely ignored the request, or postponed it from day to day.

The Governor of Van went to the front, leaving an assistant in his place, and by his patriotic exertions he re-organised the Turkish Army. He succeeded in winning to the side of the Turks the rebellious Kurds and even Smgo the Chief, who lived under Russian protection. This news was immediately telegraphed to Van and Constantinople. Djevdet Bey, the lion general of the Turks, with his reorganised army, followed the Russians up to Tabriz, and occupied it. It is unnecessary to repeat that the Turkish Army, wherever it went, carried with it fire and sword and all kinds of terrible tortures, which were inflicted upon the "*Infidels*." Regarding this, the American missionaries are the best informed eye-witnesses.

Owing to these Turkish successes on the frontier and the Armenian volunteer movements, the Government and the Turkish public changed their attitude towards the Armenians. The Government was more civil in its demands and asked all the deserters to appear before it, although without actually promising them arms and their restoration to the Army. To all questions concerning this, the answer was: "That is for us to decide." The war taxes were doubled, and to all the petitions and objections regarding this, the answer was: "The Army is more important than the populace."

The Government began now not to attach much importance to their friends the Dashnakists, and there was a time when the Assistant Governor refused even to receive Mr. Vremyan in audience, saying: "I cannot stand his rudeness and blustering."

A little distance from Van all the country places like Nordouz, Hazaren and Boghaz-Kessen were destroyed. Part of the inhabitants were massacred, others found refuge in Van, and the remainder altogether disappeared. The horrors spread to the other districts and villages round Van. Garjgan was evacuated; the village of Pelou, which had 120 houses, and the ten villages of Gargar were sacked.

In a semi-civilised country it is an easy matter for a Government to find pretexts for its acts, when the Governor so desires. For instance, in Pelou a drunken young man had a fight with a gendarme, pulled out his revolver and killed him. In the mountains above the village of Shoushantz, six Kurdish deserters were killed—but none of the authorities ascertained by whom they were killed, or who they were. These and similar events gave cause and pretext to the Turkish Government for censuring the Armenians. But no one was censured for the massacres and general unrest at Sarai, Bashkalé, Nordouz, Hazaren and Boghaz-Kessen. Then new army corps and machine guns were brought up to Van to be transferred to the frontier; all the Turkish and Kurdish citizens from 15 to 60 years of age were armed with these weapons, and when the Armenian Bishop protested to the Government, the answer was: "We are arming them to organise them into militia; after a little while we will collect them all and put them into barracks. If the Armenians are also willing to volunteer and come to the barracks, let them come and we will give them arms."

After the events at Pelou and Gargar, it was reported that a Turkish mob from Bitlis had devastated the district of Garjgan with fire and sword, and was advancing on Kavash and Haiotz-Tzor, and that after destroying these places they would proceed towards Van. Upon the arrival of this report, some Dashnakists went out towards Ankegh and Antanan in Haiotz-Tzor and destroyed the bridge near Ankegh, to prevent the Turks sending help to the mob which was advancing from Bitlis, and also to stop the mob from marching upon Van. After this the Armenians also killed a few gendarmes and Kurds. Among those killed was reported to be the Judge of Vostan. As far as I remember, seven persons were killed at this time. This event caused fear among the Turks and Kurds. The Government therefore sent Mr. Vremyan as a mediator. Mr. Vremyan settled the question, putting the blame on the Kaimakam of Vostan, who had sent for the mob from Bitlis. The Government superseded the Kaimakam of Vostan and promised to find and return the booty from Pelou and to restore the people who were deported to their homes. This was never done. An Armenian proverb says that "A thief is afraid of himself," and the Turks also were afraid of themselves on account of what they had done. While travelling through Haiotz-Tzor and Kavash they assumed Armenian names. Yet the officials, whenever they got a chance, protested to foreigners that the Armenians were ungrateful, that they furnished volunteers to the Russians, and wanted autonomy; "And therefore," they said, "we will not leave this country to them. Let the Russians take the country, but we refuse to let the Armenians rule over our families and our kin." It is unnecessary to add that there were as many Moslem volunteers as Armenian in the Russian forces.

The Turkish Government was very prudent. So long as it was weak it flattered the Armenians and praised them to their faces; the leaders of the Dashnakists, Vremyan, Aram and Ishkhan, were treated as advisers of the Government. The Armenians on their part tried not to be the cause of any disturbance in the country. The only ground for anxiety in the relations between the Government and the Armenians was the question of the Armenian deserters. After the Armenian soldiers were disarmed, they did not dare to remain in their posts, and used to desert. When it was discovered that the Turkish Government had armed all the male Mohammedans from 14 to 60 years of age, they were no longer willing to give themselves up, and decided to die with their wives and children. A few Turkish officials confessed that it was wrong to disarm the Armenians because there were more Kurdish deserters than Armenian, but the Government refrained from attaching as much blame to the Kurds as they did to the Armenians.

To consider all these problems, a meeting was called under the presidency of Yeznig Vartabed, the Assistant of the Bishop, in which all sections of the Armenian population of Van were represented. The meeting was held at the house of Kevork Agha Jidajian, and came to the following conclusions: That the Turkish Government was treating the Armenians with suspicion; that all work, trade, and farming had stopped; that certain districts such as Nordouz, Gargar and Garjgan had been cleared of their inhabitants, and that the Armenians of Sarai and Bashkalé had been annihilated when the Russian army retreated; finally, that in case of a revolution the Armenians at Van would be able to hold out for some time, but that, taking into consideration the whole of Armenia, it was necessary to maintain peace with the Turks at all costs.

As certain deserters could not give themselves up at the moment for important reasons, they decided to ask the Government to accept exemption money for them. The meeting decided to negotiate on these lines through Mr. Vremyan as their Deputy, with Avedis Effendi Terzibashian as an adviser experienced in Turkish psychology. The meeting also proposed to open negotiations through some merchants on similar lines. A week later the Armenians held a joint conference with the Turks at Jidajian's house. At this conference they decided to live together as neighbours without taking account of any changes of policy in the Government. The Turks promised to ask the Government not to give any cause for revolution.

However, the situation was far from being satisfactory, and unrest was in the air. All the workmen were working for the Government; the tradesmen would go to their shops, hear rumours, and go home again, to stay at home for four or five days; and the attitude of the Government kept changing like a weathercock, in conformity with the successes or failures at the front. Sometimes it was very severe and unreasonable, and sometimes very smooth and peaceful. Everyone was uneasy, as they did not know how long such a situation would last. We were afraid of massacres. We were afraid of the retreating Turkish army, which would undoubtedly devastate everything on its way. We were afraid of famine, as the Government had not given the people a chance of provisioning themselves, and we knew that the villages and farms had been robbed. A part of the working class was in the army. The cattle and sheep belonging to the refugees had been confiscated and sold. Many people confided to me that they wished that whatever was going to happen would happen quickly and relieve them from their suspense. Meanwhile, the people of Van armed themselves, and kept secret watch day and night at different street corners, to be prepared for any eventuality.

About the beginning of spring, rebellion started in the district of Van-Dosb, or Timar, a few hours' distance from Van. The inhabitants of the village of Erer in this district were massacred. When the turn came for the village of Bairak, the local Armenians defended themselves with the help of the Armenians in Van against the Kurds and the gendarmes. When the Government saw that people were getting ready and that things would drift from bad to worse, it went to the Bishop and expressed its regret for the events that had taken place, and asked the Armenians to send their representatives to stop the fighting at Bairak. This was immediately done. Some blamed the Vice-Governor, who had taken Djevdet's place, for these affrays. Mr. Vremyan and the Vice-Governor fell out, the Vice-Governor having refused to receive Mr. Vremyan in audience, but as Mr. Vremyan was a Deputy (Member of the Ottoman Parliament) he was allowed to remain in the district with the sanction of the Government. Mr. Vremyan blamed the Vice-Governor for the situation, and sent a telegram to this effect to the Governor, Djevdet, who was at the front. Djevdet answered him thanking him, and asking him to preserve peace until his return, when he would put everything in order, "Inshallah" ("God willing").

It was the last week of Lent when Djevdet Bey reached Van with 400 trained soldiers, called Lez[39], and a few field guns, and was received by the Armenians with royal honours; but while passing through Armenian villages he shut his eyes to the barbarous behaviour of his soldiers towards the Armenian women. In the new village of Upper Haiotz-Tzor a number of women were violated, a man was killed, and others were beaten almost to death, on the pretence of having arms. For this, one of the young men wanted to follow Djevdet and kill him, but the Armenian revolutionists did not allow him to do so. As soon as Djevdet Bey reached the city, he thanked Vremyan and all those who had done their best for the peace of the city, and started negotiating with the Armenians concerning the deserters. He persuaded the Armenians to give themselves up, or at least a certain part of them, so that he might have less difficulty in getting back the Turkish and Kurdish deserters.

During Passion Week the negotiations with the Government were postponed on account of a terrible snowstorm. At this time there was an army of 4,000 with some artillery in Van. There was no special cause for anxiety, but everybody felt there was something in the air, which turned out to be the case. After Easter, when the negotiations were taken up again with the Government, it was reported that there had been conflicts at Shadakh. The general impression was that the Government was behind it. The Government wanted to arrest a member of the Dashnakist party called Joseph. The Armenians would not allow him to be arrested, and that started the trouble. Shadakh is about 24 hours' journey from Van, towards the south, on one of the tributaries of the Tigris. During the massacres of 1895 and 1896, the Armenians of Shadakh had succeeded in defending themselves with great success and honour. After that, the Government had wanted to trap the Armenians and massacre them, and fill their places with Kurds and Turks, but it was not successful, and now in April the massacres had started from there. The liberty-loving Armenians of this place defended themselves bravely for about two months, until the end of May, when the Volunteers went to their assistance.

Djevdet Bey asked the Dashnakists to send a delegate and put a stop to these occurrences. The members of this deputation were Mr. Ishkhan and three young Armenians, a Turkish Prefect of Police, and a few gendarmes. On the evening of the 16th April, in the Kurdish village of Hirj, the Armenian delegates were all assassinated—a trap laid by the Government. Some trustworthy people from Haiotz-Tzor (Armenian Valley) reported that the very day that Mr. Ishkhan was going to Shadakh as a peace delegate, the Armenians of Upper Haiotz-Tzor came to him and said: "For how long shall we endure it? They have not spared anything. There was only Shadakh left, and they massacred even the people of Shadakh." Mr. Ishkhan, who was a fighter by nature, had declared to the Armenian villagers that they must keep the peace *at all costs*, and had ordered them to give the Government everything that was asked for; if one village was burnt, they were ordered to escape to another village.

Here I would like to explain in parenthesis the reason why I always mention the Dashnakist party. They were the people who were mixed up with politics; they were the friends and advisers of the Young Turk Party, and, having formed a "bloc" with them, they always sided with the Turks in parliamentary conflicts. The Government on their part wanted to keep them on their side, knowing that they had great influence over the villagers, in the Episcopal

Court, and in the Chancery of the Catholics of Aghtamar. The Ramgavars (Democrats) were not mixed up with politics. They had their own paper, "Van-Dosp," and were busy with their own propaganda and their own trade and teaching, only once in a while fighting against the Dashnakists. They did not, like the Dashnakists, have special members who gave all their time to political affairs. The Hunchakists were very few in number, and during mobilisation their leaders, Messrs. Ardashes Solakhian and Proudian, were arrested and afterwards killed.

On Saturday morning, the 17th April, Djevdet Bey asked the following leaders of the Dashnakists—Messrs. Vremyan, Aram, Avedis Effendi Terzibashian (a merchant), and Kevork Agha Jidajian—to visit him for a conference. Aram could not go, for one reason or another; the others went and were retained. After that it was reported that all those that went as peace delegates were killed by the Government. This started a panic among the Armenians, and young men under arms took up special positions. Father Nerses of the New Church, Set Effendi Kapamajian and myself went to the American missionaries to ask them to intercede with the Government on our behalf to maintain peace. Before the missionaries had reached the Government Building, Terzibashian and Jidajian were freed, so that they could advise the Armenians to go and surrender, but Vremyan was kept to be sent to Constantinople. Djevdet Bey told the missionaries that he had already sent for them. He also added that, as the peace of the country was disturbed, the American missionaries must make room for 50 soldiers for their own protection. If they could not do that, then they must all go to the Government Building, with their whole households. The missionaries came back with the impression that everything was over, and that Djevdet Bey had changed altogether. The same night the Armenians had a meeting in the New Church, where Terzibashian Effendi told them what Djevdet Bey had said and communicated to them the result of the negotiations. He said that it was impossible to influence Djevdet; sometimes he was quite reasonable, and at other times he was harsh and immovable and wanted all the deserters to surrender either that day or the following, and all the Armenians to give up their arms. Again it was decided to ask him to accept part of the deserters and receive exemption money for the rest. Signor Sbordone (the agent of the Italian Consul), the American missionaries and the Armenian merchants made proposals to Djevdet Bey to this effect, but they were unable to find out what his intentions were. Sometimes he declared on oath that he would not bring dishonour on his father, Tahir Pasha, who ruled over Van in peace during a time of great disturbances, and sometimes in a fury he would say: "There will either be nothing but Turks or nothing but Armenians left in this city. After I have finished Shadakh I will overthrow Van. I will not leave a single house standing except the house of my father. I will not spare either male or female, youth or old age. The Armenians must give up their arms and their deserters, and they must pass in front of my window to go to the barracks. If I hear the report of a gun or revolver, I will consider that a signal to carry out what I have just told you."

On Monday, the 19th April, Djevdet Bey was in a slightly different mood. He issued an order for everybody to go about their business, saying that nothing would happen. We had been isolated for a whole week from the districts outside the town and were ignorant as to what was going on there, and we did not even know that we were surrounded by Turkish trenches and troops. On the very day that Djevdet Bey told us that "All was well," Agantz, a big town in the district of Van, was sacked and ruined. Prominent inhabitants of Agantz, like Abaghtzian, Housian and Shaljian, were invited to go to the Government Building to receive orders from the Kaimakam. The other Armenians were collected from the streets and from their houses. At night, after dark, they took these men in groups of fifty with their hands tied behind their backs, brought them to the river bank at the back of the city, and there killed them all. Only three were able to unloose their hands and escape at night, after pretending to be dead. One of them went to an Armenian village near by and was the cause of this village's escape; another of them went to the boats that were on the shore and saw that most of the sailors had been killed, but told the rest about it, who thereupon launched their boats into the open lake and rowed for the Monastery Island. The third disappeared altogether.

Haroutune Agha Housian was wounded in three places, but escaped to his home. When the Turkish officers counted the wounded, however, they found, by their list, that Mr. Housian was missing, and when they found him in his house they killed him. All the male inhabitants of Agantz were killed except these three, and, by the permission of the Government, the Armenian households—that is, the women and children and property—were divided among the Turks. In order to secure their property, the Turks betrothed themselves to Armenian girls and women, with the intention of marrying them.

Djevdet Bey announced to everybody that "Asayish ber Kemal der" ("Peace was perfect"), and at the same time he put pressure on the American missionaries either to sign a statement that they had refused the protection of the Government, or agree to accept a guard of 50 soldiers for the missionary compound. He laid more emphasis on this latter proposition, saying that he would send the same number of soldiers to the German missionaries. The American missionaries were so considerate as to ask the advice of the Armenians, and the latter, especially Mr. Armenag Yegarian, saw in the proposal a plot to seize the Armenian quarters and homes. Accordingly they made the missionaries understand that the only thing which would protect them would be the American flag and the order of the

Government, and that, even if 5,000 soldiers were there, it would be impossible to be protected against the Government. With this in view, they told the missionaries that, if Djevdet sent more than 10 or 12 soldiers, they would be obliged to open fire on them and would not let one into the Armenian quarters. Taking all these points into consideration, the missionaries informed the Government that they were willing to accept as many soldiers as the Government sent them, but that they would not be responsible for their safe arrival and were very unwilling to start a conflict on that account. "We are not afraid of the Armenians," they said, "and we think that 10 or 12 soldiers and an order from you will be sufficient to protect us."

On Tuesday morning, the 20th April, at six o clock, some Turkish soldiers saw a few Armenian women coming to the city from the village of Shoushantz, half-an-hour's distance from Van. They attempted to violate them, and when two Armenian young men went to remonstrate with the Turkish soldiers, the latter opened fire on them and killed them. This was not very far from the German Mission, and the Principal of the German missionaries, Herr Spörri, and his wife witnessed this incident. He also was kind enough to write explicitly to Djevdet, stating that it was the Turkish soldiers who attempted to violate the women and then killed the Armenian young men who had tried to save the women's honour.

But Djevdet had received his signal, and as soon as the reports were heard from Ourpat Arou (where the women had been violated), artillery fire was opened upon the Armenian quarters of Aikesdan, and was also turned upon the inhabitants of the Market-place, which was surrounded by Turkish quarters.

Then we understood that we were really surrounded, and so the armed Armenian young men held the street corners and did not allow the Turkish or Kurdish mobs to enter. The Armenian lines protected an area of about two square miles, which was held by 700 Armenians, 300 only of whom had regular arms and a certain amount of military training. The others were simply civilians who had revolvers and a few ordinary weapons. All the fighters had decided to fight to the bitter end in defence of their families.

Even the American missionaries confessed that they could not conceive how a Government could display such meanness and treachery towards citizens who had been so faithful in their duties. It is important to mention that the sympathies of the American missionaries had been with the Armenians at all times. They not only opened the doors of their compounds and houses, but also placed families and property in security, and began to give their personal services to the sick and the children.

All the people of Van, without exception, began to work with one soul. Those who had arms and were able to fight rushed to take their stand and stop the Turks from entering the Armenian quarters, and those who were able to work took spade and shovel to go and strengthen the fighting men's positions by constructing trenches and walls. The little boys worked as scouts, the women and girls undertook the care of the sick and the children. Besides that, the women did all the sewing and cooking for the fighters.

With the object of caring for the wounded, a Red Cross detachment was raised with the assistance of Dr. Sanfani (Khosrov Chetjian) and Dr. Khatchig. To secure law and order, a local Government was formed, with judicial, police and sanitary branches. Its administration was conducted in perfect order the whole month through. The Americans said that Van had never had such a good Government under the Turkish rule. An end was put to revolutionary disputes; only such expressions as "Armenian soldier," "Armenian Self-defence Committee" and the like were heard; and they named their positions "Dévé Boyi," "Dardanelles," "Sahag Bey's Dug-out," and so on.

For the better organisation of the defending forces they appointed a military council, which was formed of the representatives of the revolutionary parties and the non-party Armenians, and which carried on the work very successfully. This body was in communication with the lines and supplied soldiers wherever and whenever it was necessary. The Supply Committee also did good work in supplying food and beds for those who were working in the different stations. Under the presidency of Bedros Bey Mozian, the ex-Mayor of Van, and with the leadership of Mr. Yarrow, they formed a Relief Society whose object was to collect supplies and provide the necessaries of life for those who were destitute and had lost their homes. This committee was a great assistance to the fighting forces.

One of the local papers began to publish the news of the fighting and distribute it to the people. The Normal School band, under the leadership of Mr. K. Boujikanian, played Armenian military airs, the "Marseillaise," and other tunes, to hearten the fighters. The greater the intensity of the Turkish artillery fire and the louder the roar of the guns, the louder the band played, and this made Djevdet more furious than the bullets of the Armenians; he did not even restrain himself from expressing his feelings in his bulletins.

During the first days of the fighting, the Military Committee, by special bulletin, made a public appeal to the Turks, reminding them of their pledges to one another, and proclaiming that Governments change but the people always remain neighbours, and that there was no reason why they should be at enmity with one another. By this they put the whole of the blame on Djevdet, who possessed nothing else in Van but a horse, "and he could ride off on that and escape." After making this point, the proclamation suggested to the Turkish inhabitants that they should force Djevdet to desist from the bloodshed. I do not know the result of this announcement.

The Military Committee also gave orders to the Armenian soldiers not to drink, not to blaspheme the religion of the enemy, to spare women, children and unarmed men, to respect neutrals, and to prevent anyone from entering their compounds under arms. They also ordered that all the wounded should be taken to the American Hospital, and that only true reports should be given.

During these dark days the Armenian people were very full of life. Everybody did his or her best. They all had good hope that Djevdet would not succeed in annihilating the Armenians of Van. The spirit of the fighters was enough to inspire those that were in despair. I have seen young men who had fought the enemy day and night, without sleeping. Their eyesight had been so affected that they were practically blind, and they were transferred to the Red Cross Station to be treated. Even then they were very cheerful. While the shrapnel was raining upon Van, the Armenian children were playing soldiers in the streets.

Armenag Yegarian, with his cool and able leadership; Aram, with his constant presence and advice; P. Terlemezian, with his great heart; Krikor of Bulgaria, with his indefatigable industry and inventive genius—they were very able leaders. To save their lives and honour all the Armenians of Van had placed then services at the disposal of the Military Council, who awarded crosses and medals to encourage those who were worthy of them. I was present when a little girl received one of these medals. During the retaking of a position in Angous Tzor she bravely went ahead, spied out the ground and brought back news that the Turks had laid no traps for the advancing Armenian soldiers.

From the very first day of the fighting the Turks burned all the Armenian houses that were outside the Armenian fighting zone, but the village of Shoushantz and Varak Monastery were still in the hands of the Armenians. Mr. H. Kouyoumjian was in charge of the entrenchments at Varak, and he came down to Aikesdan once in a while to report everything that was going on there.

After a week all the Armenians in the surrounding country came in to Aikesdan by way of Varak and Shoushantz, bringing with them famine, sickness and terrible news. Those that came from Haiotz-Tzor (Armenian Valley) reported that two Turkish armies had passed through the Armenian villages with artillery. The first army paid for everything that they took, and the people were encouraged by this act to issue from their retreats, but the second army surrounded them and massacred them. The Government carried out its work on such a well-planned system that villages were massacred without having had warning of the fate of their neighbours only a mile away. All the inhabitants of the villages that surrendered were massacred. There were villages that succeeded in removing their people and taking them to the mountains, but in general we must confess that the villagers did not prove very brave. They were not able to co-operate for their common defence, and there were even some who did not like to oppose the Government. In comparison with the city people they were short of ammunition, and they managed to convoy their families into the city by simply firing in the air, which was one of the reasons why the city people rather looked down on them. But the fact is that if they had had enough ammunition and the right leaders, they would have been able very easily to drive the enemy out of Haiotz-Tzor, Kavash and Tamar.

During the first two weeks the Government massacred the men and had all the women kidnapped, and deported the remainder from village to village to give the Turkish population a chance of wreaking their vengeance. But afterwards, in order to strike at the defensive powers of Van and to starve the Armenians into surrender by making them use up their provisions, they collected all the survivors from the villages and sent them to Aikesdan and to the city proper. The people in the city refused to pass anybody through the lines of defence; the enemy therefore sent them to Aikesdan, telling them that those who returned would be shot. The people of Aikesdan recognised their terrible straits and took them in; there were a large number of wounded among the women and children. I saw a woman from the village of Eremer, whose husband was serving in the Turkish army and whose twelve-year-old boy was slain before her eyes. She was wounded herself, as well as her two remaining children, one four years and the other eleven months old. I shall never forget the drooping look of the little one and the wounded arm that hung by his side, nor the woman herself, who was almost mad. All these were given over to Dr. Ussher, who treated them immediately. I also remember a woman who had lost seven of her children and had gone out of her mind. She lay on the ground clutching her hair. She threw dust on her head and cursed the Kaiser all the time.

The American Hospital, which could accommodate only 50 patients, had 150 sick, and they were obliged to fill every available place with the wounded. Scarlet fever, whooping cough and smallpox carried off many of the little ones.

Besides the fighting and working forces, we had to supply food for about 13,000 people. At the beginning it was possible to give one loaf of bread to each individual every day, but afterwards we were obliged to cut it down to half a loaf, supplemented with other food. All the oxen and cows in the city were slaughtered, and when we had lost all hope of procuring cattle from outside there were even people who suggested killing the dogs. The lack of ammunition was also severely felt, so that in Aikesdan for every thousand rounds fired by the Turks the Armenians could only reply with one.

After a few days the Turks occupied the positions of Shoushantz and Varak, and burned the library of old manuscripts at Varak Monastery. All the Armenians and Syrians from these occupied villages came over to the city and consequently increased the famine and plague. Up to this time women between 65 and 70 years old carried letters backwards and forwards between Djevdet and the Austrian banker Aligardi, Signor Sbordone, and the German and American missionaries. These women carried a white flag in one hand and the letter in the other, and passed to and fro in safety, with the exception of one who was shot by the Turks because she was unfortunate enough to fall down and lose the flag, and another one who was wounded by the Turks. Djevdet tried to discourage the Armenians by descriptions of Turkish successes, and also suggested that they should give up their arms and receive a complete amnesty, like the people of Diyarbekir. In a letter addressed to Mr. Aligardi, the Austrian, he wrote: "Dear Aligardi, Ishim yok, keifim tchok ("I have nothing to do but amuse myself"). In another, addressed to Dr. Ussher, he said: "I will parade the prisoners and guns I have taken from the Russians in front of His Majesty Dr. Ussher's fort, so that he may see and believe."

But the Armenians did not let Djevdet do as he pleased. They severed communications and did not allow any more letters to pass through the lines. Then, under the direction of Professor M. Minassian, they succeeded in making smokeless powder, cartridges and three guns, whose reports were heard with great rejoicings by all the Armenians. They made about 2,000 cartridges a day, and the blacksmiths made spears, so that, if necessary, they could fight with spears when the ammunition was all gone. The Armenians also dug underground passages, through which they blew up certain Turkish barracks and entrenchments.

Thus they burned and destroyed the great stone barracks of Hamoud Agha; the Telegraph and Police Station of Khatch Poghotz (Cross Street); half the police station of Arar, and the English Consulate, which was one of the chief Turkish strongholds. This encouraged the Armenians a great deal, so that there was a time when Djevdet was obliged to send 500 soldiers against a position held by only 44 Armenians, who after fighting for three or four hours left 33 dead on the field and retired. A young man called Borouzanjian, the only son of his widowed mother and the support of his orphan sisters, resigned his post as hospital orderly and went to fight in the trenches. He killed four Turkish soldiers and was finally killed himself. He praised God while dying that he had done his duty, and asked his comrades to sell his revolver and other personal belongings and to give the proceeds of them to his mother, so that she could live on them for a little while.

During this time they sent word to the Armenian Volunteers in Russia, asking them to come to their aid.

When the villagers came to Aikesdan and thus increased the number of labourers and fighters, the trenches were elaborated and increased in number, so that they now covered two square miles. When the Turkish artillerymen destroyed one line they found a second fortified line at the back, which was stronger than the first. Besides this, the Armenians had organised a body of cavalry, so that they could send help in all directions. Not only Aikesdan was defended with success, but also the city proper and Shadakh. The Americans, seeing the spirit of the Armenians, declared that it would not be far wrong to say that this beat Marathon.

The Turkish soldiers were good shots, especially the artillerymen, who could direct their shrapnel by accurate sighting upon the desired point. Who could imagine that their commanders were civilised and Christian Germans! This fact became known to the Armenians after the fall of Van.

On the 9th and 10th May we saw the white sails of boats on the Lake of Van. Without heeding the flying bullets, the people flocked on to high ground to watch them. We did not know whether they were some of the Turkish population or officers who were escaping. They continued the shooting until next morning. After the 10th May the fighting became more intense, both during the daytime and at night, and on the 15th and 16th May the guns were directed upon the American Institutions, where all the people were. Although during the whole period of fighting they had fired upon the American compound, the Hospital, the Church and Dr. Ussher's home, and wounded thirteen people, it was only during the last two days that the bombardment was confined to the compound alone. It was then that a bomb struck Dr. Raynold's house and killed Mr. Terzibashian's three-and-a-half-years-old daughter.

On the evening of the 17th May the Armenians succeeded in destroying the upper and lower barracks of Toprak Kalé, which raised their spirits vastly; but in the evening the joy of the Americans surpassed that of the Armenians. About midnight, in a strong attack, the Armenians seized and burned the largest Turkish barracks, Hadji Bekir's Kushla, which dominated the American compound. At midnight the town criers went through the town crying victory: "We have taken all the Turkish positions; they have run away: come out." On this report the Armenians, especially those who were in a starving condition, came out and attacked the Turkish quarters to rob and burn them. The revenge of centuries was being taken. The Armenian soldiers did not participate in this movement for twenty-four hours, but held their positions so that the enemy might not take them by surprise. The booty that the people took from the Turks consisted mostly of wheat, flour and bread.

I asked one of the villagers to show me her booty. She did so, and I was surprised to see that it consisted of clothing that the Turks had robbed from Armenian women and girls. They found in the house of Mouhib Effendi, a member of the Ottoman Parliament, a chalice and other sacred vessels from an Armenian Church. The Turks were in such a panic that some left their tables laid and took to flight. The hungry women of yesterday were carrying away booty without stopping, with a new strength. It was the story of the seventh chapter of the Fourth Book of Kings that was repeated word for word. The American compound was now deserted except for the boy scouts, who, with the help of one of our teachers and Neville Ussher, remained to look after the sick.

The whole city was in an uproar. Some went to look at the entrenchments; others went to look at the burned Turkish quarters, and others to look at the booty. There were others also who visited the fortress, which was captured that same night, and over which a flag with a Cross on it was waving. No Government was left, no authority. The soldiers had marked out their position from Arark to Khatch Poghotz as a military centre. They took away all the valuable vessels and property from the people. They were afraid that there would be fighting, but fortunately nothing happened. In Aikesdan there were still armed Turks in certain positions, who killed some Armenians, but they were finally found and killed. It was very pitiful to see Armenian soldiers leading Turkish women and children and unarmed men to the American compound for safety, and saying to them: "Do not cry; nothing will happen to you; we are only looking for Djevdet, who destroyed both your homes and ours." Nobody touched these Turkish women, some of whom had from £30 to £95 (Turkish) on their persons. Some of the Armenians went to look for their wounded in the Turkish hospitals, and when they did not find them they were so infuriated that they killed some of the Turkish wounded and burned the building. Mr. Yarrow asked me to go and wait there until he came. I stayed there. The scene was dreadful. For four days the Government had given them no bread and no care, so that many of them had already died from neglect. Interspersed among the dead there were also some still living, but the Armenians did not raise their hands to touch them. Before the arrival of the Americans, many came and helped me to put out the fire and attended to those that were alive. Mr. Yarrow, seeing all this, said: "I am amazed at the self-control of the Armenians, for though the Turks did not spare a single wounded Armenian, the Armenians are helping us to save the Turks—a thing that I do not believe even Europeans would do."

The scene in the prison was dreadful, as all the Armenian prisoners had been massacred. The wife of Mr. Proudian had completely lost her reason, and cried out: "Show me at least the bones of my dear one." The unveiling of these dreadful deeds of the Turks so hardened some of the Armenians that they followed the doctrine of "an eye for an eye and a tooth for a tooth," to the great sorrow of the others.

38. See Doc. 21

39. Of Lazic nationality (?)—*Editor.*

18. VAN AFTER THE TURKISH RETREAT: LETTER FROM HERR SPÖRRI, OF THE GERMAN MISSION AT VAN, PUBLISHED IN THE GERMAN JOURNAL "SONNENAUFGANG," OCTOBER, 1915.

There lies Artamid before us, adorned by its delicious gardens; but how does the village look? The greater part of it is nothing now but a heap of ruins. We talked there with three of our former orphan protégées, who had had fearful experiences during the recent events. We rode on across the mountain of Artamid. Even in time of peace one crosses the pass with one's heart in one's mouth, because the Kurds ply their robber trade there. Now it is all uncannily still. Our glance swept over the magnificent valley of Haiotz-Tzor. There lay Antananz before us, now utterly destroyed like the rest. We gave shelter, at the time, to the people from Antananz who had managed to escape. Further on in the magnificent green landscape lay Vostan. At first sight one might call it a paradise, but during these latter days it has also been a hell. What rivers of blood must have flowed there; it was one of the chief strongholds of the armed Kurds. At the foot of the mountain we came to Angegh. There again there were many houses destroyed. We found here a young woman who, after many years of widowhood, had married a native of the village. Things have been going well with her; now her husband, too, was slaughtered. One hundred and thirty people are said to have been murdered thus. We pitched our camp here in face of the blackened ruins. Straight in front of us stood an "amrodz," a tower built of cakes of manure—a common enough sight in these parts. We were told that the Kurds had burnt the corpses of the slaughtered Armenians in it. Horrible! And yet that is at least better than if the corpses of the slain, as has happened in other places, are allowed to lie for an indefinite period unburied, so that they are devoured by dogs and poison the air. There we were met by some soldiers; they were Armenian "Volunteers" who had come from Russia and were now fighting on the side of the Russians for the liberation of their Haiasdan. They were coming now from the neighbourhood of Bitlis, where heavy fighting was in progress. They had brought some sick back to the town, and proposed to rest here awhile. After that we rode on to Ten, where people we already knew came out to meet us from the village and informed us of what had happened there. There, too, the scenes of our former activity, the school and the church, lay in ruins, and many dwelling houses as well. The man who used to put us up was also among the slain; his widow is still quite distraught. Here about 150 are said to have been murdered. There were so many orphans in the place, they said to us—Should we now be inclined to take charge of any again? We were unable to give them any definite answer. As we rode on and on over the mountains, the splendid air did us much good and we thanked God for it, for little by little we have come to be in sore need of recuperation. We had a wonderful view from the mountain heights, but everywhere in the villages one sees blackened and ruined houses.

19. VAN AFTER THE MASSACRES: NARRATIVE OF MR. A.S. SAFRASTIAN, DATED VAN, 2nd DECEMBER, 1915, AND PUBLISHED IN THE ARMENIAN JOURNAL "ARARAT" OF LONDON, JANUARY, 1916.

"I have seen the ravages of the Crimean war, the Russo-Turkish war of 1877-78, the Armenian massacres of 1894-96, and the reign of terror which then followed until the year 1914; but the massacres which have been going on since April of the current year are simply appalling, and by far the most terrible blow which the Armenian nation has ever been subject to throughout the course of its long history."

So spoke to me Hagop Boghossian, an old Armenian peasant of Van, a sturdy octogenarian who, after three forced flights from his home in the rear of the Russian Army, was once more returning to his home to tide over the winter in his native village north of Lake Van; and as he was walking along the muddy pathway, he was telling me the story of the recent massacres as he knew them, and as he understood them from his own point of view. His account in its main outline corresponds with what has been proved beyond all doubt. Before arousing any suspicion among the Armenians residing in the central provinces of Asiatic Turkey about its intentions, the Turkish Government wanted to dispose of the "rebellious" Armenians of Van, which lay far away from its grip, and the Armenian element of which had generally been considered by the Turks as a doubtful quantity. One Djevdet Bey, a brother-in-law of Enver Pasha, happened to be the governor and the military commander of Van. In February he was routed in the battle of Diliman and Khoi, in Azerbaijan, a battle in which the Armenian volunteers under Andranik played some part. When he returned to Van, he told his friends that while he was at the front he had to battle throughout the time against Armenians, both as regular troops of the Russian army and as volunteers. The report says that Enver Pasha, the Minister of War, expressed almost the same opinion when his army was defeated early in January in the battles of

Sarikamysh and Ardahan. However exaggerated these estimates may have been, they seem to have served well the purpose of the Turkish Government in its efforts to destroy the Armenian population within its territory; and Djevdet Bey was commissioned to begin the massacres at Van, where the best relations existed between the Armenians under Vremyan, the Deputy for Van in the Turkish Chamber, and Djevdet himself, who for years had enjoyed the hospitality of the natives.

On the 15th April the young Armenians of Akantz, north of Lake Van (Ardjish), were mustered by the gendarmes to the sound of the bugle, to hear the recital of an order which had just arrived from the Sultan. At sunset these 500 young men were shot outside the town without any formality. During the following two days the same process was carried out with heartless and cold-blooded thoroughness in the 80 Armenian villages of Ardjish, Adiljevas, and the rest of the district north of Lake Van. In this manner some 24,000 Armenians were killed in three days, their young women carried away and their homes looted. After that, Djevdet Bey immediately proceeded to destroy the able-bodied Armenians on the south side of the Lake in the same way. Kurds were let loose upon the peasants of the *Kazas* of Moks and Shatakh, but there these hardy mountaineers proved somewhat hard nuts to crack. They put up a stout resistance and frustrated the Turkish plan.

In the town of Van itself the Armenians had already made all the concessions they possibly could to conciliate the Government in the matter of deserters from the army and the military requisitions. Djevdet, however, demanded unconditional surrender; he treacherously caused the death of four Armenian leaders, and detained Vremyan, who was killed later. These acts, in combination with the massacres of Ardjish, cleared up all doubts. The Turks had made up their minds to annihilate the Armenians by all the means in their power, as they had shown by killing thousands of absolutely innocent peasants in Ardjish. The experience of the past had taught the Armenians of Van that an appeal to arms was the only argument which could save their life, honour and property, and they collected together all the arms they possessed. From the middle of April they were besieged by a Turkish army of about 6,000 men, equipped with artillery and reinforced by numberless Kurds of all types. Twenty-five thousand Armenians of the town, who had only some 400 good rifles and double that number of arms of a medley character, fought for four weeks against great odds. They organised all their resources through an improvised staff and various committees for medical help and distribution of relief. They constructed some mortars and made smokeless powder to repel the furious Turkish attacks. Every man, woman and child did their bit to help in the work of liberation; they held their positions to the last and captured several enemy positions by blowing up barracks in which the Turks had entrenched themselves in the middle of the

Armenian quarters. After seeing something of their positions and walking over the scenes of the fight, one can well understand that it must have been a heroic battle indeed. The Turks under Djevdet despaired of overcoming Van and fled hastily at the approach of the Armenian volunteers followed by the Russian army. Van was captured by the Armenians, who saluted the entry of the Russian army by the booming of the guns they had taken from the Turks. An Armenian provisional government was established in the town and the province from early June. Excesses of an avenging nature could scarcely be avoided under the circumstances; yet such excesses by no means overstepped the passion excited at the moment.

During June and July, almost the entire Armenian population of Bitlis, Moush, Diyarbekir, and the remaining provinces of Turkish Armenia was ruthlessly massacred or deported. Of this unparalleled tragedy the later events at Van, which suffered the most lightly of all, may serve as an illustration.

After two months of self-government in Van, the fortunes of war turned against the Armenians. Towards the end of July the Turks took the offensive on the Transcaucasian front. The Russians retreated from the Euphrates and Moush towards their own frontiers in order to counter-attack the enemy under more favourable conditions. But in this game of strategy, the quarter of a million Armenians of Van, Alashkerd, etc., the last remnant of the Armenian element in Eastern Turkey, had also to retreat towards the Russian frontier. Men, women and children, who had bravely defended themselves against the Turks, fled in a panic under the most adverse circumstances. There were no means of transport, except a few ox-carts, horses, donkeys and cows, and the distance to be traversed varied from 100 to 150 miles through a waterless and trackless country; while only a few hours' notice was given to the unsuspecting people to quit their homes, abandon all they possessed, and walk to Transcaucasia. Every one burdened himself with some clothing and provisions, and, followed by exhausted women and children, walked for 10 days under the burning August sun, smothered in dust and overcome by thirst and fatigue. On the Bergri bridge (north of Lake Van) the rear of the caravan was attacked by mounted Kurds. A frightful panic ensued, in which women and girls threw themselves into the river Bendimahu, while others threw away their infants in the effort to escape, and entire families were precipitated into the waters owing to the rush caused by the panic. The sick, the infirm, and hundreds of children were abandoned on the roadside, where they died in lingering agony or were massacred by the Kurds.

On my way to Van along the north-eastern shore of the Lake, I witnessed revolting evidence of the recent events. Several search parties had already buried the dead and cleared the ground; nevertheless, here and there I saw remains of human bodies, of men and women, under piles of stones or scattered about the roadside. I discovered decomposing and horribly disfigured bodies of children; and on the shores of the lake and on the banks of streams skeletons, pieces of clothing, bones of human beings and animals lying all around. The stench of putrefaction was simply sickening. The country from Igdir to Van had indeed been a slaughter-house but a few months before. Entire villages had been completely wiped out. Except for some casual travellers, not a single human soul was to be seen there—there were but vultures and howling dogs who fed upon the putrefied human remains.

The town of Van itself is mostly a heap of ruins. Since last August it has changed hands several times; all churches, schools and the best houses have been burnt down. The pulse of life seemed to have ceased from beating, where a few months ago the natives had turned it into a beehive after capturing it from the Turk. On the other hand, the remnant of the Armenians from Turkey is being greatly diminished owing to destitution and sickness across the borders of Transcaucasia. The whole country is devastated beyond any description. Perhaps nowhere on the European battlefields has the civil population been so sorely tried as in the Armenian highlands, and no race has suffered so much as the Armenians in Asiatic Turkey. At present only some 200,000 of them can be accounted for; and these are dying by hundreds in Transcaucasia in consequence of the terrible sufferings they have gone through since last spring.

20. VAN: INTERVIEW WITH A REFUGEE, MRS. GAZARIAN, PUBLISHED IN THE "PIONEER PRESS," OF ST. PAUL, MINNESOTA, U.S.A.

A story of the flight of terror-stricken Armenians from the city of Van, from the persecution of the Turks who massacred thousands of Armenian women and children and forced the men into their armies, was told last night by Mrs. Sylvia Gazarian. She has just arrived from Armenia after suffering great hardships and persecution during a journey through Russia, and is with her son, Levon Gazarian, a North St. Paul piano builder.

Mrs. Gazarian during her flight saw her husband die of typhoid fever, and left seven of her grandchildren lying along the roadside, victims of starvation and exhaustion. Her son Edward, a Red Cross surgeon, made the journey with Mrs. Gazarian. He is at his brother's home here.

Mrs. Gazarian founded the Christian school at Van, and devoted many years to educating Armenian children. Her story, which is perhaps the first uncensored news of the cruelties inflicted by the Turks in Armenia, was told through Arsen K. Nakashian, an interpreter:—

"I spent a month in Van while our school was the target of the Turks. I saw them kill, burn and persecute," she said. "I saw our town become a part of a barren waste. I saw Turks bury Armenian victims with the dogs, divide the women among them as wives and throw babies into the lake. The school was burned, the missionaries fled, and 35,000 of the 75,000 inhabitants of the Van district were killed or starved to death.

"Djevdet Bey, Governor-General of Van, started the whole trouble when, early in April, 1915, he demanded that the Armenians should support the Turkish army.

"When the Armenians resisted, Djevdet Bey ordered them to be shot. He demanded that we and the American and German missionaries should leave Van and seek protection from the Turkish Government. We all refused. Our valley had been a garden. The Turks did their worst to make it a morgue.

"For miles around the Armenians congregated at Van, drove out the Turks and made trenches. Stones, earth and sand-bags were piled over the school buildings. The Turks attacked, and for more than a month in April and May kept up a steady fire.

"Finally the Russians came. We were under their protection for a month. The Turks, fleeing before the Russians, killed all Armenian prisoners and wounded.

"Russian treachery became evident when they evacuated the town. They pillaged every standing home. When we demanded that they should stay and protect us, the general said: 'If you don't want us to leave you, come along.'

"Only old men and feeble women refused the invitation. Fifteen grandchildren of mine, three daughters and their husbands, my son and myself made up our forlorn party. We travelled towards Russia on foot. There was no other way to go. We walked for twelve days—like dead men and women. As far ahead as we could see, there were women carrying or dragging their babies and wounded men staggering along at their sides. Death was common.

"First one and then another of the children died. Typhoid was doing its work everywhere. We buried the babies where we happened to be. Seven of them in all died on the journey. When we arrived at Tiflis my husband died.

"More than a month ago my son and I started for Northern Russia. Round the Caucasus mountains, across the Russian steppes and into Moscow, where the Russian troops were assembled in thousands, we went by train.

"Every Russian official wanted money, and we paid. We reached Archangel on the Arctic ocean and started for America."

Just as the woman finished her story her son Edward came in.

"Germany is responsible for the cruelty in Armenia," he declared: "She is not a friend but an enemy of Turkey. She covets the Dardanelles. She aims at making Turkey a German province; but she knows the power of the Armenians, and she wants Turkey without them. That is why she permits the Turks to burn, murder and ravage. The young Turks are educated criminals. They are worse than the older ones. America is beautiful and peaceful. We will always live here."

III.
VILAYET OF BITLIS.

The Vilayet of Bitlis lies due west of Van, across the Lake. The chief Armenian centres in the province were the town of Bitlis itself, commanding the principal pass leading from the lake-basin to the upper valley of the Tigris; the town and villages of Moush, situated in the only considerable plain along the course of the Mourad Su or Eastern Euphrates; and the semi-independent highland community of Sassoun, a group of Armenian villages in the massif of mountains which separates Moush from the headwaters of the Tigris and the lowlands of Diyarbekir.

The extermination of the Armenians in these three places was an act of revenge for the successful resistance of the Armenians at Van and the advance of the Russian forces to their relief. There was no pretence here of deportation, and the Armenians were destroyed, without regard for appearances, by outright massacre, accompanied in many cases by torture.

21. THE NORTH-EASTERN VILAYETS: STATEMENT COMMUNICATED BY THE REFUGEE ROUPEN, OF SASSOUN, TO THE ARMENIAN COMMUNITY AT MOSCOW; PUBLISHED IN THE RUSSIAN PRESS, AND SUBSEQUENTLY REPRINTED IN THE "GAZETTE DE LAUSANNE," 13th FEBRUARY, 1916.

At the beginning of the European war, the "Dashnaktzoutioun" Party met in congress at Erzeroum in order to decide on the attitude to be observed by the Party. As soon as they heard of this congress, the Young Turks hastened to send their representatives to Erzeroum to propose that the Party should declare its intention of aiding and defending Turkey, by organising an insurrection in the Caucasus in the event of a declaration of war between Turkey and Russia. According to the project of the Young Turks, the Armenians were to pledge themselves to form legions of volunteers and to send them to the Caucasus with the Turkish propagandists, to prepare the way there for the insurrection.

The Young Turk representatives had already brought their propagandists with them to Erzeroum—27 individuals of Persian, Turkish, Lesghian and Circassian nationality. Their chief was Emir Hechmat, who is at present organising bands of rebels at Hamadan (Persia). The Turks tried to persuade the Armenians that the Caucasian insurrection was inevitable; that very shortly the Tatars, Georgians and mountaineers would revolt, and that the Armenians would consequently be obliged to follow them.

They even sketched the future map of the Caucasus.

The Turks offered to the Georgians the provinces of Koutais and of Tiflis, the Batoum district and a part of the province of Trebizond; to the Tatars, Shousha, the mountain country as far as Vladivkavkaz, Bakou, and a part of the province of Elisavetpol; to the Armenians they offered Kars, the province of Erivan, a part of Elisavetpol, a fragment of the province of Erzeroum, Van and Bitlis. According to the Young Turk scheme, all these groups were to become autonomous under a Turkish protectorate. The Erzeroum Congress refused these proposals, and advised the Young Turks not to hurl themselves into the European conflagration—a dangerous adventure which would lead Turkey to ruin.

The Young Turks were irritated by this advice.

"This is treason!" cried Boukhar-ed-Din-Shakir, one of the delegates from Constantinople: "You take sides with Russia in a moment as critical as this; you refuse to defend the Government; you forget that you are enjoying its hospitality!"

But the Armenians held to their decision.

Once more before the outbreak of war between Russia and Turkey, the Young Turks tried to obtain the Armenians' support. This time they opened their *pourparlers* with more moderate proposals, and negotiated with the Armenian representatives of each Vilayet. At Van, the *pourparlers* were conducted by the provincial governor Tahsin Bey, and by Nadji Bey; at Moush, by Servet Bey and Iskhan Bey (this latter is at present a prisoner of war in Russia); at Erzeroum, by the same Tahsin Bey and by others.

The project of an Armenian rising in the Caucasus was abandoned. Instead, the Ottoman Armenians were to unite themselves with the Transcaucasian Tatars, whose insurrection was, according to the Young Turks, a certainty.

Once more the Armenians refused.

From the moment war broke out, the Armenian soldiers had presented themselves for service at their regimental depôts, but they refused categorically to form irregular bands. On the whole, up to the end of 1914, the situation in Armenia was quiet. But when the Turks had been expelled from Bayazid and driven back in the direction of Van and Moush, their fury turned upon the Armenians, whose co-religionists in the Caucasus had formed themselves into volunteer legions under the leadership of Andranik and other patriotic leaders, and had been giving aid to the enemy.

It was then that the disarming of Armenian soldiers, gendarmes and members of the other services began. The disarmed Armenian soldiers were formed into groups of a thousand each, and sent into different districts to build bridges, dig trenches and work at the fortresses.

At the same time the wholesale massacres began. The first victims fell at Diyarbekir, Erzeroum and Bitlis. Soldiers, women and children, both in the towns and villages, were slaughtered *en masse*. By the end of last January the massacres had extended over the whole of Armenia. In the Armenian villages, the whole male population above the age of twelve was led out in batches and shot before the eyes of the women and children.

The first movement of revolt declared itself towards the beginning of February, at Koms. Seventy Turkish gendarmes had arrived there with orders to massacre the chief men of the place, and among them Roupen and Gorioun. When the Armenians learned their purpose, they threw themselves upon the gendarmes and killed them all. They proceeded to take the local governor prisoner, and found on him the following order from the governor of Moush:—

"Execute the decision communicated verbally to you."

On the same day the leading Armenians retired into the mountains, where they were joined by the young men under arms from the district of Moush.

Two thousand Turks, commanded by Mehmed Effendi, took the offensive against them, but were annihilated by the Armenians.

This was how the revolt in Armenia began.

The Government saw that the insurrection was spreading, and announced the suspension of the process of disarmament, rescinding at the same time the order for the deportation and extermination of the people of Sassoun. A commission of enquiry was appointed, consisting of Essad Pasha, the Kaimakam of Boulanik, the President of the Military Tribunal at Moush, and Mr. V. Papazian, an Armenian member of the Ottoman Parliament.

The commission found that the gendarmes were the whole cause of the trouble between the Armenians and the Turks, and the Government promised to put an end to the reprisals. Talaat Bey telegraphed from Constantinople that the representatives of the Armenians were not to be molested.

Quiet was re-established for the moment, but in the month of May the Turks attempted to force their way into Sassoun, and at the same time the massacres began again without warning at Harpout, Erzeroum and Diyarbekir. The Armenians repulsed the Turks and took up a position round the town of Moush, where a large number of Turkish troops were concentrated. This was the situation when the Turks perpetrated the great massacre of Moush at the end of June. Half the inhabitants of Moush were massacred, the other half were driven out of the town. The Armenians never knew that at that moment the Russian troops were only two or three hours' distance from Moush.

The massacres extended over the whole plain of Moush. The Armenians, who had managed to retreat on to the heights of Sassoun with a remnant of their forces and a slender supply of munitions, attacked the Turks in the valleys and gorges of Sassoun, and inflicted considerable losses upon them. A fraction of the Armenians who escaped the massacre broke through the Turkish lines and reached Van, which was already in the hands of the Russian troops.

The number of Armenian victims is very large. In the town of Moush alone, out of the 15,000 Armenian inhabitants there are only 200 survivors; out of the 59,000 inhabitants of the plain hardly 9,000 have escaped.

22. BITLIS, MOUSH AND SASSOUN: RECORD OF AN INTERVIEW WITH ROUPEN, OF SASSOUN, BY MR. A.S. SAFRASTIAN; DATED TIFLIS, 6th NOVEMBER, 1915.

At the moment of writing, there is very little doubt that during the months of June and July last the Turks have almost completely wiped out about 150,000 Armenians of Bitlis, Moush and Sassoun.

When a detailed account of the horrors which accompanied these massacres is fully disclosed to the civilised world, it will stand out in all history as the greatest masterpiece of brutality ever committed, even by the Turk. A short description of these horrors was given to me by Roupen, one of the leaders in Sassoun, who has miraculously escaped the Turkish lines after long marches across Moush and Lake Van and has been here for the last few days. As soon as the Turks went into the war, they entered into negotiations with the Armenian leaders in Moush and Sassoun with a view to co-operating for the common defence. The Turkish representatives, however, laid down such conditions as a basis for agreement that the Armenians could scarcely entertain them as serious. Until January things had gone on fairly smoothly, and the Armenians were advised by their leaders to comply with all legitimate demands made by the authorities. On the failure of negotiations, the Turks adopted hard measures against the Armenians. They had already ruthlessly requisitioned every commodity they possibly could lay hands on, and now they demanded the surrender of their arms from the peasantry. The Armenians said that they could not give up their arms while the Kurds were left armed to the teeth and went about unmolested. Towards the end of January, a Turkish gendarme provoked a quarrel in Tzeronk, a large Armenian village some 20 miles west of Moush, where some 70 people were killed and the village destroyed. Soon afterwards, another quarrel was started by gendarmes in Koms (Goms), a village on the Euphrates, where the Turks wanted to raise forced labour for the transport of military supplies. As a previous batch of men employed on similar work had never returned home, the peasants grew suspicious and refused to go. Local passion ran high, and the Turks desired to arrest one Gorioun, a native of considerable bravery, who had avenged himself upon Mehmed Emin, a Kurdish brigand, who had ruined his home in the past. All such conflicts of a local character were settled in one way or another by negotiation between the authorities and the leaders of the Dashnaktzoutioun party. In the meantime, Kurdish irregulars and Moslem bands, who were just returning from the battle of Kilidj Geduk, where they had been roughly handled by the Russians, began to harry the Armenians all over the country to the limit of their endurance. In answer to protests, the authorities explained away the grievances and gave all assurances of good-will towards the Armenians, who naturally did not believe in them.

The Massacres at Sairt and Bitlis.—Towards the end of May, Djevdet Bey, the military governor, was expelled from Van, and the town was captured by the native Armenians[40] and then by the Russo-Armenian forces. Djevdet Bey fled southwards and, crossing the Bohtan, entered Sairt with some 8,000 soldiers whom he called "Butcher" battalions (Kassab Tabouri). He massacred most of the Christians of Sairt, though nothing is known of the details. On the best authority, however, it is reported that he ordered his soldiers to burn in a public square the Armenian Bishop Yeghishé Vartabed and the Chaldean Bishop Addai Sher. Then Djevdet Bey, followed by the small army of Halil Bey, marched on Bitlis towards the middle of June. Before his arrival, the Armenians and Kurds of Bitlis had agreed upon a scheme for mutual protection in case of any emergency, but Djevdet Bey had his own plans for exterminating the Armenians. He first raised a ransom of £5,000 from them, and then hanged Hokhigian and some 20 other Armenian leaders, most of whom were attending the wounded in field hospitals. On the 25th June, the Turks surrounded the town of Bitlis and cut its communications with the neighbouring Armenian villages; then most of the able-bodied men were taken away from their families by domiciliary visits. During the following few days, all the men under arrest were shot outside the town and buried in deep trenches dug by the victims themselves. The young women and children were distributed among the rabble, and the remainder, the "useless" lot, were driven to the south and are believed to have been drowned in the Tigris. Any attempts at resistance, however brave, were easily quelled by the regular troops. The recalcitrants, after firing their last cartridges, either took poison by whole families or destroyed themselves in their homes, in order not to fall into the hands of Turks. Some hundred Armenian families in the town, all of them artisans or skilled labourers badly needed by the military authorities, were spared during this massacre, but since then there has been no news of their fate.

It is in such "gentlemanly" fashion that the Turks disposed of about 15,000 Armenians at Bitlis; and the Armenian peasantry of Rahva, Khoultig, and other populous villages of the surrounding district suffered the same fate.

The Massacres in Moush.—Long before this horror had been perpetrated at Bitlis, the Turks and Kurds of Diyarbekir, followed by the most blood-thirsty tribes of Bekran and Belek, had wiped out the Armenians of Slivan, Bisherig, and of the vast plain extending from Diyarbekir to the foot of the Sassoun block. Some thousands of refugees had escaped to Sassoun, as the only haven of safety amid a sea of widespread terror. They told the people of Sassoun and Moush of the enormities which had been committed upon themselves. The line of conduct to be adopted by the Armenians was now obvious. The Turks were resolved to destroy them, and therefore they had to make the best of a hopeless situation by all means at their disposal. Roupen tells me that they had no news whatever as to the progress of the war on the Caucasian front, and that the Turks spread false news to mislead them. The general peace was maintained in the Province of Bitlis until the beginning of June, when things came to a climax. The outlying villages of Boulanik and Moush had already been massacred in May. Now Sassoun was attacked in two main directions. The Kurdish tribes of Belek, Bekran, and Shego, the notorious Sheikh of Zilan and many others were armed by the Government and ordered to surround Sassoun. The 15,000 Armenians of these mountains, re-inforced by some other 15,000 from Moush and Diyarbekir, repelled many fierce attacks, in which the Kurds lost heavily, both in men and arms; whereupon the Government again entered into negotiations with the Armenian leaders, through the Bishop of Moush, and offered them a general amnesty if they laid down their arms and joined in the defence of the common fatherland. And, as a proof of their genuineness, the authorities explained away the massacres of Slivan, Boulanik, &c., as due to a deplorable misunderstanding. Oppressions suddenly ceased everywhere, and perfect order prevailed in Moush for about three weeks in June. A strict watch, however, was kept over the movements of the Armenians, and they were forbidden to concentrate together. In the last week of June, one Kiazim Bey arrived from Erzeroum with at least 10,000 troops and mountain artillery to reinforce the garrison at Moush. The day after his arrival strong patrols were posted on the hills overlooking the town of Moush, thus cutting all communication between Moush and Sassoun. Kurdish bands of "fedais" and gendarmes were commissioned to sever all intercourse between various villages and the town of Moush, so that no one knew what was going on even in the immediate neighbourhood.

Early in July, the authorities ordered the Armenians to surrender their arms, and pay a large money ransom. The leading Armenians of the town and the headmen of the villages were subjected to revolting tortures. Their finger nails and then their toe nails were forcibly extracted; their teeth were knocked out, and in some cases their noses were whittled down, the victims being thus done to death under shocking, lingering agonies. The female relatives of the victims who came to the rescue were outraged in public before the very eyes of their mutilated husbands and brothers. The shrieks and death-cries of the victims filled the air, yet they did not move the Turkish beast. The same process of disarmament was carried out in the large Armenian villages of Khaskegh, Franknorshen, &c., and on the slightest show of resistance men and women were done to death in the manner described above. On the 10th July, large contingents of troops, followed by bands of criminals released from the prisons, began to round up the able-bodied men from all the villages. In the 100 villages of the plain of Moush most of the villagers took up any arms they possessed and offered a desperate resistance in various favourable positions. In the natural order of things the ammunition soon gave out in most villages, and there followed what is perhaps one of the greatest crimes in all history. Those who had no arms and had done nothing against the authorities were herded into various camps and bayoneted in cold blood.

In the town of Moush itself the Armenians, under the leadership of Gotoyan and others, entrenched themselves in the churches and stone-built houses and fought for four days in self-defence. The Turkish artillery, manned by German officers, made short work of all the Armenian positions. Every one of the Armenians, leaders as well as men, was killed fighting; and when the silence of death reigned over the ruins of churches and the rest, the Moslem rabble made a descent upon the women and children and drove them out of the town into large camps which had already been prepared for the peasant women and children. The ghastly scenes which followed may indeed sound incredible, yet these reports have been confirmed from Russian sources beyond all doubt.

The shortest method for disposing of the women and children concentrated in the various camps was to burn them. Fire was set to large wooden sheds in Alidjan, Megrakom, Khaskegh, and other Armenian villages, and these absolutely helpless women and children were roasted to death. Many went mad and threw their children away; some knelt down and prayed amid the flames in which their bodies were burning; others shrieked and cried for help which came from nowhere. And the executioners, who seem to have been unmoved by this unparalleled savagery, grasped infants by one leg and hurled them into the fire, calling out to the burning mothers: "Here are your lions." Turkish prisoners who had apparently witnessed some of these scenes were horrified and maddened at remembering the sight. They told the Russians that the stench of the burning human flesh permeated the air for many days after.

Under present circumstances it is impossible to say how many Armenians, out of a population of 60,000 in the plain of Moush, are left alive; the one fact which can be recorded at present is that now and then some survivors escape through the mountains and reach the Russian lines to give further details of the unparalleled crime perpetrated in Moush during July.

The Massacres in Sassoun.—While the "Butcher" battalions of Djevdet Bey and the regulars of Kiazim Bey were engaged in Bitlis and Moush, some cavalry were sent to Sassoun early in July to encourage the Kurds who had been defeated by the Armenians at the beginning of June. The Turkish cavalry invaded the lower valley of Sassoun and captured a few villages after stout fighting. In the meantime the reorganised Kurdish tribes attempted to close on Sassoun from the south, west, and north. During the last fortnight of July almost incessant fighting went on, sometimes even during the night. On the whole, the Armenians held their own on all fronts and expelled the Kurds from their advanced positions. However, the people of Sassoun had other anxieties to worry about. The population had doubled since their brothers who had escaped from the plains had sought refuge in their mountains; the millet crop of the last season had been a failure; all honey, fruit, and other local produce had been consumed, and the people had been feeding on unsalted roast mutton (they had not even any salt to make the mutton more sustaining); finally, the ammunition was in no way sufficient for the requirements of heavy fighting. But the worst had yet to come. Kiazim Bey, after reducing the town and the plain of Moush, rushed his army to Sassoun for a new effort to overwhelm these brave mountaineers. Fighting was renewed on all fronts throughout the Sassoun district. Big guns made carnage among the Armenian ranks. Roupen tells me that Gorioun, Dikran, and 20 other of their best fighters were killed by a single shell, which burst in their midst. Encouraged by the presence of guns, the cavalry and Kurds pushed on with relentless energy.

The Armenians were compelled to abandon the outlying lines of their defence and were retreating day by day into the heights of Antok, the central block of the mountains, some 10,000 feet high. The non-combatant women and children and their large flocks of cattle greatly hampered the free movements of the defenders, whose number had already been reduced from 3,000 to about half that figure. Terrible confusion prevailed during the Turkish attacks as well as the Armenian counterattacks. Many of the Armenians smashed their rifles after firing the last cartridge and grasped their revolvers and daggers. The Turkish regulars and Kurds, amounting now to something like 30,000 altogether, pushed higher and higher up the heights and surrounded the main Armenian position at close quarters. Then followed one of those desperate and heroic struggles for life which have always been the pride of mountaineers. Men, women and children fought with knives, scythes, stones, and anything else they could handle. They rolled blocks of stone down the steep slopes, killing many of the enemy. In a frightful hand-to-hand combat, women were seen thrusting their knives into the throats of Turks and thus accounting for many of them. On the 5th August, the last day of the fighting, the blood-stained rocks of Antok were captured by the Turks. The Armenian warriors of Sassoun, except those who had worked round to the rear of the Turks to attack them on their flanks, had died in battle. Several young women, who were in danger of falling into the Turks hands, threw themselves from the rocks, some of them with their infants in their arms. The survivors have since been carrying on a guerilla warfare, living only on unsalted mutton and grass. The approaching winter may have disastrous consequences for the remnants of the Sassounli Armenians, because they have nothing to eat and no means of defending themselves.

40. See preceding section.

23. MOUSH: STATEMENT BY A GERMAN EYE-WITNESS OF OCCURRENCES AT MOUSH; COMMUNICATED BY THE AMERICAN COMMITTEE FOR ARMENIAN AND SYRIAN RELIEF.

Towards the end of October (1914), when the Turkish war began, the Turkish officials started to take everything they needed for the war from the Armenians. Their goods, their money, all was confiscated. Later on, every Turk was free to go to an Armenian shop and take out what he needed or thought he would like to have. Only a tenth perhaps was really for the war, the rest was pure robbery. It was necessary to have food, &c., carried to the front, on the Caucasian frontier. For this purpose the Government sent out about 300 old Armenian men, many cripples amongst them, and boys not more than twelve years old, to carry the goods—a three weeks' journey from Moush to the Russian frontier. As every individual Armenian was robbed of everything he ever had, these poor people soon died of hunger and cold on the way. They had no clothes at all, for even these were stolen on the way. If out of these 300 Armenians thirty or forty returned, it was a marvel; the rest were either beaten to death or died from the causes stated above.

The winter was most severe in Moush; the gendarmes were sent to levy high taxes, and as the Armenians had already given everything to the Turks, and were therefore powerless to pay these enormous taxes, they were beaten to death. The Armenians never defended themselves except when they saw the gendarmes ill-treating their wives and children, and the result in such cases was that the whole village was burnt down, merely because a few Armenians had tried to protect their families.

Toward the middle of April we heard rumours that there were great disturbances in Van. We have heard statements both from Turks and from Armenians, and as these reports agree in every respect, it is quite plain that there is some truth in them. They state that the Ottoman Government sent orders that all Armenians were to give up their arms, which the Armenians refused to do on the ground that they required their arms in case of necessity. This caused a regular massacre. All villages inhabited by Armenians were burnt down. The Turks boasted of having now got rid of all the Armenians. I heard it from the officers myself, how they revelled in the thought that the Armenians had been got rid of.

Thus the winter passed, with things happening every day more terrible than one can possibly describe. We then heard that massacres had started in Bitlis. In Moush everything was being prepared for one, when the Russians arrived at Liz, which is about 14 to 16 hours' journey from Moush. This occupied the attention of the Turks, so that the massacre was put off for the time being. Hardly had the Russians left Liz, however, when all the districts inhabited by Armenians were pillaged and destroyed.

This was in the month of May. At the beginning of June, we heard that the whole Armenian population of Bitlis had been got rid of. It was at this time that we received news that the American Missionary, Dr. Knapp, had been wounded in an Armenian house and that the Turkish Government had sent him to Diyarbekir. The very first night in Diyarbekir he died, and the Government explained his death as a result of having overeaten, which of course nobody believed.

When there was no one left in Bitlis to massacre, their attention was diverted to Moush. Cruelties had already been committed, but so far not too publicly; now, however, they started to shoot people down without any cause, and beat them to death simply for the pleasure of doing so. In Moush itself, which is a big town, there are 25,000 Armenians; in the neighbourhood there are 300 villages, each containing about 500 houses. In all these not a single male Armenian is now to be seen, and hardly a woman either, except for a few here and there.

In the first week of July 20,000 soldiers arrived from Constantinople by way of Harpout with munitions and eleven guns, and laid siege to Moush. As a matter of fact, the town had already been beleaguered since the middle of June. At this stage the Mutessarif gave orders that we should leave the town and go to Harpout. We pleaded with him to let us stay, for we had in our charge all the orphans and patients; but he was angry and threatened to remove us by force if we did not do as instructed. As we both fell sick, however, we were allowed to remain at Moush. I received permission, in the event of our leaving Moush, to take the Armenians of our orphanage with us; but when we asked for assurances of their safety, his only reply was: "You can take them with you, but being Armenians their heads may and will be cut off on the way."

On the 10th July Moush was bombarded for several hours, on the pretext that some Armenians had tried to escape. I went to see the Mutessarif and asked him to protect our buildings; his reply was: "It serves you right for staying instead of leaving as instructed. The guns are here to make an end of Moush. Take refuge with the Turks." This, of course, was impossible, as we could not leave our charges. Next day a new order was promulgated for the expulsion of the Armenians, and three days' grace was given them to make ready. They were told to register themselves at the Government Building before they left. Their families could remain, but their property and their money were to be confiscated. The Armenians were unable to go, for they had no money to defray the journey, and they preferred to die in their houses rather than be separated from their families and endure a lingering death on the road.

As stated above, three days' grace was given to the Armenians, but two hours had scarcely elapsed when the soldiers began breaking into the houses, arresting the inmates and throwing them into prison. The guns began to fire and thus the people were effectually prevented from registering themselves at the Government Building. We all had to take refuge in the cellar for fear of our orphanage catching fire. It was heart-rending to hear the cries of the people and children who were being burnt to death in their houses. The soldiers took great delight in hearing them, and when people who were out in the street during the bombardment fell dead, the soldiers merely laughed at them.

The survivors were sent to Ourfa (there were none left but sick women and children); I went to the Mutessarif and begged him to have mercy on the children at least, but in vain. He replied that the Armenian children must perish with their nation. All our people were taken from our hospital and orphanage; they left us three female servants. Under these atrocious circumstances, Moush was burnt to the ground. Every officer boasted of the number he had personally massacred as his share in ridding Turkey of the Armenian race.

We left for Harpout. Harpout has become the cemetery of the Armenians; from all directions they have been brought to Harpout to be buried. There they lie, and the dogs and the vultures devour their bodies. Now and then some man throws some earth over the bodies. In Harpout and Mezré the people have had to endure terrible tortures. They have had their eye-brows plucked out, their breasts cut off, their nails torn off; their torturers hew off their feet or else hammer nails into them just as they do in shoeing horses. This is all done at night time, and in order that the people may not hear their screams and know of their agony, soldiers are stationed round the prisons, beating drums and blowing whistles. It is needless to relate that many died of these tortures. When they die, the soldiers cry: "Now let your Christ help you."

One old priest was tortured so cruelly to extract a confession that, believing that the torture would cease and that he would be left alone if he did it, he cried out in his desperation: "We are revolutionists." He expected his tortures to cease, but on the contrary the soldiers cried: "What further do we seek? We have it here from his own lips." And instead of picking their victims as they did before, the officials had all the Armenians tortured without sparing a soul.

Early in July, 2,000 Armenian soldiers were ordered to leave for Aleppo to build roads. The people of Harpout were terrified on hearing this, and a panic started in the town. The Vali sent for the German missionary, Mr. Ehemann, and begged him to quiet the people, repeating over and over again that no harm whatever would befall these soldiers. Mr. Ehemann took the Vali's word and quieted the people. But they had scarcely left when we heard that they had all been murdered and thrown into a cave. Just a few managed to escape, and we got the reports from them. It was useless to protest to the Vali. The American Consul at Harpout protested several times, but the Vali makes no account of him, and treats him in a most shameful manner. A few days later another 2,000 Armenian soldiers were despatched via Diyarbekir, and, in order to hinder them the more surely from escaping, they were left to starve on the way, so that they had no strength left in them to flee. The Kurds were given notice that the Armenians were on the way, and the Kurdish women came with their butcher's knives to help the men. In Mezré a public brothel was erected for the Turks, and all the beautiful Armenian girls and women were placed there. At night the Turks were allowed free entrance. The permission for the Protestant and Catholic Armenians to be exempted from deportation only arrived after their deportation had taken place. The Government wanted to force the few remaining Armenians to accept the Mohammedan faith. A few did so in order to save their wives and children from the terrible sufferings already witnessed in the case of others. The people begged us to leave for Constantinople and obtain some security for them. On our way to Constantinople we only encountered old women. No young women or girls were to be seen.

Already by November[41] we had known that there would be a massacre. The Mutessarif of Moush, who was a very intimate friend of Enver Pasha, declared quite openly that they would massacre the Armenians at the first opportune moment and exterminate the whole race. Before the Russians arrived they intended first to butcher the Armenians, and then fight the Russians afterwards. Towards the beginning of April, in the presence of a Major Lange and several other high officials, including the American and German Consuls, Ekran Bey quite openly declared the Government's intention of exterminating the Armenian race. All these details plainly show that the massacre was deliberately planned.

In a few villages destitute women come begging, naked and sick, for alms and protection. We are not allowed to give them anything, we are not allowed to take them in, in fact we are forbidden to do anything for them, and they die outside. If only permission could be obtained from the authorities to help them! If we cannot endure the sight of these poor people's sufferings, what must it be like for the sufferers themselves?

It is a story written in blood. Two old missionaries and a younger lady (an American) were sent away from Mardin. They were treated just like prisoners, dogged continually by the gendarmes, and were brought in this fashion to Sivas. For missionaries of that age a journey of this kind in the present circumstances was obviously a terrible hardship.

41. 1914.

24. MOUSH DISTRICT: NARRATIVE OF A DEPORTED WOMAN, RELATED BY HER TO MR. VARTKES OF MOUSH[42], RECORDED BY HIM ON THE 25th JULY, 1915, AND PUBLISHED SUBSEQUENTLY IN THE ARMENIAN JOURNAL "VAN-TOSP."

To-day I heard a terrible story. All the Armenians who were deported from Moush were either killed or drowned in the Mourad River[43]. Among these were my mother and three sisters with their children. This news was brought to us by a woman who came here at midnight. We thought she was a ghost, as she seemed like one coming from the grave. She had saved her two-year-old boy.

She immediately asked for bread. We had not any, as we were living on raw grain and meat, but we gave her what we had. After she had had enough, we asked her all kinds of questions. She was from the village of Kheiban, and was one of the deported. This is what she told us:

"The Turks collected all the women and children of the villages of Sordar, Pazou, Hassanova, Salekan and Gvars, and after keeping them for five days they brought them to Ziaret. Here the inhabitants of Meghd, Baghlou,

Ourough, Ziaret and Kheiban joined them, and they were all taken towards the bridge over the Mourad River. On the way the families from the villages of Dom, Hergerd, Norag, Aladin, Goms[44], Khashkhaldoukh, Souloukh, Khoronk, Kartzor, Kizil Agatch, Komer, Shekhlan, Avazaghpur, Plel and Kurdmeidan joined the party, making altogether a company of 8,000 to 10,000 people.

"All the old women and the weak who were unable to walk were killed. There were about one hundred Kurdish guards over us, and our lives depended on their pleasure. It was a very common thing for them to rape our girls in our presence. Very often they violated eight or ten-year-old girls, and as a consequence many would be unable to walk, and were shot.

"Our company moved on slowly, leaving heaps of corpses behind. Most of us were almost naked. When we passed by a village, all the Kurdish men and women would come and rob us as they pleased. When a Kurd fancied a girl, nothing would prevent him from taking her. The babies of those who were carried away were killed in our presence.

"They gave us bread once every other day, though many did not get even that. When all our provisions were gone, we gathered wheat from the fields and ate it. Many a mother lost her mind and dropped her baby by the wayside.

"Some succeeded in running away, and hid themselves in the fields among the wheat until it was dark. Those who were acquainted with the mountains of that region would thus escape and go back to seek their dear ones. Some went to Sassoun, hearing that it had not yet fallen, others were drowned in the Mourad River. I did not attempt to run away, as I had witnessed with my own eyes the assassination of my dear ones. I had a few piastres left, and hoped to live a few days longer.

"We heard on our way from the Kurds that Kurdish Chettis (bands of robbers) had collected all the inhabitants of Kurdmeidan and Shekhlan, about 500 women and children, and burnt them by the order of Rashid Effendi, the head of the Chettis.

"When we reached the Khozmo Pass, our guards changed their southerly direction and turned west, in the direction of the Euphrates. When we reached the boundary of the Ginj district our guards were changed, the new ones being more brutal. By this time our number was diminished by half. When we reached the boundary of Djabaghchour we passed through a narrow valley; here our guards ordered us to sit down by the river and take a rest. We were very thankful for this respite and ran towards the river to get a drink of water.

"After half-an-hour we saw a crowd of Kurds coming towards us from Djabaghchour. They surrounded us and ordered us to cross the river, and many obeyed. The report of the guns drowned the sounds of wailing and crying. In that panic I took my little boy on my back and jumped into the river. I was a good swimmer and succeeded in reaching the opposite shore of the Euphrates with my precious bundle unnoticed, and hid myself behind some undergrowth.

"By nightfall no one remained alive from our party. The Kurds left in the direction of Djabaghchour. At dusk I came out from my hiding place to a field in the vicinity and found some wheat, which I ate; then I followed the Euphrates in a northerly direction, and after great difficulty I reached the plain of Moush. I decided to go to the mountains of Sourp Garabed, as I had heard that there were many Armenians there. During the nights my boy was a great comfort to me. I felt that a living being was with me and fear lost its horror. I thank God I have seen the faces of Armenians again."

The poor woman ended her story, and our hearts were stricken with sorrow, for we had loved ones among the unfortunate people of her convoy. Two days later her boy died from lack of nourishment, and after five days she was found by a party of patrolling Kurds and killed.

25. MOUSH: RESUMÉ OF INFORMATION FURNISHED BY REFUGEES IN THE CAUCASUS AND PUBLISHED IN THE CAUCASIAN PRESS, ESPECIALLY IN THE ARMENIAN JOURNAL "MSCHAK"; COMPILED BY MR. G.H. PAELIAN, AND COMMUNICATED BY HIM TO THE ARMENIAN JOURNAL "ARARAT," OF LONDON, MARCH, 1916.

The following reports concerning the massacres and deportations in the region of Moush and Sassoun have come to hand from completely independent sources, yet it is remarkable to note how they confirm one another.

The massacres of Moush began on the 28th June (11th July), Sunday morning, and lasted until Monday night. They were organised by the Governors of Van and Bitlis and carried out in the presence of their representatives, among whom were Abdoullah Bey of Sipuk, Topal Ibrahim of Moush (tax collector), Hassan (tax collector), and the police hakim. Before the massacres, all the prominent Armenians underwent indescribable sufferings. They were flogged and their limbs twisted until their thumbs began to bleed. The day the peasants were arrested they wished to take Holy Communion first, but were refused. The monks of Saint Garabed and the prominent Armenians of the villages of Gvars, Sortra and Pazou were assassinated in the monastery. The perpetrators opened the tomb of Bishop Nerses Kharakhanian, with the hope of finding money. They took his shroud and put the body back in the tomb. Mehmed Effendi, the Ottoman deputy for Gendjé[45], collected about 40 women and children and killed them. Two hundred of the inhabitants of Moush were brought to the village of Shekhlan and thrown into the Mourad River. One hundred men from Sassoun, who surrendered, were imprisoned without food or drink. When they begged for bread, the Turkish inhabitants could not stand their wailing, and asked the Government either to give them bread or kill them. They were all killed about the middle of November.

Then the Government looked for the Armenians who had found refuge with some Kurds, and finding about 2,000 of them massacred them all. The fact is confirmed that Kegham Der Garabedian, the Ottoman deputy for Moush, was hanged. The property of the Armenians of Moush and Bitlis was sold by the Government, and all their sheep and cattle which were left with the Kurds were requisitioned by the army of Halil Bey.

According to reports from the Caucasus, the Turks gathered together about 5,000 Armenians by treachery and deception from 20 Armenian villages round the monastery of Saint Garabed at Moush and massacred them. This took place near the wall of the monastery. Before the massacre began, a German officer stood on the wall and harangued the Armenians to the effect that the Turkish Government had shown great kindness to, and had honoured, the Armenians, but that they were not satisfied and wanted autonomy; he then, by the report of a revolver, gave the signal for the general massacre. Among the massacred were two monks, one of them being the father superior of Sourp Garabed, Yeghishé Vartabed, who had a chance of escaping but did not wish to be separated from his flock and was killed with them. From the Sahajian district about 4,000 Armenians found refuge in the forests of the monastery, and fought against the attacking Turks and Kurds. They kept themselves alive on wheat, raw meat without salt, turtle, frogs, etc. Some of them finally surrendered, but no one knows the fate of the remainder. The monastery of St. Garabed was sacked and robbed. The Turks opened the tomb of St. Garabed and destroyed everything. They also discovered some secret chambers. Turkish chiefs took up their quarters in the monastery with imprisoned Armenian girls.

According to another report no one was spared in Moush, not even the orphans in the German Orphanage. Some of these were killed and others deported. The Rev. Krikor and Mr. Marcar Ghougasian, teachers in the German Orphanage, were killed, and only two escaped death, Miss Margarid Nalbandian and Miss Maritza Arisdakesian. These were graduates of the German Seminary at Mezré, and owe their lives to a kind German lady.

According to the reports of some Armenians who had found refuge in the forests of Sourp Garabed and finally made their way to the Caucasus, Hilmi

Bey was appointed for the purpose of clearing the Armenian provinces of Armenians. This man reached Erzeroum on the 18th May, and then went to Khnyss, Boulanik, Khlat, etc., massacring every Armenian in these places. According to a letter, dated the 19th June (3rd July), written to one of these refugees, Hilmi Bey had three army corps (?) with him, a body of gendarmes, and the volunteers of Hadji Moussa Bey and Sheikh Hazret, who had come to Moush to massacre the Armenians. To these forces were added the Turkish mob of Moush, the Turkish refugees from Alashkerd and Badnotz, Keur Husein Pasha and Abd-ul-Medjid Bey. The massacres were directed by Governor Djevdet of Van, Commander Halil of Diliman, Governor Abd-ul-Khalak of Bitlis, and Governor Servet Bey of Moush. The order for massacre was given on the 28th June (11th July). According to Turkish Government statistics 120,000 Armenians were killed in this district.

42. At that time in hiding in the forests of Sourp Garabed.

43. Eastern Euphrates.

44. Koms.

45. Ginj (?)

26. BITLIS: LETTER DATED 14th OCTOBER, 1915, FROM A FOREIGN RESIDENT AT BITLIS TO A GERMAN OFFICIAL; COMMUNICATED BY THE AMERICAN COMMITTEE FOR ARMENIAN AND SYRIAN RELIEF.

From having seen you yesterday, I am assured that you will receive with kindly consideration what I feel obliged to write to you. It is about the women and children who still remain with us.

It might be well to relate first a few of the recent events bearing on the matter.

On the 23rd June the Armenian men of the city, including those on our premises, were led to prison. A few days later, when they began to take the women from the city, I called on the Vali and told him that I could not give up the girls of our school and the women who had come to me for protection. He said that Halil Bey had decided the matter in regard to the women, and that he himself had no power to alter that decision, but that he would leave those on our premises till the last. I wrote a letter to Halil Bey with the consent of the Vali, to whom I sent a copy. I received no answer.

The women and girls are now employed in the hospitals, and by this means we have been able to keep them until now. We have spoken with Djevdet Bey recently, but he gives us no assurance of their ultimate safety, and says that the children must go. Of our Protestant community, we have twenty-five teachers and pupils, twenty-five women and twelve children. Apart from these there are other women who are employed in the hospital, and about thirty orphans. The first orphans whom we received were brought to the school by Turkish officials, and since it appeared that the Government did not disapprove, we have received others and provide them with food and shelter. Much as we should like to save them all, we feel that we can only insist on keeping those of our community.

My heart is full of this subject. It is not my desire in any way to oppose the Government. Our superiors give us very definite instructions on this point before we come out. We all agreed here that since the Government thought it a necessary war measure that the men should be taken into exile, we could not refuse to give them up. But since that time I have witnessed so many things that seemed unnecessary, that the giving up of those entrusted to my care now seems a different matter. I am not saying that we can prevent their being taken—some of our women have already been taken from us—no one realises more than we do our own helplessness. But we are trying by every means in our power to save them. I plead with you for your help in this. I have wanted very much to see the Vali, but owing to Miss A.'s being ill I have had no interpreter.

We received word recently from Constantinople that the Government had informed our Ambassador that Protestant communities would not be molested, and that he had notified the consuls to that effect. But such orders have not been carried out here.

These women and children who are with us cannot possibly do harm to the Government—why must they be sent away to such a fate? If the hospital were removed, we could then be responsible for their support, until such time as it would be fitting to take them with us to Harpout. My first plan, in the event of their trying to take our girls, was to barricade the school building, and compel them to force their way in or set fire to the building. Death in that form would have been welcome to the girls under those circumstances. The plan was not practicable, and I am telling you only that you may understand how much we dread the fate that awaits them. When I suggested the plan to my associates, I met with some opposition, but Sister B. said: "If I were in your place I would do the same thing," and suggested that she should take some of the women whom I could not accommodate in the school, to another building, and remain with them there. Her sympathetic understanding at that time was a great help to me. I have always had a great faith in Germany. Through Miss C. I learned to love her country. Somehow, I trust you as I trusted her, and I feel that you will do for us what she would have done had she been able. Both Miss A. and myself entreat you most earnestly that you will use what influence you can exert here, that we may keep these women and children with us.

Your companions are here and inform us that you will leave to-morrow. We regret that we shall not see you again, but enjoyed the opportunity of meeting you the one time.

IV.
AZERBAIJAN AND HAKKIARI.

The province of Azerbaijan lies immediately east of Van, across the Persian border, and consists principally of another and still larger inland basin, shut in by mountains which drain towards the central Lake of Urmia.

Though Azerbaijan is nominally a part of Persia, there are practically no Persians among its inhabitants. The majority of them are Shiah Mohammedans, speaking a Turkish dialect; but the parts west of the Lake, and especially the districts of Urmia and Salmas, are occupied by a Semitic Christian population, variously known as "Nestorians" (from their religion), "Syrians" (from their language) or "Chaldoeans" (from their race). They are descended from the former inhabitants of Mesopotamia, who were pushed into and over the mountains by Arab encroachment. A larger number of them is still left on the Ottoman side of the watershed, in the Hakkiari district round the headwaters of the Greater Zab, and further west, again, near the confluence of the Tigris and the Bohtan. In the two latter districts they are now in a minority as compared with their Kurdish neighbours, and Kurds are also interspersed among the Nestorians in the Urmia basin, especially towards the southern end of the Lake, but also on the west (Tergawar).

When, in the winter of 1914-15, the Turks took the offensive against the Russians on the Caucasian front, they sent a subsidiary army, reinforced by Kurdish tribesmen, into Azerbaijan. The weak Russian forces occupying the province retired northwards at the beginning of January, and the Turco-Kurdish invaders penetrated as far as Tabriz, while the Nestorian villages on the western side of Lake Urmia remained in their possession for nearly five months. The Russians were followed in their retreat by a considerable part of the Christian population, who suffered terrible hardships on their winter journey. Those that remained behind flocked into the town of Urmia, and were subject to all manner of atrocities during the twenty weeks that the Turks and Kurds controlled the place. The Russians completed the re-occupation of Azerbaijan in May, 1915; they entered the town of Urmia on the 24th May, five days after their first entry into Van, and freed the people of Salmas and Urmia from their oppressors. But they could not save the communities in the Zab district, who suffered in June the same fate as the Armenians of Bitlis, Moush and Sassoun; and when the Russians were compelled to evacuate Van again at the end of July, the panic spread from Van to Urmia, and a fresh stream of Nestorian refugees swelled the general exodus of Christians into the Russian Provinces of the Caucasus.

27. URMIA: STATEMENT BY THE REV. WILLIAM A. SHEDD, D.D., OF THE AMERICAN (PRESBYTERIAN) MISSION STATION AT URMIA; COMMUNICATED BY THE BOARD OF FOREIGN MISSIONS OF THE PRESBYTERIAN CHURCH IN THE U.S.A.

Persia is not in the war, but the war has been in Persia ever since its beginning. Indeed, the military movements of Russia and of Turkey date back several years before its outbreak. The Turks in 1906 occupied a strip of territory along the Persian border extending from a point south-west of Soujboulak to a point west of Khoi. The purpose was no doubt to secure a boundary-line making it more possible to move troops from the Mosul region into Trans-Caucasia, as well as to make it easier to hold the frontier against any Russian attack. In 1911, the Turks evacuated this strip of territory and the whole boundary question was submitted to a mixed commission, on which the British and Russian Governments were represented as well as the Turkish and Persian. When war began in August, 1914, this commission had completed its work from the Persian Gulf to Salmas. The Russians, in connection with internal disturbances in Persia, occupied with their troops a number of cities in northern Persia. Tabriz was occupied in 1909; Urmia and Khoi in 1910. This measure enabled the Russians not only to control Persia, but also to secure the road from their rail-head at Djoulfa to Van through Khoi. When the Great War began, Russia was therefore in occupation.

Disturbances at once began along the border and at the beginning of October, 1914, a determined attack was made on Urmia, ostensibly by Kurds. It was afterwards clear, from statements made by Persians and Turks who were engaged in the attack, that the nucleus of the fighting force was made up of Turkish soldiers and that the attack was under the command of Turkish officers. It was also clear from statements made by Persians friendly with the Turks and unfriendly towards the Russians, that the result of success in this attack would have been the looting of the Christian population, with probable loss of life.

About a month after this attack, war was declared between Russia and Turkey. About the same time the Russians closed the Turkish Consulates at Urmia, Tabriz and Khoi, and expelled the Kurds and other Sunni Moslems from the villages near Urmia. Arms were given at the same time to some of the Christians. The Turks in response expelled several thousand Christians from adjoining regions in Turkey. These refugees were settled in the villages vacated by the Sunni Moslems who had been expelled. Turkish and Kurdish forces gathered along the frontier and especially to the south in the Soujboulak region.

In the latter part of December, two engagements took place—one 20 miles south of Urmia between Kurdish and Russian soldiers, in which the latter were successful; the other was at Miandoab, at the south end of Lake Urmia, in which the Russian forces, with some Persians, were routed by Turks and Kurds. About the same time Enver Pasha invaded Trans-Caucasia from Armenia at Sarikamysh in the Kars region. This threatened to cut off Russia's communications with Persia, and orders were given for the evacuation of Tabriz, Urmia and Khoi. The evacuation of Urmia took place on the 2nd January, that of Salmas a day or two later, and that of Tabriz on the 5th. Meanwhile, the military situation in Trans-Caucasia had changed with the rout of Enver Pasha's army, and Khoi was not evacuated.

For convenience it may be well to summarise the military events from the 1st January to the 1st June. Tabriz was occupied by the Turks and Kurds, but, about the 1st February, a crushing defeat a few miles north of Tabriz led to its sudden evacuation and to the flight of the Turkish forces back to Miandoab. The American Consul at Tabriz, the Hon. Gordon Paddock, with the very effective co-operation of the German Consul, who had previously been in the American Hospital under the protection of the American Consul, kept the city of Tabriz from loss of life and to a large extent from loss of property. The Turks collected large Kurdish forces from the Soujboulak region and from districts in eastern Turkey; these, together with a smaller force of Turkish regulars, moved through Urmia and Salmas against Khoi, joining Turkish forces from Van under Djevdet Bey. This campaign against Khoi lasted until the 1st March, and was unsuccessful. In March the Russian forces drove the Turks from Salmas and occupied this region. Affairs remained in this condition until April. In April the Van campaign of the Russians, with the aid of Armenian volunteers, began. A Turkish force of approximately 18,000 men with mountain guns under Halil Bey, an uncle of Enver Pasha, reached Urmia on the 16th April. They had come over the mountain passes from Mosul, having been sent from Constantinople by way of Aleppo to Mosul. Halil Bey was defeated in Salmas, and in May retreated towards Van. The Turkish forces were finally withdrawn from Urmia on the 20th May, and the Russians re-occupied that city on the 24th May. The region of Soujboulak was occupied by the Turks for some months longer, but the campaign in that region has no bearing on the Christian population, since there are no Christians in the region.

The Christian population in this region is partly Armenian and partly Nestorian—or Syrian, as they call themselves. The Armenian element consisted of four or five thousand in Tabriz, ten thousand or more in Salmas, a small number in Khoi, and some six or seven thousand in the Urmia district. The Nestorians, except for less than 2,000 in Salmas, all lived in the Urmia district. Including refugees from Turkey and the Armenians, there were in Urmia, at the beginning of 1915, not far from 35,000 Christians. The Syrians or Nestorians include not only members of the old Nestorian Church but also Protestants, members of the Russian Orthodox Church, and Roman Catholics—or Chaldeans, as the last are generally called. In Maragha there is a colony of Armenians numbering some hundreds. Excepting the Christians in Tabriz, Maragha, and the city of Urmia, the last numbering not more than 2,000, all these Christians live in villages, Mohammedans and Christians sometimes sharing a village between them and sometimes living in separate villages. These Mohammedan villagers belong to the Shiah sect but speak the Turkish language.

The evacuation of the Russians put all the Christians in peril. The Salmas Christians (except about 800), most of the Christians of Tabriz, and eight or ten thousand from Urmia fled with the retreating Russians. They left on the shortest notice, without preparation and in the heart of winter. Many perished by the way, mothers dying in childbirth, old men and women and little children falling by the way side from exhaustion. This fleeing army of refugees, increased in numbers by several thousand from the regions in Turkey between Khoi and Van, passed over the Russian border and scattered in the villages and towns of Trans-Caucasia. Many of them died of disease due to the privations and exposures of flight and life as refugees.

This flight left some 25,000 Christians in Urmia. All of these sought shelter from massacre. On the one hand the Kurds were pouring into the plain, urged on and followed by Turkish officers and troops; on the other hand the Moslem villagers set to work robbing and looting, killing men and women and outraging the women. Several thousand found refuge with friendly Mohammedans. Great credit is due to no small number of Moslems, most of them humble villagers and some men of higher rank, who protected the imperilled Christians. In some cases safety was bought by professing Mohammedanism, but many died as martyrs to the faith. In several places the Christians defended themselves, but the massacring was not confined to these. Villages that deliberately gave up their arms and avoided any conflict suffered as much as those that fought. The mass of the people fled to the city, and all, including the city people, took refuge in the mission compounds. The French Roman Catholic Mission sheltered about 3,000, and the compounds of the American Presbyterian Mission about 17,000. The latter were enlarged by joining up neighbouring yards and so enclosing in one connected compound, with only one gate for entrance and exit, some fifteen to twenty yards. The American flag was placed over the compounds of the American Mission, and here people were safe from massacre. The villages, in the meantime, with three or four exceptions, were a prey to plunder and destruction. Everything movable that possessed the least value was either carried away or destroyed.

During the months of Turkish occupation there was never a moment of real safety for the Christians. The most unremitting efforts on the part of the missionaries secured comparative safety within the city walls, so that the people were scattered to some extent from the Mission Compound; and a few villages, including two that were not plundered at the beginning, were kept comparatively safe through the efforts of the Persian Governor. Beyond these narrow limits the Christians could not go. This was shown by constant robberies and murders when Christians ventured forth. During this period the Turks were guilty not only of failure to protect the Christians effectively, but also of direct massacres under their orders. One hundred and seventy men thus massacred were buried by the American missionaries, their bodies lying in heaps where they had been shot down and stabbed, tied together and led out to be murdered by Turkish agents. These massacres took place on three different occasions. Once men were seized by Turkish officers in the French Mission and sent out from the Turkish headquarters to be killed; once there were men seized in a village which was under the protection of Turkish soldiers and had had its safety pledged repeatedly by the highest Turkish officials; and once there were men from just over the border in Turkey who had been forced to bring telegraph wire down to Urmia and were then taken out and killed. In each of these cases some escaped and crawled out, wounded and bloody, from the heaps of dead and dying, to find refuge with the American missionaries. Besides these, the Armenian soldiers in the Turkish army, previously to the arrival of Halil Bey, were shot. In Urmia, the total losses of this period, from the evacuation of the town by the Russians on the 2nd January until their return on the 24th May, were the murder of over one thousand people—men, women and children; the outraging of hundreds of women and girls of every age—from eight or nine years to old age; the total robbing of about five-sixths of the Christian population; and the partial or total destruction of about the same proportion of their houses. Over two hundred girls and women were carried off into captivity, to be forced to embrace Islam and to accept Mohammedan husbands. The Salmas district suffered quite as much as Urmia, excepting that the mass of the people fled with the Russian troops, and consequently the crimes against women were not so numerous. About 800 who remained in Salmas, most of whom were old people, with some of the poorer and younger women, were gathered together by Djevdet Bey before his withdrawal from Salmas and were massacred. This happened early in March. The Salmas villages were left in much the same condition as those of Urmia.

The relief work began before the evacuation. Unsettled conditions had frightened people, and many had brought their goods for safe keeping to the American missionaries. With the evacuation many more brought their property, whatever they could save from the general riot. The protection of those under the American flag and of others in the city and in Mohammedan homes was accomplished only by the most constant vigilance during all those months. It was necessary to feed thousands of the people, and over ten thousand people were fed for about six months. Many of the girls and women who were taken captive were found and returned to their homes; information was secured as to others, which led to their subsequent rescue. Conditions of life were such that it was impossible to prevent epidemics, those that carried off the largest number being typhoid and typhus. Both of these diseases were probably brought by Turkish soldiers cared for in the American Hospital. The total number who died of disease during the period of Turkish occupation was not less than four thousand. Of eighteen adults connected with the American Mission, thirteen had either typhus or typhoid, and three lost their lives. The French missionaries suffered just as severely, and were in greater peril of violence.

To assign guilt and analyse the causes of this terrible loss of life and property is not an altogether easy task. There is no class of Mohammedans that can be exempted from blame. The villagers joined in the looting and shared in the crimes of violence, and Persians of the higher class acquiesced in the outrages and shared in the plunder. The Kurds were in their natural element. The Turks not only gave occasion for all that happened, but were direct participants in the worst of the crimes. On the other hand, individuals of every class deserve credit. There were many villagers who showed only kindness. The Persian Governor made it possible, by his co-operation, for the American missionaries to do what they did; the Kurds responded to appeals for mercy and, in some cases, returned captive girls unsolicited and did other humane service. A few individual Turkish officers and a number of their soldiers took strong measures to keep order. One such officer saved the city from loot when riot had already begun. There were various causes; jealousy of the greater prosperity of the Christian population was one, and political animosity, race hatred and religious fanaticism all had a part. There was also a definite and determined, purpose and malice in the conduct of Turkish officials. It is certainly safe to say that a part of this outrage and ruin was directly due to the Turks, and that none of it would have taken place except for them.

The duty of Americans, and especially the missionaries, is not so much to apportion the blame as to repair the damages. The task in Persia is very great, but the opportunities are equally as great. The number of destitute persons has been increased by the influx of forty or fifty thousand refugees from Turkey—Nestorians who lived in the mountain region between Urmia and Van, and who were forced to flee from their homes by the Turks and Kurds. In outlying districts the men have been massacred, and those who have survived are mainly women and children; but from the mountain valleys, where the bulk of these people live, they were able to escape *en masse*.

28. FIRST EXODUS FROM URMIA, JANUARY, 1915: REPORT DATED 1st MARCH, 1915, FROM THE REVEREND ROBERT M. LABAREE, OF THE AMERICAN MISSION STATION AT TABRIZ, TO THE HON. F. WILLOUGHBY SMITH, U.S. CONSUL AT TIFLIS; COMMUNICATED BY THE BOARD OF FOREIGN MISSIONS OF THE PRESBYTERIAN CHURCH IN THE U.S.A.

In view of your interest in the welfare of the Persian Christian refugees here in the Caucasus, and your efforts in their behalf, may I submit to you a report on their condition as I have seen it in my journey hither from Tabriz? Commissioned by the American Presbyterian Mission of West Persia to investigate the affairs of the many thousands who have fled recently from Persia into Russia in order to escape the cruel vengeance of the Kurdish border tribes, I left Tabriz over two weeks ago and have spent the intervening time visiting the various centres where these refugees are congregated. It is hard to estimate exactly the number of these refugees from Persia, for mingled with them are a multitude of fugitives from Turkey. The total number of all these unfortunates in the district of Erivan, where most of them have found refuge, was stated by a good authority to be seventy thousand. The Persian contingent is pretty consistently estimated at from fifteen to twenty thousand. The refugees from Turkey are almost entirely Armenian, and are being taken care of by the wealthy Armenians of this province through their well organised relief committees. Those from Persia are less fortunate, for a majority of them are Syrian; and, although the Armenians have been very generous to them also, they have no influential friends to speak in their behalf and minister to their needs. It is also safe to say that the fugitives from the Urmia plain are the most sadly in need of assistance, for they had no previous warning of the impending disaster, and most of them have come out without any preparation whatever for their prolonged sojourn in a strange land.

I doubt whether the story of that awful flight can ever adequately be told. Few tales that I have ever heard can compare with it in heart-rending interest. The whole northern section of the Urmia plain learned of the departure of the Russian troops about ten o'clock on the night of Saturday, the 2nd January (1915). By midnight the terrible exodus had begun, and by morning the Christian villages of that district were practically deserted. People left their cattle in the stables and all their household goods in their homes, just as they were, and hurried away to save their lives. If anyone possessed a horse or a donkey or any other beast of burden he was fortunate, and if he happened to have ready cash in his home he was even more so; but, well-to-do as a man may be, cash is not always on hand in the villages, and so many who, according to the standards of the country, were rich, started on their long journey with a mere pittance, and the vast majority of men and women and children were on foot. Before the seven days' hard walking through the slush and mud to the Russian border was accomplished, all encumbrances were cast aside, quilts, extra clothing, and even bread, for it became a question with the poor, tired, struggling crowd which they would carry—their bedding or their babies. Of course, very many of the weaker ones never reached Djoulfa at all, but lay down by the roadside for their last long rest, and those who did reach the Russian border were so haggard and emaciated that their own friends did not recognise them. Almost worse than the weary tramping by day, in the most terrible mud, were the nights in the villages by the way. Every possible shelter was so crowded that there was no room whatever to lie down, and the air became so foul before morning that the occupants were nearly suffocated; and yet those who could find no shelter and lay out all night in the wet were even more miserable. As one has heard the same sad story repeated a score of times with only a difference in details, one has wondered what human flesh and blood can stand in a great crisis like this. I should like to give two instances that have come under my personal knowledge; such stories might be multiplied a thousand times.

One old man with two daughters-in-law and six grandchildren started on that fatal night from the village of Karagöz. All were afoot, and the women carried their little ones by turns, while the old man stumbled along as best he could, unable to carry any burden. He at last gave out, lay down by the roadside and died. The two women and their little charges pressed on for a day or two longer, when one of them gave birth to a baby, also by the roadside. The mother tore off her dress, wrapped the baby in the pieces and resumed the weary tramp. Fortunately for them, the two women found their husbands waiting for them in Russian Djoulfa; but, alas, in the new complications arising from the coming of the baby two of the other children were separated from the party and lost. Two days the parents waited in Djoulfa, until a wagon-load of little waifs was brought in by kind-hearted soldiers. They found their two little ones among the number, but so emaciated by their hardships that they died shortly afterwards. People dying and children being born by the way are commonplaces of this journey; but it is not every one that has had a combination of such misfortunes.

Here, again, is another instance no less sad. The pastor of our Cosi congregation set out, as others did, in the dark, together with his wife, married daughter, and five-year-old granddaughter; but he became separated from them very soon, so that the women were compelled to make the journey alone. They reached the town of Nahichevan, in Russian territory, with hundreds of others in a wholly exhausted condition. All three of them were sick and were taken to the local hospital, where a few days later the father of the family found them. But shortly afterwards, when the thousands of refugees were cleared out of the town and scattered in the villages, he was forced to leave, and his family have not seen him since. The daughter and grandchild were dismissed from the hospital, and the old mother, rather than remain alone, sick as she was, left also. For five days they stayed with a crowd of others in the railway station, when they were moved on to another village; and there, the old woman's dysentery having become so bad and the little girl having developed the prevailing scarlet fever, they were taken to the village hospital. I found them there a couple of weeks later, or rather the younger woman and her child; the mother had passed away two hours before I arrived. I buried the dear old woman, in whose house I have been many times. I gave her a better funeral than most of the other dying refugees; but it was only a rough coffin with shavings as a pillow for her poor tired head. And then, with a little money put into the hand of the daughter and a promise to do what I could to find her father, I left her, dazed as a woman in a dream, and came away. The father cannot be found, and I fear that he has dropped down in some unknown spot and died.

I have wondered time and time again whether this panic-stricken flight was not some terrible mistake, and whether the people had not better have stayed at home and cast themselves on the mercies of the Kurds and their Moslem neighbours; but as the stories of the sufferings of those who remained behind begin to reach us—stories of bloodshed and forced apostacy, and of women and girls carried off to a life worse than death—I have revised my judgment. Even all this untold misery by the way and in a strange land is better than the fate of those who remained at home.

But I must pass on to report the conditions as they now exist among the refugees. In my effort to get the facts, I have had interviews with the Exarch (the Metropolitan Bishop of Tiflis), the Governor of the Erivan district, the Armenian Bishops of Tabriz (now in Nahichevan) and of Erivan, members of the various relief committees and the village elders, who act as local relief committees, together with a very large number of the refugees themselves in various sections of the province. Whatever one may find to criticise in the administration of relief, one cannot but recognise the tremendous burden that has descended upon the people of this region and the serious problems they have had to face. While one cannot say that there has been an adequate effort to grapple with the difficulties, yet much has been done. The Government officials have given free railway transportation to the interior, and they have wisely had the people scattered among the villages, where they can best be taken care of. The energetic Armenian committees have taken care of their own people, and have been unexpectedly generous to the Syrians who are quartered in their midst. In Tiflis the Syrians themselves have done much for their own race in that city, and have had an efficient committee working in conjunction with the municipal relief committee. But more worthy of praise than any or all of these together are the humble kind-hearted villagers themselves, who have carried the heaviest end of the burden, taking in the homeless wanderers, giving them shelter and even bedding, and furnishing them with food. Had it not been for this unorganised relief, the misery would have been many times more intense. In one village, of 50 houses, I found 307 refugees; and in another, of 100 houses, 850 dependents. In the former place all that had been received from outside sources had been 220 roubles, and in the latter the extent of outside relief had been about six pounds per head of poor flour. But the farmers of that section have had a bad year of it, and are themselves feeling the pinch of poverty; and the burden of all this multitude of destitute people is getting to be almost intolerable. At best, too, what has been done by all agencies combined has failed to save the wretched refugees from their sad plight. With often twenty of them in one room, sleeping on the grass, destitute of bedclothing and having unwholesome-looking bread to eat, their lot is not to be envied. No wonder that after the hardships of the journey scores and hundreds of them have died, pneumonia and enteric troubles and scarlet fever having carried off a multitude. The scarlet fever has been especially virulent, and there was scarcely a house which I visited where from two to five little ones had not been carried out to the cemetery. One could hardly hope to save a man with dysentery on the five kopecks (1¼d.) a day given for his support, or with the coarse flour given in other districts. While one cannot but pity all, yet one's especial sympathy goes out to those whom one has seen in their own country living in comfort and, for this country, even in luxury, yet here, in this strange land, dependent on the dole of bread given them.

With such conditions I have not dared to do anything in the way of relief, except to leave here and there small sums for the sick and for those particularly suffering. As long as I have not found anyone that has died or is dying from hunger I did not think it justifiable to expend our little funds in the hopeless task of making men comfortable. More and more am I persuaded that we must reserve our efforts to the time when these people begin to return to their homes. If the way opens for such a return, it must be our first endeavour to restore them to their villages; for very many of them have their wheat-fields and vineyards, and if these are not looked after this spring, the relief problem of the future becomes many times more serious. But how are these unfortunates to get home? Some of them had a little money when they came out and some reserve strength; now both funds and physical force are gone, and after the hard journey back they will reach homes plundered of everything, and in many cases burnt. Officials here have declared that there is no question but that the Government will send them back by rail to Djoulfa free of charge; but, when they are once in Persia, then all relief committees save our own cease to act. It is on this basis that I wish to make my appeal to the American public. In a report which I subjoin, Dr.

Shedd, of our Mission in Urmia, gives us a picture of the conditions there among those who, to the number of ten to fifteen thousand, have found shelter in our Mission yards. Up to the 25th January I learn that he has spent over eight hundred pounds sterling in their support; and he names £3,000 as the minimum of what is needed for the people there. He himself considers this an under-estimate, looking at the problem only from the limited knowledge he had at his command; and I am sure that it is. Five thousand for those in Urmia and five thousand for those who have fled, seems to me a more reasonable estimate. Ten thousand pounds is a big sum to ask, especially at this time, when so many other portions of the world are stretching out their hands to our country for aid; but most of these have many eloquent tongues to voice their cry, while for this people, that have lived so far away among fanatical Moslem masters, who is there to speak? I can only hope that this little story of their sufferings may bring some relief, even if it is not the sum asked and so much needed. I wish I might hope that others would help in this work; but the French Mission has little assistance to give, and the Orthodox Mission, that has made a big bid for the friendship of this people, seems to have completely flattened out. I doubt whether anything can be hoped for from that source, and I am very sure that nothing will be given in a large unsectarian way. And so it appears to me that we of America are the only ones that can be relied upon to come to the assistance of this old historic people, who have now endured the heaviest blow that has fallen upon them for centuries.

There is one other matter. I have said that we must reserve our help for the time when these people return home; money given them here, unless it be in very large sums, can do no good. You, however, have suggested that £200, given through me to the heads of the Relief Committees of the Caucasus to be used for these Persian refugees, might do more than anything else to quicken their own assistance to this unfortunate people. The reasons you have given for this judgment have seemed to me strong ones, and I have telegraphed to-day to our headquarters, stating the facts. If any such funds are sent, I shall ask you to help me in giving the money in such a manner as shall produce the best results. In the meantime I wish to thank you most cordially for all that you have done to assist me in this good work.

29. AZERBAIJAN, BEHIND THE RUSSIAN FRONT: EXTRACTS FROM A SERIES OF LETTERS BY THE REV. ROBERT M. LABAREE; COMMUNICATED BY THE BOARD OF FOREIGN MISSIONS OF THE PRESBYTERIAN CHURCH IN THE U.S.A.

(a) Letter dated Tabriz, 12th March, 1915 (to Mr. Labaree's mother).

Sad news. The Kurds driven back from Khoi massacred 800 Syrian and Armenian men with cruel torture. This in the plain of Salmas. In Urmia the largest and wealthiest Syrian village, Gulpashan, which had been spared by payments of large sums of money, was given over to plunder by the returning Kurds. The men of the village were all taken out to the cemetery and killed; the women and girls treated barbarously. Sixty men were taken out of the French Mission, where they had taken refuge, and shot. Others have been hanged. The Swiss teacher of the missionaries' children has died of typhoid. I have been asked to go to Urmia, but every way is blocked. Please let Mr. Speer know facts.

(b) Letter dated Tabriz, 13th March, 1915 (to Mr. Speer).

Dr. Shedd's latest communication speaks for itself and reveals a terrible condition of things at Urmia. This condition, I fear, has been rendered even more acute in the two weeks since the letter was written by the defeat of the Turks and Kurds near Salmas. At that time all the remaining Christian refugees in Diliman (the chief town of Salmas) suffered terribly. All the males above twelve years of age were taken to two neighbouring villages, tortured and shot. Their number is estimated at 800. The women were to be made Moslems, but the entrance of the Russians into the town the next day prevented that. I doubt not but that the retreating Kurds will wish to do the same thing as they pass through Urmia. One is perfectly helpless at such a time. The Consuls are acting in concert, but what can they do? The only salvation seems to be that the Russian army may advance soon to Urmia, but for military reasons this may be out of the question.

My own visit to Urmia has been stopped for the present by events. There is no possible way of my reaching Urmia, unless the Consul should go and I should accompany him.

(c) Letter dated Diliman, 19th April, 1915 (to the Presbyterian Missions Board, New York).

There seems no more prospect now than when I last wrote of any measures being taken by the Russian authorities to relieve the Urmia situation. If any plans are afoot for the occupation of the city they are not at all in evidence, and I am persuaded that a good many things must happen elsewhere before the local conditions will be materially changed.

Recently a Mr. McGowan, a reporter of the Associated Press, fresh from America, arrived here—all interest over the situation. He was most anxious to reach Urmia, if any way could be found to get in and any assurance be given that he could return. We decided upon a perfectly open policy. With the consent of the Russian officers here, we secured a messenger and sent him directly to the Turkish Consul in Urmia, asking for guards and safe conduct, from a point just beyond the pass to the city, and return. In our letter to the Consul we enclosed an open letter to Will Shedd, asking his advice in the matter. Indirectly we hear that our messenger was put under arrest (lest, I suppose, he should undertake to return), and no answer has been sent to our request; while, on the other hand, horsemen were despatched to a midway point to escort into the city some Persians who had sent a request very much like our own by the same messenger. It is no use making any more efforts to get inside this chestnut burr, until through God's Providence it opens itself. I am here to render what help I can, and while as yet I have been able to do nothing, yet perhaps it will be given me later to give some little assistance to our poor, tired, beleaguered friends in Urmia. Mr. McGowan has gone back to the Caucasus. It was a pleasure to get sight of an American face and have a fresh whiff from the outside world. The news that comes to us from across the Turkish border is far from pleasant. The many hundreds (and perhaps some thousands) of Armenians and Syrians in the region of Bashkala have been massacred. The Armenians and Kurds in and about Van have begun to fight. In the mountains Mar Shimun is said to have gathered the independent tribes about him, and they are battling for their lives against great odds. These are the near-by places. What is going on inside Turkey, God only knows.

Yesterday I assembled about fifty Armenians from the neighbourhood of Bashkala in a near-by village for a service. They were all men in the employment of the Russian army when it withdrew from there several months ago. They had to come away with the troops, leaving behind their families and all that they possessed. They feel certain that their wives and children have been massacred or else taken away to a captivity worse than death. When one stands before such an audience, the words that are so easy to speak at other times fail one. Is there any balm in Gilead for such wounds? Is there any power to take away from the hearts of these men the sorrow and the rankling spirit of revenge? May God never put me in a position like that, or else may he give me more grace than I how possess.

When one knows that three-fourths of the Moslems of this district, if not nine-tenths of them, were implicated in the plunder of Christian villages, and that many of them were parties to worse crimes, it is hard to have the same zest for work among them. But now that the way to Urmia seems barred for the present, I am planning to plunge into that work. Just now the Moslems here are so alarmed lest they suffer for what they have done that they are ready to listen to almost anything a Christian may say. It is a pity that in so many cases this willingness has no higher motive.

(d) Letter dated Tabriz, 6th May, 1915 (to the Presbyterian Missions Board, New York).

Just a word to report that I am safe at home. My departure from Salmas was most sudden and exciting. An overwhelming force of Turks and Kurds attacked the place, and in the course of manœuvres we were nearly caught between the two firing-lines. It is not an experience that often comes to one, nor is it one that one wants repeated. With hundreds of other refugees, now twice plundered, we made our way to Djoulfa, and from there I came here.

30. TABRIZ: LETTER DATED TABRIZ, 17th MARCH, 1915, FROM THE REV. F.N. JESSUP; COMMUNICATED BY THE BOARD OF FOREIGN MISSIONS OF THE PRESBYTERIAN CHURCH IN THE U.S.A.

On the 1st November (1914) Turkey declared a "Djihad," or Holy War, against the Allies, and it was soon evident that she would try to stir up other Moslem nations. In December a small force of Turkish troops crossed into Persia at Soudjboulak, south of Urmia, but we thought nothing of it, knowing that the Russian forces here would be able to cope with them. But on the last day of December it became evident that the Russians were actually about to withdraw from here, and there was a panic among the Armenians and other native Christians. Day and night the poor Armenians fled out of the city towards the Russian border, and out of 750 or more families only about 250 were left, most of these being the poorest people. From the first we were beset by people asking to be allowed to take refuge with us. We had permission to admit those who were connected with us, and, in addition, had to make arrangements to receive all the Europeans who might need protection. It was decided that all the missionaries should come to this compound, where the Memorial School and men's dispensary are located. You can imagine the rush and work of the first days of January—all the school-rooms to be cleared of everything so as to be ready for the crowds of people so anxious to get in, people to be interviewed day and night, rules to be made as to who and what were to be admitted, our own houses to be made ready for the advent of the missionary families. For example, my house, in which I had been living alone on Friday, by Saturday night contained five families, consisting of ten adults and seven children; and whereas up to that time Dr. Vanneman and I had been having our meals alone, now in my dining-room all the Americans ate together, nineteen adults and a number of children! By this time almost all the Europeans had left the city, including the

Consuls of the Allied Powers; the banks were closed and the Indo-European telegraph office was shut. The Europeans who were left in the city came to us for refuge, all except one family of Italians and a few Germans, Austrians and Turkish subjects who thought they would be safe. But even these asked to have a place reserved in case of need, for no one knew what might happen when a horde of undisciplined Kurds entered the city. Not only this, but a number of prominent Mohammedans came to ask protection, and very many more left the city to flee to Teheran, knowing that they might be molested or blackmailed.

On Tuesday, the 5th January, the Russian troops left the city and encamped on its outskirts; the next day they started north towards Djoulfa, and on Friday, the 8th, the Turks and Kurds entered. For the next three weeks they were in possession of Tabriz. We were cut off from the outside world, without news of what was occurring elsewhere, practically shut up in this compound with the four hundred who had taken refuge with us. We had as our guests Belgians from the Customs and Finance Departments, French Catholic Sisters with forty or fifty of their school-children, two German ladies who had been sick and unable to go with the rest of the German colony, a Russian lady, and two American Seventh Day Adventist missionaries from Maragha, but most of the people were Armenian and Nestorian. As you see, they were of all nationalities and religions, but all lived together in the greatest goodwill, and things moved with a remarkable lack of trouble or friction.

We had planned to observe the regular Week of Prayer with nightly services in our church, but our church had to be abandoned, for almost every Christian from that quarter of the city had fled, and no one dared to stir out of doors after dark. But we were given a greater opportunity. Instead of a week's services attended by fifty or sixty people, we had Evangelistic services in the assembly room of the Memorial School every night for a full four weeks, with a hundred to a hundred and fifty in attendance, and all listening with the most earnest attention. And as we had with us refugee families from Soudjboulak, Maragha and other places, we had a chance to preach the Gospel to those rarely, if ever, reached by the truth. Instead of having to seek a congregation, we had it ready within our gates, and one composed of those whose hearts were softened in the fact of our common danger and life together.

As the time went on, the blackmail and plundering on the part of the Kurds grew worse and people became more anxious. It was indeed a welcome day when the sound of cannon and machine guns was heard to the north, and it appeared that the Russians were returning to deliver the city. This they did on the 30th January, and so well had the campaign been arranged that the fleeing Kurds were cut off from the city after the battle, and so could not loot or kill on their retreat, as many had feared they might. And thus in God's providence the city was relieved, and we and the many lives entrusted to us were kept safe from harm during that trying time.

When the roads were once again open and word reached us from other places, we began to hear of the terrible plight of the Christians of other places, especially Urmia and Salmas. When suddenly and unexpectedly the native Christians of those places heard that the Russian army was immediately to be withdrawn, they knew that their only safety from the cruelties of the approaching Kurds lay in flight. Men, women and little children were obliged to start off at once, in mid-winter, most of them on foot, unable to make preparation or to carry sufficient food, clothing, or bedding, and to flee in terror of their lives through snow and deep mud, wading through streams and toiling over the mountains and across plains covered with almost impassable mire, till at last they might reach Djoulfa on the Russian frontier, nearly 150 miles away. The story of the horror of that flight will probably never be fully told. From Urmia 17,000 or 18,000 must have fled. When they reached the Salmas plain, their numbers were swelled by thousands of Armenian Christians fleeing thence. Men who went through the experience tell us that the events of those days are indescribable. On the edge of the Salmas plain multitudes could find no lodging and had to sleep in the snow. Some children were carried off by wolves, and many more died before morning. And then the march of those days! Up before daylight, struggling in the snow and slush and darkness to find and keep to the road through the mountain passes, hurrying on ever, knowing that at the end of the day only those who first arrived could be sure of finding shelter for the next night; parents becoming separated from each other and from their children in the darkness or in the mass of hurrying people, unable to find them again, but hoping that they might meet at the end of the day; people throwing away the quilts or other necessary bedding they had brought because physically unable to carry them; the road strewn with abandoned goods; the weak and sick falling by the wayside, many never to rise again; men become as beasts in the common struggle just to live. At night many would arrive long after dark at the appointed stopping-place only to find every caravanserai and lodging so full that they would be forced to spend the night out of doors. Those within fared little better, crowded in so tightly that often they could neither lie nor sit down, but had to remain standing all night in rooms with every door and window shut, and the air so foul that the winter's cold without seemed preferable. And at such stopping-places exhausted mothers and fathers were anxiously going from house to house and group to group, seeking their lost children. The fugitives have many terrible tales to tell. By the time they had reached Khoi their plight was desperate, but beyond Khoi their sufferings were increased by the deep mire through which they had to struggle. One of our Christian workers from

Urmia told me that with his own eyes he saw a man go up to his mother, who had sunk exhausted in the mud, and shoot her through the head, rather than leave her to die by degrees or to be killed by wolves. They tell of a family who started from Urmia—an aged father and his two married daughters, each carrying two children, one on her back and the other in her arms. There, in the mire beyond Khoi, the father could no longer go on and had to be left, and one of the women gave birth to a child. She wrapped the new-born babe in a piece of cloth torn from her dress, and taking it in her arms struggled on, but the other two children had to be abandoned like their grandfather. On arriving at Djoulfa these women found their husbands, who had been in Tiflis and had hurried down to meet the fugitives. There for several anxious days they waited, hoping for news of the lost children. The fathers had been away long, and could not be sure of recognizing them, and the mothers were too exhausted to return. At last some soldiers came in with a waggon full of lost children whom they had rescued, and among them were the two little ones. But they had suffered so from exposure that in a few days they both died. The grandfather had perished in the mire.

Mr. Labaree, of our station, left for the Caucasus as soon as the way was open, to find out conditions and see what we could do to help the poor refugees. There are 70,000 or more reported in those regions, not only from Persia, but from Turkey and the border. The Armenians of the Caucasus had organised relief committees, and the Government was also helping. The average grant was about 2*d.* or 1½*d.* per adult a day. The villagers among whom those thousands of absolutely destitute strangers were distributed were very kind, but the burden was very heavy for them. Mr. Labaree said that the poor fugitives were in a pitiable state. Sickness had followed the exposure and strain—scarlet fever and other diseases—and in almost every room he visited he heard of four or five children who had died.

But the condition of those who did not, or could not, flee from the Urmia and Salmas plains has been even worse. In Urmia about 12,000 took refuge in the three compounds belonging to our Mission, while 3,000 more were in the French Catholic Mission. Here most of them have remained since the 1st January, but some have withdrawn to yards adjoining ours, some have been taken out by force and killed by the Turks, and many have died. Urmia has been entirely cut off from us. A few letters and messages they have succeeded in sending through, and from these we have learned something of their condition. At the first arrival of the Kurds and Turks, most of the people remaining in the Christian villages fled to the Mission for protection. Of those who stayed in the villages, many girls and women were carried off by the Mohammedans and many men killed. In those first days of January, about ten thousand were crowded into our compound at Urmia city. In the church there were three thousand, so many that they could not lie down to sleep. At the beginning from ten to twenty-five were dying daily in our city compound, and a little later the mortality increased to from twenty-five to forty a day. At first it was not possible to take the bodies out of the grounds for burial. Later, when they were able to secure some adjoining yards, conditions became a little better. Dr. Packard, hearing that a large Christian village was being attacked by the Kurds, rode out there and, at the risk of his life, made his way to the Kurdish chiefs and then to the village, and persuaded the Kurds to spare the lives of the people on condition of their surrendering their goods. Thus, by his influence with the Kurds, won by many medical services in the past, he was able to save nearly a thousand poor people from massacre and conduct them that night to the city.

All these thousands have had to be fed and cared for. It has meant a daily expenditure of from £50 to £55 sterling for the three tons of bread distributed each day. Some of the wealthy fugitives to Russia left money with the Missionaries on their departure, with permission to borrow it and use it if necessary, and in this way they were able to get on up to the last reports, for we have been unable in any way to reach them or send them money. But it is now nearly a month since we have received authentic news from the Missionaries at Urmia. At that time they reported the situation as very grave. We have heard that a Turkish officer and several men entered our Mission grounds by force, beat Mr. Allen twice because he could not tell them of the whereabouts of some men they sought, and carried off several men to kill them. From the Catholic Mission, in the same way, some forty men were taken and massacred. In a village whose people had from the first been peaceful and had paid a large sum for protection, 51 (others report 85) men were seized, taken outside and butchered, and then the soldiers returned to outrage the women and girls, not even little children being spared.

For three weeks Mr. Labaree has been in Salmas, hoping that a Russian expeditionary force might be sent to rescue the Urmia Christians and that he might be able to go over to help the Missionaries, who must be greatly worn by the strain and by their work. But as yet he has neither been able to go nor to send or receive any word, nor are there any signs of a rescue.

This is the most awful calamity which has befallen the Nestorian people in the ninety years of our mission work among them. About 1,000 had been killed and 2,000 had died of disease or fear up to the middle of March, just in Urmia itself, and the Nestorians here estimate that perhaps as many more died on the flight to Russia or have died since. This would mean a fifth or a sixth of the 30,000 Nestorians who live on the Urmia plain. Their prosperous villages have all been pillaged and most of them burned, and their churches destroyed. Of the survivors, half are refugees in great want in the Caucasus, the rest remain in Urmia in conditions of peril and fear and need which wring one's heart. Already over £4,000 sterling must have been spent by the

Missionaries in Urmia to preserve the lives of those taking refuge with them. As soon as it becomes in the least safe, they must be helped to return to their ruined homes and villages to make a fresh start. Two months ago Mr. Labaree appealed to America for at least £10,000 sterling as the smallest sum required, and as time goes on it becomes evident that more will be needed. Thus far about £2,400 has been received from the American Red Cross and our Board, £30 from our missionaries in Hamadan, and £20 from the English missionaries at Ispahan. Of course we here are trying to help too. These poor distressed Nestorians are the especial charge of our American Presbyterian Church, which has laboured so many years for their good, and there is little hope of help for them in this hour when so many nations are in trouble, except in so far as *we* help them.

And it is not only the Christians of Urmia that are in great need. Those of the village of Miandoab (Armenians, these), have similarly lost everything. The Kurds still occupy their town, and they are refugees in Maragha and Tabriz. At Maragha the Armenians have suffered greatly, for most of them had to flee, and now they have the burden of all the refugees from Miandoab and other villages. And in Salmas it is worse. All the Christian villages on that plain have been smoked. Most of the Christians fled when the army withdrew in January, but some remained behind and these sought the protection of their Moslem neighbours. But a few days before the return of the Russian army to Salmas, when the Turks saw that they would be compelled to flee, they secured the names of all Christians by a ruse, pretending that all who registered would be protected. Then they gathered all the men into one place and carried them out in companies of about twenty-five, each to be shot down in cold blood. Others were tied with their heads sticking through the rungs of a ladder and decapitated, others hacked to pieces or mutilated before death. In this way practically every Christian man remaining in Salmas was massacred. You can imagine the fate of girls and women. The most detailed report received, signed by a number of men now on the ground, stated that from 712 to 720 men were thus killed in Salmas.

31. URMIA DURING THE TURCO-KURDISH OCCUPATION: DIARY OF A MISSIONARY, EDITED BY MISS MARY SCHAUFFLER PLATT, AND PUBLISHED BY THE BOARD OF FOREIGN MISSIONS OF THE PRESBYTERIAN CHURCH IN THE U.S.A.

Urmia, Persia, Saturday, 9th January, 1915.

I want to start a letter telling you of the events of the last week, though I cannot tell when it will reach you. As you know, the Russians had taken possession of this part of Persia, and were maintaining order here, so that for the last year conditions were more orderly, peaceful and prosperous than for long years before. They had a consul here who was very capable, and tried to do justice to all.

When war was declared between Russia and Turkey, we knew that this meant war for Urmia, for we are right on the Turkish border, and only a few years ago Turkey tried to get this section for herself, but failed. We were told by the Russians in authority here that they would hold Urmia against all odds, so the city was fortified by trenches and defences on every side, and several thousand reinforcements came.

On New Year's Day, according to our custom, we received our friends. As many as a hundred and forty of our Moslem and Christian friends, men and women, called "to bless our New Year." On Saturday, the 2nd, like a thunderbolt from a clear sky, we were informed that the whole Russian army was withdrawing; some had gone in the night, the rest would leave immediately. There was a panic at once among the Christian (Syrian and Armenian) population.[46] The Osmanlis, or Turks and Kurds, were but a few miles away, and the Christians were absolutely defenceless.

At once, as soon as the Russians had gone, with large numbers of Syrians and Armenians leaving at the same time, the evil-minded Moslems all over the plain began to plunder the Christian villages. When the people were trying to flee to the missionaries in the city, they were robbed on the roads of everything they had, even of their outer clothing. In some of the villages the Moslem masters placed guards to prevent the people from going themselves or bringing their possessions to the city, saying they would protect them. When they tried to get away, these same guards robbed and stripped them.

The crowds had begun to pour in at our gates on Sunday; the city people were taken in by night and many others from near by. On Sunday morning we put up the American flags over the entrances. On Monday morning Dr. Packard, with American and Turkish flags, accompanied by two Syrians, started out to meet the leading Kurdish chief. He arrived at Geogtapa in time to prevent a terrible massacre. The people of Geogtapa who had not fled to the city had gone to our church and the Russian church, both of which are situated on a high hill formed of ashes, a relic of Zoroastrian times. The churchyards are enclosed by high mud walls. All finally went to the Russian church, which was on the highest ground. They barricaded the strong doors, and, when the Kurds attacked, the men defended the fort with their guns and the women crowded like sheep into the church. When Dr. Packard arrived, a lively battle was going on, with little chance for the Christians. He had great difficulty in getting to the chiefs without being shot; but he finally reached them, and they knew him. Some of these Kurds had spent weeks in our hospital and had been operated upon by Dr. Packard, so they listened to him while he pleaded for the lives of the people inside. After several hours' entreaty, they agreed to let the people go with him if they would give up their guns and ammunition.

I was talking yesterday with Layah, our Bible Woman, who was inside the church. She said that when Dr. Packard first tried to signal to them, they did not know him and kept on firing, but when they recognized him a shout went up: "It's the Hakim Sahib! Thank God! We are saved!" I asked her what the Kurds did when they came out, and she said they stood by and helped them, saying: "Come on! Come on! Don't be afraid!" In the rush, Layah fell and broke her arm, and is now lying on Miss Lamme's sofa resting.

All Monday the refugees had been coming in, until it seemed that every room and storeroom was full, many of the rooms not lying-down full but sitting-up full. But that night, when Dr. Packard came, he brought over fifteen hundred more with him, and they had to be stowed away. This is Saturday, the sixth day these thousands have been here in our yards, not less than ten thousand—perhaps twelve or fourteen thousand. We have taken several small yards and houses adjoining ours, and the English Mission yard adjoining the seminary yard is also full. Of course, the two Englishmen of the English Mission had to leave with the Russian army, and with them a large number of prominent Syrians who had been sympathizers with Russia. Here in the city there has been plundering and some destruction of property, but no general disorder—unless it be in the Armenian quarter. The fine brick quarters which were built as barracks for the Russian army I understand have remained intact, because the invaders are afraid to go near them for fear they may be mined.

From the first the Sheikh promised protection to us and our people, and when the Osmanli officers came they immediately took possession of the city, and have tried to keep order and prevent plundering by Moslems. The other day a Moslem, terribly wounded by a Turkish guard while robbing, was brought here for treatment. This is an illustration of our position: Here is a Mussulman thief, plundering Christians, shot by the Osmanli guard, and then brought to us by his friends that we might care for him.

Although we were promised safety for all within our gates there is no certainty. On Wednesday morning I lay in bed a little longer than usual, and about half-past seven suddenly an awful cry of fear and despair went up from thousands of throats, and the crowds rushed toward the church, then swayed back, not knowing whither to fly. From the church, where human beings are packed in like sardines, they began jumping from the windows. My first thought was that the Kurds had broken in through our back gate, which opens into the Moslem quarter, and that the massacre was about to begin; but the poor, terrified people soon quieted, and before I could get dressed I knew it must have been a false alarm. The poor, hunted creatures think that if they can only hold to the skirts of a missionary they will be safe.

On Thursday, Hannah, the wife of one of our pastors, reached us after great suffering and exposure. They lived in Nazi, and heard the report that the Russians were leaving. They couldn't believe it, but on Sunday afternoon Kurds from the west came and began plundering. The people all fled to a walled village, because they thought they might be safer there and because our preacher there, Kasha Oner (Preacher Abner), had many friends among the Kurds, being a mountaineer. On Monday, a Kurd visited them, pretending that he had been sent by the Turks from the city, telling them they need have no fear, as they would be protected; but it became evident that he was a spy. Afterwards a band of Kurds came, demanded the guns, and drank tea with the people; then others came and they began robbing and killing. The people gathered together like a flock of frightened sheep, and many were slaughtered. The greater part of them got through the great gateway while the Kurds were plundering, and that night they spent in the mountains without food or shelter and with very little covering. One of our girls, Katie, who had gone home on Friday for her Christmas vacation, was among them. She saw her mother murdered and had to leave her body lying by the gate as they ran. The next morning more than four hundred of them started towards the city, cold, hungry, exhausted; many, having lost their shoes in their flight, had frozen and bleeding feet. Hannah came here, her feet were dressed, and she is lying comfortably on a mattress on Miss Lamme's floor. Her husband and daughter were already here. The rest of the party were taken in at our College compound, two miles west of the city.

The pitiful tales we hear of murder, of narrow escape through snow and mud, hungry, sick and cold, are numberless.

Monday, 11th January, 1915.

Several families from Degala are camped in our parlour, and the night before last Victoria, one of the women, came to me and said an old woman had just come in who didn't seem able to answer anything she asked her. I found her crouched in a corner of the hall. She said she was so cold. At first she couldn't eat, but after drinking some tea she improved. We had absolutely no place but a stone floor for her; but we took up a carpet from my bedroom, rolled her up in it in the upper hallway, and she went to sleep. She was the janitress of our church in Barbaroud, fifteen miles to the south. The Kurds did their worst there several days ago, and she had escaped, barefooted, almost naked, and without food. She died a day or two later.

One poor woman, who had both husband and son killed, has gone crazy, and we haven't any place to put her but a dark closet under the stairway. At midnight I was awakened by her pounding on the door. She has a nursing baby. Thank God, to-day they took her to the hospital, where they can care for her a little better than here. (She died two days later.) At the College compound, where the hospital is, they have only about two thousand, and we have perhaps twelve thousand, and every day more are coming. Those who have been hiding with Moslem friends are coming to us day by day, and we haven't any place to put them. We have not been able to take the dead from our yards, so we are burying them in the little yard by the side of the church—twenty-seven so far. Some die every day, and there is no shroud or coffin for them.

Evening.

We have just had a Praise Meeting in the parlour with fifty or sixty who could gather from the halls and rooms near, and we feel more cheerful. We thought if Paul and Silas, with their stripes, could sing praises in prison, so could we.

Wednesday, 13th January.

Since Monday, the 4th, we have been giving out bread. In the morning we sell to those who have money, and in the afternoon give free bread to those who cannot buy, disposing of over four tons of bread a day. Practically all the refugees from the city have their own food, and some from the villages, too. We buy our bread from the bazaar (market), and a very efficient and willing young Syrian has been attending to the weighing and giving out, while groups of other young men have been selling and distributing. The only things we have had for carrying the bread are our clothes-baskets and old tin bath-tubs, and they are doing good service. We have received some gifts of food for the refugees from Moslems. One man gave over six hundred pounds of meat, which we cooked and gave out in one section, but it is very difficult to distribute anything except bread among so large a number. I am speaking only of what we are doing here in this compound, where by far the larger number of refugees are. They are doing similar work in Sardari (the Boys'-School premises) and at the College compound. Mr. McDowell is looking after sanitary conditions and the streams of water flowing through the yards, which furnish the only drinking water for the crowds, and conditions are much improved.

There are hundreds of mountaineers who have no place to go to. Before this affair they were distributed among the villages, and we had established a number of schools especially for them. These people had been driven from their homes by the Kurds early in the autumn. Many of them seem little better than animals—dirty, lazy, satisfied with any hole to lie in and just enough bread to keep their stomachs comfortable. Of course, they are not all of this sort, but we have several hundred that are. They are chiefly crowded into the church and our large school-room. The people who are suffering most are those who have been accustomed to the comforts and decencies of life, who are crowded together like cattle, without sufficient clothing or food.

The day after the flight from Geogtapa we went with a basket of bread to one of the larger rooms of the Press, which was filled with self-respecting people who had the day before been in comfortable circumstances, but who had fled with nothing, or had been robbed of whatever they had tried to bring with them. When they saw the bread for distribution, they began to cry and cover their faces, and we had to drop the bread into their laps—they didn't reach out for it. Of course, we assured them that under such circumstances, it was no shame to eat the bread of charity.

When the people began to flee, they wanted to deposit their money with us, and our Treasurer accepted it on condition that we could use it without interest and repay it when normal conditions are restored. It is with this money that we have been enabled to buy bread and save these people from starvation.

Children are being born every day. We have managed to give two small rooms to these women, many of whom haven't even a quilt. Children were born even in the crowded church. One of the women who was reporting these cases complained in a very aggrieved tone that some were "even bringing two," as if one wasn't enough to satisfy anybody under existing circumstances.

This is the first day that we have been able to get donkeys to haul away the refuse. I hope we shall soon be able to take the dead to the cemetery.

Thursday, 14th January.

Mr. Allen returned last evening from his journey to the villages of the Nazlu river. Several thousand fled towards Russia; many have hidden with Moslems, who are now trying to force them to become Mohammedans and to give their girls in marriage to Moslems. In Ada perhaps as many as a hundred were killed, most of them young men. It is told that they were stood up in line, one behind another, by the Kurds, to see how many one bullet would kill. I went down to see the woman in the room under mine who had received word of the killing of her brother in Karadjalu. Everywhere there is wailing and sadness, and her lamentation for her dead brother is the wail of thousands of hearts:—

"Oh, Yeremia (Jeremiah), my brother!

The pillar of our house; a father to us all, ah, Yeremia, Yeremia!

Thou didst comfort us all! A giant in body and giant in spirit.

Oh, Yeremia, my brother, oh, my brother, Yeremia, my heart is broken for thee!

My brother! Oh, my brother, thy house is left desolate; thy little ones orphans.

Oh, Yeremia, Yeremia! thou wert a righteous man, merciful to the poor!"

Saturday, 16th January.

Yesterday some Abijalu people were in, asking for bread, although a week ago they were among the well-to-do. The same story of robbery, exposure and horror. When a Kurd tried to carry off Shamasha Sayad's daughter, she jumped into the well and stayed there for hours in water up to her chin. Some one said a few days ago, "Blessed are the dead," and I echoed the sentiment.

Monday, 18th January.

In the midst of panic, distress and death, we have had two weddings. Both had been arranged to take place on the Syrian New Year, the 14th January. Dr. Shedd performed the ceremony in both cases. Both brides had their trousseaux ready, but felt these were not proper times for the display of finery, so wore ordinary dresses.

These last few days a number of the city families have returned in fear and trembling to their homes, taking just a very few things with them. This is relieving the overcrowded rooms somewhat, and Miss Schoebel this afternoon is trying to drive the people out into the sunshine long enough to have the rooms swept—or, rather, shovelled. It consumes all one's energies to try to get anyone to do anything. All the responsibility and much of the actual labour has devolved upon the missionaries. Of course, many of our best men fled to Russia, and among those who are left there are few leaders. There are some notable exceptions, though, both here and at the College— *e.g.*, Jacob David, who without missionary assistance has charge of eight hundred and fifty refugees and is doing finely. Another, a young shopkeeper, has had charge of the weighing and distribution of bread, with much of the buying, from the beginning. He has done the work with surprising efficiency and self-devotion. Bands of young men have been ready, day after day, for distributing bread. The nights have been divided into three watches, and groups of men have taken their turns in acting as watchmen. Mr. Nisan, who has charge of the English Mission yard, one night found the watchmen asleep, so the next day they were tied to trees, and a placard placed over them with the inscription: "Unfaithful Watchmen," as a warning to others. Guarding the streams is a very necessary and a very difficult task. Mr. McDowell finds it extremely hard to get anyone among the hundreds of Syrians here who can be trusted to oversee such work, or who can be kept on a job longer than an hour or so at a time.

We are urging some now to return to their homes. Many are so afraid, and we cannot give them assurance of safety. Some Kurds have gone, but many are still about. The people come to the individual missionaries and beg for just one small room for their families, each one with his own special plea. When we tell them the greatest danger for them just now is to remain crowded in such narrow bounds, it makes little or no appeal to them. They are nine-tenths fatalists any way, and think that it all depends upon the "will of Allah." They say: "Let us die by the hand of God and not of the Kurds."

We have been having unusually fine weather; only two bad days, and they were not cold. A Mohammedan was heard to say: "Do you see how God loves these Christians? Who ever saw such weather in the middle of winter?"

Dr. Shedd is the representative of our station before the Government; he and Dr. Packard have had that end of the work, daily pleading before Persian and Osmanli authorities for the Christian population. It was told us that a prominent Moslem had said: "Dr. Shedd is the best Christian in the city! Just see how he comes every day through the deep mud to plead for those people!"

Wednesday, 20th January.

A few people from the city went to their homes, and our hopes began to rise; but yesterday and to-day others came in from the Nazlu river and from Tchargousha. Thirty-six dead were carried to the trench in Mart Maryam[47] (St. Mary) churchyard yesterday; the larger part of them were children.

Lucy, daughter of Kasha (preacher) David of Ardishai, came in yesterday with her baby from Gulpashan, where they had been refugees for some time, living in terror of Kurds by day and night. They also feared the Moslem neighbours and the Turkish guards sent in to protect the village. Her own village was Tchargousha. In terror the people fled to the roofs as the village was surrounded by Kurds, and there was no avenue of escape. The Kurds came up on to the roofs and commanded the people to go down. Lucy, with one Kurd below her on the ladder and two above her, her baby on her back, got down. In the yard she saw her younger sister, Sherin, a pretty girl of about fifteen, being dragged away by a Kurd. She was imploring Lucy to save her, but Lucy was helpless. When she was telling me this with tears and sobs, she said: "Every night, when I try to sleep, I hear her entreaties, 'Oh, Lucy, I'll be your sacrifice, Save me, Lucy!' I called to her, 'Pull your head-kerchief over your face; don't look into their faces.' She tried to conceal her face, and daubed it with mud, but she has such beautiful dark eyes and rosy cheeks! The Kurds grabbed the young women and girls, peering into their faces, till each one found a pretty one for himself, then dragged her away. If they had only killed my sister we could say, 'She is dead, like many another—it is finished'; but that she should be in the hands of a Kurd—we cannot bear it!" Some of these captives have been recovered, but there is no word of Sherin.

Saturday, 23rd January.

Yesterday we counted three thousand three hundred in the church, and many have gone out, so there must have been four thousand people there these last two weeks. Is it any wonder that children are dying by the score? Morning and afternoon there are burials; at other times the bodies are collected and laid in a room near the gate. To-day Mr. McDowell succeeded after long efforts in getting a cart for scavenger work. It came but one day. We have not been able to get even donkeys, except five or six. The scavengers would not come into the yards of Christians for such work, even though Mr. McDowell offered to pay well. We cannot open our back windows, the stench is too dreadful. I suppose the mere mention of such things is quite shocking even to read; but we have been living in such surroundings for nearly three weeks, and see only a little light ahead. We are hoping we can distribute some of the mountain refugees in empty houses here in Mart Maryam and the Christian quarter.

Many Moslems who pretended to accept food and goods of Christians for safe keeping, are now claiming them as their own. One of our preachers, after having been plundered of practically everything by his Moslem neighbours, was received as a refugee into one of their houses and was fed from his own dishes, of his own food, and put to sleep in his own bed.

Dr. Packard has been gone for several days to the Nazlu villages, to gather together the remnants of the people scattered in Moslem villages, or in hiding, and to see if it be possible to put them into a few of their own places again. Most of the Kurds have left, but the Syrians are unarmed, and, just as from the beginning, their Moslem neighbours are their greatest enemies. If it isn't a Djihad (Holy War), it is very near it. It must have been planned beforehand, for there has been concerted action from one end of the plain to the other, though here and there some Moslems have been friendly throughout, have done many kindly deeds and saved many lives.

Later.

Just at this joint we had an interesting diversion. A band of Turkish soldiers came into our yard and said they wanted to search our premises for wounded Russian soldiers. They searched the houses of the Allens, the Müllers, and our house; then the schools and all outside buildings and storehouses, even to the smallest closets. You might have thought they were searching for a lost hair from Osman's beard! I have an idea they thought we were concealing arms or ammunition, though ten days ago we collected all we could find anywhere among the people, and gave them up to the Osmanli commander.

As we had nothing hidden, of course we had nothing to fear, though some of the people were scared.

A dozen times a day I pray: "Oh, Lord, how long?" All the first days it seemed as if it must be a horrible dream from which I would awake; but it has become a three weeks' reality, with little hope of a near dawning. It looks as if our long night might stretch out till the dawn of peace in Europe. And for these things who shall answer, if not the Powers of Europe?

We have read that America has done so much for the sufferers in Europe; surely they will not be too poor to help this little corner of misery, with its twenty-five or thirty thousand sufferers, and with absolutely no one on earth to look to but the American Mission! For months we have not been permitted to write of conditions here, and now we are entirely shut off from the world, even from Tabriz. Anything we write "must be in French, just to say we are well." Our last word from Tabriz, the nearest mission station and residence of the American Consul, was written on the 31st December, and this is the 23rd January.

Sunday, 24th January.

The fourth Sunday, but no Sabbath. To-day nearly all the people were taken out of the church and distributed among the empty houses near the Russian Mission and in the old church. I went with some of the young men who are helping with the distribution of the bread to count the people in each place. In one house there were two hundred and fifty; these are all mountaineers. We give to each one sheet or loaf of bread per day; about ten ounces. Not very extravagant feeding, you see!

Tuesday, 26th January.

On Sunday a Jew brought us word from Usknuk that Kasha David's daughter, Sherin, is there in the house of a Kurd, and that every effort is being made by gifts, persuasion and threats, to make her turn Mohammedan, but that she always answers "You may kill me, but I will never deny my faith." We are making plans to try to get her back. Dr. Packard reported on his return from the Nazlu villages that in one place practically the whole population has become Moslem and have given up their church to be a mosque, while some even cursed their former faith. But, of course, such people never had any religion, and changing the name of it is a matter of convenience.

Wednesday, 27th January.

Miss Lamme and I went to-day to the Jewish quarters to look up Syrian refugees there. We found them in large numbers in the Jewish houses, where they had been kept and in some cases fed. Yesterday the French Mission sent away from their yards two hundred and fifty or more persons, who first went to the Governor. He telephoned to Dr. Shedd, and we had to receive them. They were put into Dr. Israel's house in Dilgusha, outside the city walls. All the houses there have been completely plundered; many have been robbed of doors and windows. No one thinks of returning to homes there, but a great many have returned to Mart Maryam.

Later.

Everywhere about the yards people are basking in the wonderful sunshine, which is more like April than January. The common sight everywhere is the everlasting hunt for vermin, friends and neighbours graciously assisting one another. I suppose it is a vulgar subject to mention, but "we've got 'em," and must go on living in hourly contact with thousands of others who swarm with them.

Friday, 5th February.

We can't complain of the monotony of life, for we never know what will happen next. On Tuesday morning I had a wedding in my room here. The boy and girl were simple villagers. He had gone to Russia and brought back a little money, with some foreign clothes. Then his folks began to look round for a wife for him. He was betrothed several months ago to Anna of Ardishai, and, according to custom, gave her the money to buy her trousseau. For several weeks she had been sewing, until at last the wonderful silk dress, white silk head-kerchief, veil and all the necessaries, were ready. The wedding was fixed for the Syrian New Year; but—the Kurds came and carried off wedding clothes and everything else in the house. They all fled here, and were married in the old, dirty garments they were wearing when they ran for their lives, for this was a month ago. In the flight the bride's mother was lost, probably killed, as nothing has been heard of her since. Their only present was a little tea and sugar that I tied up in a kerchief and gave to the bride, that they might invite a few friends to drink tea instead of eating the dinner they had intended giving.

There are a great many people who have been accustomed to good living heretofore, but for months have had no cooked food, so I invited a number of these to dinner on Wednesday. We had a meat stew, bread, cheese, pickles and tea, all they could eat. There were thirty-five for dinner, and twenty for supper. There was enough left over to feed fifty or more poor and sick ones outside. The whole thing cost about four dollars and fed a hundred people. We spread long cloths on the parlour floor and ate with wooden spoons from enamel plates borrowed for the occasion from the school. The matron and school-girls did the cooking and serving.

But for our next-door neighbours the scene quickly changed again from weddings and dinners to one of terror and flight by night. The house of Dr. —— adjoins ours, and the roofs are continuous. For several days there had been rumours that their house would be plundered by the Turkish authorities, and they had not dared to undress and go to bed in peace, but on Wednesday they felt more safe and went to bed early. I myself had gone to bed, but not to sleep. Just before eleven o'clock I heard loud knocking on their gate, and then a rapid trampling of feet on the roof over my room. Pretty soon there was quite a commotion in our front yard. I jumped up, and saw in the yard a dozen or more Turkish soldiers, who entered through our front door and went up to the roof through our halls. I dressed as quickly as I could and went to Miss Coan's room on the roof, to find that some of the women from Dr. ——'s family were already there. In a few minutes the rest of the women and children from there climbed the wall or slid from the roof on to our balcony, and I let them in through the window into our parlour. They were crying and frightened nearly to death, but kept quiet. The Turks searched the house, but took nothing, saying they had come to take evil men, not things. They came back through our house again. The orders have been in our yard that the gate should never be opened at night but by one of the gentlemen; so, when they first knocked, the guard came and called Mr. Allen. He let them in and went with them to Dr. ——'s house. In the meantime, a Syrian had aroused Mr. Müller, and when he tried to get out of his front door he found a Turk guarding it. He tried to push out, saying that he was the master of the house, but the Turk struck him and refused to let him pass. When the gang returned from our neighbours', they insisted on searching Mr. Müller's house, even going into the bedroom where Mrs. Müller was in bed and Ruth was sick. Meanwhile a second band came and pounded on our gate, but our guards had run away, and finally one of the men climbed a telephone pole to the roof, got down inside and opened the gate. The officer tied up the Persian guards as a punishment for not opening the gate. Afterwards they went into the Allen house and even asked to have the piano played. It is maddening to have our premises and houses invaded in this way, and by such a lot, but we are helpless, and, for the sake of what we may be able to do for the safety of the people, our gentlemen have to smile and try to turn away their wrath with soft words, even though they are threatened and called liars by the representatives of the invading Government. I don't believe the Mission in the seventy-five years and more of its existence has ever been placed in so difficult and humiliating a position.

Still the ghastly procession of the dead marches on. Between seven and eight hundred have died so far. A great many are able to get plain wooden coffins for their dead now, but the great mass are just dropped into the great trench of rotting humanity. As I stand at my window in the morning I see one after another of the little bodies carried by, wrapped mostly in a ragged piece of patch-work; and the condition of the living is more pitiful than that of the dead—hungry, ragged, dirty, sick, cold, wet, swarming with vermin—thousands of them! Not for all the wealth of all the rulers of Europe would I bear for one hour their responsibility for the suffering and misery of this one little corner of the world alone. A helpless, unarmed Christian community turned over to the sword and the passion of Islam!

This morning my attention was called to a girl of twelve, who was too sick to be kept any longer in a room with other people. A young Syrian woman, who was helping with the sick, wanted to put her into that closet under the stairway from which none ever come out alive. I said: "She will die in there." She replied: "Of course she will die, but we shall have to find a place for her until she does." We put her there temporarily until we found a small room where there were only *twenty*. These we distributed among other crowded rooms, brought Margareta there, laid her on some matting and covered her with an old carpet. Poor child, she has a sweet face, but life has treated her cruelly.

Dysentery has been bad for a long time, and when the sick get helpless and their condition offensive, it is almost impossible to get anyone to care for them unless they have near relatives. Dysentery and measles have both been epidemic for a long time, and nearly all deaths are directly due to one or both of these diseases.

We had a real respectable funeral in the front yard this afternoon. A good old woman from Degala died, and her pastor had a service for her. This is only the second real funeral service I have seen, though a preacher is always present at the two burials daily, and conducts a service at the cemetery.

Friday, 12th February.

To-day we have begun a new method of giving out bread. We have printed forms, which we fill in and ask the heads of families to sign, promising to pay us later for the bread. All day thousands have been crowding the big tent in the yard, where a number of young men have been filling in and giving out these tickets for bread. The problem is a big one. Undoubtedly some could find bread who are taking it free, but we cannot decide most of the cases. Then we are spending thousands of borrowed money, and as yet no response to our cablegram sent long ago to America! The numbers asking for bread are increasing daily, but if we should refuse it, hundreds would die of starvation.

Again the yards are wet and muddy from melting snow. The last two days have been very hard for the thousands without fuel and with very little clothing. One of the verses that helps to keep my faith steady these days is: "He that spared not His own Son."

The death-rate has been considerably reduced; for two weeks or more it averaged over thirty a day.

Mr. Allen is off on a tour to the villages of the upper Nazlu river, to see what is left there, and to give help or encouragement to anyone who may be left. A while ago when Mr. Allen visited the villages on the Baranduz, one of our Bible Women told him of a certain spot she wished him to visit. She lived in Kurtapa, and as she was about to flee with a bag containing nine tomans[48] of money, the robbers appeared at the door. She quickly threw the bag down beside a broken earthen tub and the thieves did not see it. Mr. Allen went to that village, found the room and the broken tub with the bag of money beside it, and brought the money to its owner.

Last week, the Shahbanda, or Turkish Consul, who is now the chief authority, demanded six thousand tomans of the Syrians. With great trouble this was partly collected and partly borrowed by the help of the Sirdar (Persian Governor), who demanded six hundred more for his share. The Shahbanda promised that, if this were given, the shops and houses of the Syrians in the city would not be disturbed. It remains to be seen how much his word is worth.

To-morrow completes six weeks of this siege and semi-siege condition. We keep on praying, but see no signs of deliverance. We are shut off from the world, and thousands are held in this bondage by a few hundred Osmanli troops and a few wandering Kurds. I realize now that Persia is dead—or worse; she has no manhood nor moral character left.

Wednesday, 17th February.

A few days ago the Turkish Consul arrested all the men at the French Mission. After some examination, a hundred were sent away, leaving about sixty-three at the Consulate. A gallows with seven nooses was erected at the "Kurdish Gate" of the city, the one near us, and on Sunday the ropes were put in place. The people here on Sunday were very badly scared. The women of the men under arrest came and wept and besought Dr. Shedd to do something, but he could do nothing. That evening the people gathered in the church for prayer, and continued praying until midnight. Each night since similar meetings have been held. As yet no one has been hanged, but the Turkish Consul is demanding money for their release. The second day after the arrest of these people, a Turkish soldier was sent to us to ask us to send bread for the prisoners, and we have been feeding them ever since. When their women-folk went to see them they were charged two krans (ninepence) admission. It has been reported that the prisoners have been tortured in various ways known to the Turks, in order to extort money from their families.

The Turkish Consul has demanded the ten thousand tomans of English bank money committed to us when the bankers fled. The matter has been referred to our Consul in Tabriz. If it should have to be surrendered, we should be in straits, for that is all we have to buy bread with for these thousands of hungry people. Weeks ago we appealed to America, both to the Red Cross and to our Board, but there is no reply.

It was reported to me that there were refugees here who had stores of flour, meat, butter, etc., and yet were taking bread from us, so yesterday I made an investigation and found small quantities; but if the whole were sold, it would not amount to twenty dollars, and the owners would be reduced to nothing but dry bread, and, though this might do for a limited time, they cannot "live by bread alone" week after week. Undoubtedly this terrible epidemic of dysentery which has carried off hundreds is due largely to lack of proper food and want of variety of food. As I made the rounds of our own yards yesterday and visited the people herded together in one of the dark storerooms of our Persian Girls'-School, it seemed to me that their condition of cold, hunger, filth and sickness was about as miserable as they could get in this world. One great difference that was apparent in all the rooms was the absence of small children, hundreds having died during these last months.

The evangelistic work is now well organized, and everywhere there are at least daily meetings for everyone. The women workers under Miss Lamme visit outside places. Mrs. McDowell, with native women, also visits outside places where there are large numbers of refugees herded together. Mr. McDowell tries to keep the preachers at work, too.

Last week a group of one hundred and fifty or more mountaineers who are staying at Sengar, two or three miles from the city came down with one of Kurdu's men, asking us to feed them They said that heretofore they had been provided for by Kurdu, a Kurdish chief, for whom they had been working, carrying away for him the plunder he had collected here, and that now he was leaving and we must feed them. We put them off several times, but finally accepted the additional burden. Every one who gets tired of his job of charity or responsibility throws it upon us. There seems no end, and this is the seventh week.

Thursday, 18th February.

Yesterday afternoon I went out to the College compound for the first time since Christmas. We had to drive under the gallows at the city gate. It creates rather unpleasant feelings to think that perhaps some of our friends may be suspended there.

Our Mission is being treated with more consideration than at first, and we are hoping that perhaps the Turkish Consul has heard from Constantinople, and that our own Government has been exerting influence at Berlin and Constantinople. For weeks we have had no word from the outside world; but we "rest in Jehovah and wait patiently for Him."

Friday, 19th February.

This has been a snowy day again. The people have been making it a day of fasting and prayer—as if every day were not a fast day!

Saturday, 20th February.

All day negotiations have been going on in regard to the English bank money. When Dr. Shedd and Dr. Packard were called to the Turkish Consulate, they found there the former Urmia Consul, who had fled from here last autumn when war between Russia and Turkey was first declared. He had gone south to Soujboulak. It looks as if he were perhaps fleeing now in this direction, which would mean that the Russians were in Soujboulak; we have heard this report. It is being reported that the Kurds were making preparations to-day for leaving here. It may be that the Consul's haste to get this money is another evidence that he is expecting to leave soon. He told the gentlemen to-day that he thought that, as Americans, they ought to make a contribution toward the cause of Turkey. They have felt that a compromise on the ten thousand is the best way out, and suggested that he take two thousand; but he refused to take less than five thousand, and promised that he would not take it before to-morrow, so if something does not develop before to-morrow we shall probably be the poorer by that amount. We are hoping that it may be taken without any show of force or violence. Of course, we cannot make any resistance.

To-day we finished going over all the bread tickets, arranging the names according to villages. Then we called in responsible men from each village and went over the lists, to find out those who would be able to help themselves soon, and those who had reported more members of families than they have. I am sorry to say that we found scores who were cheating in various ways, and now we have to get hold of all of them—a big business for some days to come. We are distributing 14,000-15,000 loaves of about ten and a half ounces each day; but there are so many getting more than a loaf each that there are probably not more than eleven thousand persons receiving.

An epidemic of typhoid has broken out at the College among the refugees—twenty-seven cases. To-day, even in the midst of our troubles, the Evangelistic Board met to consider a reorganization of the work. When the people are able to return to the villages, they will probably have to settle temporarily in a few of the larger ones.

Sunday, 21st February.

To-day there are three or four services in the church. This morning it was packed for a communion service and many were turned away. Another communion service is arranged for this afternoon, and then again next Sunday, to give an opportunity for all communicants.

Tuesday, 23rd February.

Last night one of the most terrible things that has yet happened occurred. In the evening ten or a dozen of the prisoners from the French Mission, taken ten days or more ago by the Turkish Consul, were discharged, and we all felt that probably the rest would soon be set free, as there was no special charge against them. But this morning five men, two of them Moslems, were found hanging from the gallows at the Kurdish Gate, and forty-eight others were shot beyond the Tcharbash Gate. No one has dared to go out yet and get the bodies, though Dr. Shedd has asked permission of the Turkish Consul. For two days we had felt so much more hopeful, but to-day a terrible fear has fallen on the people. There is much silent weeping, but little violent demonstration, though the mothers, wives and families of the murdered men are here. The question in everybody's mind is: "What will the Turks do next?" Forty or fifty shots were distinctly heard in the night between one and two o'clock, but no one guessed what they meant. We had begun yesterday to take their bread-tickets away from a few of the people to try to force them to go to their villages or find money in some way to provide for themselves; but now they are too frightened to leave and everything is set back again. Two or three days ago the Turks took some things from the French Mission property here, carpets, etc., and we hear that they are plundering more to-day. On Sunday we received a card from Tabriz saying that everything was quiet there, that £1,000 relief had been received, and that Mr. Labaree was going to the Caucasus to relieve the refugees who had fled from Urmia to Russia.

Wednesday, 24th February.

The French missionaries and the nine nuns were very much alarmed for their personal safety. They asked that one of our men should go there and put up an American flag; but, of course, we could not do that. Yesterday the Turkish Consul sent word that if we wanted the bodies of the three Christians hanging at the gate, we had permission to take them. Mr. McDowell and Mr. Allen went with some Syrians, took down the bodies, and buried them. There has been a little more disorder than usual, and the people are terrified again. I have had to give back many of the bread tickets that we had collected. There are hundreds of people who have fields and vineyards, but who cannot borrow a dollar. These tickets are really promissory notes which they have signed, promising to pay later, but we need *cash* now, and our bread queue does not decrease—rather, increases. I wonder what a trained Red Cross worker would do with a mob that will not stand in line or stay where you put them; who, when you go over the case and give the answer, refuse to take it, but stand about and weep briny tears by the hour. They have no sense of honour, don't know how to tell the truth, can't tell the same story twice, and do not know much about anything except that their stomachs are empty. They try to get bread under the names of the dead, and when accused of evading the truth, will declare in the most injured tones: "We wouldn't lie." There is much that would be funny in these investigations if it did not get monotonous.

Saturday, 27th February.

When Mr. McDowell returned from the burial of those shot on Jewish Hill, he reported that they had found forty bodies and identified all but five or six.

On Wednesday night, a still more horrible deed was committed at Gulpashan. This village and Iriawa had been shielded, partly through the efforts of a German; but on Wednesday night a band of Persian volunteers, arriving from Salmas or beyond, went there, took fifty men, and, according to reports, shot them in the graveyard near by. They then plundered the village, took girls and young women, outraged them, and acted in general as one might expect Satan to do when turned loose.

The horror and sadness of everything has been brought nearer to us by the death of Mlle. Madelaine Perrochet, a young Swiss girl who came with the Coans four months ago to teach the missionary children. She was only twenty-one, so bright, so pretty, that we had all learned to love her dearly. She spoke English well, and, of course, French and German. She died on Thursday, after dinner, and yesterday (Friday) we had the funeral service in Dr. Coan's living room, led by Mr. McDowell. We could not take her out to our little cemetery at Seir, so she was buried in Dr. Coan's garden, just at the right of the entrance to the long grape-arbour. In his prayer Mr. McDowell used the words: "We are not only walking in the valley of the shadow of death, but we are dwelling there in these weeks."

Just now two of the young Syrians who are the chief men in helping with the bread came in and told me that they had received warning secretly that they had better leave here and hide with some friendly Moslems, as the Turkish Consul is going to take out all the young men from our yards and other places in the city and kill them—"wipe them out." I cannot believe that it can be true, but we cannot know. If they enter our yards by force and murder men, then there is no further safety for any of us. As one of these young men said just now: "Let us commit everything into the hands of God, and then wait and be ready for whatever comes."

Typhus is raging at the College. Yesterday there were seventy cases at the College compound, and over a hundred others on diet, with the probability of a large part of them developing typhoid. It is impossible to take care of so many cases or feed them properly under such conditions. At the hospital they are buying all the milk and mesta (matzoun) they can get. Mrs. Cochran has had charge of the feeding there, as well as doing much else, and yesterday she went to bed; to-day there are symptoms of typhoid. Mrs. Coan and Miss Coan took care of Mlle. Perrochet, and the last week or two had the help of a Syrian woman who has had a nurse's course in America, Miss George. She has proved very efficient and a great help and comfort.

Saturday Night.

There was a great deal of anxiety lest something should happen here; but we woke on Sunday morning in safety and saw a rainbow in the northern sky, though there was no rain. The reports of Mr. Allen from Gulpashan were too black to be written. The soldiers sent out by the Consul to protect the villages against Kurds and Moslem looters left unviolated hardly a woman or girl of those remaining in the village, and a number of girls were carried off. It seemed quite apparent that they understood that the whole business of protecting was to be a farce. When on Sunday morning Mr. Allen returned and wanted to bring people with him, he was not permitted. Those who had been murdered in the cemetery a few nights previously had been buried under a few inches of earth, and when he wanted to have them uncovered to identify them and bury them deeper, he was refused. The soldiers had made them all sit down on the ground and then shot at them. They then looked them over, and any who were found to be breathing were shot the second time. The only reason for all this was that they bore the name of "Christian." What has the Christian world to say?

Mr. McDowell went to Iriawa and found similar conditions there. We were very glad to see him and Mr. Allen safely back, for they undoubtedly were in jeopardy themselves and were treated insolently by the soldiers.

Mrs. Cochran is better, and we feel now that she will not have typhoid. It is a tremendous relief. Only seven died here in this quarter yesterday. The death list here has passed the thousand mark, and, including the Boys'-School yard and the College, fifteen hundred. All the past week three young men and myself have been kept busy all the morning and into the middle of the afternoon examining bread tickets, hearing pleas, and giving out new tickets as the new refugees have come in. The last several days we have purchased, without counting the College, nearly ten thousand pounds of bread daily.

Friday, 5th March.

Mrs. Cochran has typhoid, but so far in a light form. Mrs. Coan and Miss Coan are taking on her work as best they can, and caring for her too, with the help of the Syrian nurse, Miss George. Dr. Packard has been in bed two or three days, but we do not know if it is typhoid or not. Mr. Allen went to Gulpashan with permission from the Turkish Consul, to bury those who had been murdered. He found fifty bodies. When he came back, a crowd of sixty-four, mostly women and girls, came with him. Our yards and rooms, including the church, are crowded again, but with cleaner people. Most of the mountaineers are out. Two families of mountaineers who are friendly with the Kurds started out yesterday for their homes. It is spring now, and time for ploughing and sowing, and unless the people can soon get to their villages there will be a dearth of wheat and other grain next year. There are repeated reports of the approach of the Russian army, and some Germans here have said that they were soon expecting to go on a journey. If the Turks should have to flee, there is no telling what they might do before going; but we do not dare to let our hopes of deliverance rise, for it makes the long wait harder.

A few days ago the ex-Turkish Consul sent word that if there were any girls held captive that we wanted to get, he would find them for us. That looks as if there had been a quarrel—or perhaps it is a trick to trip us into being unwise. It takes the wisdom of the serpent as well as the simplicity of the dove!

Saturday, 6th March.

Dr. Packard has developed typhoid. There is only Mrs. Packard to take care of him, and she is far from strong, and there are four lively boys to care for and keep out of mischief and danger. Since Mlle.'s death, it leaves the children's education on the mothers' shoulders, and Mrs. Packard has been trying to take the bulk of it.

This morning I made out the second month's report of the bread funds which have passed through my hands. So far we have spent approximately £1,500. Over £120 has been collected in sales, which leaves nearly £1,400 debt for us. This does not include College or Boys'-School yard. All of this has been spent on dry bread alone, two hundred and twenty-three and a half tons, all brought in on the backs of carriers. About one hundred and fifty pounds is a man's load. This month we have distributed four and a quarter tons a day.

Evening.

There is considerable fear to-night among the Christians that the Turks may strike a blow before they go. We have twenty-five extra guards of Persian soldiers. All day Moslem villagers have been fleeing to the city in fear of what the Russians may do when they come. We do not know how near they are, for we have no means of communication. It would seem strange to lie down in quiet and peace, knowing that all fear and terror to these poor people were passed.

Sunday, 7th March.

Dr. Packard is very sick with typhoid; yesterday his temperature was 105. He seems quieter to-day. Dr. Pera, former hospital assistant, has promised to take care of him every day from 9 a.m. to 4 p.m., and Mrs. Packard will be night-nurse. Mrs. Cochran seems to be getting along quietly. Thirty cases of typhoid are reported in one of the houses in the suburbs, which a few days ago we filled up with refugees brought from the College compound. They probably brought the germ with them. The only reason it is not raging here is the eternal vigilance of Mr. McDowell in looking after sanitary conditions and the watercourses. He has frequently to appeal to the Governor to get donkeys for carrying off refuse, though he pays well. As the church is full of refugees, two meetings are held daily in the Seminary yard. Kasha Moshi of Geogtapa makes a fine outdoor preacher.

Just now, as I came from dinner, a woman met me, leading a little girl by the hand, and in her most wheedling tones tried to present her to me as a gift, saying she was her great-grandchild. I laughed and said I already had one hundred such gifts. She felt that I was not properly appreciative! There are scores of people who would like to dump their responsibilities under these conditions. We have had a number of cases of relatives deserting old and helpless women and leaving them for us to care for until they died.

Monday, 8th March.

Yesterday there was general fasting and prayer until noon for Dr. Packard's and Mrs. Cochran's recovery. There is a beginning of what we hope may be a deep and permanent spiritual awakening. In such times one lives in the presence of eternal realities, and Heaven seems quite near. It is marvellous how the Word of God speaks to us in every condition and experience through which we pass.

Tuesday, 9th March.

On Sunday a Mohammedan orator made a speech in a garden in Dilgusha to a crowd of several thousand people, practically all Moslems. He said that Italy and Persia had joined in the alliance with Germany, Austria and Turkey, and, of course, are in the way of victory. America had taken no part in this war, but is doing good all over the world without regard to race or religion, caring for the sick and wounded, feeding the hungry and befriending the needy. The American missionaries here, he said, have done and are doing this, and everyone should honour them and stand up for them. At this there was great applause.

Last night a body of askars entered the house of Dr. ———, whose yard adjoins ours, and demanded Mar Elia, a Russian Bishop, who has been in hiding these last weeks. They didn't find him, but took about forty pounds' worth of money and jewellery and frightened the people nearly to death. Our watchman called Mr. McDowell and Mr. Allen and they tried to go over to the help of the women. Mr. McDowell climbed the ladder from this side to go over into their yard, but at the top met a gun in the hands of an askar, who demanded his retreat. Mr. McDowell, out of respect for the gun, didn't insist on having his way. That yard is not in our hands and we have no flag there, so, of course, we couldn't do anything. This has scared the people again. This morning one woman brought me some jewellery and papers to keep for her. She had been in America and only returned last spring, and was bewailing her stupidity in returning. She says she is only waiting for a way to open for her to go back, never to return. Hundreds are saying the same thing, and I think there will be a large emigration to America when the way opens. I wouldn't mind emigrating myself for a while!

Friday, 12th March.

We cannot complain of the monotony of life for these last two or three days. It was on Monday night that the Turks tried to get the Bishop, but he escaped over the church roof. The next afternoon they suddenly appeared again, and this time found him hiding on the church roof behind a parapet. He tried to get down an old ladder standing by the wall, but the askar who was at the other end of the roof raised his gun and told him he would shoot if he attempted to run, so he was captured. It is said that he had two thousand tomans in gold and Russian paper money on his person. This, of course, was taken. The most unfortunate incident of that capture was the arrest at the same time of Dr. Lokman. At Mr. McDowell's request, Dr. Lokman (Syrian) had gone over the wall into Dr. ———'s house to find out if there were any typhoid cases there, and was caught by the askars. Our mission at once began to make efforts to secure their release. The Turkish Consul demanded £200 for Dr. Lokman and £2,000 for the Bishop. In the evening he sent word that unless they were immediately redeemed they would be shot at midnight. He ordered the Persian Governor to send eight men to assist at the shooting. In the meantime they had gotten hold of another man or two. When word came about Dr. Lokman there was some hustling to find the money. "Brides" (young married women) were asked to give up the gold pieces from their dowry, and in a short time the £200 was sent. When Dr. Lokman was notified of his release he was sleeping soundly without any realization of the doom hanging over him. When he reached our yards and his family and friends congratulated him, he felt like one raised from the dead. Just as soon as he heard that the others were still in danger, he said: "Well, we must try to do something to release them." He is one of the most prominent Syrians here and influential with the Persian Government. From the first day of these troubles he has been on hand to help in governmental affairs in every way possible. All day yesterday efforts were being made to get money to redeem the others.

These last two nights our yards have been overflowing with people from the Christian quarter here, and already the Moslems from the villages are crowding into the city for fear of the Russians. As one of our bakers said yesterday: "The city gates cannot let them in fast enough." The city is in a panic for fear of what the Russians will do to the Moslems when they arrive. Heaven grant that they will act in the spirit of Christ and not of Mohammed! Everywhere the Moslems are now anxious to show themselves friends of Christians. David gives expression to my sentiments concerning the wicked in Ps. 59.

The Germans, I understand, have already left, except one of the leaders, and he is ready to go in haste. Yesterday I had to stay in bed with a headache, and it seemed to me that the very air was vibrating with expectation and excitement. Ten thousand times a day the petition arises, "O Lord, deliver us." Ten weeks to-morrow! It seems impossible to hold out much longer. "O Lord, deliver us from the hand of the wicked." Dr. Packard is still quite sick. Mrs. Cochran seems to be getting along slowly. They have so many cases of typhoid at the College that they have put up the big tent in the School yard there for a hospital.

Tuesday, 16th March.

To-day our hearts are heavy and sorrowful. Dr. Packard is very sick indeed, and it seems now as if Miss Coan has typhoid or typhus, whichever this sickness is. Mrs. Cochran appears to be getting along all right. We want Dr. Vanneman from Tabriz, but there seems to be no way to get a message through to him. Dr. Shedd asked the Turkish Consul to help us get a messenger through, but he said he couldn't. The Russians are between Urmia and Tabriz. We have twenty-five or thirty cases of typhoid here in this compound. Mr. McDowell is trying to empty a few rooms to put the sick in, but it is very difficult.

Last night there was great fear again in Mart Maryam lest the new arrivals might devise some new evil for them, and many wanted to crowd into our yard, but every place is full. We are feeding 15,000 persons daily, one loaf each. A note by secret messenger came from Dr. Vanneman a few days ago, saying that they had received £1,200 for relief. This means a great deal, but it will pay only a third of the debt we already have. The Turks still hold Shamasha Lazar and Mar Elia (Bishop) for a big ransom. Our funds are getting low, and Mr. Müller has borrowed some money at 24 per cent. interest. Last week our hopes of deliverance were high, but hope so long deferred makes the heart grow faint. Mr. McDowell was trying to get some sick people out of the big school-room when he saw a tired and weary woman, with a baby in her arms, sitting in one of the seats, and said to her: "Where do you stay?" She said: "Just here." "How long have you been here?" "Since the beginning (two months)," she replied. "How do you sleep at night?" "I lay the baby on the desk in front of me, and I have this post at the back to lean against. This is a very good place. Thank you very much."

The men don't dare to go outside our yards for fear of being arrested and held for ransom. One of the Syrian physicians was asked by a missionary to go outside and see some sick. He laughed and said: "I'll go if you will pay the bill."

Thursday, 18th March.

It is such a relief to have Dr. Packard come to himself again, though he is very weak. Miss Coan's fever still continues, and Miss Lamme has gone to the College to help there. This morning Mr. McDowell is down with fever, but we hope it is only malaria. Shamasha Lazar, who has been a prisoner for a week at the Turkish Consulate, was released on payment of one thousand tomans cash on the condition that he finds the other £400 within two days.

If there were a mail or some other way open to Tabriz, we could sell orders on Dr. Vanneman, our Mission Treasurer in Tabriz, but the bankers will not buy such orders now because they can't dispose of them until a way to Tabriz is opened. The day before yesterday we tried to make a bargain with our twenty or more Mohammedan bakers, who are supplying us with about six tons of bread daily, to let us have it on twenty days' credit. They agreed to do it on condition that at the end of ten days we would pay half; but after they left here they agreed among themselves that they would not deliver bread yesterday, though they didn't tell us. In the morning, when we found that no bread was coming, we sent out and got other bakers to deliver for cash. When our regular bakers found we were buying elsewhere, they came back, and after a long discussion they promised to deliver for twenty days, if we would pay half every five days. So it stands; we shall see if they stick to their bargain. Fortunately, yesterday we had half a day's supply on hand, and managed to buy enough to finish out. There is a cash famine, and anyone who has any money wants to hold on to it in such uncertain times.

This morning, a little after five, we were aroused by shouts and a commotion near by. The askars with their officers had entered the English mission yard by climbing a ladder from the street over the wall into the yard of a Mr. ———, who is a Syrian, but an English subject. The watchman gave the alarm, and Mr. Muller and Mr. Allen were soon on the spot. Of course they couldn't do anything but reassure the women. Eight or ten men were arrested and taken away, probably to be held for ransom. That property has been connected with ours from the beginning of these troubles, and the American flag has been over the entrance. Mr. Allen said to the officer: "You don't intend to respect the American flag?" He replied: "The Turkish flag is also there." (It is under the American flag.) This makes one feel doubtful for the safety of our own yards. It is wonderful how quiet these thousands of people can keep while such things are going on. A number of women and girls sleep in the parlour adjoining my room, and I opened the door and told them not to leave the room. They said: "No, we are only dressing"; but it was evident that they were trembling with fear; and this is the state we have lived in for eleven weeks.

One of the most pitiful objects of humanity that I have ever yet seen came into the room to ask for a ticket—a boy of about twelve or fourteen, wasted to a mummy-like skeleton by hunger and sickness, so weak that he could hardly stand or speak, unbathed for these many months. I asked where he had been staying. He said: "In the school-room."

The Turks have demanded ten thousand suits of shirts and pyjamas for the army. Eight thousand were demanded from the Moslem women, and two thousand from the Christian or Syrian women. As the latter are practically all here with us and in the Christian quarter, it fell upon the missionaries to take the responsibility, so Miss Schoebel took charge. So far fifty-five bolts of calico have been sent; Miss Schoebel gave out the material to responsible women, and they in turn found others to help with the sewing (mostly by hand) and about eight hundred of the shirts are ready. How would you like to sit down and make clothes for Turks and Kurds who had robbed you, burned your homes, murdered your husbands, brothers, and fathers, dishonoured your women, and carried your girls into captivity?

Saturday, 20th March.

The prisoners taken from the English Mission yards by the Turks were kept about twenty-four hours, examined, and to the great and unexpected joy of everyone were set free without ransom. The Turks said they had heard that a Russian spy was being kept in that yard, and when they found no evidence of this, they set the men free. Another thing may have had something to do with it. The night before last several Turkish soldiers who were sick with typhoid went to the College compound. When informed that there was absolutely no place for them, they returned to the Consulate, which is in the former Russian Mission. The Shahbanda then sent for Dr. Shedd. It was after nightfall and we didn't know why he was sent for, but were fearful lest another blow might be about to fall upon us. But he asked him if we would be willing to care for their sick, a dozen or more, who have typhoid. He was told that there was no room in the hospital or College building adjoining, which are already crowded full of sick, but that we would do what we could. This probably had something to do with the dismissal of the prisoners. For two days no other arrests have been made, and only the Bishop is now a prisoner. The last ransom they asked for him was fifteen thousand tomans. The Shahbanda has said that he is going to take down all the American flags except the one over our main entrance. We have several other properties adjoining ours which are full of refugees, and several of the naturalized citizens have American flags up.

We are happy this morning that all our sick are better. Mr. McDowell was up yesterday and Miss Schoebel has no fever this morning, so it looks as if she had only malaria. Mrs. Cochran is getting along finely; Dr. Packard we hope has passed the crisis; Miss Coan seems to be having a fight case. Our rooms, hallways, and every place are crowded to the limit again. The men are afraid to stay anywhere else for fear of arrest. The Turks have given out word that several thousand troops are coming, and are demanding houses in Mart Maryam, and those turned out have nowhere else to go.

We are having trouble in getting bread, as the bakers refuse to deliver without cash on the spot. They say the "blue eyes" (Russians) will return, "and then you will not pay us." Mr. Müller will try to-day to get wheat on several months' credit, and we shall use that instead of cash if possible. I am realizing what a wonderful thing money is, and what a dreadful thing it is to be without it, especially under such circumstances. As long as we could pay cash we couldn't stop some of the bakers from bringing more than we wanted. We feel, with so many of our number sick, so many others busy caring for them, the end of our money in sight, and our physical strength almost exhausted, that surely deliverance must be near. Through eleven weeks we have looked for it in vain.

I have just paid a visit to the school dining-room, which is one of our hospital rooms. If there is another spot on this earth of more concentrated human misery, I hope I may never know it. One boy had just died. The mother looked up at me so pitifully, and said: "Lady, he is dead." Another baby was lying on the floor dying, under the influence of khash-khash (opium). The mother has no milk for lack of food, and the baby is dying of starvation. The mother said: "Khanum, I am so sick, what shall I do?" I could only reply: "I do not know." Twenty others were lying on the floor, without bedding, in various stages of misery, groaning, weeping and appealing for help. One child was lying on his father's coat with a hard bundle under his head, with the marks of slow starvation upon him. To-morrow he too will probably be gone, and we shall thank God that it is so. They are so many, our strength and our means are so limited, the rooms are so crowded, we can do little for them and death is their best friend. One of our Bible Women is lying here, with her two daughters on one side of her and her sister on the other. Her boy died a few weeks ago. When I spoke to her she tried to raise herself up and tell me about some of the other sick in the room. We have been furnishing matting for the sick to lie on, and using Mr. Sterrett's supply of wood for fires in the sick room; the rest have had to do without fires except the few who have been able to get wood for their rooms. In one of the typhoid rooms yesterday I noticed a pile of charred wood in the corner and asked about it. They said they had sent to the village and brought in the half-burned beams of their homes for fuel. That was all that was left of their house, except a pile of mud. Others have done the same thing.

Yesterday Rabi Nanou, one of our Bible Women, went out as usual to hold meetings in the places where large numbers of refugees, mostly mountain people, are huddled together. She was stopped in the street by an askar who demanded her long coat. She told him she had been stripped of everything when she first fled from her village, and that the coat had since been given her by one of the missionary ladies. He said, nevertheless, it was not necessary for her, and demanded that she should take it off. Just then another askar came up who had been a guard at our gate. He interfered, saying that he knew her as a deaconess who went out every day to preach to the people, and she was allowed to go on with her coat.

A while ago I took some soft-boiled eggs and several pieces of bread to the sick ones in the dining-room, and to Rabi Surra and her family. They are very grateful for everything. I've no doubt that, if they were properly fed, most of them would be up in a week.

Sunday, 21st March.

Yesterday Mr. McDowell called a meeting of all the native doctors to try to get them to help in the responsibility of caring for the increasing number of typhoid cases. There are a number of doctors who do practically nothing and find excuses when anything is asked of them. It is hard to understand how they can spend hours every day sitting in their rooms or walking up and down the pavement here while they might be doing something to help in the care of the scores of sick people and in the effort Mr. McDowell is making for the preservation of the health of the community. Our assistant physician, Dr. Daniel Werda, is sick with typhoid, and Dr. David, of Soujboulak, who went out to the hospital to help, has been brought home sick. Dr. Pera, our former assistant, is at the College compound now, helping with the sick missionaries and a few special cases, and Dr. Joseph Khoshaba has consented to go out there to help. Dr. Theo. Mar Yosep has been our stand-by from the very beginning, and is the only native doctor here in the city yards who has really worked. He has been on hand every day.

Tuesday, 23rd March.

Sunday evening was the beginning of the Persian New Year, *Noruz*, and as soon as the cannon went off to announce that the New Year had begun there was a great firing of guns and torpedoes, more than usual. It was kept up for half-an-hour or more, and many of the people were badly frightened, thinking that perhaps a battle was on. We heard the next day that the Shahbanda was scared, not knowing what it was.

The Shahbanda sent forty-eight bolts of muslin for pyjamas, and the women under Miss Schoebel's directions are now sewing on them, having finished eight hundred and fifty shirts.

The smells in our backyards are almost unbearable. I can't open my back window at all. The sun is quite hot and dries things up; it also brings out the awful smells. Last night the Shahbanda gave us permission to send a messenger to Tabriz for Dr. Vanneman. Our sick are all getting along fairly well. Dr. Packard has passed the crisis and each day seems a little bit better. There are about twenty-five Turks in the hospital now.

Thursday, 25th March.

We are trying to send away some of the people by taking back their bread tickets to-day; but we cannot give them any assurance of safety. They are so crowded here, and there is so much sickness, and money is so scarce, that it seems the lesser of two evils to send some of the people away, even though a few be killed.

Yesterday we gave each of the sixty sick persons in the school dining-room a soft-boiled egg, and in the afternoon tea, which was served by two or three school-girls. Sugar and tea are so expensive, about three times the regular price, that it costs about six shillings just to treat that one room to tea. The big school-room is in just as bad a condition as the dining-room, only with so many more tenants that it seems impracticable to do anything there. I've no doubt that if hundreds of these people were properly fed for a week they would be on their feet, but it is beyond our means and our strength. Just now the voice of Kasha Moushi Douman of Geogtapa comes to me through the open window of the paved school court where he is preaching. Twice a day preaching exercises are held in the school yard, and besides there are a number of preachers and women who go round daily to rooms and other yards for services.

Monday, 29th March.

We have had two or three rainy days, which are very hard for the people. Some of the sick are lying on the balcony with almost no covering or bedding. I saw one of the most awful sights I have yet seen on the school balcony yesterday—a woman stretched out on the bare bricks, half-naked, in the throes of death, the damp cold air blowing over her, friendless, helpless. The whole school-room, aisles, desks, corners, and platform is filled with the most miserable of the starving sick. We made the man who has charge of our tea-stand take the samovars there yesterday, Palm Sunday, and give each of the one hundred and fifty people two large glasses of tea. It costs about twelve shillings, but eight shillings were given me by Syrians. With the thousands of dollars of debt just for dry bread, we don't feel we can borrow money for special food for the sick ones, except in limited quantities for typhoid patients. We need space more than anything else, rooms where we could put the sick on straw mats with at least a quilt over them, a fire and a little food besides dry bread, which many are too sick to eat. It seems dreadful to think of two thousand people dying here in this way, but after twelve weeks of it we cannot but feel glad every time one more of these helpless suffering ones finds rest. Sometimes for days I seem to be hardened past feeling, and then again the horror of it all sweeps over me. We pray and pray and cry out to God for deliverance, but no help comes. We seem shut off from the rest of the world and left to our fate. Nothing from the outside world for three months! We hear many reports, but few materialize. We are told that word has come that the Crown Prince has arrived in Tabriz and that Urmia should celebrate, so there has been a great deal of firing of cannon, display of banners, and decoration. We have had our entrance decorated with banners and rugs. There is a great deal of rejoicing among the Persians, who desire to see the Persian Government strong enough to turn out both Turk and Russian.

A few days ago, Mr. Müller managed to borrow a thousand tomans from a merchant in the bazaar. It was counted out in two-kran silver pieces. This he was bringing home on the back of a porter, he walking close behind with a Persian soldier. Suddenly he found himself surrounded by six Kurds, armed to the teeth with guns, cartridge belts, and daggers. Two walked ahead and punched the money-bag to assure themselves that it was really money; the others pressed close behind Mr. Müller as they followed him through the streets. They asked him where he was taking the money, but he walked on in dignified silence, not deigning to answer, though trembling for the safety of the money. They reached our gate in safety, and as he turned in, Mr. Müller thanked the Kurds for their safe escort. They laughed and passed on. Some of the young Syrians who guard the gate report that a few days ago a bunch of Kurds in passing stopped to talk and said: "We came down here to the plain with the intention of killing you all, not one of you would have escaped, but (pointing to the Stars and Stripes over the gate) we don't dare pass under that flag!" Everybody feels that had we not been able to give refuge to the Christians, there would have been few left to tell the tale; and so even yet we do not dare to force the people out, and they all say: "We would rather die here of hunger and disease than take our chances with the Kurds and Turks."

Our sick missionaries all seem to be getting along well, and we are very thankful. The typhoid here in the city is usually light, and there are few deaths from it, though many from dysentery. Measles almost disappeared some time ago.

Thursday, 1st April.

Rabi Nannou of Geogtapa, our best Bible Woman, has died of pneumonia, after a few days' illness. For the three months that she has been a refugee here she has been a fearless and faithful worker, going out daily for religious meetings to the houses where the mountaineers have been huddled, looking after the sick, not hesitating to go to any place where she could help. For several years she has supported from her small salary her brother's four orphan children, and has been to them both father and mother. Herself unmarried, she has given her means and love unselfishly to these as if they were her own children. There is no one to fill her place.

We have started to buy wheat on credit, as our cash is very low and we are not able to get more money. We have just bought four hundred bushels from Rabi David of Degala for part of his debt to us. When he was in prison and fined one thousand tomans to save his head, we furnished part of the cash and took his note. He can't pay cash now, so he is paying in wheat, which we will have ground to give to the hungry. What credit we can get for bread is for a few days only. Most of the bakers need the money to carry on their business.

Friday, 2nd April.

Bertha Shedd, ten years old, has been sick with typhoid for several days, and now Miss Lamme is beginning; the latter went out to the hospital about two weeks ago to help there when Miss Coan went down with it. Dr. Packard, Mrs. Cochran, and Miss Coan are getting well. Oraham Badel, our financial agent and general assistant in the City Compound, is very low this morning—just as I was writing he died, leaving a wife and four little ones.

Several hundred Turkish troops have come into the city, evidently in retreat, as there are wounded among them. It is not evident from which direction they came. Last evening one of the Turkish officers came rushing in here in great distress. He had taken poison by mistake and came in here to be saved. He was given an emetic, and his life was saved. They have heard of germs and are very much afraid of typhoid, and had some corrosive sublimate in a glass for washing hands. This man saw it and, thinking it was wine or whiskey, poured it down his throat. He was terribly scared, and after being relieved of the poison, it was suggested that, as his life had been saved, he should try to save other lives.

Sunday, 4th April.

This journal is fast becoming an obituary. At first the hundreds who died were the poorest and the weakest, but now many from among our best are going. Yesterday Dr. Daniel Werda, Dr. Packard's assistant, died of typhoid. For three days Mrs. McDowell has been in bed with high fever. It is not evident yet that it is typhoid. Last night our cook went to bed with typhoid. Miss Schoebel is now trying to make her comfortable and makes her old mother look after her. All day we have been trying to get something to eat for the hundreds of sick who have nothing for Easter. Easter is the Syrian "Great Feast," and is to them what Christmas is to us. They say: "The Little Feast (Christmas) was black, and now the Great Feast is black too." They had hoped so much that deliverance might come before the feast. We have given eggs and soup to about five hundred sick, and before evening I hope a glass of tea will be given to as many more. To-morrow we plan to give soup to several hundred more that we didn't reach to-day. We don't use relief money for anything but bread, and so have only personal funds for the sick—a very little.

Tuesday, 6th April.

We have dwelt so long in the valley of death with the sick, the starving, the dying, with the unending procession of little bodies sewn up in a piece of cloth, friendless corpses carried out on ladders, with gaping mouths and staring eyes, crude unpainted coffins, coffins covered with black chintz, the never-ceasing wail, and eyes of the mourners that are never dried, hands outstretched for what we cannot give, and now so many of our own number are down. I felt on Sunday as if I ought to get my own burial clothes ready so as to make as little trouble as possible when my turn came, for in these days we all go about our work knowing that any one of us may be the next to go down. And yet I think our friends would be surprised to see how cheerful we have kept, and how many occasions we find for laughing; for ludicrous things do happen. Then, too, after dwelling so intimately with death for three months, he doesn't seem to have so unfriendly an aspect, and the "Other Side" seems very near and our Pilot close beside us. It is at such times that one finds out just how much faith in the unseen he has, and just how much his religion is worth. I find the Rock on which I can anchor in peace are the words of Christ Himself: "Where I am, there ye may be also." "If any man serve Me let him follow Me, and where I am, there shall also My servant be." That is enough—to be where He is. Recently, as I have read sermons or books written for the trying times of life, I have found them tame and insufficient for the occasion; our own experiences are so much more intense and go so much deeper that nothing but the words of God Himself can reach to the bottom. I have been re-reading Browning's *Prospice*, but it doesn't thrill me as much as it did, for I have something better: "For I know whom I have believed...." and "I am persuaded that Death cannot separate us from the love of God which is in Christ Jesus our Lord."

Afternoon.

This morning Mrs. McDowell's rose-spots appeared, and now we know that she has typhoid or typhus (it was typhoid). Rabi Ister Alamshah has consented to help in the care of Mrs. McDowell. Miss Schoebel and I were perfectly willing to nurse her, but it would mean throwing our work on some other missionary already loaded up. Mr. McDowell will give up some of his work and help in nursing Mrs. McDowell. There are now six of our number sick, and it is impossible not to feel that someone else will go down in a few days unless it becomes possible to send the crowds away.

Evening.

To-day Miss Lamme's rose-spots appeared, so her case is pronounced typhoid.

* * * * * *

Thursday, 3rd June.

Almost two months since I last wrote in my journal. On Sunday, the 11th April, I went to bed with typhoid or typhus, and three days later Miss Schoebel went down with it also. Rabi Elishua, a teacher of the Persian Girls'-School, came to nurse me at once. She kept up for three weeks and saw me through the worst of my sickness; then she took the disease. Three of the other Seminary teachers in succession came to care for Miss Schoebel, and each one went down with the disease in turn. Miss Bridges, of the American Orphanage, came to help us during the day, and in twelve days went to bed with typhus. She is just getting about again. All the teachers who helped to care for us have recovered, though one of the other teachers died. We were all surprised to find how competent these untrained, inexperienced girls were as nurses when there were no available missionaries left to nurse us. We were dependent upon them and got along finely without any complications. When the last one went down we knew that she was the last *intelligent* nurse we should find, and after that we were dependent upon ignorant village women.

A great many things happened during the two months of our illness and convalescence. A very large number of our Syrian friends died. Of our own circle Mrs. McDowell died on the 16th April, and Mrs. Shedd on the 17th May. We can't take in yet what their loss will mean to us when we get to living under normal conditions. Mrs. Müller attended Miss Schoebel and me for two and a half weeks; then she took the fever. Her little boy was born in a few days, but only lived overnight. This is the fourth grave we have out in Dr. Coan's orchard by the grape-arbour. It hasn't been possible to take them to our cemetery at Seir. This week Mr. Müller went to bed with typhus. His fever has been high. He is the thirteenth out of eighteen missionaries to get the fever, besides two of the children, Bertha Shedd and Ruth Müller. On Monday, Mr. Labaree, with two nurses, Miss Easton of the Tabriz hospital and Miss Burgess, who had reached Tabriz on her way to Urmia, arrived. Mr. Labaree had been trying for weeks to get through, but was unable until the Russian army opened the way. Yesterday, the 5th June, Dr. Lamme arrived and began work last evening. One of the hard things during these five long months was our isolation from the outside world. Of course we knew that our friends were thinking of and praying for us, but it is a great help to have the tangible evidence in the shape of these friends and of letters from many others.

On Sunday, the 24th May, the advanced guard of the Russian army entered Urmia, and in the afternoon the commander came to call on our gentlemen. When we learned that the army would not remain, but were ordered to follow the enemy, there was consternation and great fear. And when the army moved on, the Moslems immediately began to annoy and rob the Syrians who had returned to their villages. There was great fear of a Moslem uprising against the Christians, and hundreds fled in the direction of Salmas. Finally the Russians left a small guard of about two hundred men. Three days ago about six thousand Russian troops, with artillery, came in from the south and marched through the city. We watched them from our roof, and it was a goodly sight to us besieged people. We shall try now to empty our yards of refugees. A few days ago there were still about one thousand left in our own yards and in one yard adjoining, which we have been renting for refugees, besides many others in surrounding yards. The stench in our back yard is almost unbearable. I don't know how we can get rid of the smells or disinfect the ground, which must be soaked for two or three feet, as that yard has been used as a latrine for hundreds of people for more than five months.

Yesterday two Red Cross nurses, who have come with the Russian army from Mongolia, asked to be our guests for a few days until the army moved on in the direction of Erzeroum. They say that from there they will go to Jerusalem. When travelling they dress like the Cossacks, but wear their nurses' costumes in the house.

A few days ago a number of prominent Syrians, who had fled when the Russians evacuated Urmia, returned, many of them to broken and badly damaged homes. We had a service of thanksgiving in the church yesterday, the first time for many months, as it had been occupied by refugees. Thousands have lived in such terror and want, it is a wonder that many have not lost their minds. It has seemed sometimes as if our tears were all dried up and our emotions were dead, we have seen and felt so much. I suppose it is nature's way of saving brain and nerve. When I look at these poor wretched creatures and little children like skeletons, I find I still have some feelings left. It is estimated that four thousand people have died from disease, hunger, and exposure, and about a thousand by violence. The suffering can never be told, nor is it ended. Hundreds, yes thousands, are destitute, and even if we empty our yard there is no one left but the missionaries to save them from starvation, and we look to America. In the name of all Christians we have tried to witness for Christianity before this Moslem people. Will the Christians of America pay the bill?

---

46. Note by Miss Platt.—The term Syrian, as used here, applies to the Christian nation who speak the Syriac language, and who are Nestorians by religious belief. In America they call themselves Persian-Assyrians.

47. Christian quarter of the city, adjoining the mission property.

48. A *toman* is about four shillings.

32. URMIA AFTER ITS EVACUATION BY THE TURKS AND KURDS: LETTER DATED URMIA, 20th MAY, 1915, FROM MRS. J.P. COCHRAN TO FRIENDS IN THE UNITED STATES; COMMUNICATED BY THE BOARD OF FOREIGN MISSIONS OF THE PRESBYTERIAN CHURCH IN THE U.S.A.

It seems almost too good to be true to think that we are going to get in touch once more with the outside world, and may be it is. But, anyway, the Governor says he will send a messenger over to Tabriz to-morrow to carry letters and perhaps he will get through safely.

I have no idea what has leaked through to civilisation since we fell out of the world, but I will give you as much of an account of the last four months and a half as the brief time allowed before the messenger goes will permit.

On New Year's Day we had our usual day of receiving callers in the city; all our Syrian and some Moslem friends called and things seemed fairly safe, though we knew we might be on the edge of war, as there was an army of Turks and Kurds within a day's march of us. They were said to be coming on to fight the Russians, who with a little force, of two thousand, perhaps, were strongly entrenched here.

The next morning the Russians rose and left in haste, and many of our Syrian men and others who were known to be their supporters here left with them. Our teaching force here at the College, our newspaper and printing press work, and even our city church work was terribly crippled by the exodus, as it took away some of our best workers.

The Russians' departure was the herald for the Kurds to pounce upon the prey they had so long been held at bay from, and, even before they arrived, the Moslem neighbours in all the surrounding villages flew upon the spoil, killing Syrians, running off with their cattle and household goods and even stripping those who were trying to run away from them of their money, bundles and any clothes they took a fancy to. They also carried off women and tried to force Christians to become Moslems, keeping them safely if they would deny their faith or repeat the sentence which constituted the acceptance of Islam. In some cases they were successful in this, though, of course, many would not and some of them were killed for it.

Then came the rush of the Kurds. They came in hundreds from every Kurdish quarter, sore against the Christians for having joined forces with the Russians, who had armed them and drafted them for military service whether they would or not.

They, being armed, put up a fight and killed a good many Kurds in the battles at some of the villages, though there were a couple of thousand Syrians killed too in the villages, before they escaped to the slender protection offered by six unarmed American men in our mission compound. Our flag was put up, not only on our own property here in the city but on all the adjoining block of Christian property in the city; doors were made or holes in the walls between all that adjoining property, to bring it under our control, and only our principal big street-gate was allowed to be opened, all others being barricaded. There in the city between ten and fifteen thousand, many thousands of them destitute, congregated and sat huddled in rooms, a hundred in a room or more, sometimes unable to lie down at night on account of the crowding.

We had a good deal of money entrusted to us by the people who had to flee, and as most of it is in silver ten-penny pieces, there being no paper money in circulation here, they could carry away but little, and we took charge of large sums without interest, to be used by us if necessary and repaid when banking was resumed. With this we began to feed the people. It was the system in the city to sell bread until noon, and after that to distribute one of the thin sheets of bread to every one who had nothing to eat and no money to buy anything. This distribution took a force of about twenty or thirty men seven hours to get through.

The city church is in the enclosure under the American flag, and it held three thousand ill-smelling people with their few earthly possessions remaining to them.

Here at the College we had about two thousand, and as we have few buildings the housing was a problem.

We had five hundred in the hospital. Our largest ward has only ten beds in it, and by putting people on the floor between the beds we could get in about twenty, but in two other large wards that we took the bedsteads out of, over a hundred apiece sat huddled together on the floor, without fire or lights, as we could not afford them for them. We had those who were destitute here; those who had escaped with their cattle and a sack of flour or some bedding or a carpet we put over on the other side of the avenue in the College buildings.

I fed those on the hospital side besides attending to the regular hospital routine, which was heavier on account of the wounded Christians who were being brought in every day.

My own rooms consist of my dining room and sitting room, in one of which I have a couch to sleep on, a kitchen and a little room downstairs for my man.

I reserved one room for myself for living, dining and bedroom combined, and took in seven of the College boys, students from the mountains, who are here all the year round and whom I knew pretty well, to bring their native beds to live in my dining room. Seakhan had the kitchen full of her people and friends, seven or eight of them, and Choban took two families into his room downstairs.

The boys helped me by distributing the bread in the hospital and holding evening prayers in the different rooms in the hospital.

Then we all began to get the typhoid fever. We had some Turkish soldiers in the hospital with it, and the people were ignorant and careless, so we had an epidemic of it. We have seven hundred new-made graves in our compound here at the College, as the result of it.

I have had it and recovered, and am as strong and well as ever, though somewhat thinner, fortunately. I had a Syrian trained nurse, the only one in Urmia, as I was the first missionary to go down with it, being in the most direct contact with it in the hospital (though Dr. Packard went down the day after I did). He also recovered. The little Swiss governess the Coans brought out with them was the first to die of the foreigners, and then followed the death of Mrs. McDowell and, this week, my dear Louise Shedd, my best friend here—a friend of fifteen years' standing from the time we were together in charge of the seminary. All my boys went down too, and my favourite one died—such a simple, sweet Christian boy. Others of the missionaries who have had it or are having it are Dr. Coan and Elizabeth, Bertha Shedd and Mrs. Müller. Mrs. Müller gave birth to a seven months' baby boy, who lived a day, and then she went on to have typhoid. Besides these there were Miss Lewis, Miss Schoebel, Miss Lamme and Mr. Allen.

In the hospital there was a time when the head physician-assistant, Dr. Daniel (who died of it), the matron, the druggist, all the nurses, the cook and the bake-woman, the steward and the washer-women were all down together, and two hundred and fifty patients to be taken care of. You can imagine, or rather you can't begin to imagine, the disorganisation of the place. Elizabeth Coan took my place at first, and in two weeks was having it. Then Miss Lamme came to take her place and in two weeks she, too, was on her back. The Syrian woman who came next to fill the vacancy is still at it, though I am back at some work, being now safe from infection. My man had it, but my woman has weathered the gale so far, and after three months we have to record to-day that for ten days past not one new case has come down here. One of the boys, Seakhan's mother and two of the men in Choban's room have died of it in my "family."

In the city it was even worse. It is raging in our big compound, though from the first they had from ten to forty deaths a day from cold, privation, illness of one kind and another, and perhaps shock from fright. In another part of the city, where we have a big school building for our Moslem boys'-school, three thousand people were rescued and brought in by Dr. Packard's valiant intervention, when he rode up to the Kurdish chief in the thick of a fight between Kurds and the villagers entrenched in Russian trenches and fighting for their lives, begged the lives of the inhabitants, and after parleying awhile succeeded in buying the souls of the people in exchange for their guns. He rode back to the city with them after the sun had set on a January night, reaching the city about nine o'clock, their homes being robbed and burned behind them by the Kurds.

Turkish rule and Kurdish plundering have reduced the inhabitants to the verge of starvation, and as yet the end is not in sight.

Yesterday the Turks and Kurds arose and departed, and it is supposed that the Russians are about to return. They are only a day's journey distant, having just been successful in a long fight with a Turkish army that came from Constantinople via Mosul, and after a three months' march was cut to pieces by the Russians near Gavilan, a day's journey from here. There were twenty thousand or more of them, well equipped, but the Russians had the advantage of a fortified position, a knowledge of the lie of the land and perhaps superior numbers. We don't know anything definite about that.

We haven't had a word of war news during 1915 so far, and feel as if we were in the bottom of a well as far as seeing what is going on about us is concerned.

No mail has penetrated the veil that hides the world from us, but we have had a telegram from the American Ambassador in Constantinople inquiring for our safety, and have sent telegrams saying we had not been disturbed personally, which is one of the miracles of missions, by the way. Just now things are very tense here; the Moslem Governor is doing well in trying to control things, but the Moslems hate the Christians, so that they are killing some of those who have gone back to their ruined villages to live.

There is no power of description that can overdraw the picture, that is and has been before our eyes constantly, of misery and distress. Instead we have to veil it, for details are too horrible, too revolting to try to convey to people who are not called upon by God to go through it. But whatever the end may be for me, I am sure I can only be thankful God has given me such an unlimited opportunity for service as these past months have been.

If the Russians come back or the Turks stay away, we shall have a mail system established again, if there is such a thing going on across the world nowadays. Since last July we have had little mail on account of the war, but some did leak through till the 1st January (1915), since when we have been like Moses when the light went out.

We are still feeding thousands of people—just enough bread every day to keep life in their bodies—and have saved the Syrian nation but have accumulated thirty or forty thousand dollars (six to eight thousand pounds sterling) of debt, which we don't know where to find money to repay. We only know of six thousand dollars (£1,200 sterling) that were telegraphed as relief two or three months ago. But we hope the Red Cross Society and charitable people in America will send us money.

We haven't even been able to get our money from the Board sent to Tabriz, but even what could be paid on our regular salaries has been paid out of these borrowed funds. However, when things settle down a little we can get at that if there are any of us left by that time.

Just now I have regularly one school-boy and often a few others at my table, as they are all hungry with the hunger that comes after typhoid and the College fare is reduced to bread and cheese.

The one who eats with me all the time is a boy from the village Dr. Packard delivered, Geogtapa, and his father was killed and his house burned and goods carried off or destroyed. Their food supplies were left, mostly, as the robbers got their fill and could only destroy the rest. For instance, a cellar had jars of molasses smashed and into that was thrown their flour, and on that pickles by jars-full—the big earthen pointed-bottomed jars that household supplies are all stored in here. Into this pudding were thrown their books, few in number, perhaps, but all the more valued for that. Then this boy, because he belongs to a village where soldier guards have been placed and some degree of safety assured, was told that he must go home. That was a general rule, and when I learned the state of things I told him he could eat with me till things cleared up. Then they have fields and vineyards that can be worked, and he has older brothers in America and Tiflis who will look after him. He is about eighteen, the youngest of the family and the only one left at home. He is only one case out of thousands equally at a loss just now. He has his room at the College and sleeps over there with other students.

I hope you have all been kept in safety during these months and will write to me all about yourselves and the world at large.

33. URMIA: LETTER, DATED URMIA, 25th MAY, 1915, FROM THE REV. Y.M. NISAN TO THE REV. F.N. HEAZELL, ORGANISING SECRETARY OF THE ARCHBISHOP OF CANTERBURY'S ASSYRIAN MISSION.

The day after the departure of our missionaries from Urmi, that is, the 3rd January (1915), the Kurds and Turks, and with them a great number of the Moslems of Urmi, began to raid and kill and to make captives from a large part of the Christian villages.

The majority of the Christians, to the number of about 25,000, took refuge in the courtyards of the Americans and French and in our own premises. Up to the present time there is a large number of the Syrians in our yard; another portion, we do not know how many, fled to Russia with the Russian army. The besieged people here were provided with bread, one portion each per day, by the missionaries; but many have not escaped death. People died from the following causes:—(1) From fear; (2) from their bad dwelling places; (3) from cold; (4) from hunger; (5) from typhoid fever—the dead up to now from this disease, as far as we can tell, are from 800 to 1,000. Those who died from the slaughter and raiding of villages numbered 6,000. Many died in the houses of their refuge from the causes mentioned above. About 2,000 died of those who fled (to Russia), either on the road or after their arrival there. In our house my daughter Beatrice died from fright, and, 25 days after Beatrice, Mrs. Nisan died from grief at the loss of her daughter; also Michael, nephew of Khan Audishu, my relative, and to-day his wife, too. Nanajan, my daughter-in-law, and her two sisters are now in bed with typhoid fever.

One day 48 people were seized in the yard of the French Mission. Mar Dinkha, bishop of the Old Church, was one of them. As they were keeping him in prison some days, I tried to buy off Mar Dinkha with the promise of 50 gold pieces, but they asked 100. I was outwitted at that time, for as often as I raised my offer they would advance the price. Then they carried them outside, and when they were bound arm to arm they were all shot.

Once they went to the village of Gulpashan and demanded a sum of money; they took money and carried off everything else as well; 45 men who were on the watch were killed that night.

At the beginning of events, the Turks demanded, in the name of the Persian Government, every kind of weapon for hewing and cutting (instead of knives); these were all seized in the name of the Persian Government. Afterwards two Osmanli officers and some soldiers came to the houses and searched for weapons and men in our yards, and so to every room and cupboard. Boxes were opened and examined, and the people were in the greatest fear.

One day afterwards they entered the yard and seized Mar Elia, the Russian Bishop and Doctor Lokman. After a long imprisonment the Bishop was ransomed for 6,500 tomans, and the doctor for 2,000 tomans. The Melet Bashi of the French was taken from their yard and afterwards ransomed for 3,000 tomans. Shamasha Lazar, whose house is just by the American gate, was seized and bought off for 4,500 tomans. The enemy had one list of 80 names, written by their own hand, of men who were doomed to be killed, or bought off at a great price.

Audishu Khan fled from our house to the house of a Moslem friend, and remained hidden for two months, but by the rogues of the village and the commander here he was robbed of 27,000 tomans.

One night two Turkish officers with some soldiers descended by means of a ladder into our yard; they seized Mr. George, our neighbour, and the brother-in-law of Mr. Comin, who was groom in his house; also Jawar, our gatekeeper, and Babu our cook and his son; also Kasha Pilipus, *natir kursi* of Mar Yohannan, and Asakhan my servant. At that time, because I had two persons very ill, I was watching from the balcony of my house so that they might not enter my rooms. Twice they came beneath the balcony and looked up, and when they saw me they went away. There is no doubt that the angels were watching over us and sent these men away.

At first Jawar's brother and his son were seized, when carrying bread for him (Jawar). After an imprisonment of two nights and one day we got them out by paying 68 tomans for the two of them. A friend of mine worked this for my sake.

The Osmanlis and the Kurds left Urmi two days ago. The Russian army is now a little way from Urmi. To-day we are very confused and fearful; they are saying that the Russian army will return. One part of the Syrians have fled and left Urmi.

One letter previous to this one—I doubt if it has reached you. I shall be glad if you will let me know quickly what is to be my work here in the future, because just now I am like a bird without a nest and without companions. There is no word from Samuel my son, and I do not know where he is.

34. URMIA: NARRATIVE OF DR. JACOB SARGIS, RECORDED IN A DESPATCH, DATED PETROGRAD, 12th FEBRUARY, 1916, FROM THE CORRESPONDENT AT PETROGRAD OF THE AMERICAN "ASSOCIATED PRESS."

Dr. Jacob Sargis, an American Methodist medical missionary, who has arrived in Petrograd after narrowly escaping death at the hands of the Turks and Kurds in Urmia, Persian Armenia, asserts that among the outrages committed against the Christian refugees was the burning to death of an American doctor named Simon, or Shimmun, as he was known there. His identity was not further established, but the story of the outrage, as told by Dr. Sargis, was as follows:

"Dr. Shimmun was in the village of Supurghan when the Turks attacked that place. He was among those who took refuge on a mountain near the lake. He was captured and told that since he had been a good doctor and had helped the wounded, they would not kill him, but that he must accept the Mohammedan faith. He refused, as almost all Christians did. They poured oil on him, and, before applying the torch, they gave him another chance to forsake his religion. Again he refused, and they set his clothes afire. While he was running in agony from the flames, the Turks shot him several times. After he fell to the ground unconscious, they hacked his head off. Mr. Allen, an American missionary, who went from village to village burying the victims of this butchery, found the body of Shimmun half eaten by dogs.

"The Catholic Mission there took 150 Christians of all sects, and kept them in a small room and tried to save them; but at least 49 of them, among them one Bishop Dinkha, of the Episcopal Mission, were bound together one night, taken to Gagin mountain and there shot down."

Mr. Sargis was born in Persia, but went to America in 1893, and was educated there by the assistance of Dr. W.F. Oldham, former Bishop of India. He is a graduate of Ohio Wesleyan and Ohio Medical University, and was for a time resident physician of the Protestant hospital at Columbus, Ohio.

Dr. Sargis was doing relief work in Urmia on the 1st January last year when the Russian army retired from that city, followed by 14,000 refugees from Urmia and a hundred surrounding villages. The hardships and sufferings endured by those refugees were described in Associated Press despatches. There were still left in Urmia and the villages 45,000 persons, chiefly Armenian refugees, when the Turks and Kurds entered. The latter at once began the work of exterminating the Christian population. In one town alone, Gulpashan, in one night, according to Dr. Sargis, 79 men and boys were tied hand to hand, taken to a hill outside the village and shot. Their wives and daughters were distributed among the Turks, Kurds and Persian Mohammedans.

Dr. Sargis' story continues:

"On the second day after the Turkish officers came, they had a good many wounded and sick. As soon as they heard that I was an able physician, they took me, gave me a bodyguard, and put me in charge of Urmia Hospital. That was how I came to learn most of their secrets; I helped their wounded and sick. One day there were sixty men brought from Bashkala, all well-to-do citizens, some of them noted men of that place. They were used as beasts of burden and forced to carry rolls of barbed wire into Urmia. The next day they were all taken to the Castle of Ismayil[49] and every one was shot or hacked to death.

"About that time Nuri, the governor of Gawar, told me that he had received word from the Turkish commander to kill all the Armenian soldiers in the Turkish army. He said that, for my sake, he would not do it, but that somebody else would. Twenty-nine were killed about fifteen miles from Urmia, at Karmad. We had eight of them in the city, fine fellows, some of them educated in Beirout. They had been disarmed, and one night they took them to the suburbs and shot them. But one of them, named Aslam[50], escaped. He dropped with the others, but was not hit. After the butchers left, he made his way to the Presbyterian mission college. I was notified and asked to take care of him. I kept him until the Russian army came. He joined, and is now fighting with them.

"In the First Turkish corps, commanded by Halil Bey, there were about 400 Armenians. One of them, Gulbenkian, a graduate of Beirout, told me that they were all doomed to be butchered. When they appointed me head physician of the hospital, they gave me plenty of helpers, including seven Christian nurses, six Arabs and one Greek. Gulbenkian told me that if I did not help them they would be killed. An Arab doctor, Bahadin Effendi, was appointed to work under my direction. My Greek nurse warned me that Bahadin had already killed more than fifty Armenian Christians, and cautioned me to watch him. One night about ten o'clock, Bahadin sent for me, saying that he was sick. Fortunately for me, the Greek and two Armenian nurses went with me. When I reached the hospital, I found that Bahadin was not sick at all. He said to me: 'What business have you to disturb me at this time of the night? Your coming shows that you have some designs upon my life.' I told him that it was a mistake, that I had been told he was sick, and went away. At the bottom of the stairs I was overtaken by an officer, who said that the doctor had not done with me. I protested, but was ordered to go back. So I put my trust in the Lord and went.

"The doctor greeted me with the question: 'Who gave you permission to leave the room?' and continued: 'You are a prisoner, and you will never see the light of to-morrow's sun.' I told him that I was an American citizen, and that I was helping the wounded for the sake of humanity. He cut me off by saying: 'This is wartime. The top of your cap is green. That means that you are a descendant of the prophet, and it will give me pleasure to destroy your life to-night. I must think how I shall kill you. I could throw you out of the window, but that would be too quick. I could shoot you, but that also is too good for you. I shall have to use my sword. You sit down there in that corner, and these Turkish nurses will sing your funeral before I begin to cut you up.'

"The Turks began to sing a droning chant and I had no choice but to sit and listen. My bodyguard, the Greek nurse Theodore and two Armenian soldiers, the latter my servants, stood outside the door, and when they heard the chanting they thought it was all over with me. The Greek, who was a shrewd fellow, told my bodyguard to enter, and, if he saw me, to say that the patients wanted to see the doctor. All of a sudden I saw him enter with a lantern. He saluted the effendi and said: 'The patients want the doctor.' I didn't give Bahadin a chance to say a word. I was up and out and down in the street in about two seconds. When I got to the outpost they yelled from the window to stop me, but they were too late. My bodyguard and the Armenians and the Greek followed close behind me, and I got away. I reached home at midnight. My wife and children thought I was already dead."

Dr. Sargis turned the tables on the Arab doctor by alleging that he was insane, and having him put under guard and on a milk diet, notwithstanding that he was a doctor in Halil Bey's army.

"Soon after the Russians left Urmia a German machinist, Neumann, who came in with the Turks, announced himself as German Consul. By his orders a Christian of the name of Moushi was hanged. Neumann had promised me to release Moushi, but overnight he sold him to the Turks for £50. An Englishman named Jonathan George, well known in Tabriz, a relative of my wife, was whipped on Neumann's orders. In the village of Karadjalu a young Christian with a wife and two children was killed by a Mohammedan. The murderer took the wife and children, promising to protect them; but while crossing a bridge he threw the children into the river. At Ardishai 75 women and girls ran into the sea[51] to escape the Turks. They refused to trust promises of safety if they came out, and were all shot as they stood in the water. Eight thousand five hundred died in the vicinity of Urmia in five months; 1,500 were killed, and the rest died of cold and hunger.

"During the days of the Turkish occupation it was no unusual sight to see an old woman carrying the body of her daughter or son to a place of burial, digging the grave herself or with the aid of other women."

---

49. Ismael Agha's Kala. See page 162 below.

50. Arslan (?).

51. *i.e.*, Lake Urmia.

35. URMIA: EXTRACTS FROM THE ANNUAL REPORT (FOR THE YEAR 1915) PRESENTED BY THE MEDICAL DEPARTMENT AT URMIA TO THE BOARD OF FOREIGN MISSIONS OF THE PRESBYTERIAN CHURCH IN THE U.S.A.

A sad case was that of the mother of a girl of twelve who was being taken away to a life of slavery. The mother protested and tried to save her child, who was ruthlessly torn from her. As the daughter was being dragged away the mother made so much trouble for her oppressors, and clung to them so tenaciously, that they stabbed her twelve times before she fell, helpless to save her little girl from her fate. This woman recovered from her wounds. Some people were shot as they ran, and children that they were carrying were killed or wounded with them. In some cases men were lined up so that several could be shot with one bullet, in order not to waste ammunition on them.

At the height of the epidemic not less than two thousand were sick. The mortality reached forty-eight daily, and the fact that four thousand died, besides the one thousand who were killed, will help to make vivid the terrible conditions that prevailed in our crowded premises. All ranks have suffered—preachers, teachers, physicians, etc., as well as the poor—for all had to live in the same unhygienic surroundings.

One of the most terrible things that came to the notice of the Medical Department was the treatment of Syrian women and girls by the Turks, Kurds and local Mohammedans. After the massacre in the village of ——, almost all the women and girls were outraged, and two little girls, aged eight and ten, died in the hands of Moslem villains. A mother said that not a woman or girl above twelve (and some younger) in the village of —— escaped violation. This is the usual report from the villages. One man, who exercised a great deal of authority in the northern part of the Urmia plain, openly boasted of having ruined eleven Christian girls, two of them under seven years of age, and he is now permitted to return to his home in peace and no questions are asked. Several women from eighty to eighty-five years old have suffered with the younger women. One woman who was prominent in the work of the Protestant Church in another village was captured by eighteen men and taken to a solitary place, where they had provided for themselves food and drink. She was released the next day and permitted to drag herself away. Later she came to the city to accuse her outragers, and practically did not get a hearing from the Government.

There is little to relieve the blackness of this picture. The Government gave some assistance in the finding and returning of Christian girls. A few have been brought back by Kurds. In one case eleven girls and young women, who had been taken away from Geogtapa, were sent to me by the chief of the Zarza tribe of Kurds. Several companies have been sent also by the Begzadi Kurds to Targawar. Since the return of the Russians to Urmia some of the Kurds have tried to curry favour by returning prisoners that they have held for months, but quite a number are still held by them, some of them women who have been married to some of the principal servants of the chiefs.

It would not be right to close this report of medical work in Urmia without a word about the native physicians. One of them received a martyr's crown early in January in the village of Khanishan. Four died in the epidemics. One had been a worker for many years in the plain of Gawar, two days' journey to the west of Urmia. One of them was a companion in the attempt to find Karini Agha at the very beginning of the troubles here that resulted in the rescue of the people of Geogtapa. One was the assistant in the hospital. He had been in the hospital since his graduation in 1908, and was a most faithful and efficient man. During the awful first days of fear, murder and rapine, it was his hands that dressed and re-dressed most of the wounded, with the help of medical students. He thought little of himself and wore himself out until he could not eat, keeping on at his work for three days after he began to be ill. His life was given in the noblest self-sacrifice, and many people will remember him with deep affection. The fourth was one of the refugees in our yard who, though he was not very active, frequently prescribed for a number of patients. His wife, who is a graduate in medicine in America, in spite of the death of her husband and two children, kept bravely on with her work, trying to relieve some of the suffering. She had charge of the maternity cases and examined many of the outraged women and girls after they finally reached us.

The most diabolically cold-blooded of all the massacres was the one committed above the village of Ismael Agha's Kala, when some sixty Syrians of Gawar were butchered by the Kurds at the instigation of the Turks. These Christians had been used by the Turks to pack telegraph wire from over the border, and while they were in the city of Urmia they were kept in close confinement, without food or drink. On their return, as they reached the valleys between the Urmia and Baradost plains, they were all stabbed to death, as it was supposed, but here again, as in two former massacres, a few wounded, bloody victims succeeded in making their way to our hospital.

The testimony of the survivors of the massacre at Ismael Agha's Kala is confirmed by the following extract from a letter, dated 8th November, 1915, from the Rev. E.T. Allen of Urmia:—

Politically, things are in apparently good order. People are easily frightened and are nervous, but we have good hopes. Yesterday I went to the Kala of Ismael Agha and from there to Kasha, and some men went with me up the road to the place where the Gawar men were murdered by the Turks. It was a gruesome sight—perhaps the worst I have seen at all. There were seventy-one or two bodies; we could not tell exactly, because of the conditions. It is about six months since the murder. Some were in fairly good condition—dried, like a mummy. Others were torn to pieces by the wild animals. Some had been daggered in several places, as was evident from the cuts in the skin. The majority of them had been shot. The ground about was littered with empty cartridge-cases. It was a long way off from the Kala, and half-an-hour's walk from the main road into the most rugged gorge I have seen for some time. I suppose the Turks thought no word could get out from there—a secret, solitary, rocky gorge. How those three wounded men succeeded in getting out and reaching the city is more of a marvel than I thought it was at the time. The record of massacre burials now stands as follows:—

At Tcharbash, forty in one grave, among them a bishop. At Gulpashan, fifty-one in one grave, among them the most innocent persons in the country; and now, above the Kala of Ismael Agha, seventy in one grave, among them leading merchants of Gawar.

These one hundred and sixty-one persons, buried by me, came to their death in the most cruel manner possible, at the hands of regular Turkish troops in company with Kurds under their command.

36. URMIA, SALMAS AND HAKKIARI: STATEMENT[52] BY MR. PAUL SHIMMON[53], PUBLISHED IN THE ARMENIAN JOURNAL "ARARAT," OF LONDON, NOVEMBER, 1915.

Seeing that *Ararat* is truly a searchlight on all the sufferings of Eastern Christians, a comforter to the broken-hearted and a fighter for their rights, I have felt it my duty and privilege to write just some bare facts of the past and present position of the Syrians in Urmi (Urmia) and Salmas in Persia, and in the Kurdistan mountains south of Van. What I will say of Urmi and Salmas applies equally to the Armenians of the two places, in the latter of which they predominate.

The Russian troops had been in occupation of Azerbaijan, north-western Persia, for a number of years, and their presence meant safety, prosperity and security of person and property both to Christians and Moslems alike. Under the conditions then prevailing, the Kurds had been restrained entirely from their occupation of plunder, and the Turks were deprived of prominence in that part of Persia which they have coveted for years. The Persians also have been restless, and their attitude towards the Christians was somewhat doubtful. On the 2nd January, 1915, it was suddenly known that the Russian army, consulate and all, were leaving Urmi—and not that alone, but it was found later that they were withdrawing from all northern Persia. It came like a thunderbolt, for it had been positively stated all along to the Christian population that the Russian army would under no circumstances withdraw from Urmi. Here, then, in the heart of winter, some 45,000 Christians, from nine to ten days' journey from the nearest railway station to the Russian border, found themselves in a very precarious position. No conveyances, horses, &c., &c., could be had for love or money. Roughly speaking, one-third of the people who happened to know of this withdrawal, through whose villages the army was to pass, left for Russia. The great majority simply left their homes and walked out. Some only heard of the withdrawal during the night, and so could hardly make any provision for the journey. A good number of people from Tergawar and Mergawar, and outlying districts, who were already refugees in Urmi—having been plundered on two or three occasions previously—left with the army. So there was a concourse of over 10,000 people, mostly women and children, walking in the bitter cold, scantily provided, sore-footed, wearied, that had to make their way to the Russian frontier over mountains and along miserable roads and through swamps. Their cries and shrieks as they walked were heart-rending. The people of Salmas had left two or three days earlier and under somewhat better conditions. There was a swamp between Salmas and Khoi where people actually went knee-deep, where oxen and buffaloes died of cold, and where there was no real resting place and provisions could only be procured from a distance of some ten miles. The agonies of the children were inexpressible. Some mothers had two or three children to take care of, and they dragged one along while they carried the other on their shoulders. Many died on the roadside, many lost their parents, many were left unburied, many were picked up by the Russian cossacks and were taken to the Russian Caucasus to be there cared for by Armenians and others. Such was their plight when they reached Russia, and in some way or another were provided for in the Syrian and Armenian villages in Erivan and in Tiflis, where they passed their time till the spring, when they again wearied of their lives and returned to Urmi and Salmas in the months of May and June.

About two-thirds of the people who stayed behind at Urmi had the cruellest of fates. No sooner had the Russian forces withdrawn than the roads were closely guarded, and no one was permitted to come in or go out of Urmi for over four months. The Kurds poured in from every quarter, and the Persian Moslems joined hands with them. They engulfed the Christian villages; plunder, pillage, massacre and rape were the order of the day. Every village paid its share. First they killed the men, then they took the women—those who had not escaped—and carried them away for themselves or forced them to become Moslems, and finally they plundered and burned the villages. In one village 80 were killed, in another 50, in a third 30, and so the thing went on in varying degrees among the 70 odd villages in Urmi. About one thousand people were disposed of in this way. In the meantime all that were able escaped to the city to the American mission quarters, whose premises were soon filled to suffocation, and altogether some 20,000 people or more found shelter in the American and French mission quarters, while some hid themselves among Moslem friends and landlords. These refugees, in their flight, were repeatedly robbed on the way by soldiers and officers sent for their protection, and by civilians as well. Many a woman came terror-stricken, shrieking, and bleeding, and almost naked; and many were forced to become Moslems. Some 150 cases or more of these unfortunate women came under the notice of the American missionaries, who tried to restore them to their own folk. One woman had two sons, four and six years of age, who were thrown into a brook to freeze, while the brute of a mullah set to work to force their mother. She at last escaped and took away the children alive, but they died of exposure the next morning.

Thus in the course of a fortnight all the 45,000 Syrians and Armenians were plundered—not one village escaped. There was no exception. The village of Iriawa was in the keeping of an Armenian—a Turkish subject. He, with twelve other Armenian soldiers, was shot, and the village plundered. Gulpashan was the last to be attacked, when, on the 1st February, 51 of its elders were taken during the night to the graveyard and there murdered most horribly and their brains knocked out. The orgies committed on women and tender girls can be left only to the imagination. I have known the village from childhood and all its inhabitants.

The refugees in the French and American mission yards remained there for over four and a half months, in daily terror and fear of their lives; the quarters were crowded to suffocation, and no man dared leave the premises. Seeing that a few houses of Christians were left in the city which were not plundered, the dozen or less of Turkish officials, who had control of things, began to fleece the people. They forced them to pay a fine of 6,600 *tomans* (a *toman* is about one pound sterling[54]), on the pretext that the Christian stores, offices and shops in the city would be saved from plunder. But no sooner was this sum extracted through the kindly offices of the American missionaries than they began to put up to auction and dispose of all the shops, offices and stores. Not satisfied with what they had done, they obtained 5,500 *tomans* as blood money for Mar Elia, the Syrian Bishop, whom they found in hiding on the roof of a house, and threatened to kill him unless the money was paid. Then, again, such prominent men as Shamasha Lazar, Shamasha Babu and Dr. Isaac Daniel had to pay 3,000, 2,000 and 1,000 *tomans* respectively to save their lives. Such was the perpetual terror in which the whole community lived.

Soon disease broke out, typhoid played havoc, and over 4,000 died of the epidemic alone. There was scarcely any life left in the remnant of the people when the Russians retook Urmi in May. They were worn out and so emaciated that one could hardly recognise them. It was the first time for months that they were able to crawl out of their filthy winter quarters and to inhale fresh air. The Americans, who had fed these people all through the winter, now gave the men and women spades and sickles to return to their villages, and some flour to start life in their ruined homes. I have seen villages turned to ashes, where not one window, door or any woodwork was to be found. Indeed, one day a woman came and said to me: "I have one room out of seven left on the second storey, but what shall I do? There is not a single ladder in all the village that I can borrow so as to mount to it." What they had left in their "homes," these people found on their return to have been eaten by dogs and cats. They have not sown anything this autumn, nor were they able to do any sowing or cultivating in the spring. Ninety per cent. of them have absolutely nothing left, and they sleep on the bare hard earthen floor, with no bedding or any other protection beyond their ordinary rags. This is their second winter!

The majority of the Salmas Christians had left for Russia by the time the Urmi people reached Salmas. But there were some left who had hidden themselves among kind Moslems here and there. When the Turks took possession of Salmas, they used every means to find out the whereabouts and number of all the Christians that had remained behind, and one night during March last they took some 723 Armenians and Syrians to the fields in Haftevan and mangled and butchered them in a most brutal manner. Three days later the Russians retook Salmas and buried these people in some trenches which they dug for them. The same fate was awaiting the women, and perhaps worse, but the advent of the Russians saved them.

The troubles of Mar Shimun's independent tribes of Tiari, Tkhuma, &c., in Kurdistan, south of Van, began last June. Mar Shimun's seat in the village of Quodshanis was attacked by regular troops and Kurds, destroyed and plundered. Most of the people escaped to Salmas. Mar Shimun at the time was in the interior with the main body of his congregation. A regular Turkish force with artillery and some 30,000 Kurds, &c., marched on the Christians. The forty villages of Berwar, those nearest towards Mosul, were destroyed first, and only some seventeen of them are known to have escaped. The women of many of the others have been forced to become Moslems. For forty days the people defended themselves against superior forces, and that only with flintlocks and antiquated rifles. At last, unable to withstand the onslaught of modern artillery, with which the Turks also bombarded the

Church of Mar Sawa, the people withdrew to the interior of the mountains with the Patriarch's family in their centre; and here they subsisted on herbs and some sheep they had taken with them, while many were daily dying of starvation. Mar Shimun came to Salmas—I had an interview with him there, and he has sent me to speak for him and his—to effect the escape of his people, or at least of as many of them as could be saved. All this happened in the latter part of September, when, according to the telegram received here from H.B.M. Consul Shipley at Tabriz, some 25,000 had already arrived, and with them Mar Shimun, himself as destitute as the rest, while 10,000 more were to follow. The condition of the remnant, for in all there are over 100,000, is very precarious, but let us hope not hopeless. Assistance can be sent to them through Mar Shimun and through H.B.M. Consul Shipley.

The Archbishop of Canterbury's Mission and the Armenian (Lord Mayor's) Relief Fund have sent £500 and £550 respectively to these people. I understand that the Lord Mayor's Fund is telegraphing a further £500 for the relief of the Christians in Persia, for which I for one feel infinitely grateful, as it cannot but assuage some of the terrible suffering that exists.

Let us now survey the whole situation. As over 90 per cent. of the Christians at Urmi are destitute, and the condition of some 10,000 to 15,000 Armenians and Syrians in Salmas is not much better, we have at once some 80,000 people and more who must be assisted, if they are not to starve during the coming winter. In this we are not taking into account the remnant of Mar Shimun's people or any Armenians that might have found their way to Persia, where the Russians are now in occupation, and where the condition of the Christians will be, so far as personal safety goes, more hopeful. The turn events are taking politically in Persia seems also favourable, but one must never be too confident of the political situation there.

I am delighted to see such a magnificent spirit of response from all corners of the world whence Armenians themselves are coming to the help of their countrymen. We have to cheer each other up in our misfortunes in every way we can, till God in His own way shall solve the problem. And with such noble friends as we have in England, among whom are the Primate, Lord Bryce, and Members of Parliament like Mr. Aneurin Williams and Mr. T.P. O'Connor, and I am sure in America as well—people who would do anything for us—let us be patient and prayerful, hoping for recompense and release from this tyranny that has had us in its grip ever since Mohammedan rule began in our country.

---

52. For a fuller version of Mr. Shimmon's statement see p. 577 below.

53. Mr. Shimmon is a graduate of Columbia University, New York, and has been resident at Urmia for the past fourteen years. He was an eye-witness of the events he relates; and, after the retreat of the Turks and Kurds, he was appointed Commissioner for the Baranduz District of Urmia (under the authority of the Russian Consul and the Persian Governor) for the restoration of plundered Christian property. He has since undertaken a mission to Great Britain and the U.S., as the representative of His Beatitude Mar Shimun, the head of the Nestorian Church.

54. 1 toman = 10 krans, and its actual value in English money is about 3*s*. 4*d*.—*Editor*.

37. HAKKIARI: FURTHER STATEMENT BY MR. PAUL SHIMMON, PUBLISHED IN THE "CHURCHMAN" NEWSPAPER, AND SUBSEQUENTLY ISSUED AS A PAMPHLET; COMMUNICATED BY MRS. D.S. MARGOLIOUTH, OF OXFORD.

The following is the story of how a Bishop, nay, an Archbishop, at the risk of his own life, saved 35,000 souls—one-third of his flock—from the pursuing Kurds and Turks, and from impending starvation on the heights of the Kurdistan Mountains. He was already in the zone of safety, where he could well have stayed; but he turned back, saying: "I am going back to die with my people." By so doing, he rescued a multitude of his people from almost certain massacre.

It will be remembered that the Assyrians (better known in Church history as the Nestorian or Syrian Christians) dwell on both sides of the Turco-Persian frontier. The bulk of them live in the very inaccessible mountains of Kurdistan, east of Mosul, which is in Mesopotamia, and south of Lake Van; while a goodly number live in the beautiful plains of Urmia and Salmas in north-western Persia and in the adjacent country districts bordering on Turkey. Over the former district Mar Shimun, the Patriarch, is the supreme ecclesiastical and civil ruler.

Early last June the Turkish forces with irregular Kurds, under the leadership and direction of the Kaimakam, made an attack on the court of Mar Shimun in Quodshanis—a Turkish governor making an attack on peaceful subjects of the Turkish Empire for the simple reason that they were Christians. Quodshanis is an isolated place. The Patriarch and members of his court were in the interior with the main body of his church, so the people of the village could hardly be expected to make more than a bare resistance. For two days they fought from within the church, but soon their ammunition was exhausted, and the women and children were in a desperate position. At night they set out for the plains of Salmas in Persia, where I saw them in a most pitiable condition. The Patriarchal house, the English mission, and the larger part of the place was plundered and burned. Even the tombs of former Patriarchs were violated.

In the meanwhile a formidable army was being gathered against the independent dwellers in the valleys of Tkhuma, Tiari, Baz, &c. Both Turkish regulars and Kurds, it is said, to the extent of some 30,000, made a combined attack on the people who had kept their independence since Tamerlane and Ghengis Khan had driven them to the craggy mountains, where in some places they have to carry soil on their backs to make artificial fields. For the first time in the life of the people, artillery was brought up to bombard their ancient and venerable churches, while they themselves made a stout resistance with flintlocks and ammunition of their own make.

For forty days they carried on an unequal warfare against tremendous odds, until at last with their families they took refuge on the top of a high mountain in the Tal country. The Patriarchal family took shelter in the famous church of Mar Audishu, and the others who had been able to effect an escape surrounded them, making a big camp. The Turks and Kurds, after having destroyed the Christian villages in the valleys below, carrying away the crops and plundering everything, endeavoured to starve the fugitives out. Near the church mentioned above there is a small fountain gushing from a rock which was hardly enough to supply drinking water, and for washing and bathing they would often steal at nights to the valleys beneath. The people stayed here for nearly three months, never taking off their clothes and always on the lookout for an attack by night. The few sheep that they had taken with them on their flight were almost eaten up now—they had no salt at all, and soon hunger and sickness began to make their ravages. There was no necessity to deport this Christian population. Its mere starvation in the mountains was all that was needed to make an end of the oldest Apostolic Church in existence.

In the meantime Mar Shimun, the Patriarch, with a few brave men, had stolen out by night and made his way to the Russian army operating in Salmas, Persia. He was received with great distinction, but it was found out after many precious weeks of delay that it might not be possible to send any relief for the people in the interior who were not in the line of march. Later on, the Russians sent their army to Van, and then Mar Shimun with a few faithful followers and good rifles—he himself is an excellent shot—set out again for the interior to reach his flock and his brothers and sisters. They soon made ready to take the congregation through the valleys and defiles to the plains of Persia.

The last day of their stay was the saddest of all. On that day Ishaya, a brother of the Patriarch, died of fever. Mar Shimun, hearing of his illness, had come over the day before. The enemy was then very near, and they could hear the sound of the guns in Tkhuma. Just when the funeral of his brother was to take place, Surma and Romi, his sisters, and Esther, his sister-in-law, were compelled to leave the place, lest they should be caught by the enemy. Mar Shimun, two priests and a few laymen remained behind at this time of danger to bury Ishaya. The burial service was quickly said and the body hastily interred, and Mar Shimun hastened after the fleeing women and children. They were only just in time, for, a few hours after their departure, the Turks arrived and made straight for the church, having heard that the Patriarch's household was there.

I shall not dwell on the horrors of those caught and slain on the way nor on the many beautiful villages ruined and the women taken captive, nor on the thousands of others who have met the same fate. In one district of forty villages, its Bishop said to me, only seventeen had been able to make an escape, and he knew but very little of the fearful fate of the rest. I want only to speak of the living who are anxious to die, but to whom death does not come. They arrived in Persia at places already ruined; they camped out in the plain of Salmas (4,000 feet above sea level) sleeping in the fields with no clothes to cover them at night, clad in the rags which they have worn for many months, without food or shelter. Some assistance has gone to them from America and England. Some quilts were bought to be distributed, one for each family of five persons, to serve as cover in the bitter cold. Some families have as many as ten members, indeed one had twenty-eight. These are the people who have been living on one dollar a month, and to whom flour is served in quantity barely sufficient to allow each person one small loaf a day and nothing more. I dare say that even their Bishops and other clergy are in not much better condition than their flock.

Assistance, however, can now be sent out to them and will reach them immediately. Urmia and Salmas are now in the zone of safety, where there are many Russian troops, and these have been very kind to the suffering Christians. Money is being sent through the American Consul, the missionaries and the Patriarch, and is at once distributed to the sufferers. The Rev. Y.M. Nisan, who is still alive, although he has lost his wife and daughter, is on the distributing committee. The defeat of the Turks at Erzeroum means peace and safety of life for all Armenia and Persia. In the latter country there are over 80,000 destitute, the majority of them Assyrians, and some Armenians as well. Money is distributed to all without discrimination.

I have purposely avoided saying anything of the horrors that we have suffered at Urmia and the agonies we have passed through, simply because I have felt that the condition of these mountaineers is even more pitiable. I hope Christian people will be moved at once to make an effort to save them from the clutches of starvation. The gallant Patriarch has saved them and brought them out of Turkey, where relief will get to them. I therefore appeal to all my friends and to others who may be so disposed to help rescue this ancient Church.

38. REFUGEES FROM THE HAKKIARI DISTRICT: SERIES OF EXTRACTS FROM LETTERS BY MEMBERS OF THE AMERICAN MISSION STATION AT URMIA; COMMUNICATED BY THE BOARD OF FOREIGN MISSIONS OF THE PRESBYTERIAN CHURCH IN THE U.S.A.

(a) Extract from a letter, dated 8th November, 1915, from the Rev. E.T. Allen (?).

As you know, the first attack by the combined force of Turks and Kurds was made in June and was partially successful. The people were driven out of their valleys into the high mountains central to Tiari, Tkhoma, Tai and Baz. In this movement not many lives were lost, but many villages were destroyed. The hostile forces were for some reason withdrawn, and for some weeks there was comparative quiet, broken only by spasmodic attacks by local forces. About three weeks ago there was another concerted attack made by the Turks and Kurds on their stronghold in the mountain top, and they were driven out. Between fifteen and twenty thousand, with great difficulty, made their escape, part of their road being held by the Kurds. They came down the Tal and Kon Valleys, followed by the Kurds, and attempted to turn up the Zab to get out by way of Djoulamerk. They found the Kurds in force at the Djoulamerk bridge, and were forced to turn down stream. At the head of Tiari they crossed the Zab and went up into the hills, which they found deserted by the Kurds, who had gone to war. They then made their way round behind Djoulamerk, meeting no hostile force until they reached the ridge between Quodshanis and the Zab. Here again they found a force of Kurds waiting for them. They had quite a sharp fight with them and the Kurds were worsted. From there on they had no more trouble, reaching Bashkala in safety, and later coming down to Salmas.

These are the people I found in Salmas. They number, according to my estimate, between fifteen and twenty thousand. Among them are Mar Shimun and his family and all our helpers, with one or two exceptions. (Mar Shimun is the Patriarch of the Nestorian Church.)

With reference to those who were left in the mountains, perhaps a thousand more succeeded in getting through. There are still some thousands shut up there, and their fate is still uncertain. How many were killed in this last attack, I have found no one who could give even an estimate, but undoubtedly the number must be large. This is in reference to those in Salmas. All the facts cannot be given out, but this is their case in brief. The mass of them are without shelter of any kind and also without bedding. They are sleeping on the bare ground without covering. The rains have begun and the winter promises to set in early. What all this means to these thousands who are without shelter, you need not be told.

Since coming down a great many of them have been taken sick with a peculiar form of bowel trouble, such as the mountaineers have been having here. Dr. David Yohannan estimates that there are as many as one thousand cases. The fatality is not as great as might be expected, but there are a great many deaths. One tribe reported forty deaths within a week. I have seen the dead lying on the roadside, and the women carrying their dead, orders to move on giving them little time to die decently or to be buried with respect. I gave no relief while there. Along the road they had gathered up a little grain; the Russians were giving out 1,200 loads, and help was being given on the threshing floor and from door to door. I have been making a complete list, so that when we are ready to begin we shall have them classified and shall be able to handle them. We shall give flour or wheat in weekly allowances. The cost per head will be about five shahis (1*d.*). I shall refrain from giving as long as I see they can subsist on what they get from other sources.

Bedding is needed as badly as food. There is not much choice between dying from hunger or dying from cold. We shall have to supply several thousand outfits, cost of each about three-and-a-half tomans (12*s.*). You may rest assured that I shall use the utmost caution in the giving of relief.

There is no further word from those left in the mountains. There is still hope that some of them may succeed in getting through, but undoubtedly many will be lost.

(b) Extract from a letter, of later date, from a missionary.[55]

About 150 or more of the Mutran's[56] people came down. Some of the children were a sight to see for destitution. I had a tableful of women to breakfast with me the next morning, including one of our own pupils who was married into the Mutran's family. They said that 200 Turks had been living off them since a year ago, but that their flocks had been so multiplied that they were able to sustain the burden. At last the Turks began sending twenty men every day with packs on their backs to Mosul, loaded with the spoils of their houses, so they feared their own end or deportation might be near; they found a chance to escape one day when their guards were a mile or two away, and silently stole away with some of their possessions.

(c) Extract from a letter, of later date, from a missionary.[57]

Some of the refugees in Salmas had flocks and possessions, but all were ravaged by disease, so that even if they had work they could not do it. A boy who was with me found his relatives among the people. One uncle of his had been living in the barracks. He had lost his three children one after the other, and then his wife died and he had no one to care for his affairs but himself. He was so weak he could not do anything—reduced to skin and bone himself—but he got a rope and tried to carry the body of his wife on his back to bury her somewhere. He had not even strength enough to dig her a grave. There the story ended. The boy said the man broke down and could not tell any more, and he did not have the heart to ask what had become of her.

Another of our preachers has lost three of his four children, and the last was very ill when we saw her. His wife had lost her brother and two sisters—one of them a pupil in the Fiske Seminary.

---

55. Name withheld.

56. A dignitary of the Nestorian Church, second in rank to the Patriarch, Mutran (or Matran) = Metropolitan.

57. Name withheld.

39. REFUGEES FROM HAKKIARI: LETTER, DATED 26th SEPTEMBER/9th OCTOBER, 1915, FROM A RELATIVE OF MAR SHIMUN, THE PATRIARCH; COMMUNICATED BY THE REV. F.N. HEAZELL.

I have not written to you for a long time. I think you will know the reason is that the war with Turkey has stopped the post to Europe. As you know, during past years there have been difficulties between the Turks and ourselves, but now the truth of the matter is made clear. When we saw many Christians of Gawar and Albek killed without reason, we thought our turn would come. Every kind of warfare commenced, and since then, for months, we have been fighting in the mountains; in the end we were not successful, because the Kurds were helped by the artillery of the Turkish Government. Of course when our cartridges were exhausted we could not stand before the great force of Turkish artillery. Then first of all Tiari was destroyed; we then thought we could flee to the mountains in the hope of victory, but soon the Turks came to the entrance of Tkhoma and our hope was destroyed—either we must deliver ourselves to Turkey and be killed or flee to save ourselves. We did the latter, but even then half the nation was left behind.

Now we are here in Diliman, Salmas; but the larger part of Tiari and Tkhoma is conquered. Up to the present time we have no news of those people; whether they are alive or have been destroyed, we know not.

Many of the refugees who come here are dying of hunger; they have no bedding, and many men just died on the way here. Would you were here to see with your own eyes our state; your sympathy would indeed be aroused. All the houses have been destroyed (also Mar Shimun's house and your Mission house in Quodshanis) and burnt and robbed; we are in rags and hunger and in a strange land. Many of the houses where you have spent the night as a guest have no bedding, the house of Malik Ismail, for instance, and the house of Khiyu.

Of all these the condition of the Tkhumnai is the most miserable; they are quite destitute. If some help is not forthcoming for the nation all hope of survival is at an end, for three parts will die of hunger. Our thanks are due to the Russian Consul, who is taking care to distribute the people among the villages to prevent them dying of cold, for all are under trees and in fields in the open.

In the course of February, Esther and I and her children went down to Malik Ismail's house in Tiari, for we thought it would be safer there. Then we soon moved from Tchumbar to Dadush, a small village of Tiari. When the Turkish army drew near that place we fled to the Church of Mar Audishu of Tal. In each place we were obliged to leave behind some of our clothes and our bedding; many times we were hungry; we made our journeys by night, and Esther's little children would fall asleep on the road. Three months we stayed in Mar Audishu, the whole time the fighting drawing nearer. Our brothers are fighting in Dizan, and there every three or four men are sleeping together for want of quilts at night. We sleep with our clothes on, ready to start when it may be necessary. In Mar Audishu the food was good, but the provision for sleeping and bathing was bad. Soap there was none; water could be had for drinking and cooking only. Sometimes we would go down to one of the Tal villages to wash our clothes and to bathe.

From Quodshanis everything we possessed was carried off and our house destroyed. A few quilts we brought to Dizan; these we could not bring away with us because we had no mules, for the Kurds had carried them off, and I think they will now remain for our neighbours (the Kurds). Of clothes to wear we had only enough for the road, but not enough for the cold of the winter. When we came here, on the road, we saw some women who had never known want entirely naked; we divided our clothes among them, giving them just enough to prevent them dying of cold. During all these years our state has been, glory to God, that only our souls have been chastened, but finally one thing has befallen us which we can never forget. I recall the last days that I stood in the Church. I had gone down to Dizan because Paulus, my brother, was sick and Ishaya[58] was ill with fever in Mar Audishu. It was at the time when the guns of the Turks were drawn up before Tkhuma and were moving forward—then it was he sickened and died. Mar Shimun had arrived there a little before. Romi[59] and Esther[60] and her children, at that very time of great sorrow, when they least wished to leave, had to set out, weeping, with their families. Only Mar Shimun with two priests and a few men remained in the Church for the funeral service, for as quickly as they could they had to place the body of Ishaya in the grave and hasten after their families. Going quickly on foot they arrived at Darawar, where Malik Ismail was. Those little children (God bless them) went on foot, without a servant, accompanied by Romi and Esther. That day, if our families had delayed in Mar Audishu, they would have been prisoners now in Turkey. The day after they left, the Turkish army entered the Church, for they knew we were there. But, thanks be to God, we had escaped.

Paulus is better, and now our family is with Mar Shimun in Diliman. Up to the present time we have not hired a house, for we do not know where we shall settle down. There is a Church here.

Mr. McDowell came from Urmia to see us and they hope to help this people as much as they can with food and clothing.

Of all the things that were left in our house I am sorrowing most of all for my English books that have gone. Those of our own language are hidden; I do not know whether they will be safe or not. I only left about forty in Dizan.

---

58. Youngest dearly loved brother to Surma.

59. Surma's sister.

60. Sister-in-law; her eldest little boy, Theodore, will succeed his uncle as Patriarch.

40. REFUGEES FROM HAKKIARI: LETTER, DATED DILIMAN, 1st/14th APRIL, 1916, FROM SURMA, THE SISTER OF MAR SHIMUN, TO MRS. D.S. MARGOLIOUTH, OF OXFORD.

I was very glad to get your sweet letter, for which I was longing and looking forward, my dearest friend. I know how you loved Ishaya, and he always asked after you. I wonder if you ever got his letter that he wrote to you in Syriac.

I wrote to you while at Quodshanis (before the war) but got no answer; I wondered if you might be away from home. I wonder if Mr. Wigram and Mr. Heazell got my letters, written since we came to Diliman; I am afraid you won't get yours, the address was incorrect.

You most kindly asked after Hormizd. I wish we knew his fate, dear boy; we have no news of him since the 20th February (5th March), 1915. I asked Mrs. Wigram if she would be able to tell us something of him by way of Dr. Wigram's letters; we are most anxiously looking forward to the answer.

The hospitals which are endowed by great Russia to help the sick are a great help. Now the people get nursed well, and, of course, the sickness is growing less. But outside the hospitals, although they do get help from Russia (recently some clothes, too), England and America, still their miseries are great, and their living very poor.

I trust and hope you will read the report recently written by Mr. Paul Shimmon. A copy has been sent to Mr. Heazell. It is all quite true, and there you will see our nation's wretchedness. Really, Russia couldn't have done more than she has by helping with hospitals, money and clothes.

Now the Russian Government wants us all to go up to Bashkala—the people to be provided with oxen and wheat to be able to plough land for themselves. Of course, Mar Shimun is quite willing to make the people do what they are ordered, and what is best for them. It really is a very good thing, but I am much afraid it won't come to pass, for two reasons—first, the difficulty of finding enough oxen and corn, and, secondly, because it is getting too late for sowing. Soon after Easter Mar Shimun intends to go to Khoi and talk the plan over with General Tchournazoukov.

I wanted very much to go to England, but Mrs. Wigram wrote to me that my friends didn't think it advisable. I don't understand well what you say in your letter about directing to me through Mr. Shipley. If it is anything to help the poor, it is most welcome.

One can't help longing to read the London *Times* and the *Church Times*, especially the Bishop of London's sermons. What will be the end? Is the world being refined? Who will endure to the last? We can only pray for mercy. His will be done. My heart is yearning to hear that "England has conquered"; pray God it will prove so—although one does feel for all the young men's lives, whether friend or foe, no difference, and for the world's misery.

Last October David and I went down to Urmia and stayed with dear Mr. Nisan. His house seemed to me quite desolate with no Beatrice or her mother, but he was the same, cheering and helping others. His daughter-in-law Nanajan is very nice, and, with her little dear boy, she will be a comfort for his old age. Samuel is still in America; it is rather hard for the young wife. I have twice written to Mr. Nisan to send service books, which he kindly sent. We often wonder what our church would have done if it were not for English printing presses? Nearly all our church books are gone. Mar Shimun has consecrated little tablets, and nearly every priest in Diliman has one to celebrate on for the people; it is the same in Urmia and Khoi.

You will like to hear that David, Zaya, Paul and Ishaya fought most bravely in Dizan. Twice the Kurds were driven away with twelve killed, and the third time Paul and Zaya alone with four servants fought against the foe and saved the little ammunition they had. I intend to write a report of all that happened (what I saw and heard) in the mountains. But really I can't, as long as I am with ten children playing in the small yard and making as much noise as a herd of the Kurds, poor little kids. I don't think you know that David is father of two boys and four girls, and Romi is mother of three girls and two boys. Are not they old? The children are as happy as children ought to be, only they are disappointed at not having as many new clothes as they used to have at home, and especially the boys, for they are not going to have any new clothes for Easter as they had theirs at Christmas, and now it is the girls' turn for Easter. The market is another difficulty for them—seeing new toys and sweets (they were free from that in Quodshanis) and with no money to buy them. However, they get used to it, poor dears.

I teach the four boys for two hours a day; they are promising pupils if properly taught. The little girls read their alphabet, too.

Romi and Esther have suffered very much under the circumstances. It was too much for them, although they have gone through it quite bravely, especially Esther, who was with child all this time, and during the last days of flight was expecting the child every hour. However, God was merciful, and the baby girl was born nearly a fortnight after we arrived in Diliman. She is baptised Helena. I am rather uneasy about Esther. She is very weak, and after Easter she will go to Urmia, both to visit her father's house (the Mutran's brother) and see the doctor.

I can't say it was too much for me; if it were not for certain reasons I should have been rather enjoying the struggle between the Kurds and Turks and us. Thank God we are very well at present, except for being over anxious for our poor nation's misery. The living here is very hard for us; we simply have no money for our ordinary necessities, and at times we have people coming to our door who can hardly stand on their feet for hunger; how could one turn them away?

However, all the world is suffering, and so must we and our nation.

Would you kindly tell Mr. Heazell that Mar Shimun got the £50 which he sent. I never wrote to him that the Mutran was let free by the Turks and has come to Urmia safely, although quite broken and very weak.

I rather enjoy the plan of going up to Bashkala after we have lost our country and home. It will suit us to turn into nomads, like the Israelites—Mar Shimun for Moses; can't make David into Aaron, he has no beard, so dear old Peter for Aaron, with his white beard; I suppose I must be Miriam, and we must take a tent, too, for celebration, which we will call the "Assyrian Tabernacle"; and very likely we shall always be having skirmishes with the Canaanites to get to our fathers' land. Wouldn't you like to come and see us, the new Israelites?

The houses in Bashkala are all ruined.

Mar Shimun sends his blessing to you and Professor Margoliouth, and we our best regards.

41. THE NESTORIANS OF THE BOHTAN DISTRICT[61]: LETTER, DATED SALMAS, 6th MARCH, 1916, FROM THE REV. E.W. McDOWELL, OF THE URMIA MISSION STATION, REPORTING INFORMATION BROUGHT BY A YOUNG MAN (WITH WHOM MR. McDOWELL WAS PREVIOUSLY ACQUAINTED) WHO HAD ESCAPED THE MASSACRE; COMMUNICATED BY THE BOARD OF FOREIGN MISSIONS OF THE PRESBYTERIAN CHURCH IN THE U.S.A.

There was a general massacre in the Bohtan region, and our helpers, preachers, teachers and Bible-Women, with their families, fell victims to it among the rest. The man who brought the word is known to me personally. This young man tells the story of how, by order of the Government, the Kurds and Turkish soldiers put the Christians of all those villages, including Djeziré, to the sword. Among those slain were Kasha (Pastor) Mattai, pastor of the church in Hassan; Kasha Elia, one of our oldest and most honoured pastors, recently working as an evangelist; Kasha Sargis, superannuated; Muallin Mousa, pastor of our church in Djeziré, and his sixteen-year-old son Philip. There are three preachers not heard from, and one of them is probably killed, as his village, Monsoria, was put to the sword; another, Rabi Ishak, is possibly alive, as there is a report that his village had been preserved by the influence of a Kurdish agha. It is to be feared, however, that this agha would not be able to protect them for long, as from every source comes the word that the Government threatened such friendly Kurds with punishment if they did not obey orders. The third man is reported as having fled to Mosul. Whether he reached there or not is not known. The women and children who escaped death were carried away captive. Among these were the families of the above mentioned brethren. The wife and two daughters of Muallin Mousa, the daughters of Kasha Elia, and Rabi Hatoun, our Bible-Woman, were all school-girls in Urmia or Mardin. Kasha Mattai was killed by Kurds in the mountain while fleeing. Kasha Elia and Kasha Sargis, with other men of the village of Shakh, were killed by Turkish soldiers who had been stationed in their village by the Government.

The three villages of Hassan, Shakh and Monsoria were Protestant, and it is to be feared that they were wiped out, as were all the other Christian villages of the plain. Many of the women of Monsoria threw themselves into the river (Tigris) to avoid falling into the hands of the Kurds. Mar Yohannan and Mar Akha were still safe at the time my informant fled. The terrible feature about it was that, after the first slaughter, there were Kurds who tried to save some of the Christians alive, but the Government would not permit it. My informant had found refuge with an agha and was working for him, when a messenger from the Government came with orders to the Kurds to complete the work or be punished. Word was brought to my informant in the field, and he with a few others fled to the mountain and made their way to Van, and so came here. The villagers of Attil, where we had work also, all escaped to Van. Their Kurdish agha, who was a warm friend of our preacher and of our work, gave them warning that he would not be able to protect them, as the massacre was being pressed by the Government. It was their pastor who fled to Mosul. His way would take him to Djeziré and Monsoria, the home of his wife. They may have been killed there. There is no word about them.

This terrible calamity grieves me more than I can tell you. And more than those who died, the fate of those carried off into captivity weighs upon me. I think of them so often—Sarah, Hatoun, Priskilla and little Nellie and others, young girls whom I knew in the home almost like my own children. What is their condition? This word of my informant is confirmed by a woman of Djeziré, who made her escape also to Van and thence hither. She tells us that Sarah and her two daughters were released and were last seen on the plain beyond Djeziré, wandering in a destitute condition.

---

61. Before the War, there were three main groups of Nestorians in the region between Lake Urmia and the Tigris, each group numbering about 30,000 souls. There were the villagers of the Urmia plain, the mountaineers of the Zab, and these other plainsmen in the Bohtan district, round the confluence of the Bohtan River and the Tigris. The present document describes the general massacre of many, or perhaps nearly all, the Nestorians of this third group, whose chief settlements were at Djeziret-ibn-Omar on the Tigris, Mansouria (Monsoria) and Shakh.

42. SECOND EXODUS FROM URMIA: LETTER DATED TABRIZ, 20th AUGUST, 1915, FROM MR. HUGO A. MÜLLER (TREASURER OF THE AMERICAN MISSION STATION AT URMIA); COMMUNICATED BY THE BOARD OF FOREIGN MISSIONS OF THE PRESBYTERIAN CHURCH IN THE U.S.A.

On Thursday, the 5th August, the rumour spread that the Russian troops were again to be withdrawn from Urmia. This very naturally frightened the entire Christian population, and on Thursday evening all Christians, except those already on the road and those physically unable to be on the road, were in the streets of the city and on the roads leading northward from the city, waiting for the departure of the foot-soldiers, with whom they intended to leave. Knowing the probable fate of any who might stay behind, we were, of course, not ready to discourage the people from going. Still, we had no official word of the anticipated evacuation, and were, therefore, perplexed as to our own duty. The breaking up of a good proportion of our missionary work, the removal of the bulk of the relief work to a different place, and the uncertainty of America's future position all contributed to indicate that a portion at least of the Station should move in case of an evacuation. On Friday morning we learned that the foot-soldiers had left, and one of our men, on visiting the Russian Consul, was told that all who were going should be off by 2 p.m. that day. The Station felt that its force should be reduced to the minimum, and that at least all women and children should leave. Very hasty preparations were made. Mr. McDowell, Mr. Labaree and Dr. Packard volunteered to stay in Urmia, and all the rest were to leave. When we got on the road, however, we found that Mrs. Packard and her children and Miss Burgess were not of the party. Mrs. Packard had decided to brave the Station vote and stay by her husband, and Miss Burgess stayed to be with Mrs. Packard and to assist the medical work. The fugitive party, therefore, consisted of Dr. Shedd and his two daughters, Mr. and Mrs. Allen with their two sons and one daughter, Dr. and Mrs. Coan, Mrs. Cochran, Miss Lewis, Miss Lamme, Miss Schoebel, and Mrs. Müller and myself with our daughter. We went in carriages, using some donkeys and horses bought the last two hours before our departure.

At the end of our second day's journey we reached a village, Kudchi, where we found perhaps 20,000 or 30,000 Syrian refugees, whose further flight had been arrested by the Russian commanding officer with the good news that a decisive victory had made the evacuation of Urmia unnecessary. All were told to go back. Unless the missionaries would return, however, the natives were unwilling to trust themselves alone. Nothing was left but for some to return, especially since this was requested by the officer in command of the troops there. Dr. Shedd and his daughters, Mrs. Cochran and Dr. and Mrs. Coan consequently turned back. This gave the crowd heart and they, too, went back. But the tables were soon turned again, and before the foot-sore crowd reached the city they were again turned back with the word that there was fighting with the Kurds on Mount Seir. The missionaries had reached the city and were there during the fighting on Mount Seir. It seemed advisable for them to leave again, as conditions were very uncertain, in spite of the fact that the Russian Consul with a number of Cossacks had stayed by his post during all this time. They, that is Dr. Shedd and his two daughters, and Dr. and Mrs. Coan, left for the second time on Friday the 13th August. This time Mrs. Cochran stayed behind.

Meanwhile, those of us who had continued on our journey from Kudchi arrived in Tabriz on Friday the 13th August, after a journey free from mishaps, but nevertheless wearing for us who were still typhoid and typhus convalescents. Every one in the party with the exception of Mrs. Allen and the Allen children had recently had the fever.

43. SECOND EXODUS FROM URMIA: NARRATIVE OF A NESTORIAN VICTIM, THE WIFE OF THE REV. DAVID JACOB, OF URMIA, PUBLISHED IN THE ARMENIAN JOURNAL "ARARAT" OF LONDON, JANUARY, 1916.

As a native of Urmia and myself a refugee who has fallen into great trouble, I am writing a few short details about my unfortunate nation. For centuries as Christians we have been crushed by the enemies that surround us. Our best looking girls have been forced to deny their creed; our men have been killed, our homes plundered, and our property has been robbed.

In all these troubles we lived under the Persian Government, and obeyed their rules; we have never been untrue to them, or disobedient. For the past seventy years the only help we have had has come through the English and American Missions that have been in Urmia. When the Russians arrived at Urmia it was a delight to us, we thought our rights would be more clearly established; of course, things were much better than before; all the country was safer than it ever had been. This was like a dream for a few years; all of a sudden, when this terrible war began, we felt almost certain that it would harm us, although we never dreamed that it would bring us under such a curse.

In the cold January, when even the beasts do not wish to go out from their caves, the people were left homeless, bleeding, impoverished and starving. This all happened when the Russian forces withdrew from Urmia; very many left their beloved and comfortable homes, and started with them on an endless journey, which caused the death of many dear souls from cold and hunger. The rest of the Christians crowded into the American Mission compounds, with nothing left; here they were fed on a morsel of bread which came through the kindness of the Missionaries. There is a great deal to tell of the misery of the people during the last winter; it was a life too wretched for humanity. Those that were used to comfortable beds now slept on the bare ground. For five months of captivity we lived expecting death every minute, surrounded by sick people who needed help; our little children died of measles; our young and strong ones could not stand the terrible epidemics of typhoid and typhus, while the elderly people could not live such a hard life; they died in the first weeks, of dysentery. Now the villages were plundered and mostly burned, a good many people killed, and our little girls and women wickedly tortured (very many even now have not been found; they were mercilessly carried into captivity); through all this long time of anxiety and expectation, during which our time was given to weeping, we prayed that God would once more save us by sending the Russians to our rescue.

It was a great relief when we heard that the Russians, for their own interests, were coming to Urmia once more. After their coming the people were at liberty, and were able to go out into the country once more. For three months they tried to live in the villages, though a very poor and wretched life it was, with everything gone and most of the buildings burned. In these hard times we were thankful to the American Missionaries and the Russian Consul who helped us in settling down. Although at this time we did not do any evil to our enemies who had treated us so unkindly, we heard them say that if once more the Russian army should leave Urmia, no Christian would be safe.

On the 4th August the peasants crowded into the city of Urmia; they had heard indirectly about the armies leaving. It was a sight that could not be described. The sick, helpless little children were terrified. All night and the next day the road that led towards the Russian border was full of refugees, although the Consul assured us that he would not leave without warning us; but the fear was so great that nothing could keep us back.

In the first invasion of Urmia[62] some of those that dwelt inside the city gates were in more security than the villagers, although they were fined a great deal and suffered many hardships and losses of property, and there had been deaths in almost every home; but this second attack meant that we must leave all and flee. On Friday morning, with sober face and heavy heart, I left my dear home. I am grateful to God that until now my home had not been robbed, so that it was very hard for me to leave its comfort and start out into the world with no hope of returning again. With many other comrades in the same plight, we began our dreadful journey. For two families we had a little cart in which we put a few necessary coverings, a little bread, and my three little children. It was very hard for us to leave our property, but life is dearer than all the riches of the world.

On the way we met all classes of people, the rich and poor were reduced to the same level; very few had carriages, because our neighbours would not hire us any, some had horses and donkeys, but the majority had to walk with great bundles on their backs. We were quite unused to such a hard journey; some sat on the roadside and wept from sore feet; it was hard to walk in shoes, and without shoes the sun burned them until the blood came; dear, innocent children died on the way; it broke the parents' hearts to part with them; old and feeble men and women were left behind; little unlucky babies were born in the sight of the passers-by; everyone was in need of help, but no help could be found. We were like the Israelites scattered in the desert, only they had Moses to conduct them to Canaan, while we had no one.

The first night we were so tired and exhausted that we stopped in a place that had very little water, a dry, dusty place; our bed was the ground, our pillow a stone, the sky our quilt. The little excited children cried all night; large crowds of people were coming all night; while some rested and went on, others from behind took their place. The next day we were so tired and hopeless that we wished we had died at home and had not started on such an endless and aimless pilgrimage.

It broke my heart when I met a little girl; her feet were sore and she could walk no further. She cried, "Oh mother! Oh, God!" The mother had a heavy load and could not carry the child, the father was killed, they had no friends. I carried the little girl on my back for about half-a-mile, but could not any further. It was too heart-breaking. Why should innocent children suffer so?

Our next stop was a better place; it had splendid, cool water, and shade; but the people were so many that bread was scarce, starvation was upon us. A great many were sick by this time and could not move. This was a Moslem town; they did not like to have us there, but they could not turn us out on account of the Russian soldiers being near. There were Christian villages on our way, but by this time they had all been destroyed. Here we stopped a few days. We heard that the Cossacks had not left Urmia entirely; they had moved their headquarters a few miles, so that we had hope that we would not lose all. From here some of us went to Tabriz, which is a larger city, and a little safer than other places. Now we are a nation scattered like the flock without a shepherd, some living here and some there, a miserable existence. Some have gone back to Urmia; most of them have found all their crops gone. If we had not left Urmia this second time, our condition would not be so hard as it is now, the places near the city having mostly been kept safe by the kindness of the Russian Consul, who did not leave Urmia; but in the more distant places the crops and vineyards have all been destroyed. We are more than grateful to the Americans, who have ransomed our lives from death by the money that has been spent for us the last winter. We hope and pray for the victory of the Allies, that through their kindness the rest of us might live.

So far one-third of our nation has perished, and even we who survive are so broken by the strain we have suffered that sometimes we are hopeless. Now we are facing a winter of famine and wretchedness, homes without bedding and clothes. Of course nobody can supply all our needs. In addition to our own trouble, our countrymen from Turkey are taking refuge in the Urmia district, and their condition is worse than ours.

---

62. By the Turks and Kurds.

44. URMIA DISTRICT: REPORT ON THE DISTRIBUTION OF RELIEF, COVERING THE PERIOD 1st JUNE TO 31st DECEMBER, 1915; COMMUNICATED BY THE AMERICAN COMMITTEE FOR ARMENIAN AND SYRIAN RELIEF.

At the beginning of June, 1915, when the people emerged from our premises emaciated from sickness and malnutrition and crushed by the blow that had fallen upon them, they were confronted by a seemingly hopeless situation. Practically all their household furnishings and food supplies had been plundered; the same was true of their domestic animals, on which they depended in large measure for their subsistence. Their houses were without any doors and windows, and probably a full third of them had been demolished. They were in terror about going back to their villages; they feared their Moslem neighbours, who had despoiled them of their property, outraged their wives and daughters, and killed many of their relatives; they feared, too, lest the Russian troops might again withdraw and leave them to the mercy of their enemies; and they were anxious lest the missionaries who had sheltered them for the previous months might forget them when they were out of sight. Everything tended to make them cling to our Mission compounds or their vicinity. To permit them to do this was of course out of the question. Our efforts, however, to scatter them to their village homes formed one of the most pitiful phases of our relief work. The people had to go, but as long as they received their bread from our yards they would not; and so we had no choice but to cut off the food supply, after giving each family sufficient flour to support them a week. At the same time, with the help of the newly arrived Russian Consul, pressure was brought to bear upon the landlords of the Christian villages to support their tenants until harvest. Some of these could not, because they themselves had been plundered; others would not, in spite of Consular pressure; and others promised to give the needed assistance, but delayed it from day to day with all the ingenuity of excuse for which the Orient is notorious. The result was that our yards were thronged daily with hundreds of people clamouring for food. To give way would have nullified all our efforts to get the people on to their own feet;

and only when it was absolutely clear that nothing could be gotten from the landlords of any one village did we assume any degree of support for the people of the village. Little by little progress was made, and although the villagers were wretchedly miserable, the approaching harvest made subsistence by their own effort possible, and virtually all food distribution ceased for a period of three months.

There was another form of relief, however, that was imperative. In the vast majority of villages there was not a spade to use in repairing their houses, in ridding their vineyards of weeds or in burying their dead, and there was not a scythe or sickle with which to reap their harvest. The best and surest way to help the people was to give them these implements, and so for upwards of a month we virtually subsidised all the blacksmiths of the city in our endeavour to get these instruments in time for the harvest. When we closed this department of our relief work, we had distributed 2,661 scythes and sickles and 1,129 spades at a cost of 18,909.90 krans. (The exchange value of a silver kran is approximately 4½d.)

By the beginning of August the situation was considerably more hopeful. The people with Consular help had succeeded in collecting a good deal of their plundered property, including bedding, household utensils and a few cattle; the harvest was good, although the acreage was below the average, and the promise of the vineyards was excellent. Then fell another blow, what seemed an inexplicable Providence. Events in another section of the war necessitated orders for a sudden withdrawal of the Russian troops, and the evacuation was actually carried out with the exception of a small force which remained with the Consul on the hills outside the city. With the going of their protectors the whole Christian population of the plain, with the exception of some 200 sick and aged who again took refuge in the Mission yards, fled, some only to the northern edge of the plain, but many to Salmas and Khoi and even Djoulfa. Fortunately it was summer time, but even so the misery was intense, and cholera and want and hardship claimed many victims in those few weeks. Worse still, much that the people had reclaimed of their stolen property and gathered from their fields was taken once more by their Moslem neighbours; and so, after nearly a month of miserable hardship and uncertainty, the poor Syrians and Armenians returned to their twice plundered homes. Very little relief, however, was given during the next few weeks; for from the fields and vineyards much could still be secured in the way of food.

At this time we calculated that about 10,000 to 15,000 of the Christian inhabitants would have to be supported during! the winter months, and we were making our plans accordingly, when a new and overwhelming burden descended upon us. For months the Syrians of Kurdistan had been holding their own in their mountain fastnesses, hoping for succour from the

Russians. When this failed and their enemies increased on every hand, they had to flee—many, many perishing in the attempt. Some 30,000 of them arrived at last in Salmas and the neighbourhood in almost absolute destitution. A few succeeded in bringing a part of their sheep, but most came with nothing, half-naked, and without any means of livelihood. This army of wretchedness was halted by the authorities on the plain of Salmas and on the hills surrounding it, until their location should be determined upon. Mr. McDowell of our Relief Committee, who has had years of experience among these people, left at once for Salmas and grappled with the serious problem of their immediate relief. But for the assistance given by our Committee there, hundreds of them would have perished from hunger. As it was, cholera, typhoid and pneumonia did their worst among a people wasted by hardship, unprotected from the cold and without shelter. Shortly the streams of suffering humanity began to pour across the pass that separates the Salmas from the Urmia plain, and to scatter themselves in the villages of this section. A few weeks before we had been wondering how the inhabitants of the plain would find shelter for themselves in their half-ruined villages; but from the accompanying statistical report[63] it will be seen that they have made room for nearly 16,000 refugees from other districts. For example, the village of Geogtapa has doubled its population, having received as many of these guests as it had inhabitants of its own.

About the middle of October we began to take steps in preparation for our winter relief work. The first thing was to buy up all supplies of wheat that we could secure while the price was low—the lowest for years, for the purchasers were few and the owners anxious to turn their crops into cash before any more untoward events might transpire. The wheat thus secured was stored in different parts of the plain accessible as distributing centres. The doing of this required quite a force of reliable men, who could act as wheat buyers and weighers.

The next step was to get accurate lists of the actually destitute in every village. This was no easy task, for many felt themselves entitled to assistance who were not wholly destitute, and to discover who were really in want, among the hundreds of poverty-stricken, plundered inhabitants of each village, required both tact and firmness. The task was made doubly hard by the constant stream of new arrivals from Salmas. On the basis of these lists tickets were issued for bedding and for food—the two most crying needs.

For bedding it was decided to issue large wool quilts, large enough to cover several persons. These we found could be made for three or three and a half tomans (12*s.*) per quilt. Under the efficient direction of Miss Lewis, and later of Miss Lamme, a quilt factory was started, which in time employed over a hundred needy women in carding wool and sewing the quilts. This factory during its three months' existence consumed over 84,000 yards of calico,

35,000 pounds of wool, and some 1,500 pounds of cotton, and expended over 18,000 tomans; it taxed the resources of the dry goods merchants to supply our demand and it quite exhausted the wool supplies of the city. Our plan was to give only one quilt to four persons, families of over four to receive two or more according to the number of members; but after the issue of tickets we found that we could not possibly supply the need, and so regretfully we had to limit our giving to one quilt to a family. The inadequacy of this relief was seen when we began to distribute to the families of mountaineers; for with them all the brothers and their wives and children form one family, and it was not uncommon to have families of over 20, one being as high as 35. But in spite of their inadequacy, the 5,510 quilts issued have saved the lives of many, for literally thousands were facing the rigours of winter without any bedding whatever.

Our wheat distribution, too, had to be of the most economical nature. We issued what was supposed to be a two months' supply at one time, giving a Russian pood and a half per capita for this period, that is, about 50 pounds. To the widows and orphans and to the new comers from the mountains we gave flour instead of wheat, the actual cost of this assistance in food at current prices being two and a half shahis per day to a person, or between a half-penny and three-farthings. But even with this small gratuity, the total amount given of wheat and flour was 4,000 poods, or about 140,000 pounds, costing about the same as the quilts, that is, about 18,000 tomans.

With these small gifts to individuals amounting in the aggregate to large figures, and with the similar work that has been done in Salmas and Khoi, and even for the district of Albek, our funds have been exhausted, and we are waiting now to see what the generosity of America will do about it. Had it not been for this generosity, many would have died of hunger and cold the last two months, for, apart from what our Committee has done, very little has reached the people from any other source. We are grateful indeed to acknowledge the receipt of considerable sums from his Grace the Archbishop of Canterbury for the Syrian refugees from the mountains, but still the largest part has come and must come from America. We shall have to look to our friends in America for their continued aid, if this unfortunate people, the victims of Mohammedan hate, are to be kept this winter and established in their homes once more.

63. Omitted here.

45. AZERBAIJAN: STATEMENT, DATED TIFLIS, 22nd FEBRUARY, 1916, BY MR. M. PHILIPS PRICE, WAR CORRESPONDENT FOR VARIOUS BRITISH AND AMERICAN NEWSPAPERS ON THE CAUCASIAN FRONT; COMMUNICATED TO ANEURIN WILLIAMS, ESQ., M.P., AND PUBLISHED IN THE ARMENIAN JOURNAL "ARARAT," OF LONDON, MARCH, 1916.

In the October of last year I came to Diliman on the plain of Salmas in northwest Persia. I had been in Urmia during September and had seen the condition of the Assyrians (mostly Orthodox, Catholic and Protestant) in the low country round that lake. The American missionaries of Urmia were doing a great deal, and on the whole the condition of the country was not so very bad. There was housing accommodation and a good deal of corn, and it seemed as if the Americans would keep the situation in hand. But in Salmas there was a very different state of affairs. At the end of September, 25,000 mountain Nestorians from the Tkhuma, Baz and Tiari regions, who had been fighting with the Kurds all summer and had had to flee for lack of ammunition, came pouring into the plain led by their Patriarch, Mar Shimun, and began to plant themselves down in the orchards and gardens round the villages. All the villages of the plain were already occupied, and, as the winter was just setting in, their condition without housing, food and clothing was desperate. I sent a message to Mr. Shipley, the British Consul at Tabriz, telling him of the situation, and he telegraphed to the Archbishop of Canterbury for financial assistance. Meanwhile relief committees were organised under the Russian Consul Akimovitch, the Armenian Bishop Nerses, who lent funds from the Armenians of the Caucasus, and an American Missionary from Urmia, Mr. McDowell, with funds from America, and they began to organise relief during November and December. The method adopted was to distribute to all the refugees, Armenians and Assyrians alike, a daily allowance of 10 kopecks a day, since increased to 15 kopecks, and to distribute warm quilts and coats from materials purchased in the bazaars of Diliman and Khoi. Some medical detachments of the Russian Red Cross and *Soyus Gorodof* were sent with medical aid to combat typhus and dysentery, which was beginning to and still is taking many in toll of the refugees. As regards the medical side of the relief, I am inclined to doubt the possibility of making effective provision under the circumstances. There are not sufficient skilled doctors, and it is impossible to get drugs through from the Caucasus in sufficient quantity to do much good.

I did not observe on my return to Salmas after a journey to Van in November any real improvement in the health of the refugees. Every day a hundred or more Assyrians and Armenians were dying in the villages round Diliman, and the same thing is going on now.

It seems to me (and these friends of mine, who have also been there and have seen the conditions, agree with me), that it is impossible under the circumstances to combat the disease by medical assistance. The hardy mountaineers from the headwaters of the Great Zab and Tigris can best be helped by giving them the means to resist disease. Once disease has hold of them, no half measures of medical relief can help. I am therefore strongly of opinion that, if more relief is sent, it should take the form of money, which should go to increase the daily allowances of the refugees, enabling them to buy for themselves, from the Persians of Diliman, food and clothing, which alone will enable them to resist disease.

The position is now as follows. When I left Diliman for Van at the end of October, I saw in the regions round Bashkalé another 5,000 or 6,000 Assyrian and a sprinkling of Armenians living in caves of the rocks or in the open, and feeding on raw grains of wheat, which they were picking from the ruined corn-fields. On my return in January most of these were in Salmas, and so I think about 30,000 Assyrian and Armenian refugees are now there—that is, after deducting 15 per cent. as loss from disease in the last three months. The Russian and American relief organisations which are working there of course stand in need of more money to carry on their work effectively. In order to save the refugees from starving, doles of money must be given out to them till next harvest at least. I should certainly think that the Americans, whose committee is centred in Tabriz, under the American Consul there, are doing the best work with the means at their disposal. With the Russian organisation there is more delay and greater leakage. Relief is being given impartially by the Americans to Assyrians and Armenians of all denominations. This cannot always be guaranteed for the Russian organisation.

I would therefore strongly appeal for further help for the distressed refugees of this ancient Assyrian Church, together with their brethren of the Armenian Gregorian, Catholic and Protestant faiths, and should suggest that it be sent to the British Consul at Tabriz to distribute with the American missionaries in the form of increased daily allowances for food and clothing.

V.
THE REFUGEES IN THE CAUCASUS.

For two months—June and July, 1915—the Armenians of Van enjoyed an autonomous national government under Russian protection. But in the last days of July the Ottoman armies on this front received strong reinforcements, and were able once more to take the offensive. The Russian troops began to fall back from Van on the 30th July, and practically the entire Armenian population of the Vilayet accompanied them in their retirement.

The retreat was unexpected. The refugees had few conveyances and hardly any provisions; and, though their rear was protected against the descents of the Kurds by the heroic fighting of the Cossacks and the Armenian Volunteers, the suffering and mortality, during their flight over almost trackless mountains, was appalling.

At Etchmiadzin and Erivan, across the Russian frontier, the Armenian refugees were joined by the stream of Nestorian fugitives from Urmia, and the total number of Christian exiles in the Caucasus rose to over a hundred and eighty thousand.

The Turks only retained their hold on Van for a few weeks, but that was sufficient for their purpose. They did what they had done at Bitlis, Moush and Sassoun; and when the Russians returned, they found that all the inhabitants who had stayed behind had been massacred, and all the towns and villages burnt to the ground, including Van itself.

As soon as security had been re-established, the refugees began to return, slowly, to build up their ruined homes. But the majority of them still remained in the Caucasus, where they had arrived in utter destitution. The Caucasian Armenians rose magnificently to the occasion. The brunt of the relief work fell upon them, and their organisation was as admirable as their generosity. They were subsequently reinforced by aid from London, Boston, and, above all, from Moscow; but the magnitude of the task was overwhelming, and the need continued to be very great.

46. THE FLIGHT TO THE CAUCASUS: DESPATCHES TO THE ARMENIAN JOURNAL "HORIZON" OF TIFLIS, FROM MR. SAMPSON AROUTIOUNIAN, PRESIDENT OF THE ARMENIAN NATIONAL COMMITTEE OF TIFLIS, WHO WENT IN PERSON TO MEET THE REFUGEES.

(a) Despatch dated Etchmiadzin, 12th August, 1915.

The road from Igdir to Etchmiadzin (about 30 kilometres) is choked with groups of sick and destitute refugees. They have now waited there several days exposed to the full heat of the sun, although they have passes authorising them to proceed to Etchmiadzin. There is urgent need for a special body of workers to organise and forward these refugees.

(b) Despatch dated Etchmiadzin, 13th August, 1915.

Between the Turkish frontier and Igdir (the first Russian village), the whole countryside is filled to overflowing with refugees. Further on, between Igdir and Etchmiadzin, all the gardens and vineyards are full of them. At Igdir, the first arrival depot, a mass of 20,000 has accumulated, and another of 45,000 at Etchmiadzin; from these two centres they are being distributed in groups to other districts. At Etchmiadzin a hospital has been installed, as well as baths and a hospice for the orphans. Between Igdir and the Turkish frontier there are patrols of horsemen searching for the children, the sick and other stragglers, and seeing to the removal of the corpses. About fifty orphans arrive every day at Igdir; part of them are kept there, the others are sent on to Etchmiadzin.

The refugees from Van and the surrounding country have traversed the whole distance on foot. The majority of them are sick and starving, having been able to take nothing with them at the moment of departure. In the course of their journey they have not been attacked except at Bergri-Kala, where a band of Kurds cut the defenceless column and headed off about 20,000 people at the rear end of it, whose fate we do not know. As a result of famine and fatigue, a large number of the refugees have been more or less severely attacked by various epidemics, especially by dysentery.

The stream flows without ceasing, and it is impossible to estimate the numbers with any exactitude. At Igdir, with the assistance of Aram, ex-Governor of the province of Van, and other representatives of the refugees, we fixed them approximately at the following figures:

Van district, 203,000; Melashkerd, 60,000, not including those who reached here at an earlier date. The average mortality amounts to 15 deaths a day at Igdir, and 40 at Etchmiadzin.

The care of all these refugees falls upon the Armenian organisations, principally upon the Committee of Fraternal Assistance at Etchmiadzin and the National Committee. The relief available is utterly inadequate to such boundless misery. The refugees need food, medical aid and clothing, especially linen and boots. There is a dearth of travelling kitchens, tents and carts. To stamp out the contagious diseases, it is indispensable to install medical stations in all the villages.

(c) Despatch dated Etchmiadzin, 13th August, 1915.

Hundreds of thousands of refugees are arriving at Etchmiadzin from Turkish Armenia. There seems no end to these solid columns moving forward in a cloud of dust. The majority are women and children, barefoot, exhausted and starving. Their accounts of the atrocities committed by the Turks and Kurds reveal indescribable horrors. The panic which set these poor people in flight came upon them absolutely unawares; parents lost their children, and children their parents. A great number of these lost children, without food and worn out as they were, were unable to keep up and died on the road. Others have been, picked up by rescue parties, and there are now at Igdir and Etchmiadzin about 500 of these little motherless creatures. We make an urgent appeal to all Armenian ladies to come to the aid of these abandoned little ones.

(d) Despatch dated Erivan, 21st August, 1915.

The stream of refugees still flows, but with a slacker current. At the present moment more than 35,000 of them have accumulated at Etchmiadzin, and 20,000 at Erivan. In spite of all the zeal displayed by the Relief Committee of Etchmiadzin, under the presidency of the Prelate Bagrad, and by the National Committees of Tiflis and Moscow, with their numerous affiliated Committees, the situation is extraordinarily harrowing. There is an absolute shortage of bread, hot food and medical assistance. The majority of the refugees are ill. At Etchmiadzin and Erivan several hospitals have been installed, which are providing for about 1,500 sick people; yet there are still great numbers of the seriously sick lying out under walls, in open courtyards, or even in the streets. They are suffering terribly from dysentery. The mortality is enormous; the day before yesterday they buried 103 people at Etchmiadzin, and yesterday 80.

At the Etchmiadzin Secondary School, 3,500 children who have lost their parents are huddled together. They sleep on the floor. Yesterday evening I visited the building; in the big hall I counted 110 babies lying on the floor absolutely naked; some of them were sleeping, others were crying. The effect was so harrowing that one could not restrain one's tears. The sight was too terrible for me to stand, and I fled from this hell. But in the courtyard an equally painful scene awaited me. Under the walls and in the corners there were refugees lying everywhere. One heard the cries of the sick; here and there one saw corpses. In front of the monastery gate I found the lifeless bodies of three children. The women of Vaharshapat and other places are sewing clothes and preparing bedding material, but such aid is quite insufficient. Professor Kishkin, the representative of the "Homo-Russe Society," has just arrived from Moscow to inspect the condition of the refugees and organise all the relief available. He told us that beyond Erivan a supply station has been established at Arkhta[64], where the refugees are receiving dry bread, and still there is not enough of that to go around. Wherever the refugees stop, there is sickness, but no medical aid. Professor Kishkin gave the necessary orders for the immediate installation of properly-equipped medical stations between Etchmiadzin and Aghstafa, and has written to the Central Committee at Moscow for doctors, travelling kitchens, clothing, linen, etc.

64. Nijni Arkha (?).

47. THE FLIGHT TO THE CAUCASUS: DESPATCH FROM THE SPECIAL CORRESPONDENT OF THE ARMENIAN JOURNAL "AREV" OF BAKOU.

The immense procession, sinking under its agony and fatigue, forces itself along and moves forward without respite. The head of the column came to a standstill some time ago at Igdir; reduced to utter despair, it is fluctuating aimlessly hither and thither. No pen can describe what this tragic procession has endured, or what experiences it has lived through, on its interminable road. The least detail of them makes the human heart quail, and draws an unquenchable stream of bitter tears from one's eyes. In the act of writing this, my pen trembles in my hand, and I inscribe these lines with my tears.

Each fraction of the long procession has its individual history, its especial pangs. It is impossible to describe or record them all. Here is a mother with her six little children, one on her back, the second clasped to her breast; the third falls down on the road, and cries and wails because it cannot drag itself further. The three others begin to wail in sympathy, and the poor mother stands stock still, tearless, like a statue, utterly powerless to help.

Here is the road again and a broken cart on it, the sole hope of a large family. The sick mother has been laid upon it, as well as the children and the provisions. The father, an elderly man, gazes in despair at the cart he must abandon. In that moment he lived through a whole tragedy. But, come what may, they must always move forward.

And here is another mother, quite young and clad in rags. She wraps her dead baby in a shawl, puts it down out of the traffic, hugs it for the last time, and goes on her way without looking behind her.

Another scene—a mother once more with little children. She was carrying two of them in her arms; the third was clinging to her skirts, weeping and crying to be taken up in her arms like the rest. Tears were pouring in streams from the young mother's eyes. She made a sudden movement, shook off the child who was hanging to her skirts, left it on the road and walked off quickly, so as not to see its agony or hear its wailing. From behind rose the cry: "Who has lost her baby?" The cry reached the mother's ears, but she stopped her ears and hurried on.

Here is a whole group of women with white hair, bent double, all of them, and marching in silence and with bowed heads. Where are they going? They do not know. They are going wherever the vast procession carries them.

Oh! these mothers, the mothers of Armenia—are there anywhere in the world other mothers who have borne the indescribable sufferings which have fallen upon them?

And so one scene succeeds another, each more fearful than the last. Often one closes one's eyes to shut them out. The fact that one is powerless in the face of such suffering prostrates one's spirit. The procession moves forward at a surprising pace, under the imperious goad of terror. In the rear the Kurds had swarmed down from the mountains and opened fire on the column of refugees. Strung to the fullest stretch of anguish and terror, the procession pushes forward across the lofty mountains and the deep valleys, devoured by thirst under a burning sun. There are many in that company who curse the day of their birth.

Now, exhausted by privation and broken by fatigue, the procession halts at Igdir, floods the streets, fills every corner, and mounts up along the river bank and into the open fields.

48. MEMORANDUM ON THE CONDITION OF ARMENIAN REFUGEES IN THE CAUCASUS AND ORPHANS AT VAN: COMPILED IN THE BRITISH FOREIGN OFFICE FROM INFORMATION, DATED 9th DECEMBER, 1915, WHICH WAS FURNISHED BY MR. STEVENS, BRITISH CONSUL AT BATOUM.

In order to secure reliability in the application of funds collected in the United Kingdom to the immediate and actual relief of Armenian refugees who have sought shelter in the Caucasus, it is generally agreed that remittances should be sent to the "Armenian Central Relief Committee for Victims of the War" at Tiflis. The President of the Committee is Mr. Sampson Aroutiounian, and the Treasurer Mr. G.M. Zurinov. A Special Refugee Committee is working under the ægis of this body, and is stated to have representatives on the spot attending to the immediate needs of the refugees. Apart from this, the Central Committee has Branch Committees in all those principal towns of Transcaucasia where the Armenian element predominates. They are all engaged in collecting for relief work.

It is a task of the greatest difficulty, in existing circumstances, without visiting the localities where refugees are now concentrated and investigating matters on the spot, to obtain an absolutely correct description of the extent of the alleged distress amongst refugees within the Armenian refugee pale. That distress is acute—indeed, very acute—is, however, universally admitted. No two opinions differ on this point: suffering everywhere, the outlook dark and the need for relief work, and above all pecuniary aid, urgent.

Attention is also called to the urgent necessity for winter dwellings, fuel, and warm clothing, and to the inadequate staff of competent doctors, nurses and assistants to deal with the exceptional amount of illness which exists among the refugees; and, in general, to the insufficiency of medicines, medical accessories, equipment, disinfectants, and every other kind of commodity required for securing a minimum degree of comfort for the refugees.

Sums of Rs. 250,000 (£25,000), Rs. 10,000 (£1,000), and Rs. 700 (£70) have just been remitted to Bakou, Elizavetpol, and Igdir, respectively, for the maintenance of the refugee lazarettos at those places.

Rs. 25,000 (£2,500)—a donation by a rich Armenian gentleman named Mantashev—have recently been spent by the Mayor of Tiflis in procuring warm bedding, as for instance mattresses, quilts, and pillow cases, which have been sent to Igdir, Delijan, Novo-Bayazid and Elizavetpol for the use of refugees.

With the available funds at the disposal of the various organisations in this country, which are not relatively proportionate to the heavy expenditure called forth by the urgent requirements of the refugees from Asia Minor, relief work obviously cannot be undertaken by them in the needed degree, owing to the very considerable numbers of fugitives who are finding their way to the Caucasus from many parts of the Empire, and whose claims on the moneys belonging to the Societies are as urgent as those of the Armenian refugees.

The unsatisfactory character of the conditions obtaining in regard to the question of relieving the refugees has been recognised by the various Armenian Refugee Committees in the Caucasus, and an Extraordinary Meeting of the Bakou Branch was convened quite recently. At this meeting it was decided to endeavour to improve relief work within as short a period as possible, and several modifications in the existing system have, it appears, been recommended. It is reported that the principal feature of the changes that are to take place is the issue of rations, which in future are to be partly in kind and partly in the form of a cash allowance—the latter at the rate of 20 copecks (about 4d.) per adult and 15 copecks (about 3d.) per child per diem. A further cash allowance of two roubles per adult per month is to be issued for rental.

Mr. Papadjanov, Member of the Imperial Duma for the Armenian constituencies, who is on a special visit to the Caucasus for the purpose of gaining a close knowledge of conditions on the spot, was present at the above meeting and has been furnished with full details in regard to the situation and the working of the several Relief Committees. He has since visited the Viceroy and is reported to have proceeded to the districts situated within the refugee pale. After this visit, he will better be able to form an opinion as to the needs of the refugees; and, before he returns to Petrograd, in all probability, a conference of delegates of all the Armenian Refugee Committees in the Caucasus will be held at Tiflis for the final discussion of the urgency of the situation.

The funds at the disposal of the Tiflis Central Committee are apparently exhausted, and Rs. 2,000 (£200) have recently been advanced by the Tiflis Municipality to meet the immediate requirements of the refugees. The Provincial Governor has been requested by the Mayor to give his support to the negotiations which are in progress for a grant of £1,000 by the State, until further funds can be raised for the more urgent needs of the refugees.

Meanwhile, it is reported that the Katholikos has received 120 bales of warm clothing from America, and Mr. Hatisov, Mayor of Tiflis, another 11 bales of the same kind of wearing apparel from London, for distribution among the refugees.

A large quantity of warm clothing, a portion of which has recently been sent from Moscow to the Caucasus and another lot prepared by the Ladies' Committee of the Central Refugee Committee, has been quite recently forwarded to Djoulfa, Diliman and Van for the refugees. Warm clothing for the use of fugitives has also been sent, by the Central Committee, to Aghstafa and Alexandropol.

From Van it is announced in the "Kavkazskoyé Slovo" that only about 1,600 Armenians remain there, but that many refugees are returning from the Caucasus. About 4,000 fugitives are in the country adjacent to Van. Great difficulty is being experienced in procuring bread and meat, and all other commodities required for domestic purposes are unobtainable. Everything has to be brought from Khoi over very bad roads, the journey occupying five to six days. Motor traffic on the roads is impossible. In view of the deplorable conditions obtaining in the town, the establishment of a hospital at Van is strongly disadvised; in fact, a measure of the kind is stated to be outside the bounds of possibility. In view of the anti-sanitary condition at Van, sickness of every kind is prevalent among the orphans of massacred Armenians, large numbers of whom have now accumulated at Van and in its district. The children are fatherless and motherless. They are in a terrible condition. Most of them are starving, and have become so emaciated that they look more like skeletons than human beings. All buildings at Van have been destroyed by fire. No places of refuge exist for the infants. The Field Lazaretto of a Russian regiment has taken some of these orphans under its care and protection, and they seek warmth and shelter under the overcoats of the Russian soldiers.

From subsequent reports which have been received, it appears that the numbers of refugees from Turkish Asia Minor and the Urmia district who have taken refuge in the Caucasus are approximately as follows:—

(*a*) *In the Government of Elizavetpol:*—2,788 men, 4,031 women and 3,853 children of both sexes, or a total of 10,672 souls, of whom only 154 are in the town of the same name, the other refugees having found accommodation in the villages of the province.

(*b*) *For the Government of Erivan* the approximate figures are:—In the town 17,000, at Alexandropol 7,000, and in the villages of the province 76,000 refugees, or a total of 100,000.

(*c*) Besides the above, 29,000 Nestorian Christians and Armenians have taken refuge at *Russian Djoulfa*. They are reported to be natives of Salmas and the adjoining districts.

The total number of Armenian and Nestorian refugees in the Caucasus is therefore about 140,000 men, women and children. The above figures are, of course, only approximate and subject to correction.

As regards the refugees at Djoulfa, it was decided at a recent meeting, at which there was present the Nestorian Patriarch Mar Shimun, to open a central hospital for 50 beds at Diliman, another for 25 beds at Haftevan, and dispensaries in the neighbourhood of this latter village.

A sum of £5,000 had been sent to these refugees by the Viceroy of the Caucasus, and was calculated to suffice till the 18th December. A further sum of £10,000 a month is required to keep the refugees supplied with food, while other needs included £8,500 for the supply of beds and warm clothing, and £1,500 for the equipment and maintenance of the hospitals and dispensaries at Diliman and Haftevan. It is feared, however, that the above estimates for pressing needs at Djoulfa will have to be largely increased in the event of a further influx of refugees from Bashkala, an eventuality which is considered probable.

49. MEMORANDUM ON THE CONDITION OF ARMENIAN REFUGEES IN THE CAUCASUS: COMPILED IN THE BRITISH FOREIGN OFFICE FROM INFORMATION, DATED 29th DECEMBER, 1915, WHICH WAS FURNISHED BY MR. STEVENS, BRITISH CONSUL AT BATOUM.

Although the considerable sums that have recently been finding their way to Russia are being applied to the relief of Armenian refugees in the Caucasus, and the numerous consignments of clothing placed by various organisations at the disposal of the Relief Committees are being served out to them, the need of the refugees for further urgent help is reported to be still very great.

Prince Argoudinsky-Dolgoroukov, the Acting Representative of the Caucasian Section of the Urban Union, after having visited the refugee camps at Bambak and Delijan, furnishes the following report on his tour of inspection:—

Four thousand refugees are concentrated in the 26 villages which he visited in the districts named above, the more wealthy villages housing a greater number of fugitives than the less important ones. He found that, as a rule, two refugees are quartered in each house. In the whole of this district, excepting at Karakeliss, the refugees are everywhere gratuitously lodged. The same rations are issued to the refugees in all the villages; they consist of one-and-a-half pounds of flour and a cash allowance of five copecks (one penny) per diem per person. Children under two years old receive no rations or money allowance; they are, however, very few in number. Most of the children coming under this denomination have died from hunger, cold and the other fearful sufferings to which the refugees have been subjected since last summer.

At Karakeliss all dwellings are in satisfactory condition. In some of the villages fuel—mainly wood procured in the neighbouring forests—is served out to the refugees. In this district the latter possess about 1,000 head of cattle.

The exceedingly well organised Relief Committee of the Karakeliss Brotherhood is very attentive to the needs of the refugees. Their registration has been admirably arranged by this Committee. Full particulars of the refugees, and the relief received, are entered in the register book kept by the Committee. The latter has two representatives who periodically visit the refugee villages, attend to the issue of rations, and inquire into the urgent needs of the refugees and their other requirements. The Committee further endeavours to find work for the refugees.

The Committee has recently prepared two hundred stoves and a quantity of warm clothing for the refugees. They are daily furnished with boiling water and sugar. An unsatisfactory feature of relief work at Karakeliss is the difficulty experienced in receiving flour and money from Alexandropol. At times it takes twenty days to obtain them. Owing to the short cereal crop of 1915 in the district, no local flour is procurable; consequently the refugees frequently remain in a practically starving condition. The Prince Argoudinsky was surprised to find that no means had yet been devised by which the transport of flour and the transmission of money over so short a distance could be accelerated.

The Urban Union maintains a fairly well organised and equipped hospital for fifty beds at Karakeliss. This establishment, however, lacks an operating room, a mortuary and a disinfecting camera.

An orphanage managed by the Petrograd Armenian Committee has also been opened at Karakeliss. It accommodates 170 beds. The premises are good—well kept and clean. The children belonging to the orphanage are taught at the Church School at Karakeliss. They are all well dressed, but do not get sufficient food. This affects their outward appearance, and the orphans are consequently pale and somewhat emaciated. Prince Argoudinsky was informed that at times some of the children would wake up at night and search for remnants of bread left about during the day.

The Tairov Asylum for Orphans, maintained at the personal expense of Mrs. U.M. Tairov, impressed the Prince very favourably. The Orphanage is equipped for 25 orphans belonging to soldiers, and for 25 fatherless and motherless refugees. The children are well accommodated with plenty of room, in a fine and spacious building. They are made to work. They tidy up and clean the rooms, wash their own linen, wash up crockery, pans and utensils, lay the tables, assist in cooking and perform all other domestic work. They are taught to read and write, and also various trades. The children sing in Armenian and Russian to the accompaniment of a piano. They are well dressed and shod. Their robust and healthy appearance testifies to good conditions of life, and also points to the fact that Mrs. Tairov and the whole of the personnel of the establishment put a good deal of energy into their work, and are much concerned in the welfare of the children.

The conditions obtaining in the district of Kazakh are not so satisfactory as they are at Karakeliss. The need for methodical organisation in supervising relief work and introducing a defined plan of action is everywhere noticeable.

About 4,500 refugees are concentrated in this locality, viz.:—3,145 Armenians, 805 Nestorians and 550 Armenian orphans. The latter are accommodated in the Orphanage of Delijan.

Up to the 23rd November last, the above refugees were receiving a cash allowance of 10 copecks (2d.) per person per diem. On that date, however, this cash allowance was increased to 15 copecks (3d.) a day. Until the 20th November the Urban Union maintained feeding stations at the more important refugee centres, but, to the great disappointment of the refugees, these stations were then closed, and victualling was taken over by the police authorities and the village committees, which continue to perform these duties. The refugees here receive relief at the rate of 1 lb. 32 zol. (about one English lb.) of flour, and a cash allowance of 7 copecks (1¼d.) per diem per person. Fuel is not distributed to all the refugees. Some of the latter have had warm clothing, supplied by the Armenian Benevolent Society, served out to them; others have been furnished with iron stoves.

No special committee which could take over the management of relief work exists in this district. The Delijan Committee partly performs the duties which would devolve on such a body. No properly organised system of administering relief is provided. Very few individual refugees are unwilling to find employment. The invariable excuse put forward for refusing work is the absence of proper clothing for taking on open air work; also, that no food is procurable where work is offering, in consequence of which the refugees have to starve. Up to the 2nd December, the refugees were supplied with tea and sugar by the Urban Union. For some unknown reason, this allowance has recently been discontinued.

Hospital arrangements are good in this district. The hospital is maintained out of funds supplied by the Urban Union.

The ground floor of a wing of an unoccupied barrack building has been adapted to accommodate refugees. The building, although spacious, is gloomy and dark, and is exceedingly badly ventilated. The upper floor is temporarily occupied by 123 orphans, who are cared for by the Armenian Central Committee. The children go about barefoot.

At Delijan four asylums for children exist. Prince Argoudinsky was only able to visit one of these establishments. The one inspected by him is managed by Princess Toumanov, and is maintained out of funds furnished by the Armenian Benevolent Society. After their dinners, the children go to school. They look strong and healthy, and their appearance shows care and kind treatment in every respect. According to information obtained by Prince Argoudinsky, the other three asylums at Delijan are likewise well managed and kept.

The relief extended to the refugees at Delijan is only of a primitive nature; the same remark cannot, however, be applied to the unsatisfactory conditions obtaining in this connection in the district of Kazakh. Here the question of housing the refugees is one of the most painful features of the relief work undertaken. In a large number of villages in this district, the refugees are mostly accommodated in derelict sheds and shops—dark, unheated and overcrowded. For some unaccountable reason warm clothing has not been issued to them. They do not receive their rations of flour and cash allowances with regularity, and no Central Organisation to inquire into their immediate and urgent needs exists on the spot.

The Bakou Refugee Committee has just forwarded several further consignments of 10,000 quilts, 12,000 mattresses and sacks, 12,000 pillow cases, 600 jackets, 3,000 shirts, 3,000 pairs of drawers; and the Tiflis

Committee, 400 quilts, 4,000 mattresses, 4,000 pillow cases, 200 jackets, 1,000 shirts and 1,000 pairs of drawers, to the Governors of Elizavetpol and Erivan, to be served out to the refugees. The latter Committee has also sent several bales of clothing to Persia and to Turkish Asia Minor for the refugees, but according to the newspapers a large proportion of the fugitives are still in utmost poverty—destitute, to a very great extent, of the absolute necessities of existence.

Seventy-six railway truck loads of flour, of which 53 were for the needs of the Armenian Refugees in the Government of Erivan and 23 for the use of those in the Government of Elizavetpol, left Gulevich in the Northern Caucasus a few days ago. These trucks, under ordinary conditions, should already have reached their respective destinations.

Owing to anticipated heavy snow drifts at the Akhta Pass (Kars-Karakeliss direction), the Zemstvo Union gave orders a few days ago that all its refugee victualling and provisioning stations should be moved to Igdir.

According to information obtained by Mr. Sarebey, the Dragoman of the Vice-Consulate at Van, from the Armenian Bishop of Erivan and from various other data he has been able to procure on the spot, the number of Armenian refugees in the Caucasus is 173,038, of whom 105,000 are from the Province of Van; 48,000 from the districts of Alashkerd, Bayazid and Passin; and 20,038 from Moush, Boulanik, &c., &c.

They are housed as follows:—

Government of Erivan:—

Town of Erivan	18,820
Villages in the neighbourhood of Erivan	14,680
Market town of Vaharshapat	5,360
Villages of the district of same name	22,730
Town of Nahichevan	271
District of Nahichevan	468
Igdir	1,028
Surmalin	7,342
Town of Alexandropol	8,450
Villages in the neighbourhood of Alexandropol	14,121

Sharori	268	
Town of Novo-Bayazid	1,164	
Villages of Novo-Bayazid district	10,336	
		105,038
Government of Elizavetpol:—		
Town of Elizavetpol	12,000	
Villages, district of Elizavetpol	5,000	
District of Karabagh	1,000	
		18,000
Province of Kars:—		
Town of Kars and adjacent villages	26,000	
Karakeliss	4,000	
		30,000
Government of Tiflis:—		
City of Tiflis	5,000	
Villages of the district of Tiflis	3,000	
		8,000
Northern Caucasus (probably the Armenian town of Nahichevan-on-Don)		12,000
Grand total		173,038

The number of refugees in the Caucasus from Khoi and Salmas is small, about 1,000. They are housed principally at Nahichevan and a few at Erivan.

The foregoing figures differ from those obtained from an official source, which put the number of refugees in the Caucasus, in round figures, at 140,000. The data now procured by Sarebey, who is on the spot, originating as they do from Armenian sources and being in greater detail, are likely to be more correct than the information then furnished.

Reports received through the newspapers from Colonel Termen state that the situation at Van has recently improved. It would appear that 6,000 refugees have returned to the town, which has been subdivided into four police districts. Strict measures to prevent further pillage and destruction of property have been introduced at Van. Ordinary necessaries of life are procurable, although only in very small quantities. Some threshing machines and four or five flour mills have resumed work in the district, with the result that several bakeries have reopened.

All persons, organisations and other bodies in the Caucasus and elsewhere that have Armenian orphans from Van and its district in their care, have been requested to furnish particulars to the Governor of Van in regard to the names, ages, parentage and native places of the orphans in their charge. Also, where possible, information is asked for as to any property their deceased parents may have possessed, in order to enable the authorities to institute a search for, and appoint guardians to protect, such property.

The spread of disease has been stayed. The town has assumed a cleaner and more orderly appearance. In some streets the restoration of buildings has been commenced. Ten or twelve shops and stores have resumed trade.

The Armenian newspaper *Horizon* states that the news from Salmas is very unsatisfactory. Bishop Nerses' urgent appeal for warm clothing has hitherto remained unheeded. Only a small quantity of clothing forwarded by the Tabriz Women's Committee has reached him, but the articles sent are like a drop in the ocean. The cold is excessive.

50. REPORT ON THE ACTIVITY OF ARMENIAN REFUGEE RELIEF ORGANISATIONS IN THE CAUCASUS AND TURKISH ARMENIA; ENCLOSED IN A DESPATCH (NO. 1), DATED BATOUM, 3rd JANUARY, 1916, FROM MR. CONSUL STEVENS TO THE BRITISH FOREIGN OFFICE.

The Armenian organisations in the Caucasus which have been so active in relieving Christian refugees since the first arrival of the latter in this country in the early days of July last, still continue their good work.

The number of victims of the war who took refuge in the Caucasus from Turkish Armenia and Persia, in roughly estimated figures, is 150,000. The influx of refugees, however, continued for some time after July. There is, therefore, good reason to believe that the number of refugees who crossed the Russian border was in excess of the figures quoted above.

The refugees for the most part settled in the Government of Erivan, and principally at and about the town of Etchmiadzin. Housing accommodation for such large numbers could not here be provided, and the refugees, in the circumstances, had to be accommodated without cover in yards and open spaces, in the neighbourhood of the Monastery of Etchmiadzin.

Daily telegrams from Etchmiadzin to the Principal Relief Committee at Tiflis depicted a truly painful situation, and reported that from 350 to 400 deaths were daily taking place, owing to the destitute and starving conditions that prevailed amongst the refugees.

At this time relief work was in the hands partly of the "Chief Caucasian Committee for Succouring Victims of the War," and partly in those of the Red Cross Society. Shortly after, several other public bodies joined in relief work.

The combined efforts of these various organisations had little effect in improving the situation. The funds at their respective disposals were small, and quite out of proportion to the enormous numbers of the refugees, whose ranks kept on swelling, especially after the heavy fighting that took place last summer on the Caucasian front.

Meanwhile the insanitary condition of the refugees, in view of the very hot weather, was daily becoming more and more appalling. Dysentery, spotted fever, typhoid, measles, diphtheria, and subsequently cholera, all of which were assuming epidemic form, were thinning the numbers of the refugees at a very rapid rate; and yet, despite this alarming situation, the funds necessary to cope successfully with the deplorable conditions were not forthcoming.

Finally, the Caucasian Section of the All Russia Urban Union, after a hurried investigation of matters, prepared a rough estimate of the money needed for the immediate relief of the refugees, and a grant of Rs. 1,103,250 (£110,325 about) was asked for by the Section from its Principal Organisation. This money was shortly afterwards remitted to the Caucasus, and the urgent needs of the hordes of refugees were then and there met. The temporary measures of relief adopted gave the Caucasian organisations a short time to think matters over, and to decide on further action in connection with relief work.

Accordingly, steps were taken to bring the pressing needs of the refugees before the public, and, in response to appeals made throughout the Caucasus, in Russia and abroad, moneys were collected privately; the Russian Government contributed important sums, and latterly funds have been flowing in from the United Kingdom and America. With these moneys relief work is being extended on a wider scale, and the requirements of the refugees are being more closely attended to; but the needs of the fugitives are still very great, and more and more moneys are required.

The necessity for substantial additional sums is, to a great extent, due to a new series of tasks the Urban Union has taken upon itself to carry out, together with the heavy responsibilities it has had to accept in connection with refugee relief work outside the confines of the Caucasus.

A comparatively large number of refugees have latterly been returning to their homes, and the Djoulfa-Van and Igdir-Van roads have had to be placed under the immediate supervision of the Caucasian Section of the Urban Union. A number of kitchen and housing stations have had to be opened at various points on these two routes, which the Union will have to maintain at its own expense for a considerable period, in view of the increasing tendency among the refugees to return home, in reliance upon the restoration of security in their own country.

The organisation of the kitchen and housing stations in the Djoulfa-Van direction is reported to be proceeding apace under the guidance of the Representative of the Caucasian Committee of the Urban Union, and the work is being carried out in complete harmony with, and according to the directions and indications of, the military authorities.

The Urban Union has also undertaken to equip and open a hospital for 200 beds for refugees at Van, which it will also maintain at its own expense.

The duties of the Urban Union do not end here, for it has been called upon by the Viceregal authority to perform many other functions connected with refugee relief work; the difficulties they present have to be faced with as much energy and resource as all the other duties taken over by this body.

The following is a list of the medical and kitchen stations which have been opened by the Union and are at present serving the needs of the refugees in the areas mentioned above:—

I.

HOSPITALS.

1. *At points at which the refugees originally settled.*

(*a*) *At Etchmiadzin.*—A hospital consisting of several buildings belonging to the Monastery and to its Academy, which have been temporarily adapted to accommodate 570 beds for patients of both sexes and for children.

A cholera ward, No. 5, in which, owing to the disappearance of the disease, no cases are at present under treatment. The vacant beds of this ward (70) are now being used for cases of spotted fever.

A flying medical column (consisting of a medical officer, his assistant and several competent attendants) has been provisionally formed to attend to those sick refugees who are within the limits of Monastery territory.

Three miles distant from the Monastery, on the road to the railway station of Etchmiadzin, a medical quarantine station has been established. At this point healthy refugees are subjected to a quarantine of four to five days, before they are allowed to proceed to the station for the purpose of entraining en route to the Government of Elizavetpol. On their journey, the refugees are accompanied by a medical officer and two professional assistants.

(*b*) *At Igdir.*—A hospital, in temporarily occupied buildings, accommodating 100 beds; and, three and a half miles from this point, at a village named Plour, a hospital for 50 beds.

(*c*) *At Erivan.*—A hospital, in private houses provisionally rented, which provides 200 beds. A quarantine station of a temporary type has also been opened in connection with this hospital. Two assistant medical officers are placed in charge of the latter establishment, and they accompany refugees by rail to their places of settlement in the Government of Elizavetpol.

(*d*) *At Alexandropol.*—A hospital, in premises rented temporarily, accommodating 200 beds to which an isolation section has been added.

Within the limits of the district of Elizavetpol several stations have been established with assistant medical officers in charge.

2. *Along the refugees' line of advance.*

(*a*) *Nijni-Akhti.*—A hospital for 50 beds.

Assistant medical officers' stations at Elenovka and Tchibouhli.

(*b*) *Delijan.*—A hospital for 50 beds.

3. *In places where refugees have more or less settled.*

(*a*) *Novo-Bayazid* (*Erivan*).—A hospital for 50 beds.

(*b*) *Annenfeld.*—A hospital for 80 beds.

(*c*) *Kedabek.*—A hospital for 50 beds.

The total number of beds provided—including the 70 belonging to the cholera ward at Etchmiadzin—is 1,450.

NOTE: Funds furnished by the Urban Union are at present being employed for adapting a building—ceded to the Military by the Katholikos—to the needs of the refugees.

II.

KITCHEN STATIONS.

1. *On the railway lines used by refugees.*

At the quarantine station near Etchmiadzin and at the stations of Aghtalia and Annenfeld.

2. *On the metalled roads (chaussées) used by refugees.*

At Parakar, Erivan, Novo-Nikolaievka, Ailar, Suhoi Fontan, Nijni-Akhti, Elenovka, Tchibouhli, Delijan, Tarsa-Tchai, Karavan-sarai and Uzuntal.

Bread and hot food are served out to the refugees at these stations. The refugees are quartered during their stay at these points in sheds rented for the purpose which are properly roofed.

A separate kitchen station has been opened at Djoulfa out of funds—Rs. 10,000 (£1,000)—placed by the Urban Union at the disposal of Bishop Nerses, for the use of Nestorian refugees.

III.

With a view to improving the insanitary conditions obtaining in the refugee settlements, and also the hygiene of the refugees:

1. *Three disinfecting stations have been opened.*

The first of these is now operating at Etchmiadzin. The station undertakes to disinfect cemeteries, refuse-dumping grounds, hospitals (in the event of infectious disease), and premises of every other type, and to operate the disinfecting camera.

The officials of the station perform their duties under the guidance of a sanitary medical officer.

The second station is at Igdir, and the third at Erivan.

The duties of the latter two stations are identical with those of the first-named station, and each is worked by a similar personnel.

2. *Detachment for erecting buildings.*

This detachment has to attend to the building of bath and wash (laundry) houses of a provisional type in the refugee settlements. It consists of a chief, two assistants, an instructor, two stove-building masons (petchniks), two fitters, a tin smith, and two rough carpenters.

The detachment has erected a bath-house (Turkish) and laundry at Annenfeld, a similar bath-house at Tchibouhli, and a Turkish bath and laundry at Kedabek.

New work of the same description is in immediate prospect for the detachment at Delijan, Elenovka, Nijni-Akhti, Igdir, Etchmiadzin and its neighbourhood, and at Alexandropol. The detachment has also been ordered to take in hand work connected with the erection of a series of steam-formaline disinfecting cameras. A camera of this type is in course of construction at Erivan.

3. Under-garments and warm clothing have been served out in various places to the refugees. Wearing apparel, as stated above, was purchased at a cost of Rs. 66,000 (£6,600), out of moneys contributed by a number of organisations and individuals; and warm clothing costing Rs. 11,996 (£1,200), assigned by the Principal Committee of the Urban Union, has also recently been distributed to the refugees.

Apart from the more or less completed organisation of relief work described above, necessity has compelled the Urban Union to take over relief work in Persian territory, and a hospital for 110 beds is under equipment at Salmas.

Further duties connected with the relief of the refugees will shortly be taken over by the Urban Union, when it is proposed to open small hospitals and dispensaries in all refugee settlements.

It is estimated that between 11,000 and 12,000 refugees have returned to the valley of Alashkerd and to the Vilayet of Van, and that from 2,000 to 3,000 refugees belonging to the middle classes have settled in the Governments of Tiflis and Bakou.

The cost to the Union of feeding the refugees is estimated at between 18 and 19 copecks (4d.) per head per day.

The following are the rations issued to the refugees:—

Bread, 108 lbs.	Rs.	7·20
Meat, 20 lbs.	"	3·00
Rice, 10 lbs.	"	1·20
Potatoes, onions, salt, pepper	"	0·60
Fuel (wood, peat or coal)	"	1·70
Tea, ⅛ lb.	"	0·25
Sugar, 4½ lbs.	"	1·13
Rental for accommodation	"	1·00
Administrative expenses	"	2·00

Rs. 18·08 per 100 refugees per diem, or 18·08 copecks per head.

The Government ration is 1½ lbs. per person per day, or an allowance in cash, in lieu of rations, at the rate of 15 copecks a day or Rs. 4·50 per month. The Government method of sending provisions to points of distribution is, however, very erratic. Owing to the lack of railway facilities and to delays in remitting moneys by the Principal Committee, the refugees dependent on relief from this source have frequently to go without their bread for days and at times for weeks.

The following is a list of other organisations engaged in relief work in this country:—

- The Etchmiadzin Brotherhood;
- The Tiflis Armenian Central Committee;
- The Moscow Armenian Red Cross Committee;
- The Russian Red Cross Society; and
- The Communes of the various villages in which the refugees have settled.

The Etchmiadzin Brotherhood, under the chairmanship of the Katholikos, maintains branches of its organisation at Igdir, Erivan, Alexandropol, Kars, Nahichevan, Novo-Bayazid, and Karakeliss. Relief work was undertaken by the Brotherhood in March, 1915. Since that date, apart from the large quantities of clothing, medicines and other comforts served out to the refugees, a medical detachment has been organised at Igdir, and, in all, the Brotherhood has spent Rs. 900,000 (£90,000) in relief work. This, in the main, has been obtained by voluntary contribution from persons of Armenian nationality all over the world, but especially in the Russian Empire (at Petrograd, Moscow, Kharkov, &c.). The Brotherhood serves out with punctual regularity flour rations, money allowances, and clothing to the refugees. It has all along maintained kitchens at Igdir, Etchmiadzin, and Alexandropol, as well as hospitals in various places; has organised a proper system of medical aid; and has opened refugee orphanages, schools and workshops for the children. In short, the organisation is thorough, and this is one of the most important relief societies engaged in work in the Armenian refugee pale.

The Tiflis Armenian Central Committee has also been carrying out relief work for nearly ten months. This body maintains its own hospitals and kitchens, and hitherto has expended Rs. 200,000 (£20,000) in connection with the relief of Armenian refugees settled in the Government of Erivan. The necessary funds are raised by voluntary contributions collected from members belonging to Armenian society in the Caucasus.

The Moscow Armenian Committee of the Red Cross.—The relief work of this organisation is confined to the Government of Erivan. The Committee commenced operations in April last, when four medical and kitchen stations (viz. at Etchmiadzin and at the villages of Markar, Ashtarak, and Arzap) were opened. A staff consisting of a medical officer, two assistants, and several competent attendants and nurses, besides several sanitary officers and other employees, is appointed to each of these stations. The organisation affords relief when and as urgent occasion requires. This Committee has spent Rs. 300,000 (£30,000), all of which has been contributed by the Armenian colony at Moscow. An orphanage is maintained by the Committee at Ashtar, together with a school and workshop. The organisation likewise keeps a flour store and stocks of other provisions at the last-mentioned place. Refugees are fed by the Society at Markar and at eight other villages situate in the valley of Alashkerd. The above remarks apply only to the more important duties that devolve on the Committee, but it also attends to the needs of the refugees in many other ways. A hospital at Arzap is also maintained by the Committee.

In August, 1915, *The All Russia Red Cross Society* entered the field of refugee work by opening a medical observation point at Igdir. The staff here consists of a superintendent, a medical officer, two assistants, and 19 sanitary officers. In September last, alone, this body served out 18,598 dinners and 16,775 portions of tea, and rendered medical aid to 4,652 refugees. In October, 1915, the Red Cross Society daily fed from 850 to 900 refugees in the district of Igdir. The stations of this Society are well organised, the staffs strictly disciplined, and their work is effected with neatness and punctuality. The Society maintains a dispensary and victualling store at Igdir. The estimated cost of the dinners and tea served out to the refugees by the Society is between 17 and 18 copecks (3d.) a day per head.

The Village Communes.—The peasants of each of the villages in which refugees have been settled have undertaken to accommodate them, gratuitously, in their houses. In these the refugees find warm shelter, and are not infrequently fed as well out of the slender resources at the disposal of their hosts. Whilst seemingly unimportant, the relief extended to the refugees by the peasantry is of the greatest value. An accurate idea of this benevolence can only be formed when all the good deeds of the peasantry are taken into consideration. Undoubtedly, this aid relieves the contributory public from responsibilities amounting to several hundreds of thousands of roubles. In other words, the charitable disposition of the by no means affluent peasant effects an enormous saving of money, which under other conditions would have to be provided by the various organisations.

On the recommendation of Prince A.M. Argoudinsky-Dolgoroukov, who has recently been on a tour of inspection through the refugee districts, it has been decided to improve the work of relief by adopting the following measures:—

1. That the present accommodation at the hospital at Annenfeld be increased by an additional 30 beds. That the bath-houses in course of construction at Barsoun and Kedabek be forthwith completed, and a bath-house built at Tchardahli.

2. That a medical officer, two assistant doctors and two nurses, as well as another assistant medical officer and three nurses for the 30 additional beds, be immediately appointed to the hospital at Annenfeld. That all equipment required for the additional 30 beds at this hospital, and the necessary undergarments and clothing for outgoing patients, be at once supplied.

3. That should a further evacuation of refugees from Erivan to the Government of Elizavetpol be ordered by the authorities, additional warm and roofed-in buildings should be rented at Annenfeld and Evlakh, and be furnished with some comfort for the refugees, even if only of a very primitive nature.

4. That kitchens for refugees on the move be opened at Annenfeld, Evlakh, and Elizavetpol.

5. That small hospitals be opened at the village of Tchaikent in the district of Elizavetpol, and one each in the districts of Djevanshir and Shousha.

6. That movable sanitary detachments and kitchens be organised in the refugees' districts of settlement.

7. That permanent dispensing stations be established in the colony of Annenfeld and at the railway station of Evlakh.

8. That the question of the restrictions in force at Elizavetpol and on the road leading through Annenfeld regarding the passage of refugees, be at once brought before the notice of the competent authorities.

9. That the cash allowance to refugees in the Government of Elizavetpol be brought up to 15 copecks per day per head.

10. That the authorities whom it may concern be requested, when settling refugees on new lands, to take into consideration the previous conditions of life of such refugees, and allot to those coming from highland districts identical localities in this country, and *vice versa* in regard to refugees who have been inhabitants of lowland districts. Further, that in defining the number of refugees to be temporarily domiciled in villages, the degree of prosperity or poverty of the villages be taken into consideration.

11. That warm clothing, blankets, bast-shoe leather, iron stoves, kerosene and (if possible) tea, sugar and soap, if only in small quantities, be immediately served out to the refugees.

12. That the question of the supply of fuel to the refugees be brought to the notice of the forestry authorities of the Caucasus.

13. That the question of the supply of flour to the refugees through the Central Organ, and of the accumulation of stocks of the same commodity in villages or groups of villages for the winter, be forthwith decided.

14. That local administrative offices be requested to give the Committee timely notice of the dates and hours of dispatch of trains conveying refugees.

15. That the Caucasian Principal Committee be requested to entrust the Urban Union with the task of feeding refugees on the spot. Should this prove impossible, to ask that steps be taken to introduce modifications in the present system of distributing food.

16. That a representative of the Committee be appointed to each of the localities where refugees have been settled, in order that these representatives may communicate to the Committee when there is urgent need of relief in any given locality.

51. REFUGEES IN THE CAUCASUS: LETTER DATED ERIVAN, 29th DECEMBER, 1915, FROM REV. S.G. WILSON TO DR. SAMUEL T. DUTTON, SECRETARY OF THE AMERICAN COMMITTEE FOR ARMENIAN AND SYRIAN RELIEF.

We have just returned from a tour of some of the Armenian villages where refugees are living, and are ready to report on their condition from personal observation. In this district or Governorship of Erivan there are 105,000 Armenian refugees, besides Nestorians and Yezidis. Of these, 18,000 are in the town of Erivan; of these, again, many are scattered in the homes of the people and others gathered in large buildings, orphanages, etc. We visited the barracks where 420 were living. Room after room was full—in some rooms 40, in some half the number. The lucky ones were those that had a plank platform or board floor on which to sleep and sit. Many of them were in the kitchens and store-rooms on the bare ground. Most of them had insufficient bedding, and many of them scarcely any. Some were lying four under one coverlet, head to feet. One man told us how he sat and shivered in the night till his teeth chattered. Another man stayed in bed during the daytime because he had no clothes. One room contained, among others, two Protestant families from Van; the fathers had both died lately of disease, the mother of one group was lying sick. Seven or eight was the number of each household, lying in rags on hay and with scarcely enough cover for two people. The atmosphere of the rooms was foul in the extreme. These people were from the city of Van and had lived comfortably.

The condition in the villages is even worse. At Somaghar, 15 miles from here, we were taken about by the elder of the Protestant Church. Sad indeed were the sights that we saw. Some, too, were comforting in a measure. This good man had taken into his household, already of sufficient size, two women refugees, who were clothed cleanly and neatly and fed as his own. Many of the Armenian villagers have taken in and cared for the destitute refugees. Others have given them the use of their spare rooms, bake-houses, stables and barns. Fortunate are those who are in the bake-houses, for the heat in bread baking is a free gift to them, albeit mixed with smoke. Fortunate, too, those who have stables, for they have steam-heat from the oxen and buffaloes; for those in the other store-rooms and out-houses have no stoves or fires. These uplands of Armenia have a severe winter. The ground is now covered with snow. Ararat, with its two grand peaks, is always in sight, and but a few miles away. Cold winds from the Caucasus range blow over the plain. The sight of these multitudes with neither clothing for day nor bedding for night is a great draft on our sympathies, and this is intensified by their pitiful stories. We entered one bake-house. One young man appeared among 15 women and children. They had been a prosperous patriarchal family of 36 persons—father, three sons and their wives and children. Of these, 21 were killed, including all the men except this young fellow, who threw himself into the arms of a Kurd and was saved in some freak of mercy. This was a Protestant family from a village called Perkhous. We saw families of 13 and 16—mothers, daughters, brides and children—with no man among them. We asked: "Where are your men?"—"They were all killed;" or, "Out of 70 men but one escaped;" or, "We were 100 men in the village, but only 20 escaped;" or, "There were 450 households in our village, but 20 or 30 men alone escaped."—"Were the women taken away?"—"Yes, our pretty girls were carried off."—"How many?"—"Four out of nine; we too were stripped naked." As to the rest of their sufferings and outrage, they were silent.

We addressed the one surviving man and asked: "How are you here?" He replied: "I was off as a soldier in the Turkish army. I heard of the massacres, and by bye-ways through the mountains I returned to find our village destroyed. I escaped to Russia and found them here." Another woman, from Ardjish, near Van, said: "All our men were collected from the bazaars and taken before the Government. After dark, we heard the shots which killed them. We fled in the night."

In the village of *Kourpalou*, with 300 houses, there are 900 refugees. Of these, 300 are from the first exodus of January to April, 1915, and 600 from the second in July and August. The first were able to bring with them some of their property; many of the men came safely. The second was the terrible flight after the massacres; of these, 40,000 are said to have died of disease after reaching Russian territory. The condition of the later refugees is most heart-rending. Let me give a few glances at conditions in Kourpalou. A woman surrounded by seven or eight persons, with scarcely beds for all, and rags as their clothes, said: "I escaped by throwing myself in the mud, a dead child lying over my head. There were 50 in our household. Nine women and boys were taken captive by the Kurds." In a stable the oxen and buffaloes were crowding up close; at their side a flock of sheep was huddled; the air was stifling. Three families of 18 persons were crowded at one end, in a space so small that it seemed impossible for them to lie down. Some had improvised a couch in the manger. A hammock for a baby was stretched above on two posts. Of these 18, a blind youth was the only man. In the bake-house were 27 persons, one youth, one very old man. Six men of their household had been taken as soldiers, the rest were massacred. Of the 600 refugees of the second exodus who are in this village, about 30 are men. Some are escaped soldiers who were in the army when the atrocities occurred. One had dragged himself out from under a mass of dead bodies.

Nor did all the women escape death. Women were wantonly slain; those with child ripped up with swords; the breasts of others cut off. Some threw themselves and their children into the streams and over the precipices to escape outrage. One woman lately arrived who was captured some years ago by a Kurd. She had escaped now. after killing the Kurd, and brought her two children with her.

Mouandjik.—Also many refugees. As in all other places, great lack of clothing and especially of bedding. Twenty-two persons in one room, two of them men. Mostly sleeping on the ground, with bedding enough for one-fifth of their number. In another room 10 persons, no men, 15 of this connection killed, girls carried away, one boy saved by hiding under skirt of mother; clothes in tatters, bedding lacking.

Veri Ailaulou.—This village of 70 houses is sheltering 370 refugees, in wretched condition. Three families of 22 persons are in one bake-house, one side of which is filled with dried manure. Their village in Turkey had 70 men, one escaped alive; 4 girls and 3 brides carried off. Another hut contains 4 women and some children, the remnant of a family of 24. All the men of their village were killed. They are living in a wretched condition. Bread and water have been the chief food of these refugees for months past.

We are doing what we can to relieve this distress, supplementing the work of local and Government committees. Ready-made clothing in any large quantity is not to be found, nor blankets. Comforters we have purchased in small quantities. We are organising some sewing circles and will contract for clothing in Tiflis, where we succeeded in buying about 7,000 garments. They are hard to find, and transport is difficult when they are ready, as the army has the first right to the trucks.

I have not time to tell you of our reception by the Grand Duke Nicolas and his good wishes for the success and progress of our relief work, nor of our visit to the Katholikos at Etchmiadzin and his warm thanks for the sympathy and help of the American people for his people in their distress. We were entertained by him over-night. Governors, Bishops and Press have all bidden us God-speed.

Warm clothing and bedding will save many from sickness and death. The pitiable condition of these wretched people should appeal strongly to our American people in their comfortable homes and in the enjoyment of ten thousand blessings.

After organising relief committees here in several places, one or both of us will return to Tiflis for supplies of clothing and bedding.

52. REPATRIATION OF REFUGEES: LETTER, DATED ERIVAN (?), MARCH, 1916, FROM THE REV. S.G. WILSON; COMMUNICATED BY THE AMERICAN COMMITTEE FOR ARMENIAN AND SYRIAN RELIEF.

Events have moved rapidly since I sent my appeal of the 18th February. In the intervening month the Russian army has made splendid progress and driven the Turks back many miles beyond Erzeroum and Van. The capture of Bitlis, Moush and Mamahatoun (Derdjan) has given assurance to the Government, to the Armenians and to us all. The return of the refugees to the Van province has been officially authorized. Men are hastening back even while the snow is on the ground. The 12,000 already there will soon be 20,000 and 30,000. Reports say: "Men are going in large numbers."—"Every day caravans of those returning to the fatherland enter," via Igdir. Most of these have returned from the Erivan province to Van. Others, of whom 500 are women, have settled in Alashkerd. Fifty-three hundred have gone back from Russian Passin to the Turkish province of the same name. The Governor of Kars reports that from Olti and that region refugees are returning to the districts of Erzeroum, and that many of them are women and children. In Bashkala there are nearly 3,000 refugees, said to be in great wretchedness and in need of daily sustenance.

Besides these, numbers are coming forth from their places of concealment, or from the houses of certain friendly Kurds, or from their captivity in Moslem harems. These are indeed but hundreds compared with the thousands who have been massacred or driven into the wildernesses. But it is a gratification to hear that from Sassoun 160 men came forth; that in Khnyss there have appeared more than a thousand new refugees; that in Riza on the Black Sea more than 200 Armenian children were discovered after the taking of the town by the Russians; that in Bitlis men, women and children have come forth in large numbers (2,800); that in Moush nearly 3,000 souls have been freed. Erzeroum seems to have been dealt with most savagely. Less than 200 Armenians out of 20,000 in the city itself escaped death or deportation, that is, exile. Of these, thirty were saved in the house of Mr. Stapleton. The Armenians report that when the Moslems came and demanded that these girls should be delivered over to them, Mr. Stapleton replied: "You must kill me before you can touch them." Recent reports say that in the villages round Erzeroum Armenian women and children are appearing, singly and in groups, and are in the greatest need. Whose heart is not moved with pity for and desire to preserve these remnants who have escaped from the greatest destruction! Our opportunity is a wonderful one—to save the remnant, to aid in the restoration, to prepare for the return of the 200,000 fugitives now in Persia and the Caucasus.

Our call to help is both general and specific. A specific and unusual call has reached us from the Russian Governor of Van, Mr. Alfred Teremin.

Now we have telegraphed to the Governor that we are coming, as we telegraph to the American Committee of our entrance upon the new work. Fortunately we have a considerable balance on hand, and we are going in the faith that America will support us generously. Large funds will be necessary, to put roofs over the heads of the people, to supply seed-corn, ploughs, oxen, carts, etc.; to set at work carpenters, blacksmiths and other artisans; to help the most needy till harvest time. We shall buy the necessary things here or in Persia or from the Kurds, and will do our part in assisting the returning exiles to cultivate their fields, so that harvest may be abundant. Fortunately the time of spring sowing in the highlands of Armenia does not close till June, so we have yet time. A letter from Van says: "The important thing is that material help should be received quickly. If delayed, it will lose half its value. It is necessary to hasten. Every day is precious."

VI.
VILAYET OF ERZEROUM.

The Vilayet of Erzeroum lies due north of Bitlis and Van, and is likewise a border province. It consists principally of the upper valleys of the Kara-Su (Western Euphrates) and the Tchorok. The fortress-city of Erzeroum itself is situated in a plain which collects the head-waters of the former river; Erzindjan, a place of almost equal importance, lies further west, about 120 miles down stream; while Baibourt, in the Tchorok valley, is the most important place on the high road from Erzeroum to Trebizond. The districts north of the Kara-Su are as civilised as the rest of Anatolia; but south of the river, in the great peninsula enclosed by the two arms of the Euphrates, lies the mountain-mass of Dersim, inhabited by wild, independent tribes of Kizil-Bashis and Kurds, who played an active part in the destruction of their Armenian neighbours.

In the Vilayet of Erzeroum the deportations began at the end of May and during the first days of June. Reports from a particularly trustworthy source state that, by the 19th May, more than 15,000 Armenians had been deported from Erzeroum and the neighbouring villages, and that, by the 25th May, the districts of Erzindjan, Keghi and Baibourt had also been "devastated by forced emigration." Our information concerning Erzeroum itself was at first somewhat scanty, but since its capture by the Russians it has been visited by representatives of various relief organisations in the Caucasus, who have obtained circumstantial accounts of what happened in the city and the surrounding villages. They report that, out of an Armenian population estimated at 400,000[65] souls for the Vilayets of Erzeroum and Bitlis, not more than 8,000-10,000 have survived,—in other words, that 98 per cent. of the Armenians in these vilayets have been either deported or massacred.

We are also particularly well informed with regard to Baibourt and Erzindjan, and the documents in this section may be noted as a clear case in which independent testimonies exactly bear one another out.

---

65. The author of Doc. 57 estimates them at 300,000 only; but consult Annexe D. to the "Historical Summary."

53. ERZEROUM: RECORD[66] OF AN INTERVIEW BETWEEN THE REV. H.J. BUXTON AND THE REV. ROBERT STAPLETON, A MISSIONARY OF THE AMERICAN BOARD, RESIDENT AT ERZEROUM FROM BEFORE THE OUTBREAK OF WAR UNTIL AFTER THE CAPTURE OF THE CITY BY THE RUSSIANS.[67]

Up to 1914 the population of Erzeroum was between 60,000 and 70,000, of whom 20,000 were Armenians.

In 1914 Tahsin Bey was Vali of Erzeroum (whom Mr. H.J. Buxton had met, as Vali of Van, in 1913).

On the outbreak of war with Turkey (November, 1914) the British Consul, Mr. Monahan, received his passport; the Russian Consul was ejected; the French Consul was absent. All their servants and interpreters were Armenians; these were ejected likewise, and were sent to Kaisaria as prisoners. The three Armenian servants of the Russian Military Attaché were hanged. The wife of one of these was sitting up, knitting socks and putting things together for her husband's departure, when news came to her, early in the morning, that he was hanging on the scaffold.

In the spring of 1915 Passelt Pasha was Military Commandant of Erzeroum, and he suggested that all Armenian soldiers should be disarmed, withdrawn from combatant service and put on road gangs (yol tabour). These were men who had been conscripted, and, owing to the friendly relations between Turks and Armenians in this district (for the past ten years), had joined readily.

Teachers in the schools were first of all put into hospitals to do the work of dressers and nurses among the wounded. They were men with a good education, and did their work with intelligence. Then came the order that they were to be put on to the road gang, and they were replaced by totally incompetent men, so the soldiers had very poor attention in the hospital.

All through this period, up to May, 1915, military service could be avoided by men of all races and parties upon payment of an exemption tax of £40 (Turkish).

Even Turks themselves obtained exemption on these terms, and for a period (of, say, twelve months) the terms were faithfully observed; but, of course, eventually the need for soldiers made the authorities come down even upon exempted persons. In any case, this exemption only applied to military duties, and afforded no shelter to Armenians in the final crisis.

Stapleton managed to get one Armenian exempted by the payment of this tax.

19th May, 1915.

There was a massacre in the country round Khnyss. As the Russians advanced from the east a large number of Kurds fled in front of them, bent on vengeance, and carried out a raid on the peasantry which was quite distinct from the organised massacres later on.

Some of Stapleton's teachers, boy and girl students, were at Khnyss on holiday, and perished in this massacre.

6th June.

The inhabitants of the one hundred villages in the plain of Erzeroum were sent away by order of the Government at two hours' notice. The number of these must have been between 10,000 and 15,000. Of this number very few returned, and very few reached Erzindjan. A few took refuge with friendly Kurds (Kizilbashis), but all the rest must have been killed.

They were escorted by gendarmes, but the people responsible for the massacres would probably be chettis or Hamidia.

One of the Kurds was charged in court for murder, pillage and rapine, and he thereupon produced a paper and laid it before them, saying: "These are my orders for doing it."

It is not certain who gave these orders, but the presumption is that they originated with the Government at Constantinople.

About this time definite orders arrived, by which Tahsin Bey was instructed that all Armenians should be killed. Tahsin refused to carry this out, and, indeed, all through this time he was reluctant to maltreat the Armenians, but was overruled by *force majeure*.

On the 9th June

he issued an order that the whole civic population were to leave Erzeroum, and many Turks and Greeks actually did leave (the latter being hustled out).

The German Consul was now aware of what was coming, and wired protests to his Ambassador; but he was told to remain quiet, as the Germans could not interfere with the internal affairs of Turkey.

This is what he said to Stapleton, and his goodwill is borne out by his evident intention to help the Armenians. It is an established fact that, in the days following, he used to send bread tied up in large sacks to the refugees outside the city, conveying these large supplies in motor cars.

16th June.

The first company of Armenian deportees left Erzeroum on the 16th June, having got leave to go to Diyarbekir by Kighi. These were forty families in all, mostly belonging to the prosperous business community.

First of all, after starting, all their money was taken from them, "for safety." After a short halt, when some alarm was expressed, they were reassured of the complete security of their journey, and shortly after resuming their journey (somewhere between Kighi and Palu) they were surrounded and a massacre took place. Only one man and forty women and children reached Harpout.

Evidence of this massacre comes from various sources: (1) letters to Stapleton from women survivors; (2) evidence of Americans who were living in Harpout at the time of the arrival of the survivors, and cared for them; (3) evidence of a Greek, who passed the scene of the massacre shortly after it took place and described it as sickening.

19th June.

About five hundred Armenian families left Erzeroum, *via* Baibourt, for Erzindjan; they were allowed time for preparations—a concession granted throughout the deportations from the town itself. At Baibourt there was a halt, and the first party of about 10,000 people was joined by later contingents, bringing the number up to about 15,000. A guard of gendarmes (up to 400) was provided by the Vali, and these doubtless took their toll of the Armenians in various ways, licentiously and avariciously.

The Vali went to Erzindjan to see after their security, and it is known that about 15,000 reached Erzindjan. Up to this point the roads were good enough to allow transport by bullock carts (arabas), but after Erzindjan, instead of being allowed to follow the carriage road *via* Sivas, they were turned aside to the route *via* Kamakh, Egin and Arabkir, where there were only footpaths. The arabas had, therefore, to be left behind, and no less than 3,000 vehicles were brought back to Erzeroum by an Armenian in the transport service, whom Stapleton met on his return.

At Kamakh, twelve hours from Erzindjan, it is reported that the men were separated and killed, their bodies being thrown into the river. Beyond this place letters come from women only, though Stapleton's account leads us to suppose that, from among thirty families of which he has news, ten men survive. Letters from women to Stapleton do not, of course, give details of what occurred; they only indicate what happened by such phrases as: "My husband and boy died on the road." The destinations reached by these Armenians, as definitely known to Stapleton in January, 1916, were Mosul, on the east; Rakka, on the south; Aleppo and Aintab, on the west. The need in these places has been urgent. German Consuls in Aleppo and Mosul are known to have assisted in distributing relief funds sent by Stapleton, per the Agricultural Bank at Constantinople, to Mesopotamia—in all about £1,000 (Turkish).

Stapleton had previously been able to distribute a sum of about £700 (Turkish), received from America, to poor Armenians before their departure. This he did in co-operation with the Armenian Bishop.

November, 1915.

Certain Roman Catholic "lay brothers and sisters" (Armenians), claiming to be under Austrian protection, were permitted to remain until November,

1915, when they left Erzeroum in arabas. They were known to have reached Erzindjan, and probably Constantinople, in safety, where they were housed in the Austrian schools[68].

From twelve to twenty families of artisans were left to the last, as they were doing useful work for the Government. Also fifty single masons, who were building a club-house for the Turks, being compelled to use gravestones from the Armenians' cemetery.

February, 1916.

These masons were sent to Erzindjan, where they were imprisoned for some days and then brought out and ordered to be shot. Four, however, escaped by shamming death, and one of them saw Stapleton on the 16th February and gave an account of what had happened.

The fate of the artisans is thought to have been similar, but we have no details, except that three families were able to return.

One of those to leave the town in the early days was a photographer. He would not wait. Ten hours out from Erzeroum he was surrounded by forty chettis, stripped naked and stoned to death. They mutilated his body. One child was brained. Of the other children, a girl was taken away and only escaped many months later when the Russians came. Very reluctantly she poured out her story to the Stapletons, from which it appeared that she had been handed round to ten officers after the murder of her husband and his mother, to be their sport.

Thirty-five families of Greeks remained in Erzeroum until near the end. They were then hustled out when the Russian approach was imminent, the Turks virtually saying to them: "We are suffering. Why should not you?"

These deportations went on in an almost continuous stream from the 16th June to the 28th July, when the Armenian Bishop left. He is supposed to have been put to death near Erzindjan.

The part which Stapleton took during these events may now be described. In addition to what we have already said about his relief work, he and Mrs. Stapleton sheltered eighteen Armenian girls. It was by the permission of the Vali that these were allowed to stay with him, and on only one occasion was his house actually threatened. This was just on the eve of the Russian arrival, when he was warned by the German Consul that a plot had been made to burn down his house and, in the subsequent rush of panic, to seize the girls. Nothing could have stopped this but the Russian entry, which took place on the very day for which it was planned. This plot, however, was an isolated act, and, on the whole, Stapleton speaks highly of the general conduct of the Turks in Erzeroum itself.

The Last Days.

On Sunday, the 13th February, the German Consul left. On Monday, the 14th February, the Persian Consul was forced to go with the Turks to Erzindjan. They maintained that, as he was a representative accredited to the Government, he must go with them when the Government moved its headquarters. He went reluctantly, as he was anxious to look after his fellow-countrymen.

On Monday evening (the 14th February) Stapleton was sent for by the Vali, and he went, expecting to be told to leave the town. The Vali said that he and the Turks were leaving on the morrow, but that Stapleton might remain.

Tahsin Bey requested him to ask the Russian Commander to spare the population of the city, as, in general, they had had nothing to do with the deportations.

And that is a fact.

On the 15th, Stapleton was asked by a deputation of all ranks of Turks in the town to go out (three hours' distance) and meet the Russian Commander. He refused to go, but he delivered Tahsin's message the following day, when the Russians entered the city.

On the 15th, Turkish troops fired the Armenian episcopal residence and the market. They also burned schools and arsenals, and looted in the city.

Wednesday, the 16th February.

The first Russian to appear was a Cossack with a white apron. He was accompanied by Russian and Armenian soldiers, who shouted: "We are Armenians. Are there any here?" Then the Cossack came into Stapleton's house, and wrote his name in the book as "the first Russian to enter Erzeroum." The house was soon filled, and Stapleton lent eight beds to Russian officers, and also supplied food.

When the Grand Duke came, a few days later (the 20th), the Russians asked for another bed; but this was refused.

Mr. H.J. Buxton asked Stapleton: "Was there a good deal of looting by the Russians?" Stapleton said: "No, I should not say a good deal of looting. They were very hungry, and the stores were all open; but, for an invading army, they were quite mild. For the first twenty-four hours they were very short of food."

Armenian Volunteers began to search the city for Armenians, and they did not find very many. Four girls were held by Turks, and these, together with the eighteen with Stapleton, made the full quota of twenty-two Armenians in the town.

The appointment by the Russians of an "Old Turk" (a former agent of Abd-ul-Hamid at Bukarest, who had subsequently been banished by the Young Turks to Erzeroum) is now giving considerable satisfaction to the Moslem population.

In August, 1915, the Turkish Government appointed and despatched a Commission from Constantinople, ostensibly to protect the property of the deported Armenians. During August this Commission took possession of, and sold, this property, including valuables left with Dr. Case (Stapleton's colleague at that period). Stapleton asked the police for their authority, and was turned off his own premises by a high-handed secretary. However, he wired to his Government, and got the official removed, and from that time he was treated with respect and was able to exert considerable influence with the Vali; in fact, he remonstrated with him on the brutal treatment of the women at the hands of the zaptiehs and Kurds on the road from Erzeroum.

Stapleton is not a Consul, but a Missionary. To the foreigner a "Missionary" always means a Government representative; and as Stapleton was the only American in Erzeroum, he was, *de facto*, Consul. In many ways he was able to do far more than if he had been officially a Consul, knowing the ways of the country and exactly how far he could go, but yet free from official fetters.

---

66. Undated.

67. Mr. Stapleton's total period of service at Erzeroum is thirteen years. For a letter from Mr. Stapleton himself, see Doc. 149, page 589.—EDITOR.

68. See Doc. 62

54. ERZEROUM: REPORT, DATED 25th SEPTEMBER, 1915, DRAWN UP BY THE AMERICAN CONSUL-GENERAL AT TREBIZOND, AFTER HIS RETURN FROM A VISIT TO ERZEROUM; COMMUNICATED BY THE AMERICAN COMMITTEE FOR ARMENIAN AND SYRIAN RELIEF.

I left Trebizond on the 12th August on horseback, accompanied by kavass Ahmed and a katerdji with my travelling outfit, also two mounted gendarmes furnished by the Governor-General. I reached Erzeroum about midnight on the 17th August, and was allowed to enter the city gate only after communicating with the Commandant.

I found the two American families well. The Rev. Robert S. Stapleton, who is the director of the American Schools and Treasurer of the Mission Station, is living with his wife and two daughters in the upper storey of the Boys'

School building. The lower part is used as a Red Crescent Hospital for lightly wounded or convalescing soldiers, accommodating on an average about 75 patients. Dr. Case and wife and two small children were living in the upper part of the Hospital building, the lower part being used as a Red Crescent Hospital for about 30 patients. The Girls' School building, with the exception of two rooms belonging to the teachers, which are locked up, is also used by the Red Crescent for lightly wounded soldiers, accommodating on an average about 200. These three fine buildings are on the same street, about 100 yards apart. The Red Crescent flag flies over the three buildings, and on Fridays and holidays the Turkish flag is also raised over the Girls' School building, which is entirely devoted to the Red Crescent work, with the exception of the two rooms mentioned above. Over the other two buildings, which are partly occupied by the Americans as residences, the American flag is hoisted, in addition to the Red Crescent flag, on Sundays and holidays, and there seems to be no difficulty raised by the authorities now in regard to the flag question.

I called upon the Governor-General, Tahsin Bey, accompanied by the Rev. Mr. Stapleton and Dr. Case, and the Bey received us very cordially. He informed me that he had just received a report from the military authorities that the Russians, upon evacuating Van, had destroyed every building in the city, including the American buildings, in order that the Turkish army should not find shelter for the winter, and had taken the Americans from Van with them on their retirement towards Russia. This information I telegraphed to the Embassy on the 18th August as follows:

"All American buildings reported destroyed by Russians upon their withdrawal from Van, and Americans now in Russia."

He also informed me that all the Americans at Bitlis had gone to Diyarbekir.

The Vali said that, in carrying out the orders to expel the Armenians from Erzeroum, he had used his best endeavours to protect them on the road, and had given them fifteen days to dispose of their goods and make arrangements to leave. They were not prohibited from selling or disposing of their property, and some families went away with five or more ox-carts loaded with their household goods and provisions. The Missionaries confirm this.

Over 900 bales of goods of various kinds were deposited by 150 Armenians in Mr. Stapleton's house for safe keeping. There are also about 500 bales in Dr. Case's house and stable. The value of the bales is estimated by Mr. Stapleton at from £10,000 to £15,000 (Turkish). He has a good American combination safe belonging to the Mission in his house, and two safes of English make left by merchants, which he filled with paper and silver roubles and jewellery deposited by Armenians, for safe keeping. He gave no receipts and assumed no responsibility, however. The gold deposited by Armenians amounted to £5,559 (Turkish), and of this amount £5,000 (Turkish) was sent to Mr. Peet through the Imperial Ottoman Bank in Erzeroum by telegram. The roubles, however, the Bank refused to transfer, and so they were left in his safes in the shape received, namely, tied up in handkerchiefs or made up in small packages. Afterwards these packages were all opened, and an itemized list was made of the contents of each package. The paper roubles and jewellery were then packed into tin boxes and sealed with the Mission seal and deposited in the Imperial Ottoman Bank in Mr. Stapleton's name for safe keeping....

Many policies of insurance in the New York Life Insurance Company were found in these packages, upon which a separate report will be made. There were also deeds to house and lands, promissory notes and other valuable papers, which no doubt have now lost much of their value.

The Gregorian Armenian Cathedral and the Catholic Armenian Church at Erzeroum were filled with goods of various kinds which had been entrusted to the Imperial Ottoman Bank by the Armenians before they were deported. These goods were entrusted to the Bank, and the keys are in the possession of the Bank....

The Vali of Erzeroum informed me that he had received instructions from Constantinople to allow the Protestants and Catholics to remain where they were for the present. One of Mr. Stapleton's valuable teachers, Mr. Yeghishé, was taken some time ago for military service, and was working upon the roads near Erzeroum. Mr. Stapleton needed this man as an interpreter, since he himself knows very little Turkish. The Vali promised me he would give Mr. Yeghishé a vesika or permit to remain in the city, if his military exemption taxes were paid. I attended to this matter, and on my way to Trebizond found Mr. Yeghishé at Ilidja, three hours from Erzeroum, and delivered to him the vesika, which gave him freedom to return to Erzeroum and remain there.

I also asked for the return of another Protestant teacher who was thought to be in Erzindjan, but this the Vali declined to allow, saying that the order did not permit their return, but simply allowed them to remain where they were. In case they had already been sent away he could not recall them.

Mr. Stapleton has twenty Armenians in his house now; four of them are women and the balance girls. Dr. Case had six Armenians in his house when he left Erzeroum. Four of these went to Mr. Stapleton, and one he takes with him to Constantinople, and one he expects to leave at Marsovan for training in the Hospital. The Vali granted a special permit for these two girls to travel with Dr. Case, and also handed to him a letter of appreciation for the work he had done in his hospital for Turkish officers.

Mr. Stapleton's relations with the Vali, Tahsin Bey, are good, and indeed the latter, who was Mutessarif of Pera a few years ago, impressed me as being a very reasonable man, who desired to do the right thing and entertain good relations with the Americans....

55. ERZEROUM: ABSTRACT OF A REPORT BY MR. B.H. KHOUNOUNTZ, REPRESENTATIVE OF THE "ALL-RUSSIAN URBAN UNION," ON A VISIT TO ERZEROUM AFTER THE RUSSIAN OCCUPATION; PUBLISHED IN THE ARMENIAN JOURNAL "HORIZON," OF TIFLIS, 25th FEBRUARY, 1916.

There are between 80 and 100 Armenians left in Erzeroum—according to other reports 130—and about 25,000 Turks, who dare not come out of their houses. The sanitary condition of the city is deplorable. Mr. Khounountz had interviews with a number of Armenian and foreign eye-witnesses. He met an Armenian officer who had escaped from the Turks, who told him of the deportation and massacre of the Armenians. He said that the attitude of the Turks towards the Armenians was more or less good at the beginning of the war, but it was suddenly changed after the Turkish defeat at Sari-Kamysh, as they laid the blame for this defeat upon the Armenians, though he could not tell why.

After that, they separated the Armenian soldiers from the Turks as a dangerous element, and removed them from the fighting line. They put them on the roads to work as ordinary labourers.

At the same time terror reigned in the city. Mr. Pasdermadjian, a well-known Armenian, was assassinated, and a number of prominent young men were hanged or exiled. A number of Armenians were forced to go to the cemetery and destroy the statue which was erected to the memory of martyred Russian soldiers in 1829. They were also forced to open hospitals for the wounded Turkish soldiers at their own expense.

On the 5/18th April, by an order received from Constantinople, the Turks held a big meeting in which the hodjas (religious heads) openly preached massacre, casting the responsibility for the defeat upon the Armenians. The Armenians appealed to them and implored for mercy, but in vain. The Vali was rather inclined to spare the Armenians, but the order from Constantinople had tied his hands.

The deportation of all the Armenians in the Vilayet of Erzeroum began on the 4th June. It was carried out promptly, and took the Armenians by surprise. Gendarmes were sent to the Armenian villages at night, who entered the houses, separated all the men from their families and deported them. The deportation of the men of Erzeroum—the city proper—was carried out less cruelly, the Vali giving them 15 days' notice.

But as the refugees were escorted by brutal gendarmes and chettis (bands of robbers) many of them were massacred in a most cruel manner, and very few of them reached their destination, which was the district of Kamakh, west of Erzindjan.

According to the officer, the plan of deportation was exactly the same as in other vilayets. None were spared, not even certain women teachers—Protestant and Roman Catholic—who were foreign subjects and had taught in foreign colleges.

Only 15 skilled labourers were left, with their families, as they were needed for war work. These were massacred before the Turks left Erzeroum.

56. ERZEROUM: ABSTRACT OF A REPORT BY DR. Y. MINASSIAN, WHO ACCOMPANIED MR. KHOUNOUNTZ TO ERZEROUM AS REPRESENTATIVE OF THE CAUCASIAN SECTION OF THE "ALL-RUSSIAN URBAN UNION"; PUBLISHED IN THE ARMENIAN JOURNAL "MSCHAK," OF TIFLIS, 8th MARCH, 1916.

Dr. Minassian gathered his information from the following sources: The American Vice-Consul at Erzeroum, Mr. Stapleton; Mrs. Stapleton; Dr. Case of the American Mission Hospital; an educated Armenian lady—Zarouhi—from Baibourt, who escaped the massacres by a miracle; an Armenian soldier who had accepted Islam; an old man from Erzeroum; and many others.

Before Turkey's entry into the war, the Young Turks saw that war between them and Russia was inevitable, so they tried to win the Armenians over to their side by promising them all kinds of privileges.

As soon as war was declared, they confiscated everything from the shops of the Turks, Greeks, Armenians and Syrians, without any distinction of race or religion. The Armenians lost more than the other nationalities, as they were the wealthiest commercially.

The Turks asked the Armenians to join with them, but they declined, saying that if they fought against the Russians they would endanger the lives of their brothers in Caucasia. This seemed reasonable to the authorities, and on the surface, at least, they left the Armenians in peace.

The Armenians performed their civic duties faithfully and opened a hospital for the Turkish wounded; later on they were forced to open others.

Everything went smoothly until the first Turkish defeat, which occurred at Keutag. It was then that the Turks found out that the Armenian volunteers were fighting side by side with the Russians. This was announced everywhere and excited the Turks; but no steps were taken until it was reported that Garo Pasdermadjian, a member of the Ottoman Parliament and one of the deputies for Erzeroum, was commanding a body of volunteers in the Russian army. The result was that Mr. Pasdermadjian's brother was assassinated. Then Djemal Effendi from Constantinople, with another Turk, Saifoullah, incited the people to massacre the Armenians.

The Governor saw that the excitement was growing, so he called a conference of all the prominent Turks. This was held at Pasha-Kiosk, and Djemal and Saifoullah took part. These demanded an immediate massacre, but the Governor requested them to hold their hand until he could communicate with Constantinople about it.

After this the authorities disarmed and removed all the Armenian soldiers from Erzeroum, and put them on the roads to work as unskilled labourers. A number of wealthy Armenians were forced to destroy the statue which was erected in memory of martyred Russian soldiers in 1828, and transfer its stones to another place to build a club-house for the Young Turks. Some could not stand the hard work, yet could only obtain release from it by paying large sums.

Then the rich Armenians were asked to vacate their homes and to transform them into hospitals. This was done willingly, and the Armenians undertook to care for the wounded.

Then an order came to some Armenians to leave their homes and go. But they begged to remain, and were allowed to do so on payment of £1,500 (Turkish).

A week later, all the rich and educated men were imprisoned; many of them died in prison under terrible tortures.

Then it was announced that they would all be deported. When the Governor was asked where they would be sent, he replied: "To a safe place, where the mob cannot hurt you."

The Armenians packed all their valuables and left them at the American Consulate, the missionary schools, and at the Armenian Church.

To obviate any possibility of resistance, the villagers were first deported towards Kamakh, and when the Erzeroum Armenians followed them they saw heaps of ruins in place of prosperous villages.

The deportation of the Armenians of Baibourt was more terrible. They were all taken by surprise at midnight.

"Where are you taking us?" they asked. "To a safe place," was the reply, "away from the Turks, where the mob cannot massacre you. It is the duty of the Government to protect its subjects. You will remain there until peace is re-established."

The Armenians believed them and followed the gendarmes without resistance. After they had travelled several miles, they noticed that the attitude of the guards changed and that they had been deceived. By and by they were asked to pay fifty pounds, which they paid. Towards nightfall they asked for two girls. The next day they asked for five hundred pounds. They had to pay that also. That night they asked for five girls and took them. Then every day they were robbed. They lost all their valuables and provisions. The Turkish villagers stole the best looking girls and boys.

Just before they reached Erzindjan, their outer clothing was taken away from them and they were left in their underclothes. When they reached Erzindjan they protested to the Kaimakam. The Kaimakam promised to accompany them. The next day they started for Kamakh.

After they had travelled a few miles, they were attacked by chettis from all sides. The Armenians wanted to run back to Erzindjan, but the gendarmes opened fire on them. Many of them were thus massacred, and the remainder were driven towards Kamakh.

It was discovered that these chettis had been organised by Djemal Effendi, and it was by deliberate design that all the refugees were left in their white underclothes, so that no one could run away or hide himself.

When the refugees reached a gorge of the Euphrates River they were attacked again, and many of them were drowned in the river.

Zarouhi—who related the above story—said that the river was filled with corpses. She also was thrown into the river, but clung to a rock behind some bushes and remained there until the gendarmes and chettis had gone away.

Coming out of the river she met a kind Kurdish shepherd, who wrapped her in a blanket and took her to the house of a Turk who knew her. The Turk took her to Erzeroum and kept her in his home.

In speaking of the responsibility of the Germans for the massacres and deportations, Dr. Minassian says that, before the deportation, the Armenians went to the German Consul and asked his assistance. His answer was: "I do not want to mix in other people's affairs, and I have no authorisation to do so from my Ambassador at Constantinople."

The German officers at Erzeroum helped the Turks to organise the deportation, and also took their share of the booty. Almost every one of them had kidnapped Armenian girls.

An officer called Schapner, for instance, took with him four girls; another called Karl, two girls; and so on—there was a long fist of names which the reporter could not remember.

57. ERZEROUM: STATEMENT BY MR. A.S. SAFRASTIAN, DATED TIFLIS, 15th MARCH, 1916.

Since last October, when the Armenian atrocities were disclosed to the world at large, we had hoped against hope that, in spite of overwhelming evidence to the contrary, all that was said to have occurred might not be confirmed; that there might have been outlying districts in Turkish Armenia where the local Armenians had been spared the horrors that had accompanied their destruction in areas situated on the main roads. Unfortunately, now that the entire provinces of Erzeroum and Bitlis have been cleared of the Turk and one is able to see for oneself what actually has taken place, one is simply staggered at the depth and extent of the great crime, and the unprecedentedly cruel means by which the Armenians were cleared out of those two provinces, as well as the adjacent districts.

After seeing something with my own eyes in Erzeroum and Van, and compiling the facts about Bitlis, Moush and Khnyss from Russian official and other sources, my impression is that, out of the 250,000 Armenians of the Erzeroum and Bitlis Vilayets that remained under the dominion of the Turk in April, 1915 (exclusive of some 50,000 who saved themselves last summer, either by fighting their way out or by the advance of the Russians, and are now in Trans-Caucasia), only some 10,000 can be accounted for since an estimate was made possible by the death-blow which the Turks suffered last month. The remaining 240,000 or so have apparently perished under circumstances of the most extreme violence and inhumanity of which any human being is capable.

I am now in a position to state that all the accounts of Armenian atrocities which have been published in Europe and the United States are not only completely true, but that they represent merely such facts as have come under the eyes of consular officers or missionaries of neutral states; whereas the most ghastly and heinous crimes have been committed in the unfrequented parts of the country, out of sight of any observer.

The city of Erzeroum, the great military stronghold in Turkish Armenia, contained some 50,000 inhabitants before the war, of whom 20,000 were Armenians. The so-called plain of Erzeroum, a fertile alluvial plateau extending north-west of the city, contained some 60 Armenian villages with at least 45,000 inhabitants, almost all of them belonging to a sturdy race of peasants.

As soon as the European war broke out, the Central Committee of the Young Turks sent one Boukhar-ed-Din-Shakir-Bey, one of the Committee leaders, to Erzeroum, to organise the annihilation of the Armenians. Another, Djemal Effendi, a fanatic of the foulest type, was sent later on to help him in the work. These two Committee stalwarts sent from Constantinople were assisted in their fiendish business by two notorious natives—Edib Hodja and Djafer Bey.

At Erzeroum, as everywhere else, the Armenians in particular were ruthlessly robbed of most of the goods they possessed under the cloak of military requisitions. The Turkish defeat at Sarikamysh in January, 1915, and the exaggerated accounts of the part played by Armenian Volunteers in that battle, envenomed relations at Erzeroum. A Turkish officer who returned from Sarikamysh told the Armenian Bishop Sempad at Erzeroum that they chiefly met Armenians on the battlefields: "Many of our soldiers were shot by Armenians," he said, "and it was the Volunteers who destroyed our villages and scouting parties."

Subsequently a campaign of slander and provocation was started by the Young Turk leaders against the Armenian people. Armenian soldiers in the Turkish army were disarmed and sent to labour battalions, and further severe measures were taken to squeeze every available asset out of the helpless people. A great mass meeting was held by the Turks on the 18th April just outside the city, in which the Armenians were publicly denounced as "traitors" and "dangerous to the Empire" and as supporters of the enemies of Turkey. Strict orders were issued to all Moslems who were inclined to shield their Armenian friends that they would be punished as severely as their protégés if they dared to protect them.

Fully aware of the fate that awaited them, the Armenians of Erzeroum made desperate appeals to Tahsin Bey, the Vali of the province, for protection. The latter's reply was that he could not defy the instructions sent by the Central Government. The answer of Herr Anders, the German Consul at Erzeroum, to whom the Armenians appealed again for protection, seems to have been still more brutal. He definitely stated that the persecutions levelled by the Turkish Government and the mob against the Armenians were quite lawful, and that he could not interfere in the matter.

By an exercise of imagination one may perhaps visualise to some extent the anguish and agony those poor Armenians suffered during April and May. Trapped on all sides by the ruthless enemy and deprived of all means of armed or legal protection, they attempted to make the best of an unprecedentedly tragic situation. Almost all the intellectual leaders and teachers were openly done to death in prison under horrible tortures. Pilos, Atrouni and several others have never been heard of since their imprisonment. Pasdermadjian, a leading citizen of the town, was shot dead in the streets. This reign of terror also prevailed in the villages of the plain.

The capture of Van by the Armenians on the 16th May and the entry of the Armenian Volunteers, followed by the Russian Army, made a great impression on the Turkish authorities at Erzeroum. On the same day, the Armenians of Khnyss and of the neighbouring 38 villages were butchered almost to a man, and the women and children distributed among the Kurds. During the recent capture of Khnyss by the Russians, some 3,000 women and children were rescued in and around Khnyss. Apparently these represent the remnant of the 22,000 Armenians of the Sandjak of Khnyss.

In the meantime the Russians were advancing towards Melazkerd and Bitlis, and the Turks deported the Armenian peasants from Melazkerd and Passin and drove them towards Erzeroum. These half-starved peasants, exhausted and harried by forced marches, were not allowed to enter Erzeroum; they were kept out in the rain for seven days. Their situation became so shocking in May (1915) that even the German Consul was moved at the spectacle, and took some clothing and bread in his own car to distribute among "these rebellious scoundrels." Later on they were driven towards Erzindjan and drowned in the Euphrates.

On the 4th June, the first batch of Armenian peasants from the plain of Erzeroum, amounting to some 15,000 persons, were forced by the gendarmes to leave their homes and proceed to Mamahatoun, west of Erzeroum. They were escorted by chetti (Moslem Volunteer) bands consisting of criminals released from prison since the proclamation of the Holy War. In the ankle-deep mud and along the rugged roads, children and weak women fell by the wayside amid the laughter of the chettis. Every evening a forced tribute was levied upon the peasants. Gradually they were robbed of everything they possessed—money, clothing, horses, etc. Girls and women were distributed among the Turks as they passed through Turkish villages. A few hours' distance beyond Mamahatoun, at the entrance of a valley called the Kamakh gorge, this convoy was "ambushed by unknown robbers." The signal was given by a revolver shot, whereupon a volley of fire was poured upon the Armenians. One of the survivors of this batch, a lad of 18 whom I saw in Erzeroum, told me that the shrieks and cries of the women and weeping children under fire were distracting. Many attempted to escape, but they were fired upon by their own escort. In two hours' time the valley had become a vast cemetery of unburied human bodies. Out of the 15,000 thus disposed of, a few escaped and reached Erzeroum in the guise of Turkish peasants.

On the 18th June it was the turn of the city. A fortnight's time-limit was given to the Armenians for settling their affairs; they packed their property in boxes and bales and stored them with Mr. Stapleton, the head of the American Mission, and in the Armenian Cathedral. The Governor took £1,000 (Turkish) from them in payment for a safe-conduct before their departure. A hundred and sixty leading families were selected first for deportation. They were all people of means and education. The German officers in Erzeroum behaved in an outrageous manner towards the Armenian women torn away from their men. The Germans, in fact, seem to have set the example of wrenching women from their homes. One Captain Schapner (?) is said to have forced Miss Tchilingarian, a handsome girl, to follow him. On her resisting and crying, she was dragged about in the streets and roughly handled. This worthy German also carried off Mrs. Sarafian, a young woman educated in Switzerland. Another German lieutenant, Karl (?), dragged five women to his rooms, and so on.

The convoy of 160 families started out with carriages and some luggage, and were sent off in the same direction as their predecessors—towards Mamahatoun and Erzindjan. As they travelled they were robbed of everything and even stripped of their clothing. They are reported as having skirted the town of Erzindjan, but beyond that nothing has since been heard of them.

Bishop Sempad was sent off alone in his own carriage to Erzindjan, and never heard of again.

In the last week of June, several parties of Erzeroum Armenians were deported on successive days and most of them massacred on the way, either by shooting or drowning. One, Madame Zarouhi, an elderly lady of means, who was thrown into the Euphrates, saved herself by clinging to a boulder in the river. She succeeded in approaching the bank and returned to Erzeroum to hide herself in a Turkish friend's house. She told Prince Argoutian (Argoutinsky), the representative of the "All-Russian Urban Union" in Erzeroum, that she shuddered to recall how hundreds of children were bayoneted by the Turks and thrown into the Euphrates, and how men and women were stripped naked, tied together in hundreds, shot and then hurled into the river. In a loop of the river near Erzindjan, she said, the thousands of dead bodies created such a barrage that the Euphrates changed its course for about a hundred yards. Several Armenians of this last party, however, seem to have survived this dreadful journey. Recently some of them wrote from Rakka, in northern Syria, to Mr. Stapleton imploring money and help, as they were in the direst distress.

After the recent capture of the city by the Russians, there were some 100 Armenians altogether in Erzeroum and some 25,000 Turks. Thirty girls and women were protected by Mr. Stapleton in his house. A certain number of women are gradually being rescued from the Turks in the city, and perhaps thousands more may be saved, if the military authorities take the necessary measures and help the Armenians to discover their own people.

Most of the children converted to Islam are quite used to Moslem habits; they speak and behave as if they were Turks by birth. They are now changing these habits again in Armenian hands.

When one stood at the gate called Kars Kapou, the eastern entrance to the city, and looked at the panorama it presented in March, 1916, Erzeroum did not seem to have suffered great changes in its general aspect. But I suffered a rude shock in the interior of the city, when I saw Armenian houses occupied by Turks still gloating over their booty, the city deprived of its Armenian element, and the dome of the Cathedral broken away at its base.

The Armenians of Erzeroum to whom I have talked here about their prospects are consoling themselves—though it is a poor consolation—with the thought that thousands of them had left the city before the war, and that they will all return home and take possession of their property as soon as the conditions there become better defined.

58. ERZEROUM: STATEMENT BY THE KURD ALI-AGHAZADÉ FARO, PUBLISHED IN THE ARMENIAN JOURNAL "MSCHAK," 19th DECEMBER, 1915.

Ali-Aghazadé Faro, a Kurd, related to some Armenians of St. Garabed, who reached Caucasia as refugees, that he had gone to Erzeroum last September to sell sheep, &c., and to get his share of the booty from the Armenians if possible. Faro remained in Erzeroum for five or six days, during which time he did not see a single Armenian. He only saw Turks sitting in the shops of the Armenians. When he asked how it was that they were in these shops, some answered that they had bought them, while others said that they were gifts to them from the Government.

Faro spent the night in a Turkish house, and asked his host what had become of the Armenians. The latter replied as follows:—

"It was at the end of May when the Governor asked all the leaders and prominent Armenians to go to him. He told them that they were obliged to abandon the city to the enemy, consequently the army would retreat from the place. Therefore he instructed them to get ready and join him within twenty-four hours. They had to get ready, but as all means of transport had been requisitioned, they could take practically nothing with them. Before the twenty-four hours were up, they all gathered near the Government Building without knowing what was impending. Several hundred gendarmes surrounded them immediately and drove them out of the city towards the west. They were taken as far as Charuk-Dersim (Doujik). The Kurds of Dersim had already received their orders. They attacked them and killed every one. Another batch of Armenians was deported towards Sivas. They were seen passing through the Kamakh Pass, but what happened to them afterwards has never been known. A few hundred of their most beautiful girls were captured by certain Turks, and the Government was still looking for them."

59. BAIBOURT: NARRATIVE OF AN ARMENIAN LADY DEPORTED IN THE THIRD CONVOY; COMMUNICATED BY THE AMERICAN COMMITTEE FOR ARMENIAN AND SYRIAN RELIEF.

A week before anything was done to Baibourt, the villages all round had been emptied and their inhabitants had become victims of the gendarmes and marauding bands. Three days before the starting of the Armenians from Baibourt, after a week's imprisonment, Bishop Anania Hazarabedian was hanged, with seven other notables. After these hangings, seven or eight other notables were killed in their own houses for refusing to leave the city. Seventy or eighty other Armenians, after being beaten in prison, were taken to the woods and killed. The Armenian population of Baibourt was sent off in three batches; I was among the third batch. My husband died eight years ago, leaving me and my eight-year-old daughter and my mother a large property, so that we were living in comfort. Since mobilization began, the Ottoman Commandant has been living in my house free of rent. He told me not to go, but I felt I must share the fate of my people. I took three horses with me, loaded with provisions. My daughter had some five-lira pieces round her neck, and I carried some twenty liras and four diamond rings on my person. All else that we had was left behind. Our party left on the 1st/ 14th June, fifteen gendarmes going with us. The party numbered four or five hundred[69] persons. We had got only two hours away from home when bands of villagers and brigands in large numbers, with rifles, guns, axes, etc., surrounded us on the road, and robbed us of all we had. The gendarmes took my three horses and sold them to Turkish mouhadjirs, pocketing the money. They took my money and the gold pieces from my daughter's neck, also all our food. After this they separated the men, one by one, and shot them all within six or seven days—every male above fifteen years old. By my side were killed two priests, one of them over ninety years of age. The brigands took all the good-looking women and carried them off on their horses. Very many women and girls were thus carried off to the mountains, among them my sister, whose one-year-old baby they threw away; a Turk picked it up and carried it off, I know not where. My mother walked till she could walk no farther, and dropped by the roadside on a mountain top. We found on the road many of those who had been deported from Baibourt in the previous convoys; some women were among the killed, with their husbands and sons. We also came across some old people and little infants still alive but in a pitiful condition, having shouted their voices away. We were not allowed to sleep at night in the villages, but lay down outside. Under cover of the night indescribable deeds were committed by the gendarmes, brigands and villagers. Many of us died from hunger and strokes of apoplexy. Others were left by the roadside, too feeble to go on.

One morning we saw fifty or sixty wagons with about thirty Turkish widows, whose husbands had been killed in the war; and these were going to Constantinople. One of these women made a sign to one of the gendarmes to kill a certain Armenian whom she pointed out. The gendarmes asked her if she did not wish to kill him herself, at which she said "Why not?" and, drawing a revolver from her pocket, shot him dead. Every one of these Turkish hanoums had five or six Armenian girls of ten or under with her. Boys the Turks never wished to take; they killed them all, of whatever age. These women wanted to take my daughter, too, but she would not be separated from me. Finally we were both taken into their wagons on our promising to become Moslems. As soon as we entered the araba, they began to teach us how to be Moslems, and changed our names, calling me X. and her Y.

The worst and most unimaginable horrors were reserved for us at the banks of the Euphrates[70] and in the Erzindjan plain. The mutilated bodies of women, girls and little children made everybody shudder. The brigands were doing all sorts of awful deeds to the women and girls that were with us, whose cries went up to heaven. At the Euphrates, the brigands and gendarmes threw into the river all the remaining children under fifteen years old. Those that could swim were shot down as they struggled in the water.

After seven days we reached Erzindjan. Not an Armenian was left alive there. The Turkish women took my daughter and me to the bath, and there showed us many other women and girls that had accepted Islam. Between there and Enderessi, the fields and hillsides were dotted with swollen and blackened corpses that filled and fouled the air with their stench. On this road we met six women wearing the feradjé[71] and with children in their arms. But when the gendarmes lifted their veils, they found that they were men in disguise, so they shot them. After thirty-two days' journey we reached our destination.

---

69. "4000-5000"—Doc. 2

70. *i.e.*, the Kara Su.

71. Moslem veil.

60. BAIBOURT: STATEMENT, REPRODUCED FROM THE ARMENIAN JOURNAL "HORIZON," OF TIFLIS, IN THE ARMENIAN JOURNAL "GOTCHNAG" OF NEW YORK, 18th MARCH, 1916.

On the 15th May, some of the prominent Armenians of Baibourt—north-west of Erzeroum—Hadji Simon, Hamazasb, Arshag and Drtad Simavonian, Hagop Aghparian, Vagharshag Lousigian, Garabed Sarafian, Garabed Duldulian, and the Bishop were arrested. They were then taken to a place called "Ourbadji Oghlou Déré" and killed. When the Armenians heard of this they were terrified, but the Government declared that these were traitors, that they had sent money to the enemy and tried to persuade the people to revolt—that consequently they were punished, but that nothing would happen to the other Armenians. They were, in fact, really left in peace for some time, but after the retreat from Van Turkish soldiers came and disarmed them. They were then deported and massacred.

Forty armed young men from the village of Lsounk and 20 from Varvan escaped to the mountains. They were pursued by regular soldiers and forced to fight. Both sides lost heavily, and finally 12 of the Armenians, by the help of Greek villagers, reached Caucasia.

61. BAIBOURT, KEGHI, AND ERZINDJAN: LETTER[72], DATED ERZEROUM, 25th MAY/7th JUNE, 1915; COMMUNICATED BY THE AMERICAN COMMITTEE FOR ARMENIAN AND SYRIAN RELIEF.

The districts of Erzindjan, Keghi, and Baibourt have been devastated by forced emigrations. The Armenian population of the city of Erzeroum has also received categoric orders to leave the city. They will be deported *en masse*; 160 merchants are already *en route* with their families. The Government has confiscated their goods. We have no information about the deported people; they say they will be sent to Mosul.

---

72. Name of author withheld

62. ERZINDJAN: STATEMENT BY TWO RED CROSS NURSES OF DANISH NATIONALITY, FORMERLY IN THE SERVICE OF THE GERMAN MILITARY MISSION AT ERZEROUM[73]; COMMUNICATED BY A SWISS GENTLEMAN OF GENEVA.

In March, 1915, we learnt through an Armenian doctor, who died later on of typhus, that the Turkish Government was preparing for a massacre on a grand scale. He begged us to find out from General Passelt whether the rumour were true. We heard afterwards that the General (a gallant officer) had his own fears of it, and asked, for that reason, to be relieved of his post.... We fell sick of typhus and ... in consequence of a number of changes in the hospital staff ... we were obliged to leave Erzeroum. Through the good offices of the German Consul at Erzeroum, who also possessed the confidence of the Armenians, we were engaged by the Red Cross at Erzindjan, and worked there seven weeks.

At the beginning of June, the head of the Red Cross Mission at Erzindjan, Staff-Surgeon A., told us that the Armenians had revolted at Van, that measures had been taken against them which would be put into general execution, and that the whole Armenian population of Erzindjan and the neighbourhood would be transported to Mesopotamia, where it would no longer find itself in a majority. There was, however, to be no massacre, and measures were to be taken to feed the exiles and to secure their personal safety by a military escort. Wagons loaded with arms and bombs were reported, he said, to have been discovered at Erzindjan, and many arrests were to be made. The Red Cross staff were forbidden to have any relations with the exiles, and prohibited any excursions on foot or horseback beyond a certain radius.

After that, several days' grace was given to the population of Erzindjan for the sale of their property, which was naturally realised at ludicrous prices. In the first week of June,[74] the first convoy started; the rich people were allowed to hire carriages. They were to go to Harpout. The three succeeding days, further deportations followed[75]; many children were taken charge of by Moslem families; later on, the authorities decided that these children must go into exile as well.

The families of the Armenians employed in our hospital had to go with the rest, including a woman who was ill. A protest from Dr. Neukirch, who was attending her, had no effect except to postpone her departure two days. A soldier attached to our staff as cobbler said to Sister B.[76]: "I am now forty-six years old, and yet I am taken for military service, although I have paid my exemption-tax regularly every year. I have never done anything against the Government, and now they are taking from me my whole family, my seventy-year-old mother, my wife and five children, and I do not know where they are going." He was especially affected by the thought of his little daughter, a year and a half old; "She is so sweet. She has such pretty eyes"; he wept like a child. The next day he came back; "I know the truth. They are all dead." And it was only too true. Our Turkish cook came to us crying, and told us how the Kurds had attacked the unhappy convoy at Kamakh Boghaz[77], had pillaged it completely, and had killed a great number of the exiles. This must have been the 14th June.

Two young Armenian teachers, educated at the College of Harpout, whose lives were spared, related that the convoy had been caught under a cross-fire by the Kurds on the flanks and the Turkish irregulars in the rear. They had thrown themselves flat on the ground and pretended to be dead; afterwards they succeeded in finding their way back to Erzindjan by circuitous paths, bribing some Kurds whom they met on the way. One of them had with her her fiancé in woman's clothes. He had been shielded by a Turkish class-mate. When they reached Erzindjan a gendarme tried to abduct the girl and her fiancé interfered. He was killed, and the girls were carried off to Turkish houses, where they were treated kindly but had pressure put upon them to change their religion. They conveyed this news to us through a young doctor who attended some Armenian patients in our hospital, and was thereby enabled to get into touch with us; he brought us an appeal from them to take them with us to Harpout. If only they had poison, they said, they would poison themselves. They had no information whatever as to the fate of their companions.

The day after,[78] Friday, the 11th June, a party of regular troops (belonging to the 86th Cavalry Brigade) were sent out "to keep the Kurds in order."

We heard subsequently from these soldiers how the defenceless Armenians had been massacred to the last one. The butchery had taken four hours. The women threw themselves on their knees, they had thrown their children into the Euphrates, and so on.[79] "It was horrible," said a nice-looking young soldier; "I could not fire, I only pretended." For that matter, we have often heard Turks express their disapproval and their pity. The soldiers told us that there were ox-carts all ready to carry the corpses to the river and remove every trace of the massacre.[80]

Next day there was a regular *battue* through the cornfields. (The corn was then standing, and many Armenians had hidden in it.)

From that time on, convoys of exiles were continually arriving, all on their way to the slaughter; we have no doubt about their fate, after the unanimous testimony which we have received from many different quarters. Later, our Greek driver told us that the victims had their hands tied behind their backs, and were thrown down from the cliffs into the river. This method was employed when the numbers were too great to dispose of them in any other fashion. It was also easier work for the murderers. Sister B. and I, of course, began at once to think what we could do, and we decided to travel with one of these convoys to Harpout. We did not know yet that the massacre on the road had been ordered by the Government, and we also thought that we could check the brutality of the gendarmes and stave off the assaults of the Kurds, since we speak Kurdish and have some influence over the tribesmen.

We then telegraphed to the Consul at Erzeroum, telling him that we had been dismissed from the hospital, and urging him, in the interests of Germany, to come to Erzindjan. He wired back: "Impossible to leave my post. Expect Austrians, who are due to pass here the 22nd June...."

On the evening of the 17th June, we went out for a walk with Mr. C., the druggist of the Red Cross Staff. He was as much horrified as we were at the cruelties that were being perpetrated, and expressed himself very plainly on the subject. He also received his dismissal. On our walk we met a gendarme, who told us that, ten minutes' distance away, a large convoy of exiles from Baibourt had been halted. He narrated to us, with appalling vividness, how one by one the men had been massacred and cast into the depths of the gorge[81]: "Kezzé, kezzé, geliorlar! (Kill, kill, push them over)." He told how, at each village, the women had been violated; how he himself had desired to take a girl, but had been told that already she was no longer a maid; how children had had their brains battered out when they cried or hindered the march. "There were the naked bodies of three girls; I buried them to do a good deed," was his concluding remark.

The following morning, at a very early hour, we heard the procession of exiles passing in front of our house, along the high road leading in to Erzindjan. We followed them and kept up with them as far as the town, about an hour's walk. Mr. G. came with us. It was a very large gang—only two or three of them men, all the rest women and children. Many of the women looked demented. They cried out: "Spare us, we will become Moslems or Germans or whatever you will; only spare us. We are being taken to Kamakh Boghaz to have our throats cut," and they made an expressive gesture. Others kept silence, and marched patiently on with a few bundles on their backs and their children in their arms. Others begged us to save their children. Many Turks arrived on the scene to carry off children and girls, with or without their parents' consent. There was no time for reflection, for the crowd was being moved on continually by the mounted gendarmes brandishing their whips. On the outskirts of the town, the road to Kamakh Boghaz branches off from the main highway. At this point the scene turned into a regular slave market; for our part, we took a family of six children, from three to fourteen years old, who clutched hold of us, and another little girl as well. We entrusted the latter to our Turkish cook, who was on the spot. She wanted to take the child to the kitchen of Dr. A.'s private house, and keep her there until we could come to fetch her; but the doctor's adjutant, Riza Bey, gave the woman a beating and threw the child out into the street. Meanwhile, with cries of agony, the gang of sufferers continued its march, while we returned to the hospital with our six children. Dr. A. gave us permission to keep them in our room until we had packed our belongings; they were given food and soon became calmer. "Now we are saved," they had cried when we took them. They refused to let go of our hands. The smallest, the son of a rich citizen of Baibourt, lay huddled up in his mother's cloak; his face was swollen with crying and he seemed inconsolable. Once he rushed to the window and pointed to a gendarme: "That's the man who killed my father." The children handed over to us their money, 475 piastres (about £4), which their parents had given them with the idea that perhaps the children, at any rate, would not be shot.

We then rode into the town to obtain permission for these children to travel with us. We were told that the high authorities were in session to decide the fate of the convoy which had just arrived. Nevertheless, Sister B. succeeded in getting word with someone she knew, who gave her the authorisation to take the children with her, and offered to give them false names in the passport. This satisfied us, and, after returning to the hospital, we left the same evening with baggage and children and all, and installed ourselves in a hotel at Erzindjan. The Turkish orderlies at the hospital were very friendly, and said: "You have done a good deed in taking these children." We could get nothing but one small room for the eight of us. During the night there was a frightful knocking at our door, and we were asked whether there were two German ladies in the room. Then all became quiet again, to the great relief of our little ones. Their first question had been, would we prevent them from being made Mohammedans? And was our cross (the nurses' Red Cross) the same as theirs? After that they were comforted. We left them in the room, and went ourselves to take our tea in the hotel café. We noticed that some discharged hospital patients of ours, who had always shown themselves full of gratitude towards us, behaved as if they no longer recognised us. The proprietor of the hotel began to hold forth, and everyone listened to what he was saying: "The death of these women and children has been decreed at Constantinople." The Hodja (Turkish priest) of our hospital came in, too, and said to us, among other things: "If God has no pity on them, why must you have pity? The Armenians have committed atrocities at Van. That happened because their religion is *ekzik* (inferior). The Moslems should not have followed their example, but should have carried out the massacre with greater humanity." We always gave the same answer—that they ought to discover the guilty and do justice upon them, but that the massacre of women and children was, and always will remain, a crime.

Then we went to the Mutessarif himself, with whom we had not succeeded in obtaining an interview before. The man looked like the devil incarnate, and his behaviour bore out his appearance. In a bellowing voice he shouted at us: "Women have no business to meddle with politics, but ought to respect the Government!" We told him that we should have acted in precisely the same way if the victims had been Mohammedans, and that politics had nothing to do with our conduct. He answered that we had been expelled from the hospital, and that we should get the same treatment from him; that he would not stand us, and that he would certainly not permit us to go to Harpout to fetch our belongings, but would send us to Sivas. Worst of all, he forbade us to take the children away, and at once sent a gendarme to carry them off from our room.

On our way back to the hotel we actually met them, but they were hurried past us so quickly that we had not even a chance to return them their money. Afterwards we asked Dr. Lindenberg to see that this money was restored to them; but, to find out where they were, he had to make enquiries of a Turkish officer, and just at the moment of our departure, when we had been told that they had already been killed, and when we had no longer any chance of making a further search for them, the aforementioned Riza Bey came and asked us for this money, on the ground that he wanted to return it to the children! We had already decided to spend it on relieving other Armenians.

At Erzindjan we were now looked askance at. They would no longer let us stay at the hotel, but took us to a deserted Armenian house. The whole of this extensive quarter of the town seemed dead. People came and went at will to loot the contents of the houses; in some of the houses families of Moslem refugees were already installed. We had now a roof over our heads, but no one would go to get us food. However, we managed to send a note to Dr. A., who kindly allowed us to return to the hospital. The following day, the Mutessarif sent a springless baggage cart, in which we were to do the seven days' journey to Sivas. We gave him to understand that we would not have this conveyance, and, upon the representations of Dr. A., they sent us a travelling carriage, with the threat to have us arrested if we did not start at once. This was on Monday, the 21st June, and we should have liked to wait for the Austrians, who were due to arrive on the Tuesday morning, and continue the journey in their company; but Dr. A. declared that he could no longer give us protection, and so we started out. Dr. Lindenberg did us the kindness of escorting us as far as Rifahia[82]. During the first days of our journey we saw five corpses. One was a woman's, and still had clothes on; the others were naked, one of them headless. There were two Turkish officers on the road with us who were really Armenians, as we were told by the gendarme attached to us. They preserved their incognito towards us, and maintained a very great reserve, but always took care not to get separated from us. On the fourth day they did not put in an appearance. When we enquired after them, we were given to understand that the less we concerned ourselves about them the better it would be for us. On the road, we broke our journey near a Greek village. A savage-looking man was standing by the roadside. He began to talk with us, and told us he was stationed there to kill all the Armenians that passed, and that he had already killed 250. He explained that they all deserved their fate, for they were all Anarchists—not Liberals or Socialists, but Anarchists. He told the gendarmes that he had received orders by telephone to kill our two travelling companions. So these two men with their Armenian drivers must have perished there. We could not restrain ourselves from arguing with this assassin, but when he went off our Greek driver warned us: "Don't say a word, if you do ..."—and he made the gesture of taking aim. The rumour had, in fact, got about that we were Armenians, which was as good as to say condemned to death.

One day we met a convoy of exiles, who had said good-bye to their prosperous villages and were at that moment on their way to Kamakh Boghaz. We had to draw up a long time by the roadside while they marched past. The scene will never be forgotten by either of us: a very small number of elderly men, a large number of women—vigorous figures with energetic features—a crowd of pretty children, some of them fair and blue-eyed, one little girl smiling at the strangeness of all she was seeing, but on all the other faces the solemnity of death. There was no noise; it was all quiet, and they marched along in an orderly way, the children generally riding on the oxcarts; and so they passed, some of them greeting us on the way—all these poor people, who are now standing at the throne of God, and whose cry goes up before Him. An old woman was made to get down from her donkey—she could no longer keep the saddle. Was she killed on the spot? Our hearts had become as cold as ice.

The gendarme attached to us told us then that he had escorted a convoy of 3,000 women and children to Mamahatoun (near Erzeroum) and Kamakh Boghaz. "Hep gildi, bildi," he said: "All gone, all dead." We asked him: "Why condemn them to this frightful torment; why not kill them in their villages?" Answer: "It is best as it is. They ought to be made to suffer; and, besides, there would be no place left for us Moslems with all these corpses about. They will make a stench!"

We spent a night at Enderessi, one day's journey from Shabin Kara-Hissar. As usual, we had been given for our lodging an empty Armenian house. On the wall there was a pencil scrawl in Turkish: "Our dwelling is on the mountains, we have no longer any need of a roof to cover us; we have already drained the bitter cup of death, we have no more need of a judge."

The ground floor rooms of the house were still tenanted by the women and children. The gendarmes told us that they would be exiled next morning, but they did not know that yet; they did not know what had become of the men of the house; they were restless, but not yet desperate.

Just after I had gone to sleep, I was awakened by shots in our immediate neighbourhood. The reports followed one another rapidly, and I distinctly heard the words of command. I realised at once what was happening, and actually experienced a feeling of relief at the idea that these poor creatures were now beyond the reach of human cruelty.

Next morning our people told us that ten Armenians had been shot—that was the firing that we had heard—and that the Turkish civilians of the place were now being sent out to chase the fugitives. Indeed, we saw them starting off on horseback with guns. At the roadside were two armed men standing under a tree and dividing between them the clothes of a dead Armenian. We passed a place covered with clotted blood, though the corpses had been removed. It was the 250 roadmaking soldiers, of whom our gendarme had told us.

Once we met a large number of these labourers, who had so far been allowed to do their work in peace. They had been sorted into three gangs—Moslems, Greeks and Armenians. There were several officers with the latter. Our young Hassan exclaimed: "They are all going to be butchered." We continued our journey, and the road mounted a hill. Then our driver pointed with his whip towards the valley, and we saw that the Armenian gang was being made to stand out of the highroad. There were about 400 of them, and they were being made to line up on the edge of a slope. We know what happened after that.

Two days before we reached Sivas, we again saw the same sight. The soldiers' bayonets glittered in the sun.

At another place there were ten gendarmes shooting them down, while Turkish workmen were finishing off the victims with knives and stones. Here ten Armenians had succeeded in getting away.

Later on, in the Mission Hospital at Sivas, we came across one of the men who had escaped. He told us that about 100 Armenians had been slaughtered there. Our informant himself had received a terrible wound in the nape of the neck and had fainted. Afterwards he had recovered consciousness and had dragged himself in two days to Sivas.

Twelve hours' distance from Sivas, we spent the night in a government building. For hours a gendarme, sitting in front of our door, crooned to himself over and over gain: "Ermenleri hep kesdiler—the Armenians have all been killed!" In the next room they were talking on the telephone. We made out that they were giving instructions as to how the Armenians were to be arrested. They were talking chiefly about a certain Ohannes, whom they had not succeeded in finding yet.

One night we slept in an Armenian house where the women had just heard that the men of the family had been condemned to death. It was frightful to hear their cries of anguish. It was no use our trying to speak to them. "Cannot your Emperor help us?" they cried. The gendarme saw the despair on our faces, and said: "Their crying bothers you; I will forbid them to cry." However, he let himself be mollified. He had taken particular pleasure in pointing out to us all the horrors that we encountered, and he said to young Hassan: "First we kill the Armenians, then the Greeks, then the Kurds." He would certainly have been delighted to add: "And then the foreigners!" Our Greek driver was the victim of a still more ghastly joke: "Look, down there in the ditch; there are Greeks there too!"

At last we reached Sivas. We had to wait an hour in front of the Government Building before the examination of our papers was completed and we were given permission to go to the Americans. There, too, all was trouble and sorrow.

On the 1st July we left Sivas and reached Kaisaria on the 4th. We had been given permission to go to Talas, after depositing our baggage at the Jesuit School; but when we wanted to go on from Kaisaria, we were refused leave and taken back to the Jesuit School, where a gendarme was posted in front of our door. However, the American Missionaries succeeded in getting us set at liberty.

We then returned to Talas, where we passed several days full of commotion, for there, as well as at Kaisaria, there were many arrests being made. The poor Armenians never knew what the morrow would bring, and then came the terrifying news that all Armenians had been cleared out of Sivas. What happened there and in the villages of the surrounding districts will be reported by the American Mission.

When we discovered that they meant to keep us there—for they had prevented us from joining the Austrians for the journey—we telegraphed to the German Embassy, and so obtained permission to start. There is nothing to tell about this part of our journey, except that the locusts had in places destroyed all the fruit and vegetables, so that the Turks are already beginning to have some experience of the Divine punishment.

63. KAMAKH AND ERZEROUM: STATEMENT[83] PUBLISHED IN THE NEW YORK JOURNAL "GOTCHNAG," 4th SEPTEMBER, 1915.

The Armenian villages of the Kamakh district have been visited with the most ghastly horrors. The Turks began by perpetrating massacres, and subsequently deported the survivors to various places—the men in one direction and the women in another. The houses and property belonging to the Armenians have been taken possession of by the Turks and Kurds, who have come to this district as refugees from the Vilayet of Van.

The Armenian villages in the plain west of Erzeroum have all been cleared of their inhabitants. After all the men who were physically fit had been mobilised, the remainder were deported. The Armenian houses are being handed over to Turkish immigrants. The Archimandrite Kevork Tourian, Metropolitan of the Armenians of Trebizond, has been brought to Erzeroum, where he will be tried by court-martial.

---

73. They were at work in the German hospital at Erzeroum from October, 1914, to April, 1915.—EDITOR.

74. 7th June—*Allgemeine Missions-Zeitschrift*, November, 1915.

75. Amounting to about 20,000-25,000 people in all—*Allgemeine Missions-Zeitschrift*, November, 1915.

76. One of the two authors of the present statement, which has been drafted in the first person by the other witness, but represents the experiences of both. The Editor is in possession of the drafter's name, but does not know the identity of Sister B., Dr. A., or Mr. G.—EDITOR.

77. A defile, 12 hours' journey from Erzindjan, where the Euphrates flows through a narrow gorge between two walls of rock.

78. *i.e.*, after the departure of the last convoy of exiles from Erzindjan (10th June), *not* after the narrators were informed of the massacre by their cook and by the two Armenian girls. The passages about the cobbler, the cook, and the two girls are evidently in parenthesis, and interrupt the sequence of the narrative.—EDITOR.

79. The further details are given in the *Allgemeine Missions-Zeitschrift*, November, 1915: "When we exclaimed in horror: 'So you fire on women and children!' the soldiers answered: 'What could we do? It was our orders.' One of them added: 'It was a heart-breaking sight. For that matter, I did not shoot.'"—EDITOR.

80. On the evening of the 11th, we saw soldiers returning to town laden with loot. We heard from both Turks and Armenians that children's corpses were strewn along the road.

81. Every day ten or twelve of the men had been killed and thrown into the ravines.—*Allgemeine Missions-Zeitschrift*.

82. This was not the route followed by the convoys of exiles.

83. Source unspecified.

VII.
VILAYET OF MAMOURET-UL-AZIZ.

This province lies south-west of Erzindjan, where the Kara-Su bends from west to south and effects its junction with the Mourad-Su, to form the united stream of the Euphrates. The remnant of the convoys from the Vilayet of Erzeroum passed through this district on their way to Mesopotamia, and the Armenian inhabitants of Mamouret-ul-Aziz itself were sent after them in the first weeks of July.

The great advance of the Russians in the winter of 1915-6 brought this province within the immediate war zone, and apparently provoked a second outburst of persecution. On the 24th February, 1916, the Paris journal "Le Temps" published the following telegram from Rome: "According to information that has reached the Vatican, the Turks have carried fire and sword through the region of Mamouret-ul-Aziz, killing all the Christians, including the Catholic Armenian Bishop, Mgr. Ivraklon, who was subjected to prolonged and fearful tortures."

The name of the town to which most of the documents in this section relate is, for obvious reasons, withheld.

64. H.: STATEMENT MADE BY MISS DA., A DANISH LADY IN THE SERVICE OF THE GERMAN RED CROSS AT H., TO MR. DB. AT BASLE, AND COMMUNICATED BY MR. DB. TO LORD BRYCE.

Sister DA. left the German Red Cross Mission at H. in April, 1916, travelling through Ourfa to Aleppo, and thence by road and railway across Anatolia to Constantinople. Mr. DB. met her at Basle, on her way from Constantinople to Denmark, in the house of a mutual friend.

Sister DA. told Mr. DB. that on the 16th March, 1915, the German Vice-Consul appointed provisionally to Erzeroum (the Consul himself being interned in Russia) was passing through the town of H., accompanied by two German officers, and arranged to dine that evening with the German Red Cross Staff, after paying his respects to the Vali. At the hour fixed, only the two officers appeared. They said that they had called, with the Vice-Consul, upon the Vali, but that after a time the Vali had shewn signs of being irked by their presence, and so they had taken their departure, leaving the Vali and the Vice-Consul together. The company waited for the Vice-Consul about two hours. He arrived about 9.30 p.m., in a state of great agitation, and told them at once the purport of his interview. The Vali had declared to him that the Armenians in Turkey must be, and were going to be, exterminated. They had grown, he said, in wealth and numbers until they had become a menace to the ruling Turkish race; extermination was the only remedy. The Vice-

Consul had expostulated and represented that persecution always increased the spiritual vitality of a subject race, and on grounds of expediency was the worst policy for the rulers. "Well, we shall see," said the Vali, and closed the conversation.

This incident occurred on the 16th March, 1915, and Mr. DB. points out that it must have been practically simultaneous with an interview given by Enver Pasha at Constantinople to the Gregorian Bishop of Konia in the course of February, 1915, Old Style. In this interview the Bishop had asked Enver whether he were satisfied with the conduct of the Armenian soldiers in the Ottoman Army, and Enver had testified warmly to their energy, courage and loyalty—so warmly, in fact, that the Bishop at once asked whether he might publish this testimonial over Enver's name. Enver readily consented, and the Gregorian Patriarchate at Constantinople accordingly circulated an authorised account of the interview to the Armenian, and even to the Turkish, press.[84] Thus, in the latter part of February, 1915, the Central Government at Constantinople was advertising its friendly feelings towards its Armenian subjects, while by the 16th March, less than a month later, it had given its representative in a remote province to understand that a general massacre of these same Armenians was imminent.

To return to Sister DA.'s narrative—she told Mr. DB. that between February and the beginning of May, 1915, about 400 Armenians had been arrested and imprisoned at H. They were the young men, the strong in body and the intellectuals. Most of their kind had been taken for the Army in the mobilisation of the previous autumn, but these 400 had been left, and were now thrown into prison instead of being conscripted.

At the beginning of May, the Vali of H. sent for the head of the German Protestant Mission Station in the town, and requested him to tell the Armenians that they must surrender their arms. Otherwise, he said, the most stringent measures would be taken against them. The missionaries must persuade them to deliver up the arms quickly. The head of the Mission Station called a meeting of Armenian notables, and put to them what the Vali had said. The Armenians decided to consult with their Turkish fellow-townsmen, and so a mixed meeting was held of all the Turkish and Armenian notables of H. At this meeting the Turkish notables urged the Armenians to give up their arms and promised that, if they did so, they themselves would guarantee their security, and would see that they suffered nothing at the Government's hands.

This promise induced the Armenians to comply. They collected their arms and presented them to the Vali, but the Vali declared that all had not been brought. The newest and most dangerous weapons, he said, had been in the hands of the 400 prisoners. These must be surrendered also, or the penalties he had threatened would still be inflicted on the whole Armenian community at H. So the notables went to the men in prison, and besought them to reveal where their arms were hidden; all the Gregorian priests went, and the head of the German Mission Station went with them. The 400 were obstinate at first, but it was represented to them that, if they refused, they would be responsible for the destruction of the whole community, and at last they gave in. They revealed the hiding-places, and the arms were duly found and delivered up to the Vali.

The Vali immediately had photographs taken of all the arms collected, and sent them to Constantinople as evidence that an Armenian revolution was on the point of breaking out at H. He asked for a free hand to suppress it, and an order came back from Constantinople that he was to take whatever measures he considered necessary on the spot.

After that, the 400 young men were conveyed out of the town by night and never heard of again. Shots were said to have been heard in the distance.

Three days later, the rest of the Armenian community at H. was summoned by bugle to assemble before the Government Building, and then deported. The men were first sent off in one direction, and later the women and children, on ox-carts, in another. They were only given a few hours to make their preparations, and Sister DA. described their consternation as being terrible. They tried to dispose of their property, which the Turks bought up for practically nothing. Sewing-machines, for instance, sold for two or three piastres (4*d.* to 6*d.*). The process of deportation was extended to the whole Vilayet.

The Armenian children in the German Orphanage at H. were sent away with the rest. "My orders," said the Vali, "are to deport *all* Armenians. I cannot make an exception of these." He announced, however, that a Government Orphanage was to be established for any children that remained, and shortly afterwards he called on Sister DA. and asked her to come and visit it. Sister DA. went with him, and found about 700 Armenian children in a good building. For every twelve or fifteen children there was one Armenian nurse, and they were well clothed and fed. "See what care the Government is taking of the Armenians," the Vali said, and she returned home surprised and pleased; but when she visited the Orphanage again several days later, there were only thirteen of the 700 children left—the rest had disappeared. They had been taken, she learnt, to a lake six hours' journey by road from the town and drowned. Three hundred fresh children were subsequently collected at the "Orphanage," and Sister DA. believed that they suffered the same fate as their predecessors. These victims were the residue of the Armenian children at H. The finest boys and prettiest girls had been picked out and carried off by the Turks and Kurds of the district, and it was the remainder, who had been left on the Government's hands, that were disposed of in this way.

As soon as the Armenians had been deported from H., convoys of other exiles began to pass through from the districts further north. Sister DA. did not see these convoys, because they made a detour round the town, and she never left the town precincts; but she talked with many people who did see them, and they gave a terrible description of their plight. The roads near the town, they said, were littered with the corpses of those who had died of sickness or exhaustion, or from the violence of their guards. And these accounts were confirmed by her own experience last April (1916), on her journey to Aleppo. On the road to Aleppo from Ourfa she passed numbers of corpses lightly buried under a layer of soil. The extremities of the limbs were protruding, and had been gnawed by dogs. She was told by people she met that unheard-of atrocities had been committed, and that there were cases of women who had drowned themselves to escape their tormentors.

It was Sister DA.'s impression that the deportation and massacre of the Armenians had ruined Turkey economically. The Armenians had been the only skilled workers in the country, and industry came to a standstill when they were gone. You could not replace copper vessels for your household; you could not get your roof re-tiled. The Government had actually retained a few Armenian artisans—bakers, masons, &c.—to work for the Army, and whatever work was still done was done by these and by a few others who had gone over to Islam. But though the sources of production were cut off, the Turks had not begun to feel the pinch. Having laid hands on all the property of the Armenians, they were richer, for the moment, than before. During the past year bread had been plentiful and cheap, cattle and meat had been abundant, and there were still enough supplies, she thought, to last for some time yet. Under these circumstances, the Turkish peasantry were well content—except for the women, who resented the absence of their husbands at the war. The dearth of men, Sister DA. said, was everywhere noticeable. She had been told, however, that some Kurdish tribes had refused to furnish recruits, and that the Kizil Bashis of the Dersim had furnished none at all. The Government had been preparing an expedition against the Kizil Bashis to extort a toll of conscripts, but the plan had been thwarted by the Russian advance. In the Turkish villages agricultural work was being largely carried on by the Armenian women and children, who had been handed over to the Moslem peasants by the authorities. Sister DA. saw quantities of them everywhere, practically in the condition of slaves. They were never allowed to rest in peace, but were constantly chivied about from one village to another.

As she came down to Aleppo she found the country under good cultivation. Great stores of bread had been accumulated for the army in Mesopotamia.

In Anatolia, on the other hand, the fields were neglected, and she thought that there famine was not far off. But it was not till she reached Constantinople that she found any present scarcity. In the provinces only sugar and petrol had been scarce; at Constantinople all commodities were both scarce and dear.

Sister DA. was told at Constantinople that Turks of all parties were united in their approval of what was being done to the Armenians, and that Enver Pasha openly boasted of it as his personal achievement. Talaat Bey, too, was reported to have remarked, on receiving the news of Vartkes'[85] assassination: "There is no room in the Empire for both Armenians and Turks. Either they had to go or we."

---

84. This incident was communicated to Mr. DB. by DC. Effendi, a gentleman who had held high office under the Ottoman Government till the outbreak of the War.

85. Mr. Vartkes was an Armenian deputy in the Ottoman Parliament, who was murdered, together with another deputy, Mr. Zohrab, when he was being escorted by gendarmes from Aleppo to be court-martialled at Diyarbekir (see Docs. 7 and 9).—EDITOR.

65. H.: REPORT, DATED 11th JULY, 1915, FROM A FOREIGN RESIDENT AT H.; COMMUNICATED BY THE AMERICAN COMMITTEE FOR ARMENIAN AND SYRIAN RELIEF.

If it were simply a matter of being obliged to leave here to go somewhere else, it would not be so bad, but everybody knows that it is a case of going to one's death. If there was any doubt about it, it has been removed by the arrival of a number of convoys, aggregating several thousand people, from Erzeroum and Erzindjan. I have visited their encampment a number of times, and talked with some of the people. A more pitiable sight cannot be imagined. They are, almost without exception, ragged, filthy, hungry and sick. That is not surprising, in view of the fact that they have been on the road for nearly two months, with no change of clothing, no chance to wash, no shelter and little to eat. The Government has been giving them some scanty rations here. I watched them one time when their food was brought. Wild animals could not be worse. They rushed upon the guards who carried the food, and the guards beat them back with clubs, hitting hard enough to kill them sometimes. To watch them, one could hardly believe that these people were human beings.

As one walks through the camp, mothers offer their children and beg one to take them. In fact, the Turks have been taking their choice of these children and girls for slaves, or worse. In fact, they have even had their doctors there to examine the more likely girls and thus secure the best ones.

There are very few men among them, as most of them have been killed on the road. All tell the same story of having been attacked and robbed by the Kurds. Most of them were attacked over and over again, and a great many of them, especially the men, were killed. Women and children were also killed. Many died, of course, from sickness and exhaustion on the way, and there have been deaths each day that they have been here. Several different parties have arrived, and, after remaining a day or two, have been pushed on with no apparent destination. Those who have reached here are only a small portion, however, of those who started. By continuing to drive these people on in this way, it will be possible to dispose of all of them in a comparatively short time. Among those with whom I have talked were three sisters. They had been educated at —— and spoke excellent English. They said their family was the richest in Erzeroum and numbered twenty-five when they left; but there were now only fourteen survivors. The other eleven, including the husband of one of them and their old grandmother, had been butchered before their eyes by the Kurds. The oldest male survivor of the family was eight years of age. When they left Erzeroum, they had money, horses and personal effects, but they had been robbed of everything, including even their clothing. They said that some of them had been left absolutely naked, and others with only a single garment. When they reached a village, their gendarmes obtained clothes for them from some of the native women. Another girl with whom I talked is the daughter of the Protestant pastor of Erzeroum. She said that every member of her family with her had been killed and that she was left entirely alone. These and some others are a few survivors of the better class of people who have been exiled. They are being detained in an abandoned school-house just outside the town, and no one is allowed to enter it. They said that they were practically in prison, although they were allowed to visit a spring just outside the building. It was there I happened to see them. All the others are camped in a large open field, with no protection at all from the sun.

The condition of these people indicates clearly the fate of those who have left and are about to leave from here. I believe nothing has been heard from any of them as yet, and probably very little will be heard. The system that is being followed seems to be to have bands of Kurds awaiting them on the road, to kill the men especially, and, incidentally, some of the others. The entire movement seems to be the most thoroughly organised and effective massacre this country has ever seen.

Not many men have been spared, however, to accompany those who are being sent into exile, for a more prompt and sure method has been used to dispose of them. Several thousand Armenian men have been arrested during the past few weeks. These have been put in prison, and each time that several hundred had been gathered up in that way they were sent away during the night. The first batch were sent away during the night of the 23rd June. Among them were some of the professors in the College and other prominent Armenians, including the Prelate of the Armenian Gregorian Church. There have been frequent rumours that all of these were killed, and there is little doubt that they were. All Armenian soldiers have likewise been sent away in the same manner. They have been arrested and confined in a building at one end of the town. No distinction has been made between those who had paid their military exemption-tax and those who had not. Their money was accepted, and then they were arrested and sent off with the others. It was said that they were to go somewhere to work on the roads, but no one had heard from them, and that is undoubtedly false.

The fate of all the others has been pretty well established by reliable reports of a similar occurrence on Wednesday, the 7th July. On the Monday many men were arrested, both at H. and G., and put in prison. At daybreak on the Tuesday morning they were taken out and made to march towards an almost uninhabited mountain. There were about eight hundred in all, and they were roped together in groups of fourteen each. That afternoon they arrived in a small Kurdish village, where they were kept overnight in the mosque and other buildings. During all this time they were without food or water. All their money and much of their clothing had been taken from them. On the Wednesday morning they were taken to a valley a few hours distant, where they were all made to sit down. Then the gendarmes began shooting them, until they had killed nearly all of them. Some who had not been killed by bullets were then disposed of with knives and bayonets. A few succeeded in breaking the rope with which they were tied to their companions and running away, but most of these were pursued and killed. A few succeeded in getting away, probably not more than two or three. Among those who were killed was the treasurer of the College. Many other estimable men were among the number. No charge of any kind had ever been made against any of these men. They were simply arrested and killed as part of the general plan to dispose of the Armenian race.

Last night several hundred more men, including both men arrested by the civil authorities and those enrolled as soldiers, were taken in a different direction and murdered in a similar manner. It is said that this happened at a place not two hours distant from here. I shall ride out that way some day when things become a little quieter, and try to verify it for myself.

The same thing has been done systematically in the villages. A few weeks ago about three hundred men were gathered together at AT. and BG., two villages four and five hours distant from here, and then taken up into the mountains and massacred. This seems to be fully established. Many women from those villages have been here since and told about it. There have been rumours of similar occurrences in other places.

There seems to be a definite plan to dispose of all the Armenian men; but, after the departure of the families during the first few days of the enforcement of the order, it was announced that women and children with no men in the family might remain here for the present, and many hoped the worst was over. The American missionaries began considering plans to aid the women and children, who would be left here with no means of support. It was thought that perhaps an orphanage could be opened to care for some of the children, and especially those who had been born in America and then brought here by their parents, and also those who belonged to parents who had been connected in some way with the American mission and schools. There would be plenty of opportunity, although there might not be sufficient means, to care for children who reached here with the exiles from other vilayets, and whose parents had died on the way. I went to see the Vali about this matter yesterday, and was met with a flat refusal. He said we could aid these people if we wished to do so, but the Government was establishing orphanages for the children, and we could not undertake any work of that nature. An hour after I left the Vali, the announcement was made that all the Armenians remaining here, including women and children, must leave on the 13th July.

66. H.: MEMORANDUM[86] FORWARDED BY A FOREIGN RESIDENT AT H. (THE AUTHOR OF THE PRECEDING REPORT); COMMUNICATED BY THE AMERICAN COMMITTEE FOR ARMENIAN AND SYRIAN RELIEF.

On the 1st June[87], 3,000 people (mostly women, girls and children) left H., accompanied by seventy policemen and a certain Turk of influence, K. Bey. The next day they arrived at AL., safely. Here K. Bey took 400 liras from the people, "in order to keep it safe till their arrival at Malatia," and promised to accompany them, for their protection, as far as Ourfa; but that same day he ran away with all the money.

The third day the convoy of exiles reached AM. There the Arabs and Kurds began to carry off the women and girls, and this went on till they reached the first railway station at Ras-ul-Ain, on the Bagdad line. The policemen given to them for their protection incited the half-savage tribes of the mountains to attack them in order to rob, kill and violate their women or else carry them away, and they themselves many times violated the women openly.

The fourth day they arrived at AN., where the policemen killed three of the prominent men. The ninth day they came to AO., where the horses, hired and paid for in full for the journey as far as Malatia, were taken and sent back. So they had again to hire ox-carts to carry them to Malatia. Here many were left without any beast of burden, only a few being able to buy donkeys and mules, which were also stolen in their turn.

At AO., a policeman carried off Mrs. L. and her two daughters and ran away.

The thirteenth day the caravan was at Malatia, but for one hour only, for they returned to the village of AP., two hours from Malatia. Here the policemen deserted them altogether, after taking from them about 200 liras in toll for the protection they had given them that far, and the people were left to the mercy of the beastly Bey (claw-chief) of the Kurds of Aghja-Daghi.

On the fifteenth day they were again toiling on their way through the steep mountains, when the Kurds rounded up 150 of the men of all ages from fifteen to ninety years. They took them some distance off and butchered them; then they came back and began to rob the people.

That day another convoy of exiles (only 300 of whom were men) from Sivas[88], Egin and Tokat, joined the convoy from H., thus forming a bigger convoy of 18,000 people in all. They started again on the seventeenth day, under the so-called protection of another Kurdish Bey. This Bey called out his people, who attacked the convoy and plundered them. They carried off five of the prettiest girls and a few Sisters of Grace from Sivas. At night some more girls were stolen, but they were returned after being violated. So the journey began once more, and on the way the pretty girls were carried off one by one, while the stragglers from the convoy were invariably killed. On the twenty-fifth day they reached the village of Geulik, and all the villagers pursued the convoy for a long distance, tormenting and robbing the exiles. On the thirty-second day they found themselves at the village of Kiakhta. Here they remained two days, and again many girls and women were carried off.

On the fortieth day the convoy came in sight of the river Mourad, a branch of the Euphrates. Here they saw the bodies of more than 200 men floating in the river, with traces of blood and blood-stained fezes, clothes and stockings on the banks.

The chief of the neighbouring village took one lira in toll from each man, as a ransom for not being thrown into the river.

On the fifty-second day they arrived at another village, and here the Kurds took from them everything they had, even their shirts and drawers, so that for five days the whole convoy marched completely naked under the scorching sun. For another five days they did not have a morsel of bread, nor even a drop of water. They were scorched to death by thirst. Hundreds upon hundreds fell dead on the way, their tongues were turned to charcoal, and when, at the end of the five days, they reached a fountain, the whole convoy naturally rushed towards it. But here the policemen barred the way and forbade them to take a single drop of water. Their purpose was to sell it at from one to three liras the cup, and sometimes they actually withheld the water after getting the money. At another place, where there were wells, some women threw themselves into them, as there was no rope or pail to draw up the water. These women were drowned, and, in spite of that, the rest of the people drank from that well, the dead bodies still remaining there and stinking in the water. Sometimes, when the wells were shallow and the women could go down into them and come out again, the other people would rush to lick or suck their wet, dirty clothes, in the effort to quench their thirst.

When they passed an Arab village in their naked condition, the Arabs pitied them and gave them old pieces of clothes to cover themselves with. Some of the exiles who still had money bought some clothes; but some still remained who travelled thus naked all the way to the city of Aleppo. The poor women could hardly walk for shame; they walked all bent double.

Even in their nakedness they had found some means of preserving the little money they had. Some kept it in their hair, some in their mouths and some in their wombs; and when the robbers attacked them some were clever enough to search for money in those secret places, and that in a very beastly manner, of course.

On the sixtieth day, when they reached Viran Shehr, only 300 exiles remained out of all the 18,000. On the sixty-fourth day they gathered together all the men and the sick women and children and burned and killed them all. The remainder were ordered to continue on their way. In one day's journey they reached Ras-ul-Ain, where for two days, for the first time since they started, the Government gave them bread. The bread was uneatable, but for the three succeeding days they did not have even that.

Here a Circassian persuaded the wife of the Pastor of Sivas, as well as some other women, with their children, to go with him to the station, promising to send them to Aleppo by train. In spite of all the warnings of their friends, these women followed the man, as they and their children were no longer capable of finishing the journey on foot. The man took them in the opposite direction from the station, explaining that he would borrow money from his friend, near by, for the tickets; but after a short time he came back to where the convoy was halted. The women and their children were no more.

The governor of the place demanded three liras for himself and one lira for the railway ticket from each of them, before he would let them go by train.

On the seventieth day, when they reached Aleppo, 35 women and children were left out of the 3,000 exiles from H., and 150 women and children altogether out of the whole convoy of 18,000.

---

86. Name of author withheld.

87. July?—EDITOR.

88. See Doc. 78.

67. H.: NARRATIVE OF AN ARMENIAN REFUGEE FROM H.; COMMUNICATED TO LORD BRYCE BY THE CORRESPONDENT OF THE LONDON "TIMES" AT BUKAREST.

Much has been written in the Press about the Armenian massacres, and especially about the horrors of the wholesale deportations, by which the Armenians were forcibly removed from their native homes. At the same time no precise or concrete description has yet been given of the monstrous excesses of which the Armenian nation has been the victim. But a young Armenian, an eye-witness who escaped by a miracle from the atrocious butchery at H., has related to us in all their appalling detail the events that took place at this town. His narrative gives a clear idea of the enormity and the ignoble cruelty of the crime committed, not only at H., but in all the other provinces of Armenia. We can easily discern from these facts the criminal tactics of the Young Turkish Government.

"At H.," says this witness, "the deportation of the Armenians lasted three months. In June the most prominent members of the Dashnaktzoutioun Committee were arrested, including Messrs. DE., DE., DG., DH., and DJ., as well as various others. They were subjected to unheard-of tortures, to extract from them supposed secrets concerning the alleged project of an Armenian revolution. No result was obtained from this inquisition.

"The Armenian population was simple enough to believe that this harsh persecution was only directed against the members of the Dashnaktzoutioun Committee, and it therefore displayed no uneasiness on its own account. But shortly afterwards the arrests were extended in scope and began to assume formidable proportions. All the Armenian young men in the town were arrested and terrorised by infernal torments. About 13,000 Armenian soldiers, too, who were serving among the Ottoman troops at H., were stripped of their arms and transferred to the "Red Palace" at G. They were kept there under stringent guard, and hunger and thirst were left to do their work upon them. The friends and relations of the prisoners were rigorously debarred from any communication with them. A week later all the prisoners were brought out again and despatched to an unknown destination, under a strong escort of gendarmerie with fixed bayonets. They were told that they were going to be transported to Ourfa, to work on the roads and lines of communication, but when they reached BP. Han, near BQ. village, they were all shot and their corpses shovelled into a great trench, which had been specially prepared for them. The majority of the young Armenians who were treated in this way were pupils of the American College, the French College, and the Central Armenian School. Other prisoners were subsequently led away in the same direction in gangs of five and shot. Twenty of these unfortunates succeeded by a miracle in escaping, and have related the details of this awful butchery.

"Next came the turn of the imprisoned members of the Dashnaktzoutioun Committee; but they had guessed the fate that was awaiting them and offered a desperate resistance, which ended in their setting fire to the building in which they were confined, since they preferred being burnt alive to becoming the prey of Turkish barbarity. (There were from twenty-five to thirty of these Dashnakists, but the young refugee was ignorant of their names, with the exception of those which we have mentioned above.)

"In July all Armenian families of any standing in G. were compelled to emigrate. The arrests of the young men had been effected at night time, but the deportation of these wealthy families was carried out in full daylight.

"These exiles from G. were taken to the villages of AN. and AO. On their way they were overtaken by a gendarme riding post-haste with an order from the Vali, which directed the return of a score of individuals among the party. These individuals were taken a distance of twenty kilometres and then slaughtered without pity, like cattle, on the banks of a river and their corpses thrown into the water. As for the rest, the men were separated from the women and cruelly murdered by blows of the axe. The women and girls were carried off by the Kurds and Turks.

"This was followed by the general deportation. The people were deported in several convoys, and in different directions. These convoys were massacred openly and without discrimination, some below the hill of AU., others on the summit of BR. Hill and on Mount BS.

"A few men and women in the service of the Turkish and Kurdish beys were allowed to live until the end of the harvest. The compulsory emigration was even forced upon Armenians who had been converts to Islam since the massacres of 1895. These were deported in October.

"All the professors and schoolmasters were also imprisoned and subsequently assassinated, at the same time as the young men. Those, however, who were connected with German institutions were happily excepted.

"The American Consul did not see fit to intervene in favour of these unfortunates—not even when they were American citizens. We do not know the motive of this passive attitude of his.

"Out of a numerous convoy of exiles from Erzeroum and Erzindjan, nothing but a handful of women and children succeeded in reaching H., after abandoning on their way many of their number who could no longer bear up against the misery and starvation. Those who have reached H. are in an absolutely deplorable condition. They hardly look like human beings, and roam about the streets seeking for a morsel of dry bread, until they fall fainting from exhaustion and are picked up next day half dead by the municipal scavenger carts. These scenes are repeated daily.

"The massacre of the entire population of the Province of Sivas has been effected in the same fashion. Everywhere one passes corpses lying unburied in the open. On my journey I saw heart-rending incidents—women in their last agony lying on the ground with their sucklings, already dead, beside them.

"The Turkish and Kurdish villages are full of Armenian women and girls. Some of the villagers have taken possession of dozens of them. Eimen, the head of the 'German Oriental Mission,' remarks, as if that completely justified everything, that now the Armenians will realise for the future the serious consequences of conspiring against Germany and her Allies. A considerable number of Armenians from H. and the neighbourhood have taken refuge among the mountains of Dersim, where the native Kurdish mountaineers have offered them generous hospitality."

Another Armenian, who succeeded in escaping from Der-el-Zor, in Arabia, describes the miseries endured there by the Armenian women. They are not only suffering from the ravages of disease, but from the lawlessness of the Arabs, who come again and again to snatch victims for their bestial lust.

68. MAMOURET-UL-AZIZ: NARRATIVE OF AN ARMENIAN LADY DEPORTED FROM C. (A PLACE HALF-AN-HOUR'S DISTANCE FROM H.), DESCRIBING HER JOURNEY FROM C. TO RAS-UL-AIN; WRITTEN AFTER HER ESCAPE FROM TURKEY, AND DATED ALEXANDRIA, 2nd NOVEMBER, 1915;

PUBLISHED IN THE ARMENIAN JOURNAL "GOTCHNAG" OF NEW YORK. 8th JANUARY, 1916.

Shortly after last Easter (1915), the Turkish officials searched the Armenian churches and schools of G., H., C., AQ., AR., AS. and the surrounding villages, but without finding anything incriminating. Afterwards they took the keys of these buildings, and filled them with soldiers. They also searched private houses on the pretence of looking for arms and ammunition, but they did not find anything. After that the Town Crier announced that all arms were to be handed over to the Government, and by this means a number of arms were collected.

After that, they arrested from the town of C. the following persons: Professor B., Mr. H. and his brother J., Mr. O. and his son P., Mr. Q., the brothers R., the brothers S., and T. Effendi, as well as many others, old and young. They took them to the house of V. Agha, stripped them one by one and gave them 300 lashes on their backs. When they fainted, they threw them into a stable and waited until they had revived, in order to beat them again. The men who performed these cruel acts consisted of the following Turks: Commissary (Gendarme) W. Effendi the son of Commissary X., V. Agha, V.'s cousin Y., Z. Agha, Hadji CA. Bey the son of CB. Effendi, CD., and CE. the son of V. Agha. Among the Kurds implicated were the son of CF., CG., etc. The above-mentioned CF.'s son and another Kurd beat Mr. CH. until he was half dead.

After beating T. Effendi in H., and tearing out his finger nails and the flesh of his hands and feet, they put a rope under his arms, dragged him to C., and threw him into prison. Then they entered his house, and, on the pretence of searching it, made his wife, who was in indifferent health, lie on the ground; a soldier sat on her, and they began to beat her on her feet, asking her where they had hidden their arms. After a few days her husband died in the prison.

In C. they beat many young men to get their arms, so that they were obliged to buy arms from the Turks and give them to the Government[89].

When the Government was convinced that they had no more arms to surrender, they stopped tormenting them; but after a few days' interval they took the young men to G., imprisoned them there for a time, and then deported them in May. Meanwhile the women of C. went to the German missionary, Dr. U., at G. and begged him to defend them. Dr. U. came to C. and spoke in a church; he advised the Armenians to trust the Turks absolutely.

When I was in C. I heard that in H. they had beaten CI. Agha, who subsequently disappeared.

They plucked out the hair and nails of some of the professors. They dug out their eyes and branded them with red hot irons, so that some of them died immediately, and others first lost their reason and died thereafter.

The Bishop of H., CJ., and other prominent Armenians were imprisoned and suffered many cruelties.

On Friday, the 2nd July, they deported part of the Armenians of G. Their destination appeared to be Ourfa *via* Diyarbekir.

On Saturday, the 3rd July, they deported all Armenians domiciled in the houses belonging to CL. in A. Street, in the town of G. Again their destination was supposed to be Ourfa, but *via* Malatia in this case.

We ourselves were deported on the 4th July in the direction of Ourfa *via* Diyarbekir.

The Town Crier proclaimed that on the following Tuesday those from B. and C. Streets in the Town of H. would be deported, on Wednesday the Armenians from AQ., on Thursday those from AR., and so on.

CJ. and two hundred other Armenians were deported ten days before we were, that is on Wednesday, the 23rd June; we do not know their destination. Their party started at midnight. Some of them dropped cards asking for money, and at AT. money was conveyed to them. But the following Monday, the 28th June, when the Armenian women of AT. went to the river, they saw some Turkish women washing blood-stained clothes. The Armenian women took the clothes from the Turkish women and brought them to the Governor at G. The Governor on hearing this went to AT. and found that the Bishop and the 200 Armenians had been killed.

Up to the day we started, the Syrians had not yet been deported, and the women who had no husbands were also allowed to remain, but later on CK. Aghassi said that not a single Armenian would be left. After the Armenians were deported, the Government locked their houses and sealed them up. The men of CL.'s factory were also deported with their families. In C. some of the tradesmen were not deported, as, for example, CM. Agha the son of CN. Agha, the baker CO. and his family, and the two brothers, CP. and CQ. Aghas, the sons of Q. Agha. CQ. Agha became a Moslem, while the father was deported with the Bishop.

All the people of C. started the same day. I think we were about 600 families. We had with us all our cattle and all our property. The first night we reached AU. and slept that night in the fields. The next day we passed many corpses heaped together under bridges and on the road; their blood had collected in pools. Probably these were the Armenians that were killed with the Bishop, for the corpses were all those of men. We spent the night near AV. in a valley, and that night we had to drink water polluted with blood. We promised our guards money if they took us a better road and gave us clean water. The third day they again made us travel past corpses, and on Wednesday we reached A.

The same morning the gendarmes that were accompanying us, W. Effendi and the other Turkish effendis that were with him, put down their chairs in front of our han, and sat down. Then they turned to us and told us that they had received telegrams from H., and that instead of going to Ourfa some of us would go to Yermag and the rest to Severeg, so that our journey would thus be shortened. "Only it is necessary," they added, "that your men should come and register themselves at the han at A., and state which way they would like to go. Thank the Sultan, who has made your journey shorter." After these words they all clapped their hands and forced us to do the same. Our men, being simple-minded, were deceived, and they even left their hats and coats to go to the han in question. None of those that went returned. Then the rest of those above 16 years of age and all the old men were arrested and taken to the same place. After this the gendarmes beat the women and forced them to continue their journey. The women said: "We will not go unless our men go with us. You may kill us if you want to." But the Turkish officials told us that our men would follow us in a little while, and forced the women and children to march on, so they marched on crying and wailing. After half-an-hour's journey they made us sit in the fields, and all the Turkish officers returned to A. except one. The same day some Arab women (that is, Armenian gipsies) brought us bread, in spite of the officers' efforts to prevent them, and when they heard that we were crying because our men had been killed, they told us that they had seen them all passing by roped together. Again we went on under the hot burning sun, still crying. The sixth day they made us stop in a Kurdish village, where we spent the night. Next morning we saw that all the gendarmes that had returned to A. had now rejoined the convoy.

Then Gendarme W. Effendi and the other Turks with him beat us and forced us under threat of death to give them all our money and ornaments. They said that, if we did not give them up, they would violate us and exile us to different places. We were afraid, and gave them everything we had. Then they gave us back from five piastres (10d.) to one medjidia (3s. 2d.) each, at the same time stating that our money and everything else would be returned to us at Diyarbekir, and that they had only taken our jewellery and money for safety.

The ninth day, they took us to the top of a mountain, and the same Effendi and the other gendarmes searched us all over in a shameful manner; they took all the silk-stuffs and everything else of value in our clothes and bedding. Half-an-hour later we reached a Kurdish village. There I met a Turkish soldier from Malatia, called CR., whom I knew. He pitied me, and told me that it was all over with us. "I would advise you," he said, "to leave your company and look after yourself."

We were already within a short distance of Diyarbekir when two soldiers came from the Governor, to find out where we had been during the last nine days. Here the gendarmes that were with us took away all our cows and cattle; they also kidnapped one woman and two girls. Outside the walls of Diyarbekir, we had to sit in the burning sun for 24 hours. That same day a number of Turks came from the city and kidnapped our little girls. Towards evening again we went on, still crying; more Turks came to carry off our girls and young brides, and would not let us even open our mouths to protest. Then we left all our cattle and everything we had, to save our honour and our lives. It was already night when the Turks from Diyarbekir attacked us three times and carried off the girls and young brides who had fallen behind. After this we lost all sense of time. The next morning again the gendarmes searched us all over, and then made us march six hours. During these six hours we found no drinking water, and many women sank on the way from thirst and hunger. The third day after that they robbed us, and violated us near a place where there was water. Some days after, two Turks dressed in white coats followed us, and, every time they had a chance, carried off still more of our girls. The wife of CS. Effendi from C. had three daughters, one of whom was married. A coloured gendarme who was with us wanted to take these girls. The mother resisted, and was thrown over a bridge by one of the Turks. The poor woman broke her arm, but her mule-driver dragged her up again. Again the same Turks threw her down, with one of her daughters, from the top of the mountain. The moment the married daughter saw her mother and sister thrown down, she thrust the baby in her arms upon another woman, ran after them crying "Mother, mother!" and threw herself down the same precipice. Some said that one of the Turkish officers went down after them and finished them off. After that Mrs. CS.'s remaining daughter and I disguised ourselves, and, each taking a child in our arms, abandoned everything and walked to Mardin. There our party joined us again. We stayed there eight days. There was an artificial lake there, and every night they opened the sluices and flooded the ground, so that in the panic they might kidnap some of the girls. They also attacked us every night and kidnapped little children. At last, one evening, they drove us on again and left us among the mountains. They wounded a woman because she did not wish to give up her daughter. When they were going to carry off another girl, I asked CT. Tchaoush, a Mardin man, to help us. He stopped them at once, and did not let them take her away. He told us to stay there and not to start until further notice. The Kurds from the surrounding villages attacked us that night. CT. Tchaoush, who was in charge of us, immediately went up on to the heights and harangued them in Kurdish, telling them not to attack us. We were hungry and thirsty, and had no water to drink. CT. took some of our vessels and brought us water from a long way off. The wife of my brother-in-law, the tailor CU., had a baby born that night. The next morning we started again. CT. left some women with her and kept an eye on her from a distance. Then he put the mother and the new-born child on a beast, and brought her to us in safety. Again we marched six hours without water. Here a Turk kidnapped the son of the woman who had been thrown down the mountain side. Finally, in the last stages of hunger and exhaustion, we reached Viran Shehr. Many had already been left on the road.

We had nothing more to eat until we reached Ras-ul-Ain. A fourth part of our convoy had already perished of starvation. Just before reaching Ras-ul-Ain we marched through the whole of one night. We passed three wells choked with corpses up to the brim. The women that went before us encountered three wounded women who crawled out of these wells and asked for bread. These three women went on in our company towards Ras-ul-Ain. Two of them died on the way, and the third was sent to Der-el-Zor with the convoy. It was here that CV., the sister of CW., a girl about 18 or 19 years old, fell down because she could not walk any further. Her mother and sister-in-law kissed her, crying, and left her. We were forced to leave her by herself, because the soldiers would not let any one stay behind with her.

We did not see a single Armenian until we reached Ras-ul-Ain. There we found many deported Armenians who had come from Erzeroum, Egin, Keghi, and other places. They were all on their way to Der-el-Zor. At Ras-ul-Ain we suddenly met CX. Agha of H. He had come from Aleppo to help us. He wanted to save at least a few of the party and take them to Aleppo. He advised us to go to the house of CY. Bey, a Circassian, or to the house of his son-in-law, so that he might convey us into safety from there. At Ras-ul-Ain a great many of the Armenians found refuge in the houses of some Tchetchens (a tribe akin to the Circassians), but afterwards the Government removed them all from the Tchetchens' houses to deport them to Der-el-Zor. Only my batch, consisting of forty-one people, were left in the house of this CY. Bey, and we were safe here because the Bey and his friends were Government people. The first moment that we saw CX. Agha we thought we had seen an angel from Heaven, and cried to him: "CX. Agha, save us." When the Tchetchens heard his name, they discovered that he was an Armenian, and immediately attacked him. He was almost killed, but withstood them by his bravery and address; he told them that he had been sent there specially by the Government, and turning immediately to us, he gave us to understand that those who went to CY. Bey's house would be saved.

CX. Agha took the next train and returned to Aleppo. He tried every means to save us, and after fifteen days he came back. The Circassians (or

Tchetchens) endeavoured to force us to become Moslems, but we answered them: "We will throw ourselves into the water and die, but we will not become Moslems." The Tchetchens were surprised at these words, and said they had never seen people like this, so zealous for their honour and their religion and so devoted to each other. CX. Agha found this out and went to the chief of the Tchetchens; he bribed him, and then, with superb courage, conducted us to the railway one by one, the station being about two miles from where we were. It was Saturday evening when we reached Aleppo. Here for the first time we met some Armenian soldiers, who were almost crazy with joy when they saw us. We could hardly believe they were Armenians, until CX. Agha's father came after dark with some of these soldiers, carrying no lights, and took us to the Armenian Church. There they told us that if the Government should discover us and inquire how we came, we were to tell them that we had travelled at our own expense. They immediately brought us bread; we had not eaten anything for twenty-four hours. There were a number of deported Armenians in the Church; they came from different places and had been travelling for four months. They were so exhausted that about forty of them were dying every day. The priest who performed the ceremony could not drag himself home. From the deported Armenians in Aleppo we learned that the husbands of many of the women had been roped together and taken to Sheitan Deressi (Devil's Valley)[90], where they were slaughtered with axes and knives. Here we gave up all hope of seeing our husbands again, being convinced that they were all killed. We heard that in some places they made the Armenians dig their own graves before they killed them. An Armenian soldier from Tchemesh-Getzak told me that the Turks were killing the Armenians and throwing them into the Euphrates, when six of them managed to cross the river and get away, after three days' journey through country littered with corpses.

On Sunday morning I went to see the American Consul at Aleppo, and asked him to save me, as I was an American citizen. He asked me where my papers were. I told him they were taken from me on the way; I told him all the circumstances, and he promised to help me. I went to him again the next day and told him how my parents were American citizens, and my husband also, and how my husband had lived in America for 18 years; I told him he could prove it by asking the American Consul at H. or even the Washington Government. After five days had passed, he sent for me and made me tell my story in the Turkish language. He put my name in his book, and placed me in his kavass's house. Then he gave me a passport and sent me to Alexandretta in the company of some Russian subjects. We stayed fifteen days in Alexandretta. From there we reached Alexandria on board the American cruiser "Chester," on the 22nd September, 1915.

While I was in Ras-ul-Ain, we saw some Armenian girls in the houses of some Tchetchens. One of them was married to one of the Tchetchens. They begged us not to forget them if we were ever saved. J. Agha's wife and children reached Ras-ul-Ain. A Kurd came and said to them: "I am from the village of Karer; you come with me, and I will take you to Karer until the end of the war." They believed him, and went to his house. Afterwards CX. Agha tried to save them, but they had already gone. H. Agha's wife and three daughters went to Der-el-Zor.

The Turkish Government did not provide any food for us on the way; one day only, at Diyarbekir, they gave us one loaf each, and again for about eight days at Mardin, but the bread was so hard that it cut our mouths. The son of Prof. B., his married daughter, and his future daughter-in-law, as well as the wife and two daughters of Mr. CZ., reached Aleppo in safety. CC. Agha's daughter and his little boy were kidnapped by the Turks. Only two of the boys were left with the mother, who reached Aleppo safely. Besides the gendarmes, Kurdish irregulars also followed us on the way, to kill those that were left behind. The clothes of those who underwent this deportation were all rotted by the end of the journey, and the exiles themselves had almost lost their reason. When they were given new clothes they did not know how to put them on, and when their hair was washed it came off bodily from their scalps.

69. H.: STATEMENT BY THE PRINCIPAL OF THE COLLEGE, DATED 19th JULY, 1915; COMMUNICATED BY THE AMERICAN COMMITTEE FOR ARMENIAN AND SYRIAN RELIEF.

I shall try to banish from my mind for the time the sense of great personal sorrow at losing hundreds of my friends here, and also my sense of utter defeat in being so unable to stop the awful tragedy or even mitigate to any degree its severity, and compel myself to give you concisely some of the cold facts of the past months, as they relate themselves to the College. I do so with the hope that the possession of these concrete facts may help you to do something there for the handful of dependants still left to us here.

Buildings—Seven of our big buildings are in the hands of the Government, only one remaining in our hands. The seven buildings in question are empty, except for twenty guards who are stationed there. I cannot tell you exactly the amount of loss we have sustained in money by robberies, breakages and other means, and there is no sign that the Turks will ever return these buildings to us.

Constituency.—Approximately two-thirds of the girl pupils and six-sevenths of the boys have been taken away to death, exile or Moslem homes.

Professors.—Four gone, three left, as follows:—

Professor A.—Served College 35 years; representative of the Americans with the Government, Protestant "Askabed," Professor of Turkish and History. Besides previous trouble, arrested May 1st without charge; hair of head, moustache and beard pulled out, in vain effort to secure damaging confessions; starved and hung by arms for a day and a night, and severely beaten several times; taken out towards Diyarbekir about June 20th, and murdered in general massacre on the road.

Professor B.—Served College 33 years, studied at Ann Arbor, Professor of Mathematics. Arrested about June 5th, and shared Prof. A.'s fate on the road.

Professor C.—Taken to witness a man beaten almost to death; became mentally deranged; started with his family about July 5th into exile under guard, and murdered beyond Malatia. Principal of Preparatory Department; studied at Princeton; served College 20 years.

Professor D.—Served College 16 years, studied at Edinburgh; Professor of Mental and Moral Science. Arrested with Prof. A. and suffered same tortures; also had three finger nails pulled out by the roots; killed in same massacre.

Professor E.—Served College 25 years. Arrested May 1st; not tortured, but sick in prison; sent to Red Crescent Hospital, and after paying large bribes is now free.

Professor F.—Served College for over 15 years, studied in Stuttgart and Berlin, Professor of Music. Escaped arrest and torture, and thus far escaped exile and death, because of favour with the Kaimakam secured by personal services rendered.

Professor G.—Served College about 15 years, studied at Cornell and Yale (M.S.), Professor of Biology. Arrested about June 5th, beaten about the hands, body and head with a stick by the Kaimakam himself, who, when tired, called on all who loved religion and the nation to continue the beating; after a period of insensibility in a dark closet, taken to the Red Crescent Hospital with a broken finger and serious bruises. Now free.

Instructors, Male.—Four reported killed on the road in various massacres, whose average term of service is eight years.

Three not heard from, probably killed on the road; average term of service in the College, four years.

Two sick in the American Hospital.

One elsewhere.

One, engaged in cabinet work for the Kaimakam, free.

One, owner of house occupied by the Kaimakam, free.

Instructors, Female.—One reported killed in F.; served the College over 20 years.

One reported taken to a Turkish harem.

Three not heard from.

Four started out as exiles.

Ten free.

Total Loss.—About seven-eighths of the buildings, three-quarters of the students, and half the teaching staff.

Of the Armenian people as a whole we may estimate that three-fourths are gone, and this three-fourths includes the leaders in every walk of life—merchants, professional men, preachers, bishops and government officials. And there is no certainty for those who are just now free. The Vali has said that *all* must go. It is only temporary measures, such as bribes or special favours, that have secured postponement. Since we know the fate to which they go, since we have seen the pitiable plight of the stragglers who have survived the journey from Erzindjan and Erzeroum, since we find ourselves forbidden to aid them except in insignificant ways, and since we are forbidden to accompany them to aid them on the way, we are the more eager, if possible, to save those who are left with us.

It seems to us possible that something can be done to save these few. Permission has recently been obtained through the German Embassy for those connected with the German Mission, teachers and their families, orphans and servants, a circle of several hundred, to remain in G. I therefore beg of you to take what steps are possible to secure the permission through our Ambassador for the handful of dependants still with us to remain in H.

If such permission is not secured, we shall probably be called upon to see the very members of our households dragged off to decorate the harems of those who have not as yet secured as many girl slaves as they wish. Nothing can be done locally. The Kaimakam and his coterie in H. are more powerful here than the Vali, and take pleasure in flaunting our impotence in our faces.

I have said enough. Our hearts are sick with these sights and stories of abject terror and suffering. The extermination of the race seems to be the objective, and the means employed are more fiendish than could be concocted locally.

The orders are from headquarters, and any reprieve must be from the same source.

70. H.: STATEMENT BY THE PRINCIPAL OF THE COLLEGE, DATED 19th JULY, 1915, RELATING TO THE DEPORTATION OF ARMENIANS FROM VILLAGES IN THE NEIGHBOURHOOD OF H.; COMMUNICATED BY THE AMERICAN COMMITTEE FOR ARMENIAN AND SYRIAN RELIEF.

From the village of E., 212 individuals set out, of whom 128 (60 per cent.) reached Aleppo alive; 56 men and 11 women were killed on the road, 3 girls and 9 boys were sold or kidnapped, and 5 people were missing.

From the same place another party of 696 people were deported; 321 (46 per cent.) reached Aleppo; 206 men and 57 women were killed en route; 70 girls and young women and 19 boys were sold; 23 were missing.

From the village of D. a party of 128 were deported, of whom 32 (25 per cent.) reached Aleppo alive; 24 men and 12 women were killed en route; 29 girls and young women and 13 boys were sold; and 18 were missing.

71. H.: LETTER DATED 10th NOVEMBER, 1915, FROM THE PRINCIPAL OF THE COLLEGE AT H. TO MR. N. AT CONSTANTINOPLE; COMMUNICATED BY THE AMERICAN COMMITTEE FOR ARMENIAN AND SYRIAN RELIEF.

The difficulty of securing local permission to start out for America, as well as the scarcity of wagons, has delayed our party for some days. We have been grateful, in the meantime, that we have heard from you approving our plans. We hope to start in a day or two. We do not anticipate the journey with relish, but we feel that it will be better to go now than to wait. I am apprehensive for those who stay, though nothing definite threatens citizens of our country at present.

Following your circulars of information as to the attitude of the authorities at the capital, we opened our girls' department two weeks ago, and planned soon to open the boys' department also. The registration of the girls reached about 150, of which number about one-third are in the kindergarten. More than another third are boarders, mostly those who have been with us from the time school closed. There are very few day-pupils above primary age.

Last Thursday afternoon, the 4th November, a raid was suddenly made on the Armenian population. Men, women and children were arrested that afternoon in G. and taken to the police station. The next morning the same thing occurred here in H. Most of those arrested in H. were women and children, and they were nearly all of them released the same day, when they showed their papers. In G., however, many were kept over a day or two and then sent off on the road, probably to be butchered as other parties had been. The season is now so late that it is preposterous to suppose a safe journey to be possible when the exiles are allowed no preparation whatever. By far the largest number sent off seem to have been from the villages, where the people were pretty well cleared out. Estimates run as high as a thousand for those who were sent off in one night.

The panic resulting from this wholly unexpected raid can hardly be pictured. Those pupils who were coming to us from outside have stopped coming pretty largely, and many advise us to close the school. Those exiles who had managed in various ways to escape from the convoys and had settled down to normal life, are now plunged in terror. We have had to guard our gates and walls to prevent the public from pouring in on us.

During this recent event the Government has turned its attention to us once more. On Friday the police came, with a sufficient force, to arrest all the men on our premises. They were polite, but expressed the belief that we were hiding many. I went with the handful of men and boys available, and the next day my brother presented those who were not in evidence that day, and they were all sent back to our premises safely. The Commandant personally asked the Consul to write to us and warn us against harbouring any fugitives in our grounds. We assured him that it had been our settled policy all along to refuse such requests, and that we had no such persons with us. The Kaimakam refused to believe that we had no fugitives with us, but I think he has been persuaded more or less of the truth of this. Two of our teachers, who live in their own houses off from our compound, did not appear on Friday before the police. Afterwards, when they found that the others had been released, they also appeared. They were then put in prison, where they still remain. One of them, I hope, will soon be released, but I have fears for the other, because he was so intimately connected with the former Kaimakam, and there seems to be evidence against him that he was a tool in securing bribes for the said Kaimakam—of course under fear of death.

We have had frequent interviews with the Kaimakam and the Commandant, who is *locum tenens* for the Vali at present. Both of them have been courteous, and assure us that there are no further measures in store for those who have been allowed to stay by order of the Government. But our faith in such promises has been sadly shaken this summer. At two different times the Kaimakam has said that Armenian was no more to be taught in our schools. We have expressed our desire to make the language of the school English, and have assured him that we are working to that end.

As I wrote to you, our curriculum has been submitted to the Mearif, and has been largely approved verbally. We are still in correspondence over some minor details regarding texts. We shall not be able to open work for the few boys who are available at the present, and I confess my deep apprehension lest they and their male teachers should all be rounded up, to go the same road that their comrades followed in July.

It is hard for us to leave just at this juncture. Yet there seems no advantage in our staying compared with the difficulties of leaving later. We shall try to keep you informed of our curriculum.

VIII.
VILAYET OF TREBIZOND, AND SANDJAK OF SHABIN KARA-HISSAR.

The Vilayet of Trebizond lies between Erzeroum and the Black Sea, and consists of a long, narrow littoral, shut off from its hinterland by a wall of mountains on the south. The town of Shabin Kara-Hissar is situated about seventy miles west of Baibourt, near the upper course of the Kelkid Irmak.

The population of this region is very mixed. The substratum is Lazic (a Caucasian race) and Greek; but advanced guards of the Kurdish migration have penetrated into the mountains overlooking the coast, while the towns and ports have been occupied, since the Ottoman conquest in the fifteenth century, by large colonies of Armenians and Turks, who lived there peaceably side by side for four centuries—until June, 1915.

The deportations began in the last week of that month. Their nominal destination was the same as that of the convoys from the Vilayet of Erzeroum, but in this case there seems never to have been any intention of conducting the Armenians alive to their journey's end. At Trebizond, a number of them were herded on to boats and drowned in the open sea. Such convoys as started by land were massacred within a day's journey of the city, and their fate was shared by the convoys from Kerasond. The Armenians of Shabin Kara-Hissar took warning, and resisted the Government's decree. Troops were sent against them, and every Armenian in the town and district was put to the sword.

72. TREBIZOND: REPORT FROM A FOREIGN RESIDENT AT TREBIZOND, COMMUNICATED BY THE AMERICAN COMMITTEE FOR ARMENIAN AND SYRIAN RELIEF.

Passages included between brackets are inserted from the version of the same document published in the brochure "Quelques Documents sur le Sort des Armeniens, 1915" (Geneva, 1915).

On Saturday, the 26th June, the proclamation regarding the deportation of all Armenians was posted in the streets. On Thursday, the 1st July, all the streets were guarded by gendarmes with fixed bayonets, and the work of driving the Armenians from their homes began. Groups of men, women and children, with loads and bundles on their backs, were collected in a short cross-street near my residence, and when a hundred or so had been gathered, they were driven past my residence on the road toward ———, in the heat and dust, by gendarmes with fixed bayonets. They were held outside the city until a group of about 2,000 had been collected, and then sent on. Three such groups, making about 6,000 altogether, were sent from here during the first three days; and smaller groups from —— and the vicinity, sent later, amounted to about 4,000 more.

The weeping and wailing of the women and children was most heart-rending. Some of these people were from wealthy and refined circles. Some were accustomed to luxury and ease. There were clergymen, merchants, bankers, lawyers, mechanics, tailors, and men from every walk of life. The Governor-General told me that they were allowed to make arrangements for carriages, but nobody seemed to be making any arrangements. I know of one wealthy merchant, however, who paid £15 Turkish (about £13 10s. sterling) for a carriage to take himself and wife to ——, and when he arrived at the station where they were being collected, at ——, about ten minutes' distance from the city, they were commanded by the gendarmes to leave the carriage, which was sent back to the city.

The whole Mohammedan population knew that these people were to be their prey from the beginning, and they were treated as criminals. In the first place, from the date of the proclamation, the 25th June, no Armenian was allowed to sell anything, and everybody was forbidden, under penalty, to buy anything from them. How, then, were they to provide funds for the journey? For six or eight months there has been no business whatever in Trebizond, and people have been eating up their capital. Why should they have been prohibited from selling rugs or anything they had to sell, to secure the needed money for the journey? Many persons who had goods which they could have sold if they had been allowed to do so, were obliged to start off on foot without funds and with what they could gather up from their homes and carry on their backs. Such persons naturally soon became so weak that they fell behind and were bayoneted and thrown into the river, and their bodies floated down past Trebizond to the sea, or lodged in the shallow river on rocks, where they remained for ten or twelve days and putrefied, to the disgust of travellers who were obliged to pass that way. I have talked with eye-witnesses, who state that there were many naked bodies to be seen on snags in the river fifteen days after the affair occurred, and that the smell was something terrible.

On the 17th July, while I was out on a ride with a German resident, we came across three Turks digging a grave in the sand for a naked body which we saw in the river near by. The corpse looked as though it had been in the water for ten days or more. The Turks said they had just buried four more further up the river. Another Turk told us that a body had floated down the river and out into the sea a few moments before we arrived.

By the 6th July (Tuesday) all the Armenian houses in Trebizond, about 1,000, had been emptied of their inhabitants and the people sent off. There was no inquiry as to who were guilty or who were innocent of any movement against the Government. If a person was an Armenian, that was sufficient reason for his being treated as a criminal and deported. At first all were to go except the sick, who were taken to the municipal hospital until they were well enough to go. Later, an exception was made for old men and women, pregnant women, children, those in Government employment and members of the Roman Catholic Church. Finally it was decided that the old men and women and the Catholics must go too, and they were sent along towards the last. A number of lighters have been loaded with people at different times and sent off towards <Samsoun>. It is generally believed that such persons were drowned. During the early days, before the deportation commenced, a large caique or lighter was loaded with men supposed to be members of the Armenian Committee, and sent off towards <Samsoun>. Two days later, <a certain Vartan,> a Russian subject, who had been one of those who started in the boat, returned overland to Trebizond, badly wounded about the head and so crazy that he could not make himself understood. All he could say was "Boom, boom." He was arrested by the authorities and taken to the municipal hospital, where he died the following day. A Turk said that this boat was met not far from Trebizond by another boat containing gendarmes, who proceeded to kill all the men and throw them overboard. They thought they had killed them all, but this Russian, who was big and powerful, was only wounded and swam ashore unnoticed. A number of such caiques have left Trebizond loaded with men, and usually they return empty after a few hours.

Totz, a village about two hours from Trebizond, is inhabited by Gregorian and Catholic Armenians and Turks. Here, according to a reliable witness, a wealthy and influential Armenian, <Boghos Marimian,> and his two sons were placed one behind the other and shot through. Forty-five men and women were taken a short distance from the village into a valley. <The wife and daughters of an Armenian named Artes>[91] were first outraged by the officers of the gendarmerie, and then turned over to the gendarmes to dispose of. According to this witness, a child was killed by beating its brains out on a rock. The men were all killed, and not a single person survived from this batch of forty-five.

The plan to save the children by placing them in schools or orphanages in Trebizond, under the care of a committee organized and supported by the Greek Archbishop, of which the Vali was president and the Archbishop vice-president, with three Mohammedan and three Christian members, has been abandoned, and the girls are now being given exclusively to Mohammedan families and thus scattered[92]. The suppression of the orphanages and the scattering of the children was a great disappointment to us and to the Greek Archbishop, who had worked hard for the plan and secured the support of the Vali; but <Nail Bey,> the local head of the Committee of Union and

Progress, who was opposed to the plan, succeeded in thwarting it very quickly. Many of the boys appear to have been sent to ———, to be distributed among the farmers. The best looking of the older girls, who were retained as caretakers in these orphanages, are kept in houses for the pleasure of members of the gang which seems to rule affairs here. I hear on good authority that a member of the Committee of Union and Progress here has ten of the handsomest girls in a house in the central part of the city, for the use of himself and his friends. Some of the younger girls have been taken into respectable Mohammedan houses. Several of the former pupils of the American Mission are now in Mohammedan homes near the Mission, and have not been visited by <Nail Bey,> but of course the majority of them are not so fortunate.

The 1,000 Armenian houses are being emptied of furniture by the police one after the other. The furniture, bedding and everything of value is being stored in large buildings about the city. There is no attempt at classification, and the idea of keeping the property in "bales under the protection of the Government, to be returned to the owners on their return," is simply ridiculous. The goods are piled in without any attempt at labelling or systematic storage. A crowd of Turkish women and children follow the police about like a lot of vultures, and seize anything they can lay their hands on, and when the more valuable things are carried out of a house by the police, they rush in and take the balance. I see this performance every day with my own eyes. I suppose it will take several weeks to empty all the houses, and then the Armenian shops and stores will be cleared out. The commission which has this matter in hand is now talking of selling this great collection of household goods and properties, in order to pay the debts of the Armenians. The German Consul told me that he did not believe the Armenians would be permitted to return to Trebizond, even after the end of the war.

<Arab merchants, under British protection, were included in the deportation, as well as all Armenians with Russian, Persian or Bulgarian passports. Ovhannes Arabian, the Dragoman of the British Consulate, could take nothing with him but the clothes he stood in.>

I have just been talking with a young man who has been performing his military service on the "inshaat tabouri" (construction regiment), working on the roads out toward Gumushkhané. He told me that 15 days ago all the Armenians, about 180, were separated from the other workmen, marched off some distance from the camp and shot. He heard the report of the rifles and later was one of the number sent to bury the bodies, which he stated were all naked, having been stripped of clothing.

A number of bodies of women and children have lately been thrown up by the sea upon the sandy beach below the walls of the Italian Monastery here in Trebizond, and were buried by Greek women in the sand where they were found.

---

89. See Docs. 82, 94 and 122.

90. See Doc. 9, page 21.

91. "The women."—*American version.*

92. *The origination of this plan is recorded in an earlier (undated) report from the same hand, from which the following sentences are a quotation:*—

"The children attending the American school conducted by ——, also those children left with them by persons being deported, have all been taken and placed in a school organised by a local committee, of which the Vali is president and the Greek Metropolitan vice-president. Into this school all the Armenian children, females up to fifteen years and males to ten years of age, are being placed as soon as the parents are sent off. Children above these ages go with their parents."

73. TREBIZOND: EXTRACTS FROM AN INTERVIEW WITH COMM. G. GORRINI, LATE ITALIAN CONSUL-GENERAL AT TREBIZOND[93]. OF ROME, 25th AUGUST, 1915.

For over four years I was Consul-General at Trebizond, with jurisdiction over practically the whole Black Sea littoral, from the Russo-Turkish frontier to the neighbourhood of Constantinople, and over five provinces in the interior of Asia Minor (Eastern Anatolia, Armenia and Kurdistan)—districts chiefly inhabited by Turks, Armenians and Kurds, with a considerable sprinkling of Persians, Russians, Greeks and Arabs. For the last ten months, moreover, I had also been responsible for the protection of the very numerous Russian subjects and Russian interests, as well as the Greek and Montenegrin, and also, to some extent, the French, the English, and the American, with others of minor account....

As for the present internal condition of the Ottoman Empire, I can only answer for my own district. In my district the present condition of things is almost desperate. The population is showing true Moslem resignation in the way it is bearing the existing situation—the ruin and desolation of individuals and community, the holocaust of all and everything for a war which no one desired, but which was forced upon them by Enver Pasha, and which will lead to the ruin and dismemberment of all that still remains of the Ottoman Empire. But the Moslem and Christian populations can do nothing more— they have reached the extreme limit of their effort. The oxygen is being administered by the Germans, who are trying to prolong the agony of the dying Empire, but will not be able to perform the miracle of restoring life to a corpse. Apart from a few lunatics, a speedy peace, even if it involves the foreign occupation of Ottoman territory, is the prayer of all. There is no courage for a rebellion. The Germans and the "Committee of Union and Progress" are hated and detested by all, but only in the intimacy of the heart and in confidential conversation, for the Germans and the Committee constitute the one genuine, solid organisation at present existing in Turkey— a masterly and most rigorous organisation, which does not hesitate to use any weapon whatever; an organisation of audacity, of terror, and of mysterious, ferocious revenge....

As for the Armenians, they were treated differently in the different vilayets. They were suspect and spied upon everywhere, but they suffered a real extermination, worse than massacre, in the so-called "Armenian Vilayets." There are seven of these, and five of them (including the most important and most thickly populated) unhappily for me formed part of my own Consular jurisdiction. These were the Vilayets of Trebizond, Erzeroum, Van, Bitlis and Sivas.

In my district, from the 24th June onwards, the Armenians were all "interned"—that is, ejected by force from their various residences and despatched under the guard of the gendarmerie to distant, unknown destinations, which for a few will mean the interior of Mesopotamia, but for four-fifths of them has meant already a death accompanied by unheard-of cruelties.

The official proclamation of internment came from Constantinople. It is the work of the Central Government and the "Committee of Union and Progress." The local authorities, and indeed the Moslem population in general, tried to resist, to mitigate it, to make omissions, to hush it up. But the orders of the Central Government were categorically confirmed, and all were compelled to resign themselves and obey.

The Consular Body intervened, and attempted to save at least the women and children. We did, in fact, secure numerous exemptions, but these were not subsequently respected, owing to the interference of the local branch of the "Union and Progress Committee" and to fresh orders from Constantinople.

It was a real extermination and slaughter of the innocents, an unheard-of thing, a black page stained with the flagrant violation of the most sacred rights of humanity, of Christianity, of nationality. The Armenian Catholics, too, who in the past had always been respected and excepted from the massacres and persecutions, were this time treated worse than any—again by the orders of the Central Government. There were about 14,000 Armenians at Trebizond—Gregorians, Catholics, and Protestants. They had never caused disorders or given occasion for collective measures of police. When I left Trebizond, not a hundred of them remained.

From the 24th June, the date of the publication of the infamous decree, until the 23rd July, the date of my own departure from Trebizond, I no longer slept or ate; I was given over to nerves and nausea, so terrible was the torment of having to look on at the wholesale execution of these defenceless, innocent creatures.

The passing of the gangs of Armenian exiles beneath the windows and before the door of the Consulate; their prayers for help, when neither I nor any other could do anything to answer them; the city in a state of siege, guarded at every point by 15,000 troops in complete war equipment, by thousands of police agents, by bands of volunteers and by the members of the "Committee of Union and Progress"; the lamentations, the tears, the abandonments, the imprecations, the many suicides, the instantaneous deaths from sheer terror, the sudden unhingeing of men's reason, the conflagrations, the shooting of victims in the city, the ruthless searches through the houses and in the countryside; the hundreds of corpses found every day along the exile road; the young women converted by force to Islam or exiled like the rest; the children, torn away from their families or from the Christian schools, and handed over by force to Moslem families, or else placed by hundreds on board ship in nothing but their shirts, and then capsized and drowned in the Black Sea and the River Deyirmen Deré—these are my last ineffaceable memories of Trebizond, memories which still, at a month's distance, torment my soul and almost drive me frantic. When one has had to look on for a whole month at such horrors, at such protracted tortures, with absolutely no power of acting as one longed to act, the question naturally and spontaneously suggests itself, whether all the cannibals and all the wild beasts in the world have not left their hiding places and retreats, left the virgin forests of Africa, Asia, America and Oceania, to make their rendezvous at Stamboul. I should prefer to close our interview at this point, with the solemn asseveration that this black page in Turkey's history calls for the most uncompromising reproach and for the vengeance of all Christendom. If they knew all the things that I know, all that I have had to see with my eyes and hear with my ears, all Christian powers that are still neutral would be impelled to rise up against Turkey and cry anathema against her inhuman Government and her ferocious "Committee of Union and Progress," and they would extend the responsibility to Turkey's Allies, who tolerate or even shield with their strong arm these execrable crimes, which have not their equal in history, either modern or ancient. Shame, horror and disgrace!

74. TREBIZOND: NARRATIVE OF THE MONTENEGRIN KAVASS OF THE LOCAL BRANCH OF THE OTTOMAN BANK, PUBLISHED IN THE ARMENIAN JOURNAL "AREV" OF ALEXANDRIA, 2nd OCTOBER, 1915.

The Kavass of the Local Branch of the Ottoman Bank at Trebizond, a Montenegrin, who left Trebizond in Signor Gorrini's company[94] and is at the present moment in Cairo, has made the following statement to Mr. Malezian, Secretary of the General Armenian Union of Benevolence:—

"The very evening of the day on which the order arrived from Constantinople, they threw into the sea about forty of the intellectuals and the members of political parties, saying to them: 'You are to be sent into exile by the sea route.'

"At the present moment there is not a single Armenian left at Trebizond except two employees of the Ottoman Bank, who will also be deported as soon as other persons arrive from Constantinople to take their place.

"Children have been converted to Islam and handed over to Mohammedan families. Those who cry and do not keep quiet have their throats cut.

"After the Armenians had gone, their houses were confiscated.

"The whole thing was organized by the members of the Committee of Union and Progress.

"The exiles were not allowed to take with them either money or clothes or provisions. Five hundred Armenian soldiers were disarmed, and then deported and massacred on the road. As for the other exiles, they must have been massacred without exception, for the news received from Djevizlik (a village six hours from Trebizond, on the one and only road leading to Gumushkhané) makes it certain that the exiles were seen passing that place in batches, while beyond Djevizlik no one has seen them pass. At the same time, the river Yel-Deyirmeni brought down every day to the sea a number of corpses, mutilated and absolutely naked, the women with their breasts cut off."

---

93. Signor Gorrini left Trebizond on the 23rd July, 1915, in the interval between the Italian declarations of war against Austria-Hungary and against Turkey. He hired an open motor-launch with a Lazic skipper and crew, and took with him two servants and the Montenegrin Kavass of the local branch of the Ottoman Bank. The coastwise voyage from Trebizond to Constantinople took seven days and nights. They touched at Kerasond, Samsoun, Sinope, Ineboli, Kidros, Zonguldak, Zacharia, Chilé and Faro d'Anatolia, without landing, however, at any of these places. From

Constantinople Signor Gorrini travelled via Dedeagatch and Palermo to Rome, where he gave this interview to the representative of "Il Messaggero."

94. "I hired the motor launch for myself and three members of my household, one of them a Montenegrin kavass who was under our protection.—*The Italian Consul, Signor Gorrini, in the interview published in the Rome journal "Il Messaggero," 25th August, 1915.*

75. KERASOND (KIRESOUN), TREBIZOND AND SHABIN KARA-HISSAR: EVIDENCE COLLECTED BY AN ARMENIAN GENTLEMAN FROM EYE-WITNESSES NOW IN ROUMANIA; COMMUNICATED BY THE CORRESPONDENT OF THE LONDON "TIMES" AT BUKAREST.

Kerasond.—Much has been written lately about the Armenian massacres in Turkey, but it is only now that we are receiving more precise and detailed information, from eye-witnesses who, by some means or other, have escaped the scene of the most horrible atrocities ever known in this world.

The atrocities of Kerasond are described by a prominent Greek of that town, who succeeded in obtaining a passage on board a Greek ship bound for Roumania with a cargo of nuts. On her voyage across the Black Sea, this ship was met by two Russian torpedo boats, which took on board the crew and this gentleman among them, sank the ship, transported the crew to Sevastopol, and there set them free. This gentleman had been an eye-witness of all that happened in Kerasond, and he describes the atrocities as follows:—

"It is impossible to express in words the humiliations and atrocities that the Armenians of Kerasond have had to undergo. One morning the Government announced, through the public crier, that every male Armenian, old or young, must immediately go to the Government Building, where an important communication was to be made to them. Those who neglected to comply with this order were threatened with imprisonment. The Armenians obeyed, as there was no alternative in a town where they were in minority; but as soon as they had arrived at the Government Building, they were surrounded by hundreds of gendarmes and driven straight to prison. At midday their families, seeing that nobody returned, collected together and went in a body to the Government Building. They demanded that their husbands should be set free. The gendarmes replied with the bayonet, and dispersed the crowd, while those who still insisted in their protest were sent to join their husbands in prison. That night was passed by the poor Armenians in the prison, while all night long their families mourned and wept. I visited several Armenian neighbours and tried to calm them, but they were all convinced that they would never see their people again, as they had guessed latterly, from the attitude of the Turks, that some plot was being prepared against them. Next morning the prisoners were told that they were to be exiled to Kara-Hissar (a town inland from Kerasond) and that they were only to take with them provisions for five days. Their wives were notified of this, and in the afternoon, under the escort of hundreds of gendarmes, they were marched out of the prison on to the road leading to Kara-Hissar, and divided up into several separate batches. Several days passed, and then a few telegrams reached various families, signed by their husbands or brothers and announcing that they had arrived in safety at Kara-Hissar. But unfortunately these telegrams were merely forged by the Government in order to calm down those left behind, who had not yet ceased to demand the return of their dear ones. Their true fate was very different. A fortnight later, I met a friend who told me that he had given protection to a young Armenian who had escaped from the party of Armenians that were sent to Kara-Hissar, and that this young man gave horrible descriptions of their experiences. I went to see this young man at my friend's house. He was an honest business man in the town, so that I do not question for a moment the honesty of his declaration in the present case, which he made to the following effect:—

"Our party consisted of 350 men, mostly young fellows. The next day after our departure from Kerasond, we reached a spot on the banks of the River Kara Su. It was lunch time, and the gendarmes ordered us to stop and eat. We had just begun to do so when guns were fired on us from all sides, and I saw many fall dead. I was wounded myself in the arm and collapsed on my side from the pain. The firing continued, and I fainted. I only recovered consciousness to find myself in the river with hundreds of dead bodies floating round me. My wound did not prevent me from swimming, so that I struggled out of the river, and at night-fall walked back to the town. I was afraid to go to my family, so I asked shelter of my friend here; but as my prolonged presence may bring him harm, I am going home to-night."

In fact, the Government had announced that any Turk or Greek giving protection to an Armenian would be punished with death. So that night the young man went to his house; but he was soon found out, and under the pretext of sending him to hospital for his wound they took him away and he has never been heard of since.

This was the end of the male population. The women were dealt with in the same fashion. They were likewise herded by force into the prison, and marched under escort in batches along the same road leading to Kara-Hissar. They were not massacred, but treated with extreme brutality and forced to walk for long hours, so that many died of exhaustion, and many others committed suicide by throwing themselves into the river with their children in their arms. Some went mad through inability to endure the brutalities and humiliations inflicted on them by the gendarmes and by the Turkish villagers they met on the way. The small children under three years of age were allowed to be carried along by their mothers, but the children between the ages of three and fifteen, both girls and boys, were all distributed among Mohammedan families, with instructions to convert them to Islam. The Armenians' houses were sealed with the Government's seal, but it is clear that they were first stripped of their furniture and placed at the disposal of Turkish immigrants. This is the tragic history of the extermination of the 3,000 Armenians of Kerasond.

One old Armenian only escaped death by embracing the Mohammedan religion; but that only served to save his own life, as his son and wife were sent off with the rest.

Kara-Hissar is a town three days inland from Kerasond, Kerasond being its port. The Armenian population of this city, guessing the intentions of the Turks, took up their arms and fled into the mountains surrounding the town. The gendarmes and soldiers sent in their pursuit had several encounters with them, but they failed every time to drive them out of their mountain positions. In my opinion their positions are good and can resist attacks, but their supply of food may soon come to an end, and in their isolation they may starve, if no help reaches them[95].

Trebizond.—During the last massacres (1896) Trebizond suffered the most, and this time also it has been the scene of the most fiendish atrocities. These are described by a young Armenian girl who was an eye-witness of them. She was saved through the protection of the late Italian Consul at Trebizond, who was allowed to leave in a motor boat for Constantinople[96], whence he went to Italy and sent this girl to some relatives of hers in Roumania. She gives the following account of her experiences:—

"In the morning my father, a Russian subject, was summoned by a gendarme and taken away to the Government Building. A few hours passed, and my mother went to find out what had happened to him. She did not return either, and, being thus left alone in the house, I went to our neighbour, the Italian Consul, and asked for his protection. He immediately disguised me as a servant girl in the Consulate. Every day I used to see hundreds of Armenians, men and women in separate batches, passing our house under escort— mothers carrying their children on one arm and a package of provisions on the other. That was all they were allowed to take. The Kavass of the Consulate used to come in every day and report to the Consul all that was going on in the town. Business was at a standstill, all the shops were closed, and you met nothing in the streets but Armenians escorted by gendarmes. Many young girls were forced to marry Mohammedans. All the children were collected and distributed to Turkish families to be brought up, as

Mohammedans. Several leading Armenians committed suicide by throwing themselves down from the windows of their houses. All the Armenians who were Russian subjects (there were forty-five of them) were put on board a sailing ship bound for Kerasond, but on the way they were thrown into the sea and shot at by the gendarmes sent with them. This we verified later on, when the Consul was allowed to leave Trebizond in a motor boat, in which I accompanied him as servant girl. On the way a sailor on the launch, in answer to a question from the Consul, said that he had refused to take those forty-five Russian subjects in his sailing boat because he knew what fate was marked out for them on the way; and, in fact, when we arrived at Kerasond, we discovered that not only had those forty-five people never arrived (though they were put on board the boat under the pretext that they were to be exiled to the districts inland from Kerasond), but that not a single Armenian was left in the town itself. We were told the same thing all along the coast—at Tireboli, Ordou, Samsoun, Ineboli, etc.[97] The wife of the late Secretary of the British Consulate at Trebizond (himself a British subject) was forced to marry a Turk; the rest of the family—the Secretary, his brothers, his uncles, etc., who were all British subjects too—were exiled to the interior of the country, and nothing has been heard of them since. Many women have offered to become Mohammedans but have been refused. Only one family in Tireboli, called A., obtained leave to remain by turning Mohammedan."

This is confirmed by a telegram received lately by a gentleman in Constantinople, who has business connections with the family in question. The telegram was signed "A. Zadé Mehmed Sirry."

The plan of the Government has been the same everywhere—to convert the children to Islam, and to march the male and female population under escort into the interior of the country, until the last of them has dropped dead with exhaustion. As to their houses, the furniture was distributed among the officers and soldiers. Pianos, side-boards, and other objects too luxurious for soldiers' houses were sold by auction, where the best buyers, in many districts, were Jews, who considered the price of 50 piastres too high for a piano, and tried to buy them at 10-15 piastres. The houses thus emptied were given over to Turkish immigrants or paupers. The copper kitchen utensils, and, in fact, everything made of copper, were carefully packed, and sent, by different means, to Constantinople, where the Germans were anxiously waiting for them as their share of the plunder.

It is only in Constantinople and Smyrna that the Armenians have not been exiled; but that does not mean that they there escape their share of the general misfortune. Most of the leading Armenians there, including doctors, deputies, wholesale merchants, journalists, etc., were exiled to the interior, and nothing has been heard of them since. The requisitioning officer takes away anything he finds in an Armenian shop, and many have thus been reduced to closing their shops, having nothing left to sell. Only one man among those deported from Constantinople was brought back, having consented to become a Mohammedan. This is Mr. B. of the B. Bros. firm, the largest export and import business in Constantinople. He has been forced to pay £5,000 for the building of a Mosque in Kaisaria, to build a Turkish school in Constantinople, to wear a turban, and to pray seven times a day, as a proof of his sincere devotion to his new religion.

95. This was written before it was known that the Armenians of Kara-Hissar had been overwhelmed by force and massacred to the last woman and child, with their bishop at their head.—EDITOR.

96. "I hired the motor launch for myself and three members of my household".—*Signor Gorrini in the Rome journal "Il Messaggero," 25th August, 1915.*

97. "Of the 200 Armenian families at Ordou, 160 have embraced Islam, under pressure of threats and violence. Of the 400 Armenian families at Kerasond, 200 have embraced Islam to escape persecution; the rest have been deported."—*New York Journal "Gotchnag," 28th August, 1915.*

76. TREBIZOND AND ERZEROUM: DESPATCH FROM THE CORRESPONDENT OF THE LONDON "TIMES" AT BUKAREST, DATED BUKAREST, 18th MAY, AND PUBLISHED ON THE 22nd MAY, 1916.

Since the entry of the Russian troops into Trebizond it has become possible to lift the veil of mystery that has hitherto shrouded the fate of the Armenian population in this prosperous port. The troops on their arrival found all the Armenian houses plundered and for the most part in ruins. Doors, windows, shutters, and all woodwork had been carried away. There was no opposition on the part of the authorities.

The deportation of the Armenians, which began in June, was carried out here, as elsewhere, in accordance with instructions from Constantinople. The leading families were the first to suffer. Some 300[98] of these received the order to prepare for emigration and purchased a number of wagons for the transport of their property, but four days after their departure all the wagons were brought back to the town. The emigrants had been massacred and their property plundered.

Other groups, each of several hundred families, followed. This process went on for some time, but eventually new methods were adopted. The police entered the houses of the remaining Armenians, forcibly expelled them, drove them through the streets, and locked up the houses. The whole Armenian population of Trebizond, numbering some 10,000 souls, was thus exterminated. It is hoped, however, that some hundreds of persons may yet be found hidden in the villages in the neighbourhood.

At Erzeroum, where the Armenian population was considerably greater, being estimated at 35,000, practically the same programme was carried out. The proceedings, which began in the middle of May, were inaugurated by the arrest and imprisonment of 400 young Armenians.

Many families, after being expelled from their houses, were kept waiting for several days in the streets before being taken to their fate. At the entrance to the town the processions of exiles encountered tax-gatherers, who insisted on the payment of arrears of taxation, although the unfortunate people had left all their property behind them. Only a few artisans, who were required to work for the Army, were allowed to remain in the town. By the beginning of August the whole Armenian population had disappeared from Erzeroum. Only the Bishop remained. On the 5th August two police officers appeared at his house and communicated the order for departure. The Bishop had taken precautions to secure some horses for the transport of his effects, but these were now stolen. He tried to purchase others, but at the last moment he was informed that he was not allowed to take anything with him. He was then removed to an unknown destination.

German officers stationed in the town and the German Consul manifested open approval of these proceedings. Among the spoils which fell to the Turks were several Armenian girls, and a share in this living booty was conceded to the Germans.

98. Including Muggerditch Zarmanian, a contractor employed by the Ottoman Army.—*Information furnished to the writer by Armenian refugees in Roumania.*

IX.
SIVAS: THE CITY AND PARTS OF THE VILAYET.

The Vilayet of Sivas lies immediately to the west of the Vilayet of Erzeroum. It includes the upper basins of two rivers—the Kizil Irmak (Halys), on the banks of which the City of Sivas itself is situated, and the Yeshil Irmak, further towards the north-west and nearer the Black Sea coast.

The province is less mountainous and much richer than its eastern neighbours. Agriculture is flourishing, the nomad shepherd is comparatively rare, and there are a number of populous towns, with the beginnings of local manufactures.

The peasant population is predominantly Turkish, interspersed with important Greek enclaves, which have held their own from the first Seljuk invasions to the present day; but there are also a number of Armenian villages, and the Armenians constitute—or constituted before June, 1915—about half the population of the towns. The rising trade and industry was almost entirely the product of these Armenians' initiative, and they themselves had risen with it in education and civilisation, till in all essentials they were on a level with the corresponding commercial and professional classes in Western Europe.

This peaceful, progressive community was entirely uprooted by the Deportation Decree. The villages were cleared in June; the City of Sivas suffered its first deportation on the 5th July.

77. SIVAS: LETTER FROM A FOREIGN RESIDENT AT SIVAS, DATED 13th JULY, 1915; COMMUNICATED BY THE AMERICAN COMMITTEE FOR ARMENIAN AND SYRIAN RELIEF.

To begin with the all-important fact, which may have reached you by now, the Armenians of the interior are being deported in the direction of Mosul. At the time we left Sivas, two-thirds of them had gone from the city, including all our Protestants, our teachers and pupils, and all our side of the city. Those left were the orphan girls and teachers and a few boarding girls, three nurses and two orderlies in the hospital, D. Effendi and his family and a few women servants. According to my best knowledge and opinion, with the exception of Armenian soldiers and prisoners (all of whose families have been sent) and a very few exceptions in the case of people who, for various reasons, were necessary to the Government, all Armenians are gone from Sivas. According to what I consider good authority, I believe it to be true that the entire Armenian population from Erzeroum to (and including) Gemerek, near Kaisaria, and from Samsoun to (and including) Harpout has been deported. There is also a movement in the central field which had not become general yet when I left, but will doubtless become so later. More than 100,000 Greeks from the Marmora and Mediterranean coast have been deported.

We heard many rumours of massacres, but I have no evidence on the subject. To my knowledge, no general massacres have occurred in the Sivas Vilayet. Not a few men have been killed in one way and another.

This general movement against Armenians began months ago in arrests for alleged revolutionary activity and in searches for guns and bombs. In Sivas the winter passed rather quietly, and it was late spring before much was done. About two months ago a general endeavour was made to imprison all leading Armenians, and within a week more than 1,000 were arrested. I estimate the whole number of Sivas men in prison to be between 1,500 and 2,000. The only person taken from our circle was H. Effendi, who was taken by name the first day—not, we think, as from us, but as a resident in the city. Strict orders were given not to molest us or our people, though all our efforts to do anything for H. Effendi failed. Up to the time of our departure from Sivas these men had been in prison a month. They were well, and as comfortable as could be expected in a Turkish prison; but no examinations had been held, no charges made, and no one knew what was to be done. The Vali assured me again and again that they would be released and sent with their families; but this was not done for at least ten days after the deportation was begun, and I have no confidence that it will be done at all. We could not believe that this outrage would really take place, but when, on Monday, hundreds of families were loaded on to ox-carts and sent off, and our Protestant people were told that they were to start on Wednesday, Miss Graffam said she was going to try to go with them, and in this she succeeded. She bought a spring wagon, a common wagon, eight ox-carts and six donkeys, so that our pupils and teachers went by their own conveyance. The Government furnished on an average an ox-cart to a family, but how far they went that way and how soon they were obliged to walk we do not know.

The advice of the Vali was that the orphans should remain for the present, and we have no idea what they will do to them in the end. This was one of our motives in getting to Constantinople. I represented to our friends there the fear we had that, after all the others were gone, these girls might be forcibly taken from us and put into Turkish families. I talked with Mr. N. about the possibility of bringing them all out of the country. Mr. Morgenthau promised to have strict orders sent to Sivas for their protection. I presume you will hear from Mr. N. on the subject, if his letter gets through. At the time we left Sivas the orphanage circle (female) was complete with the exception of Miss O., who went with the Protestants. I think they deemed it wise to keep as few teachers as necessary. Miss P. and Miss Q. expect to go with them if they go, and take care of them if they remain. We understand that, since we left, the orphans have been moved up to the college building with the ladies; probably the old building is vacant, and very likely sealed by the Government to ensure its safety. The Y.'s are probably sleeping in our house and going to the city for hospital work in the daytime.

The only men besides Dr. Y. are G., our kavass, D. Effendi and two or three orderlies in the hospital, of whom you will remember only our old teacher, Z. Effendi, of Divrig. All the Protestants except R. the Greek and his family, most of the boarders (boys and girls) and all our teachers excepting H. Effendi, who was in prison, and K., who is with us, went on the road together on Wednesday afternoon, the 7th July. Six or eight of the larger boys ran away a day or two before, and we got no word from them. S. Effendi and T. Effendi went with their families, and the others—U., V., W. and X.—went the same day.

After we had seen thousands of people start out, and especially after ours had actually gone, we came to the conclusion that if anything could be done to stop this terrible crime, which impresses us as ten times worse than any massacre, it would be done in Constantinople. Our work in Sivas seemed to be terminated, at least for the present, and our furlough was due; so it was decided that Dr. Y., because of his knowledge of Turkish and his medical work, should remain, and that the rest of us should go. We had been getting neither letters nor telegrams for some time, and I did not believe that those we sent arrived. In Constantinople we found that the whole plan of deportation originated from the Central Government, and that no pressure from the Embassies had been able to effect anything. Mr. N. felt that the most we could do now was to work for raising relief funds for the Armenians, and, in view of the uncertainty of travel from Constantinople to the border, he was anxious for us to get out of the country as soon as possible. So we started at once on receiving our passports.

We believe there is imminent danger of many of these people (whom we estimate for the Sivas, Erzeroum and Harpout Vilayets to be 600,000) starving to death on the road. They took food for a few days, but did not dare take much money with them, as, if they did so, it is doubtful whether they would be allowed to keep it. From Mr. N. we understood that the Rockefeller Foundation people are in Geneva or Berne, and we hope that everything possible will be done to make them recommend relief appropriations at once. Mr. N. and our Ambassador promised to do what they could, and gave me some hope that some relief funds might be sent to Harpout at once. It is questionable whether relief work will even be allowed, but it ought to be undertaken if possible. We shall do all we can in the United States, with the aid of the American Missions Board....

I started out from Sivas with several hundred addresses of people to whom we promised to give word about their friends. Then there was my own list of some 700 names of my constituency that I brought, but we were obliged to leave them all in Constantinople. It was impossible to carry out of Turkey a single address or a scrap of writing of any kind. I bought an empty account book, and started a new travelling expense account after crossing the border.

We met on the road near Talas the people of two villages journeying on foot with less than a donkey to a family, no food or bedding, hardly any men, and many of the women barefooted and carrying children. A case in Sivas worthy of notice was that of T. Effendi's sister. Her husband had worked in our hospital as a soldier nurse for many months. She contracted typhus, and was brought to our hospital. Her mother, a woman of sixty to seventy, got up from a sick-bed to go and take care of their seven children, the oldest of whom was about twelve. A few days before the deportation, the husband was imprisoned and exiled without examination or fault. When the quarter in which they lived went off, the mother got out of bed in the hospital and was put on an ox-cart to go with her children.

78. SIVAS: LETTER[99] WRITTEN FROM MALATIA BY MISS MARY L. GRAFFAM, PRINCIPAL OF THE GIRLS' HIGH SCHOOL AT SIVAS, TO A CORRESPONDENT AT CONSTANTINOPLE; REPRINTED FROM THE BOSTON "MISSIONARY HERALD," DECEMBER, 1915.

When we were ready to leave Sivas, the Government gave forty-five ox-carts for the Protestant townspeople and eighty horses, but none at all for our pupils and teachers; so we bought ten ox-carts, two horse arabas, and five or six donkeys, and started out. In the company were all our teachers in the college, about twenty boys from the college and about thirty of the girls'-school. It was as a special favour to the Sivas people, who had not done anything revolutionary, that the Vali allowed the men who were not yet in prison to go with their families.

The first night we were so tired that we just ate a piece of bread and slept on the ground wherever we could find a place to spread a *yorgan* (blanket). It was after dark when we stopped, anyway. We were so near Sivas that the gendarmes protected us, and no special harm was done; but the second night we began to see what was before us. The gendarmes would go ahead and have long conversations with the villagers, and then stand back and let them rob and trouble the people until we all began to scream, and then they would come and drive them away. *Yorgans* and rugs, and all such things, disappeared by the dozen, and donkeys were sure to be lost. Many had brought cows; but from the first day those were carried off, one by one, until not a single one remained.

We got accustomed to being robbed, but the third day a new fear took possession of us, and that was that the men were to be separated from us at Kangal. We passed there at noon and, apart from fear, nothing special happened. Our teacher from Mandjaluk was there, with his mother and sisters. They had left the village with the rest of the women and children, and when they saw that the men were being taken off to be killed the teacher fled to another village, four hours away, where he was found by the police and brought safely with his family to Kangal, because the tchaoush who had taken them from Mandjaluk wanted his sister. I found them confined in one room. I went to the Kaimakam and got an order for them all to come with us.

At Kangal some Armenians had become Mohammedans, and had not left the village, but the others were all gone. The night before we had spent at Kazi Mahara, which was empty. They said that a valley near there was full of corpses. At Kangal we also began to see exiles from Tokat. The sight was one to strike horror to any heart; they were a company of old women, who had been robbed of absolutely everything. At Tokat the Government had first imprisoned the men, and from the prison had taken them on the road. The preacher's wife was in the company, and told us the story. After the men had gone, they arrested the old women and the older brides, perhaps about thirty or thirty-five years old. There were very few young women or children. All the younger women and children were left in Tokat. Badvelli Avedis has seven children; one was with our schoolgirls and the other six remained in Tokat, without father or mother to look after them. For three days these Tokat people had been without food, and after that had lived on the Sivas company, who had not yet lost much.

When we looked at them we could not imagine that even the sprinkling of men that were with us would be allowed to remain. We did not long remain in doubt; the next day we heard that a special kaimakam had come to Hassan Tchelebi to separate the men, and it was with terror in our hearts that we passed through that village about noon. But we encamped and ate our supper in peace, and even began to think that perhaps it was not so, when the Mudir came round with gendarmes and began to collect the men, saying that the Kaimakam wanted to write their names and that they would be back soon.

The night passed, and only one man came back to tell the story of how every man was compelled to give up all his money, and all were taken to prison. The next morning they collected the men who had escaped the night before and extorted forty-five liras from our company, on the promise that they would give us gendarmes to protect us. One "company" is supposed to be from 1,000 to 3,000 persons. Ours was perhaps 2,000, and the greatest number of gendarmes would be five or six. In addition to these they sewed a red rag on the arm of a Kurdish villager and gave him a gun, and he had the right to rob and bully us all he pleased.

Broken-hearted, the women continued their journey. Our boys were not touched, and two of our teachers being small escaped, and will be a great help as long as they can stay with the company. The Mudir said that the men had gone back to Sivas; the villagers whom we saw all declared that all those men were killed at once. The question of what becomes of the men who are taken out of the prisons and of those who are taken from the convoy is a profound mystery. I have talked with many Turks, and I cannot make up my mind what to believe.

As soon as the men left us, the Turkish drivers began to rob the women, saying: "You are all going to be thrown into the Tokma Su, so you might as well give your things to us, and then we will stay by you and try to protect you." Every Turkish woman that we met said the same thing. The worst were the gendarmes, who really did more or less bad things. One of our schoolgirls was carried off by the Kurds twice, but her companions made so much fuss that she was brought back. I was on the run all the time from one end of the company to the other. These robbing, murdering Kurds are certainly the best-looking men I have seen in this country. They steal your goods, but not everything. They do not take your bread or your stick.

As we approached the bridge over the Tokma Su, it was certainly a fearful sight. As far as the eye could see over the plain was this slow-moving line of ox-carts. For hours there was not a drop of water on the road, and the sun poured down its very hottest. As we went on we began to see the dead from yesterday's company, and the weak began to fall by the way. The Kurds working in the fields made attacks continually, and we were half-distracted. I piled as many as I could on our wagons, and our pupils, both boys and girls, worked like heroes. One girl took a baby from its dead mother and carried it until evening. Another carried a dying woman until she died. We bought water from the Kurds, not minding the beating that the boys were sure to get with it. I counted forty-nine deaths, but there must have been many more. One naked body of a woman was covered with bruises. I saw the Kurds robbing the bodies of those not yet entirely dead. I walked, or, rather, ran, back and forth until we could see the bridge.

The hills on each side were white with Kurds, who were throwing stones on the Armenians, who were slowly wending their way to the bridge. I ran ahead and stood on the bridge in the midst of a crowd of Kurds, until I was used up. I did not see anyone thrown into the water, but they said, and I believe it, that a certain Elmas, who has done handwork for me for years, was thrown over the bridge by a Kurd. Our Badvelli's wife was riding on a horse with a baby in her arms, and a Kurd took hold of her to throw her over, when another Kurd said: "She has a baby in her arms," and they let her go. After crossing the bridge, we found all the Sivas people who had left before us waiting by the river, as well as companies from Samsoun, Amasia and other places.

The police for the first time began to interfere with me here, and it was evident that something was decided about me. The next morning after we arrived at this bridge, they wanted me to go to Malatia; but I insisted that I had permission to stay with the Armenians. During the day, however, they said that the Mutessarif had ordered me to come to Malatia, and that the others were going to Kiakhta. Soon after we heard that they were going to Ourfa, there to build villages and cities, &c.

In Malatia I went at once to the commandant, a captain who they say has made a fortune out of these exiles. I told him how I had gone to Erzeroum last winter, and how we pitied these women and children and wished to help them, and finally he sent me to the Mutessarif. The latter is a Kurd, apparently anxious to do the right thing; but he has been sick most of the time since he came, and the "beys" here have had things more or less their own way, and certainly horrors have been committed. I suggested that they should telegraph to Sivas and understand that I had permission to go with these exiles all the way, and the answer is said to have come from Sivas that I am not to go beyond here.

My friends here are very glad to have me with them, for they have a very difficult problem on their hands and are nearly crazy with the horrors they have been through here. The Mutessarif and other officials here and at Sivas have read me orders from Constantinople again and again to the effect that the lives of these exiles are to be protected, and from their actions I should judge that they must have received such orders; but they certainly have murdered a great many in every city. Here there were great trenches dug by the soldiers for drilling purposes. Now these trenches are all filled up, and our friends saw carts going back from the city by night. A man I know told me that when he was out to inspect some work he was having done, he saw a dead body which had evidently been pulled out of one of these trenches, probably by dogs. He gave word to the Government, with the result that his two servants, who were with him, were sent for by under-officers, saying that the Pasha wanted them, and they were murdered. The Beledia Reis here says that every male over ten years old is being murdered, that not one is to live, and no woman over fifteen. The truth seems to be somewhere between these two extremes.

My greatest object in going with these exiles was to help them to get started there. Many have relatives in all sorts of places, to whom I could write; and

I could, in my own estimation, be a channel by which aid could get to them. I am not criticising the Government. Most of the higher officials are at their wit's end to stop these abuses and carry out the orders which they have received; but this is a flood, and it carries everything before it.

I have tried to write only what I have seen and know to be true. The reports and possibilities are very many, but the exact truth that we know, at best, calls for our most earnest prayer and effort. God has come very near to many during these days.

79. EXTRACTS FROM A LETTER, DATED MASSACHUSETTS, 29th AUGUST, 1915, FROM ANOTHER FOREIGN RESIDENT AT SIVAS TO MR. G.H. PAELIAN.

You may be surprised to get a letter from me from America, and I am surprised myself that I am really here. It is seven years and our time for a furlough; but as there was no one to leave the College with, and the children were small, we decided to wait a year or two. But when they deported the Armenians and left us without work and without friends, we decided to come home and get our vacation and be ready to go wherever we could after the war.

You will want to know about Sivas and about your family in particular. In general, the Sivas Armenians are gone, but there were a few exceptions when we came away—the Swiss Orphanage, the Sanasarian School, the people in prison (1,500 of the best men), and the Armenians in the army who were employed in making roads, building houses, tailoring, shoe-making, &c., for the army. Then there are Dr. A. and Dr. B., the C.'s, a few tent-makers and people who were necessary to the Turks, a few nurses in our hospital, and D., our druggist.

The others were all deported on ox-carts on the 5th July and the succeeding ten days. In general, there was one ox-cart to a family, and they could take whatever they wished to on that. The Vali allowed the Protestants all to go on the same day, although they were scattered all over the city, and the others were sent by quarters. Our teachers and boarding pupils went with the Protestants.

E. and her children went with the Protestants too. I bought a cow for her, and gave it to her and another woman who could take care of it. I thought that F. must have milk. I did not get down in time to see them off, but Miss Graffam went with them to help what she could.

The morning after they started out, we sent G. on horseback to see how they were. They had spent one night without any accident, although they had not slept much.

All our teachers went except H., who was in prison. We do not know why they imprisoned him, but we think some enemy of the family must have told some lies about them, because they imprisoned his brother, too, and J. We tried every way to get him out, but it was of no use.

Have you heard that he is engaged to K., a girl who has been in our family a great deal? She was a teacher in the girls'-school, studied one year in Smyrna, and then taught one year more. She usually spends the summer in our family, and was to do the same this year. When the Armenians were deported, the Vali allowed us to keep three girls as servants, and, as she was to be with us, we kept her with two others who were already with us, and we brought the three to America with us, saving these three from the general deportation.

Since coming to America and hearing about what happened in other places, it seems that the deportation from Sivas was very humane, but at best it was awful. I cannot describe the sadness of having all our friends taken away from us in one day and not knowing where they were going or whether we should see them again. The College was full of boys, teachers, carpenters, servants, &c. The L.'s, &c., were camping. In a single day they went, and only our family was left, with G. We were not afraid; we did not care what happened.

Now we do not know what has become of them, or what has become of the prisoners or the soldiers.

80. SIVAS: NARRATIVE OF A NATURALISED OTTOMAN SUBJECT, DATED NEW YORK CITY, 10th MARCH, 1916; COMMUNICATED BY THE AMERICAN COMMITTEE FOR ARMENIAN AND SYRIAN RELIEF.

When the majority of the Armenian people were exiled from Sivas, I was in Talas, but when I heard what had happened I started back at once, thinking of course that my relations would also be sent away, and wishing to accompany them. It was with great difficulty that I obtained permission from the officials in Kaisaria to go back; they claimed that the road was very dangerous, and that it would be impossible for a woman alone to travel over it. Finally, the head official of the Military Transport, who was living in Sivas and had taken possession of Dr. AB.'s house there, telegraphed to Kaisaria that I might travel under the protection of the Menzel, and I started with two officers who were in a wagon behind me and who warned me that I must keep close to them, as the road was very dangerous. The road until we reached Sharkishla, two days' journey from Kaisaria, was very quiet, and we met almost no one. At Sharkishla the plain was black with exiles from different parts of Anatolia; they had been waiting there for about a week and new recruits were coming in every day. At that time they did not seem very unhappy. The weather was beautiful, the plain was covered with trees, and many of the wealthy people had tents and wagons, while there were a great many boys and men in the party.

Later, when they reached Malatia, or even before, the men were separated from them, their wagons and goods were taken from them, and they were only allowed to take what they could carry on their backs over the narrow mountain pass through which they went. I know this because Miss Graffam met these same people later on, while she was on the road with the Sivas people. I was not very near them, but I could see them from the han window. The handji, an Armenian, told me he was sure they were all to be killed, and the officers told me the next day that they had visited them at night, and that the men were to be killed; they said they were sorry for the women and children, but one of them added: "This is what happens to people that want a kingdom of their own."

I had a few unpleasant experiences on the road, but I will not stop to tell them. I found my relations safe, and the Vali had told them they might stay— I believe because of the influence of some powerful Turkish friends they have in Constantinople, who had telegraphed to the Vali to save Dr. AB. and his wife. The prisons at that time were filled with our Sivas men—several thousand; these men we visited every day, taking food to some of them and trying to cheer up the others. Their wives and children had gone with the exiles, and it was pretty hard work to be brave when they did not know their fate, but it was surprising how really brave they were. Some of the gaolers were very brutal men, and would be as disagreeable as possible to us, but others were polite and willing to let us see the prisoners, even allowing selected ones to come into the yard and talk with us. About a month later these men were taken out in batches of a hundred at night; they were told that they were to be taken to the railway near Angora to work on it; the rich men were allowed to hire wagons from Turks, at a big price, to travel in. They were all taken very early in the morning, several hours before daylight, and they were seen, those on foot, to go over the mountain into the valley, where we are pretty sure they were killed, as the soldiers returned with clothes, and the wagons always came back three or four hours later filled with clothes. The soldiers, moreover, described how many of the men met their fate, some bravely, some otherwise, and we think they spoke the truth, for they told of men we knew intimately, and who would have been apt to do and say just what they said they did, in the face of death. It was hard to see so many of our fine young men go off in this way, and many of them had no idea they were going to their death. Some of them took money with them, thinking they might meet their wives and children. When they heard that Miss Graffam was returning, they were so anxious to see her and hear of their families. Most of them were gone when she got back, but she was allowed to go into the prison and tell those that were left something about the journey she had made. They were thankful to hear that their wives and children were still alive, as they had heard they had all been massacred a few days' distance from Sivas. Miss Graffam said that although they were robbed on the road and almost everything they had was taken from them, still the girls and women were not outraged or treated badly as far as Malatia. After that, we heard from boys that had escaped from the party and come back to Sivas that many of the girls were carried off by the Kurds a few days after Miss Graffam left them.

After all our Sivas men had been taken from the prisons, other men kept coming in from other cities and towns like Angora and Yozgad. They were kept in prison for a few days and then taken out as our men had been. We were not permitted to see these men. Many of them when they reached Sivas were in carriages. We heard that they, too, were killed in the mountains, and that Sivas was being called the "Great Slaughter House." The last of our young men that remained in prison were three young doctors. One of them, Dr. AC., had been educated by Mrs. AD.; he had been brought up in the Orphanage at X., and was a splendid young man, full of enthusiasm for his work, which was in the military hospital. Another of the three was the son of a wealthy Divrig family, who had been educated in Germany and had many strong German friends among the high German officials in Constantinople, who either would not or could not do anything to save him. They were executed while I was in Constantinople. I had taken with me letters to a high German official from Dr. AE., asking him to save them; and later Miss Graffam telegraphed to me that they were in great danger, and begged me to do all I could to save them—to go to the Germans. I did so, but was told they had gone to Enver Pasha before, and that he would do nothing for them.

About thirty or forty families in Sivas, all of them wealthy, had become Moslems, having the promise that, if they did so, their lives and property would be safe. A few weeks later, all of them, with the exception of two or three merchants, were told they had to go, and, as soon as they left, their property was confiscated by the Government. The Vali's family doctor, an Armenian, was told that he was to stay, and he asked if that meant he was to become a Moslem. The Vali said: "No, I am tired of these people becoming Moslems."

At two different times our orphanage children were ordered out; both times Dr. Y. went to the Vali and begged that they might stay, telling him how small many of them were, only three or four years old, and how they would certainly die on the road, for at that time even ox-carts could not be found. He seemed to be touched and said they might. There seemed always to be friction between the police and the Vali; he would give permission for them to stay and the police would come and say they were to go; several of the police officers came to the older girls and teachers, and asked them to become their wives and stay, saying that they would be carried off on the road anyway, and that they might as well accept them and remain. Many hundreds of little girls were being brought back to Sivas before I left; some were being placed in Moslem families and some in empty houses. We were not allowed to see them. Many of the Turkish officers had seized one or two of these little girls and were planning to take them on to Constantinople with them. Some of our orphanage teachers were able to interview some of the older girls that were brought back from Kara-Hissar (one of the places where the Armenians tried to defend themselves). These girls tell horrible tales of what they saw there. A great many of these girls were being married to Turks; the Turks were saying they were not forcing them; they wanted them to become their wives willingly. A number of women and children who had been in hiding were also beginning to come out of hiding when I left, and the Missionaries were taking them into the orphanage and the hospital, trying to save them.

Several Armenian soldiers from the Samsoun region had also fled to the hospital for protection; they had started with their regiments from Samsoun, and the Armenians, who numbered a thousand or more, had been attacked by the guards and the majority killed or left for dead. The men that came to Dr. Y. had been among those left for dead; one of them had a horrible wound across the back of his neck, where he had been cut by an axe; they usually used axes, saying they did not want to waste powder and shot on them. Some others came from a lonely barracks on the Marsovan road, where they and their comrades, all Armenians (soldiers), had been shut up for three days without food or water. Finally a young Turkish officer heard the noise as he passed, and came and let them out. These men said that they were put in this building towards evening. They were tied together by threes and called out in succession. Those that went out never returned, and they found that they were being butchered with axes. One of the men succeeded in untying the cord that he and his two companions were tied with; they closed and barricaded the door, and when the soldiers, who were only a few in number (Turkish), found that they could not get in, they fastened it on the outside so that the Armenians should not get out. They were afraid, indeed, to go out even after the Turkish soldiers had left, until this officer appeared and sent them on to Sivas; he said that the men that did these things would be punished, but they were not. We believed that they were allowed to do pretty much as they pleased with the Armenians, and so, when they happened to be brutal, they did this kind of thing, with the result that many of the

Armenians that had gone through it had become nervous wrecks. Dr. Y. had seen and talked with a number of these men, and I also saw those who had fled to the hospital.

In Tokat the girls, small and large, were left in the houses alone. The daughter of the Badvelli there managed to send a letter to her uncle, who was a nurse in our hospital (a soldier), saying that she and her four little sisters were in the house alone and had nothing to live on, and that the city was full of girls in the same condition; up till that time, which was a month after their parents had left them, they had not been injured by the Turks. A Turk brought the letter.

On the 1st October, when I left Sivas to go up to Constantinople, I had some difficulty in getting permission to start, as the Vali was away. I had to wait until he returned. He said he would see that I got as far as Talas safely, and he told me which places to stop at; but because of some trouble with the driver, I was unable to stop at the hans he told me to stop at, and the first night the han was filled with Armenians who were being deported from X., both men and women. They were wealthy people who had become Moslems. My driver told me that they had not become true Moslems and for that reason were being sent away. The soldiers with them were very evil-looking men. I noticed that they had many beautiful rugs and carpets in their wagons. In the next room there were some Turks who were talking of the killing of the Armenians; however, nothing happened to them that night. The second night I had to stop at a han which had been very prosperous a few months before, but was now half wrecked and deserted. It was dark and we could not go on, and we found that the son and brother of the former handji had become Moslems, and that the Government had allowed them to take charge of the han on condition that they turned over all the money they made to the Government. These two men were in the most pitiable condition from fear, and they both told me horrible tales of how the men of Gemerek had been killed; this han was outside the town of Gemerek. They said they had hidden in the mountains for three weeks until driven out by starvation, and then had given themselves up to the Government and become Moslems, but they added: "We are only Moslems with our mouths, but Christians in our hearts." Still, they were very fearful, and not at all sure that they would not be killed later. In the village of Gemerek, they said, most of the girls had been forced into marriage with the Turks, and many of the old women had been killed and the rest deported. I had seen them on my way to Sivas going out, so I knew this to be true. The next night I heard two hodjas talking, under my window, of a terrible massacre of the Armenians that had just taken place in the mountains; they seemed to be very sorry about it and spoke of it with horror; they did not know, of course, that I was listening. When I reached Talas, the people had almost all gone from there and from Kaisaria. The

Kaisaria Protestants, or at least a number of Protestant families, were sent out to Talas and given houses there, while the Talas Protestants were sent to neighbouring villages; but their condition was much better than that of any of the Armenian people in our Sivas region. The Girls'-School was filled with girls from Kaisaria, most of them the daughters of wealthy Gregorian and Catholic families. The Kaisaria people had been allowed to leave their daughters behind. While I was there, a woman and two men arrived from one of the Kaisaria out-stations and told of the terrible massacre of the whole village. First the little boys up to ten were taken outside the village and killed. There were only a few men in the village, so the women dressed as men and held the village against the Kurds and Turks for three weeks, keeping them off with stones; they had fled to the hills. These people said that the Turks used to call to them to come down and become Moslems and their lives would be spared; this they refused to do. Later, the village Turks were reinforced by the soldiers from Kaisaria, who shot them down, only these three people escaping. They had been weeks reaching Talas, having to hide by day and travel very slowly at night for fear of being caught. This village had many of our Protestant people, and among those killed was the mother of one of the teachers and the wife of another. We heard that all the villages in that region were treated in this way, instead of being deported. While in Talas I had a telegram from Sivas asking me to wait for a professor of the Sanasarian College, who was coming from Sivas with his wife and little boy. The Vali had given them permission to go on to Constantinople; he had been educated in Vienna and his wife in this country; they were very fine people. I waited several days and they did not come. I found that they had left Sivas as they planned and disappeared between Sivas and Talas—they have never been heard from. I know a number of people that disappeared in just this way on that road, after the Vali had given them permission to travel and the promise of a safe escort.

The rest of the way from Kaisaria to the railway I went under the protection of the Military Transportation Company. I passed through many deserted towns, but saw no dead bodies on the road, only one between Sivas and Talas. On the railway we passed truck-load after truck-load of Armenians—exiles being sent into the interior. All were in cattle-trucks, huddled together like animals. We met these trucks every day; often they were shunted on the siding. All along the Konia plain were tens of thousands of people; some had tents, many of them had nothing. The weather at that time was warm, so they were not suffering specially from the cold. Later, while in Constantinople, we heard that these people on the Konia plain were being sent into the interior and not allowed to take any food with them, so that they would die quickly.

On the train, in the compartment with me, was the wife of the Mutessarif of Erzindjan. She had several Armenian girls with her—one of them in the compartment with us to wait on her children. She was kind to this child, who was only about nine years old, but she treated her like a little slave. She told another Turkish woman that her parents had been sent away and she had taken her from the streets. The Armenians in Constantinople had not been deported, only the men who were suspected of revolutionary tendencies, but there is great suffering among them for lack of food, and they need work. Professor —— told me, the week before I left, that the Turks in Constantinople were saying: "The Armenians from Constantinople must go," and that great pressure was being brought to bear upon them by the Turks to become Moslems and stay. We had a number of Armenian young women employed in the Red Cross work, and they all showed a most beautiful Christian spirit, were always kind and gentle to the soldiers, and never showed in any way that they felt any bitterness toward them. Several of them had come from the interior and had relatives that had been deported; one of them was from Trebizond, where there had been that terrible massacre of children, and her little baby of seven months was, she fears, among them. This young woman went into exile with her husband, and lost everything and everyone in Trebizond. She was a most beautiful Christian, and was loved and respected by the people that worked with her.

81. SIVAS: THE ADVENTURES OF MURAD; NARRATED BY "S.H.S.," IN THE JOURNAL "THE NEW ARMENIA," OF NEW YORK, 1st MARCH, 1916.

In December, 1914, Murad was peacefully at work in his native village of Govdoun. Then he was apprised of the troubles brewing in the city of Sivas, the capital of the Vilayet. He hastened there to find the Armenians panic-stricken. All the Armenians of military age, as well as all the prominent Armenian business men, had been imprisoned on the pretext that the bread supplied to the Turkish soldiers was poisoned by the Armenian bakers. The Armenian physicians in the city went to the military commander and protested against this outrage, offering to prove that the accusation was false. As the military commander was not on good terms with the Vali, he ordered some of the bread to be brought, and the physicians ate it before him without any bad results. Then he ordered the prisoners to be released. However, matters grew steadily worse, persecution increased, and spread finally to the surrounding villages.

Murad, with a group of brave Armenians, resisted the outrages of the Turkish Government for several months, until he was obliged to take refuge in the mountains. In March, 1915, Turkish soldiers were sent to capture Murad and his band, but they were defeated and repulsed. The Armenians fought their way slowly over the mountains in a continual guerilla warfare. The Government became so exasperated that it placed a price on Murad's head.

Murad was stricken with typhus as a result of the privations and hardships the band endured, and his comrades had to carry him from snow-clad mountain to mountain, and from cave to cave, in order to save him from capture. At Mount Sachar Murad and his comrades were surrounded by three hundred Turkish cavalrymen, but they succeeded in escaping to an Armenian village in Khantzart. The peasants nursed Murad, and said: "Remain here, and we will die by hundreds to protect you." Murad did not wish to expose them to danger. When he heard that the Turkish cavalry were approaching, he requested his comrades to remove him to the mountains.

In the milder weather of May, Murad began to recover. A company of Turkish cavalrymen renewed the search for the little band of Armenian warriors. Murad and his seven men opened fire upon the Turks, wounding several of them. The Turks beat a hasty retreat, but returned soon with reinforcements. These also were put to flight by the Armenians. Murad then withdrew from the mountain and travelled for some days through the woods and valleys.

Because of the extraordinary prowess of the Armenians, it was rumoured that Murad had a thousand men with him. The Vali of Sivas determined to capture him at any cost. At a place called Telouk-Khaina a hundred Turkish infantry advanced upon Murad's army of eight, but Murad decided to save his ammunition, and retreated. Near Tedjir a Turkish regiment with seven guns advanced to give battle to the supposed Armenian army, but the Armenians again used discretion. Murad's men had armed themselves well at the beginning, and replenished their stock of ammunition constantly from the soldiers whom they killed. They frequently found on the slain Kurds and Turks jewelry and other ornaments that had belonged to Armenian women, and Murad still has in his possession some of these jewels.

After numerous victorious encounters and skirmishes with the Turks, Murad turned toward Samsoun, in the autumn of 1915. His band had been increased by seven Armenians and three Greeks. Having reached the village of Tchamulan, not far from Samsoun, they were welcomed by a prominent Greek named Constantine. The Turks had burned and destroyed all the boats owned by Constantine, who was also subjected to other persecutions. Defying the Turks, he harboured the eighteen rebels in his house, and defended them. One day three hundred Turkish soldiers surrounded the Greek's house and opened fire. The besieged band so successfully defended itself that the enemy could not approach the house. Every new attack was repulsed successfully, and many of the Turks were killed. In the evening the siege was raised and the enemy withdrew. Murad and his comrades, together with Constantine and his family, evacuated their stronghold and proceeded toward Samsoun.

The party finally reached the woods of Hodjadagh, near the Black Sea. There they remained in hiding, and sent scouts to reconnoitre the country and find a way of escape. Having replenished their stock of food and ammunition, the brave warriors hastened one night to the sea coast. They found there a Turkish sailing vessel at anchor, and captured it with its Turkish crew of five. They loaded the vessel with their supplies and set sail, taking with them the Turkish crew to man the boat.

After eight days and nights on the Black Sea, their water supply was exhausted and they were compelled to make bread with sea-water. Meanwhile they suffered terribly from thirst. The vessel passed Samsoun and Kerasond, and approached Riza. While they were still about three or four hours' distance from the Russian coast, two Turkish motor-boats were seen pursuing. The Turks had learned of Murad's escape and had dispatched a force to capture him at sea. The Turks opened fire on the rebels. The Armenian sharpshooters replied effectively. The motor-boats turned back after many of the soldiers had been killed. In Murad's party brave Yegho was killed, and one of the Greeks wounded.

A heavy storm arose, and the superstitious Turkish sailors begged that the body of Yegho might be thrown into the sea, because they feared that the boat would be wrecked if the corpse remained on board. The vessel finally reached Batoum, and the party landed safely on Russian soil. Murad buried Yegho and then went to Tiflis, where he joined the other Armenian Volunteers.

82. SIVAS: RECORD OF AN INTERVIEW GIVEN BY THE REFUGEE MURAD TO MR. A.S. SAFRASTIAN AT TIFLIS.

Once more the curtain drawn over the heinous details of Armenian massacres in Asia Minor is raised by that well-known fighter, Murad of Sivas, the Armenian leader of the province. Starting from Sharkishla, some twenty miles south-west of Sivas, with a small force, he opened his way to Divrig, lying about sixty miles south-east of Sivas; and after a great number of encounters with regular Turkish troops, he eventually entrenched himself on the heights of Yaldiz Dagh, north-east of Sivas, where, surrounded by large numbers of the enemy, he kept up desperate fighting for eight days. Most of his comrades were killed in this unequal combat. He himself, however, succeeded in breaking through the Turkish lines and emerged on the coast, somewhere near Samsoun. Here he forced some Turkish boatmen to set sail in the direction of Batoum. On the voyage, his boat was chased by Turkish motor launches and fired on, and in this encounter one of his comrades was killed by a bullet. He has just reached here to throw more light upon the horrors which have been committed in the Vilayet of Sivas and in parts of Harpout and Western Dersim.

For about twenty years Murad (a brother-in-arms of Andranik, the organiser of the present volunteer regiments) has been in the front ranks of the Armenian movement as a leading fighter, and the circumstances of his struggle since last March, and the story of his adventurous escape to Russia when all was over, would fill volumes. He has come to tell the outside world the news that, of 160,000 Armenians inhabiting the province of Sivas, there remain now, or, rather, remained a month ago, when he left, some 10,000, who have either been spared as useful artisans toiling in the labour battalions and the prisons, or were old people left in their homes. The remaining 150,000 souls have either been massacred outright or deported to the area bounded by the right bank of the Euphrates and Northern Mesopotamia.

The story which Murad gave me reveals once more the thorough organisation of these massacres by an overmastering hand, and the ruthless processes by which the details were carried out. Anybody listening to Murad, who had been cut off from the rest of the world for eight months, would at once have thought it to be the story of the massacres at Bitlis or one of the other places, there is such a striking resemblance of detail in the work of destruction.

The persecutions began with the outbreak of the Turkish war. The Armenians of Sivas did all they could to help the Red Crescent work of the Turkish army, either by personal service or contributions. Notwithstanding all these efforts, the Armenian element in particular was unscrupulously robbed under the cloak of military requisitions. In the meantime, the Turks of Sivas did not conceal their intention of settling old scores with the Armenians, who had applied to Europe for reforms.

The storm broke over the question of Armenian deserters from the Turkish army and the disarming of civilian Armenians. The Divisional Commander of Sivas had ordered that able-bodied men above thirty-three years of age and liable to service should get a permit from the military authorities for temporary exemption from entering the field; whereas Muamer Pasha, the Vali of Sivas, looked upon such a step as a sign of Armenian disloyalty. During December and January most Armenian soldiers in the Turkish service were either disarmed and sent to the labour battalions, or were imprisoned as 'suspicious' characters. The treatment they received in the army was of a most unenviable kind. A Holy War had been proclaimed by the Caliph, and the fate of the Infidels was in the Moslems' hands. To mention an instance: on an unfounded charge of desertion six Armenians were hanged in Gurin, three of them being brothers, who were absolutely innocent.

For disarming the Armenians, the Turks employed the most fiendish methods. The order for delivering up all arms in the possession of civilians was nominally universal, but in fact it was directed against the Armenians. In Khourakhon, a village near Sivas, one man (Harutune) was actually shod like a horse, one (Muggerdich) was castrated, and another (Puzant) was done to death by putting a red-hot iron crown on his head. Under threats of such tortures many Armenians were compelled to buy arms and give them up to the authorities. The tragi-comical part of the whole business was that the Turkish officials entrusted with the mission of collecting arms were themselves selling them to Armenians at a good profit[100]. The object of these infamous proceedings seems to have been the wish of the Turkish Government to place the Armenians in the category of rebels, and accuse them of having hidden arms in spite of official warnings.

Then, again, with a view to striking terror among the Armenians, four or five of the leading men in every town or village were mysteriously shot, while most of the Government officials of Armenian nationality were dismissed without any reason. Nishan Effendi, the sub-governor of Kotchesur[101] (Province of Sivas), a man of good record, was peremptorily dismissed from his post with many others.

Towards the end of January last (1915), Odabashian Vartabed (the Armenian bishop-elect of Sivas) was proceeding to his post from Angora, when he was attacked on the way and killed in his carriage. It has now been proved beyond doubt that the plot was hatched with the cognisance of Muamer Pasha, the Governor, as among the murderers were Mahil Effendi of Zara, his aide-de-camp, Tcherkess Kior Kassim, his chief hangman, and two others.

During the course of February, Armenian soldiers on active service and Armenian bakers were accused by the authorities of having poisoned the soldiers' bread and food. The subsequent medical inquiry instituted by Turkish and Greek doctors easily proved the baselessness of so gross a charge.

The billeting of Turkish soldiers upon Armenians throughout the province, and their uninterrupted movement from one front to the other[102], Sivas being on the main road between Angora and Erzeroum, caused indescribable suffering to the defenceless population. Like famished wolves, the Turkish soldiers ate up everything they saw, and took everything they could lay hands on. In Ketcheurd, an Armenian village east of Sivas, the women were horribly outraged by the soldiers, six of the best-looking of them being so atrociously treated that they succumbed before the very eyes of their tormentors; and this is only a typical example.

Another incident of a quite impersonal character greatly embittered the relations between the Armenians and the Turks. About 1,700 Russian prisoners of war, captured by the Turks in February, were brought to Sivas in a deplorable condition. The Russian soldiers of Moslem origin had already been released at Erzeroum, most of the Armenians had been killed, and the Russians were stripped of their clothing. On their way to Sivas they were grossly insulted, spat on by every Moslem passer-by, and whipped by their escort into quicker march. Half their number reached Sivas almost naked, covered with filthy rags, their feet swollen and in some cases with their sheepskin coats glued to their sore bodies. In face of such an outrageous treatment of these Russian prisoners, the Armenians of Sivas provided them with medical help and various comforts. This trivial manifestation of humane feeling displayed by the Armenians, however, caused great resentment among the Moslems. In spite of all such efforts, only some sixty Russians survived out of the contingent of 1,700 prisoners. The Turks picked quarrels with the Armenians when the latter tried to bury the Russian dead.

In the last days of March, Murad and other Armenian leaders were asked by the Vali of Sivas to attend a meeting for the deliberation of some important questions. Murad had, however, been privately informed by some Turkish friends that there was a plot against him and his comrades, so he very naturally failed to comply with the Vali's request. The consequence of this was that the relatives of these men were subjected to shameful treatment at the hands of the Turks. Nevertheless, the Armenians throughout Sivas, Erzindjan, Harpout,

Tchemesh-Getzak and the other districts thought it wise to endure these persecutions, so as not to give any grounds for harsher measures. Fresh contingents of troops were sent to each village in April to collect an imaginary number of arms, and such arms were provided for the authorities in the manner already described. Courts-martial were set up in many places and people were summarily tried and sentenced. Hovhannes Poladian, Vahan Vartanian, Murad of Khourakhon and twelve other leaders were shot. Men belonging to the *Dashnaktzoutioun* and the *Huntchak* parties were subjected to 110 strokes each. These terrorising methods were carried out in thorough earnest in Oulash, Sharkishla, Kotchan, Gemerek, Gurin, Derenda, Divrig, and other districts.

More dreadful days for the Armenians began in June. On the assumption that every Armenian soldier was a deserter, and that his people at home had secreted numberless arms, the Turks never relaxed their policy of squeezing out of the Armenians every *piastre* they could get by employing the most brutal means. Towards the end of June and the beginning of July, massacres on a far vaster scale were carried out in various parts of the area referred to. The methods pursued in these massacres were precisely the same as everywhere else in Armenia. The men were separated from their women, and the latter driven in a south-easterly direction. The able-bodied men were first imprisoned and then massacred in small batches under blood-curdling circumstances. For the space of two weeks, Murad thinks, 5,000 Armenians were daily disposed of in the various districts of the province. At Maltepé, a village an hour's ride east of Sivas, some twenty Armenian officials in the Government service were hacked to pieces with pointed and spiked hatchets. At Duzasar, another Armenian village near Sivas, 32 Armenians were done to death in the same manner.

At Habesh, near Zara, east of Sivas, 3,800 Armenians of the neighbourhood were poleaxed, stoned or bayoneted in a fiendish manner. In Khorsan, the headman of the village, named Nigoghos, was hanged upside down on the Boghaz bridge near the village. At Gotni, another village with 120 Armenian families, Turkish bashi-bazouks, mostly released convicts organised into "Chetti" bands, gloried in the achievement of having killed every male above twelve and outraged every woman above the same age.

At Herag, a village near Sivas, the men were killed, the young women carried away and about 600 children detained by the Vali, perhaps to be converted to Islam. The women of Malatia were stripped naked and driven out from their homes, amid the gibes and jeers of the Moslem rabble; many young women actually went mad, others resorted to hideously painful means to put an end to their lives. At Niksar, north of Sivas, most of the young women were distributed among the Turks, and the remainder were deported to the south.

During his wanderings Murad happened to see that only 300 children and old people were left in the town of Tchar-Shamba, near the coast, where there was a large, prosperous colony before. The young people of both sexes had been either killed, abducted or deported from their homes; no child above ten years of age remained among the survivors.

In the territory extending from Amasia, north-west of Sivas, to Erzindjan and Harpout, the Armenian element has been reduced to the same condition. In certain centres like Arabkir, Tchemesh-Getzak, etc., some families escaped persecution by adopting Islam.

About 15,000 Armenians of Erzindjan and the surrounding district were for the most part drowned in the Euphrates near the Kamakh gorge; the Armenians of Baibourt are also reported to have suffered the same fate in the river Kara-Su, a tributary of the Euphrates. With the exception of some thirty Armenian families at Samsoun, all Persian subjects, and a few other families spared here and there, Murad states that all along the Black Sea coast the industrious Armenian element has been uprooted from its homes and its property distributed among local or immigrant Moslems.

In the town of Sivas itself, which comprised some 25,000 Armenians, many of the important inhabitants have either been killed or deported to the deserts. There remain now some 120 Armenian families in the town, consisting mainly of children and elderly folk.

Amid this general scene of unopposed slaughter and destruction, however, there are brave deeds to record and stories of death faced heroically by both men and women.

The Armenians of Duzasar, Gavra, Khorsan, Khantzod, &c., all places in the Province of Sivas, made every possible sacrifice with a view to preventing an inter-racial outbreak in the early stages of the war; but when they were convinced that the attitude of passive resistance they had adopted did not avail in any way, they took up arms, and, supported by their compatriots of Gurin, Gemerek, Divrig, Ketch-Magara, Mandjaluk and other places, fought for days against the Moslem soldiers and bands and repaid the enemy in their own coin.

The Armenians of Shabin Kara-Hissar and Amasia, exasperated at the unaccountable savagery of the Turks, took to reprisals. They burnt down the Moslem quarters and the Government Buildings in their respective towns and temporarily drove the Turks from them. Later, however, they were overwhelmed by large Turkish forces, and died fighting to the last.

Sirpouhi and Santukht, two young women of Ketcheurd, a village east of Sivas, who were being led off to the harem by Turks, threw themselves into the river Halys, and were drowned with their infants in their arms. Mdlle. Sirpouhi, the nineteen-year-old daughter of Garabed Tufenkjian of Herag, a graduate of the American College of Marsovan, was offered the choice of saving herself by embracing Islam and marrying a Turk. Sirpouhi retorted that it was an outrage to murder her father and then make her a proposal of marriage. She would have nothing to do with a godless and a murderous people; whereupon she, and seventeen other Armenian girls who had refused conversion, were shamefully ill-treated and afterwards killed near Tchamli-Bel gorge.

The rich Shahinian family of Sivas, father, sons and one daughter, the fourteen-year-old Khanum, escaped the authorities, who wanted to capture them, and fought for four hours at the entrance of a narrow mountain pass against considerable odds. They were all killed, however, when they ran short of their cartridges.

I could prolong the story of these acts of desperate bravery on the one side and of murderous frenzy on the other. The grim reality of these horrible crimes was forcibly brought home to me when, in the course of my interview with Murad, some girls and young men, Armenians of Sivas, who were anxious to hear something of the dear ones they had left before the war, came to see Murad. They inquired about their relatives and friends, and Murad told them how and when they had been killed or deported. The percentage of murders, at any rate in the cases inquired into on this occasion, was much higher than that of the deportations. One of the girls present, on being told that everyone she had inquired about had been killed, was terribly overcome; yet she succeeded in suppressing her strong emotion, and nerved herself to take a solemn oath of remembrance, which was shared by all present.

X.
SANDJAK OF KAISARIA.

The Sandjak of Kaisaria is an outlying sub-division of the Vilayet of Angora. It lies under the shadow of the Erdjies Dagh (Mount Argaios), and bestrides the course of the Kizil Irmak immediately below Sivas.

We have comparatively little testimony concerning the occurrences in this district, but the documents contained in this section show in sufficient outline what happened at Kaisaria itself, as well as at Everek and K., the only other centres of importance.

83. KAISARIA: STATEMENT BY A TRAVELLER[103] FROM KAISARIA, PUBLISHED IN THE ARMENIAN JOURNAL "BALKANIAN MAMOUL," OF ROUSTCHOUK.

The Armenians of the Kaisaria district, with the exception of Talas, have been deported. At the end of July the Government issued the following manifesto to the Armenians of Talas and Kaisaria:—

"(i) All the Armenians are to leave in batches of 1,000—the men, separated from the women, in one direction and the women in another.

"(ii) No one is to take with him more than 200 piastres (£1 13s. 4d.). If, after examination, anyone proves to have more than this, he will be brought before a Council of War.

"(iii) No one has the right to sell his property, etc.[104]"

After urgent petitions this latter condition was modified as follows:—

"Anyone who has no ready money is authorised to sell property up to a maximum of 300 piastres."

Up till now more than 80 persons have been hanged at Kaisaria, including doctors and other notables such as Hampartsoum and Boyadjian Mourad of the Huntchakist Party.

The relations of the victims themselves were compelled to take down the corpses from the gallows.

Only the women and girls were permitted to go over to Islam. When the Governor was petitioned to allow the infants to be entrusted to charitable Moslem families, to save them from dying on the journey, he replied:—

"I will not leave here so much as the odour of the Armenians; go away into the deserts of Arabia and dump your Armenia there."

99. Date unspecified.

100. See Docs. 68, 94, and 122.

101. Kotch Hissar.

102. As the Russian fleet had blockaded the Black Sea ports and transport by water was difficult, the Turks appear to have been using the Anatolian Railway to Angora, the terminus of the line, for their communications, proceeding thence to Erzeroum through Sivas by horse and camel.—[Note by the interviewer.]

103. Name withheld.

104. For other versions of the official proclamation see Doc. 120 and Annexe C. to the "Historical Summary."

84. EVEREK: STATEMENT[105] PUBLISHED IN THE ARMENIAN JOURNAL "GOTCHNAG," OF NEW YORK, 28th AUGUST, 1915.

At Everek a bomb explosion was the signal for a terrible persecution of the Armenians. The German who narrates this adds that the Governor of Everek was a good man, and was therefore relieved of his duties and replaced by a Circassian of violent character. There had been numerous arrests and atrocities in this district. After that, the wholesale deportations were begun.

---

105. Source unspecified.

85. K.: LETTER FROM A FOREIGN RESIDENT AT K., DATED 16th NOVEMBER, 1915; COMMUNICATED BY THE AMERICAN COMMITTEE FOR ARMENIAN AND SYRIAN RELIEF.

I wish to confirm my telegram in Turkish dated the 12th November, stating that the authorities had begun to send away our Armenian teachers, and that we did not understand the reason for this.

I must now add to this that all our Armenian teachers have been deported, having left for the south by wagon yesterday. Two of them had been started in another direction last week, but were brought back to go south. One of these, however, had become insane from fright, and is left temporarily in our hands. It is doubtful whether he can recover under present conditions.

Our local Mudir gives us assurances that our school and pupils will not be interfered with, and we are going on as best we can, loading most of the extra work on to ourselves and our Greek teachers. Children of Armenian parents who have changed their faith are leaving, but so far others remain. What to do with children left on our hands without support is a serious problem.

The head of the orphanage at J. has left also, and I understand that the institution is in a very precarious, chaotic condition. What the outcome will be I do not know.

The members of our Armenian circle are well, but the long-drawn-out nervous strain is telling on some. Routine school work has not been stopped for an hour, and goes on quietly, as if nothing whatever were happening about us. But to accomplish this, some quick shifts have had to be made, and, as our Turkish friends say, "Idaré-i-maslahat."

XI.
THE TOWN OF X.

We are better informed as to what happened in this town than in regard to any other place where the Ottoman Government's design against the Armenians was put into execution. The documents relating to it, contained in this section, are so full of personal detail that it has been necessary, in consideration for the safety of those concerned, to conceal the town's identity, though in this case, as in others, it is almost impossible to disguise it effectively to anyone acquainted with Asiatic Turkey.

The people of X. were a very typical Armenian urban community, and the story of their destruction represents, in its main features, what happened to innumerable other Armenian communities throughout the Ottoman Empire. The only peculiar feature at X. was the extent to which forcible conversion was attempted by the local authorities. It may also be noted that here, as at Trebizond, there was no intention of forwarding the exiles to their nominal destination. The convoys were butchered en masse *as soon as they reached the next town on the road.*

86. X.: NARRATIVE OF THE PRINCIPAL OF THE COLLEGE AT X., COMMUNICATED BY THE AMERICAN COMMITTEE FOR ARMENIAN AND SYRIAN RELIEF.

The trouble for the Armenians began, as for all other nationalities, with the collection of soldiers. The Government swept off all men possible for military service. Hundreds of the bread-winners marched away, leaving their wives and children without means of support. In many cases, the last bit of money was given to fit out the departing soldier, leaving the family in a pitifully destitute condition. A number of Armenians were quite well off and paid their military exemption fee. A much larger number escaped in one way and another, so there were more Armenians than Turks left in the city after the soldiers had gone. This made the Government suspicious and fearful. The discovery of Armenian plots against the Government in other places added to this feeling.

The special Armenian troubles began in the beginning of May. In the middle of the night, about twenty of the leading men of the national Armenian political parties were gathered up and sent to where they have been imprisoned ever since. In June the Government began looking for weapons. Some of the Armenians were seized, and, by torture, the confession was extracted that a large number of arms were in the hands of different Armenians. A second inquisition began. The bastinado was used frequently, as well as fire torture (in some cases eyes are said to have been put out). Many guns were delivered up, but not all. The people were afraid that, if they gave up their arms, they would be massacred as in 1895. Arms had been brought in after the declaration of the Constitution with the permission of the Government, and were for self-defence only. The torture continued, and under its influence one fact after another leaked out. Under the nervous strain and physical suffering, many things were said which had no foundation in fact. Those inflicting the torture would tell the victim what they expected him to confess, and then beat him until he did it. The college mechanic had constructed an iron "shot" for the athletic games, and was beaten terribly in an effort to fasten the making of bombs on to the college. Some bombs were discovered in the Armenian cemetery, which aroused the fury of the Turks to white heat. It should be said that it is very probable that these bombs had been buried there in the days of Abd-ul-Hamid.

On Saturday, the 26th June, about 1 p.m., the gendarmes went through the town gathering up all the Armenian men they could find—old and young, rich and poor, sick and well. In some cases houses were broken into, and sick men dragged from their beds. They were imprisoned in the barracks, and during the next few days were sent off towards Y. in batches of from thirty to one hundred and fifty. They were sent on foot, and many were robbed of shoes and other articles of clothing. Some were in chains. The first batch reached Y. and sent word from various places. (It is said that this was a scheme of the Government in order to encourage the rest. None of the rest have been heard from. Various reports have been circulated, the only one generally accepted being that they were killed. One Greek driver reported seeing the mound under which they were buried. Another man, in touch with the Government, in answer to a direct question, admitted that the men had been killed.)

Through the intervention of a Turk, the college was able to free those of its teachers already taken, and obtain a stay of proceedings against all its teachers and employees, by the payment of the sum of 275 Turkish liras. Later, this same Turk said that he believed that he could obtain the permanent exemption of the entire college group by the payment of a further sum of 300 liras. The money was promised, but after some negotiations, which showed that no definite assurance of exemption would be forthcoming, the matter was dropped.

Following the sending of the batches of Armenians in the direction of Y., criers went through the streets of the town announcing that all male Armenians between the ages of fifteen and seventy were to report at the barracks. The announcement further stated that their refusal to obey would result in their being killed and their houses being burned. The Armenian priests went from house to house, advising the people to obey this announcement. Those reporting at the barracks were sent away in batches, the result being that within a few days practically all the Armenian men were removed from the city.

On the 3rd or 4th July, the order was issued that the women and children should be ready to leave on the following Wednesday. The people were informed that one ox-cart was to be provided by the Government for each house, and that they could carry only one day's food supply, a few piastres, and a small bundle of clothing. The people made preparation for carrying out these orders by selling whatever household possessions they could in the streets. Articles were sold at less than 10 per cent. of their usual value, and Turks from the neighbouring villages filled the streets, hunting for bargains. In some places these Turks took articles by force, but the Government punished all such cases when detected.

On the 5th July, before the order for the expulsion of the women was carried out, one of our staff went to the Government to protest against the execution of this order in the name of humanity. He was told that this order did not originate with the local officials, but that the orders had come from those higher up not to leave a single Armenian in the city. The commandant, however, promised to leave the college to the last, and gave permission for all people connected with the American institutions to move into the college compound. This they did, and at one time over three hundred Armenians were living on the college premises.

The population had been ordered to be ready to start on Wednesday. But on Tuesday, about 3.30 a.m., the ox-carts appeared at the doors of the first district to be removed, and the people were ordered to start at once. Some were dragged from their beds without even sufficient clothing. All the morning the ox-carts creaked out of the town, laden with women and children and, here and there, a man who had escaped the previous deportations. The women and girls all wore the Turkish costume, that their faces might not be exposed to the gaze of drivers and gendarmes—a brutal lot of men brought in from other regions. In many cases the husbands and brothers of these same women were away in the army, fighting for the Turkish Government.

The panic in the city was terrible. The people felt that the Government was determined to exterminate the Armenian race, and they were powerless to resist. The people were sure that the men were being killed and the women kidnapped. Many of the convicts in the prison had been released, and the mountains round X. were full of bands of outlaws. It was feared that the women and children were taken some distance from the city and left to the mercy of these men. However that may be, there are provable cases of the kidnapping of attractive young girls by the Turkish officials of X. One Moslem reported that a gendarme had offered to sell him two girls for a medjidia.[106] The women believed that they were going to worse than death, and many carried poison in their pockets to use if necessary. Some carried picks and shovels to bury those they knew would die by the wayside. During this reign of terror, notice was given that escape was easy—that anyone who accepted Islam would be allowed to remain safely at home. The offices of the lawyers who recorded applications were crowded with people petitioning to become Mohammedans. Many did it for the sake of their women and children, feeling that it would be a matter of only a few weeks before relief would come.

This deportation continued at intervals for about two weeks. It is estimated that, out of about 12,000 Armenians in X., only a few hundred were left. Even those who offered to accept Islam were sent away. At the time of writing, no definite word has been heard any of these batches. (One Greek driver reported that, at a little village a few hours from X., the few men were separated from the women, beaten and chained, and sent on in a separate batch. A Turkish driver reported seeing the convoy two days journey from X. The people were so covered with dust that features were scarcely distinguishable.) Even if the lives of these exiles are being protected, it is a question how many will be able to endure the hardships of the journey over the hot, dusty hills, with no protection from the sun, with poor food and little water, and the ever-present fear of death, or some worse fate.

Most of the Armenians in the X. district were absolutely hopeless. Many said that it was worse than a massacre. No one knew what was coming, but all felt that it was the end. Even the pastors and leaders could offer no word of encouragement or hope. Many began to doubt even the existence of God. Under the severe strain many individuals became demented, some of them permanently. There were also some examples of the greatest heroism and faith, and some started out on the journey courageously and calmly, saying in farewell: "Pray for us. We shall not see you again in this world, but sometime we shall meet again."

---

106. About 3*s*. 2*d*.

87. X.: ADDRESS DELIVERED IN AMERICA, 13th DECEMBER, 1915, BY A PROFESSOR FROM THE COLLEGE AT X.; COMMUNICATED BY THE AMERICAN COMMITTEE FOR ARMENIAN AND SYRIAN RELIEF.

On the 1st June of this year (1915), the town in Asiatic Turkey from which I come had a population of 25,000, half of which was Armenian and the other half Turkish. When I left X. on the 18th August, the 12,000 Armenians, who comprised the Armenian half of the city's population, had either been driven into exile or done to death. What happened to the Armenians of X. is but a specimen of what has happened to these poor people in every other city of Asia Minor and Armenia.

Over fifty years ago, the American Board of Commissioners for Foreign Missions established a mission station at X., which during the intervening years had grown into an important religious, educational and medical centre. We had there a boys' college with 425 students, nearly all of whom were boarders, who came from all parts of Asia Minor, from the Balkan States and from Russia. We also had a girls' boarding school with 276 pupils enrolled. Besides these we had a large hospital, which had recently been newly equipped at great expense. Here the American physician and the Armenian nurses, in addition to the ordinary large work of the hospital, were caring for sick soldiers of the Ottoman Army under the auspices of the American Red Cross Society. About half the constituency of these three institutions was Armenian. More than half the teachers and professors in the schools and nearly all the nurses of the hospital belonged to that same race, which all through the Christian centuries has been the vanguard of Christian civilisation on the frontiers of Christendom against the heathen and Mohammedan hosts of Asia, and which has been the first to respond to and co-operate with modern missionary effort in the Near East.

Now there remains not a single Armenian teacher or pupil in our mission college at X., out of the more than 200 who were there before the war began. All have been sent away by the order of the highest Government authorities, into exile or to death. With unspeakable brutality, the innocent young women teachers and pupils of the girls' school, who were remaining in the school for the summer vacation on account of the difficulties of travelling to their homes, were carried off by the Turkish gendarmes under Government orders; but with equal heroism and courage the American principal of the girls' school rescued 41 of them from death, or a condition worse than that, after nearly a month's pursuit over rough and dangerous roads.

With insensate cruelty and wickedness, the young women nurses of the hospital, who were risking their lives in nursing soldiers of the Turkish Army sick with the deadly typhus fever, were driven away by the gendarmes just like the rest of their unfortunate sisters. The American physician in charge of our hospital begged the Turkish officers in charge of the deportation to spare the nurses who were serving their own soldiers. These officers declared that they were ordered by their superiors to make no exceptions whatsoever; but, because the doctor begged so hard, four out of the dozen nurses would be allowed to remain temporarily and continue their work of mercy. That left the doctor to perform the heart-rending task of selecting those who should go and those who should remain. It was like casting pearls before swine when he made them draw lots to decide their fate. Some of the best and most experienced nurses drew lots to go. One who held a diploma from one of the leading London hospitals, who was a pioneer in the nurses' profession in Asia Minor, and who was known as the Florence Nightingale of Armenia, was taken away with the young women of the girls' school. She was not rescued with the 41 fortunate ones. Though great in soul, she was lame and not comely in form, and on this account she has probably been allowed to perish by the way instead of being reserved for a life of shame.

It is now my purpose to show you, as best I can, by narrating facts out of my recent experience at X. in connection with these events, how the work of this great mission station in Asia Minor, a work in which I have been engaged as a missionary for ten years, a work in which hundreds of our American people have a deep and personal interest, and in which they have invested hundreds of thousands of dollars of their hard-earned money and the life work of a score of devoted missionaries, was suddenly and brutally interrupted by the Turkish Government on the 10th and 12th August of this year. You will see, incidentally, how this work of destruction illustrates the deep laid and carefully executed plans of the Turkish Government for the assassination and annihilation of the Armenian people. You will see how that Government scorned and flouted all the efforts of the missionaries and of the diplomatic representatives of our Government to save the lives and the honour of innocent women and girls. You will also see how it is possible for Christian men and women to bear faithful witness to their faith in this twentieth Christian century in a persecution not less in intensity, and greater in magnitude, than any that was ever inflicted on the early Christian martyrs by the most cruel of the pagan Roman emperors. It may astonish you to hear it, but it is true nevertheless, that there are living in the world to-day men who are the equals of Nero in cruelty.

On my way from X. to Constantinople,[107] I saw at least 50,000 people, three-fourths of whom were women and children, who had been torn from their homes and all their earthly possessions, and driven into the fields along the railway line without any shelter or any adequate means of subsistence, hungry, sick and perishing, awaiting the conveniences of the railway traffic to be crowded like sheep into the goods trucks, to be carried away eastward to die in the deserts, if they did not perish or disappear in Turkish harems on the way. I saw hundreds of mothers whose hearts were being broken by the cries of their hungry children, whom they had no hope of being able to succour or to save. The officials of the German railway were co-operating with the corrupt officials of the Turkish Government to extort all the money they could from this doleful throng. The 50,000 whom I saw represented but a brief section of the procession which has been passing along that way for months.[108] A very moderate estimate of the number of people who have perished in this way places the figure at 500,000; and still they go on!

I have received the farewell kiss and parting embrace of men, cultured Christian gentlemen, some of whom held university degrees from our best American institutions in this country, men with whom I have co-operated and at whose side I have laboured for ten years in the work of education in that land, while at their side stood brutal gendarmes, sent there by the highest authorities of the Government to drive them away with their wives and children from their homes, from their work, and from all the associations which they held most dear, into exile or to death, and some of them to a condition worse than either. We had no better friends in this world than those people were. To part with them under such circumstances was harder than I can say, and yet but few tears were shed on either side. Our feelings were too deep for idle tears! I have often seen pictures of the early Christian martyrs crouching together in the arena of the Coliseum, expecting at any moment to be torn in pieces by the hungry lions which were being turned loose upon them, while the eager spectators were watching from their safe seats, and waiting to be amused by that spectacle. And I had supposed that such cruelties and such amusements were impossible in this twentieth Christian century. But I was mistaken. I have seen 62 Armenian women and girls, between the ages of 15 and 25, huddled together in the rooms of the principal of our American girls' school at X., while outside were waiting men more cruel than beasts, ready to carry them off; and these men were demanding, backed by the highest authorities of the Government, that we should deliver these defenceless girls into their brutal hands, for them to do with them what they would. I had supposed that there was no man in the world to-day who could be amused by such a spectacle as that. In this, too, I was mistaken, for when the wife of our American Ambassador at Constantinople made a personal appeal to Talaat Bey, the Minister of the Interior in the Turkish Cabinet—the man who more than anyone else has devised and executed this deportation of the Armenians, and who has boasted that he has been able to destroy more Armenians in 30 days than Abd-ul-Hamid was able to destroy in 30 years—when she made an appeal to this Turkish Minister, begging him to stop this cruel persecution of Armenian women and girls, the only answer she got from him was: "All this amuses us!"

I will now narrate some of the more important events leading up to this climax.

We were surprised on the morning of the last Wednesday in April to learn that the professor of Armenian in our college had been arrested during the previous night along with a number[109] of the other leading Armenians of the city. We found upon inquiry that all these men were or had been members of one or the other of the Armenian nationalist societies, the Hunchakists or the Dashnakists[110]. These societies had a legal existence under the Turkish Government. They had up till quite recently been on good terms with the Government of the Young Turks. They co-operated with the party of Union and Progress in overthrowing the tyranny of Abd-ul-Hamid in 1908. They desired to co-operate with the Turks in establishing an enlightened constitutional Government in Turkey. But recently, when the policy of destroying the Armenians was determined upon, it seems that the Government thought it advisable to hit the leading members of the Armenian nationalist societies first. A number of the prominent members of these societies were hanged in Constantinople. Those arrested in our city were held in prison for a few days. Then they were sent to the capital of the province, where they were tortured and exposed to the contagion of typhus fever. Within six weeks of their arrest, their families received notice through the Government officials that not any of them remained alive. The wife of our professor was a cultured young woman, who had taught for years in our girls' school. She was left a widow with one child, a little girl. She remained alone in her home, but not for long; for, some weeks after, when all the people were deported from her quarter of the city, she was carried away along with the rest. I saw her, dressed in the costume of a Turkish woman, leading her little girl by the hand as she passed by our college gate on the morning she was driven out, with hundreds of other women and children, on to the roads, to be captured or to die.

During the month of May, the Government was active in enlisting into the Army the Armenian young men whom they had not already enrolled. The majority of them were already serving under the colours, having been called out in the early months of the war. Some of our Armenian students had already been advanced to the position of officers in the Turkish Army because of their superior education and intelligence. Those who remained were now being called out and sent away. Some, who could afford it, paid the exemption tax of £44 (Turkish—about £40 sterling), and remained at home. Those who went with these last contingents, as a rule, were not allowed to bear arms, but were forced to do menial labour, such as building roads and carrying baggage, most of the horses and donkeys which had been requisitioned from the poor people in the early months of the war having died from rough usage or neglect.

In the month of June the Government repeatedly published an edict, by criers in the streets, ordering all the people to give up their weapons of every kind to the police. It was not at all strange that the Armenians should possess some weapons. It was the custom of the country, because of the insecurity of life and property there, for all who could afford it to possess some means of self-defence. It was obvious that this order was intended only for the

Armenians, as they alone were compelled to obey it, whereas their Mohammedan neighbours, who possessed at least as many weapons as they did, were not compelled to obey it. This fact aroused the suspicions of the Armenians, because they remembered that on previous occasions, when the Turks contemplated a massacre of Armenians, they began by disarming them. Many Armenians hesitated on this account to give up their arms, and none of them would have done so if they had suspected what plans the Turks had in store for them. However, the Government took special pains on this occasion to reassure the Armenians, promising them protection and security if they would give up their arms. They were told that they could prove their loyalty only by obeying the order, and they were threatened with the severest punishment if they should refuse. In spite of many misgivings, most of the Armenians gave up their arms; and some of them, to prove their loyalty, actually assisted the Government in disarming their own people. Only a very few held out against the order and hid their weapons in their houses or in their gardens. Persons suspected of doing this were arrested and taken to the Government Building, where they were subjected to the cruellest forms of torture. Usually they were bound and bastinadoed until they became unconscious. Boiling water was often poured on the soles of the feet, to increase the pain of the bastinadoing. The victim was usually ordered to confess that he was guilty of conspiracy against the Government. Often he was ordered to implicate others; and to escape the terrible pain of the torture they would say almost anything they were told to say. These declarations made under torture were used as evidence against others. At least two men of our city died under this torture. Two of our own employees were subjected to it, the one a gate-keeper and the other a blacksmith, who did general repair work about our premises. I saw two gendarmes leading this man out of our front gate one afternoon in June. They took him to the Government Building. There they bound him, and four brutal men stuffed his mouth with filth and beat him with rods all over the body until he became unconscious. As soon as he regained consciousness, they repeated the process. Apparently their intention was to kill him by torture, and they would have done so if it had not been for the timely intervention of a friendly gendarme, a Circassian, who had been in our employment and who knew the Armenian who was being tortured. He intervened and rescued the man from his tormentors, and carried him home on his own back after it was dark enough to escape observation. He was saved, but not for long. When he had recovered, a month after[111], he was carried away, with his wife and two small children, in the general deportation. We learned afterwards that the occasion for this man's torture was that he was seen casting a 16-pound shot, which we had ordered him to make for our college field-day sports this year. The man who saw him reported to the police that he had been making bombs!

After having weakened the Armenians to the extent of having sent most of the young men into the Army, and of having terrorised the rest, one night, toward the end of June,[112] suddenly, without any warning, the houses of almost all the Armenians who still remained in the city were forcibly entered by the police and gendarmes. The men were arrested and held as prisoners in the soldiers' barracks at one side of the city. The whole number amounted to 1,213. Two more of our leading Armenian professors were arrested on this occasion.[113] After being held a few days, a very few, by paying very large sums of money[114] as bribes to the officials, were allowed to become Mohammedans, and were let out, to be sent away in a few days in the opposite direction to the rest. The rest were told that they were to be sent away into exile to Mosul, in the deserts of Mesopotamia, six or seven hundred miles away.

Now the Government did not intend that any of these men should reach that destination. Its purpose was extermination, not simply deportation. While they were still held in the barracks, the commander of gendarmerie, who had the business of their deportation in charge, called at the mission compound, and talked freely about the deportation of the Armenians in the presence of all the American men in our station. He said that not one out of a thousand would ever reach Mosul, and that if any of them did arrive there they could not survive, because of the hostility of the nomads in those regions, and because of the impossibility of gaining a livelihood there when deprived of all their resources, as these Armenians had been. "Orada Christiyanliq olmaz" was the Turkish expression which he used, which means: "Over there Christianity is impossible." The Government's purpose was to get rid of Christianity in the Ottoman Empire by getting rid of the Christians. The mayor of our city told our American Consular Agent[115] that the Government intended first to get rid of the Armenians, and then of the Greeks, and finally of the foreigners, and so to have Turkey for the Turks. Enver Pasha said the same thing to our Ambassador. These 1,213 men of whom I spoke, after being held for a few days, were bound together in small batches of five or six men each and sent off at night, in companies of from 50 to 150, under the escort of gendarmes. Some 15 miles from the city[116] they were set upon by the gendarmes and by bandits called *chettis*, and cruelly murdered with axes. These *chettis* were criminals who had been turned loose from the prisons of Constantinople and the cities of the interior, and set upon the roads for the express purpose of preying upon the Armenians, as they were being driven along the roads. One of the gendarmes who helped to drive these 1,213 men away, boasted to our French teacher that he had killed 50 Armenians with his own hands, and had obtained from their persons £150 Turkish. The chief of the police at X. stated that none of these 1,213 men remained alive. Our Consular Agent visited the scene of this slaughter in August,[117] and brought back with him Turkish "nufus teskeriés," or identification papers, taken from the bodies of the victims. I personally saw these papers. They were all besmeared with blood.[118]

The motive which the Government claimed for all these cruelties was military necessity. They said that the Armenians were a disloyal element in the population, which it was necessary to weaken in order that they might not hit them in the back while they were engaged in war with the foreign foe. This was only a pretext. The real motive was a compound of religious fanaticism, jealousy, greed for loot and bestial lust. This was evident from what followed. If their motive had been to weaken the Armenians in order to protect themselves from attack, they had succeeded in doing this in a most thorough manner. The Armenians were now quite helpless. All the strong men had been sent into the Army, or killed, or sent into exile. All that now remained were the women and children and old men. But when the Government had reduced the Armenians to this helpless state, they decided to exterminate the rest. Criers were sent through the streets[119] announcing to the people that all the Armenians were to be deported. Not a single person with an Armenian name, whether rich or poor, old or young, sick or well, male or female, was to be left in the city. They were to have three days to prepare to go.

This announcement produced great consternation among the people. They came in great numbers to the mission compound, begging us to advise them what to do, bringing their money, jewels and other valuables and asking us to keep them for them. Some of them offered to give us their children, knowing that it would be impossible to keep them alive on that terrible journey. The promise of three days was not kept. The very next morning, the local police with gendarmes well armed with Mauser rifles began to enter the Armenian houses, drive the women and children into the streets, and lock the doors of their homes behind them and seal them with the Government's seal, thus dispossessing them of all their worldly possessions. They then assigned four or five persons to each of the ox-carts which they had brought with them to send the people away with. The carts were not intended to carry the people. They had to walk beside them. The carts were for carrying a pillow and a single bed-covering for each person. When they had gotten from five hundred to a thousand persons ready in this manner, they were set moving, a doleful procession, driven by gendarmes along the roads toward the east. Morning after morning, during the month of July, we saw groups of this kind pass by the college compound, the women carrying their babies in their arms and leading their little children by the hand, without anything left in this world, starting on a hopeless journey of a thousand miles into the wilderness, to die miserably or to be captured by Turks. By the end of July the city had been emptied in this manner of its 12,000 Armenian inhabitants. Only the Armenians in the mission compound remained. Fearing for their safety, we had tried to get into communication with Constantinople. All our telegrams for this purpose were intercepted by the Government. When we complained to the Governor that he was cutting us off from communication with our Ambassador, he frankly informed us that we would not be allowed to communicate with our Ambassador. This had a sinister meaning to us. It was a threat not only against the Armenians in our compound, but also against us. The Governor had declared consistently from the beginning that he would deport all the Armenians in our compound as soon as it suited his convenience. All channels of communication having failed, we sent off to Constantinople one of our Greek tutors, and following him one of our English tutors, to carry information of our situation to our Ambassador in Constantinople. They reported the Governor's threats to Mr. Morgenthau. He promptly visited Talaat Bey, the Minister of the Interior, and Enver Pasha, the Minister of War, and obtained from both these men their unqualified assurance that they would send orders to the local authorities at X. ordering them to exempt the Armenians in our schools and hospital from the general deportation. He sent repeated telegrams to this effect to our Consular Agent, whom he had ordered to come to X. to look after our interests. In this matter these ministers seem to have told a direct lie to our Ambassador, or else their subordinate officers refused to obey their orders, in which case the country would have been in a state of anarchy. But there was no sign of any anarchy in all these transactions and dealings with the Armenians. There were no mob outbreaks. Everything seemed to be under perfect control and to be carried through with military precision. When our Consular Agent showed the telegram from our Ambassador to the local Governor, he stated that he had received the exact contrary orders, and that furthermore he knew that he would not receive any other orders. Our Consular Agent, desiring to make a full report on the situation to the Ambassador, left for his post at L. on the 9th August.

The next morning, the 10th August, there appeared at the front gate of our mission compound the chief of the police of the city, with the local police force and a company of gendarmes and ox-carts. They demanded that we should admit them to the compound and should order the Armenians in our premises to come out and get ready to leave. The President of the college reminded them of the assurances we had received from Constantinople, and said that we could not allow them to enter our premises with our consent. If they wished to enter, they would have to use force and accept the responsibility therefor. They replied that if we dared to resist their authority in any way, we would be hanged just like any Ottoman subject. The Capitulations had now all been abolished, and we no longer had any rights or special privileges. They hesitated, however, to use force for a time, and sent one of their number to the Governor, asking for instructions. We also sent our doctor at the same time to do what he could in our behalf. They met in the Governor's office. The policeman reported to the Governor that the Americans were resisting their authority. The Governor gave orders to enter the premises by force and take out all the Armenians. They gathered up a squad of some 25 more gendarmes, and returned and entered the compound by force. They drove their ox-carts in and unyoked their oxen. It was a group of nomads coming to destroy a more civilised community. The gendarmes entered the college buildings and our own American residences, and drove out at the end of their rifles all the Armenians they could find. Our professors with their families were taking refuge in our houses. In the college buildings were the Armenian servants and employees connected with the institutions. They drove out all these, with our own personal servants, some of them young Armenian women, and assigned them to ox-carts just as they had done to the people of the city in the days before. They collected 71 people on our college premises in this way. When they were ready to go, we took our last sad farewell of these people with whom we had worked for years, and among whom were some of the best friends we had in the world. They had no adequate food supply. We reminded the Governor of their needs, and he promised to detain them over-night at the Armenian monastery two miles out of the city, in order that a food supply might be got ready. The college bakery was kept busy over-night baking hard tack. Early in the morning a wagon-load was taken to the monastery, but it was found that the Governor had not kept his word. The professors and their families had been hurried on as fast as possible. They had not been allowed to stop at the monastery. They had been driven on without food. We have never heard anything about that party from our college compound from that day to this, except from some of the gendarmes who took them away. They said that the men had been separated from the women out on the road, taken to one side and killed. The women had been sent on, to be disposed of as those who went before had been.

Two days after, on the 12th August, the chief of the police, with the local police force and a few gendarmes, came to the mission compound again and demanded the young women of the girls' school. The whole forenoon was spent by the missionaries in arguing with the police, and in trying to prevent them from taking the young women away. The Principal at one time thought it would be better to have them all shot in the school garden than to give them into the hands of those brutal men. When further resistance proved useless, the girls were prepared for the journey with food, clothing and money. Their American principal[120] tried to get permission to go with them. This was denied at first. Afterwards she was allowed to go as far as Y., the first day's journey. Fourteen wagons bore away the 62 young women from the school compound at two o'clock in the afternoon of the 12th August. Some beastly looking gendarmes were escorting them. At the edge of the city the procession was halted. While they waited, the Governor sent for the

President of the college to come out and witness what was done, in order, as he said, that he might see that no undue pressure was brought to bear upon these young women to change their faith. The police asked each of the young women whether they would deny their faith and become Mohammedans, to save themselves from that terrible journey. All 62 refused. Two miles out on the road the same thing was repeated. All refused again. The first night they reached Y., and were kept in a field by the city over-night. The next morning the American principal furnished them with an extra supply of food and money, and then the Governor of Y. ordered her to leave the girls and return home. She arrived back at X. on the evening of the 13th August very sad, expecting never to see any of her girls again. After four days she was granted permission to visit the Governor of the Province at Z., hoping she might be able to persuade him to order the return of her girls. She caught up with the party just this side of Z. She found that 21 of the 62 girls had been carried away and lost—41 still remained. These she was allowed to take to the compound of the American school in Z.[121] While they were waiting there, she succeeded in persuading the Governor to allow her to take the 41 remaining girls back to X. The party arrived back there on the 6th September, after nearly a month's absence on the road. Thus these brutal men were cheated out of some of their choicest prey. These 41 girls were all that were left of the city's 12,000 Armenian inhabitants who had not been exiled or killed or compelled to turn Mohammedan. What happened at X. is but a specimen of what happened to every other town in Asia Minor.[122]

Now the question arises—What do we think about all this, and how do we feel? We all know what we think and how we feel. But the more practical question—What are we going to do about it?—is more difficult to answer. Most of these people are beyond our help. But small groups such as I have described still remain in some of our mission stations, which are accessible to help through our Board. Many have escaped to Russia, where they are accessible to help through the Armenian Relief Committee. These poor people deserve our help.

The Preliminary Report by the same author contains certain passages not included in the preceding Address, which give additional information and are therefore appended here.

(*a*) The nervous strain and mental agony which our people had to endure during the month of July was terrible. They were hanging suspended between the hope that the American Ambassador would be able to do something for them and the fear that they might at any time have to suffer the terrible fate of those that had gone on before them. This dread of what might befall his wife and daughter made one of our professors temporarily insane. All were tormented with the terrible temptation to save themselves by denying their faith. They reasoned with themselves that they could profess Islam with the mental reservation that, as soon as the storm was over, they would again outwardly profess their loyalty to their true faith. About fifty members of the Protestant church and congregation yielded to this temptation, as did also a larger number of the Gregorians. Merely declaring their wish to become Mohammedans by no means insured their safety. Only the rich and powerful, and those few whom the Governor thought he could use to advantage, were accepted upon the payment of large sums of money. He was said, on good authority, to have enriched himself by £20,000 (Turkish) in this way. Many who professed Islam and paid money were deported, but usually in the opposite direction and with the understanding that they might return to their homes after a time. Some of these new recruits to Islam seemed to have their characters completely undermined. In order to show their loyalty to their new faith, they assisted the persecutors of their own people. One of our students, the son of the richest man in the city, who became a Mohammedan, stood at our gate on the day that the professors and students were deported and actually informed the gendarmes that one of the young men who had been his fellow student was missing. They went back and found him.

(*b*) On the 11th August, a Turkish doctor, who was the medical instructor for the Vilayet of Z., called on us and stated that he did not approve of the deportation of women and children, and that he would try to save three Armenian girls by taking them with him to Constantinople. One of the teachers of the girls' school, a nurse from the hospital and a pupil of the girls' school, whose home was in Constantinople, ventured to accept his offer. They prepared themselves for the journey by dressing themselves in Turkish women's costumes, so as not to attract any attention along the road. On the first night of their journey, this doctor tried to force these three young women to become Mohammedans and enter the houses of his friends. He persisted in his arguments through the whole of the first night, but they stood firm, and then he declared that he would send them back to X., and give them into the possession of the Turkish officials there who desired them. The next morning he sent them back under the charge of his servant. On the road back to X. they met the convoy carrying away the girls from the girls' school, and made themselves known by crying out to Miss A., who went to their assistance, and learned what had befallen them during the night. They begged Miss A. to get their release, in order that they might go off into exile with the rest of the girls and teachers; and the young men who had them in charge delivered them over into Miss A.'s charge, she signing a receipt that she had received them. They declared that even exile and the terrible things that might befall them by the way seemed like heaven to them after the experiences they had gone through the previous night. I tried for a month to get permission to bring the teacher in this party with us to America before she was carried away, but even the efforts of the American Ambassador on her behalf were unavailing.

The following passage is taken from the letter (dated 1st/14th October, 1915, and written by an acquaintance who interviewed the author of the preceding Address at Athens) which has been quoted already in a preceding footnote.

Two families accepted Mohammedanism at the beginning. One was the family of Professor B. with his three grown-up daughters, who were immediately required to marry Turks; the other was the family of Mr. C., a notable of the town. Both families were Protestants. The authorities allowed D.'s family to remain at X., as they wanted D. to take photographs of the bombs and guns found in the possession of the "rebels"—all such guns and bombs having been specially placed by the authorities to be photographed. D. found life unbearable as a Christian and also accepted Mohammedanism after some time. Professors E. and F., both of whose mothers are Germans, from the German colony of M., near Y., were rescued by the German colonists, and remained with them up to the time my friend (the author of the preceding Address) left X. The Kaimakam of X. said that they had only escaped for the moment, and that he would get at them, too, in the end.

Two Turks of X. were hanged for sheltering or offering to shelter some Armenian friends of theirs.

---

107. The witness started from X. on the 18th August.—*Preliminary Report dated 7th October, 1915, from the witness' hand.*

108. "At Mirkedjia alone, the station-master told us there were 30,000 exiles. Many were weak from hunger, others almost dead."—*P.R.*

109. "Twenty-five."—*P.R.*

110. "This Professor had relinquished his association with this society before entering our employment."—*P.R.*

111. "He remained unconscious for a day, and could not walk for a month."—*P.R.*

112. "The 26th June."—*P.R.*

113. "Professors E. and FF."—*P.R.*

114. "£275 Turkish, in all."—*P.R.*

115. "Mr. AL."—*P.R.*

116. "On the road to W."—*P.R.*

117. "A German farmer reported to our Consular Agent that he had seen 50 Armenian corpses in a well, and long trenches on the mountain side where other victims had been buried."—*P.R.*

118. *The author of the present address gave further particulars of these men's fate to an acquaintance who interviewed him at Athens on his way from Turkey to the United States. This gentleman is the author of the letter dated Athens, 8th/21st July, Doc. 8 of this collection. The information he obtained from his interview with the author of the present document is presented in a subsequent letter, dated Athens, 1st/14th October, 1915, from which the following paragraph is taken:—*

"The Kavass of the College, a Circassian, who was ordered to accompany the deported Armenians, returned a day or two afterwards and told how these 1,200 men or more were roped together in rows of five, and were marched towards Y. On each side rode zaptiehs with fixed bayonets. Those who could not walk were flogged, and finally, when any one of the five in a batch could walk no further, the whole five would be made to fall out of the procession and several zaptiehs would remain with them, who, after ten or twenty minutes, would rejoin the column with the ghost of butchery shining in their eyes. Somewhat more than half the prisoners reached Y. On their arrival at that town a fire broke out in the Armenian quarter, and the Turks began looting and massacring the women of Y., while the newly arrived prisoners were accused of being the incendiaries, and were all led out of the town to a place already prepared. Here the prisoners were halted and led in successive batches of five to what appeared to be tents. Groans were heard from within, and the prisoners outside, realising what was happening, tried to break through the cordon. But they were bound hand to hand, and when one or two in any batch had been shot, the survivors could only trail the corpses along with them until they gave up the effort in exhaustion. They were all picked up afterwards and carried off to be butchered. They were butchered with axes."

119. "On the 2nd July."—*P.R.*

120. "Miss A."—*P.R.*

121. "At Z. the servants were separated from the teachers and pupils and sent southwards towards V."—*P.R.*

122. "The town of L. was similarly emptied of its Armenian population; also Y., BT. and U."—*P.R.*

88. X.: STATEMENT BY MISS AA., A FOREIGN TRAVELLER IN TURKEY; COMMUNICATED BY THE AMERICAN COMMITTEE FOR ARMENIAN AND SYRIAN RELIEF.

The feud between the Armenians and the Turks is of very long standing. The Armenian nation is the only one of all the peoples conquered by the Turkish nation which has not yielded to the demand of the Turkish Government that they should give up their religion and become Mohammedans. When the relations between the two nations became settled after their many wars, the Armenians were given much religious freedom, but with that freedom came also many oppressive measures which have been very hard to bear. The Armenian, through all the centuries, has been exempt from military service. In place of that, each male member of the Armenian families paid a small poll-tax. This freedom from military service gave the young men an opportunity to engage in trade.

The nation is a nation of great traders. They travel easily and are keen in every financial relation. As a result, when the young Turks came back from their military service they found in all the large cities that the young Armenians had seized all the opportunities in trade. The soldiers have always felt that they had the right to loot these unfortunate persons, and this has been most systematically done for centuries.

When *Huriet*[123] came in, the privilege of military service was given to the Armenians, and it was announced in many public meetings that the fraternity between Armenians and Turks was to be complete.

Before this time, the Armenians had not been allowed to carry arms, but the Committee of Union and Progress advised them to carry personal arms, as the Turks had done for many years. There have been among the Armenians what have been called "National Societies." These societies have been more or less revolutionary and nihilistic in character, but they have also been very useful in promoting the advancement and education of the Armenian people, and since *Huriet* their revolutionary propaganda has been very much lessened. But it was these societies that furnished arms for the men who could afford to pay for them, and it is claimed by the Turkish Government that they also hid in various cities bombs and reserve arms, which were to be used against the Turkish Government when opportunity arose.

In many cities such bombs have been found hidden. It is very difficult to find absolute evidence for the truth of political statements made by any party in Turkey, but it is true that these revolutionary societies had, in certain centres, hidden bombs for the defence of the people. Whether their plans included definite insurrection or not, I do not know; if so, they were most inadequate.

The history of the Armenians in Turkey has not merely consisted in exposure to great financial losses, but, at intervals of about 20 years, the Turks have risen against them in greater or lesser massacres. In the border towns, their daughters have been carried away; their flocks have been at the mercy of the Kurds; their houses have been taken by any powerful Sheikh who wished to do so, and they have never been allowed justice in the courts.

With this history behind them, it is not astonishing that they had no faith in the promises of fraternity from the party of Union and Progress, and their arms could easily be explained as being a means of protection against Turkish attack, should a massacre arise.

When Turkey entered this war, the Armenians were conscripted with the Turks, but a large number of the people had money with which to pay the £40 which would exempt them from military service. In X., out of the 5,000 soldiers that were sent off, 4,000 were Turks and 1,000 Armenians, while the proportion of Turks and Armenians in the population of the place is about even. It meant, of course, that many more Armenian men were left in the place than Turks. The Turks claimed that this was a menace to the safety of the city and also of the country. They began to oppress the Armenians by requisitioning from them large quantities of cloth, for clothing the Army, and food. Their stores were practically emptied of everything that could be used by the Army. Horses, wagons, donkeys were all taken, and no money was paid; a promissory paper was given, but no one valued it.

About eight months after the beginning of the war, a notice was served on all Armenians that they must give up their arms. The reason for this was stated to be that there were so many more Armenians than Turks left in the country and that the nation was known to be revolutionary. This political difficulty was being anticipated by the Government, which was in no condition to meet an inter-racial revolution.

At other times, just before a massacre, arms had been demanded from the Armenians, and so when this order was given great fear took possession of the people. The Government promised in public and private that no harm should come to the Armenians, and that this was only a war measure and a legitimate protection to the nation. The Armenians, however, gave up their arms very reluctantly and very slowly.

But suddenly one night a batch of about 20 men were arrested and sent, after a day or two's imprisonment, to Z., the seat of the Vali for the whole province. This was immediately followed by the imprisonment of other leaders among the Armenians of the city. These men were tortured cruelly. Meanwhile what was going on in X. was being duplicated in all other cities. I saw some of the men who had been released, after they had been exhausted by torture. They had been thrown into a dungeon and kept without food, then beaten on their backs and the soles of their feet, and, when the flesh was sensitive, hot water had been poured on them and they had been beaten again—all this in order to make them reveal the whereabouts of the hidden arms. When they would not tell, they were made to kneel and their arms and feet were bound together; their mouths were filled with manure and all kinds of indignities were poured upon them. Some died under the process; many went mad. Eyes and nails were torn out. Some were let go, whether they had confessed anything that satisfied the Government or not, but many others disappeared entirely. This sort of inquisition went on until late in June.

Some bombs were found in a field, and it is claimed that they had been hidden in the houses in the city and then, in fear, transferred to this field, where the Government soon afterwards found them.

The Missionaries approached the Government, asking that a Committee from the different Armenian communities—Catholic, Gregorian and Protestant—might be formed, to collect arms. The Government gave permission for this, and promised again that no trouble should be given to the Armenians if they gave up their arms. The Government told the Committee how many rifles ought to be delivered from that city, and claimed to know who had most of them. Representatives of the Committee spoke to the people in the churches, and promised that if they would deliver their arms to them their names would not be given to the Government. The requisite number of rifles were soon collected, but, almost immediately, the order for deportation was given.

First the men were taken, usually from their homes at night, and imprisoned in empty barracks. About 400 men were taken the first time. The next morning their families were notified that they were to be deported, and that, if they wished, they could furnish them with food and clothing. So the women got together their supplies and carried them to their husbands, hoping that they were providing for their needs on a long journey. They sold everything they could lay their hands on, and provided money for the men. After a few days the men were sent away. They were sent at night, bound in fours, about 50 a night. The barracks were continually filled with recruits from the city. I do not know what became of these men, but I do know that, within six hours of the city, there are long ditches and deep wells filled with the bodies of Armenians. Their clothing was taken from them, as well as those supplies that the women had so pathetically prepared, and all their money.

Officers of the Government have told our friends that the official figure for the number of men killed at X. is over 1,300. People like to tell stories in Turkey, and it may be that this is not true.

On the 4th July the deportation order for the women came. It had been hoped that they would be allowed to remain. At the same time, it was publicly announced that people could save themselves if they would become Mohammedans. Large numbers, it is said 1,000 families, put in petitions to the Government. Only a small number of these petitions were accepted; the rest of the women and children were rapidly sent away.

Ox-carts were provided, and in some cases wagons, by the Government, but the people had to pay the carriage hire; if not, they had to walk. Some people could get donkeys, but, of course, the poor went on foot. It was difficult to get wagons and carts, and so the people were not all sent out at once. The Government scheduled the houses of those who were to go in each company, and gave them notice two or three days beforehand.

Sometimes they were taken in batches of from three to four hundred up to a monastery, about an hour from the city. Here they were imprisoned, and the Turkish men and women went to take away the women and girls who could be persuaded to become Turks and live in their harems. This was said to be the only way to save their lives, for they were all assured over and over again that, if they were not killed by the gendarmes or the wild villagers, they would die from the privations of the journey.

The missionaries in X. were allowed to bring to their premises those people who belonged to their institutions, the families of professors and servants, and many girls who had been students in the school. It was vacation, and, although a Summer school had been open to other boarders who could not get home because of the war, most of the city pupils who were in their own homes were allowed to enrol themselves as boarders.

The Government soon said that they must clear the premises. Some of the professors were arrested and imprisoned, but, by a money arrangement with the Government, their Armenian friends were able to secure them their release. It was soon learned that the Armenian people in the town were beginning to offer large sums of money for their protection and for permission to remain. These offers were accepted. The women gave their jewels to the wives of the Government officers, and obtained promises that they should not be sent away, although in every case they were obliged to become Moslems. The missionaries tried in every possible way to persuade the Government to allow their people, about 350 in all, to remain upon their premises. The American Embassy in Constantinople secured permission from the Ministries of War and the Interior for these people to be protected. But these authorisations were not recognised by the local Government, and, on the 10th August, the professors and servants were sent away on ox-carts—about 173 in all. The nurses in the hospital and the sickest of the patients, together with the people in the Girls' School, were not taken at this time, but they were taken on the 12th August. The professors and servants travelled together as far as W., about a week's journey with ox-carts, over the mountains. Here the men were bound together, shoulder to shoulder, in batches of four and marched away. Their wives sorrowfully went on alone. As these women reached the high mountain pass of AZ., the Circassians rushed upon them and robbed them of coats and bedding, as well as of all the gold they could lay their hands on.

These people and all those who went from X., and indeed from the whole Vilayet of Z., travelled east as far as the village of V. Here whatever means of conveyance they had travelled with was taken away and they were obliged to find some substitute. Wagoners placed exorbitant prices on their wagons. Ox-cart drivers quadrupled their prices, and many people were unable to find any way, except to go on foot. They were then driven eastward to Kirk Göz, a small village about six hours from Malatia, on the bank of the River Euphrates.

There again their conveyances were taken away, and they could not cross the river without paying large sums of money. Many, many died here, and it is said that many were thrown into the river. From this point they went south over the Taurus mountains, and word has been received from a few at Surudj and Aleppo....

(A portion of this document has been omitted here, and printed separately as Doc. 96)

went out from Constantinople to all the vilayets stopping further deportation of Armenians, but yet the deportation has been continuing ever since. Only four weeks before I left X., a company of young Armenian brides with their little boys, all of whom had become Mohammedans, were sent away. The order had come privately, not to the Governor but to the police, that women who had boys, no matter if they were babies in arms, should be deported with their children. Of that category there were perhaps three or four hundred in the city, and about 60 wagon-loads were chosen out at this time to go. No warning was given to the people beforehand; the ox-carts were simply driven to their doors in the morning. They had made no preparation, and the women, especially mothers-in-law (who have a good deal of influence in this country) were very angry. They went to the Governor and said: "See! We have given our pearl necklaces to your wife in order to save our lives; we paid one hundred liras to be saved; we have become Mohammedans. We have sold our souls and have given our money, and now you take our lives. We will not go." One woman stood up on her cart and shouted all the Mohammedan prayers she had learned, to prove that she was a Mohammedan. It was a time of general frenzy. But they grabbed the women—bound them to the carts in many instances—and took them to the Armenian monastery. There they were imprisoned, but after much petitioning they finally got permission to send a representative from each family to the city to prepare food and get money for their journey. They sold their personal effects and in this way provided for themselves. This whole batch was killed in the mountains, on the other side of the plain from the city. Their birth certificates were found, and the burial had been so badly done that the bodies of little children were left on the ground, and the arms and legs of the corpses in the ditches protruded. Stories of this kind can, of course, be duplicated in all parts of the country, but I am only telling the things I can personally vouch for.

Many stories of wonderful bravery are told of the people who went away. In Samsoun, one of the most prominent Protestants of the place was not allowed to go with the crowd that was first sent out. The Governor came to him, and said to him: "You are a man, a real man; we do not want you to be lost. Now just say that you will be a Turk, and your life and that of your family will be saved." The man replied: "But I cannot say I believe a thing of which I am not convinced. I do not believe the Mohammedan religion; you must educate me." So they sent their teachers to him, and every few days would send in an official and ask him: "Now, are you not convinced?" Thus two weeks went by and finally the officials' patience wore out, for the man continually said: "No, I cannot see what you see, and I cannot accept what I cannot understand." So the ox-carts came to the door and took the family away. The wife was a delicate lady, and the two beautiful daughters well educated. They were offered homes in harems, but said: "No, we cannot deny our Lord. We will go with our father."

From this city the whole Protestant community went together, led bravely by the Pastor. We heard from them near Shar-Kishla, but their men had all been taken away and the women robbed terribly.

In a mountain village there was a girl who made herself famous. Here, as everywhere else, the men were taken out at night and pitifully killed. Then the women and children were sent in a crowd, but a large number of young girls and brides were kept behind. This girl, who had been a pupil in the school at X., was sent before the Governor, the Judge and the Council together, and they said to her: "Your father is dead, your brothers are dead, and all your other relatives are gone, but we have kept you because we do not wish to make you suffer. Now just be a good Turkish girl, and you shall be married to a Turkish officer and be comfortable and happy." It is said that she looked quietly into their faces and replied: "My father is not dead, my brothers are not dead; it is true you have killed them, but they live in Heaven. I shall live with them. I can never do this if I am unfaithful to my conscience. As for marrying, I have been taught that a woman must never marry a man unless she loves him. This is a part of our religion. How can I love a man who comes from a nation that has so recently killed my friends? I should neither be a good Christian girl nor a good Turkish girl if I did so. Do with me what you wish." They sent her away, with the few other brave ones, into the hopeless land. Stories of this kind can also be duplicated.

The number of Armenians in Turkey was variously estimated at from one and a half millions to two and a half millions. Most people who know this country well, think that not over five hundred thousand are now left. This, however, may be too small an estimate, for there are thousands left in the various cities who have become Mohammedans. But this "turning" is recognised by both Christians and Mohammedans as a temporary thing. There are also many in hiding, especially in Greek villages and in the mountain districts. In previous years, after massacres, people have sprung up from most unexpected quarters, and I expect that this will be the case again. Those who were left, however, have been more thoroughly stripped of all worldly possessions than has ever been the case before. The best houses are immediately occupied by Turkish officials. Furniture has been taken to furnish officers' houses and Government buildings. The disposal of the rest of the property varies in different places.

In X., the best furniture is being stored in the Gregorian churches, to be disposed of by the Commission appointed by the Government. However, almost everything that is valuable is gradually disappearing. The more common things are thrown into an empty square and auctioned or sold for a song.

X. is a city of weavers, and all the equipment for the looms was in the public square when I came away, and was ruined by rain and mud.

Whatever may be said about the revolutionary intentions of the Armenian people, a rebellious nation is not executed by its government, but is fought in fair fight, and those of us who have loved the Turks and believed that they would, in the end, work out a government that could be respected, grieve almost more over this great failure of theirs than over the suffering of their unfortunate subjects.

---

123. The Constitution of 1908.—EDITOR.

89. NARRATIVE OF MISS AA., A FOREIGN TRAVELLER IN ASIATIC TURKEY, DESCRIBING A JOURNEY FROM X. TO Z., 10th AUGUST TO 6th SEPTEMBER, 1915; COMMUNICATED BY THE AMERICAN COMMITTEE FOR ARMENIAN AND SYRIAN RELIEF.

The delay of our party in Constantinople was hard to bear there, but the circumstances found on our arrival at X. were so distressing as to make the delay heart-breaking. All the Armenian college people—professors, teachers, servants and their families, with many from the hospital—had gone on the 10th August. We arrived on the evening of the 11th, and the next morning the Government officers had wagons driven on to the premises for the girls in the A.G.S. The order was peremptory. Of course the Kaimakam was visited, but no change in the order could be obtained. The Principal and I finally went and asked that Miss A. and I might be allowed to accompany the girls. This was refused, but finally a paper was given allowing us to precede or follow them by an hour.

There were at this time 74 Armenians in the school. The children in the deaf school with two caretakers were allowed to remain in their building, and the two old ladies, Miss AG. and Miss AH., who had been connected with the school during all its fifty years of life, were also allowed to stay. (There had been some 135 people in the school for several weeks, but they had many of them gone to other cities for safety, or, in the case of girls, had gone with their mothers into exile.)

The company that left the premises consisted of 62 people—7 trained nurses, 6 teachers, 3 dressmakers, 15 servants or members of their families, and 31 students. One of the only two trained teachers in the Ottoman Empire for teaching vocal speech to the deaf, was there. Perhaps the best trained native nurse in Anatolia was there. One of the few good music teachers in the country was there. The Armenian nurse who had gone in the winter to take care of the soldiers sick with typhus was there. The Presidents of the City Y.W.C.A. and of the student Y.W.C.A., the advisory officer, and four members of the cabinet were in the company. It was indeed too precious a group to be swept into the mälström of wretchedness that makes up the unending procession of the "exiled" in Anatolia. (It is said that 91,000 have passed south through Harpout, and that 250,000 is the number that must pass south over the mountains from Malatia.)

Just before Miss A. and I left the house, an urgent order came to the Principal, summoning him to the outskirts of the city. The Kaimakam wished him to be present when the official invitation was given to the girls to become Mohammedans. The invitation was politely given to each girl individually, and no force was used; but, an hour further on, another officer was sent to urge them again and to tell them of the inevitable death that awaited them in a very short time if they did not yield; then the wagon drivers began their work, telling continually of the horrors that lay before them. This was only the beginning of the pressure brought to bear upon them. The girls say that no day passed in which at least three formal representations were not made. Men of all types, even the most disgusting, were brought to them to urge them to "turn." Whenever the officers presented the matter, they were always asked if they did not want to take "a new name." This is entirely different from the former custom of the Turks when enforcing their religion. Formerly all have been asked simply to affirm their belief in one God. This "New Name" makes one shudder, when one connects it with the Revelation. The party was most splendidly protected physically on all their journey, for, in accordance with the promises, the greatest care had been taken in choosing the gendarmes and their sleeping places; but in spite of this care on the part of the Government, several nights were spent in their wagons, so vile were the threats made to them if they should descend. However, they reached AW.-han (one day's journey beyond AX.) without any change in their number. There they were kept two nights and days, and every effort was made to terrorise them. One girl finally gave up the fight and consented to become the wife of an officer from Y. Here, also, the servants with their families and the older nurse, Miss K., were separated from the others and sent on via V., while the girls and teachers were sent on to Z. The girls say that the reason for this was the belief that the older ones in the party influenced the younger not to "turn." However, the men were finally convinced of the uselessness of their efforts when one of the younger and prettiest girls spoke up for herself and said: "No one can mix in my decisions; I will not turn, and it is I myself that say it."

The Principal decided to accompany Miss A. and me to Y. This was a great blessing to us. We passed the long line of fourteen wagons on the plain, and hastened on to find the Mutessarif Pasha if possible that night. This, however, proved impossible, and we were obliged to content ourselves with peering out of our han window at the line of wagons slowly winding through the streets of the city in the dusk to a camping place outside the town. The police of the city immediately called on us, and refused to accept our travelling papers, saying that they knew no Kaimakam's orders—that they only recognised the police. We were not received by the Pasha early, and so were blocked; but we were given permission to go to the girls with food and money. The night had been a frightful one, and it seemed as if we could never let them go alone, but orders soon drove them out and they bravely started off. It was a heart-breaking experience to all of us. We hastened back to the city for permission to follow them. The Pasha was very stiff, and would not admit that the Government needed any assistance in looking after its children. We soon saw that it was useless to do anything but send a complimentary telegram to the Vali, asking him to keep our pupils under his personal protection.

We came back to X. and for four days worked to get more satisfactory travelling papers, but were finally obliged to start off with only a note from the police saying that no papers were needed for travelling within the bounds of the same vilayet, except in the case of suspects. In Y. our papers were again refused, but we had written to the Mutessarif the nicest note we could get translated into Turkish, asking his help in securing an opportunity for us to visit the Vali in Z. Twenty-four hours went by, and then we heard that a town meeting had been called and a negative decision made to our request. We decided that that word must never officially reach us. We started for the Pasha's office, but he had gone to his harem. Here we followed him. We found his wife a real woman, with great sympathy for our desire to save our girls from the terrors of deportation, and the Pasha in his home was a transformed man. He promised to get us to the Vali if possible, and in due time this promise was made good. The police succeeded in putting enough obstacles in our way to keep us in the city another night, and so our people were six days ahead of us when we started from Y. The last annoyance was a peremptory command to sleep in a certain han. This we refused to do because of its inconvenience, and so we stayed in a han in the heart of the city, only a short distance from the recently burned district. We do not know why we were not wanted there, but the sickening odour that came into our windows till late into the night, the words which dropped from groups of men passing under our windows, and the five slowly fading fresh fire-spots on the ruins of the buildings, said to have been set on fire by the "turned" Armenians of the city, make me morally certain that a ghastly revenge had been taken that night.

Our guard was ready betimes in the morning. Our wagoner—a great Turkish thug—was on our side and ready to make time. The Pasha's paper assured the greatest courtesy at every police station, and with rising hope we started off. But hope fades in the face of the great sight of these deported people, and we soon felt that in all human reason our request must be fruitless. We passed that first day two great processions of the exiles, all villagers from the mountains of BU. A few were riding in ox-carts, but the great majority were on foot. The dust was suffocating, and the poor things all carried great burdens—sometimes little children, often cradles with babies in them, always sacks of supplies. All we could do was to hold out a little money to them. We tried most often to give to the old or to young girls. They were often too much frightened or dazed to come to our carriage and take it, but our great husky driver would shout out: "Do not fear, these will help you." Then they would come, but their fear only too plainly told of their experience. I must, however, witness to the fact that we did not see any sign of anything but patience and even kindness on the part of the gendarmes walking with these crowds. The general impression gotten everywhere is that orders are carried out, only orders, and that even the cruelties are well organised. Very few men were in the parties, but there were some. These people had been on the road more than three weeks.

We reached a lonely unfinished han three hours beyond AY. Here we found our first company of "turned" Armenians. They were from the town of L., and were going they knew not where. We met many after this; they are a little more comfortable than the Christians, and their men are with them, but they have been robbed like the others, and are full of uncertain fear of what may be coming to them, and also of remorse because their denial of what is really precious to them has brought them so little. We only stopped in AX. to send telegrams and get the story of that city. The men here, as everywhere else, had been rounded up first and sent off bound in fours, in gangs of from forty to fifty, in various directions from the city—to death, as all believe. In every city the citizens all believe this to be the fate of all men; all the gendarmes and arabadjis say it is, but all the officers deny it, saying that they send the men in this way because they have no gendarmes to handle the situation in any other way. They take all money and weapons (even razors) from them for the same reason. In AX. the women were also imprisoned and sent out without any preparation for the journey. The AX. people say that the AZ. Pass is the place where all the worst things happen, and we can well believe it. At BA. it looked ugly, and although it was quiet enough except for the coarse voices of the terrible-looking officers that were sitting about, you felt that things were wrong. A little bride and a slim young girl sidled up to our wagon to talk. In reply to our talk they told us that they were "busy taking care of the babies." We asked what babies, and they said: "O, those the effendis stop here; the mothers nurse them and then go." We asked if there were many, and were told that every house was full. We were watched too closely to make calls possible. Afterwards we found an officer ready to talk, who said: "We take them off after a while and kill them. What can we do? The mothers cannot take them, and the Government cannot take care of them for ever." That night we stopped in another lonely place with a lot of new Turks in it. We were glad to help the sick, both among them and in the Circassian village near by, though I have no doubt the Circassians belonged to the bands who rob the exiles so frequently on this mountain. In the early morning, as we climbed the AZ. Pass, we passed a great camp of exiles. We decided that we needed to save the horses, so we walked up the steep ascent. We knew that our own girls were not far ahead, and wondered if our professors were here. They were not, but the company proved to be from BC., and the pastor and people were there. As we walked by, we saw ahead of us the girl teacher who has so self-sacrificingly worked there these many years. We had prepared packages of money to give away, and as she threw her arms about us with a brave quiver of her chin and a look of agony never to be forgotten, we hid upon her person a bag of money and told her to use it for all. There was no opportunity for talk except to learn that the men were still with the party. At the top of the mountain, when we changed our guard, I went into the kitchen to buy milk and talk. It was evident that we had not been allowed to come up the night before, although we had pleaded for it. Forty prisoners had been there, and they had been taken off to the tents just the other side of the mountain in the night and disposed of in some way. We wondered if it could have been our own professors and workers. We learned later that they (our people) had been separated from their wives at W. a few days before, and that the women had been robbed on this mountain only forty-eight hours before.

We reached AW.-han about nine that morning—only the second morning from Y.—and went immediately into the town for news, though we were apparently only interested in the famous rug-industry of the place. While I was discussing this interesting industry with a man, a woman told Miss A. to hurry to the deserted factory—that our girls were there and in danger. My man had already proposed to take us there. We found no rugs and no girls. The former had been confiscated by the Government, and the latter had gone only two hours before toward Z., five hours away. A friend turned up in the street, who told us that the girls had had a hard time here and that we had better go directly to the Kaimakam. This we did. He told us a made-up story, but said that the girls would lunch at BD.-han and that we could overtake them if we would hurry. We hurried! When we rounded the last turn of the road we saw the most beautiful sight I ever expect to see—every window full of dark heads and waving handkerchiefs. The Kaimakam had telephoned that they might wait for their teachers. He was the man who had tried so hard to get a girl, and to whom our small maiden had made her confession of faith! (When you are in the Government it is just as well not to let your left hand know what your right doeth.) After a few words with the girls, we hastened on to the city, reaching there about two hours before the girls. Just as we reached the city, we said to the gendarme with us: "Why should not these girls stay with us at the American School while we wait for the Vali's decision?" He gave rather a non-committal reply, but we were scarcely settled with our friends when this man turned up, saying: "There has been a mistake; I got the permission for the girls to come here, but they have been taken to a Turkish boarding school." A visit to the Turkish school soon straightened this out, though for a while we feared our misunderstanding would be a fatal one for our cause. The Vali's sister is greatly interested in this school, which has been established for Armenian girls left in villages whose adult inhabitants had been sent on "sefkyat." The authorities thought our girls a new relay, and were a little disgusted that it was not so. One of the humorous experiences of the journey occurred before the girls were allowed to leave. In the dim light they were lined up to meet the commissioner of education, who wished to say a few words to them. They dressed like Turkish girls on the journey in white sheets, and were a weird sight in the long hall; but when the commissioner told them that they had no need to leave that fine place and go with foreigners, and asked them if they would not rather change their names and stay there, there came so emphatic a "Khyar, Effendim" from the long line, that they were immediately proved to be very lively ghosts. The Vali was away from the city attending to a Kurdish revolution in the villages, and this affair gave a very providential opportunity for a call on his sister, to apologise for the seeming lack of appreciation of her hospitality on the part of our students. She was stiff and angry, but we ended the best of friends, I saying that I wished she and all the world were

Christian, and she avowing that she wished me a Mohammedan, and each of us declaring that we were going to use our best efforts to bring about our desires.

As soon as the Vali returned, we called, and after a very pleasant talk on every subject but the one in hand, we handed him our formal petition for the return of the girls. He immediately granted it, inviting us not to hurry away, but to enjoy the hospitality of his city as long as possible. We concluded that it was better not to hasten, for we wanted an opportunity to present another petition for our professors, and to talk to him about relief for the suffering in his country. The second call was not so pleasant as the first, for the idea of his country needing any help from foreign nations under any circumstances was an absurdity. We told him that no country could live to itself in this age of reciprocity, and that in time of great trouble, whether caused by nature or by war, friendship was shown as much by accepting help as by giving it; that our country could only in these sad days offer to help the warring nations, and that it was doing it indiscriminately. He warmed a little, but said that at present there was no need and that he had not such matters in charge.

We only left our petition for the return of our other friends, and took leave after he had assured us that our journey should be facilitated in every way. This was done. He himself was on the telephone at the AZ. Pass to hear from our own lips the assurance that we were passing that dangerous place in comfort. We came in comfort, and this fact only emphasised the suffering of those we met always going in the other direction. Our driver one day voiced the thought of our hearts: "Who will give the Arzu Hal for these?" The road all along the way was marked by dead and decaying animals, and though we did not personally see human bodies, we were told of their presence under bridges and in ravines, and frequent groups of vultures gave silent witness. There were many feeble and dying in the processions we met, for the weather was very hot. In Y. we called on the Pasha and his family and the gendarmerie chief, and were very politely received and earnestly congratulated. But in the early morning, when Miss A. and I went up town to get some necessary supplies for the journey, six men hung on gallows in the streets and one old man was saying: "Why, that is my son!" So near are joy and agony in the world, and especially in this land. They were deserters from the Army.

Our findings, in regard to what we have witnessed, are as follows:—

I. The Armenians have been deported practically universally from these six vilayets. Many of them have been killed by order of the Government and many have died by the way, but many also are enduring months of travel, and are approaching the borders of the great Arabian desert, where help must be gotten to them. A large plan of relief is absolutely necessary. It must emanate from the capital and there receive authority.

II. Orders given from Constantinople are often made void by other private orders; so anything that is promised must be written, and put in the hands of the people authorised to carry it out in co-operation with the Government. Only official seals will be recognised.

III. The orders about Protestants are only partially acknowledged by a few authorities, and in most cases all Protestants have either gone into exile or have been terrorized into becoming Mohammedans. Some order providing for relief for them, either where they are this winter or after they return to their plundered homes, is necessary if any real help is to be given them.

IV. Permission for the recantation of the recently "turned" Protestants would be of the greatest help to the country, for their condition is most pitiable. They are neither one thing nor the other, and are afraid to engage in any real business, for all they possessed is soon required of them in bribes by different officers.

V. Bribe-taking has been enormous in some places, notably in X.; many have paid 2,000 liras to save their lives and then been sent into exile practically without a para.

VI. Forcible Mohammedanizing has been universal, in the assurance that death on the road is the only available alternative. Many, for the sake of trying to save wife and children a little while, have so changed their faith. The best of the Turks, however, only emphasise the national side of this change and not the religious.

VII. The Turkish houses are full of Christian children, girls and women. They are usually early registered Mohammedans and an Imam comes and teaches them some of the prayers. After a while their "nufus" teskeriés are called for and a Turkish one given in their place, and so their nationality is lost.

VIII.—*Omitted by the Editor.*

IX. What has become of the men is a profound mystery, but I am increasingly certain that the large majority of them have been killed. The soldiers are still most of them alive, I believe, though all say that in the end they will also be killed. I talked with one who had managed to crawl to the Z. hospital wounded. He was one of ten men who had escaped, when all the rest of their company of 200 had been shot by the gendarmes in a defile of the mountains.

90. X.: REPORT FROM MR. AL., A FOREIGN RESIDENT AT L., IN ASIATIC TURKEY, DATED 26th AUGUST, 1915; COMMUNICATED BY THE AMERICAN COMMITTEE FOR ARMENIAN AND SYRIAN RELIEF.

On the 14th instant I started again for X., and I returned from there on the 24th.

On the 10th instant, that is, immediately after my departure, the Turkish Government carried away, in 31 ox-carts, part of the Armenians of the College and the Hospital.

These gentlemen had been instructed by me not to allow these people to start voluntarily, and as you will see stated in the Principal's letter, they were taken by force. Besides, 63 persons were taken from the Girls' School.

As stated in the Principal's letter, the lawyer of the College said that these people could perhaps be released if a sum of two or three hundred pounds (Turkish) were given to the Kaimakam and the Gendarmerie Commander. But as I could not approve such proceedings on the part of the College, I sent you a telegram on the 13th instant, reporting on the actions of the authorities at X.

It seems that the Kaimakam, the Gendarmerie Commander and the Beledié-Reis could not agree on the sharing of the sum, so that the Kaimakam dared not accept the money from the Americans, and meanwhile the girls were sent away.

The conversion of these girls to Islam was attempted, but as they refused to change their religion, they were sent towards Y. Miss AA., Miss A., and the Principal went with them to Y. There they were not allowed to enter the city, and had to camp in the open air.

The Americans were forbidden by the Mutessarif to go further than Y., on the pretext that the vessikas which they had taken at X. were without value. They came back to X. I told them that they could have asked the Kaimakam for a vessika for Z., stating that they had to work for the American Mission at that place. On the 16th instant this was tried, but the Kaimakam did not believe the reason given, and he said that only the Mutessarif of Y. could decide about that departure. Miss AA. and Miss A. then started again for Y., on the 16th instant.

At Y. they could not at first manage to see the Mutessarif, so they called at his harem, where he came later. They succeeded in obtaining from him the promise that he would ask the Vali of Z. for that permission. Thus was the journey finally permitted.

Miss AA. and Miss A. will arrive at Z. at the same time as the 63 girls, and they will try to obtain from the Vali permission to accompany them.

These girls are accompanied by a servant from the College, and inform telegraphically of their arrival in each place.

I doubt whether Miss AA. and Miss A. will ever succeed in obtaining that permission from the Vali, because these girls are all from 12 to 18 years old, and they will assuredly be distributed among the Turkish families of Z., Malatia, etc.

Only 52 persons are left in the College and the Hospital. I gave a list of their names to the Kaimakam, requesting him to deliver them vessikas so that they may not be troubled. The Kaimakam sent that list to the Vali of Z., and he told me before I left that these people would in any case be allowed to stay. I am convinced, however, that the contrary will happen, because this is a European institution, and life is made very hard for these people. They were all ready to be sent away on the 18th or 19th instant, but my presence prevented that action. I telegraphed requesting permission for the remaining Armenians to keep their positions, because otherwise Dr. BB. would be obliged to close the hospital, because he cannot do without an apothecary or without nurses.

My opinion is that, owing to the Government's proceedings, no foreign mission will now be able to carry on its work in Turkey, because they cannot do without the Christian element....

There still remain in X. a few more Armenians who are hiding themselves, and also those who have embraced Islam, but these will assuredly be deported after they have taken all that they possess.

I called on the Kaimakam the last day, and he was very kind to me. I went also to M. I know from a reliable source that nothing disagreeable happened to the Armenians from L. on the way to Y. The Mutessarif was very kind, and gave the gendarmes strict instructions, threatening them with severe punishment in case the Armenians were ill-treated. He even asked the Commander of Gendarmerie, Latif Bey, to accompany them to BH. The latter was very kind to the Armenians, and these are very grateful both to him and to the Mutessarif.

At Y., the women were separated from the men, and the latter were bound in groups of five and carried away at night, no one knows where.

Near Y. there is a well which must contain from fifty to sixty corpses; heaps of torn clothes, fezes and papers were found near there. Part of these papers were gathered up. Not far from Y. there must also be a common grave for about 400 corpses.

A person of standing[124], who has been travelling in the interior, gave me confidentially the following details on the subject:

(1) *Samsoun, Amasia and Marsovan people*—all reached Amasia. Then all the men were taken, bound, and some of them killed, between Amasia, Tokat and Tourchal. All those who reached Tokat were directed towards Tchiftlik or Gishgisha and murdered. The women and children were taken in ox-carts to Sharkishla; then they were sent to Malatia, and finally thrown into the Kirk Göz or Euphrates.

(2) *Tokat.*—The same thing as above, with the difference that all pretty women and all children were taken off to Turkish houses.

(3) *Erbaa, Niksar, Messoudia.*—The men were bound during the night, and then part of them were thrown into the river Kelkid. The others were murdered near Tokat. The women and children were deported *via* Sharkishla and Malatia—same fate as in No. 1.

(4) *Sharkishla, Gemerek, Azizia, Tchoroum, Derenda*—all sent on foot to Malatia, same fate.

(5) *Sivas, Divrik, Kangal*—in ox-carts to Kangal, then all on foot to Malatia, men murdered en route, same fate.

(6) *Egin, Arabkir, Keban, Harpout, Malatia*—same fate.

(7) *Karahissar, Sou-Shehr, Zara, Tchavik*—all murdered.

(8) *Erzindjan, Kamakh*—part murdered, the rest thrown into the Euphrates.

Bands of Kurds from Dersim are at work in Malatia. All Armenians have been killed, according to my informant. I believe that all the men have been killed, but that the women and children have been distributed among the Turkish families of the interior. Not one Armenian is to be seen.

I wanted very much to go to M. and Y., so as to see myself what was happening, but the Kaimakam had his eye on me. I do not know that one can believe everything one is told, and it seems rather curious that none of my friends from the interior have reported these things to me.

---

124. Name given in the original—Mr. BZ.

91. X. (?): NARRATIVE OF A FOREIGN RESIDENT OF GERMAN NATIONALITY[125]; COMMUNICATED BY THE AMERICAN COMMITTEE FOR ARMENIAN AND SYRIAN RELIEF.

I was called to a house one day where I saw a sheet which originated from the prison, and which was being sent to the wash. This sheet was covered with blood, and running in long streams. I was also shown clothes which were drenched and exceedingly dirty. It was a puzzle to me what they could possibly have done to the prisoners, but I got to the bottom of the matter by the help of two very reliable persons who witnessed part of it themselves.

The prisoner is put in a room (just as was done in the time of the Romans), and gendarmes standing in twos at both sides and two at the end of the room administer bastinadoes, each in their turn, as long as they have enough force in them. In Roman times forty strokes were administered at the very most; in this place, however, 200, 300, 500, even 800 strokes are administered. The foot swells up and then bursts open, owing to the number of the blows, and thus the blood spurts out. The prisoner is then carried back into prison and brought to bed by the rest of the prisoners—this explains the bloody sheet. The prisoners who become unconscious after these blows are revived by having cold water thrown on their heads, and that accounts for the wet and dirty clothes. On the next day, or, more exactly, during the night, as all ill-treatments are carried on at night in ——, as well as in ——, the whole bastinadoing is repeated again, in spite of the swollen feet and the wounds. I was then in ——, but in that prison there were also no less than thirty prisoners, who all had their feet in such a state that they began to burn, and had to be amputated, or had actually already been taken off. Equally revolting tortures have been inflicted in ——, and also by the cruel Mutessarif in ——. A young man was beaten to death within the space of five minutes.

Apart from the bastinadoing, other methods were employed as well, such as putting hot irons on the chest. A smith, who was suspected of having forged the shells of the bombs, was let go only after his toes had been burned off with sulphur (called kezab). I have seen the wounds.

Four weeks ago we received news that the Kaimakam of —— had had ten to eighteen people shot in a district between —— and ——. Shortly after this had happened, an order was promulgated with respect to the Christians of ——, in which they were all commanded to leave the place within three-quarters of an hour. Among them were several women who gave birth to children on the way, and threw them, in their desperation, into the water. Many men were recalled, and it is impossible to say how many were secretly murdered, or how many will still be butchered.

I wish to state that the inhabitants of —— are so terribly ignorant that I really never saw the like, and I therefore feel convinced that not one single person had ever dreamt of opposing the authorities. Neither from the Turks nor from the Christians have I ever heard that one of these people had ever rebelled during the four months in question, and it is the Kaimakam alone who says so in order to excuse his deeds. And yet the Kaimakam always declares: "No one dares oppose me." When I ventured to protest to the Kaimakam in all friendliness against the bloody sheets, he replied as follows: "If the law and the Sultan were to forbid it, I would carry out these measures in spite of everything, and do as I please."

In ——, three weeks ago, when I was engaged in getting ready to go off, I noticed two gendarmes riding in the direction of the mountains with an inhabitant of —— who had been expelled and then recalled. They (the gendarmes) returned without the man and declared, as their excuse, that the man had escaped, which is, of course, out of the question, as the man's feet were completely swollen and he was on a mule, while the gendarmes were on horseback.

The German consul at Aleppo estimates the number of individuals deported to be 30,000. Five thousand people were deported to the unhealthy spot of Sultania, in the Konia district. The Government served out some bread during the first few days. When the bread was finished and they received no more, the misery was heart-rending. According to Mr. ——, ——, the rich were also deported to Sultania, and shared their bread with the poor as long as their money lasted, which was not very long, of course. Mr. —— begged the Vali for permission to supply the people with bread, but he replied that the Government attended to this, and that the people did not want any.

92. X.: LETTER, DATED NEW YORK CITY, 30th DECEMBER, 1915, FROM PROFESSOR QQ., OF THE COLLEGE AT X., TO AN ARMENIAN PROFESSOR RESIDENT BEYOND THE OTTOMAN FRONTIER.

I received your letter only yesterday. I am very glad you were in London and not in Turkey. They have been terrible days, filled with terrible events. The experiences I have had during the last six to eight months are terrible indeed. Not that I had much to suffer in person, but I suffered by witnessing the sufferings of others.

I am sending you some printed material that may interest you.

The short of it is that all the Armenians of X. have been "deported" (*sefk oloundou*)—the official word. The destination was Mosul, Der-el-Zor—sometimes Bagdad was mentioned. The very first to be arrested were twenty-five members of the Executive of Hunchak[126].... They were sent to Z. They all either died of typhus or were put to death, and it was the same with AJ. and AK. and some fifty others—all sent to Z. and finished off there. Then all the men found in the streets were arrested; many were taken out of their beds at night. These were professedly sent to Y. It is certain that they were all killed at a distance of three to four hours from X., on the W. road. I cannot give you a list; here are some of the names[127] ...; the number was officially stated as 1,215.

Then they sent away the women and children, including some old men like AW. Before the ox-carts left the town, some girls were picked out and sent to harems—M.'s daughter, a pretty girl just graduated in June; N.'s daughter, etc., etc. The women were distributed to the villagers; many would perish on the way, and perhaps some might reach Syria.

Dr. LZ., of Adana, told me the other day that many from U., T. and X. had passed through Adana. Some of the women of X. came to his home. Unfortunately he could not remember the name of anyone. Some were graduates of the American schools. They said that the men had been killed on the way; many had died of hunger, disease or exposure. They had no money. It took them three months to go from X. to Adana. They were to go on to Aleppo—then Mosul!

When they were all imprisoned at X., then the wealthy and the wise began to consult together and find means of escape. First of all, Mr. O. declared in favour of conversion to Mohammedanism as the only way of salvation. He influenced many and persuaded them to follow him. It was not so easy to persuade the officials. P., Mr. Q.'s man, our graduate, said to me: "We have lost all—our religion and our money too (Hem dinimizden oldouk, hemdé paramizdan).' He said that everyone gave large, very large sums, hundreds of pounds. Someone is said to have given £2,000. All this went into the pocket of the Kaimakam and the Commandant of the gendarmes. These two men had in their hands the people's lives, property and everything else. Many applied to become Mohammedans, but were not accepted. I saw the Kaimakam, Kadi, Mufti, etc., all sitting and examining whole piles of petitions. Perhaps some thirty to forty from among them were accepted, to mention a few names[128] ... all with their families.

X. had more converts than other places. O. told me that it was through his influence that this success was obtained. He was on good terms with the Kaimakam. If one wanted to stay in Turkey, he told me, one had to become a Moslem. He approved my decision to leave the place. A prominent official said to B.: "In these parts you will hear no more 'Kal' Iméra' or 'Pari Louis.'"[129]

Your brothers, I am sorry to say, are among those who were sent away. What happened to them, who knows? I suppose there is no hope for them, especially considering the name they bear. K. was intimate with the Kaimakam and the Commandant, as their wives had been in the Hospital; but when they found out that she was a relative of yours, they began to behave differently. She was sent away with the girls of the girls' school; Miss A. went with them as far as Z.; they were 63 in all; 23 have been sent on, chiefly servants; 40 girls came back to X., and are now in the girls' school, J.'s daughter among them. Before the girls were taken, the Kaimakam asked each one, in the presence of the Principal of the College, whether they wanted to become Mohammedans and stay, or go. They all replied that they would go. Only Miss H. became a Mohammedan, and went to live with G. Professors E. and FF. had been arrested with other Armenians, but in the name of all the teachers some £250-£300 were presented to the officials, and so they were let free—the officials said they were to go with the last batch.

Meanwhile, word was sent to Constantinople, and Ambassador Morgenthau secured a promise from Talaat that the College people would not be touched. But the Kaimakam declared to the Principal that no such order had reached X.

The Principal refused to deliver up anyone from the College premises; but the gendarmes came and broke down the big gate, and any other door that was barred, and took away all the Armenians—FF., GG., J., HH., and JJ. According to the testimony of the gendarmes, they all marched with their families for three or four hours, and then the men were separated and killed, while the women were sent on. Not a word came from any one of them.

When the girls were being sent on, Miss AA. managed to get promises for two of the inmates, Miss AG. and Miss AH., to stay on at the school, so they stayed. But the promise said "For a time." AX. and AY., the cook and steward of the College, were also allowed to remain, and four nurses were left in the hospital. All the rest—servants, nurses and patients—were taken. The two druggists of the hospital, AZ. and AI., had to become Mohammedans, and are still working with Dr. BB. All the shops and houses were seized by the Government—in one word, confiscated.

The priests were among the first to be sent off. A Turk described how KK. was killed. They stripped him of all his clothes, excepting his underclothing. With his hands bound behind his back, he knelt, with his son beside him, and they finished him off with axes, while he was praying. The same description was given of the execution of LL.—how they took off his head by hacking down into his shoulders with axes and carving the head out like a bust.

The missionaries had written on behalf of Mrs. MM. to Constantinople, so it was through Mr. Morgenthau that special orders were sent for her. After the troubles began, she stayed in the Hospital. I left X. on the 2nd August. I was detained eighteen days in the town of S., because I came from X. and was a Protestant. The difficulty was in the word "Protestant," which was taken as equivalent to Armenian. How could there be a Protestant of my nationality? At last the Vali was persuaded that there could be other than Armenian Protestants, and permitted me to go to Constantinople. I lost thirteen days in Constantinople over the same point. At last I got my papers through the American Ambassador, or rather Consul—perhaps both. It is a long story; some day I might relate it in full. Many others of my nationality were in Constantinople trying to get passports, but they did not succeed. I am very glad I got away from Turkey....

I left everything I had in X. It was no use attempting to sell the things, neither could we take them with us. But I do not regret that—even should they be lost for good—when I stop to think of what happened to my friends and colleagues. I cannot believe that it is real. How glad I am that I escaped from that hellish scene! My only fear now is about my people—relations and friends in S. and elsewhere. I am afraid that they will persecute my nationality also.

The Armenian Church <at X.> was sealed up and guarded by soldiers. The Protestant Church was just finished and ready to be used. We might not enter it for prayer, not even once. Someone said that O. had promised to bear the expense of adding the minarets to it. Of course, he may have said it to save his own position....

All the Catholics and Gregorians of S. were carried off. By that time I was in Constantinople. The men, it is said, were killed; of the women, those that had become Moslems were allowed to stay, the rest were sent on to Mesopotamia. Mosul is their ultimate destination.

You will find hardly an Armenian left in Trebizond, Ordou, Samsoun, or the districts of Marsovan, Köprü, Amasia, Tokat, Sivas, Harpout—excepting just a few who became Moslems. The vilayets of Harpout and Sivas, it seems, had the worst treatment, but I cannot say—it was bad everywhere. Again, the Protestants were left alone at S. and R.; they were likewise spared in the towns of Kaisaria and Talas, but not in the surrounding villages....

93. X.: NARRATIVE OF A JOURNEY FROM X. TO CONSTANTINOPLE, BY PROFESSOR QQ. OF THE COLLEGE AT X.; COMMUNICATED BY THE AMERICAN COMMITTEE FOR ARMENIAN AND SYRIAN RELIEF.

Under the pretext of transportation for political reasons, the Young Turks are carrying out a well-planned, systematic process of extermination. Beginning in April, they imprisoned the leaders and many other prominent people in X. In order to exact confession they used all sorts of torture, only to be paralleled in the records of Mediævalism and the Inquisition. I saw people unable to walk brought on donkeys to Dr. BB. for treatment of their wounds and sores that they got from torturing and beating. GG., a strong young man, an employee of the College, was beaten so terribly that he was unable to walk for weeks. I saw him moaning in bed.[130]

I heard from the lips of Professors FF. and E., as well as from many others, our graduates, etc., of the terrible condition of those imprisoned in a subterranean place under the barrack in X. People were literally packed there—the air suffocating. Happily they were kept there only for a short time; but—unhappily—they were taken away from there in groups and put to death, at a distance of three or four hours from X. This was openly confessed by the Turks to many Greeks. I heard it from a Greek gendarme who was compelled to take part in the killing. Axes were used for killing them. The condemned were stripped of all but their underclothing and led to the brink of a great ditch. There they knelt with their hands bound behind their backs, and were despatched by axe-blows on the head—as the scene was described by an eye-witness to Mr. NN., the representative of the Greek bishop in X. The Armenian priests were killed likewise. One of them, KK., was killed in the attitude of prayer—praying with his son beside him.

Women, children and old men were carried away on ox-carts. The sight was tragic[131]. Women of good family were dressed like peasants and driven away on ox-carts, accompanied by wild, savage-looking gendarmes and Turkish drivers. On one cart I saw the aged mother, wife, sister and two-year-old daughter of Mr. OO., one of our teachers[132]. As they passed by our door they bade us good-bye. The old mother, waving her hand upward, said to us, "Pray for us," and so they went on. The little child was smiling. On one cart there was a woman expecting childbirth. Miss K., a nurse in the Hospital, saw her as she was driven past the Hospital windows. She begged the gendarmes to let her stay in the Hospital until she was delivered, and they let her. She was delivered within a few days. Others, however, were not so fortunate and were carried mercilessly along.

I left X. on the 3rd August, accompanied by Pastor CC. with his wife and niece[133]; Mr. DD. of our College, with his wife, mother and daughter; and

Mrs. MM. with her four daughters. The first family travelled by the permission—officially given—of the authorities at X. The other two had a special permit from the Minister of War, Enver Pasha. Mr. DD. was an American subject.

Two days short of S., near the village RR., we were stopped by a gendarme. Standing near him were several men with axes in their hands. He asked me whether there were any Armenians in our company. He said all Armenians had to go back—anyone of my own nationality could go on. I tried to reason with him and pressed the point that they travelled by the special order of Enver Pasha. He replied that "he could not read, so he had to carry out the orders given him." In a few minutes 56 men came up, on horseback and armed. One of them could read. They repeated the same order—"All Armenians back."

All the arabadjis—Turks, all of them—pleaded hard with the man[134]. They all said: "These are all others and not Armenians. They had already finished off the Armenians in X. before we started." There was only one Armenian family in the group, they said, and they had the order of Enver Pasha. The document was presented to the leader, EE. He read it aloud. Then I told him that I was from S., and that I had a friend, a medical doctor, in military service in S. I described him and gave his name to the leader. It so happened that he knew my friend and regarded him with much esteem, so when he heard this he laughed and shook hands with me, and begged me to take his compliments to my friend, adding: "Excuse us, this gendarme made a mistake in stopping you. Go on." The whole party went on. We were told afterwards that this leader was a well-known criminal robber, and that the whole group were *chettis*—bandits—armed by the order of the Government and let loose to harry the Armenians. During this scene of anxiety, Mr. CC. and Mr. DD. were perspiring the cold sweat of agony. Mrs. MM. was in a tremor.

In one carriage there were a son and a daughter of Mr. AB., pastor in the city of BO.

The very day that we reached S., Friday, the Armenians of the place were being arrested. Their documentary permits for travel were taken from our companions and never returned to them. They were told by the Police that they had inquired from Constantinople about them and were awaiting orders. Mr. DD. and Mr. CC. called on the Chief (Mudir) of the Police in S., and had interviews, but to no effect. The Mudir questioned DD. on his citizenship; how was it possible for a man born in Turkey to become an American subject? Three days after our arrival, CC.and DD. were taken away at night from the hotel, and sent off with other leading Armenians of S. in carriages—hands tied. They were sent along the road towards TT. and T. Carriages were hired for a distance of four hours, as far as a lake four hours' journey from S. The driver who took our friends, a man from X. who had driven Mrs. MM. to S., told me that "those men were finished off on the way"; he was not allowed to see the dead,

but the zaptieh told him. He was sure that all those sent off were robbed on the way!

Peasants told my friend—a medical man in the military hospital at S.—that places near their villages, close to the scene of our incident with the chettis, were all blood-stained.

The drivers said they wished they had never seen the like of what they saw. One Albanian in S. boasted in the café of how he had killed 50 Armenians.

The railway stations between S. and Isnik were full of women, children and men—Armenians driven from their homes and waiting for an opportunity to enter the train. They were conveyed in goods trains—packed in like sheep. It was a pitiful, heart-breaking sight.

It seems that there was a prohibition against speaking to them. Near Isnik, in one of the wagons, I saw AC., a man from X. employed in the school at AD. I ventured to call his name as our train passed by, but could not attract his attention. Immediately the Turk near me asked me whether I was an Armenian. There was no Armenian in our train.

Turkish soldiers from T. and its villages told me at VV., on our way to S., that all the villages in their region were emptied—all the men killed. I asked them about the women; "God alone knows," was their reply.

I saw a carriage (araba) loaded with spades, shovels, etc., in front of the police headquarters in S. They were all covered up, but one could distinguish then what they were. Then a policeman started to ride off. During the loading, people were not allowed to look on. As I was passing by at that moment, and dared to glance in that direction, I was given a terrible blow by the police officer.

The Kaimakam and the commandant of the gendarmes at X. told me repeatedly that they were only tools; they had to carry out the orders given them. No Armenian is to be left. Old or young, blind or lame, or disabled—all had to go away, without any exception being granted.[135]

The Vali of S. was dismissed from office for refusing to carry out the orders. A new Vali, an inexperienced young man, was sent to take his place, who carried out the order strictly and harshly.

The Roman Catholic Armenians of S.—some 3,000 families—were all deported.

Mrs. CC., Mrs. DD. and Mrs. MM. were still in S., residing in the Protestant church building, when I left S. on the 26th August. They tried to see the Vali, but were not allowed, and their papers and permits were not given back to them. Mrs. MM. pleaded hard with my wife that we should take with us at least one of her daughters. There were similar petitions from many others, but it was impossible to do anything. We ourselves were under suspicion and liable to suffer, and it is a wonder how we escaped. It is due to the grace of God and to the kindly help of the American Embassy and Consulate in Constantinople.

94. X.: NARRATIVE OF MISS CC., COMMUNICATED BY HER TO A SWISS GENTLEMAN AT GENEVA DURING HER PASSAGE THROUGH SWITZERLAND IN DECEMBER. 1915.

It was on the 29th April that the Turkish Government began to arrest the leading Armenians at X.

Mr. OO., Professor of Armenian, was sent to Z. with sixteen other Professors; they suffered fiendish atrocities. Their hair was plucked out by the roots; they were burned with red hot irons; they were sprinkled with boiling water; they were flogged daily; some of them died in prison. Mr. OO. himself had his eyes gouged out, and was then hanged.

At X., the arrests continued, and the Armenians were flogged to make them confess to pretended revolutionary preparations. The surrender of a definite number of rifles were demanded of them; some of them bought rifles from the Turks in order to be able to deliver them up to the Government. They were tortured to make them bring in their arms[136].

The Turkish villagers were paid to flog the Armenians, because the Turkish townspeople of X. might possibly have taken pity on them.

PP., the college blacksmith, was so terribly beaten that a month later he was still unable to walk. Another was shod with horse-shoes. At Y., Mr. AD. (brother-in-law of the pastor AE., who suffered martyrdom at Sivas twenty-one years ago) had his finger-nails torn out for refusing to accept Islam. "How," he had answered, "can I abandon the Christ whom I have preached for twenty years?"

The search for rifles lasted several weeks. In the Armenian cemetery the Turks found several bombs, buried there since 1908 and now absolutely rusty and unusable.

By the end of June, all the men were in the prisons, barracks or cellars. The women, who went to visit their husbands and bring them clothes and food, were beaten and driven off by the gendarmes.

After several days' imprisonment, those who had promised to embrace Islam were released, as well as those who had paid very large sums of money. Mr. AF., a colporteur, had been willing to embrace Islam, but his wife refused to recognise his apostasy and declared that she would go into exile with the rest of the people, so he went with his wife and was killed.

The remainder were sent in batches out of the town and killed on the road. The Turks told their Armenian friends what was happening, and promised them the same fate.

No sooner were all the men disposed of, than they began to deport the women and children and even the sick; the ox-carts kept passing day and night. A Turk, the landlord of our house, told us that he had watched this procession, covered with dust and tortured by the heat and lack of water, and that he had said to himself that they would all be dead before they reached their destination. A woman who got back to X. by accepting conversion, after being on the road about ten days, gave an account of their heart-rending condition. Even mothers abandoned their children or handed them over to the Kurds; the Kurds for that matter took them by force and violated the girls, some of whom were carried off for their harems. After several days' journey, the carts turned back and the exiles had to proceed on foot.

Those connected with the American college gave the Turkish officers large sums to procure their exemption, but this brought them nothing but a postponement of their cruel fate. Meanwhile, the efforts of the American Embassy obtained for Professor DD. permission to go to Constantinople with his wife and eight-months-old baby, as well as his old mother, and my own family was permitted to leave for Smyrna. After several days travelling by carriage, we all arrived at S. There my father and mother were arrested, as well as Professor DD.

Everything we could do to get them released was in vain. It was impossible to learn anything about their fate. The Mudir said: "They have reached their destination safe and sound."[137]

Several days later all Armenians, with the exception of a few Protestant ladies, were cleared out of S.

Later, some of the missionaries from X. passed through S. and found us there in the desperate state we were in. They told the American Embassy as soon as they reached Constantinople, and that is how we obtained permission to proceed to Constantinople.

Here it took us three months to obtain a passport for America.

At X. several families made up their minds to take poison. Mr. GG. was imprisoned. He apostatized and returned home, and his wife fainted at the sight of him. Professor B. accepted Islam, and became head of the printing works. F., E., and the photographer D. have all three apostatized to Islam. There was no revolutionary movement. Frightful atrocities occurred. There was a dark underground cellar into which the Armenians were crowded, one on the top of the other. One night one of them cried out in his sleep: "Escape," and the other prisoners began to shout as well. Then the guards were given the order to fire into the living mass, but they showed some human feeling and fired against the wall.

---

125. Name withheld. It is possible that the scene of the events described by this witness may be, not X., but Cilicia.—EDITOR.

126. Six of the names here follow in the original: M., OO., AN., AO., AP., AQ., AR.

127. Four names here follow in the original: AS., AT., AU., AV.

128. Seventeen names here follow in the original: C., BC., O., B., D., BD., G., BE., BF., AN., BG., BH., BI., BJ., P., BK., BL.

129. Greek and Armenian, respectively, for "Good morning."—EDITOR.

130. *The treatment of this victim is described in more detail in a narrative subsequently published by the author of the present document.*

"Some died as a result of torture. I saw Garabed GG., who, after having been whipped and beaten a whole day and night, at intervals of two hours, was moaning in his bed with excruciating pain. He was confined to bed for weeks. He related to me how one gendarme had sat on his mouth, that he might not scream, while two others had held up and bastinadoed his feet, which were bound with ropes attached to a strong rod. Sometimes they would beat him on any part of his body, indiscriminately. The poor fellow, a strong, brave young man, the leader of the college firemen, who, in the presence of all the leading Turkish officials, had extinguished some time ago a big fire in the town, was in despair and longed to die. His body was all blue as a result of the beating."

131. *Further details in the narrative subsequently published:*

"I visited a great many Armenian families while they were preparing for this Babylonian captivity. I could not stand the sight, neither could I find any words of comfort for them. The scene varied from house to house, but everywhere there was the same feeling of suspense, dread and despair. In some houses one saw a feeling of true resignation and heroism. There was a retired pastor, sixty-eight years old. He did not pack anything in the house, but left it as it was. Taking his staff in his hand, he said: 'I am ready to go wherever they send me. The Lord is my guide!'"

132. *The fate of Mr. OO. himself is recorded in the narrative subsequently published:*

"Mr. OO. was put to death at Z. with excruciating tortures—his eyes being gouged out, and red-hot irons driven under his nails."

133. Daughter (?). See Doc 94.—EDITOR.

134. *Further instances of Turkish kindness are recorded by the writer in his subsequently published narrative:*

"The poor Armenians sold their few possessions, but the transaction was really a legalised plunder. Everything was sold at one-tenth of its value. Here is a conversation between two Turks in a coffee house: 'What a pity things were sold at such a low price! I could not stand the sight in the streets; I saw many cheap things, but my conscience would not permit me to buy anything.' The other fellow replied: 'Well done! What a conscience you have! If you really pitied them, you should have bought something and offered them a good price! If you and I do not buy, to whom will the poor people sell?' It is to their credit that many of the old school Turks really took pity on the persecuted Armenians. During the massacres of 1895 many Turks had shielded and saved Armenians, but in this instance no one dared express his feelings or do an act of kindness. It is said that a Turk was hanged in front of his own house in Vezir Köprü, in the Vilayet of Sivas, for giving shelter to an Armenian."

135. *This is brought out very clearly in the narrative subsequently published by the same writer:*

"A blind old man named CZ., whose son is a physician in the United States, was scarcely able to walk, even with the aid of a staff. The Mohammedan neighbours took pity upon him and promised to take care of him if the Government permitted. I appealed to the Kaimakam and the commandant of the gendarmes. The answer was: 'Impossible; all have to go; no Armenian is to be left behind, whether blind, deaf or paralytic.'

"The Kaimakam regretted that he found himself in office at such a time; he was sorry he had ever entered the official life. His father, a professor in the Turkish University in Constantinople, had advised him to go into business, but, as he had had no capital, he entered the Government Service."

136. See Docs. 68, 82 and 122.

137. We know from other sources that Mr. CC. was put to death.—EDITOR.

XII.
THE CITY OF ANGORA.

Angora is the capital of a vilayet, and the terminus of a branch line of the Anatolian Railway. It is the half-way house between Constantinople and Sivas, and the focus of traffic with all the provinces of the north-east. It is naturally an important centre of commerce as well as of administration, and there was a strong Armenian element in the population of the town.

Our information regarding the destruction of the Armenians at Angora is comparatively scanty—scantier, perhaps, than in the case of any other Armenian centre of equal importance in the Ottoman Empire. Yet the documents included in this section, together with incidental references in other pieces of testimony (e.g., Doc. 109, suffice to show that the Government's order was executed here in the same fashion as at Sivas and at X.

95. ANGORA: STATEMENT BY A TRAVELLER, NOT OF ARMENIAN NATIONALITY, WHO PASSED THROUGH ANGORA IN AUGUST, 1915.

While the Armenians of Sivas and other Armenian provinces were being deported, there were repeated rumours that the deportation was to be confined to the seven vilayets in which special reforms were due to be carried out. As in the case of 1894-5, the promise of reforms was followed by massacres—and that almost throughout the whole Ottoman Empire.

The Vali of Angora, a really good man, refused to carry out the orders from Constantinople to deport the Armenians of Angora, so the Commander of the Military Forces of the Vilayet and the Chief of the Police agreed with the Vali and supported him. The leading Turks of Angora, including the religious leaders, were all of the same mind. They knew that the Christians of the place were all loyal and useful subjects of the Empire.

The Armenians here were chiefly Roman Catholics, and were all truly loyal to the Turkish Government. They had no sympathy with any national aspirations. They even refused to be called Armenians. They were simply called the "Catholic Nation," and the Government so regarded them. There were some 15,000 to 20,000 of them, and they were leaders in commerce and trade. They had more outward polish than other Armenians. They spoke Turkish, and wrote it in Armenian characters.

There were also some 300 to 400 other Armenian families who were members of the National or Gregorian Church, and had settled in Angora from various parts of Turkey.

The Armenians' houses and shops were searched during July, 1915, and neither arms nor incriminating documents were found. But the central authorities in Constantinople had decreed their extermination, and, as the Vali refused to obey them, both he and the Chief of the Police were dismissed. Their successors made themselves ready tools to carry out any orders given from above. They succeeded in deporting all the Armenians of Angora.

As in other places, a number of leading Armenians were first arrested, including some Catholics. This was towards the end of July, 1915. The Catholics were soon released; those who remained in gaol were tortured terribly. Then all the Armenians of all creeds had to register their names, including women and children—without any omissions—at the police stations. For several days the police stations were packed with people. As soon as the list was completed the deportations began. This was the second week in August. Men were led to the prisons, and stripped of all valuables, watches, purses, rings, &c. They were told that these things would be taken care of by the Government and that they would find them all safe at the place of their destination. An eye-witness who had visited the Chief of the Police, saw his office choked up with piles of such articles taken from the Armenians.

Then they were sent away, principally in three directions—some along the high-road that leads to Kaisaria and Yozgad, others in the Süngürlü direction, and others westward. Reports came from all directions that these exiles were all killed after proceeding some miles from the city. It was said that one party was shot, but in all the other cases the Turks practised economy, killing their victims with axes and daggers. Some of the perpetrators of these horrible crimes boasted of it openly in the cafés, giving details of their achievements and the number of their victims. One Albanian said he had killed fifty men. Villagers from Kilidjlar, on the way to Süngürlü, spoke to many people confidentially of how the ground in their neighbourhood was soaked with blood.

Those arrested and deported first were chiefly Gregorians, with a few Protestants among them. By the middle of August these had all been deported. They were all men; the women were apparently safe. The Government in some instances began to give money for the support of the poor; but the scenes at the office of the Chief of the Police and at the entrance of the gaol were heart-rending. There were women and children anxiously waiting to make enquiries about their dear ones—husbands, or sons, or fathers, or friends. The only answers they got were vague assurances that they were all safe. Some, they were told, were already proceeding to their destination, and others were soon to leave. This was simply a war-measure, a temporary arrangement; as soon as the war was over, all would return home; any of the women desiring to follow their husbands or relations would be sent to the same place as they.

After the departure of the Gregorians (including some Protestants as well) about the middle of August, it was rumoured that Protestants and Catholics would be exempted from deportation. The promise was observed in some instances, *e.g.*, in Istanos, which is a village near Angora, within about twenty miles of the city. All the Armenians of Istanos were brought, chained, to Angora. Then, after the order for exemption, the Protestants were set at liberty to return home, whereas the Gregorians were all deported.

As for the Catholics, the leaders of the Union and Progress Party sent a special message to the Bishop and his Council stating that, if the whole Catholic community, headed by the Bishop and the priests, would accept Islam, they should all remain unmolested; otherwise the order was to be carried out. This is an ascertained fact. But they all preferred to stand firm in their faith, and rejected the proposal of the Committee.

Consequently, on the last Friday in August, 1915, all the Catholics—that is, the men—were arrested. According to one earlier report, they were then butchered at a short distance from Angora; but a later report says that, when the plans for this murder were ready, there suddenly came special envoys from the Government with instructions that the Catholics were to be deported safely. Consequently they were sent to Konia, and thence to the Adana district.

The latter story may be true, as it is a fact that the Papal Envoy in Constantinople and the Austrian Ambassador pressed the Turks hard in defence of the Catholics, and they are said to have secured promises of exemption for the Catholics from Enver and Talaat. But, however that may be, it is difficult to have any preference as between an immediate death and the slower process, for deportation is nothing but a slow process of execution.

The very day that the Catholic men were sent away, all the Armenian women in Angora were hurried off to the railway station. They were told to make haste and catch up their husbands. They were at liberty to take any valuables with them. As soon as the poor creatures reached the station, they were all packed by scores, like cattle, in the sheds and warehouses and barns there. The scenes in the town and at the station defy description. All the men were gone—no one knew where—and now the rest, the women and children, were left in anguish and sorrow, pain and despair, in the company of the Turkish soldiers.

Any of the women and children that accepted Islam were brought back to the town and given to prominent Turks. Those who refused were deported to Syria and Mesopotamia. Their fate must be similar to that of other sufferers from other regions.

A few Protestant families were left unmolested in the town. The Protestant pastor was deported, and nothing is known of his fate.

Many children were circumcised and placed in so-called orphanages.

96. ANGORA: EXTRACT FROM THE NARRATIVE (DOC. 88) OF MISS AA., A FOREIGN TRAVELLER IN ASIATIC TURKEY; COMMUNICATED BY THE AMERICAN COMMITTEE FOR ARMENIAN AND SYRIAN RELIEF.

It is strange that one can live constantly in Asia Minor and actually see very little of the crimes that are going on. As one travels across the country, he feels continually the dead silence of a situation which is surrounded by crime and from which he is continually shielded.

I have just come from X. to Constantinople, five days' journey by wagon. After waiting a week in Angora, I succeeded in getting one day further along the railway to Eski Shehr, where one must wait two days longer. And finally, on a belated train, with neither light nor heating in the first-class carriage, I arrived late on the succeeding day in Constantinople.

I came alone with a Tatar servant. An English exile, who had been for many years in business in this country, joined my company and came part of the way towards his home. The English prisoners are treated very well in the country. This man, after being exiled for more than ten months, had been allowed his freedom. There are English prisoners to be found all through the country. I met several at Tchoroum. They are allowed to have a house and servants, and are treated politely, especially those of them who can speak Turkish. They go and come in the fields, and even can go hunting if they choose, and they are only restricted at night by a rule that they must be in their house by 8 o'clock. The American missionaries have supplied them with reading and are able to be distributing agents for the allowance of money made to them by the American Embassy. They are full of praise for the American Embassy, for its generosity and care.

Some of these men had been carried in the night from Angora eastward. When they started out from Angora, they could not understand why they were taken at night; but when, in utter darkness, they passed the bridge over the river beyond Asi Yozgad, and for an hour were nearly suffocated with the odour that came to them from decaying flesh, they knew why they were not allowed to pass in the daylight. People say that the mountains round Asi Yozgad are a cemetery; I could not see evidences that would prove this, except some suspicious heaps of earth and stone that seemed to me likely to have been raised over pits that had been dug.

In Angora I learned that the tanners and the butchers of the city had been called to Asi Yozgad, and the Armenians committed to them for murder. The tanner's knife is a circular affair, while the butcher's knife is a small axe, and they killed people by using the instruments which they knew best how to use.

These stories are too horrible for repetition.

The Ottoman Bank President showed bank-notes soaked with blood and struck through with daggers with the blot round the hole, and some torn that had evidently been ripped from the clothing of people who had been killed—and these were placed on ordinary deposit in the bank by Turkish officers.

An interesting story was told of the Catholics of Angora. It had been rumoured, at the time people were deported from Angora, that the Catholics were to be allowed to be free. But the rumour was not corroborated, and the Government did not recognise it. So the Catholics were all gathered together at the station and sent off. Many of the men had been sent separately before, but this was a second large company. I think it also included women. They had reached this town, Asi Yozgad, and the people were there to kill them. The priests with them begged ten minutes for prayers and the presenting of the sacrament to them. The ten minutes were granted, and, as the whole company knelt and prayed, a horseman rode up suddenly, shaking a paper in front of him and crying: "Your freedom is given! Your freedom is given! You are not to be killed!" The officers would not send them back, but they saved their lives and sent them south instead.

The favour that had been obtained through the Austrian and American Embassies in Constantinople for Catholics and Protestants to be exempted from deportation, is in some cases being faithfully observed, but in others not at all. I was in Sivas when the rich village of Perkenik was entirely and most ruthlessly deported. It was an entirely Catholic village of perhaps one thousand homes. They had beautiful horses and great flocks of sheep. The flocks and horses were sent into the city, and the people were literally driven out with whips. When a complaint was made to the officers that this should not be done, because they were Catholics and had been especially faithful to the Government at all times, the reply was given that politics had changed, and that Italy had entered the war since this order had come from Constantinople.

In Angora I found that many Catholic women and children had been left there, but all have become Mohammedans. The Protestant women and children were also still there, though the men have practically all been taken away. A few have been heard from at Osmania.

At Süngürlü, I visited the Protestant community after I arrived in the evening. Their story was a sad one. They had been threatened that they would be deported with the other Armenians of the city, but one of their number, who was in employment elsewhere but was at home for a time on a holiday, besought the Kaimakam for the Protestants. The Kaimakam said he had no orders, but that he would wire to Constantinople and see what the orders were. In the meantime they were all taken to "hans," and families were ruthlessly broken up. However, the Protestant community managed to get together for a meeting, and, as a body, they put in a formal petition to the Government for their safety, saying that they knew it was the intention of the Constantinople Government that the Protestants should be saved. Finally the Kaimakam yielded to this request and returned them all to their homes; the Gregorians were all sent away from the city, and from several reliable sources the story has come to me that none of them got further than Yozgad alive. These Protestants and the families of a few Armenian soldiers remained in Süngürlü for a few weeks, and then all at once they were taken up and carried to different villages. Again families were broken up, and they suffered great deprivations because the Turkish villagers were afraid to feed them. However, after two weeks' absence from the city, they were allowed to come back to their homes. One large family, of the influential ones, was chosen out and compelled to accept Islam. This family included the spokesman who had been instrumental in saving them.

97. ANGORA: EXTRACT FROM A LETTER[138] DATED 16th SEPTEMBER, 1915; APPENDED TO THE MEMORANDUM (DOC. 11), DATED 15/28th OCTOBER, 1915, FROM A WELL-INFORMED SOURCE AT BUKAREST.

At the end of the month of July, all Armenian men from 15 to 70 years of age were arrested without exception, bound together in gangs of four, and despatched towards Kaisaria. Everything they possessed had first been stolen from them, except for 3½ piastres that each man was allowed to keep. In the valley of Beyhan[139] Boghazi, six or seven hours' distance from the town, they were attacked by a wild horde of Turkish peasants, and, in pursuance of the order, were all massacred with clubs, hammers, axes, scythes, spades, saws—in a word, with every implement that causes a slow and painful death. Some shore off their heads, ears, noses, hands, feet with scythes; others put out their eyes. Thus was exterminated the whole male Armenian population of Angora, including the "political prisoners" who had been brought thither from Ayash and Kingri[140], and our best poets, professors and journalists, as well as the manager of the Imperial Ottoman Bank in Angora, and all Armenian officials in the public service. The bodies of the victims were left in pieces in the valley, to be devoured by the wild beasts. The gendarmes boast about the part they played in these exploits.

Ten or fifteen days after these massacres, the Government arrested the men of the Armenian Catholic community at Angora. A convoy of 800 persons was sent off under the same circumstances as the others. Another convoy of 700 persons followed these, and so on—all bound together in gangs of four, and all deprived of food and clothing. The order had been given that these were not to be murdered *en masse*; they were to be pushed ahead until they died of hunger and fatigue. Then began the deportation of their families. In two hours, all the women were collected together in the goods-shed at the station. They were left there for from three to five days without food and at the mercy of the gendarmes' outrages. Children of rich families begged for a piece of bread when they happened to see a passenger. Part of these women had to embrace Islam; the rest, about 500 in number, were deported to Konia. The Armenian soldiers working on the railway have been forced, under threat of death, to embrace Islam. More than 1,500 soldiers have already been converted by force, and they are obliged to make their children and their other relations follow their example.

138. Name of writer withheld.

139. Beinam (?).

140. Kiangri, Etchangeri.

XIII.
THRACE, CONSTANTINOPLE, BROUSSA, AND ISMID.

These districts are divided officially into the Vilayet of Adrianople, the Sandjak of Chataldja, the Vilayets of Constantinople and Broussa, and the Sandjak of Ismid, which contains the first section of the Anatolian Railway. Together they constitute the metropolitan area of the Ottoman Empire, and for many centuries this area had attracted a strong Armenian immigration, in spite of its remoteness from the original home of the Armenian race.

At Constantinople the number of the Armenians had risen to more than 150,000, and in wealth and importance they were becoming serious rivals of the Greeks. In Thrace they had established themselves not only at Adrianople but in all the lesser towns, and seemed likely to reap the benefit of the expulsion of the Greek and Bulgarian elements, which the Ottoman Government had been effecting systematically since the Balkan War. There was a flourishing colony of them at Broussa, the chief city on the Asiatic littoral of the Sea of Marmora, and there were not less than 25,000 of them at Adapazar, in the hinterland of Ismid. This metropolitan region had practically become the centre of gravity of Armenian commerce, and the organisation of the Gregorian Church in the Ottoman Empire was centralised here as well. The Armenian Patriarch had his residence at Constantinople, the administrative centre of the Ottoman Government, and there was a Gregorian Theological Seminary at Armasha, a country town in the vicinity of Ismid.

The Deportation Scheme had emanated from the Government at Constantinople, but the home provinces were among the last to which it was applied. The smaller towns of Thrace seem to have been cleared towards the beginning of August; the clearance was more or less contemporaneous at Broussa and Ismid; the Seminary at Armasha was broken up by the wholesale exile of pupils and teachers, and the flourishing Armenian villages in the district shared the same fate; at Constantinople, the Government compiled a register of Armenian inhabitants, singling out those who were immigrants from the provinces from those actually born in the city, and a considerable number of prominent people in the former class had been deported by the middle of August. However, the Government seems either never to have intended to apply the scheme to Constantinople in its full rigour, or at any rate to have yielded, in the course of applying it, to representations from authoritative quarters. The measure was never here made universal, while at Adrianople it seems hardly to have been put into practice at all until the 10th October, though it was executed then with particular stringency.

The Armenians deported from the metropolitan districts do not seem often to have been massacred on the road—there were no Kurdish tribes or "Chetti" bands at hand. They were despatched towards the Arabian desert along the Anatolian Railway, and this, rather than any clemency on the Government's part, accounts for the two months' grace that they received. The Armenians further down the line had been sent off in June and July, and the metropolitan districts had to wait until the consequent congestion had abated. The fate of all those deported by the railway is described in the documents contained in the section (XIV.) following this.

98. THE METROPOLITAN DISTRICTS: INFORMATION PUBLISHED IN THE ARMENIAN JOURNAL "GOTCHNAG," OF NEW YORK.

(a) Thrace: Survey of the situation[141], published on the 28th August, 1915.

At Adrianople, all Armenian officials in any administrative, public or financial service have been dismissed by order of the Government. The Turkish soldiers transferred here from other districts are committing unheard-of atrocities. The Armenians are continually exposed to persecution. About fifty Armenians from the city have been imprisoned or exiled. The Armenians are forbidden to go abroad, or even to travel within the boundaries of the Province. The Armenians of Keshan have been exiled. The Armenian boatmen of Silivri have been imprisoned, on the charge of revictualling the English submarines.

The Armenian Church and Monastery at Dhimotika have been confiscated by the Government. They gave two weeks' grace to the Armenians of this locality in which to emigrate to other parts.

The Armenians of Malgara were also given two weeks' grace before their exile. Their houses are to be occupied by Turkish refugees from Serbia.

The Armenians of Tchorlu have been deported.

(b) Constantinople: Statement[141], published on the 4th September, 1915.

In all the quarters of Constantinople they have begun to make a register of the Armenians, entering on separate lists those actually born in Armenia and those whose birthplace is Constantinople. It is thought that they are going to deport the immigrants from Armenia.

Six Armenian pupils of the Normal School of Ottoman Teachers at Constantinople have been poisoned during a meal. One of them—Khosrov, born at Van—has died; the five others are under treatment in hospital. The Turkish press at Constantinople is beginning to prepare public opinion for the loss of Armenia. The *Tanin* and the *Sabah*, in particular, have devoted articles to the subject, preaching the idea that it is in Turkey's best interest to have a homogeneous population. In consequence, they argue, the Armenians must be eliminated as irreconcilable enemies.

(c) Constantinople and the neighbourhood: Statement[141] **published on the 2nd October, 1915.**

According to a despatch published in the American Press, the Armenians of the Pera quarter (of Constantinople) have taken flight. Nearly 4,000 Armenians from Constantinople have found asylum in Bulgaria. Recently there was a rumour that all the Armenians in the Scutari quarter were going to be deported. Enver Pasha has confirmed these rumours, and added that, if he chooses, he can have all the Christians of Constantinople deported within a fortnight, and leave no one there but Turks and Germans. According to another rumour, the Armenians of Scutari and Ortakeui have already been deported. The villages on the upper Bosphorus have likewise been cleared of their Armenian inhabitants. We have been informed by letter that the Armenian girls who were being educated at the American school at Constantinople have been carried off by the Turks.

At Broussa they have converted all the rich Armenians to Islam; the poor have been deported. Their children have been sold at 20 piastres each (3s. 4d.).

At Smyrna, several Armenians were recently hanged. The Austrian Consul on the spot requested the Austrian Ambassador at Constantinople to demand an explanation from the Turkish Government. He received the reply that the Armenians possess a Patriarchate, and ought to make any representations through this channel. "As for you, if you are our allies, you ought not to meddle in such questions."

---

141. Source unspecified.

99. CONSTANTINOPLE: LETTER, DATED CONSTANTINOPLE, 13/26th OCTOBER, 1915, FROM AN ARMENIAN INHABITANT; PUBLISHED IN THE ARMENIAN JOURNAL "BALKANIAN MAMOUL," OF ROUSTCHOUK[142].

You must by now have received my second letter. To-day I shall not be able to write you very much, for time is short and I am extremely depressed in spirit.

Besides, what would you have me write? For ever it is calamities, miseries and sorrows.

The last news is that the Seminarists of Armasha have been sent to Constantinople and put under the charge of the Patriarchate. The whole congregation, with its Superior at its head, has been deported and the

Convent has been confiscated; the Superior has even been robbed of the £400 (Turkish) realised by the sale of the Convent's live stock and various other properties.

A month ago they began to deport the unmarried men from the provinces who had established themselves at Constantinople. So far they have deported from four to five thousand persons, and this without warning and without giving them time to put their affairs in order. The families of those deported to Ayash and Etchangeri[143] had been given notice to leave Constantinople, but afterwards this order was reconsidered. Is this the beginning of the deportation of the Armenian population of Constantinople, for which the Government has so far shown a certain consideration?

The majority of those who had been deported to Ayash and Etchangeri have been brought back to Angora; at the present moment we have no news of them, and no news either of those who have remained at Ayash and Etchangeri. As I wrote to you in my last letter, they also have been assassinated. Indeed, a connection of the Prefect of Police actually said: "The Armenians are making demonstrations at Sofia, Roustchouk and other places, and are presenting protests. We have given them their answer by exterminating the prisoners at Ayash."

As for the deportations from Anatolia and Armenia, they are being continued systematically. The whole Armenian population of Konia and Angora is on the road, and is at present concentrated along the line of the Baghdad Railway, in the last extremity of misery. They are being sent to Tarsus and Aleppo, to be forwarded in due course to the desert.

In consequence of certain diplomatic representations, the Government had given instructions not to deport the Catholic or Protestant Armenian families, or those whose bread-winners had been mobilised. But these instructions have been very speedily withdrawn, and are only followed in a small number of places.

The families of mobilised Armenian soldiers who had got as far as the course of the Railway, had received orders to wait, but we hear now that they have been subjected to brutal treatment. These women, who were concentrated at Eregli, beyond Konia, had made representations to the Government and claimed the restoration of their mobilised sons. The result of these representations is not yet known.

The situation of the exiles in Syria is lamentable. The despatch of relief is urgently required, in order at least to save the survivors. Let the Armenian colonists abroad come to their aid before it is too late. A halfpenny saves a life. Don't disdain to give this halfpenny.

142. Date unspecified.

143. Kiangri, Kingri.

100. ADRIANOPLE: DESPATCH FROM THE CORRESPONDENT OF THE LONDON "TIMES" AT BUKAREST, DATED 18th DECEMBER AND PUBLISHED ON THE 21st DECEMBER, 1915.

I have received information in regard to the wholesale extirpation of the Armenian population of Adrianople.

On the 10th October the Turkish police arrested 45 Armenian inhabitants who had become Bulgarian subjects. The prisoners were transported to Constantinople, and thence to Asia Minor, with the exception of 10 who escaped and took refuge in the Bulgarian Legation at Pera. On the intervention of the Bulgarian Government these persons obtained liberty to return to Karagatch. In regard to the fate of the remaining 35 the Porte professes ignorance.

Shortly afterwards, all the Armenians in Adrianople—about 1,600 persons—were arrested, and the men immediately deported to Asia Minor. The women and children were detained two days in prison before removal, and were subjected to brutal treatment by their captors. Several were subsequently placed in sailing vessels for transportation to Asia Minor. Two of the vessels foundered off Rodosto and most of those on board were drowned. Some of the exiled families were sold at derisory prices, for the most part to Jews.

A deputation from Karagatch proceeded to Sofia to invoke the intervention of the Government, but have received no reply to their petition. A memorial previously addressed to the Bulgarian Government by another deputation gives a frightful picture of the sufferings of Armenian prisoners in Asia Minor at the hands of the Turkish authorities.

The document furnishes a list of 29 districts in which the whole Armenian population, numbering some 835,000 persons, have been either killed or exiled or forcibly converted to Islam. One ecclesiastic was burnt alive, five were hanged or otherwise killed, and ten were imprisoned.

101. BROUSSA: REPORT BY A FOREIGN VISITOR TO THE CITY, DATED 24th SEPTEMBER, 1915; COMMUNICATED BY THE AMERICAN COMMITTEE FOR ARMENIAN AND SYRIAN RELIEF.

It was inevitable that the Armenians, whose deportation from Broussa and the environs had been ordered a few days before my arrival, should occupy some of my attention. It is doubtful whether the full significance of this measure can be realized without a visit to the interior, where the results may be seen in all their appalling details. Words are inadequate to describe the utter misery and destitution of these hordes of emigrants who are to-day roaming all over Asia Minor. The roads are crowded with thousands upon thousands of these unfortunate wretches, considering themselves lucky if they are able to procure—at the sacrifice of a small fortune—an ox-cart for their families and a few belongings; many of them journeying on foot—men, women and children, tired, haggard, and half-starved—the pictures of want and desolation. Broussa was among the last of the more important cities to receive the order for the deportation of the Armenians, so that I had occasion to see the application of the measure from the very beginning. Thus I met the first contingents of the exiles between Broussa and Yeni-Shehr. The authorities had given them three days in which to clear out, with the result that they could not sell any of their property, even had there been buyers. All personal property, such as furniture, clothes, tools, etc., which they could not take with them, had to be left behind, and the Turks quite openly distributed them among themselves, often even in the presence of their owners! As regards the houses evacuated by the Armenians, a little more red tape was gone through, but the effect was the same. The Armenian proprietor was called before a magistrate, made to sign a document that he had sold the house to a certain individual (of course always a Moslem), and was given a roll of banknotes. No sooner had he left the room than the money was taken from him by the police and returned to the magistrate, to be used in hundreds of similar cases!

I realised, of course, that I was quite powerless—even unofficially—to interfere with these proceedings. But there were certain other points which came to my knowledge and about which I did not hesitate to speak to the Vali—always quite informally only—as they seemed to me a useless and senseless aggravation in a situation which was already trying enough. In the first place, hundreds of Catholic and Protestant Armenians had been ordered away—many of them had even left—although, according to the decision of the Government, they had a right to remain. I obtained from the Vali the promise that in future these two denominations should not be disturbed, and that those who had "by mistake" been sent away should be called back. This was done, and during the next few weeks a number of Catholic and

Protestant families returned. I then asked that those ordered to leave should be given at least a week, and in a few special cases even two weeks, in which to get ready. This enabled many families to make the most necessary preparations for the journey. A few casual remarks to the Vali about flogging and forcible conversions of women and girls to Mohammedanism seem to have put a stop also to these two outrages—at least, so I was informed at the American School, which was in close contact with everything going on in the Armenian community. I cannot but refer in this connection to the altogether admirable work done by the ladies of this institution in helping the unfortunate exiles in the most unselfish and efficient manner. But for their devotion and practical assistance, the sufferings of many families must needs have been much greater.

Unfortunately, the hardships of exile and privation are not the only dangers to which the Armenians are exposed. There can be no doubt that many of them—chiefly men—have been massacred in cold blood. Although no instances of this seem to have occurred during my stay in Broussa, I was informed by very trustworthy sources that, shortly before my arrival, about 170 of the most prominent Armenians from Broussa and neighbouring towns had been shot near Adranos, whither they had been exiled in June. I have all the more reason to credit this report because, when I made inquiries concerning two of the men, the brothers A., whose relatives live in America and who are insured with American companies, the Vali replied evasively, but finally said that he had heard that they escaped from custody and had disappeared!

However, even if no Armenians had been killed outright, the result would be the same, for the deportation as carried out at present is merely a polite form of massacre. Unless the whole movement be stopped at once, there is, I am firmly convinced, not the slightest chance of any of the exiles surviving this coming winter, except possibly the very wealthiest amongst them.

Nor do the authorities make any secret of the fact that their main object is the extermination of the whole Armenian race. The Vali admitted quite frankly: "We are determined to get rid, once and for all, of this cancer in our country. It has been our greatest political danger, only we never realized it as much as we do now. It is true that many innocents are suffering with the guilty, but *we have no time to make any distinctions*. We know it means an economic loss to us, but it is nothing compared with the danger we are thereby escaping!"

Without commenting on the truth or falsity of these remarks, the fact remains that the Turks are rapidly depleting their country of some of the thriftiest, most intelligent, and, in many respects, the most valuable elements of their population. One has only to walk through the streets of any town in the interior to realize how this deportation has wrought havoc with the life of the community. Nearly all doctors, dentists, tailors, carpenters are gone—in short, every profession or trade requiring the least skill has been stopped, not to mention the complete stagnation of all business of any consequence. Even Turks are realizing the danger, and in some villages they petitioned the authorities to allow certain Armenians to remain! It is therefore all the more surprising that the Ottoman Government persists in this shortsighted policy, for there can be little doubt that every place left vacant by an Armenian will—irrespective of the outcome of the European conflict—have to be filled by a foreigner, as the Turk has proved himself totally incapable of doing this kind of work.

102. ADAPAZAR: STATEMENT, DATED 24th SEPTEMBER, 1915, BY A FOREIGN RESIDENT IN TURKEY; COMMUNICATED BY THE AMERICAN COMMITTEE FOR ARMENIAN AND SYRIAN RELIEF.

On the 1st August the beating began in the church. The object of this was to force the people to bring in any ammunition and firearms they might have. Most of the people accepted their fate in silence, but one man said boldly: "You must answer to God in heaven for these things."

"What do I care for your God in heaven? He says you are good people and I must not beat you; but he is not good, we must kill him."

A mother threw herself in front of her consumptive son, and herself received the stripes. A German woman tried to save her Armenian husband. "Get out of the way or I will beat you," cried the Beast. "I don't care for the Emperor himself; my orders come from Talaat Bey."

Some Armenian ladies came to intercede with the Beast, and for a day or two the beatings were less vigorous.

Then came the awful Saturday, the day of darkness and horror. Women came to our house saying: "They are beating the Armenian men to death, and they are going to beat the women next!" I ran to a neighbour's house and there found men and women crying. The Protestant brethren had gotten out of the church and were telling their story. "They are beating the men frightfully," they cried. "They say they will throw us into the River Sakaria; they will send us into exile; they will make Mohammedans of us; they will beat our women next; they are coming to the house."

"Come to the school and I will put up the American flag," I said. Soon after, more women came to the school to find out if I could do something.

"We will go to the mayor; we will go to the Beast," said they, "and we are all losing our heads!"

Then our woman doctor came, crying frightfully. She had been down to the church to care for the wounded. Then the trustee came. "I want you to take my money and give it to my son if I die," said he. Then he sat down and wept, the tears rolling down his face.

At last I could endure it no longer. "I am going to the church; I do not care what you say," I exclaimed. I did not know the way and every one was afraid to show me, but I found it by inquiring. One man said: "You are going to the church? It is hell there." I arrived and walked past the guards at the gate without looking at them, and came to the door and lo, one of the trustees came to meet me. We walked up and down the church together and he remarked: "I think the police do not like to see you." I said: "They had better not; I am going to America to tell of all these things." He said there was one Turkish soldier outside the church in tears. He said he had been crying three days and nights because of the awful treatment of the Armenian people. Some of the people were shut up ten days in the church, but special favour was shown to the Protestants; none were beaten, and they had more liberty to go in and out. During all this time the Armenian shops were closed, and Armenians were not allowed to go to market to buy food or even to their gardens to gather their fruits, so that many were on the verge of starvation.

Three days after this the beating ceased and we were beginning to take courage again; a few Armenian shops were opened; but the next morning early, which was Sunday, news came that all the Armenians in Adapazar, numbering about 25,000, were to be sent into exile. They were to go to Konia by freight train, if they could pay their passage, and then to Mosul by carriage—on foot a journey of weeks and months. Such awful stories came to us about things that had happened to those who went on foot, that people sold their last possessions to get enough to pay their train passage. They were afraid to take money with them. The poor had none to take; the rich must leave all their property behind. If they took money they feared violence. By Wednesday there were no goods trains to send them by, as so many had gone, but all the people were turned out into the streets to await their turn— many for several days—except the Protestants, who were allowed to come to the Protestant church to wait, while some of the wealthy people remained in their houses. The Protestants, in Adapazar especially, were in good favour with the Government, and their condition is somewhat hopeful.

A card has been received, written three weeks after the exile began, from Eski Shehr, telling how some of the Protestants in the hotel there were allowed to have their church services on Sunday and were being well treated.

They thought it possible that they might be able to rent houses and remain there. If this is indeed true it will be a very great blessing.

103. ADAPAZAR: FULLER STATEMENT BY THE AUTHOR OF THE PRECEDING DOCUMENT; PUBLISHED IN THE JOURNAL "THE NEW ARMENIA," OF NEW YORK, 15th MAY, 1916.

For several months there had been occasional exiles from Adapazar, but we felt safe because we had a good Mayor and a good Military Commander in the city. They were our friends. The Commander frequently joined us in our daily games of croquet, while the sick soldiers watched us from the windows. We gave a garden party to all the officers. They liked us and would have spared the school and the Protestants had they been able. But one day little Arousiag, one of our youngest pupils, came to us, a refugee, with only the clothes on her back. She had been staying with relatives at Sabandja, but the whole village had been exiled. As she had been born in America, of naturalized parents, she was saved, and I was afterwards able to bring her to her parents in America.

Soon after, some villagers whom I knew came from another mountain village, Tchalgara, and from their lips I heard how for seven days the men had been shut up in the church and beaten—especially the priest—until some fainted. The Government was searching for weapons, and the men were beaten until they either produced their own or secured others to surrender. Then in Bardezag, our nearest neighbouring missionary city, similar things happened. We did not know what was going on in the interior, although occasional vague rumours had come to us.

Then horrible cruelties began in Adapazar. About 500 important men were imprisoned in the Gregorian church. Those belonging to the Socialist Party were mercilessly beaten. Most accepted their fate in silence, but one man said boldly: "You must answer to God in Heaven for these things." "You have no God but me," was the response, and the man was beaten till his feet were red with blood. "What do I care for your Mayor?" continued the Beast, as he was called: "He says you are good people, but he is no good himself. Kill me if you wish," he continued, "but ten men will come to take my place." A mother threw herself in front of her invalid son and herself received the stripes. A German woman tried to save her Armenian husband. "Get out of the way or I'll beat you," cried the Beast; "I do not care for the German Emperor himself, my orders come from Talaat Bey." But afterwards the man was released. When I heard these things I knew it was of no use for me to try to interfere; if the Beast would not listen to a German, he certainly would not to an American.

One day two of our delicate ladies went to see the Beast—to plead, like Queen Esther, for their people—saying, by this act: "If I perish, I perish." They found a man of fine appearance who had been educated in Europe, and who received them most politely. "We have heard bad things about you," they said, "but now we see that you are a good man. Can't you persuade the people to surrender their arms without beating them?" "I am glad to see you so patriotic," he responded, "and would be glad of your assistance. You go, too, to the houses and persuade the people to give up their arms, and it will be well with them." So these two ladies hired a carriage and drove up and down the city, exhorting the people to surrender all their arms.

For a day or two the beatings were less. Then came the awful Saturday—the day of darkness and horror. Someone came running to the school-house crying: "They are beating the men in the church to death, and are going to begin on the women next."

I ran over to the neighbour's house and there I found men and women crying. Two of our Protestant brethren had escaped from the church and were telling their story. "They are beating the men frightfully," they cried. "They say they will throw us into the River Sakaria; they will send us all into exile; they will make Mohammedans of us. They are going to the houses to beat the women next." I begged the women to come to the school and I would put up the American flag, but they did not wish to leave their houses to be pillaged, although they promised to come if necessary.

Soon after, more women came to the school, frantic to do something. "We will go to the Beast; we will go to the Mayor," they cried, and we were all losing our heads. Then our lady doctor came. She had been to the church to care for the wounded and the tears were streaming down her face. Then one of the school trustees came. "I want you to take my money and give it to my son if I die," he said. Then he sat down and the tears streamed down his face and mine. At last I could endure it no longer. "I am going to the church; I don't care what you say!" I exclaimed, and I put on my hat and started. I did not know the way to the Gregorian church and everyone was afraid to show me, so I had to find my way by inquiry. "You are going to the church?" asked one man: "It is hell there." I arrived. I walked past the guards without even looking at them, and there at the open door stood one of the trustees, Mr. Alexanian. "Can't I speak to the police and get you out?" I asked. The other trustees had already left. "No," he said, "I am superintendent now."

The beatings had ceased for a time, in order that leading men might go out to search for weapons. Mr. Alexanian would write down their names as they went out, erasing them when the men returned. "I am glad I was here last night," he continued, "for I have been able to help the poor people to-day." How many of us would be glad of the privilege of spending a sleepless, bedless, chairless night for the sake of being useful? He told the same sad story of awful beatings. No Protestant had been beaten. The Turks have always been favourable towards the Protestants, especially in Adapazar. This trustee told how after the beatings he went outside the church and found a Turkish soldier in tears, who said he had been crying three days and nights because of the wrongs inflicted upon the Armenian people. So you see there are some good Turks. It is the Government that is responsible, not all the people.

Soon after this, an important exile returned, the father of our two sweetest kindergarten children, and the head of a society. Great anxiety was felt on his behalf, for we feared he would be hanged and we grieved for his refined and delicate wife. He answered boldly at the trial. "Why do you punish these men? If there is any fault it is mine, and yet I also am guiltless. This society was organized with the permission of the Government. You allowed us to obtain firearms." Which was all very true. The Government was hatching a diabolical scheme to send all the Armenians into an endless exile, and wished first to disarm them.

Sunday brought new terrors but no especial troubles. On Monday the Beast left the city, and our hearts were filled with a subdued rejoicing, even though he said he would return on Wednesday. We did not believe it. We thought he had been recalled on account of his cruelties. As to the man himself, he was an ex-convict, having been implicated in a conspiracy against the Government and sentenced to a thousand years imprisonment. He was working for his liberty by carrying on this devilish work, and, to give himself courage for it, he drank heavily of the most intoxicating liquor.

During these ten days of imprisonment all Armenian shops were closed. The Armenians could not go to market to buy provisions or even to gather the produce of their gardens. Many were on the verge of starvation. On Saturday evening a few shops were opened, and we began to take heart a little. Some were fearful of exile, but I declared it would be impossible to send from twenty to thirty thousand Armenians from one city into exile, though a few would doubtless be sent. At this time the Government collected taxes from the Christians a year in advance—a bad sign. On Sunday morning I was awakened early by someone calling below my window. I put out my head and was informed that all the Armenians in Adapazar were to be sent into exile. As early as possible I went to the Mayor to intercede for the people, but it was useless. He would not even promise to protect our American property, and out of the entire city I could save only little Arousiag, who was American born.

From that Sunday onwards, the streets were full of Armenians trying to sell their possessions for a mere pittance. All was very quiet—the silence of despair. Even the Turks looked serious, for they knew that their city was financially ruined, as the Armenians are the most thrifty and skilful of all the peoples of Turkey. In spite of apparent quiet, however, robbery was not lacking. A poor servant girl was trying to sell her sewing machine—her only possession—and when she refused to sell it for four dollars, a man seized it and ran away with it. A few days later, the husband of one of our school servants was bringing their machine to our school when a man snatched it from his shoulders.

The people who had any money went to Konia (the ancient Iconium) in goods-trucks, being allowed to take only a few possessions with them. They were told to leave their possessions in the churches and they would be safeguarded, but the same promise had been made in Sabandja, and the church had been looted almost before the people were out of the city, so nobody trusted this promise. The exiles were crowded on the top of their possessions, sixty to eighty people in a truck marked for forty people. Some missionaries from the south met a train-load of these refugees and described their condition as miserable in the extreme. One girl had hanged herself on the way; others had poison with them. Mothers were holding out their beautiful babies and begging the missionaries to take them. A Turkish officer ordered the Americans off, saying: "These Armenians are dangerous people; they may have bombs."

From Konia they were to go by foot or carriage to a desert place called Mosul, in Mesopotamia. Those who had no money must make the entire journey on foot. Such dreadful stories came to their ears as to the treatment of those who walked—of how people were not allowed to sell them bread, of how they were robbed, and families separated, the men slain and the women and girls given to the Turks, the children sold to be brought up as Mohammedans—that people sold their last possession so as to be able to go as far as possible by train.

They were afraid to take money with them, lest they should be robbed by the way. They must leave all their property behind, and as soon as they vacated their houses, refugees from Macedonia took possession of them. What a lamentable condition—to be poor and in danger of starvation; to be rich, accustomed to luxury and refinement, and then suffer all these things; to be a woman, especially a pretty woman, with all a woman's dangers (some in Constantinople told me they would disfigure their faces if they were exiled); to be a man and see all these things and yet be unable to lift a finger in resistance; to be there and endure; to be here and imagine!

How can the people keep their faith in God during such trials? How many will deny and curse Him? How many will accept Mohammedanism? Or how many will remain faithful to the end, and say through their tears: "Though

He slay me—or worse than slay me—yet will I trust in Him?" Again and again they said to me: "Oh, if they would only kill me now, I would not care; but I fear they will try to force me to become a Mohammedan."

What was the meaning of all this? It was the death blow aimed at Christianity in Turkey, or, in other words, the extermination of the Armenian people—their extermination or amalgamation. And why? At the beginning of the struggle, or soon after, the Holy War was declared. This signified a purpose to kill all Christians, the reward for which is eternal pleasure in the Mohammedan paradise. At first Turkey declared that the Holy War was directed only against nations at war with herself, but later she waged it against all Christians.

The Armenians were so patient, so silent and uncomplaining. We came very near to each other in those days. "You have made our sorrows your sorrows," they said to me: "You have an Armenian heart." But as the realization of what their exile actually meant dawned upon me, I could neither eat nor sleep. One day I said to my friends: "I cannot comfort you to-day; you must comfort me. I think I feel worse than if I were going into exile myself." And they were so brave and cheerful that I did actually carry away cheer and comfort from that home.

I had planned to remain with my friends until all were gone, but that was impossible. The Protestants were given special favours; they were the last to go, and were allowed to remain in their homes or in the church, while on the Wednesday of that week all other Armenians were turned out into the streets to wait their turn to go. There they waited, with their baggage, for days, by the roadside near the station.

So, with a sad heart, on the Friday of that exile week, I bade farewell to the group of friends gathered at the school-house door, and with little Arousiag mounted on to the top of my goods in the ox-cart, fearing to trust my possessions out of my sight a moment. I put up an umbrella to protect me from the rain and the curious gaze of others. I felt and looked like an exile myself.

When we reached Constantinople, everything looked so peaceful and quiet that I felt disappointed. We had received no news from the city for some time, and thought that it must be nearly in the hands of the enemy. To see women and children all dressed in the height of fashion, and seemingly indifferent to the misery of the world, was a painful contrast.

Not only did I leave terror behind me. In Constantinople also every man's heart was failing him for fear. There were rumours that Constantinople also would be evacuated, and awful stories of the separation of families, of the Mohammedanizing of Christians, reached our ears. "This is worse than massacre," again and again they said: "Only let them kill us now." Everybody was frantic to leave the country, and the police stations were crowded with people seeking, too often in vain, for permission to go to America, Bulgaria, or Roumania. No men at all were allowed to go. They were left behind to be exiled or massacred. On some days women were given permission to leave, and on other days they were refused. It took me, an American, two days to get my papers, with help from the Embassy, and at every step I feared difficulty or refusal because of Arousiag, and also another Armenian girl whom I was bringing with me.

On the train just before we reached the boundary-line, an Armenian family was sent back. Two of our graduates joined us in Bulgaria, and they were said to be the last Armenians to leave Constantinople. I know that some American ladies who joined us later were not allowed to bring a servant with them, although she was badly needed to help them with their babies.

At last we were out of the land of the dreadful Turk, but alas! a part of us has been left behind. In all our silent hours visions float before our mental eyes. As we passed through desolate-looking provinces on our journey, I could see marching, marching, without food or water or rest, my poor friends—the sun beating down upon their heads, the cruel faces and rods of their oppressors urging them on when they were ready to faint with weariness and hunger. No place to buy bread, no bed to lie upon except the bare earth—only marching, marching always. And I wondered whether the sublime faith and courage with which they had started out would fail them in the end. And thinking of these things the words of the Psalmist became my words: "My tears have been my meat day and night, while they continually say unto me, 'Where is thy God?'"

But there is a brighter side to the picture. One Sunday on my voyage I turned to Revelation to see if I could find a message for these days, and lo! there it was in Rev. vii., 13-17:—"These are they which came out of great tribulation, and have washed their robes and made them white in the blood of the Lamb.... They shall hunger no more neither thirst any more; neither shall the sun light upon them nor any heat.... And God shall wipe away all tears from their eyes."

XIV.
THE ANATOLIAN RAILWAY.

The Anatolian Railway runs diagonally across Anatolia from the Asiatic suburbs of Constantinople to the Gulf of Iskanderoun (Alexandretta), but, beyond Konia, the line is in the hands of the Baghdad Railway Company, and the construction of this section is still incomplete. The tunnel through the Taurus Range is not yet open to traffic, and the present rail-head is at Bozanti, on the northern side of the mountains. In the Adana plain, a short section of line has long been in working order between Adana itself and the ports of Mersina and Alexandretta. But beyond this, again, there is another breach of continuity at the Amanus Range, and this second mountain barrier has also to be crossed by road before the traveller reaches the railway system that radiates from Aleppo.

The Anatolian Railway follows an ancient artery of trade, and there were important Armenian colonies in the chief places along its course, as well as in places lying off the railway towards the north-east. But the track of the line forms the general limit of Armenian expansion, and defines the Armenian "sphere of influence" in Asiatic Turkey as against the Greek. The only considerable colony of Armenians south-west of the Anatolian Railway is at Smyrna, where they seem to have suffered less severely than in other parts of the Ottoman Empire—we know no more than that a few of the leading Armenians there were hanged.

The deportation of the Armenian colonies in the railway zone appears to have been started during the months of June and July. Their numbers were soon swelled by the still larger streams of exiles from the metropolitan districts (see section XIII. above), and the traffic on the line became hopelessly congested. The hardships of travel in crowded cattle-trucks were painful enough, but now at every station on the line crowds of exiles were detrained to await their turn for transport for interminable periods. The central table-land of Anatolia, which the railway traverses, has a very high average altitude, and even in summer the climate is severe. The exiles were turned out on to the open plateau in an absolutely destitute condition, without food or shelter—here 2,000, here 5,000, here 11,000, here 12,000, here 15,000, here 30,000. These facts and figures are vouched for, by a number of unimpeachable witnesses, in the documents contained in this section. The witnesses write from half-a-dozen different points along the railway, and one of them was himself an exile, experiencing in person the horrors of a concentration camp. But the misery of detention was as nothing compared with what the exiles suffered when their turn came to be carried on to rail-head and driven across the mountains on foot. There are frightful descriptions of their condition by a witness who saw them when they had reached the Adana Plain, and still more terrible accounts of the survivors who had lived to traverse the second mountain barrier and were dragging themselves towards Aleppo.

This agonising journey along the route of the railway was protracted for more than three months. The exiles were mostly uprooted from their homes in August; the first documents date from the beginning of September, and by that date the foremost batches had hardly *begun their marches across the first mountain range; the last documents were written in November, and still the vast body of the exiles had not reached Adana, but were huddled together—stationary through exhaustion—on the south-eastern slopes of Taurus and Amanus, between the summits and the plain. One of the latest witnesses reckons the number here at 150,000.*

104. THE ANATOLIAN RAILWAY: NARRATIVE OF A JOURNEY, DURING THE DEPORTATION OF THE ARMENIANS, BY A PHYSICIAN OF FOREIGN NATIONALITY, WHO HAD BEEN RESIDENT IN TURKEY FOR TEN YEARS; COMMUNICATED BY THE AMERICAN COMMITTEE FOR ARMENIAN AND SYRIAN RELIEF.

A journey through Asia Minor even in "normal" times can be understood only by those who have had the "experience" of travel in Turkey. During war-time there is simply no accommodation at all. Passenger traffic was limited to one train a week until shortly after the time of which I write, when that was cut off too, leaving no train connection with the interior open to the civilian.

On this particular journey, not many hours elapsed before the fact was forced upon one's consciousness that things were not as they used to be. One felt the sense of unwelcomeness, the aloofness of all fellow-passengers. Conversations were in an undertone, no joviality—looks of suspicion, as if to say: "Who is that infidel who dares intrude himself in such times as these?"

At the first large station a sight burst upon my view which, although I knew and was prepared for it, was nevertheless a shock. There was a mob of a thousand or more people huddled about the station and environs, and long strings of cattle-trucks packed to suffocation with human beings. It was the first glimpse of the actual deportation of the Armenians. Our train drew up to the station, but there was no confusion, no wailing, no shouting, just a mob of subdued people, dejected, sad, hopeless, past tears—looking backward to abandoned homes, to husbands, fathers, brothers who had been torn from them; looking forward to a death in the desert, or to a living death in the hands of captors who were compelled, "by political and military necessity," to free their land of the curse of a nation which had grown powerful while they themselves stagnated. There were guards everywhere among the people, making communication with them impossible. The advent of a foreigner among them was the sign for eager enquiring looks from some, as if to say: "Can it be that he brings deliverance for us;" while others seemed to accept their lot in settled despair.

The town from which many of these had come, I learned later, was cleaned out completely, except for perhaps a dozen old women too feeble to undertake the journey. A missionary compound in the same town was left unguarded by the Government while, for four successive nights, marauders from a neighbouring village came, and, smashing doors and windows, helped themselves to such things as they could carry away.

Our train sped away, taking with us as many cattle-trucks, packed with men, women and children, as the locomotive could pull. In these trucks one could see improvised hammocks swung above the crowd squatting upon the floor, and in these hammocks the tiny babies—the only individuals in all that crowd oblivious to the horrors of the situation, but doomed nevertheless, in all their innocence, to pay the penalty of human jealousy and greed.

The scenes just described were repeated at various stations; but at the station of ——, as I looked across the fields to the river, I heard the Turkish commander say: "Yes, I have 30,000 here under my charge." Then I looked as far along the river as I could see, and it was one mass of improvised blanket tents, their only protection from the parching heat of the mid-summer sun. Where this multitude were to get food for their long journey I was unable to see, for although most of them were as yet but a few days' journey from their homes, they could take but a bit of grain and almost no money with them. Can you imagine the sanitary condition of a camp of 30,000, when absolutely no provision is made, not even as much as would be made for so many cattle?

During the weary days of travel I had as my companion a Turkish captain, who, as the hours dragged by, came to look on me with less of suspicion, growing quite friendly at times. Arrived at ——, the captain went out among the Armenian crowd and soon returned with an Armenian girl of about fifteen years. She was forced into a compartment of an adjoining railway coach, in company with a Turkish woman. When she saw that her mother was not allowed to accompany her she began to realise something of the import of it all. She grew frantic in her efforts to escape, scratching at the window, begging, screaming, tearing her hair and wringing her hands, while the equally grief-crazed mother stood on the railway platform, helpless in her effort to save her daughter. The captain, seeing the unconcealed disapproval in my face, came up and said: "I suppose, Effendi, you don't approve of such things, but let me tell you how it is. Why, this girl is fortunate. I'll take her home with me, raise her as a Moslem servant in my home. She will be well cared for and saved from a worse fate—besides that, I even gave the mother a lira gold piece for the girl." And, as though that were not convincing enough, he added: "Why, these scoundrels have killed two of our Moslems right here in this city within the last few days," as though that were excuse enough, if excuse were needed, for annihilating the whole Armenian race. I could not refrain from giving him my version of the rotten, diabolical scheme, which, however, fell from his back like water.

It was pitiful to see rough Turkish hawkers offering for sale, from wagons in the street, articles of all kinds stolen or bought for a pittance from the Armenians. As I passed by, one held up for the inspection of a number of Turkish women a child's white coat, and as I looked at it a vision flashed through my mind of a little girlie across the sea, whom I had seen in a little coat of just about that size, and who looked up into my face and called me "Daddy."

I learned here, too, of a nurse who had been in one of the mission hospitals, who two days before my arrival there had become almost crazed by the fear of falling into the hands of the human fiends, and had ended her life with poison. Were these isolated or unusual instances, it would excite no comment in this year of unusual things, but when we know of these things going on all over the Empire, repeated in thousands of instances, we begin to realise the enormity of the crimes committed. I spoke again to the captain: "Why are you taking such brutal measures to accomplish your aim? Why not accept the offer of a friendly nation, which offers to pay transportation if you will send these people out of your country to a place of safety?" He replied: "Why, don't you understand, we don't want to have to repeat this thing again after a few years. It's hot down in the deserts of Arabia, and there is no water, and these people can't stand a hot climate, don't you see?" Yes, I saw. Anyone could see what would happen to most of them, long before Arabia was reached.

Leaving the railway, I travelled several days by wagon across country. Arrived at ———, I found the process of deportation in full swing, the streets of the Armenian quarter of the city thronged with Armenians, Turkish civilians and Turkish officials. Officers standing in the street directed lesser officers in their work of turning out the households, one after another. The men of these households hurried about to find animals or wagons, paying exorbitant prices out of the little sum which represented all their savings, while others offered rugs and articles of all sorts for sale, that they might get enough money to hire a donkey. Most were unable to get animals at any price, and simply bundled together a few personal belongings and set out, in a dazed condition, not realising what it meant, except that they must go. One old Armenian gentleman, on leaving, accosted his Turkish neighbour, kissing his hand and bidding affectionate good-bye, which was reciprocated by the Turk; evidently these two had for long years been 'good neighbours.' Crowds of Turkish women were going about insolently prying into house after house to find valuable rugs or other articles. After being accosted by the police, I returned to my wagon, and, while waiting there, heard the inn-keeper call to one of his men, and say in a stage whisper: "You go out and get *rugs—rugs*, you understand, by all means get *rugs*; and, say, don't pay too much; not more in any case than two medjids (6*s.* 4*d.*)." While I waited, the man brought rugs by the armload; they were placed in a room in the inn, while the innkeeper and other men discussed their value and gloated over the purchase for a mere pittance. Four men came by, bearing a corpse covered with a black cloth. Fearing lest they might in this way smuggle out valuables, the innkeeper strode out and flung up the cloth, exclaiming: "What have you fellows got there?"

This general plan of deportation I saw carried out in several towns. Such animals and carriages as were available were loaded with goods and sent to the outskirts of the town, where they waited until all were ready; then they were joined by the crowds on foot and all went off together. It was pitiful enough as they set out, but I met group after group on the road "on the march"—and these travel-stained, worn and haggard—on and on, and on to their death. Ah, yes, one can stand almost any hardship if hope fills the breast and home and friends are at the journey's end.

We passed one group of about 900 souls and only two mounted and armed gendarmes. "Why didn't they kill the gendarmes?" has been asked me. That is easy enough, to be sure, but, having killed their guards, they remain at the mercy of the first band of armed men they meet, and they must go to villages, for the mountains of Turkey cannot support life. My wagon driver showed the tenderness (?) of his heart by remarking, as we passed this group: "Effendi, it is almost more than I can stand to see women and little children in such condition. But," he continued, "there are some fine-looking girls in that bunch. I'll get one when I get to the next town." He then started to tell me some of the atrocious things of which the Armenians are accused. I found that, as time went on and the deportation gained momentum, the common people came to believe more and more the grossly exaggerated stories and whole-cloth lies manufactured for the very purpose of exciting the sympathy of the common people towards the scheme. Arrived at ——, I found the Armenian market-place closed and the shop doors shut and sealed by the Government, although as yet but a small proportion of the Armenian population had been deported from that particular place. Fourteen prominent Armenian merchants were hanged that night in this city. Passing to ——, I found the missionaries besieged with terror-stricken Armenian friends and neighbours who were living in daily terror of orders to move. The general deportation orders came a day or two later, and the people swarmed about the missionaries, beseeching help for life and protection of property. One can scarcely understand the strain to which the missionaries were subjected; and yet how helpless they were, imprisoned, as it were, in a country which was in the throes of war and shut off from intervention by foreign powers.

Rich, proud Armenians, crushed by the blow, seemed to age years in these days. Some, with tears streaming down their faces, came beseeching us to find a way out for them. Public auction of household and private effects was held in the market square. No one was allowed to buy by private sale, and the prices had to be approved by the officials. Orders came permitting the sale of houses and lands at auction, which raised the question in their minds: "If we sell for cash, in all probability our money will be taken from us, or if for Government promissory notes, will they have any value?" An order came exempting Protestants from the general deportation, and we rejoiced at the prospect of saving even a few. The result of this favour was, however, a distribution of Protestants, five to ten families each, to surrounding Turkish villages, where, surrounded by a Moslem community, they were forced to become Moslem or to suffer terrible persecution. As far as I can learn, no one attempts to pass judgment on any Armenian Protestant or Gregorian who has so "turned." All we could do was to advise against it, realising as we did what it meant for them to marry into Moslem homes, as those who "turned" were forced to do. God alone knows the tremendous pressure brought to bear upon them, and the self-sacrificing spirit in which many of them sought in this way to save their own families from death by signing a scrap of paper. These papers were printed forms, indicating that the signer accepts of his free will and in full conscience the tenets of the Moslem faith.

When we consider the number forced into exile and the number beaten to death and tortured in a thousand ways, the comparatively small number that turned Moslem is a tribute to the staunchness of their hold on Christianity. Those who "turned" found that the Moslems were not true to their promise to leave such unmolested, for in many places these were forced to go into exile later on, although they were counted as Moslems. In one city about 1,000 families turned Moslem, but this being too large a number might be considered a menace, so they were deported all the same.

If the events of the past year demonstrate anything, they show the practical failure of Mohammedanism in its struggle for existence against Christianity—in its attempt to eliminate a race which, because of Christian education, has been proving increasingly a menace to stagnating Moslem civilisation. We may call it political necessity or what not, but in essence it is a nominally ruling class, jealous of a more progressive Christian race, striving by methods of primitive savagery to maintain the leading place.

105. ESKI SHEHR: LETTER FROM AN ARMENIAN VICTIM[144] PUBLISHED IN THE ARMENIAN JOURNAL "HORIZON," OF TIFLIS, 30th OCTOBER/12th NOVEMBER, 1915.

We shall perish of hunger; we have had to leave behind us everything we possess, and they are robbing us of the little money that we have brought with us, robbing us even of our clothes. Most of us have not a penny left. It is a cruel situation. The ferocity of the minor officials passes all limits. The evening before last, two gendarmes looted the tents of the exiles from the village of Kelidj (who had only arrived that day). Incidentally they wounded some of them with a perfect rain of blows. They also tried to carry off forty or fifty tents, and then one of them came to announce that the Tchaoush must be conciliated. We collected 400 piastres (£3 6s. 8d.) and handed it over to them on condition they left us in peace; one of the exiles sold his single blanket for 4 piastres in order to pay his share of the subscription. Most of us were plundered on the road. Before the exiles reach a station they are told: "You can start off, we will see that your baggage follows you;" and they are sent on their journey after their money, too, has been taken from them. During the journey the sick were abandoned by the roadside. Some threw their children into the rivers, others committed suicide. Why don't people at least send us some relief?

Many have lost members of their family, and no one knows where they are. The exiles from the districts of Ismid and Broussa have been exposed at each station to indescribable sufferings, and are only waiting for the approach of death. From Eski Shehr to Konia the uplands are covered with the tents occupied by the Armenians. This frightful suffering inspires no pity in the ruthless officials, who throw themselves upon their wretched victims, armed with whips and cudgels, without distinction of sex or age.

During the last two days they have begun to transport the exiles further afield—free of charge! All that has happened here is nothing compared with what has been going on beyond Eregli and Bozanti. I have seen with my own eyes the convoy that marched to Konia on foot, and I simply cannot describe the condition of the old women and children. They had ceased to be human. Having obeyed the deportation order, they had paid a toll of 300 victims, and the widows had been marched over the mountains. As for the men, there were not many of them. There were other exiles who had been forced to come on foot, from all parts, because no general order has been issued for transporting the exiles by railway. The gendarmes demand enormous sums for granting the exiles permission to encamp from place to place and rest. But whether they go by train or on foot, the exiles are condemned in any case to pillage and ill-usage.

They are now beginning to deport the people in Syria and the Lebanon as well, and the first convoy of them has reached Konia. They are filling their places with Mohammedan emigrants from Europe. They distribute thirty loaves among 130 people, and even that not everywhere.

106. AFIUN KARA HISSAR: LETTER[145] DATED AFIUN KARA HISSAR, 10th/23rd SEPTEMBER, 1915; PUBLISHED IN THE ARMENIAN JOURNAL "HORIZON" OF TIFLIS, 30th OCTOBER/12th NOVEMBER, 1915.

Some of the exiles have been sent to Konia, but on the bleak uplands of Afiun Kara Hissar, under canvas, or, in many cases, without tents at all, there are about 11,000 exiles in misery. Most of them have been reduced to an indescribable condition. They endured all kinds of hardships on their journey, and a large proportion of them died on the road. Many fathers have been compelled to abandon their children on the road. They have been obliged to march day after day on foot, pricked on at the point of yataghans and deluged with curses. In the struggle to keep up this unending journey on foot, they have been forced to abandon by the road such possessions as they had taken with them, even the most necessary articles, and they are now naked and shelterless on the frozen plateau.

This pitiful mass of sufferers is composed of Armenians from the towns and villages of Balikesri, Panderma, Erendjik, Hai Keui, Mikhalidj, Kassaba, Broussa, Gemleyik, Benli, Marmardjik, Karsakh, Gurlé, Yenidjé, Djera, Ezli, Adapazar, Karasu, Yalova, Tchoukour, Karsz, Kelidj, Shaklak, Mess Nor Keui, Tchingiler, Orta Keui and Keremet.

There are about ten priests from these villages among them.

The rich have become poor, and the poor, naked, famished and deplorably miserable, without help and without hope, are compassed by all the terrors of death. Exposed to freezing blasts and drenching rain, their life is one long agony. One would rather die than see such a spectacle.

The railway has been requisitioned for the transport of troops, so they have decided to leave this unfortunate mass of people here for an indefinite period. There is no means of escaping from this terrible life of exposure to the elements. The only means is death, and they are dying in numbers every day. There have been twelve deaths only to-day.

---

144. Name withheld.

145. Name of writer withheld.

107. AFIUN KARA HISSAR: RESUMÉ OF A LETTER[146] DATED AFIUN KARA HISSAR, 2nd/15th OCTOBER, 1915; APPENDED TO THE MEMORANDUM (DOC. 11), DATED 15/28th OCTOBER, 1915, FROM A WELL-INFORMED SOURCE AT BUKAREST.

The 16,000 deported Armenians who were living in the tents have been sent to Konia, in cattle-trucks. At night, while thousands of these unfortunate people, without food or shelter, shiver with cold, those brutes who are supposed to be their guardians attack them with clubs and push them towards the station. Women, children and old men are packed together in the trucks. The men have to climb on to the top of the trucks, in spite of the dreadful cold. Their cries are heart-breaking, but all is in vain. Hunger, cold and fatigue, together with the Government's deeds of violence, will soon achieve the extermination of this last remnant of the Armenian people, the former inhabitants of the Sandjak of Ismid, the Vilayet of Broussa and the neighbourhood. In spite of the great misery that prevails among the exiles, the Government took from them by force one hundred Turkish liras for the "Defense Nationale."

---

146. Name of writer withheld.

108. AFIUN KARA HISSAR: LETTER, DATED MASSACHUSETTS, 22nd NOVEMBER, 1915, FROM AN AMERICAN TRAVELLER; COMMUNICATED BY THE AMERICAN COMMITTEE FOR ARMENIAN AND SYRIAN RELIEF.

Mr. and Mrs. A., Miss B., a Greek student from our College who wished to come to America to study, my husband and I left BO., and, after travelling all day and night, reached Afiun Kara Hissar about nine o'clock the next morning. We had three hours to wait in Kara Hissar, so we took a carriage at the station and drove to the home of an Armenian doctor there—a well educated, fine young doctor, whom we had met on our previous visit to Kara Hissar. We found his wife and two small children at home, but the doctor had been taken a year ago to work for the wounded Turkish soldiers.

The wife had heard of the exiling of all the Armenians from different towns around her, and so she was packing a few things to take with her when her hour came to go. That hour arrived while we were in her home. All the Armenians were ordered to be at the station in twenty-four hours, to be sent—where? They did not know, but they did know that they had to leave everything—the little homes they had worked for for years, the few little things they had collected—all must be left to the plunder of the Turks.

It was one of the saddest hours I ever lived through; in fact, the hours that followed on the train, from Kara Hissar to Constantinople, were the saddest hours I ever spent.

I wish I could picture the scene in that Armenian home, and we knew that in hundreds of other homes in that very town the same heart-breaking scenes might be witnessed.

The courage of that brave little doctor's wife, who knew she must take her two babies and face starvation and death with them. Many began to come to her home—to her, for comfort and cheer, and she gave it. I have never seen such courage before. You have to go to the darkest places of the earth to see the brightest lights, to the most obscure spot to find the greatest heroes.

Her bright smile, with no trace of fear in it, was like a beacon light in that mud village, where hundreds were doomed.

It was not because she did not understand how they felt; she was one of them. It was not because she had no dear ones in peril; her husband was far away, ministering to those who were sending her and her babies to destruction.

"Oh! there is no God for the Armenians," said one Armenian, who, with others, had come in to talk it over.

Just then a poor woman rushed in to get some medicine for a young girl who had fainted when the order came.

Such despair, such hopelessness you have never seen on human faces in America.

"It is the slow massacre of our entire race," said one woman.

"It is worse than massacre!" replied another man.

The town crier went through all the streets of the village, crying out that anyone who helped the Armenians in any way, gave them food, money or anything, would be beaten and cast into prison. It was more than we could stand.

"Have you any money?" my husband asked the doctor's wife. "Yes," she said; "a few liras; but many families will have nothing."

After figuring out what it would cost us all to reach Constantinople, we gave them what money we had left in our small party. But really to help them we could do nothing, we were powerless to save their lives.

Already the Turks had taken our American school and church, and after a big procession through the streets had dedicated our church as a mosque and turned our school into a Turkish school—taken down the Cross and put up the Crescent.

Some weeks before, they had exiled our faithful Armenian pastor, who for a great many years had toiled there, as he himself told us, "to make a little oasis in that desert."

For many weeks Mr. C. of our College in BO. had stayed in Kara Hissar to try and get back our church and school, but nothing could be done. The Turks had named our church "Patience Mosque," because, they said, they had waited so many years to get it.

It was with broken hearts that we left the town, and hardly had we started on our way when we began to pass one train after another crowded, jammed with these poor people, being carried away to some spot where no food could be obtained. At every station where we stopped, we came side by side with one of these trains. It was made up of cattle-trucks, and the faces of little children were looking out from behind the tiny barred windows of each truck. The side doors were wide open, and one could plainly see old men and old women, young mothers with tiny babies, men, women and children, all huddled together like so many sheep or pigs—human beings treated worse than cattle are treated.

About eight o'clock that evening we came to a station where there stood one of these trains. The Armenians told us that they had been in the station for three days with no food. The Turks kept them from buying food; in fact, at the end of these trains there was a truck-full of Turkish soldiers ready to drive these poor people on when they reached the Salt Desert or whatever place they were being taken to.

Old women weeping, babies crying piteously. Oh, it was awful to see such brutality, to hear such suffering.

They told us that twenty babies had been thrown into a river as a train crossed—thrown by the mothers themselves, who could not bear to hear their little ones crying for food when there was no food to give them.

One woman gave birth to twins in one of those crowded trucks, and crossing a river she threw both her babies and then herself into the water.

Those who could not pay to ride in these cattle-trucks were forced to walk. All along the road, as our train passed, we saw them walking slowly and sadly along, driven from their homes like sheep to the slaughter.

A German officer was on the train with us, and I asked him if Germany had anything to do with this deportation, for I thought it was the most brutal thing that had ever happened. He said: "You can't object to exiling a race; it's only the way the Turks are doing it which is bad." He said he had just come from the interior himself and had seen the most terrible sights he ever saw in his life. He said: "Hundreds of people were walking over the mountains, driven by soldiers. Many dead and dying by the roadside. Old women and little children too feeble to walk were strapped to the sides of donkeys. Babies lying dead in the road. Human life thrown away everywhere."

The last thing we saw late at night and the first thing early in the morning was one train after another carrying its freight of human lives to destruction.

Another man on the train said that in one train he was in the mothers begged him to take their children to save them from such a death.

He said that an Armenian, a leading business man in Harpout, told him that he would rather kill his four daughters with his own hand than see the Turks take them from him. This Armenian was made to leave his home, his business and all he had and start off with his family to walk to whatever place the Turks desired to exile him to.

When we reached a station near Constantinople, we met a long train of Armenians that had just been exiled from Bardezag.

My husband and Mr. A. talked with one of the native teachers from our American school. Among other things he said that an old man was walking in the street in Bardezag when the order came to leave. The old man was deaf and did not understand what was going on, so, because he made no move to leave the town, the soldiers brutally shot him down in the street. The teacher said he could buy no food, for the soldiers kept them from buying any.

The crying of those babies and little children for food is still ringing in my ears. On every train we met we heard the same heart-rending cries of little children.

109. Q.: REPORT FROM DR. D., DATED Q., 8th SEPTEMBER, 1915; COMMUNICATED BY THE AMERICAN COMMITTEE FOR ARMENIAN AND SYRIAN RELIEF.

The conditions are so bewildering here that it is hard to know how to present a general view of the situation. The deportation is still going on in full force, and yet shows unaccountable stoppages and delays. I suppose that the *vis a tergo* emptying out the population is so out of proportion to the executive ability to keep the channels of travel open that the result is this great damming back of the current that has filled the cities from Eski Shehr to the

Taurus mountains. Beyond that I know very little. Exemptions and delays are granted with no apparent reason, often, however, with the plainest of reasons, viz., the enriching of the police. The amount of extortion practised must extend into thousands of liras.

Dr. E. will tell you of what he has seen on the way here. I will try not to duplicate what he says. The information that I have from P. is reliable. The Protestants of Q. who were there have all returned here, though many difficulties were thrown in their way. There were about 15,000 exiles in P., but there has been a steady stream pouring in that direction and the number must be larger now, except for the number sent on into the mountains from there. How many there are at Bozanti, the terminus of the railway, I have not been able to learn. Whether they are now being sent on to Tarsus and Adana, I cannot learn with certainty. Reports have it that travel beyond Adana is cut off, and so the exiles are not being sent, as before, beyond Aleppo.

In P. the exiles are encamped in the open fields in the neighbourhood of the railway station. No protection is provided for them, and they have none, except such tenting as they can make up for themselves out of carpets, coarse matting, cloaks, gummy sacks, sheets, cotton cloth, tablecloths, or handkerchiefs, all of which I have seen used here in Q. There are no sanitary arrangements for this horde, and every available spot is used for depositing excrement. The stench of the region is described as appalling. Here in Q. I have seen how the adjoining field, entirely open as it was, was so thickly covered with excrement that it seemed impossible to step anywhere, while women and girls, as well as others, were defecating there in the daytime simply because there was absolutely no screen or protection anywhere. When it is considered that diarrhœa and dysentery are rife, you can imagine the results. The region there, as well as here, is exceedingly malarial, and this is the time of year for it. I have no knowledge of how many deaths have taken place.

After a time, large numbers of the exiles at P. were allowed to find shelter in the town, where they rented houses and for a time were better off. But they were not allowed to rest in quiet. Suddenly the order would come from the police that all were to leave for Bozanti, and the whole number who were in the town, perhaps 5,000, would be driven (and I mean literally driven under the lash) into the streets with all their goods and be rushed to the encampment. There perhaps 100 wagons would be ready and 500 people find places and be sent off. The rest were then left to stay in the encampment or bribe their way back to the town again and re-rent their houses, until another alarm and driving forth. Every such onslaught meant several medjids of expense for every family for transporting their goods and bedding to and fro, and this in addition to the bribes paid to the police for the privilege of going back to the town. Such bakshishes had to be paid to the police for every favour asked, from medjids[147] to liras.[148] No one could go to present a petition to the Governor without bribing the police first. In the encampment the police would come along in the morning and order all tents in a certain section to be taken down, saying they were to start for Bozanti, and this order would be enforced instantly with scourge and club. The terror of the people, from the reports they had of that journey "beyond"—of pillage, murder, outrage, stealing of girls and starvation—was such that they were always ready to purchase a few days' respite if they had any money to do it with. No train or wagon is ready, so when enough money is brought out, the people are graciously allowed to put up their tents again twenty feet away from their former site. The sick, the aged—none were respected. The people have described to me the terror of that constantly recurring order, "Down with the tents!" with the whip behind it.

For those who did have to start, the conditions were still worse. They must hire wagons brought there for them, and the drivers charge four times the ordinary price. It must be paid, or they will be driven out to go on foot, and, of course, in that case, can take no bedding and hardly any food with them. The drivers acknowledge afterwards that the police take one half of the price paid. It is impossible for me to tell you all the means of extortion employed. I know of a family here who had to pay nineteen liras to hire a wagon and hamals and get permission from the police to move from the filthy encampment to a small, horribly crowded hotel near by. The hotel-keepers charge a lira a day for a little room with three or four dirty beds in it, and then share this with the police.

Protestants are supposed to be freed. The story of my contest with the officials here, before the Vali arrived, shows how they had planned to get all sent away before his arrival by concealing the order for exemption.

The Protestants who were already in P. were notified that they were free, yet had to pay fifty liras to the police to get their permit to leave. At the station, where they went to get third-class tickets, they were told that there were no third-class coaches left and that they must take second-class. After purchasing these tickets two-thirds of them were put into third-class coaches after all. It was merely a trick to separate them from more of their money. Of course, they were glad to have third-class coaches, for, coming here first, the exiles were compelled to pay the full fare and then packed forty or fifty together in box-trucks, cattle-trucks, or even open flat trucks. The Railway seems to be as conscienceless in wringing the money out of them as the Government or the Turks.

The whip and club are in constant use by the police, and that upon women and children too. Think what it is for people, many of them cultivated, educated, refined, to be driven about in this way like dogs by brutes. I have seen women black and blue from the beating they have received. A woman with a fractured thigh at the station was being helped by friends intending to bring her to the hospital. A commissary of police came along and ordered her to be dragged back into the carriage. A boy yesterday in the encampment here was struck on the head by a policeman and killed. The pastor of the church at O. was beaten with a whip and his forehead cut open, in a great gash, by a blow from a club, for saying that he was a Protestant and asking for his freedom. He is not freed yet in P. Two of his daughters we took into the hospital as nurses when the family first passed through here.

Dr. E. will tell you of conditions here in Q. The Vali is a good man, but almost powerless. The Ittihad Committee and the Salonika Clique rule all. The Chief of Police seems to be the real head. The Vali came here on the promise that Q. should be spared. Then he was delayed in Constantinople day after day until the deportation here should be accomplished. He was furious when he heard of it on his way here, and he is likely to resign soon. I am telling you what a close friend of his, a travelling companion, told me.

The Armenians of N. sent here were forced to come by wagon. The Circassians of the region knew of it and followed after and robbed them, and shot one girl. Gendarmes were sent out after the Circassians, but only took their turn in completing the stripping of the party.

Another party was sent in the same way and was attacked at night by Circassians, and one of the men was shot through the thigh—a horrible wound. He died here in the hospital a few hours later. We have one boy and one girl here in the hospital who were run over by trains, compelling the amputation of the leg. Three hundred families from Baghtchedjik are in Eski Shehr. About two hundred of the men were in market, nearly a mile from the encampment, when the police came on them and drove them out at once to start on foot for Q., without letting them go back to their families or get money. They are here now, begging me to try to communicate with their families. The mail is closed to all such communications. Telegrams innumerable are given in at the office, the money received and then the telegram never sent—(witness two long telegrams I sent you).

During the last four days the inhabitants of the villages above Baghtchedjik have been poured in here, and are filling the encampment. They come from a cool and well-watered region. They are thrown out here in this burning heat, without shelter and with a water supply so scanty that there is a constant struggle at the fountain to get their jars filled. The sickness that we are seeing among them is heart-rending. Many are simply overcome with the heat. Our dispensary floor is covered all day with sick in all stages. A little girl died here this morning. Others, moribund, will perhaps hardly get back to their tents.

We are trying to refresh them with yoghourt and water-melons. They are too sick to take bread.

Hardly anything makes me so hot as the thought of the soldiers' families. The men—the fathers, brothers, sons and husbands—are serving in the Turkish Army as loyally as any, and their families—their children, wives and sisters—are driven off in this inhuman manner. Soldiers' families are also said to be exempt from deportation, but in countless cases they are swept away with the rest. The wife must put in a special petition claiming her relationship. This petition has to be paid for, for she cannot write Osmanli. It must be stamped with the regular stamp, the additional stamp, the Hidjaz Railway stamp and the War-Aid stamp. Then, after the usual delays of "Go and come again," a telegram is written to the Army Post where she says the soldier is, and this she must pay for—thirty to sixty piastres[149]—and all this when she and the children are hungry for bread with no money to buy it. A woman came for treatment yesterday with three children, two almost dying. She happened to mention that she was a soldier's wife. I asked why she did not get free by that. "They wanted thirty-one piastres for the telegram and I had nothing," was her reply. Oh! I wish you could see the abominable cruelty of their treatment and the diabolical ingenuity of the ways devised to strip them of all their money before bringing them to their deaths—for that is where it will surely end for all these people, unless some means of stopping it is soon found. Whether the taking of Constantinople will be such a means or not will depend, I suppose, on whether the present Government succeeds in making its escape and continuing its rule in the interior.

An "Exiles' Commission" has come here from Constantinople. It was announced that their business was to be to settle the exiles in this vilayet and not make them go further. Telegrams from Enver Pasha were received stating this before the Commission came. Now they have come, and it appears that their duty is merely to clear the choked channels and speed up the traffic. They have announced that they have come not to settle the exiles but to drive them on. Since beginning this letter I have learned that the stream has begun to flow again from P. and Bozanti to Adana and on, and it is reported that now the destination is Arabia.

I must add a report from Angora, whence I have received to-night what I have every reason to believe to be an accurate account. Some two or three weeks ago, about two hundred of the chief Armenians at Angora were imprisoned, then taken at night in wagons, thirty or forty at a time, to the banks of the Kizil Irmak, and there killed. Eighteen of the employees of the Railway and the director of the Ottoman Bank were among these. I had this on good authority then, and it is confirmed now. Within this past week all the Armenian men, whether Gregorian, Protestant or Catholic, have been taken, stripped to shirt and drawers, tied together and taken away and heard of no more. The women and girls have been distributed to the Turkish villages, the Turks coming and looking over the girls and choosing what they wanted. I could give you the name of one of the wealthiest men in Angora, whose wife and three daughters were taken away before his eyes, and who went crazy. Three hundred boys were circumcised. The name of the railway official was told me who saw one hundred of these done, and reported it. The region from Angora to Polatlu (on the railway) is said to have been the scene of such outrages as cannot be described. It is reported that this complete extermination applies to the whole of the Angora Vilayet outside the Kaisaria Sandjak, but my accurate information does not cover this.

It is openly stated by officials here that the exemption of Protestants and Catholics is only temporary, and the trend of events seems to me to give colour to this.

The saddest part of all this is our utter impotence to do anything to stay the awful deeds that are being perpetrated.

---

147. About 3*s*. 2*d*.

148. Slightly less than a pound sterling.

149. Five to ten shillings.

110. Q.: REPORT FROM DR. E., DATED Q., 3rd SEPTEMBER, 1915; COMMUNICATED BY THE AMERICAN COMMITTEE FOR ARMENIAN AND SYRIAN RELIEF.

Although you are already well informed as to the Armenian situation in this region, I am taking the liberty to add a few notes from personal observation on the way here, chiefly from what I saw at Eski Shehr, Alayund and Tchai.

At Eski Shehr there are about 12,000 to 15,000 exiles in the fields about the station, evidently in great need and distress. The majority of them appear to be without shelter, and what shelter they have consists of the flimsiest kind of tent, improvised out of a few sticks covered with rugs or carpets in a few instances, but often only with cotton cloth—absolutely no protection from the heavy autumn rains which will soon be coming. The station-master, whom I have known as a reliable man for several years, told me that the people had been treated with every kind of brutality, the police ostensibly trying to prevent the Turks from molesting them by day, but aiding and abetting them by night. I myself noticed that in several places large groups of young women and girls were being kept separate from the rest and guarded (?) by the police, and was told that in several instances the police had allowed them to be outraged. At the present, instances of actual violence were not so common, but there was no provision made for feeding them and the people were quickly spending what little cash they had to buy provisions at exorbitant rates. Certainly they seemed to have little or nothing in the way of supplies, and many looked pinched and sickly. About thirty to forty deaths were taking place every day. Germans whom I overheard talking while on the way to Eski Shehr, and also the German hotel-proprietress at Eski Shehr, were loud in their condemnation of the whole affair as being conducted in the most brutal and horrible way.

At Alayund there were perhaps 5,000 exiles in about the same condition. They were from Broussa for the most part, and those with whom I was able to converse told the same tales. Within two weeks the Government had made two distributions of bread, neither of them sufficient for more than one day, and had given nothing else. I myself saw police beating the people with whips and sticks when a few of them, in a perfectly orderly way, attempted to talk to some of their fellow-exiles on the train, and they were treated in general as though they were criminals who had no claim to consideration of any kind. What talking I did, I had to do with them rather surreptitiously, of course.

At Tchai I saw perhaps a couple of thousand in the same condition. Here the men and women were together, and the Turks had not succeeded in carrying off more than two girls. By keeping constant guard the Armenians, although unarmed, had been able to frighten the assailants away. They said that all the men there would die rather than give up any of their women, and that, as the Turks were not so numerous, they felt safer, but dreaded what was awaiting them when the order came to move on. A heavy rain had fallen at Tchai and occasioned great suffering, followed by sickness and some deaths, especially among the children. A good many of the people had gone insane.

A conductor on the train told me that, although the order had come for the return of the Protestants and the Catholics, he had seen about 100 to 150 of the latter from Ismid re-deported towards Angora and in this direction, even after they had gone through the form of having been returned to their homes. In their second deportation they were to be scattered—a few to each Turkish village in the region.

At Q. about the same conditions exist, although we are fortunate in having a good Vali. However, he is much handicapped by some powerful men of the Committee,[150] who are opposed to him and accuse him of undue clemency. Even a prominent Armenian of this city warned him not to be too kind lest he be sent away (the above was an Armenian connected with the railway, and therefore not deported). The Protestants here are very grateful to you for securing them exemption from deportation. However, they are in much distress, for the Government has sealed up all their shops and will not let them conduct any business, so that what little cash they have is rapidly being exhausted.

All of the above and much that I might add is as nothing, however, to what the railway employees report as going on at the end of the line, where the people leave the railway and set out on foot, only to be set upon by brigands, who rob, outrage and kill all the way from Bozanti to Adana and beyond. At Angora also there has been great slaughter, according to all reports.

Whether these unfortunate people are sent on towards the east or whether they remain where they are along the road, their future is very dark, and it means annihilation for the whole race unless they can be quickly reinstated in their homes with permission to carry on their business, or else taken out of the country altogether. Even if they are left just as they are, two or three months will probably see the end of most of them. The climate of the interior is very different from that of Constantinople, and the nights are already cold. We shall do the best we can here, but can hardly touch the outer edge of the national wretchedness and misery, which is written so clearly on the despairing faces of the people, especially of the women and girls, that enquiry and investigation are almost unnecessary to confirm the horrible truth. We are using every means we can, however, to see as much as possible ourselves and get reliable information of the rest....

P.S.—I have had to wait several days to find a suitable messenger, and the delay has enabled me to get a pretty comprehensive view of the situation. There are at present in Q. about 5,000 to 10,000 Armenian refugees, mostly from the Broussa, Ismid and Bardezag regions; a few hundreds come from Eski Shehr, Ak Shehr and other places nearer by. The people are, for the most part, encamped in the fields near the railway station, much as they are at the places above described. The protection is, for the most part, very flimsy, and there is a considerable proportion of the people whose things have been stolen from them and who are simply lying out in the open with no protection from the scorching sun by day or from the dew and dampness by night. This state of affairs produces a vast number of cases of malaria and dysentery, and also of heat prostration, and one cannot walk a few paces through the camp without seeing sick lying everywhere, especially children. There are, of course, no sanitary arrangements at all, and last night the stench that came from the camp was overpowering. Conditions are ripe for an epidemic at any time, especially as these people have not, like the soldiers, received any prophylactic treatment. Until very recently the Government had done absolutely nothing for the refugees; during the last few days they have been giving the adults one piastre[151] and the children twenty paras[152] a day, which is, of course, insufficient to feed them adequately. The people have no occupation and stand and lie about listlessly; a steady stream of them passes up and down the main street, begging or peddling their small remaining stock of clothing, rugs, embroidery, &c. At night the people are not molested as much as they were at first, but this is probably due chiefly to the fact that the best of everything has been taken away from them by this time and that a vast assemblage of sickly and half-starved people is naturally comparatively safe from molestation. There are a fair proportion of the Armenians who have managed to keep some money and goods, and who are fairly comfortable for the time being in houses and rooms that they rent. These, however, have troubles of their own, for the police try to get money out of them by frightening them, saying that they are next on the list to be sent off to Bozanti, that their papers are made out wrong, &c. Numbers of anxious parents have been to us, beseeching us to take their daughters as nurses or servants in order to protect them from the Turks. We have employed as many as we dared—not that we are afraid for ourselves, but that we have to think of our own regular nurses and employees, who would be in danger if we overstepped the mark. But it is terrible to refuse asylum to girls whom we know to be in danger. Yesterday an unusually pretty and refined young girl of fifteen was brought to us by her parents; she had been pursued all the way from Broussa by an Army officer, but they had been able to elude him and the police as well. Our hospital is too public to shelter her, and we are still looking for a place for her. Most of the people in town are scared to do anything at all, foreigners included, but we do not propose to show the white feather, and are only waiting for certain official persons to return from P., where they went a few days ago in order to get larger liberties for Red Cross activities. At present our hospital has taken in all the soldiers and refugees that it can, and we are seeing sick refugees in the clinic all day long. To-day I counted 21 women and children in one of our waiting-rooms, mostly lying on the floor from sheer exhaustion, one child moribund, two others nearly so, and half the rest of the group quite likely to die in a few days, if they are allowed to remain where they are in the camp. Many of the villagers are mountaineers, and, lying out on the hot dusty plain by day and exposed to the cold of night, they quickly succumb. To-day I took a little girl into the hospital who had been perfectly well until four days ago, when everything was stolen from the mother and she had no place to lay her except on the ground, so that she quickly got up a dysentery and died a few hours after admission to the ward. The family were respectable Protestant people from Ismid. Hardly had the little girl died and the sheets been changed than another child, this time a boy, was put into the same bed; his leg had been cut off by a railway-truck and apparently there was nobody to take care of him. We found that the mother had been forcibly separated from her children further back on the road. In that same ward lies a young girl who has recently had her leg amputated for the same accident, and who to-day was crying and screaming because some friends had told her that her parents had suddenly been deported to P. without having been given a chance to see her. It is all horrible, horrible—no mere description can adequately portray the awful suffering of these unfortunate people, whose only crime is that they are Armenians.

If a few of the men have had revolutionary ideas, I am convinced that the vast majority of them have had no more idea of rising against the Government than have their helpless wives and children. The suffering we see is utterly unlike anything confronting the Americans in Constantinople. Sad as is the lot of many of the poor soldiers, they at least have the comfort of kindness and sympathy, and the realisation that the enemy is sharing the same lot. But these people are being deliberately done to death at a sufficiently slow pace to allow their oppressors the opportunity of choosing out such of their women and their goods as they care for and getting all their money away from them before they die. Dr. and Mrs. D. went through the massacres of '94 and '96, and they and Miss H. and I have been through two revolutions, one massacre and two wars since then, but we all agree that we have never seen anything like this. Another outrageous side of it is that many of the fathers and brothers of these women and children are in the Army, fighting the country's battles. Such was the case with the dying child that was brought to the clinic this afternoon, and with another who will probably be in the same condition soon.

In addition to the medical work, we have begun distributing bread and fruit at the hospital twice a day, and a few quilts to those who are most needy. But this is very inadequate, and we hope to get the Government's permission to keep a large number of the sick in the city under our supervision with a couple of Armenian physicians to assist us. Many of the people had heard of the offer of transportation to America some time before I came here, and sigh that it might be realised. Unless political circumstances allow of their speedy restoration to their homes or their *bona fide* establishment in new places, transportation to America seems their only hope, or else the nation will be annihilated, and that very soon....

---

150. Of Union and Progress.

151. Slightly more than twopence.

152. Slightly more than a penny.

111. Q.: LETTER FROM DR. E., DATED 27th OCTOBER, 1915; COMMUNICATED BY THE AMERICAN COMMITTEE FOR ARMENIAN AND SYRIAN RELIEF.

Since my writing to you last the situation has changed considerably, although the general need and suffering remain. The whole encampment near the railway has been cleared out and sent on, with the exception of some tents belonging to families with contagious cases, such as diphtheria, scarlet fever, etc., which are being attended to by the Beledié physician. There remain, however, a very large number of people in the city, some say as many as 20,000, who are still permitted to stay here—probably through bribes to the police, friends in the Government, etc. Although the above number may be an exaggeration, one sees crowds of Armenians everywhere in town, and we have the same crowd of about 500 every day to feed, and more patients coming to the clinic than we have time to see.

Soon after the great deportation that preceded the arrival of the new Vali, Miss H. and I drove out to PP. Han, the first station on the railway towards P., just to follow up the crowd, as a large number had been driven off on foot with the expectation of taking the railway later on. PP. Han is about three hours from here by carriage, and, even so near to Q. as this, we found 100 people sitting and lying about the station in utter destitution. They had been there three days; most of them had eaten up all the provisions they had and looked haggard and emaciated—veritable famine victims such as one sees in pictures of what occurs in India. On leaving Q. they had been promised food along the way, and the gendarmes there left, saying "geledjek," but the fact was that they had had no provision whatsoever made for them. The train from Q. came along while we were there, and most of the people dragged themselves to the carriages and endeavoured to get on, but were pushed back by the gendarmes, partly because they had no tickets and partly because there was no room; so the poor people turned back bitterly and hopelessly to where they had been sitting or lying about the station. There is a village an hour or two away from the station, and a Turkish baker had driven to the station to sell bread, but as there was no money to buy, the grown-up people looked at it from the distance, while the little gaunt children drew near to stare at it wistfully. I bought enough to give each person there a loaf, and many declared that it was the first food they had had for three days. Some of the people there were intelligent and educated—their sufferings were even greater than those of the villagers, who were more accustomed to hardship. There were two women there desperately sick, with puny babies tugging away at the breast and getting nothing, their pathetic cries mingled with the groans of the mothers in physical and mental anguish. Among the hundred people there were not half-a-dozen tents, and these improvised and of the flimsiest description. All the rest of the people were lying out in the open, day and night, many without even a blanket or quilt. Half-a-mile from the station I found two old women who were crawling about on hands and knees, too weak to walk; they had been carried off on a wagon, ostensibly to go to a village, but, once out of sight of the gendarmes, the driver had dropped them in the field and hurried away. All without exception looked forward to certain death by starvation, nor could we see any other future for them. A few miles further on, we found a little heap of clods that had been apparently piled together and then scattered, and near it a bundle of rags full of a child's bones. The skull, with the scalp still clinging to it, was lying a yard or two away. Evidently there had been a hasty burial, and the dogs had come and torn the grave to pieces and devoured the body. That same day we found another dead body by the roadside—an old woman wrapped in a torn quilt; also a woman about 40 years old sitting alone by the road, miles away from any city or village, with feet bare and swollen, almost pulseless, and evidently crazed from terror and exposure, muttering something about Turks who were coming to cut her throat, about her people who had left her behind, and so forth. A little further on, lying beside an empty wayside stable, we found an old woman, half-naked, pulseless, muttering in low delirium and with only a few hours to live. We lifted her into the old stable, covered her with an old quilt that we found near her, and drove back to the city, weighed down with the thought of the awful suffering that is going on all over the country, especially to the south-east of us, of which we see such terrible examples at our very doors.

Our new executive is affable and pleasant enough, but is hand and glove with the clique here and impresses me as insincere. After pushing the deportation vigorously for a few days, things have quieted down again, and the Armenians in town are having their hopes revived, although we see nothing to ground them upon. The hunger and want in the city are increasing; to-day we fed over 600. It is blessed work, even if it seems to have no future for the recipients. A lot of the exiles are well qualified to earn a living, but the police will not allow them to work.

Next time you write, I should be interested to know if the case of Vartouhi, whose sisters from Gumuldjina were abducted, was taken up by the Bulgarian Ministry.

A side-light on the rate of extermination of the Armenians is thrown by a glance at mortality statistics in our hospital, which I have been studying lately. In ordinary years the average mortality from all causes is about 4 per cent. This year, among 500 to 600 soldiers we have taken in, it has been about 6 per cent., the increase being doubtless due to the lowered vitality of the soldiers in general. The mortality among Armenians—exiles—who have been admitted to our wards has been over 30 per cent., and this in spite of the fact that we have taken in only the ordinary run of maladies and that there has been no epidemic! The nation is being systematically done to death by a cruel and crafty method, and their extermination is only a question of time.

112. Q.: LETTER, DATED Q., 25th NOVEMBER, 1915, FROM DR. E. TO MR. N. AT CONSTANTINOPLE; COMMUNICATED BY THE AMERICAN COMMITTEE FOR ARMENIAN AND SYRIAN RELIEF.

Profiting by a medical call to Bozanti to see the family of a railway employee, I have at last had a chance which I have been waiting for for some time, namely, to investigate the conditions to the south-east of us. The journey there and back was very tedious and disagreeable; the locomotives burn only wood, and the trains take just about twice the ordinary time to cover the distance. About every three or four hours the train has to stop to load wood on the tender, and when it comes to a steep grade the train has to be divided into two, the locomotive taking up half of it and then returning for the other half. There is still transportation of Armenians going on, but most of the movement is in the other direction, great numbers of raw Arab recruits being brought from Syria and the Hauran and sent on to Eski Shehr and Constantinople. The men are of the wildest type, thinly clad, many of them having neither shoes nor stockings. They suffer greatly from the cold, which is already becoming severe, and are treated with great brutality by their officers, whom I saw beating and stoning and cursing them all along the way.

Leaving on Sunday, the 21st, I spent the next day at P. There were about 2,000 exiles there, of whom about a third had permission from the Government to remain on account of being artizans or, in the cases of women and children, of being members of soldiers' families. The remainder were more or less under the ban, and were dragging out a wretched existence dodging the police, but preferring such a life to the fate of being sent on into the mountains to starve. The artizans above-mentioned were receiving a loaf of bread a day from the Government and being forced to work for nothing; also the soldiers' families were receiving rations, but in no case sufficient. I heard many stories of how the Armenians had been refused transportation by train, and had been forced to hire wagons at exorbitant rates, ten liras and more from P. to Tarsus, or else had been driven off on foot, leaving most of their belongings behind them. I saw great piles of baggage heaped up at the station, at least five or six hundred pieces, that had been abandoned, and was told that probably there had been three thousand in all. Most of this property had been confiscated as "metrouk" (abandoned) and had been partitioned among the officials or sold, while a good deal had been stolen by the Turks in the town. About a hundred children had been abandoned on account of sickness or of their being too young to walk. The Turks had taken all but about twenty of these and adopted them as Moslems, and I found the remainder of them in the care of a poor Armenian woman, who with the help of some of the Armenians in the town was trying to look after them. They were all in a dark, wretched room, about nine by twelve feet—miserable specimens of humanity they were. Seven of them in that room actually looked sick, and all of them pinched and pale and insufficiently clothed. The kind-hearted woman in charge was not only nursing a baby of her own but actually trying to make her small supply of milk suffice for two of the littlest refugees as well, who were sick and for whom there was no cow's milk to be had. Being in such wretched condition they were not much in demand, but from time to time, she told me, the Turks would come round to see if there were any worth taking off, especially girls. The Government was doing absolutely nothing for these children.

Deportation in P. was still in progress, about a hundred wagon-loads of people having been driven off a few days before I arrived. One of the parties, consisting of husband, wife, two boys and one girl, had been set upon near BE. by robbers. Upon some resistance being offered by the man, the whole party was stabbed to death, the little girl of six years having first been foully outraged. This story is authentic, and the Government is now making investigation and promises to punish the "guilty" when they are found.

Near the station I found about two hundred people who had been driven out of the town, and were crowded into a couple of abandoned and tumble-down houses, in filth and misery indescribable. I started to look at the sick, but gave it up as a bad job, as almost all were sick and no medicine would make them well as long as they were obliged to live under such conditions. There were a few tents spread outside on the frozen ground, and the condition of the people in them was about the same as that of those in the houses. In the evening, when I took the train, some of the people were trying to buy tickets, when I saw an officer deliberately pulling them away from the window and beckoning to Turks to take their places and to their friends to crowd about the window, apparently with the intention of delaying the Armenians so that they should miss the train, which now takes passengers only once a week. I managed to crowd in and buy tickets for four of them, the officer meanwhile telling the rest of them that there were no tickets for them that night. Fortunately the train was so late that I think all must have eventually gotten tickets. This in itself is a small incident, but is a sample of the continual nagging and harassing that is going on when there is no opportunity to do something worse. The regular resident Armenians of P. have for the most part been allowed to remain, through the goodwill of the Kaimakam, but are, of course, subjected to constant nagging. They are frequently invited to become Moslems, and even J. Effendi, who is a Protestant, is nagged by one of the Turkish officials, who is trying to get his youngest daughter to marry him. All Armenians there are in great anxiety and fear, and I could see that they were nervous about being seen with me, so that I had some difficulty in seeing and hearing what I wanted. In Q. they seem to take a great deal of comfort in our presence in the city and in being able to apply to us in a way that does not excite suspicion. Also, some of the police are our friends and refrain from making trouble.

Going on to Bozanti, I found only about 250 refugees. These were scattered along the long valley that leads towards Tarsus, and were altogether the most wretched of the exiles that I have yet seen. They are the remnants of the vast encampment that has been there during the past months, and are all too poor to hire any conveyance to Tarsus, eighteen hours away, while their women and children are too feeble to attempt the journey on foot. About two-thirds of the people had wretched tents of some description, and the rest had no shelter at all. They had sold what had not been stolen from them, and many were half-naked. All were famished and wretched, with despair written on their pinched and haggard faces; a large number were sick, and I counted five corpses in half-an-hour. Of the latter, two were still stretched out in the tents, one was being buried, and two had been thrown out by the roadside. There is no available shelter for these people in Bozanti, even if they had permission to use it. The Government sends some bread to them from time to time, but with no regularity. Most of them were villagers, but some from good families. I found a pretty young girl with her mother in one of the tents, whom I recognised as having seen in Q. The girl had been in danger of being abducted by the police while here, so her mother had hurried her on to Bozanti; but there the money gave out, and they had nothing left but some scanty bedding, a few dishes, a little clothing and three medjidias. Beside their tent were two others, whose occupants, like them, were people of some breeding and refinement, but in similar destitution, and with only women and children in all the three tents. In another tent I found a young girl who had been carried off by the gendarmes but rescued by the station employees at Bozanti. I was told that she had been a bright and attractive girl, but when I saw her she was thin and emaciated and had become idiotic. The valley was strewn with graves, and many of them had been torn open by dogs and the bodies eaten. I was told that considerably over a thousand people had died at Bozanti, and about the same number at P.—how many thousands all along the way from Constantinople to Mesopotamia, no one can tell. People coming from that region say that not one person in ten ever reached Zor, and that those people who have gotten there have nothing but starvation before them. From the statements of railway officials and others I should think that not less than 500,000 people must have passed through Bozanti.

At P., in addition to distributing some money, I left 30 liras to be spent for the people by J. Effendi and the Armenian Beledié physician there (a first-rate and very capable fellow), paying especial attention to the waifs above mentioned. At Bozanti I bought a donkey-load of bread and distributed it to the refugees, gave out a considerable amount of cash in small sums, hired several camels and horses that were then available to take some of the people on to Tarsus as soon as possible, and left 20 liras with my host to hire wagons next day and send on more of the people (wagons there can now be hired quite cheaply). If we get word that they reached Tarsus safely, I think we can arrange to send on the rest. Tarsus is at least warmer and better in every way than the bleak mountains among which they are staying now, and we can only hope that things may take a turn for the better before they are driven into the desert. The Vali here is now very friendly, and assures us that at least all Protestants will be allowed to remain here and will not be molested, but that others will be sent off soon to the towns (kazas), though not to the villages. We all breathe easier with the chief of police and his cronies now no longer in Q.

113. KONIA: RESUMÉ OF A LETTER[153] DATED KONIA, 2nd/15th OCTOBER, 1915; APPENDED TO THE MEMORANDUM (DOC. 11), DATED 15th/28th OCTOBER, 1915, FROM A WELL-INFORMED SOURCE AT BUKAREST.

Immediately after the recall of the Vali, Djelal Bey, who had left the exiles' tents with tears in his eyes, more than 80,000 Armenians—men, women and children—were driven away from their tents and directed towards the south, beaten along with whips and clubs. It was a heart-rending sight. The poor people, who were already in rags, had to abandon what blankets or clothes they possessed and start on foot. Parents had lost their children, women were looking for their husbands, but the wild gendarmerie flogged without mercy all those who cried or entreated. The tents were full of corpses, which dogs were devouring. More than thirty people died daily from hunger and cold. All along the railway line from Konia to Karaman, Eregli and Bozanti (the rail-head), hundreds of thousands of Armenians were herded along by the gendarmes. Tired and hungry, they begged bread from the passengers and the railway officials. The few families that had managed to remain in Konia at the cost of great sacrifices, have also received the order to leave the town. The Government has published a report on alleged crimes committed by the Christians, and especially by the Armenians, against the Moslems. By such means it deliberately exasperates the Turks more and more. On the journey the number of deaths goes on increasing.

---

153. Name of writer withheld.

114. BAGHDAD RAILWAY: DIARY OF A FOREIGN RESIDENT[154] IN THE TOWN OF B., ON A SECTION OF THE LINE; EDITED BY WILLIAM WALTER ROCKWELL, ESQ., PH.D., AND PUBLISHED BY THE AMERICAN COMMITTEE FOR ARMENIAN AND SYRIAN RELIEF (1916).

30th June, 1915.

The skies are dark here, and people have been in and out all day—these of all classes, and every one with the same question: "What of the night?" The news from BV. was not encouraging. A few influential Turks here want to help, but *dare not*. Some women went by carriage to see an influential man and his family in a vineyard; were well received. Each had her part; —— was assigned that of shedding tears, but I do not think she did so alone. It has been like a funeral here. Several families have been notified to be at the station with all their members and their beds on Monday next, when they would be told their destination. P.'s brother and Q. head the list; the others are poorer people. They are working for a week of grace in which to settle business affairs. *Isn't it awful*—and all are asking: "Who next?" Such drawn and tired faces as we have seen all day.

Half the town want to "store" things here, to be ours if they never return; rugs, coppers, etc.—but we may be blown up, who knows?

1st July.

Times here are lively. In B. people get two orders at once, and then ask which one they must obey? Conditions in BV. are hard. The Vali's brother is against the Armenians. People of all sorts and conditions come from morning until night to ask questions and to weep. The conditions here are far from cheerful.

4th July.

Several families go to-morrow (only one of them a Protestant). The Government says they will go a few at a time. I doubt their sending widows, and, for all their positive assertions, I still feel it in my bones that there will be modifications of the order. People come from morning till night to talk.

I am giving up the room downstairs for a store-room. —— says he has 5,000 liras' worth of mortgages and farms, etc., which he can't store. The R.'s have eight times as much out among the ruling race. I suspect that leading families are to go first. Every one trembles.

We had a comfortably full chapel both morning and evening, and two beautiful sermons suitable for the time. Many Greeks and Gregorians present. The Greeks are being sent from Constantinople. —— urged upon the people their going away in a right spirit, remembering the blessings of the past, opportunities as a nation for education, business and church life, to pay their debts to Moslems, to help the poor among them, to go as evangelists in faith and courage. It was comforting and inspiring.

18th July.

Eighty-three men from Kaisaria (without their families), the most influential man in the Protestant community among them, came to-day en route for Aleppo. They say that spies are everywhere now-a-days. What days these are, and when will they end?

20th July.

Last night the city districts across the river were notified to be ready. The Commissaire (chief of police) is registering families all over the city, and says they are to go at least fifty at a time and that vigorous measures will now be taken, etc. These are miserable, anxious days for everybody.

23rd July.

One does not know what to say of the situation here. There seemed to be a holding up yesterday. Some who went to be registered were sent home to wait till called for. In the meantime, Arab women were going through —— Agha's district (where word had been given the previous evening to pack up and leave), and were buying all sorts of things, rugs, coppers, etc., at one-third or one-fifth their value. Things worth a lira[155] sometimes went for a mejidia[156], etc. There is trouble in every family.

I've been out in the market getting cloth so as to give sewing to some poor women, and also to get the news. I met the Armenian priest at S.'s store. He is pretty certain there is no help for the people. However, he is going through his congregation and making out a list of all the lame and halt and deaf and blind and old and soldiers' families, to lay before the Government as exceptions. He had a *hope* of gaining their case.

A few wretched people from Zeitoun are in the churchyard. They were left behind somewhere, but are now here, and I hear that one woman was likely to be confined last night.

Streets are full of Moslem women of the common sort, buying freely, talking loudly, and, I fear, getting goods "charged." Merchants do not seem glad to see them.

Some say that Armenians in BV. have paid £10,000 (Turkish) to buy exemption; others say forty families are to leave soon.

I made several calls and saw many in the streets. It was pitiful to find the gateways blocked by crowds of Moslem women demanding what there was for sale; even pushing into houses after hearing there was nothing for sale. In one house of our congregation is a woman with three little children. The mother had sold her few decent clothes, bought coarse flour and made a pile of the hardest and poorest thin bread I've seen for many a day. She needed her clothes badly enough, but, with hungry children, she needed money more. I gave her a medjidia.

T.'s wife was at home selling and packing, quite cheerful, but says T.'s old mother mourns the years of labour given to the vineyard, etc. (naturally). Her neighbours had torn some sheets of corrugated zinc from their roofs to sell. The Government forbade it.

28th July.

Many people actually left on Monday, so that in all over forty families have gone, and many more are to go next Thursday. Our baker went on two hours' or less notice. He left bread in the oven, and gathered up wheat that was drying. He has a lame wife and three children, and his half-blind mother went also. There seems to be no help. (N.B.—The poor baker died soon on the way.)

A few families have left BV. and several men have left AE., with families to follow. The poverty and distress of the people is heartbreaking. The poor family from BM., which you gave help to and who have seven daughters, are to go next Monday. This intense heat has pulled the eldest daughter down so that she is confined to her bed. I fear it is tuberculosis. Doctor says so. The family will ask delay. There isn't much chance of their getting it.

—— (the Moslem doctor) examines people and says to the sick, "You can go," and gives a stimulant. The mother of the R. brothers is to go on Monday. I hope we can keep the boys here.

I've bought a cow for which I paid three liras (fifty-four shillings). Others would not have paid so much, but it means food and money for the journey.

Wages in the factory have been cut down, as people are willing to work at any price if they can escape exile.

2nd August.

Over forty more families left this morning. Most of them were very poor, and it was a sad sight to see them going to the station on foot, loaded down with small children, jugs, baskets and bundles. They were not laughing or talking at all; some of the children were crying; better off people went to the train by carriage, but looked no happier. Thus far soldiers' families seem to be exempt.

Sixty men from AE. were on the train as exiles this morning; more are to follow. The train runs now for military and exile service from AE. I can't even write letters, my mind is so upset.

4th August.

School is still an open question. The Turks are taking note of stock in shop to-day.

One of the ―― boys, about twelve years old, was returning home to the vineyard and was robbed and wounded a little. After the murder of young ―― ―― last week, we are thankful this boy was not seriously hurt. The incident shows the spirit of the times.

7th August.

Miss ―― has just come from AE. She saw the AE. people being loaded into carts sent by the Government, and carriages hired by themselves, to be deported. Seventy families came as far as B. in the night. ――'s family got a day longer. George was summoned in the night to help them. He went on horseback, and hasn't returned. Many are to leave here on Monday.

8th August.

Such a full day; people coming, coming, a constant stream, to deposit things, to get eye-medicine, salve for sores, to ask for help, to beg all manner of things, shoes, money, tents and so on. I did something for each asker, but not much. There was a mad rush to the station—one stream of vehicles of all descriptions, carrying goods to the station, families on top in most cases. The regular passenger train pulled out sometime before ― o'clock. The live freight was so overfull that many were left until to-morrow—among them ――, who has been ill for weeks. Their goods are at the station, and their house locked and sealed; ―― is lying under an empty goods-truck, very weak and miserable.

The people in BW. are now threatened with deportation. There are scarcely half-a-dozen mature men left in the village since the last massacre, but plenty of women and children.

A group of people from Talas have come. The women have been robbed, and some of the girls in their party had suffered terrible things. The party had sons in military service, and others in business in America.

9th August.

Miss ―― went to BV. to-day. We saw the people (put by themselves) off for AG. Besides many B. people we know, there were fifty carriages full of AE. people, including Protestants and many big Armenian families. Seventy families came up a few days ago. ――'s shop was shut up and sealed so quickly that they got only three packages out before the Government was on hand to close up. Little —— even left his coat in his haste. Between 800 and 900 liras' worth of goods were in the store. Their house is new, and newly furnished. They were to have come on last night, but six days more were granted, because of new-born baby and wife's being too weak.

There has been an uprising of Armenian runaways and Kurds, and a meeting *in conflict* near Marash. A few soldiers killed. This event has disturbed still more the minds of the Turks. The sea-coast towns are to be emptied in two weeks, they say. Turks will go to the mountains.

11th August.

There seems to be a holding up of deportation to last until after Bairam at least, and we hope longer. There is no hold up for AE.

14th August.

Dr. L. arrived here from AC. He said there was no place as quiet and safe as this region! In AC. a thousand families have been told to leave, and among them are the families of all their teachers. So there was no hope of opening the College unless something very unexpected occurred soon. There have been *extensive massacres* all through that region, at Malatia, Besné, Adiaman, etc. The Marash region is all afire—runaways stirring up to wrath and revenge being taken by massacre, the Turks *wanting an excuse* to do their worst. Nothing has been heard from Marash for some time. He knows of special trouble and killing at Fundadjak (five hours from Marash). Ourfa region is all excitement, people being exiled and made away with en route. He mentioned many killed that we knew.

One thousand Zeitoun people have died in exile, they say. The city is full now with exiles from Adapazar and that region. The son of —— of Talas died in Osmania. The family were exiled, and the hardships of the journey were too much for the professor.

Many Zeitoun people are wandering about the streets of B. They say they were driven from the Konia Vilayet. They reported to the Kaimakam here, who said he had no orders about them and would not meddle, they might do just as they pleased. (Later they were driven on). Dr. L. appealed personally to U. Pasha for permission to do general relief work. He was flatly refused. U. said the Government would attend to its own business. Dr. L. says they will do so, and *are* doing so in regions to the east, and people are dying in many ways; it's a part of the policy.

Dr. L. says the Arabs at Der-el-Zor (where Armenians are exiled) are kindly, and treat women well. The climate is hot and dry, and warm river-water is all there is to drink, and he fears cholera and typhoid, as bodies are continually seen floating down the rivers (massacre victims).

16th August.

Crowds of Zeitoun people, *sent away* from Sultania, went on to-day towards BM. I fear they go to death. Between 600 and 700 have died already of hardship and illness.

I made some Bairam calls on Turks and was well received, but one cannot be at all sure of the heart of any one these days.

Have just returned from the priest's house. I went to get a girl's story. The girl was a day-pupil of Miss V.'s[157] at X., about fifteen years old. Officers came to many houses and said they were to be exiled, but school-girls were to be excepted, and they took the girls "back to school;" not to their own school, though, but to a Turkish barracks, where they were on exhibition and chosen as the property of certain officers. This girl was claimed by one; the others, over a hundred, were carried in automobiles to Constantinople. Fifteen of them were this girl's friends. This girl was brought here with exiles from *somewhere*. She refused the attentions of the officer claiming her. The priest heard of her and went to investigate. The officer complained that not one smile had she ever given him. The priest said she would never smile on him, and left him to think over-night on the matter. In the morning he said he didn't want her against her will. The priest secured the girl, and the officer has gone his way on to Aleppo. The priest can't afford to keep her, and I have written to the BV. school about her. Perhaps we here can raise 10 liras for her and send her to school. She left her mother two months ago. Her family were exiled at once.

W., X.'s sister and her child were here an hour ago, en route from the north (where the Zeitoun people were first sent). She tells dreadful tales. What will be the end of it all? The streets are full of exiles begging for bread. —— and relatives are all here, and Partani's sister. I am buying ——'s bed to lighten her luggage and fill her purse. She tells of babies left to die on the roadside, as the mothers could carry them no longer. Many tell me this.

A young man from —— was just in. Two hundred and fifty families are en route from there. The city swarms with exiles, and many are at ——.

19th August.

Our —— boys and families are also in the procession. The Nigdé people have begun to move on from here. The Adapazar people are *à la franca* and some of them very rich. Thirty more carriages from AE. last night.

Robberies are common, and girls carried off, and three Armenians killed at BY.

20th August.

The stream of arrivals continues to flow into B. The poor people on foot simply drop down utterly exhausted, and many are dying of hunger and fatigue. Three quite large children died in the Gregorian churchyard yesterday; another is badly off with smallpox; a middle-aged man there is dying. —— Hodja has been over there this morning to minister to him. A crowd of those ill were carried off to the Turkish hospital yesterday. —— and his family are still here from BV., waiting for the rest of his family—mother and brothers and their families. The advance line has arrived and tell him that his relatives lost almost everything from their homes. Plunderers threw their goods from the windows, and partners carried off rugs, bedding, &c. and some money they had. His brothers had been in prison.

I helped yesterday a blind man (led by his wife) who had been driven from Bor; also an old woman with snowy white hair who was hungry and penniless. I got Y. to make up a dress for a young woman, and Z. made a skirt for another young married woman whose clothes were in tatters. A crowd are in our churchyard. I sent them soap for a wash and bath, and shavings, &c., for fuel.

There has been a pause in the B. deportation, waiting for the present crowd to pass on. AE. people are again on the move. I hear that only five Armenian families will be left in AE. One is the dealer in iron for the Railway, and the others are employed for business dealings with the Government.

People here are dealt with *very* gently as compared with treatment received in northern districts and to the east.

22nd August.

B. presents a strange sight these days with literally *thousands* of strangers in our streets. These are from places all the way up to Adapazar, and they are of all types and degrees of civilisation, "some in rags, and some in tags, and some in velvet gowns." The church was full this morning.

I went by the Gregorian church yesterday and looked into the yard. Such a sight! Such a pandemonium of noises! In that crowd there are deaths *every day*, from disease, hunger and exhaustion. I sent money to help a few, but any help any of us can give is but a drop in an ocean of misery.

According to a wire from our Ambassador, Catholics and Protestants are excused from exile. It seems to be true. I suppose our people in AG. will be called back now. Now for the red tape to get a full and correct list of the Protestant villages and strangers!

I have written for some relief money. One poor Zeitoun woman is too ill to travel, but her husband has been driven on—forced to leave her here. She is at the church. Some people are in our churchyard, some in hans, and some have rented houses in which to rest for a few days. The Zeitoun people are "free," but are driven from place to place. They are, as a whole, ragged, dirty and covered with vermin, and hungry, and afraid of the purpose of the Government.

Same Evening.

There is danger of cholera breaking out. Two died in the churchyard who had symptoms of it. The Government is trying to drive away the poorest of the people, chiefly Zeitoun people. They say there is cholera in Aleppo. Was there ever a year like this?

A lot of people from Nigdé were called from our service by the police to start on, this afternoon. The Government is not quite pleased over the new order for exemption of Protestants and Catholics. The Zeitoun people are watched closely, and one must not help them.

26th August[158].

———'s letters do not—cannot—exaggerate it. The state to which things have come is indicated by ———'s very casual remark last night: "Well, to-morrow we'll first go out and see who has died."—"I hope that woman in the church has."—"I wish that child would, but I'm afraid she won't."

Yesterday and the day before, most of those in the open—those absolutely too sick to move along being excepted—were driven out with whips. We fear they have but gone to BZ. (outside the town), to suffer still worse. Many have been even deprived of their bedding, or at least separated from it and forbidden to hunt it up. There is never a day but some die.

Those able to hire houses have escaped from being driven on, by keeping out of sight, as the driving is done with much cruelty but no system.

In our church a very *à la franca* family from ——— had an addition the day they arrived. They have been given a few days' grace.

I've been out to BZ., where conditions are still worse than in the city. Saw one old woman by the road, dying. People walked by her, lying out in the blazing sun, with scarcely a look. The sight is too common. Thousands are out there, and no shade or shelter of any kind, except such as the people themselves can manage to put up.

I go out with ——— every day, and come back sure I've merely had a nightmare.

2nd September.

Streams of Yozgad people have come, and the word is that 10,000 are *en route* from Constantinople. Some Broussa people are here *now*—new-comers. Yesterday was a hard day, heart-breaking. I went to the train, a long one, to see over forty B. families off, and others besides. Among the B. people were ——, ——, AB., and his *sick wife*, taken from bed to go and almost carried aboard the train. ——'s sister and husband, her daughter Akabé and Akabé's family go on Saturday, and our dear, kind, and just neighbour —— and his family. He looked white with pain at going, and his wife, well, she could talk, though far from happy. Notwithstanding ——'s assurances that —— and —— could remain as boarders, their boys were taken. The Kaimakam evidently had not been notified by the Vali. The Kaimakam seems to have a heart, but is hard pressed, I am told, by the rich and influential Turks in B., who are making life a burden for him.

Another of those *wretched* old women without money, food, friends, or bed, and ill, has finished her pilgrimage. Three remain in the Gregorian yard, and three men in the same hopeless condition. I do not see how they live. The old women raise a cry for water when I go. I sent —— with iced "iran" yesterday and to-day. The woman with a fever is better. Two girls, without beds, are now ill. I am getting excelsior beds filled for them to-day. The woman with a burnt arm has moved on. The train was to go to CD. From where will they be fed there?

3rd September.

Things get worse and worse. Mr. —— called last night and told me he saw a telegram from U. Pasha, saying: "Let not the Americans and consuls be seen helping the exiles or appearing with them at stations and public places."

——'s name is down to go to-morrow. We are doing our best to save him. I've sent to Mr. AG. for help, and may have to go myself to the Kaimakam.

4th September.

—— went to AE. yesterday with a letter to Mr. AG. about our boys and teachers. I've little hope from that quarter, but give him his opportunity. Mr. AH. put ——'s case before the Kaimakam strongly yesterday, as *our* man. The Kaimakam is well disposed, but is under heavy pressure to send *every* Armenian without exception. Anyway, I may be able to save his family.

6th September.

Crowds of people went to-day. There was only one passenger carriage, for which people paid. All others were crowded *en masse* into goods-trucks, and driven with whips like so many cattle. One old man, who had spoken and prayed beautifully in our morning prayer meeting yesterday (a Protestant from Yozgad), turned, when the police called him, to call his townsman. He was struck with a stone and asked if it was *his* business to call people. He quietly accepted the rebuke.

At BV. the proclamation was given out on Saturday from the housetops all over the city that *every* Armenian of whatever church would leave BV. without delay.

No notice has been served on the Protestants here *as yet*. The Kaimakam accepted it that they were to remain. He has assured me that he will do his best to save ——— as *our teacher*. But this morning ——— was demanded by the police and taken from our yard to be sent *at once*. You may believe it, he was fairly wild. Said he *couldn't* go at once, hadn't change of clothes, and he would write and ask for a few days' time. I signed his petition, and a boy ran to the Government while a policeman led him to the station. George gave him money and collected three blankets for him. The Kaimakam sent me greetings and the message that he would attend to the matter. At the station ——— was arrested for coming so late, and thus attempting to be left behind. The train was still there but full, and he was rushed back and put into prison! I suspected that the Kaimakam was taking this way to secure delay, and I still think so. Hence I made no enquiries, intending to do so after the train pulled out. Some time later, ——— returned all out of breath, saying he could stay until Wednesday, and he drove up to the vineyard to give his wife details. She knew nothing of the proceedings of the day.

Yesterday, after service, a nice looking middle-aged woman came to me with her arm in a sling and said it pained her, and could I do something for it. I took her upstairs and called Nurse ———, and we found a stab in her shoulder and dressed it. She said she and her son were stabbed by bashi bazouks on the way. To stop the bleeding they had stuffed in earth, and this and the blood had caked well.

I took Nurse ——— to see some other patients. The old woman who usually raises herself and asks for water seemed unconscious, and didn't answer even when I said "cold water" and put a few drops on her head. She was alive but getting cold, and died in the night. This morning the man in the corner was also released. He came only two days ago, and was in a *most wretched* condition.

The other night I found the woman with short grey hair just able to reach up and call: "Water, water." An Armenian woman lifted her head and she drank, but fell back at once, and we found her hands icy cold, and saw she was dying. We straightened out her rags, and got an old pillow under her head. She was soon released.

This morning Nurse ——— and I started out again for the churchyard. Sitting opposite the gate was the fat police commissioner who is so cruel. He called out to "Madame ———." I stopped and explained that we were only looking after a woman who had met with an accident on the road. But I was told decidedly that I was not to go into that yard again; that the Government would send *food! doctors! medicines!* and *foreigners* were not to help or interfere. So I returned.

So many young women and pretty girls come to me here and in the street, asking with tears what is to become of them.

7th September.

The woman and her son with sword-cuts came this afternoon. No one was around, so the gate-man let them in and I dressed the wounds. Both *doing well.* I gave new bandages and other needfuls, so that, if they could not come again, or were driven on the road to-morrow, they could care for the wound. They were *most grateful.* They are Protestants, and intelligent; were robbed of money. I gave them a little for food—shall give more if I see them again. AC. got through; no trouble about keeping boys in the yard now. Little fellows run for all. Massacre near Yozgad; the air heavy with the odour of unburied bodies. Some of our travellers came by them. Dr. BB.[159] and the hospital still in X. when the exiles left, but things in a bad way generally. AD.'s postcard tells of AC. BM. seems quiet at present.

—th September.

The woman I was forbidden to nurse got over here yesterday leaning on a friend and by help of a cane. George was here, and we gave the heel a good dressing but couldn't get all the broken bone out. The flesh is getting clean. The poor old woman cried and said she was hungry. I fed her and gave her a little money. She hopes to get here again to-morrow, but she suffers excruciating pain when her foot rests on the ground.

There will soon be a lull, I suppose, as the town is getting well emptied, not a Christian butcher left, and only two Moslems.

8th September.

The pot is boiling *harder* and *harder.* Another special train takes nearly all left of B. Armenians. —— and his family were all hustled off this morning as "a dangerous man who had tried to help exiles." Talas people are here now (came last night) and tell sad tales.

10th September.

R. feels helpless and it looks that way now, as things get worse every day. The powers that be have their own plans and listen to no one. On all sides one hears a wail of distress. Every man, woman, and child has come from — —, leaving most of their possessions behind. Even their preacher is here, and is ordered to "move on." I have "cabbaged" the three little fellows who were our pupils, and am keeping them here, as they were of our last year's boarders. No one will look them up. Two little orphan boys (new ones) were offered from these, but I couldn't take them. They too must "move on."

To what straits all are now reduced! The woman with a broken heel was here this morning and I took two more pieces of crushed bone from it. She bears it well. I think the loose pieces are about all out now. I did it up and made a sort of burlap outer covering as a protection. I gave her some food, for she cried and said she was dying of hunger. Only the helpless (and a few others) are now left here. The —— people are at the station. Crowds of people have been shipped off. AE. people are coming now. Poor —— is still in prison.

11th September.

We are nearly crazy with difficulties. I hardly think AJ. will be sent, but *no one knows*. AF. is here from BV., and reports that some five days ago a telegram was received from some German "sefer" ordering that *every Armenian should stay where he was*, whether at home or abroad. In BV. the Government hurried people off all the more, but now the order has leaked out, and probably is known here, as there was a lull to-day, and the Vali passed last evening to —— —— and saw the Kaimakam en route. —— and —— are to leave on Thursday. Circassians are to take the houses of the common people, and officers those of the wealthier ones.

—— reports that Marash Protestants were called back—almost compelled to come. In Adana it looks as if the deportation were an alternative for a massacre. Exiles are not wanted anywhere.

12th September.

No Christians left in Bor. Zeitoun was burned by the runaways and Fundadjak is in ruins; also Deré Keui and another neighbouring village.

14th September.

BV. is being emptied of *every* Armenian, and the foreigners fear they also may have to go, if there is an invasion on the coast. I do not think conditions are as bad here.

17th September.

Dr. —— says we must not think of Red Cross work as the Society *has not the funds*, but must let the Turks run things on their own responsibility. The Turks expect an invasion and are sending their families away.

Some rich Samsoun people here to-day. —— says that the three families among whom she is are to go to Konia.

A stranger priest died here yesterday from exhaustion and heart-break, etc.

19th September.

No exiles to-day; there seems to be a calm for a few hours.

—th October.

Life is getting fuller and fuller of problems here. Affairs here are in a very critical condition.

---

154. Mother of the "Miss B." of Sect. I., Doc. 8

155. 18s.

156. 3s. 2d.

157. The "Miss A." of Sect. XI.

158. *Note by Dr. Rockwell:*—This letter, by a man, is inserted here to reflect the situation from a man's point of view.

159. See Section XI.

115. AE., A TOWN ON THE RAILWAY: SERIES OF REPORTS FROM A FOREIGN RESIDENT AT AE., COMMUNICATED BY THE AMERICAN COMMITTEE FOR ARMENIAN AND SYRIAN RELIEF.

(a) Undated Report.

Two days ago an order was received here for the immediate deportation of the entire Armenian population of AE., consisting of about 1,800 souls. Yesterday nearly 300 persons were sent to ——, and to-day many more have been ordered to be ready to leave. In anticipation of their deportation, the Armenians are selling all their non-portable goods for a song. Sewing machines sold for 1½ medjidias, iron bedsteads for a few piastres, and so on. The Government is allowing each person only a few metaliks per day for food, and transports only a little baggage. The present destination of the deported persons is ——. Apart from their actual distress and misery, the terror of these people is indescribable. Stories of the massacre of thousands of Armenians in the interior now reach here. Some of these appear to be well founded, but I presume that you have been fully informed of what has transpired in the regions of ——.

(b) Report dated 11th September, 1915.

Thousands of additional Armenians from the North have arrived here and been transported to the Aleppo region. Six thousand have been deported from the city of Adana, without the exception supposedly given to Catholics and Protestants. The congestion of people at the various stations en route caused terrible suffering and hardships to the refugees. The authorities no longer appear disposed to grant exceptions in favour of teachers and pupils of American schools, and, despite intervention, St. Paul's College at Tarsus has been suffering in this respect.

(c) **Report dated 22nd September, 1915.**

This report opens with the mention of a fear among the Ottoman authorities at AE, that the Allies were about to make a landing there, and proceeds as follows:—

Naturally one of the first results of the above fear was a general rush to complete the deportation of Armenians from Adana. The number of Armenians sent from that city now totals about 25,000, and this is in addition to the many thousands coming from the North that pass through. The misery, suffering and hardships endured by these people are indescribable. Deaths are innumerable. Hundreds of children are constantly being abandoned by their parents, who cannot bear to see them suffer or who have not the strength to look after them. Many are left by the roadside, and cases of their being thrown from railway-carriage windows are reported. Petty cruelties by police and officials increase the sad plight of these people. Conditions in this vicinity are reported to be moderate in comparison with those between Osmania and Aleppo, where the congested masses and lack of facilities render the problem of feeding and transporting these people an impossible task. Protestant and Catholic Armenians continue to be deported, and the same measures are also applied in towns like Hadjin.

(d) **Memorandum dated 27th September, 1915.**

I submit herewith the following general details to supplement my various reports concerning the deportation of Armenians and the circumstances responsible for the sufferings and the deaths of many of these people.

(1) The lack of proper transportation facilities is the most important factor in causing this misery. The long distances not covered by railways, between Tarsus and Bozanti on the north and Osmania and Radjou (near Aleppo) to the south, and the lack of carts and carriages, compel many to go afoot. The carts are of the most primitive kind and are usually loaded with the effects of the travellers, on which they must find places to sit. Only those with ample means can afford the luxury of carriages, which for from two to four days' journey cost from £6 to £20 sterling. In addition to the payment of their 'fare,' the travellers are frequently 'held up' for more money by the driver or accompanying gendarme; otherwise they are obliged to descend and walk. While in general the Government furnishes carts, these are far from sufficient, and the railway transportation has in most cases had to be paid for

by the people themselves. The local section of the Baghdad Railway was a great convenience, nevertheless, in furthering the march of the exiles, but unfortunately of late its services have been considerably required for military transport purposes, and the Armenians have consequently had to find other means of conveyance or else to walk.

(2) While formerly cases of violence to Armenians were rare in this district, of late there have been flagrant cases of highway robbery, while reports of violations of women and girls are more numerous and apparently well founded. Forced conversions, which were formerly only reported from the interior, are now taking place here. Thus in Adana the many Armenian orphan girls whose parents were killed in the massacres of 1909 were told either to leave or become Moslems. A small number had the courage to leave, and were without any shelter or refuge. I had advised the American missionaries not to take in any too great number of outsiders into their institution, as they would thereby jeopardise their present inmates. Miss K., however, secured the consent of the authorities to place these girls in private homes, which she found for them after much difficulty. The work of the German mission at Harounia on behalf of Armenian girls must also be commended in this connection, and the benevolent attitude of His Excellency the Governor General towards girls'-schools must also be pointed out, with the hope that the same will continue.

(3) No attempt has been made of late to solve adequately the problem of feeding the Armenian exiles. This is true both of the stations along the route of deportation and in the larger cities. Thus at Osmania, where for the past few weeks there have always been from forty to sixty thousand people, the food supply is scarcely enough for one-third of that number, so that all are either on short rations or without any food at all. This is responsible for the illness which prevails and the numerous deaths which are reported. This it is which compels mothers to abandon their children, whom they cannot bear to see suffer or are too weak to carry along.

Apart from the general distress brought upon the persons deported, the effect of the deportation measures is becoming more and more apparent on the economic situation of this province. The great majority of the stores and bazaars are shut, and it is difficult to purchase one's daily requirements. Most of the merchandise belonging to Armenian merchants is in sealed stores. The creditors of Armenian merchants were in most cases able to secure the value of their outstanding credits through taking goods in payment. As the greater part of the business of this district in most lines was in the hands of Armenians, the consequences of their deportation are only too apparent for the future of the Adana Province.

(e) **Report dated 30th October, 1915.**

The stream of deported Armenians from the north continues unabated. Recent arrivals were in a terribly wretched condition, and their sufferings from insufficient food and raiment are indescribable. The police and other officials also prohibit their receiving assistance, which makes it evident that slow death is the ultimate fate of the majority.

Three rabid members of the Union and Progress Committee of Adana were expelled from that city because of the manner in which they were hounding the Armenians out of the city. It is stated that they even planned incendiary measures against Armenian houses and buildings, and among others reported to have been endangered was that of the American Mission. At the request of the missionaries, I directed the attention of the authorities to the matter.

The new law concerning the real estate and personal property of deported persons is being carried out in a manner which, I fear, will leave little if anything for the Armenians. Their houses are being inhabited by mouhadjirs, officials, etc., at ridiculously low rents. The goods of deported merchants are being taken possession of by commissions designated for this purpose, and abuses of all kinds are reported. The President of the Commission, Ali Seidi Bey, was recently removed—some say because he opposed the manner in which these measures were being applied.

Baron Oppenheim, who has been with Djemal Pasha, passed through here recently on his way to Constantinople. German reading-rooms, where all manner of literature in favour of the German cause is displayed and distributed, have been established in AE. and Adana. The Baron is their principal supporter. The German school in Adana was also re-opened recently with great éclat. The personal relations between the American missionaries and their German co-workers in this province are of the most cordial nature.

(f) **Report dated 4th November, 1915.**

The stream of deported Armenians from Anatolia to Syria continues. In enumerating the various distressing elements connected with this movement, I perhaps failed to point out the terribly insanitary conditions that prevail in the vicinity of the camps or stations near Tarsus and Osmania. These result in part from their overcrowded state, but largely also from the imperfect burial of the corpses of the victims of starvation and disease. The mortality among the deported is daily increasing in percentage, and, when the rains set in, the toll will be frightful. The feeding problem is completely neglected, and will become worse in the future, as even the regular population is beginning to suffer because of a scarcity of wheat. The crop this year was only one-half the normal yield, and there were enormous shipments to Constantinople for the army....

(g) Report dated 6th November, 1915.

An order has been received by the authorities to stop further deportations of Armenians. This, however, refers only to the few thousand natives of the towns of AE., B., and Adana, who have hitherto escaped deportation. On the other hand, the many thousands in the camp near B. were ordered to be sent away to make room for others coming from the north. An important Imperial Commissioner has also arrived to investigate the abuses of local officials regarding the taking of the personal property of the deported Armenians.

His Excellency Von der Goltz Pasha arrived at B. to-day en route for Aleppo, where he is to make his headquarters, according to reliable reports.

116. THE TAURUS AND AMANUS PASSES: EXTRACTS FROM A LETTER, DATED ALEPPO, 5th NOVEMBER, 1915, FROM DR. L., A FOREIGN RESIDENT IN TURKEY, TO MR. N. AT CONSTANTINOPLE; COMMUNICATED BY THE AMERICAN COMMITTEE FOR ARMENIAN AND SYRIAN RELIEF.

As I telegraphed to you from Adana, I had an uneventful journey. I felt that I could not give a whole week to Konia; no one met me at the train, and I did not have time to go up to the city. Very large numbers of Armenians on the road, suffering hunger, nakedness and cold. Very many of them very old or very young, or delicate women on foot, carrying burdens, or children, etc., etc. I saw Miss M. and left £100 (Turkish) with her. She can use it for the refugees en route between Osmania and Entilli. Aleppo is the great centre from which to do relief work, and the need is beyond estimate. The 150,000 or more refugees will, I suppose, pass on through here; they are now on the road between Konia and Aleppo. There are large numbers in the city now, and large numbers within reach from here. Trustworthy native friends are able to use considerable sums—in small amounts. The Katholikos is being sent from here to Jerusalem....

There is, unfortunately, no way to reach effectively the many thousands en route—10,000 between Bozanti and Tarsus; 20,000 at Tarsus; 40,000 between Osmania and Islohia (which is now the head of the rail); and 40,000 to 50,000 at Kotmo. I saw Djemal Pasha this morning about our teachers at Aintab. He seems friendly, and told me to ascertain whether any order had been sent from the Ministry of the Interior and the Vali of Aleppo. I will let you know if anything comes of it.

P.S.—Typhus has broken out here.

117. THE AMANUS PASSES: STATEMENTS BY TWO SWISS RESIDENTS IN TURKEY; COMMUNICATED BY THE AMERICAN COMMITTEE FOR ARMENIAN AND SYRIAN RELIEF.

(a) Report by Fräulein M., dated 16th November, 1915.

I have just returned from a ride on horseback through the Baghtché-Osmania plain, where thousands of exiles are lying out in the fields and on the roads, without any shelter and completely at the mercy of all manner of brigands. Last night, about 12 o'clock, a little camp was suddenly attacked. There were about 50 to 60 persons in it. I found men and women badly wounded—bodies slashed open, broken skulls and terrible knife-wounds. Fortunately I was provided with clothes, so I could change their blood-soaked things and then bring them to the next inn, where they were nursed. Many of them were so much exhausted from the enormous loss of blood that they died, I fear, in the meantime. In another camp we found thirty or forty thousand Armenians. I was able to distribute bread among them. Desperate and half-starved, they fell upon it; several times I was almost pulled down off my horse. A number of corpses were lying about unburied, and it was only by bribing the gendarmes that we could induce them to allow their burial. Mostly, the Armenians are not allowed to perform the last offices of love for their relatives. Dreadful epidemics of typhoid-fever broke out everywhere; there was a victim of it practically in every third tent. Nearly everything had to be transported on foot; men, women and children carried their few belongings on their backs. I often saw them break down under their burden, but the soldiers kept on driving them forward with the butt-ends of their rifles, even sometimes with their bayonets. I have dressed bleeding wounds on the bodies of women that had been caused by these bayonet thrusts. Many children had lost their parents and were now without any support. Three hours' distance from Osmania two dying men were lying absolutely alone in the fields. They had been here for days without food or even a drop of water, after their companions had continued their march. They had grown as thin as skeletons, and only their heavy breathing showed that there was still life in them. Unburied women and children were lying in the ditches. The Turkish officials in Osmania were very obliging; I succeeded in obtaining many concessions from them, and many hardships were remedied. I obtained carriages to pick up the dying people and bring them in to town.

(b) Report by Fräulein O. on a visit to the exiles' camp at Mamouret, 26th November, 1915.

We saw thousands of tiny low tents, made of thin material. An innumerable crowd of people, of all ages and every class of society! They were looking at us partly in surprise, partly with the indifference of desperation. A group of hungry, begging children and women were at our heels: "Hanoum, bread! Hanoum, I am hungry; we have had nothing to eat to-day or yesterday!"

You had only to look at the greedy, pale, suffering faces to know that their words were true. About 1,800 loaves could be procured. Everybody fell greedily upon us; the priests who were charged with the distribution of the bread had almost to fight for their lives; but it was by no means sufficient, and no further bread was to be had. A crowd of hungry people stood imploringly before us. The gendarmerie had to keep them back by force. Suddenly the order for departure was given. If anybody was slow in striking their tent, it was torn down with the bayonet. Three carriages and a number of camels were held in readiness. A few wealthy people quickly hired the carriages, while others less well-to-do loaded a camel with their things. The wailing of the poor, the old and the sick filled the air: "We can't go any further, let us die here." But they *had* to go on. We were at least able to pay for a camel for some of them, and to give small change to others in order to buy bread at the next station; clothes, sewn at the Mission Station in Adana, were also distributed. Soon the immense procession was moving on. Some of the most miserable were left behind (others rested there already in the newly-dug graves). As many as 200—destitute, old or sick—are said to have waited there for help to come. The misery was increased a hundredfold by the severe rain and cold that had set in. Everywhere convoys left dying people in their track—little children and invalids perishing. Besides all this the epidemic was spreading more and more.

(c) Report by Fräulein M. on a visit to the exiles' camp at Islohia, 1st December, 1915.

It had rained three days and three nights; even in our houses we were acutely sensible of the cold and damp. As soon as possible, I set out on my way. About 200 families had been left behind at Mamouret. They were unable to proceed through exhaustion or illness. In this rain the soldiers, too, felt no inclination to rouse them up and drive them on, so they were lying about in what might have been a lake. There was not a single dry thread left in their ragged bedding. Many women had their feet frost-bitten; they were quite black and in a state for amputation. The wailing and groaning was horrible. Everywhere there were dying people in their last agonies or dead bodies lying in front of the tents. It was only by "bakshish" that the soldiers could be persuaded to bury them. It seemed a comfort to them when we came with dry clothes; they could change their things and get some bread and small change. Then I drove in a carriage along the whole route to Islohia. Though I had seen much distress before, the objects and the scenes I saw here defy description. A frailly-built woman was sitting by the roadside with her bedding on her back, and a young baby strapped on at the top of it; in her arms she had a two-year-old child—its eyes were dim and it was at its last gasp. The woman had broken down in her distress and was weeping in a heart-breaking way. I took her with me to the next camp, where the child died; then I took care of her and sent her on her way. She was so grateful. The whole carriage was packed with bread. I kept on distributing all the time. We had three or four opportunities of buying fresh supplies. These thousands of loaves were a great help to us. I was also able to hire some hundreds of animals to help the poor people forward. The camp at Islohia itself is the saddest thing I have ever seen. Right at the entrance a heap of dead bodies lay unburied. I counted 35, and in another place 22, in the immediate neighbourhood of the tents of those who were down with virulent dysentery. The filth in and around these tents was something indescribable. On one single day the burial committee buried as many as 580 people. Men were fighting for bread like hungry wolves. One saw hideous scenes. With what timidity and apathy these poor people often stared at me, as though they wondered where this assistance came from! For some weeks now many camps have been provided daily with bread. Of course, everything has to be done as unobtrusively as possible. We are so thankful to God that we may at least do something.

(d) Letter from Fräulein M. to Mr. N., dated 13th December, 1915, on the way to Aleppo.

I should have written long before this, but during these last weeks I have been more on the road than at home, and the work in the camps was often so urgent that I could not find time for anything else. I suppose you have had, in the meantime, the receipt for the 200 liras you sent me. Many thanks for the quick response. I only wish you could see these poor people yourself; you would get an impression of the absolutely dreadful need and distress that these camps conceal. It is simply indescribable; one has to have seen it oneself. So far I have had no difficulty whatever; on the contrary, the officials here are most obliging, and grateful for everything we are doing for the poor people. You will find some reports enclosed which Miss O. copied for you as well; they will give you an idea of what we are doing here. Up to the present we have worked in four camps, twelve hours distant. We were often able to distribute about 10 to 20 liras' worth of bread a day; besides this, we gave flour, clothes and nirra to many sick people, to help them on the long journey. Sometimes it happened that in some places we did not have nearly enough bread—in such cases we provided the people with money to buy bread at the next bakery along the route.

Now we are on our way to Aleppo, and Miss O. will stay there some weeks, D.V., to prepare everything for another journey to Der-el-Zor. I intend to come back soon, since there is still much work to do on the Mamouré-Islohia route, and it seems to me that we ought not to give up the work among the distressed so long as any of them are left in this place, for if we did they would absolutely die of starvation. Judging by our recent experience, we shall need about 300 to 400 liras a month. Dr. L. told me to send you word about this, because I should get the money from you. It would be better not to stop the work for lack of money, because the poor people would suffer by it. If, however, you think that less money ought to be spent, or that the whole work should be given up, please send me a telegram in time, so that we may stop doing it. If not, will you please be so kind as to send me the amount. To-day I have asked you by wire to send me 400 liras—200 for Mamouré and 200 for Islohia-Hassan-Beyli.

I hope you are well. We got a message that Dr. L. is down with typhus. I hope that God will soon give him new strength. Fräulein O. and I both send you our best wishes.

118. SMYRNA—ALEPPO—DAMASCUS—ALEPPO—SMYRNA: ITINERARY OF A FOREIGN TRAVELLER IN ASIATIC TURKEY; COMMUNICATED BY THE AMERICAN COMMITTEE FOR ARMENIAN AND SYRIAN RELIEF.

I left here (Smyrna) on the 16th September, 1915, for Aleppo. I first saw the Armenians at Afiun Kara Hissar, where there was a big encampment of people—probably 10,000—who had come down from the Black Sea. They were encamped in tents made of material of all descriptions, and their condition was deplorable.

The next place where I saw them was at Konia, also a large encampment. There I saw the first brutality. I saw a woman with her baby separated from her husband. He was put on our train, while she was forcibly held back and prevented from getting on to the train. At the next place, where there were said to be about 50,000, their condition was terrible. They were camped on both sides of the railway track, extending fully half a mile on either side. Here they had two wells from which they could get water, one of which was a very long way from the encampment, the other at the railway station platform. At daybreak the Armenians came in crowds—women and children and old men—to the well to get water. They fought among themselves for a place at the well, and the gendarmes, to keep them in order, flogged several people. I saw women and children repeatedly struck with the whips and sticks in the hands of the gendarmes. Later, I had occasion to pass through the camp on the way to the town of Osmania, and had an opportunity to see the condition of the people there. They were living in tents, like those above described, and their condition was miserable. The site of the encampment had been used several times over by different convoys of Armenians, and no attempt at sanitation had been made, either by the Turks or by the Armenians themselves, with the result that the ground was in a deplorable condition and the stench in the early morning beyond description. At Osmania they were selling their possessions in order to obtain money to buy food. One old man begged me to buy his silver snuff-box for a piastre, in order that he might be able to buy some bread.

From Osmania I travelled by carriage to Radjou, and passed thousands of Armenians en route to Aleppo. They were travelling in ox-carts, on horseback, on donkey-back and on foot—the majority of them children, women and old men. I spoke to several of these people, some of whom had been educated in the American Mission Schools. They told me that they had travelled for two months. They were without money and food, and several expressed their wish that they might die rather than go on and endure the sufferings that they were undergoing. The people on the road were carrying with them practically all their household possessions, and those who had no carts or animals were carrying their goods on their backs. It was not unusual to see a woman with a big pack wrapped up in a mattress and a little child of a few months old on the top of the pack. They were mostly bare-headed, and their faces were swollen from the sun and exposure. Many had no shoes on, and some had their feet wrapped in old pieces of rag which they had torn from their clothing. At Entilli there was an encampment of about 10,000, and at Kotmo a large encampment of 150,000. At this place, adjacent to their encampment, were Turkish troops, who exacted "bakshish" from them before they would let them go on the road to Aleppo. Many who had no money had had to stay in this camp since their arrival there about two months before. I spoke with several Armenians here, and they told me the same stories of brutal treatment and robbery at the hands of the gendarmes in charge as I had heard all along the road. They had to go at least half-a-mile for water from this encampment, and the condition of the camp was filthy. From Kotmo on to Aleppo I witnessed the worst sights of the whole journey. Here the people began to give out in the intense heat and dearth of water, and I passed several who were prostrate—actually dying of thirst. One woman, whom I assisted, was in a deplorable condition, unconscious from thirst and exhaustion; and further on I saw two young girls who had become so exhausted that they had fallen on the road, and lay with their already swollen faces exposed to the sun. The road for a great distance was being repaired and paved with cracked stone; on one side of the road was a footpath, but many of the Armenians were so dazed from fatigue and exposure that they did not see this footpath, and were walking—and many of them bare-footed—on this cracked stone, with their feet bleeding as a result of it. The destination of all these Armenians is Aleppo. Here they are kept crowded together in all available vacant houses, hans, Armenian churches, courtyards and open plots. Their condition in Aleppo is beyond description. I personally visited several of the places where they were kept and found them starving and dying by the hundred every day. In one vacant house which I visited I saw women, children and men all in the same room, lying on the floor, so close together that it was impossible to walk between them. Here they had been for months, such of them as had survived, and the condition of the floor was filthy. Many were lying in their own excrement!

The British Consulate was filled with these exiles, and from this place the dead were removed almost every hour. Coffin-makers throughout the city were working late into the night making rough boxes for the dead whose relatives or friends could afford to give them decent burial. Most of the dead were simply thrown into two-wheeled carts, which made a daily round to all the places where the Armenians were confined. These carts were open at first, but afterwards covers were made for them. An Armenian physician whom I know, and who is treating hundreds of these suffering Armenians who have become ill through exposure on the journey and through hunger and thirst, told me that there are hundreds dying daily in Aleppo from starvation and as a result of the brutal treatment and exposure that they have undergone on the journey from their native places. Many of these suffering Armenians refuse alms, saying that the little money so obtained will only prolong their sufferings and that they prefer to die. From Aleppo those who are able to pay are sent by train to Damascus; those who have no money are sent by road to the interior, towards Der-el-Zor. In Damascus I found conditions practically the same as in Aleppo, and hundreds are dying every day. From Damascus they are sent still further south into the Hauran, where their fate is unknown. Several Turks whom I interviewed told me that the motive of this exile was to exterminate the race, and in no instance did I see any Moslem giving alms to Armenians, it being considered a criminal offence for anyone to aid them.

I remained in Damascus and Aleppo about a month, leaving for Smyrna on the 26th October. All along the road I met thousands of these unfortunate exiles still coming into Aleppo. The sights I witnessed on this return journey were more pitiful than those I had seen on my outward journey to Aleppo. There seems to be no end to the convoy which moves over the mountain range from Bozanti south. Throughout the day, from sunrise to sunset, the road as far as one can see is crowded with these exiles. Just outside Tarsus I saw a dead woman lying by the roadside, and further on I passed two more dead women, one of whom was being carried from the roadside to be buried by two gendarmes. Her legs and arms were so emaciated that the bones were nearly through her flesh, and her face was swollen and purple from exposure. Further on I saw two gendarmes carrying a dead child between them away from the road to where they had dug a grave. Many of these soldiers and gendarmes who follow the convoy carry spades, and as soon as an Armenian dies they take the corpse away from the roadside and bury it.

The open spaces round the hans en route are used as camping-places for the Armenians, and the ground is littered with refuse and human excrement, the stench from which is unbearable. I saw many people who had been in good circumstances forced to lie in this filth. Their clothes were rags and many had no shoes. The mornings were cold and many were dying from exposure. There are very few young men in these convoys; the majority are women and children, accompanied by a few old men over fifty years of age. At Bairamoglu I talked with a woman who had become demented from the sufferings she had undergone. She told me that her husband and father had both been killed before her eyes and that she had been forced for three days to walk without rest. She had with her two little children, and all had been without bread for a day. I gave her some money, which she told me would probably be taken from her before the day was over.

Turks and Kurds meet these caravans as they pass through the country and sell them food at exorbitant prices. I saw a small boy about seven years old riding on a donkey with his baby brother in his arms. They were all that was left of his family. Many of these people go for days without bread, and they become emaciated beyond description. I saw several fall from starvation, and only at certain places along this road is there any water. Many die of thirst. Some of the Armenians who can afford it hire carriages. These are paid for in advance, and the prices charged are exorbitant. At many places, like Bozanti, for example, where there is an encampment of Turkish soldiers, there is not enough bread for these Armenians, and only two hours from Bozanti I met a woman who was crying for bread. She told me that she had been in Bozanti for two days and was unable to obtain anything to eat except what travellers like myself had given her. Many of the beasts of burden belonging to the Armenians die of starvation. It is not an unusual sight to see an Armenian removing a pack from the dead animal and setting it on his own shoulders. Many Armenians told me that, although they are allowed to rest at night, they get no sleep because of the pangs of hunger and cold. These people march all the day through at a shuffling gait, and for hours do not speak to one another. At one place where I stopped on the road for lunch I was surrounded by a crowd of little children, all crying for bread. Many of these little tots are obliged to walk barefoot along the road, and many of them carry a little pack on their backs. They are all emaciated, their clothes are in rags and their hair in a filthy condition. The filth has bred millions of flies, and I saw several babies' faces and eyes covered with these insects, their mothers being too exhausted to brush them away. Disease has broken out in several places along the road, and in Aleppo several cases of typhus fever among the Armenians were reported when I left.

Many families have been separated, the men being sent in one direction and the women and children in another. I saw one woman who was with child, lying in the middle of the road crying, and over her stood a gendarme, threatening her if she did not get up and walk. Many children are born on the way, and most of these die, as their mothers have no nourishment for them.

None of these people have any idea where they are going or why they are being exiled. They journey day after day along the road, with the hope that they may somewhere reach a place where they may be allowed to rest, and I saw several old men carrying on their backs the tools of their trade, probably with the hope that they may some day settle down somewhere. The road over the Taurus Mountains is, in places, most difficult, and often the crude conveyances, drawn by buffaloes, oxen and milch cows, are unable to take the grades, and are abandoned and overturned by the gendarmes into the ravine below; the animals are turned loose. I saw several carts, piled high with baggage and with a number of Armenians on the top of that, break down and throw their occupants on to the road. One of the drivers, who was a Turk and who had collected his fare in advance from the people he was driving, considered it a huge joke when one woman broke her leg from such a fall.

There seems to be no cessation of the streams of these Armenians pouring down from the north, from Angora and the region round the Black Sea. Their condition grows worse every day. The sights that I saw on my return journey were worse than those on my outward journey, and now that the cold weather and winter rains are setting in, deaths are more numerous. The roads in some places are almost impassable.

XV.
CILICIA (VILAYET OF ADANA AND SANDJAK OF MARASH).

Cilicia occupies the south-eastern corner of Anatolia, overlooking the Gulf of Iskanderoun (Alexandretta), and falls into two sharply contrasted regions—the fertile, malarious coastal plain of Adana, traversed by a section of the Baghdad Railway, and the hill-country inland to the north-east of it, where the lines of Taurus are broken by the upper courses of the Sarus and Pyramus (Sihoun and Djihoun) and spread out fanwise into a maze of high valleys and mountain blocks.

Until the spring of 1915, Cilicia was one of the chief centres of the Armenian race in Turkey, and there was no region, with the possible exception of Van, which they succeeded in making and keeping so thoroughly their own. The Armenian Dispersion in north-eastern Anatolia and the suburban districts round the coasts of Marmora, numerous and wealthy and influential though it was, still constituted no more than an urban class, and even in the towns was usually in a minority. The Cilician highlands, on the other hand, were sown thick with Armenian peasant communities—small but prosperous hill towns and villages, of which the most important were Hadjin and Zeitoun in the north, but which stretched in an unbroken chain from the Taurus to the southern spurs of the Amanus, until, at Dört Yöl, they touched the north-eastern corner of the Mediterranean.

The Cilician Armenians were mainly shepherds and husbandmen, but they were also one of the most civilised and progressive sections of the Armenian race. Schools, both Armenian and American, had been established in the mountains, and the mountaineers were in close contact with Adana, Tarsus, Mersina and the other ports and cities of the Adana plain, where commerce and industry were almost entirely in the hands of the Armenian element—an element constantly reinforced from the reservoir of Armenian population in the highlands.

The Cilician Armenians seemed destined to play an important part in the future development of the Ottoman Empire. Their country was of peculiar strategical and commercial importance, for it was to be traversed by the main artery of the Empire, the Baghdad Railway, in the most vital section of its course, where it has to negotiate two mountain-barriers and approach most nearly to the Mediterranean coast. And meanwhile the Armenian population itself was here steadily increasing in numbers, while in almost every other part of Turkey it had been receding under the continuous repression to which it had been subjected since 1878. This increase was the more remarkable because Cilicia had been especially visited by the last outbreak of massacre, which occurred in 1909.

All this, however, only rendered the Cilician Armenians more obnoxious in the Ottoman Government's eyes, and the war gave it the opportunity it coveted for rooting them out. A universal deportation of all the Armenians in the Empire may or may not have been contemplated before the breach between the Turks and Armenians at Van, in the middle of April, 1915; but, as far as Cilicia is concerned, there is no doubt whatever that the scheme was devised and put in train before any of the events at Van occurred. Fighting began at Van on the 20th April; the first Armenians had been deported from Zeitoun on the 8th April, twelve days before, and by the 19th a convoy of them had already arrived in Syria (Doc. 138. The Cilician deportations, at any rate, must therefore have been planned at least as early as March, and probably earlier still.

And there is one special feature about the execution of the scheme in Cilicia which makes it evident that it was carried out deliberately and thought out far ahead. Immediately the Armenians were evicted from their villages, their houses were assigned to Moslem refugees. We have occasional evidence of the same practice, during June, in the Vilayets of Erzeroum and Trebizond; but in these cases the Moslem intruders, where we can trace their origin, generally prove to have been Turks or Kurds from the adjoining districts on the east, who had just evacuated their own homes in consequence of the first Russian occupation of Van. Their installation in Armenian houses was apparently extempore and conceivably only provisional. On the other hand, the "mouhadjirs" brought by the Ottoman Government to Zeitoun, Hadjin and the other towns and villages of the Cilician highlands, were all of them Moslem refugees from Europe—from the Roumelian Vilayets ceded by Turkey in 1913, as a result of the Balkan War. They had been on the Government's hands for over two years, and during all that time they had remained stranded in Thrace or along the Aegean littoral. But now they had been transported from these western fringes of the Empire to the other extremity of the Anatolian Railway, and by the 8th April, 1915, they were in readiness to occupy the homes of the Armenians in Cilicia immediately their rightful owners had started on their road to exile. This is clear proof that, at any rate in Cilicia, the deportation was not only planned systematically, but planned a long time in advance.

Its execution began at Zeitoun in April, and was extended to all the highland villages in the course of May and June. In the cities of the plain and the coast, on the other hand, it did not become drastic till the first week in September—a tacit avowal that the official pleas of Armenian disloyalty and strategical necessity were a pretext hardly intended to be taken seriously even by their authors.

The Zeitounlis were deported in two directions—half of them to Sultania (see Documents 123 and 125) in the Anatolian Desert, and half to the Mesopotamian Sandjak of Der-el-Zor (see Document 145). The exiles at Sultania were subsequently removed to Der-el-Zor to join the rest, and the later convoys seem all to have taken the south-eastward road. The deportation was conducted by the gendarmerie with the same brutality as elsewhere, but the Cilician country is free of nomadic Kurds, so that there was here less wholesale massacre on the way. On the last stages of their journey to Zor the exiles were harassed by the Arab nomads of the steppe, but these are a milder race than their Kurdish neighbours. The chief alleviation of the Cilicians' fate was their geographical position. The distance they had to traverse was comparatively short, and they only began to die in large numbers after reaching their destination.

119. CILICIA: ADDRESS (WITH ENCLOSURE), DATED 3rd JULY, 1915, FROM THE ARMENIAN COLONY IN EGYPT TO HIS EXCELLENCY LIEUTENANT-GENERAL SIR J.G. MAXWELL, COMMANDER-IN-CHIEF OF HIS BRITANNIC MAJESTY'S FORCES IN EGYPT.

(a) **Address from the Armenian Colony.**

We addressed ourselves recently to your Excellency to obtain your authorisation to send three emissaries to Cilicia, in order to inform ourselves of the true situation in that country.

While we are profoundly grateful to your Excellency for your courtesy in granting this authorisation, we now desire to inform you that trustworthy information, furnished by official persons who have arrived from Syria in the course of the present week, shows that the situation in Cilicia has undergone a complete transformation. On this account the despatch of the emissaries is, for the moment, postponed; the actual state of affairs calls for altogether different measures.

Cavalliere Gauttieri, the Italian Consul at Aleppo, and certain foreign residents at Alexandretta and Adana, as well as others from Bitlis and Harpout, who travelled across Cilicia and all arrived here last Monday on board a neutral vessel, give the following account of what has occurred:—

The town of Zeitoun, which was exclusively inhabited by Armenians and is famous for its heroic struggles against the Turks, took warning by the manifest intention of the Ottoman Government to take advantage of the favourable moment created by the war for effecting the extermination of the Armenian race, and revolted several months ago. Dört Yöl and Hassan Beyli (a large Armenian village half way between Marash and Dört Yöl) were preparing to take the same action. The Turkish Government tried to subdue Zeitoun by military force, but all its efforts remained fruitless; its troops were decimated, and had to beat a retreat several times over. At that stage of affairs the local authorities, by order of the Central Government, employed the following stratagem: they threatened the Katholikos of Cilicia, an old man of 75 years, that if the Zeitounlis refused to capitulate they would have the whole Armenian population massacred, while they assured the Zeitounlis that, in case they laid down their arms, they would be in no way interfered with. On the urgent recommendation of the Katholikos, the Zeitounlis, thinking that they were fulfilling a patriotic duty, laid down their arms to save their compatriots; and the inhabitants of Dört Yöl and Hassan Beyli did the same thing for the same reason. Thereupon the Government treacherously proceeded to deport the inhabitants of Zeitoun and the afore-mentioned places en masse, and to replace them by Moslem emigrants from Macedonia. At the same time they began to persecute the peaceful populations of the plains—those of Marash, Aintab, Sis and Adana, and so on—who are thus threatened now with imminent massacre. It is worth noting that the towns situated on the coast—Mersina, Alexandretta, Selefka and Kessab—continue to enjoy relative tranquillity. Notwithstanding all these persecutions, there are certain localities, scattered over the whole extent of Cilicia, where groups of Armenian fighting-men have entrenched themselves solidly in the mountains and are putting up an indefatigable resistance to the Turkish troops. Whenever they can, they leave their positions to go to the rescue of the defenceless people of the cultivated lands, always hoping that aid will come to them *from abroad*, and that, thus reinforced, they will be able to drive their historic oppressor from the country. The same hope is cherished by the whole Christian population of these regions, and one may say that the Moslems themselves are convinced that all this country will, before long, be occupied by the Allies.

That is the present situation in Cilicia, as it was unfolded to us by the official persons whom we have mentioned above.

(b) Resumé of Travellers' Reports, enclosed with the Address.

My official informants are unanimous in asserting that the object pursued in Cilicia by the Turkish Government is neither more nor less than the complete extermination of the Armenian element. The philanthropic efforts put forward by the Italian and American Consular Bodies, with a view to preventing the execution of this sinister plan, have remained without fruit, since the mandate for destruction and massacre emanated from the Central Government itself. The Turks, with the Government officials at their head, everywhere declare openly that the extermination of the Armenian element in Turkey is for them one of the necessities of national salvation, it being understood that the Allies protect the Armenians, and that they afford a permanent pretext for foreign intervention in the country's affairs. The Governor of Aleppo, a fair and liberal-minded man, who is personally opposed to this criminal policy, has avowed it to the European Consuls, declaring that the military commanders have only executed faithfully the orders received from the Sublime Porte, and emphasising this in the case of Fakhri Pasha, who is the representative of Djemal Pasha, the supreme commander of the military forces in Syria and Palestine. Among the other official persons responsible for the atrocities that have been committed, they mention the Mutessarif of Marash and the Kaimakam of Zeitoun. Latterly Marash and Zeitoun have been consolidated into an independent Sandjak by order of the Central Government, and so the above-mentioned functionaries are no longer under the control of the Vali of Aleppo.

The German Consul at Aleppo, of whom we shall have more to say below, made an extremely significant declaration to the Consul of a Power which has since joined the Allies:—

"However painful and deplorable the condition may be to which the Armenians find themselves reduced, the Turkish Government could take no other course towards them, in view of the fact that they have everywhere cast in their lot with the enemies of Turkey."

Zeitoun.—The Turkish troops which marched against Zeitoun and presided, after the capitulation, over the deportation of the Zeitounlis, were commanded by German officers. The Turks have torn from their homes in this way all the inhabitants of Zeitoun, Furnus, Alabash, Geben and the neighbouring districts, and have sent them off in batches to Der-el-Zor, to Djibal Hauran, and towards various unexplored regions of the desert. The women have been sent to Konia, an exclusively Turkish district. In place of the Armenians they had installed at Zeitoun a number of Moslem refugees from Macedonia.

Marash.—This town was relatively tranquil till a short time ago; now it is the scene of all kinds of atrocities and persecutions. Hundreds of Armenian families have been driven out and marched away, no one knows where. These atrocities have been committed in the presence and with the connivance of the German Consul at Aleppo, according to the testimony of a large number of Armenians which has been recorded by the European Consular authorities.

Hassan Beyli.—This unfortunate village, which had been already so cruelly tried during the Cilician massacres of 1909, has this time been destroyed root and branch. The inhabitants have been deported.

Dört Yöl presents the same tragic spectacle. Though there have been no massacres here in the literal sense of the word, the arrests and expulsions en masse continue without abatement. The story is already well-known of the German spy who came to Dört Yöl disguised as a British officer—how he incited them to revolt against the Turkish Government, and the arrests and partial massacre that came of it. The story of this piece of treachery is also confirmed by the Italian Consul from Alexandretta. The village of Dört Yöl, once so prosperous, is now plunged in frightful misery.

At *Aintab, Sis and Adana* the Armenians have so far been less molested and persecuted than elsewhere. The arrests are less numerous; but sinister rumours are current, which are propagated by the Turks, and the terror of imminent butchery haunts the inhabitants of these towns, who are strong in numbers but absolutely bereft of all means of defence and of all protection against the danger of extermination by which they are menaced.

Ourfa groans under a Governor of the name of Haidar Bey, who, as his own wife avows, has committed atrocities of all kinds wherever he has exercised authority. He is the notorious organiser of the butcheries at Mardin. The Armenian monastery at Ourfa has been confiscated by the authorities and transformed into an asylum for the British and Russian subjects who have been put under arrest in Cilicia.

The Turkish Forces.—The Turks do not dispose of military forces of any importance in Cilicia; the troops they have there are not a permanent garrison, and their number is not constant.

120. CILICIA: LETTER, DATED 20th JUNE, 1915, FROM DR. L., A FOREIGN RESIDENT IN TURKEY; COMMUNICATED BY THE AMERICAN COMMITTEE FOR ARMENIAN AND SYRIAN RELIEF.

The deportation began some six weeks ago with 180 families from Zeitoun, since which time all the inhabitants of that place and its neighbouring villages have been deported, also most of the Christians in Albustan and many from Hadjin, Sis, Kars Pazar, Hassan Beyli and Dört Yöl.

The numbers involved are approximately, to date, 26,500. Of these about 5,000 have been sent to the Konia region, 5,500 are in Aleppo and the surrounding towns and villages, and the remainder are in Der-el-Zor, Rakka and various places in Mesopotamia, even as far as the neighbourhood of Baghdad.

The process is still going on, and there is no telling how far it may be carried. The orders already issued will bring the number in this region up to 32,000, and there have been as yet none exiled from Aintab, and very few from Marash and Ourfa.

The following is the text of the Government order[160] covering the case:— "Art. 2nd.: The commanders of the Army, of independent army corps and of divisions may, in case of military necessity, or in case they suspect espionage or treason, send away, either singly or in mass, the inhabitants of villages or towns and install them in other places."

The orders of commanders may have been reasonably humane, but the execution of them has been for the most part unnecessarily harsh and in many cases accompanied by horrible brutality to women and children, to the sick and the aged. Whole villages were deported at an hour's notice, with no opportunity to prepare for the journey—not even, in some cases, to gather together the scattered members of the family, so that little children were left behind. At the mountain village of Geben the women were at the wash-tub, and were compelled to leave their wet clothes in the water and take the road bare-footed and half-clad, just as they were. In some cases they were able to carry part of their scanty household furniture or implements of agriculture, but for the most part they were allowed neither to carry anything nor to sell it, even where there was time to do so.

In Hadjin well-to-do people, who had prepared food and bedding for the road, were obliged to leave it in the street, and afterwards suffered greatly from hunger.

In many cases the men (those of military age were nearly all in the Army) were bound tightly together with ropes or chains. Women with little children in their arms, or in the last days of pregnancy, were driven along under the whip like cattle. Three different cases came under my knowledge where the woman was delivered on the road and, because her brutal driver hurried her along, she died of hæmorrhage. I also know of one case where the gendarme in charge was a humane man and allowed the poor woman several hours' rest and then procured a wagon for her to ride in. Some women became so completely worn out and hopeless that they left their infants beside the road. Many women and girls have been outraged. At one place the commander of gendarmerie openly told the men to whom he consigned a large company that they were at liberty to do what they chose with the women and girls.

As to subsistence, there has been a great difference in different places. In some places the Government has fed them; in some places it has permitted the inhabitants to feed them; in some places it has neither fed them nor permitted others to do so. There has been much hunger, thirst and sickness and some real starvation and death.

These people are being scattered in small units, three or four families in a place, among a population of different race and religion and speaking a different language. I speak of them as being composed families, but four-fifths of them are women and children, and what men there are, for the most part, are old or incompetent.

If means are not found to help them through the next few months, until they get established in their new surroundings, two-thirds or three-fourths of them will die of starvation and disease.

121. BM.: LETTER FROM A FOREIGN EYE-WITNESS, DATED 6th JULY, 1915, ON BOARD A STEAMSHIP; COMMUNICATED BY THE AMERICAN COMMITTEE FOR ARMENIAN AND SYRIAN RELIEF.

Central Turkey has reached a crisis in its history. There are grave problems to face. In many parts the accumulated work of years has been washed away in a few weeks by the great and terrible flood of deportation, and we are again on bed-rock. We understand that, between the middle of May and the middle of June, 26,000 people were deported, and that the number is to reach 32,000. When I left BM., on the 14th June, Zeitoun had been practically emptied of Armenians. Only one, or perhaps two families, who were originally not of Zeitoun and who were in the employment of the Government and necessary to it, were left in Zeitoun, and even they were not allowed to live in houses, but were living in a church. The place is now occupied by Macedonian Moslem refugees. They began by cutting down the fruit trees, laden with green fruit, and using them for firewood, and by cutting down the green grain and using it for fodder. One man demanded the mule that had carried him there from the Moslem katerdji, who had been asked by the Government to convey the man to Zeitoun—or Yeni Shehr, as I think it is now to be called. When the katerdji naturally demurred, the man killed the katerdji and took the mule. So lawless are they that the Government seems afraid of them, and so leaves them strictly alone. As far as I know, at that date not an Armenian was left in Albustan and all its region, in Furnus and all its region, in Geben and all its region, or in Gourksoun and all its region (I don't remember the other places that have been swept clean), and Fundadjak and Deré Keui and all that region expected to move any day. Indeed, the Government says that the plan is that all Cilicia shall be entirely cleared, except for Sis, Adana and BM., where the serving class shall be left. Some officials say that all but about three hundred rich and influential families of BM. shall be left, but no one believes them and all from the highest to the lowest are preparing to leave. The same officials say that Sis and Adana will not be touched, but we know that some from there have been taken already. As you may know, Marash was this year made an independent "Sandjak," like Ourfa, and this has made this infamous work more easy. The Vali of Aleppo resisted all efforts at deportation in his district, but the day we left Aleppo we were informed by him that he had been removed to Konia, so by this time deportation is very probably in full swing in the Aintab field. When we were in Aleppo I saw some of the first one hundred families to be deported from Hadjin, and the rest of Hadjin were expected the day we left, or within the next few days. The man who has been deporting in Diyarbekir, and, worse, has been killing people by beating or scalding them to death—one person said: "He is killing them alive!"—was transferred about the middle of June to Ourfa, with the evident purpose of letting him continue his work there. To go out into other fields, I might add that a private code telegram from Mardin received about the 24th June said that massacres had begun there.

Why is there this deportation? There are many theories. When the people asked, the answer was: "It is an order from Constantinople." One official, who is being worked nearly to death by this extra work of deportation, said one day: "It is all right for people in Europe to deport. They simply put people on a train and send them wherever they wish"—and much more along that line, which led us to believe that Germany has a hand in it. Indeed, we know that, when Turkish officials are easing up on these poor people, German officials step in and make things hard.

Where are they going? Some are being scattered, one or two families to a village, among Moslem villages, evidently with the idea of forcing them to become Moslems; others are being taken from their mountain homes and are being driven across the desert towards Baghdad. German officers, who came into Aleppo one night on their way from Baghdad to Constantinople, said that they first met this weary train two days out of Baghdad, and that the road the thousands they had met were marching along was marked or outlined by the bodies of their dead.

Who are these people? Women and children, tottering old men and babes. The men, twenty-one to thirty-five or forty years old, have practically all gone to the war, so these women are at the mercy of those in charge of them. Some soldiers are as kind to them as circumstances permit; others farm the women out for the night to the men of the villages near which they camp, or march in themselves, as a bull might into a herd of cows. This is not guesswork, but well-known fact. Some women kill themselves by jumping into the rivers, to escape, but others, for the sake of their children, endure.

Some of the circumstances that make this deportation especially cruel are these. As a general rule village people get their new clothes in the autumn. Now they are expecting to go up into the mountains with their flocks, and so will wear out the old rags of last year's clothes and be ready for the new clothes after harvest. So, at best, they are very ill-provided for a journey. Not only this, but the Government takes special pains in many, if not most, instances to prevent their taking what clothes they have. The first to be summoned were some families in Zeitoun. Early one Saturday morning, as usual, the industrious housewives donned their old washing clothes and began their Saturday's washing. Without warning, all of a sudden, a terrible knocking was heard at many doors. In a minute the soldiers came pouring in, saying that the people in those houses were wanted immediately at the Government House. Not a moment was given to don dress or shoes, but, in night-clothes or washing rags, the mothers and a few fathers snatched sleeping children out of their beds, the women throwing a shawl over their heads as they ran. Of course, many children were left behind, and there are many pathetic stories of little boys and girls, eight or nine years old, stumbling along the road, hardly able from sheer weariness to walk, yet carrying their little baby brother or sister, because, as their mother was being taken away by the soldiers, she had said: "Look after baby and never leave him (or her)."

Geben's turn came later, so the people had heard of the deportation and gotten ready, although the Government assured them again and again that that district was not to be deported. Time went on, and no order came. The Government said: "Why will you not believe? Why do you sit here waiting for that which is not coming? See, your flocks are suffering for want of pasture. Be sensible, and go to the mountains as usual." Some brave ones started out, and nothing happened. So, in great joy, the flocks started for the mountains. One morning the women were putting into the tub the clothes that had got dirty during all those weary weeks of waiting, that they might go to their mountain places with clean clothes. Such was the need of washing that they wore the fewest clothes possible, that they might take everything nice and clean. Hardly an hour had passed, or at least a very short time, before some soldiers presented themselves to these women with the command "March!" while others accosted those who had gone to the mountains with the flocks with the command "Leave all and march!" So they were forced to leave all their clothes in the tub and their flocks on the mountains, and march!

In Albustan, when friendly Moslems wished to buy things of the Armenians and so give them ready money for the road, the Government stationed soldiers in all the Armenian streets to prevent this, so all they could sell was what they smuggled out by the back door.

Another factor that adds horror to the situation is the fact that most of the horses, mules and donkeys have been taken by the Government for the use of the Army. So now the people have practically no animals to carry their own loads, and the Government can furnish few. Sometimes they force an Armenian from a distant village, who happens to have kept a poor old lame horse or two, to help transport people. He hears on the way that orders have come for the deportation of his own family. Of course, if he can steal away in the night to go to the help of his own family, he does so. Or the soldiers make a raid on some neighbouring Moslem villages and gather up the few donkeys that are left. Their owners know that, if these donkeys once reach some large centre, they will never see them again. So these poor people, who have been tramping along all day, must keep awake all night to keep the donkeys from being stolen by their *owners*, who are sneaking round watching their chance. So the mothers are obliged to walk and carry their little children as best they can. Some throw their little ones into the river or leave them under a bush by the road, that they may be able to manage those that are left. One mother threw one child in and jumped in with the other in her arms.

The heart-breaking cry is: "Won't you take my daughter and save her from the horrors of the road? She was educated in your schools; surely you can take her and save her?" Or: "My little one, my darling! Take her, take him! How can I trudge on, day after day, over the rocks or the burning sands of the desert, and carry and feed and keep my darling?"

There is not an Armenian family in BM., I suppose, but has given clothes and money and food, till now they say: "We have nothing left but what we shall need on the road when we are summoned." They could not stand the bitter cry of the mothers, and many, many have taken children, saying: "If we put a little more water in the soup, it will be enough for all," and yet they say: "When we are summoned, what is to become of these children? To be sure, they have had a few more days of security and life, but then—what?"...

Still another factor adds to the horror, and that is: a Government that is not able to feed even its soldiers, how is it to obey the beautiful paper instructions and see that the people are well fed and lack for nothing? In BM., for over a month, Christian churches have been giving two meals a day to the three thousand people to whom the Government gives two small stale loaves of bread a day, and I suppose it is safe to say that those fed are never for any two or three days running the same people. Each party stays two or three days, or even a week, but nearly every day some are coming and others going. This, as you may suppose, is a terrible drain on those from whom the Government has used nearly every means to extract the last penny, even hanging a man in the market-place because he did not pay ten pounds when asked for it! Hanging is so common in BM. now that it creates little stir. It is only when someone happens to mention having seen a man hanging in the market yesterday or the day before that we even hear of it. The people are looking into their fast-emptying larders, and asking: "How long will it last?" In Aintab the people are not even allowed to feed the refugees, who are now sent by a long detour round the town to prevent anyone's seeking to feed them. Some good Aintab people took a lot of water-bottles right out to the cross-roads two hours or more away, to give to the refugees as they started out on their desert journey; but they were not allowed to give them, and had sadly to take them home again.

And how are the people going? As they come into BM., weary and with swollen and bleeding feet, clasping their babes to their breasts, they utter not one murmur or word of complaint; but you see their eyes move and hear the words: "For Jesus' sake, for Jesus' sake!"

The Albustan people were brought by a roundabout way which no one knew, because, we think, the soldiers were afraid to follow the direct road past what used to be Zeitoun. So, instead of coming in two days they wandered for eight days in the mountains, many of them having not a morsel to eat for the last two days. After they had been in BM. for nearly twenty-four hours, Badvelli V. came up to see us. Even then he was so weary and his lips were so parched that it seemed a great effort for him to speak. Suddenly he threw up his head and squared his shoulders, and a new tone came into his voice, as he said: "I want to tell you of my great joy. As my people left their houses, their lands, their all, there was not one murmur or complaint, but with joy—yes, with joy—we left all! And I can say that I believe my people to-day to be nearer to Christ than they have ever been before."

I saw the wife of the Gourksoun preacher. She was so tired that, in spite of herself, perhaps even unknown to herself, her lips quivered as she spoke, and yet there was nothing but a smile or a cheery word to be seen or heard from those lips. Someone asked her how she came, and she said that for a few hours they hired an animal for one pound (I think that was the sum), but that most of the time she walked. I looked at her—a delicate woman, who could hardly be expected to walk three or four miles, to say nothing of all those miles, climbing up over the mountains or tramping among the rocks—and I said: "Walk! How could you?" She turned to me, and a look of almost childlike trust and wonder came into her face, as she answered: "I don't know. We felt no weariness; the road was not hard. It just seemed as though God put out His arms and carried us."...

122. ZEITOUN: ANTECEDENTS OF THE DEPORTATION, RECORDED BY THE REV. STEPHEN TROWBRIDGE, SECRETARY OF THE CAIRO COMMITTEE OF THE AMERICAN RED CROSS, FROM AN ORAL STATEMENT BY THE REV. DIKRAN ANDREASIAN, PASTOR OF THE ARMENIAN PROTESTANT CHURCH AT ZEITOUN.[161]

On the 10th August, 1914, the Turkish authorities in Zeitoun made a declaration of "seferbeylik," which in Turkish military parlance means that every man in the district under 45 years of age should be prepared to leave at short notice for active service in the Army. Every man, Moslem or Christian, was required to secure a "vesiké" or certificate from the Government stating that he had fulfilled the preliminary conditions and was ready for military service.

Hundreds upon hundreds, chiefly Moslem Turks, from the surrounding country came to the Zeitoun Government Building, and while going through the formalities were entertained hospitably by the Armenians of the town. These Armenians were also summoned, and they began seriously to consider whether it would be best to agree to this. (It is only since 1909 that any Christians have been allowed in the Turkish Army, though in ancient times the Janissaries were a very important section of the Ottoman troops.)

Many of the Zeitounlis took to the mountains to escape military service. Among these were about twenty-five thorough-going ruffians who made their living by deeds of violence. This small band, sincerely disliked and dreaded by the peaceable and thrifty people of Zeitoun, came down upon a company of new Turkish (Moslem) recruits, stripped them and enraged them by the insolence of their language. Thereupon Haidar Pasha, the Mutessarif of Marash, came out about the 31st August with 600 soldiers. He brought with him some Christian notables from Marash to "persuade" the Zeitounlis.

<The people of Zeitoun knew of this, and Yeghia Agha Yenidounyaian, one of the notables, advised Nazaret Tchaoush, his cousin, to meet Haidar Pasha with 500-600 armed young men, as he felt that Haidar Pasha's motives were not good. But Nazaret Tchaoush answered: "No, it may be that his coming means death to me; but I would rather die than see Zeitoun ruined, as I know well that this is not the time for opposition." All the party leaders were of the same opinion, for they knew that they were not ready for a prolonged struggle, and that the European Powers were not in a position to come to their help. So> no opposition was offered to this force.

The Pasha demanded the surrender of the twenty-five outlaws who had attacked the new recruits. Every one of these was secured and actually handed over to the Turkish Government. This would seem to have answered the Pasha's utmost demand, but, as a matter of fact, he was not satisfied, and made a proclamation demanding the surrender of all weapons and firearms. On the pretext of making the Armenians own up to the possession of rifles, torture and the bastinado were used with terrible cruelty. Many prominent citizens had their feet beaten into a mangled pulp. Those who had no rifles made desperate efforts to purchase some from their neighbours, in order to be able to deliver them up and escape the torture[162].

There were in all about 200 Martini rifles among the 8,000 people of Zeitoun, and some 150 of these were seized in this fashion by the Turkish officers. A quantity of old-fashioned guns and pistols were collected and confiscated. The Pasha in returning to Marash took away with him a number of the Armenian notables, allowing the soldiers to insult and beat them on the road. Certain classes of the Armenians were also taken to the Marash barracks "for military service," but after terrible experiences many of them escaped and returned to Zeitoun.

The old troubles began again. On the pretext of finding deserters, houses were searched in the most lawless manner, and relatives and even neighbours were cruelly beaten. The fathers of some "deserters" almost died under the beating, <among them Nazaret Tchaoush himself>. The women and girls in the "deserters'" families were attacked and violated. Again and again young Armenian girls were outraged by the coarse Turkish soldiers. Even the young men who were not deserters were beaten "lest they might desert later." Of course, trade had long been at a standstill, and now large quantities of private property were being confiscated on these various pretexts. Then, <about the end of February,> some ignorant hotheads met one night and planned to attack the Government Building. This plot was frustrated by the Armenian notables, <among whom was Baba Agha Besilosian, the most influential of them all,> because they felt it would be doomed to failure. The Arashnort (Armenian bishop and head of the community) felt it his duty to notify the Government of this plot.

These are the facts. How can anyone charge the people of Zeitoun with desiring or attempting an insurrection?

About twenty-five of the young men who had been brutally treated by the Turkish officers took to the mountains. These twenty-five attacked and killed nine Turkish mounted police on the way to Marash. The whole Armenian population of Zeitoun was against this, and openly said so. A night attack by this reckless band, <who had taken refuge in the adjacent monastery,> was frustrated by Government troops aided by a great mass of the Armenian people. Yet it became evident that the Government was only watching for pretexts to destroy Zeitoun root and branch.

Gradually 5,000 soldiers were gathered about the town, <and on the 24th March/6th April an Armenian delegation was sent to Zeitoun from Marash. Among these were the Rev. A. Shiradjian, Father Sahag, a Catholic monk, and Herr Blank, who persuaded the Armenians to inform the Government of the whereabouts of the insurgents and follow the instructions of the Government, to ensure their own safety and the safety of the other Armenians in Cilicia. The Armenians unanimously accepted the proposal, and told the Government that the insurgents were in the monastery.

The next day, the 25th March/7th April, the attack on the monastery began. The new Mutessarif of Marash wished to invest the monastery, but Captain Khourshid opposed him, saying that he would be able to get hold of all the insurgents dead or alive "within two hours."

The fight continued until nightfall, when the Turks decided to burn the monastery. But during the night the insurgents rushed out, killed an officer and many soldiers and escaped to the mountains, leaving only a few of their men behind them. The Turks lost between 200 and 300. On the 26th March/8th April the Turks burned the monastery, thinking that the insurgents were still there.

After this,[163]> fifty prominent families were sent into exile; a few days later, sixty more, then a whole quarter, and another and another. Finally the remainder were all sent at once. By the time the Rev. Dikran Andreasian left, no families whatever remained. Even the Armenian inscriptions over the arches of churches were hacked to pieces by order of Khourshid Bey, the commander of the troops, and the name of Zeitoun was changed to Souleimania (after a Turkish officer who was killed on the Marash road). The Turkish Mufti of Zeitoun, in his report, stated that in the course of all these events, such as the storming of the monastery, 101 Turkish soldiers were killed and 110 wounded. Over against this we may add that 8,000 Armenians who had no evil intention against the Government were outraged and despoiled beyond all endurance, and were at last driven out according to a methodical plan born of the Germans—driven out into hideous misery and suffering in the arid plains of Mesopotamia.

The Zeitounlis were longing for the Allies to carry all before them at Gallipoli. They were hoping for a sweeping defeat of the Turks; but there was no insurrection. The one or two seditious plots were opposed and frustrated chiefly by the Armenians of a saner mind. The evidence is convincing that the destruction of the people of Zeitoun was a deliberate Turco-German plan.

160. See Doc. 83 and Annexe C. to the Historical Summary.

161. The passages included between brackets are taken from the (fuller) Armenian version of Pastor Andreasian's narrative (Doc. 130, "A Red Cross Flag That Saved Four Thousand." These passages have been translated for the Editor by Mr. G.H. Paelian.

162. See Docs. 68, 82 and 94.

163. The author of Doc. 123 states (page 483, line 24) that the first batch of Zeitounlis were deported the morning following the night on which the insurgents in the monastery escaped. This would be the 8th April. The author of Doc. 121 on the other hand, states (page 475, line 44) that the first deportation from Zeitoun took place on a Saturday. This would be the 10th April, 1915.—EDITOR.

123. EXILES FROM ZEITOUN: DIARY OF A FOREIGN RESIDENT IN THE TOWN OF B. ON THE CILICIAN PLAIN; COMMUNICATED BY A SWISS GENTLEMAN OF GENEVA.

Sunday, 14th March, 1915.

This morning I had a long conversation with Mr. —— about events at Zeitoun. He has managed to obtain some information regarding the little Armenian town, although all direct communication with it has been interrupted. Turkish troops have left Aleppo for Zeitoun—some say 4,000, some 6,000, others 8,000. With what intention, one wonders? Mr. ——, who has been there himself during last summer and this winter, assures me that the Armenians have no wish to revolt and are prepared to put up with anything the Government may do. Contrary to the old-established custom, a levy was made at Zeitoun at the time of the August mobilisation, and they did not offer the slightest resistance. None the less, the Government has played them false. In October, 1914, their leader, Nazaret Tchaoush, came to Marash with a "safe conduct" to arrange some special points with the officials. In spite of the "safe conduct" they imprisoned him, tortured him, and put him to death. Still the people of Zeitoun remained quiet. Bands of zaptiehs (Turkish gendarmes), quartered in the town, have been molesting the inhabitants, raiding shops, stealing, maltreating the people and dishonouring their women. It is obvious that the Government are trying to get a case against the Zeitounlis, so as to be able to exterminate them at their pleasure and yet justify themselves in the eyes of the world.

—th April, 1915.

Three Armenians from Dört Yöl were hanged last night in the chief squares of Adana. The Government declare that they had been signalling to the British warship or warships stationed in the Gulf of Alexandretta. This is untrue; for I know, though I dare not put the source of my information on paper, that only one Armenian from Dört Yöl has had any communication with the English.

—th April.

Two more Armenians from Dört Yöl have been hanged at Adana.

—th April.

Three Armenians have been hanged at Adana. We were out riding to-day, and the train came into the station just as we reached the railway. Imagine our indignation when we saw a cattle-truck filled with Armenians from Zeitoun. Most of these mountaineers were in rags, but a few were quite well dressed. They had been driven out of their homes and were going to be transplanted, God knows where, to some town in Asia Minor. It seems we have returned to the days of the Assyrians, if whole populations can be exiled in this way, and the sacred liberty of the individual so violated.

—th April (the next day).

We were able to see the unfortunate refugees, who are still here to-day. These are the circumstances of their departure from Zeitoun, or rather this is the tragedy which preceded their exile, though it was not the cause of it.

The Turkish gendarmes outraged several girls in the town, and were attacked in consequence by about twenty of the more hot-headed young men. Several gendarmes were killed, though all the while the population as a whole was opposed to bloodshed and desired most earnestly to avoid the least pretext for reprisals. The twenty rebels were driven out of the town and took refuge in a monastery about three-quarters of an hour's distance from the town. At this point the troops from Aleppo arrived. The Zeitounlis gave them lodging, and it seemed that all was going excellently between the populace and the 8,000 soldiers under their German officers.

The Turks surrounded the monastery and attacked it for a whole day; but the insurgents defended themselves, and, at the cost of one man slightly wounded, they killed 300 of the regular troops. During the night, moreover, they managed to escape.

Their escape was as yet unknown to the town when, about nine o'clock on the following morning, the Turkish Commandant summoned about 300 of the principal inhabitants to present themselves immediately at the military headquarters. They obeyed the summons without the least suspicion, believing themselves to be on excellent terms with the authorities. Some of them took a little money, others some clothing or wraps, but the majority came in their working clothes and brought nothing with them. Some of them had even left their flocks on the mountains in the charge of children. When they reached the Turkish camp, they were ordered to leave the town at once without returning to their homes. They were completely stupefied. Leave? But for where? They did not know.

They had been unable even yet to learn their destination, but it is probable that they are being sent to the Vilayet of Konia. Some of them have come in carriages and some on foot.

—*th April.*

I heard to-day that the whole population of Dört Yöl has been taken away to work on the roads. They continue to hang Armenians at Adana. It is a point worth remembering that Zeitoun and Dört Yöl are the two Armenian towns which held their own during the Adana massacres of 1909.

—*th May.*

A new batch of Zeitounlis has just arrived. I saw them marching along the road, an interminable file under the Turkish whips. It is really the most miserable and pitiable thing in the world. Weak and scarcely clothed, they rather drag themselves along than walk. Old women fall down, and struggle to their feet again when the zaptieh approaches with lifted stick. Others are driven along like donkeys. I saw one young woman drop down exhausted. The Turk gave her two or three blows with his stick and she raised herself painfully. Her husband was walking in front with a baby two or three days old in his arms.

Further on an old woman had stumbled, and slipped down into the mud. The gendarme touched her two or three times with his whip, but she did not stir; then he gave her several kicks with his foot; still she did not move; then he kicked her harder, and she rolled over into the ditch; I hope that she was already dead.

These people have now arrived in the town. They have had nothing to eat for two days. The Turks forbade them to bring anything with them from Zeitoun, except, in some cases, a few blankets, a donkey, a mule, or a goat. But even these things they are selling here for practically nothing—a goat for one medjidia (3s. 2d.), a mule for half a lira (nine shillings). This is because the Turks steal them on the road. One young woman who had only been a mother eight days, had her donkey stolen the first night of the journey. What a way of starting out! The German and Turkish officers made the Armenians leave all their property behind, so that the mouhadjirs (refugees) from Thrace might enter into possession. There are five families in ———'s house! The town and the surrounding villages (about 25,000 inhabitants) are entirely destroyed.

Between fifteen and sixteen thousand exiles have been sent towards Aleppo, but they are going to be taken further. Perhaps into Arabia? Can the real object be to starve them to death? Those who have passed through our town were going to the Vilayet of Konia; there, too, there are deserts.

—th May.

Letters have come which confirm my fears. It is not to Aleppo that the Zeitounlis are being sent, but to Der-el-Zor, in Arabia, between Aleppo and Babylonia. And those we saw the other day are going to Kara-Pounar, between Konia and Eregli, in the most arid part of Asia Minor.

Certain ladies here have given blankets and shoes to some of the poorest. The local Christians, too, have shown themselves wonderfully self-sacrificing. But what can one do? It is a little drop of charity in the ocean of their suffering.

—th May.

News has come from Konia. Ninety Armenians have been taken to Kara-Pounar. The Zeitounlis have arrived at Konia. Their sufferings have been increased by their having had to wait—some of them 8, some 15, some 20 days—at Bozanti (the terminus of the Anatolian Railway in the Taurus, 2,400 feet above sea level). This delay was caused by the enormous masses of troops passing continually through the Cilician Gates; it is the army of Syria which is being recalled for the defence of the Dardanelles.

When the exiles reached Konia, they had eaten nothing, according to our news, for three days. The Greeks and Armenians at once collected money and food for their relief, but the Vali of Konia would not allow anything of any kind to be given to the exiles. They therefore remained another three days without food, at the end of which time the Vali removed his prohibition and allowed food to be served out to them under the supervision of the zaptiehs.

My informant tells me that, after the departure of the Armenians from Konia for Kara-Pounar, he saw an Armenian woman throw her new-born baby into a well; another is said to have thrown hers out of the window of the train.

—th May.

A letter has come from Kara-Pounar. I know the writer of it, and can have no doubt of his truthfulness. He says that the 6,000 or 8,000 Armenians from Zeitoun are dying there from starvation at the rate of 150 to 200 a day. So from 15,000 to 19,000 Zeitounlis must have been sent into Arabia, the total population of the town and the outlying villages having been about 25,000.

—th May.

The whole garrison of ―― and of Adana have left for the Dardanelles. There are no troops left to defend the district if it should be attacked from outside.

—th May (the next day).

New troops have arrived, but they are untrained.

—th May.

The last batch of Zeitounlis passed through our town to-day, and I was able to speak to some of them in the han where they had been put. I saw one poor little girl who had been walking, barefoot, for more than a week; her only clothing was a torn pinafore; she was shivering with cold and hunger, and her bones were literally pushing through her skin.

About a dozen children had to be left on the road because they could not walk any further. Have they died of hunger? Probably, but no one will ever know for certain. I also saw two poor old women without any hair left, or with hardly any. When the Turks drove them out of Zeitoun they had been rich, but they could not take anything with them beyond the clothes they were wearing. They managed somehow to hide five or six gold pieces in their hair, but, unfortunately for them, the sun glinted on the metal as they marched along and the glitter attracted the notice of a zaptieh. He did not waste any time in picking out the pieces of gold, but found it much quicker to tear the hair out by the roots.

I came across another very characteristic case. A citizen of Zeitoun, formerly a rich man, was leading two donkeys, the last remnants of his fortune. A gendarme came along and seized their bridles; the Armenian implored him to leave them, saying that he was already on the verge of starvation. The only answer he received from the Turk was a shower of blows, repeated till he rolled over in the dust; even then the Turk continued beating him, till the dust was turned into a blood-soaked mud; then he gave a final kick and went off with the donkeys. Several Turks stood by watching; they did not appear to be at all surprised, nor did any of them attempt to intervene.

—*th May.*

The authorities have sent a number of people from Dört Yöl to be hanged in the various towns of Adana Vilayet.

—*th May.*

There is a rumour of a partial exodus from Marash. It is going to be our town next.

Dört Yöl has also been evacuated and the inhabitants sent into Arabia. Hadjin is threatened with the same fate. There has been a partial clearing out of Adana; Tarsus and Mersina are threatened too, and also Aintab.

124. EXILES FROM ZEITOUN: FURTHER STATEMENT BY THE AUTHOR OF THE PRECEDING DOCUMENT; COMMUNICATED BY THE AMERICAN COMMITTEE FOR ARMENIAN AND SYRIAN RELIEF.

About the middle of April, about 150 Armenian families belonging to Zeitoun came to B. This is what they told us about the circumstances under which they had to leave their village.

After a battle that took place one day before their departure, between the Ottoman troops and 25 young men of Zeitoun, who had rebelled when they were asked to join the Army (a battle in which 300 soldiers perished, but in which the population of Zeitoun took no part), these families were called to the Government Building without any previous explanation and without any other information. Most of them were rich and went to the Government without misgivings. There they were informed that they had to leave their village instantly. They were then all obliged to abandon all that they had in their houses, their cattle and even part of their families (for, not knowing why they had been called away, many of them had left their children at home).

This is what I heard from one of the Armenian exiles in the first convoy from Zeitoun. They came to B., but when some of them went to the American Mission in this town, they did not yet know where they were to be planted. Most of them were in the greatest anxiety on account of the children whom they had left tending the cattle and whom they had not been able to take with them.

The first group was not in a very bad state, because it was composed of the first families of the city, and they could in large part provide for their immediate needs (carriages and food). But, a few days later, new bands appeared in a most deplorable condition; their number was nearly two thousand people.

Many, in fact, most of them, went on foot, getting food every two or three days, and in general lacking the most necessary clothes. The Christian population of B. tried to help them, but, whatever their efforts, what they could do was like a drop of water in the ocean. Also, they were not all allowed to enter the city; they had to sleep out of doors in no matter what weather, and the soldiers that guarded them put all sorts of difficulties in the way of the population of B., who wanted to help the refugees. We saw some of them on the road. They went slowly, most of them fainting from want of food. We saw a father walking with a one-day-old baby in his arms, and behind him the mother walking as well as possible, pushed along by the stick of the Turkish guard. It was not uncommon to see a woman fall down and then rise again under the stick. Some of them had a goat, a donkey, or a mare; when they reached B., they were obliged to sell them for five, ten, or fifteen piastres,[164] because the Turkish soldiers took them away from them. I saw one who sold his goat to a Turk for six piastres. I saw an Armenian pushing two goats; a policeman (zabit) came and carried away the animals and, because the poor man protested, beat him mercilessly, until he fell in the dust senseless. Many Turks were present; no one stirred.

A young woman, whose husband had been imprisoned, was carried away with her fifteen-days-old baby, with one donkey for all her baggage. After one day and a half on the road, a soldier stole her donkey and she had to go on foot, her baby in her arms, from Zeitoun to Aleppo.

A reporter, Mr. Y., told us that, while the refugees were on the way to Bozanti, his carriage was stopped all the time by refugees asking for bread.

The third and last band numbered 200 people. It reached B. on the 13th May, about seven o'clock. They were put in a han, where I went to visit them. They had all come on foot from Zeitoun to B., and had had nothing to eat for two days—days when it rained abundantly. Accompanied by one of my pupils, I made one or two translations from the Armenian, because we were under the surveillance of a policeman.

As soon as the Armenian refugees left their houses, mouhadjirs (Moslem refugees) from Thrace took possession of them. The Armenians had been forbidden to take anything with them, and they themselves saw all their goods pass into other hands. There must be about 20,000 to 25,000 Turks in Zeitoun now, and the name of the town seems to have been changed into that of Yeni Shehr.

I saw a girl three and a half years old, wearing only a shirt in rags. She had come on foot from Zeitoun to B. She was terribly spare and was shivering from cold, as were also all the innumerable children I saw on that day (Monday, the 14th May[165]).

An Armenian told me that he had abandoned two children on the way because they could not walk, and that he did not know whether they had died of cold and hunger, whether a charitable soul had taken care of them, or whether they had become the prey of wild beasts. I learned later that this was far from being a unique case. Many children seem to have been thus abandoned. One seems to have been thrown into a well.

As I passed through Konia, I went to see Dr. AB.[166], and this is what he told me: When the first refugees from Zeitoun came to Konia, the Christian population bought food and clothes for them; but the Vali refused to allow them any communication with the refugees, pretending that they had all that they wanted. A few days later, however, they could get the help they needed. The fact is that the Government gave them only very bad bread, and that only every two or three days. Dr. AB. told me that a woman threw her dying baby from the window of the train.

The refugees from Zeitoun have been directed to Kara-Pounar, one of the most unhealthy places in the Vilayet of Konia, situated between Konia and Eregli, but nearer the latter. Many of them have died, and the mortality is increasing every day. The malaria makes ravages among them, because of the complete lack of food and shelter. How cruelly ironic to think that the Government pretends to be sending them there to found a colony; and they have no ploughs, no seeds to sow, no bread, no abode; in fact, they are sent with empty hands.

Only part of the Zeitounlis seem to be at Kara-Pounar; the others seem to have been sent to Der-el-Zor, on the Euphrates; there their condition is still worse, and they ask as a favour to be sent to Kara-Pounar.

The Armenians of Adana received orders to leave the town, without being told where they were to go. Many of them came to B., others went to Osmania. But they were all recalled to Adana. Is it intended to send them somewhere else, or are they to remain in Adana? I could not find this out for certain before leaving B.

A great panic reigns among the Armenian population in B., because it was said that they also were to be exiled. But nothing has happened there yet.

From Konia, again, more than 200 Armenians have been sent to Kara-Pounar. Among them is Mr. AC. On Thursday, 90 people were notified to be ready to leave on Saturday, the 26th May.[167] The Armenians dare not leave their houses.

164. 1 piastre=2d.

165. The 14th May, 1915, was a Friday.—EDITOR.

166. Author of Doc. 125

167. The 26th May, 1915, was a Wednesday.—EDITOR.

125. EXILES FROM ZEITOUN: LETTER, DATED KONIA, 17th JULY, 1915, FROM A FOREIGN RESIDENT AT KONIA TO MR. N. AT CONSTANTINOPLE; COMMUNICATED BY THE AMERICAN COMMITTEE FOR ARMENIAN AND SYRIAN RELIEF.

In hope of having opportunity to send by Miss FF., I can write freely. Have you any means by which you can send me as much as fifty liras for relief of the Zeitounlis in Sultania? The Government has now left them to starve. At first, rations of bread were given; then 150 drams of flour to each per day (children under five not being counted at all); then their amount was reduced to 100 drams. It is now four weeks that this has been cut off *entirely*. The people are not allowed to scatter over the country in search of work. They can only search the fields for roots and herbs, and there have been several cases of poisoning from this food. The exiles from Konia, numbering 107 (men who have money and supplies sent to them from their homes) took up a subscription among themselves and subscribed 1,400 piastres a week towards supplying bread for the starving. I have sent personal gifts from ourselves and our friends of five or six liras a week; but these sources are becoming exhausted. Later Mr. GG., whom Dr. EE. knows, has been "pardoned" by the Vali and has returned here. He has been the leader among the exiles in trying to secure food for the Zeitounlis. I called on him this evening to get accurate information of their state. It is worse even than I knew. The number is over 7,000, 2,200 having been sent without coming through Konia, so that I had no account of them. The facts about the cutting off of all food for them are as I have stated. A bin-bashi, an Arnaout,[168] who went there on military service, was greatly moved by what he saw, and sent a strong telegram demanding rations to be given to the families of the men (about 300) who were drafted into the Labour Regiment after being sent to Sultania. This he could do in his military capacity, and it was accepted by the War Department. This provided for about 1,600, leaving, however, nearly 6,000 with nothing. The number of deaths up to last week was 305. Dr. Stepanian, of Baghtchedjik, has distinguished himself by self-sacrificing work for the poor. He testifies to seeing deaths from starvation already.

The refugees are "housed" principally in great camel stables and such like. It is a great camel region, the Government having requisitioned 4,000 of these animals from there. The cattle and animals of the Zeitounlis were mostly requisitioned by the Government en route. What they managed to conceal and bring with them has been put under requisition, but *not taken*. Meanwhile, the owners are forbidden to sell, are unable to use, and are compelled to feed these animals, because the Government holds them responsible to deliver them when called for. I have before heard of refinements of devilry, but I have seen instances this year that have burned into my soul. The manifest purpose to destroy these people by starvation cannot be denied.

I find that it is the exiles from Ak Shehr and Baghtchedjik, who are also at Sultania, who have been more generous than those of Konia in giving of their own means. The Kaimakam has been very good, giving out of his scanty purse to help and favouring the efforts of others, in spite of the official attitude in Konia. Dr. Stepanian, of Baghtchedjik, whom you perhaps know, is one of the "Commission" there for distributing all assistance that may be sent. Can you in any way get money to put at my disposal, so that I can send *ten liras a week*? With this we may be able to get enough from others here to provide *ten paras per person*. Of course, this is nothing, but may we not do something?

168. Albanian.

126. AF.: STATEMENT, DATED 16th DECEMBER, 1915, BY A FOREIGN RESIDENT AT AF.; COMMUNICATED BY THE AMERICAN COMMITTEE FOR ARMENIAN AND SYRIAN RELIEF.

The events connected with the banishment of the Armenians of the AF. region by the Turkish Government began on the 14th May. On that day the Alai Bey, or Justice of the Court Martial, arrived in AF. from Aleppo, the seat of the Court Martial. The three days following his arrival were spent in seclusion, very probably in consulting with secret agents. On the 18th, 19th and 20th May he had conferences with the elders of the city. He demanded in a very courteous manner that the city should deliver up all arms, and all deserters from the army and other outlaws. He desired that they should comply with his request within the next three days. He took an oath on his honour that, if his demands were obeyed, all would be well for the people of AF. and in no way should harm come to them. In case of disobedience, however, he said that he had at his call three thousand soldiers, who would enforce his demands.

Towards the last of the conferences, however, the Alai Bey's attitude grew threatening, and the people were filled with alarm. The elders and spiritual heads of the communities were at a loss what counsel to give. If they delivered up their arms and were betrayed, they might all be massacred; if they retained them, it would mean open opposition to the Government. A number of the leaders came to consult with Miss B. and me, and we supported the party which stood for full compliance with the requests. It was finally almost unanimously decided that this should be done, and a general response seemed to follow.

By Sunday, the 23rd May, all but three or four of the deserters had delivered themselves up and about seventy Martinis had been surrendered. C. Bey seemed pleased with the results, and the people were beginning to grow more tranquil. At three o'clock in the afternoon, about two thousand soldiers, cavalry and infantry, entered the city. The local centurion had prepared for their coming by taking forcible possession of the Gregorian Boys' School, the Monastery (which was used for orphanage purposes, the orphans being sent out as the soldiers entered), and the Protestant Boys' Academy. Miss B. immediately put in a protest at the Government House against occupying the last-named building. The cavalry was sent to another building belonging to a certain philanthropic society, for whose properties Miss B. was responsible. As the buildings were empty and not in use, it seemed best to allow this without a protest. The following morning we called upon the cavalry officer, D. Bey, were very courteously received, and were given assurances that the property should be well cared for, which assurances were kept. The Boys' Academy building was not freed of soldiers, but only a very few were stationed there, and all rooms we desired we kept locked. Guards of soldiers were placed in all conspicuous parts of the city, a squad being on duty night and day at the head of the private road which leads to the American Board Compound.

Towards evening on Monday, the 24th, the ammunition and load-animals of the troops came in. The soldiers with these were sent to a building belonging to another institution in the city. This building, though unoccupied because of the absence of the missionaries, was filled with property. Word was sent to Miss B., but before she could get there the attendant had been forced to open the door. She protested to the police in charge, and, finding it useless, sought audience with the justice of court martial. He promised to empty it the following day, and this was carried out.

On the 25th May, Miss B. again called on the Alai Bey to present several personal requests, such as permission to take flour to the mill without molestation, to have our road and premises free from the trespass of soldiers, etc. All was readily and courteously granted. She also reported the gun in our possession, which had been registered in the name of our steward. He smiled graciously and asked whether we did not want a few more; he had plenty, he said, to give us. In the days that followed there was repeated pressure, always more drastic, for ammunition of all kinds and the delivery of deserters. C. Bey gave repeated assurances that, if the deserters were delivered up, no one would be exiled. On the 27th May a large number of the leading men were imprisoned, and, after that, every day added to their numbers.

The strain upon the people was now so great that the majority could neither eat nor sleep. We were in the same case, and were up from very early until late in the evening to meet the many who came to consult with us. On the morning of the 28th, a party of women from the city besought our aid. The husbands of nearly all of them had been thrown into prison, and they and their children were left defenceless in their homes, with no suggestion of what the future held in store. At their request, then, Miss B. and I interviewed both C. Bey and E. Bey, the military commander. We besought them to distinguish between the innocent and the guilty, and asked mercy for the women and children. We were again received with entire courtesy, but had no satisfaction. The Alai Bey took pains to explain to us that, as we had come from a land of freedom, where people lived in a more enlightened way, we could not fully understand the necessary actions of the Turkish Government; that there existed a Committee among the Armenian people which was harmful to the Government, but that our hearts and minds were pure and the people easily deceived us.

The last of the deserters was delivered up on the 30th May, and the total number of guns was one Mauser and ninety Martinis. The Alai Bey, however, insisted that there were yet many more guns hidden by the people, either in the city or on the mountains. The soldiers were accordingly set at work to dig into walls and refuse heaps and search all the houses for guns. With the exception of some powder, the results were insignificant. The people of the city charged the soldiers with themselves hiding guns and ammunition in and about the walls of dwellings, for the purpose of securing convictions.

Meanwhile, the atmosphere grew worse and worse, and on the 3rd June it became known that the deportation was about to begin. In response to the desire of the people we, together with Miss F., a German lady, made a last plea before the officers. The only result was that we received permission to send telegrams. We sent messages to Mr. N. and the Ambassador, but afterwards learned that no such messages were ever transmitted. The men to be exiled the following morning were released from prison in the afternoon. Miss B. and I, together with the Protestant pastor, called upon all the families who were going. In the morning we asked permission for the school-girls of the exiled families to remain with us, and were refused on the ground that only the Vali could give such permission. We immediately telegraphed to the Vali, but, as usual, received no answer. The Alai Bey, however, personally gave us permission to keep three girls, as well as the privilege of receiving gifts from our friends who were going away.

Thirty leading Protestant and Gregorian families were marched away in the first batch. Gendarmes were placed to prevent relatives and friends from accompanying those sent out, but Miss B. and I always passed freely among them, giving aid wherever we could. Four days later G. Effendi, our steward and chief servant, received notice to go. Miss B. again interviewed the Alai Bey with respect to the case of G. Effendi. She said that we were greatly dependent upon him, and asked that he might be left among the last to be sent. The Alai Bey granted one day's delay, but his decision was not carried out in fact. The following morning he was the first to be driven from his house by the soldiers.

By the 10th June, about 150 households had been deported, and new papers were being distributed every day. Some of the men had now been imprisoned fifteen days. They were usually released the day before leaving, and had no chance of making preparations for the journey. The Alai Bey left the same day, delegating the work of further deportation to the military commander and the Kaimakam of AF. The soldiers left some two weeks later. The deportation of the people of AF. continued throughout the summer, until, by the 1st October, only a very few men and their families and about 250 widows and soldiers' families remained.

It was the intention of the Government to provide animals for those sent into exile, as the people of AF. had very few animals of their own and were obliged to journey over rough mountain roads. Horses, mules, camels and donkeys were levied upon all the surrounding villages, whether Christian or Turk. The owners were obliged to go with the animals. It can readily be seen that many of them bore the travellers no good will, and vented whatever cruelty they pleased upon them. Gendarmes were also sent along with the convoys, presumably for protection, but very often they themselves became the greatest menace, and almost never succeeded in preventing the raids made upon the defenceless exiles by marauding bands. Towards the latter part of the summer the supply of animals was so diminished, so many having died upon the road, that Circassian carts were used for transporting the people. The exiles from AF. were sent first to AG., and from there by slow degrees to Aleppo. There is a well-travelled caravan road to AG. by way of AH., which can also be used by the rude mountain cars. This, however, the exiles were not permitted to use, but were forced to travel over a stony and very difficult road leading over a high mountain pass. The entire village of Shar and the Armenian population of Roumlou were deported soon after the deportations began in AF. Being agricultural villages, they came for the most part with their own carts. When they reached the pass, they begged to be allowed to go by way of AH., so that they might have the benefit of their cars; but this was denied them. All the carts had to be abandoned at the river, and, throwing most of their possessions into the stream, they took what little they could carry, and started up the stony way on foot.

At the beginning of September a very large percentage of the remaining population of AF. was deported, consisting for the most part of the very poor, and including many widows. As very few animals and carts came in response to the call of the Government, a large number of men, women and children started on the long journey on foot, carrying on their backs or strapping to their persons the very few articles deemed most necessary.

Miss B. and I found our position in the face of such terrible events a most difficult one. We felt obliged to help the Armenian people in every way possible, and at the same time felt we could not have a break with the Government, nor give up our cordial relations with the Moslem families. We felt responsible for the American property situated in and about AF., and also had Armenian orphan teachers and girls in the compound, for whose protection our lives were not too costly. One of the great problems was in connection with the property of the exiled families. They had been told by the Alai Bey that they could place the property left behind wherever they pleased. Naturally everyone wished to put it under our care. We could have filled our whole compound full of all imaginable household articles and treasures, to say nothing of horses, cows, goats, etc. As we had no American gentleman to advise us, and, moreover, wished always to deal in such a way as not to involve the Consul or the Embassy, we decided in general against the taking of property. That which we did accept we paid for, and the purchasing was always to help those in such desperate need. The Government came to understand this, and respected us accordingly.

From the time when the first people left, in early June, until October, we were very fortunate in having the opportunity to render some financial help. Miss B. passed through the line of gendarmes guarding the villages of Shar and Roumlou, and was enabled to leave some pounds with the head men of the villages for the aid of the very poor. To the outgoing people of AF. we gave freely, according to our limited means, and even occasionally could help exiles from other villages passing through from the Kaisaria country. We succeeded also, with the aid of a Greek and a Turk, in sending some relief to the villagers of AJ. and AK. before they left. We felt confident that the authorities knew something of the extent to which we were helping the people, but we encountered no open opposition.

Our servants were nearly all sent away early in the deportation, so that extra and unaccustomed work was imposed upon us. Miss B., for example, always had to take the post in person to the Government Building. Providing for the food supply, and dealing with our shepherd and the villagers who came to sell things, often fell to us personally. A large part of the time we had no cook. Another tax upon our strength and time was the battle with the swarms of locusts which visited Syria and Cilicia. They first appeared in early June and ravaged the country till September. They destroyed our vineyards, and we had to fight day after day to keep them out of the compound. When we destroyed those hatched on our premises, their places were quickly filled by armies coming down the mountain side. When I left, many of the villages were suffering from the lack of food due to the locust scourge.

Another problem was how to relieve, in some small measure at least, the suffering in the city caused by lack of food. A great many widows and orphans and soldiers' families were left with no means of support, after the more well-to-do families had been deported. Moreover, the industrial work, which employed a considerable number of widows, was closed with the coming of the court martial officer. The two Bible Women, up to the time when they also were deported, worked heroically, with the little means that we could spare them each week, to meet and provide for the cases of greatest need. We bought large quantities of cheap wheat to help towards this end. The only shop left open was that of the druggist, so there was no way of obtaining any supplies. The lack of soap and salt was very keenly felt. As our own supply was limited, we could not give freely as we wished, but finally Miss B., in spite of all the demands upon her strength and time, made considerable quantities of soap, so that at least the women might wash their clothes occasionally. All who received it were most grateful, and the supply was never sufficient.

Miss B. and I personally never suffered any discourtesy from either the official or village Turk. Our situation was often delicate, and, in such a case as the affair connected with the Government Industrial, the Kaimakam ignored our rights and courteously took everything into his own hands; but, on the whole, we were well treated. When we asked Mr. H. to come to our aid from Marash and the Government prevented him from coming, the Kaimakam sent the chief of police to explain the case to us, and assured us that we need not fear, that we were the guests of the Government, and that not a hair of our heads should be injured. When I left AF., although I had the escort of Miss J., the Consul's kavass and their gendarme, the captain in AF. sent with me as a personal escort his best horseman. The postal official showed himself very friendly, and did us many personal favours. When money was sent us through the post office, he tried always to pay in gold or silver, and in such a way that we might get it quickly into the hands of the people. He knew we used it to help those condemned to be exiled. When the first convoys of exiles were driven out of AF. his mother was unable to leave her bed for two weeks, she was so depressed by what she saw and heard. She spoke with great vigour against the terrible events that were happening.

Our head teacher, Miss K., and her mother were with us in the compound. They have Moslem relatives, two of whom were officers' families in AF. These were especially friendly to us, and visited us frequently. They were all outspoken against the horrors. One time U. Effendi had failed to visit us, as was his custom, and, when we asked the reason, he said he was ashamed to come because he could bring us no good news. We saw Moslem women loudly wailing with the Christians when the first families were sent out. When the Alai Bey first came, he called the Mufti and asked his approval of what he was about to do; but the Mufti refused to sanction it, and said he could see no good in it. This same Mufti was a strong personal friend of one of the leading Protestant Armenians (our special friend and adviser), and he tried in every way to save him from exile, but in vain. When M. Agha left, the Mufti took possession of his house and all his properties for him. He also said he would stand as protector of the Americans and the American compound after M. Agha was gone.

Some of the village aghas also expressed themselves freely to us, both on the matter of the war and on the calamity which had befallen the Armenians. They said that such cruelty would not go unavenged, and that their day of reckoning would come. They complained bitterly that there were now no artisans or shopkeepers left to supply their wants, and that in a short time they themselves would be in desperate want. Our watchman at the summer residence showed us his foot half-naked, because he could not find a shoemaker in all AF. to mend it. All the surrounding Turkish, Kurdish and Circassian villages were in the same need.

A Kurdish Sheikh, N. Effendi, from a village not far from AF., visited the city twice only during the summer. The first time he only remained about an hour, and, with the tears streaming down his cheeks, he said he would return to his village at once; that he could not endure such sights. The second time he came to bid farewell to O. Effendi, his Armenian friend. He kissed each of his children, pressing them to his heart, and left again in tears. A Kurd also brought us the secret information that the new Shar church building had been partially destroyed by dynamite.

The Moslems of AK. and A J. were very much opposed to the exiling of the Armenians from those villages. They said they were not guilty of anything, possessed no weapons, lived peacefully and were friends with them, and were, besides, their artisans and tradesmen. Through their efforts they put off the deportation about three months; but, in the end, even they were unable to save them. The Turks of AK. ought to have special mention for their honourable attitude throughout the whole affair. Miss K.'s uncle, an officer in AK., broke a water jar over the head of a young Moslem who had entered into a room to molest an Armenian soldier's wife. He said he was obliged to defend the unprotected who dwelt under the shadow of his house. Once when Miss B. was passing through the streets of AF., she was appealed to by two gendarmes who had been ordered to expel from their home for deportation an aged man and his wife and their bed-ridden son. The gendarmes said: "How shall we do this thing?" and begged Miss B. to beseech the authorities for mercy. These are samples of faint gleams of light in the midst of four months of horrible darkness. Pages and pages might be written on the barbaric and relentless cruelty of the many.

Throughout the summer Miss B. and I were confronted with the question whether we had come to Turkey only to work for the Christians, or whether we would also be willing, now that the Armenians were gone, to take Moslem children into our school. These inquiries finally resulted in expressions on the part of several officers' families of a desire to place their daughters in our school. Every week there were inquiries as to when a decision would be made as to the opening of our school. One Moslem woman even went so far as to inquire about the clothing necessary to prepare for her daughter. Whether they were sincere or not, of course, we cannot tell; but the desire seemed to be a general one.

There is yet one more phase in connection with the summer's events. Shortly after the deportation of the Armenian families of AF. took place, about thirty families of Mouhadjirs were sent in by the Government to take their place. These unfortunate people were refugees from Roumelia since the time of the Balkan War. For two years they had been wandering, always sent on by the Turkish Government from place to place, and finally placed in the houses just vacated by those who were likewise to face months of wandering and homelessness. Four families came to live close to our end of the city. We at once decided to show them friendliness. They responded in a touching way, came frequently to call, and poured out their over-burdened hearts. When they first came, the men were too weak to work; all were subject to chills and fever, and, of the whole village from which these people had come, only two children were living. One of the women spoke with horror at having to live in a house with such associations, saying that only they knew what such suffering meant. The morning when I left and bade them good-bye, one of these Mouhadjir women threw her arms about me and begged me not to go.

Miss Vaughan and I saw the departure of hundreds of Armenians into a hopeless exile. It was heart-breaking and too awful even to imagine in detail; yet we praise the God of all mankind, whether Moslem or Christian, that we were permitted to see the spirit of Christian faith and humility manifested by so many in the darkest period of Armenian history. There may have been examples of hard-heartedness and cursing against God and an utter losing of faith, but we did not personally come in contact with them. How often did we pray together with those about to go and, with the tears streaming down our faces, beseech God to keep our faith sure! How often did men and women clasp our hands at parting, saying: "Let God's will be done. We have no other hope!" P. Effendi, the Protestant preacher, came to our compound the morning of his leaving and asked that, with the girls and teachers, we might all have worship together. His young wife, who was about to become a mother, was left to our care. Whether they were ever reunited I do not know. With entire calm he read from God's word, and prayed God's protection for all of us who were left behind. At the close he asked that the girls should sing "He leadeth me."

"Though He slay me, yet will I trust in Him."

127. AF.: RECORD OF INDIVIDUAL CASES, DRAWN UP BY THE AUTHOR OF THE PRECEDING STATEMENT, AND DATED 17th DECEMBER, 1915.

1. Q. was a young man who had graduated from the law school at Constantinople, and in the winter and early spring of 1915 had served in the Mounted Imperial Guard. Not being well, he returned to his home in AF. a few weeks before the deportation began. Upon the arrival of the court-martial and army officers, he was at once chosen to serve them as a military attendant, and was dressed in full uniform. He was in constant attendance upon them till the evening of the 3rd June, when he was roughly stripped of his uniform and told to be ready for exile in the morning. We saw him go off with the convoy on foot, not even an animal having been granted him.

2. R. was for years a Government officer at AF. At the time when the officers and army entered AF., he was away in the villages on Government business. Two days before the day set for deportation, his wife was notified. She and the four small children were left alone to prepare for the journey. The husband returned from the villages a few hours before the time when the families were deported, having had no information whatever of what was taking place.

3. S.'s husband had been in Syracuse, N.Y., for two years, and she was left alone in AF. with two small children. He intended to send for her as soon as

conditions were favourable. Her parents were deported early in the season, and, at the time, she asked permission of the Alai Bey to go with them, as otherwise she was left friendless. She even begged to go. He refused and said: "Have no fear, my daughter, you will not be sent off. Remain quietly in your place." Early in September, she was deported in company with a great many other defenceless women.

4. When the soldiers were digging for ammunition and guns in the walls and refuse heaps of AF., they found in a wall close to a house an iron ball wrapped in a piece of cloth. The woman of the house, a young bride, happened to be standing before the door, and the soldiers noticed that the cloth of her apron was the same as that in which the ball was wrapped. The woman was seized, sent to Adana and thrown into prison. This was on the last day of May, and in October she was still in prison. The Bible Woman in Adana discovered her there, and said her condition was horrible. She is confined in a small room with three or four Turkish women of desperate character, living in terrible filth and mostly without food.

5. The pastor of Tchomakly, a village near Everek, passed through AF. en route for the desert. He is a Marsovan graduate and a pastor in the Kaisaria district. He had been assured by the Everek Kaimakam that nothing should happen to him, and that, even if the village were deported, he would not be included, as he was not a native of the place. At three o'clock in the morning soldiers entered the village, roused all the inhabitants and told them to be ready to depart in two hours. When they came to the pastor's door, they said: "You also must go. You went to Talas to talk with the Americans a few days ago." His wife, not having suitable shoes, had her feet bound up in skins.

6. Lydia was the wife of a soldier who, at the time when the court-martial officer came to AF., was a deserter and in hiding. However, he surrendered to the authorities, was pardoned, and was sent to the coast with the labour gang. She was assured by the court-martial officer (and, after his departure, by many of the local officers) that she should never be deported, in consideration of her being a soldier's wife. Throughout the summer, however, they played with her. Again and again she was given notice to leave, and then, upon entering a personal petition at the Government House and stating her case, she would be assured upon their word of honour that she would never be deported. The chief of police gave us the same assurance. Finally, early one morning, gendarmes came to her door and roughly told her to be ready to go in a few hours. She again took her three small children and went to the Government House. All in vain. She was given two camels for herself, the loads and the children. A fourth child was born under the burning sun of AG., and when she arrived in Aleppo with the child dead, she was only able to reach the hospital.

7. T. was for four years in charge of the Government Industrial in AF. This was closed when deportation began. He did his work so well that this Industrial was the best business in AF. He was living quietly in the building, guarding the property and stock of the Industrial. In the middle of September, when almost all the rest of AF. were exiled, he also received notification to go. Gendarmes came in the evening after dark and drove him, his invalid wife, and four children to the Government Building. There they were to wait for animals or a cart to take them on their journey. In company with hundreds of others, they sat down on the bare ground in front of the Government Building, gathering their few possessions close to them lest they should be stolen. He and his family remained there two days and three nights before being sent on, and were exposed during one of these nights to a terrible rainstorm. They were within ten minutes of their home, but were not permitted to go there for shelter. His wife secretly made her way to our compound to ask for a little bread, as their supply for the journey was already gone.

128. ADANA: STATEMENT, DATED 3rd DECEMBER, 1915, BY A FOREIGN RESIDENT AT ADANA; COMMUNICATED BY THE AMERICAN COMMITTEE FOR ARMENIAN AND SYRIAN RELIEF.

When Turkey became a belligerent in the November of last year (1914), there were Armenians and other Christians serving in the Army under arms. Many of these came under fire both at the Dardanelles and in the expedition against Egypt. Later, the arms were taken away from the Armenians, and those in the Army were converted into "Labour Regiments," to which were attached the very considerable number of Armenians drafted into the Army later. These men were employed in road building, transport, trenching, etc., and rendered extensive and very important service. When the arms were taken from them, a feeling of anxiety took possession of the Armenians, in the thought that this action of the authorities might portend something. However, much was done in the Adana Province to reassure the people that Governmental action would be discriminating and severity exercised only against blameworthy or suspected people. In pursuance of this policy a number of men whose names had been listed during and after the massacre period of 1909 were put under arrest or surveillance.

In the early winter, the British and French war-vessels in the Eastern Mediterranean bombarded some points on the Gulf of Alexandretta, notably the town of Alexandretta and the branch line of the Baghdad Railway that runs to Alexandretta. The town of Dört Yöl—almost entirely Armenian—lies quite near the head of the Gulf on the plain of Issus about 20 miles from

Alexandretta, and is a station on the line. That branch line of the railway was put out of commission. The Government officials made charge that the Dört Yöl people had communication with the hostile ships, affording them valuable information. A number of them were brought before the court-martial and imprisoned, of whom some were executed by hanging. Men were arrested and imprisoned in other places, notably Hadjin, and brought before the court-martial. These and other acts of the Government officials increased the anxiety, but in April the exiles from Zeitoun on their way to Konia (Iconium) passed through the city of Adana. They had suffered terribly, but they had considerable property with them, and also cattle and sheep. It was announced that these people would be settled on lands in the Konia district. This was somewhat reassuring, and there was hope that wholesale deportation or massacre was not in contemplation.

However, this assurance was converted into consternation. At midnight, in the latter part of April, gendarmes went through the city rapping at certain doors, searching the houses for arms and informing the inmates that in three days they were to be deported. In the third week in May, 70 families (three to four hundred people—men, women and children) were sent off in the direction of Konia. They had not reached the Cilician Gates Pass in the Taurus Mountains when they were turned back with the announcement that they had been pardoned and were to return to their homes. The joy of their return was almost equal to the consternation caused by the order for deportation. However, exiles from north of the Taurus (Marsovan, Kaisaria, etc.) in considerable numbers were passing through Adana to the Aleppo district. The explanation given was that that was being done because of revolutionary agitation in those districts. As nothing of overt import had been done on the part of the Armenians in Cilicia, the people of the district were reassured. There was an influential element among the Moslems—including influential officials—who opposed oppressive measures. The Governor was, to all appearances, strongly opposed. Insistent orders from Constantinople forced the deportation of groups of Armenians. Early in the movement towards Aleppo, men were left free to take their families or leave them. No massacring was done, though there was an uneasy feeling that it might occur. In this way various batches were deported, from whom word was received of their safe arrival in the Aleppo district. However, the suffering of deportation—abandonment of home and property and friends, the exposure and hunger on the road, the insanitary state of the concentration camps, and the rough treatment by gendarmes, and in many cases outrage and pillage—all this, though heart-breaking in itself, was not as bad as, or rather was much less horrible than, the torture of the crowds that suffered in the north and east.

Later in the year there was a distinct effort to save many of the Armenians. This effort synchronised with the order to exempt Catholics and Protestants. It seemed a success, and everybody was greatly encouraged. But an emissary from the Committee of Union and Progress at Constantinople arrived at that time, and was able to overturn the arrangement and secure an order for the immediate deportation of all. Exception was later made of some widows, of the wives and children of men serving in the labour regiments, and of men working in mills under Government contract and in the Baghdad Railway construction.

The great drive took place in the first week of September, when two-thirds of the Armenian population of Adana City were deported. Hadjin and Dört Yöl were treated very much more harshly, both in the process of eviction and on the road. The people were allowed to dispose of some of their properties, which they did at a great sacrifice; still, they had to abandon the great mass of their properties, which was later confiscated. I would call attention to the fact that the appalling nature of the deportation is none the less appalling because there was comparatively less torture and outrage. It is only fair to state that one Moslem was scourged to death for participation in the robbery of some Christians that were being deported.

It is not merely the suffering of the outlawed and deported people that is appalling, but the effect of it all on the country. Two-thirds of the business of Adana City was dependent on Armenians, and the markets seemed deserted after they were driven out. The disaster to the whole province from the material standpoint is beyond calculation. However, it would appear that the whole scheme was intended to be a relentless effort on the part of the central authorities either to exterminate the Armenian nation or to reduce them to a condition like that of the people of Moab, as described by Isaiah in the last clause of the 16th chapter: "A remnant very small and of no account." The enormity is not so much in the torture, massacring, outrage, etc., as in the intention and effort to exterminate a nation. The Armenians have endured massacre and outrage and persecution and oppression; this, however, shatters all hope of life and a future.

The Armenian Protestant communities are all deported with the pastors and leaders, but the men deported are a tower of strength to the suffering people in their exile. Let me quote from W. Effendi, from a letter he wrote a day before his deportation with his young wife and infant child, and with the whole congregation: "We now understand that it is a great miracle that our nation has lived so many years amongst such a nation as this. From this we realise that God can and has shut the mouths of lions for many years. May God restrain them! I am afraid they mean to kill some of us, cast some of us into most cruel starvation and send the rest out of this country; so I have very little hope of seeing you again in this world. But be sure that, by God's special help, I will do my best to encourage others to die manly. I will also look for God's help for myself to die as a Christian. May this country see that, if we cannot live here as men, we can die as men. May many die as men of God. May God forgive this nation all their sin which they do without knowing. May the Armenians teach Jesus' life by their death, which they could not teach by their life or have failed in showing forth. It is my great desire to see a Reverend Ali, or Osman, or Mohammed. May Jesus soon see many Turkish Christians as the fruit of his blood.

"May the war soon end, in order to save the Moslems from their cruelty (for they increase in that from day to day), and from their ingrained habit of torturing others. Therefore we are waiting on God, for the sake of the Moslems as well as of the Armenians. May He appear soon."

129. ADANA: STATEMENT, DATED 9th MAY, 1916, BY MISS Y., A FOREIGN RESIDENT AT ADANA, RECORDING HER EXPERIENCES THERE FROM SEPTEMBER, 1914, TO SEPTEMBER, 1915.

From the time Turkey began to mobilise in the autumn of 1914, before entering into the war, fear and questioning naturally took hold of the Armenians. First there was the unreasonable and irregular way in which the men were drafted into the Army or Labour Regiments; and then there was the news concerning the harsh and cruel treatment of the male population of Dört Yöl, where all from the ages of about 16 to 70 years were suddenly sent away *en masse* to work on the roads in the Hassan Beyli district—this, on the mere rumour that fruit and food had been conveyed from Dört Yöl to one of the Allies' warships.

This was followed by a few selected men from Dört Yöl being hanged at intervals in the streets of Adana. One night in the winter (1914-15) the Government sent officers round the city into all Armenian houses, knocking the families up and demanding that all weapons should be given up, or actually searching for them. Think of the fright of many of them, thus rudely awakened; this action was the death-knell to many hearts. Soon after this, Armenians whose names had been registered as having escaped or defended themselves during the massacres of 1909, or who were found in possession of arms, or were under some other accusation, were collected and imprisoned. I am not sure what happened to these.

Then came the news of Zeitoun being deported. These hardy mountaineers were destined for Sultania, a low malarial district on the plain beyond Konia. Most of these villagers passed through Tarsus *en route*, save those who had died on the way. A Tarsus graduate from Zeitoun who had hoped to become a teacher, voluntarily followed his mother, a widow, to Sultania, for the reason that she had no one to take care of her, neither she nor his sister with her four children, as the latter's husband was imprisoned in Marash.

"Why imprisoned?" I asked. "I do not know any reason," the boy replied. This boy recounted to me how the people had to live in this sultry region. Some one hundred souls, regardless of any distinction, among them a College Professor and a few leading people from Konia, were for a time crowded into the largest house in the place. They could not sleep, many were sick, children and babies crying, the heat great. Other houses were occupied likewise; probably many people camped around. These poor people were not allowed to do anything to earn money or to go beyond a certain distance. Those who still had money for food helped the more needy as far as they could. This same student told me that while he was in Sultania 750 had died. Then the remainder were all despatched back to Tarsus to be forwarded to the Arabian desert.

I may say here that thousands and thousands of Armenians passed from the north over the Cilician plain, telling heart-rending stories of massacre or brutal treatment on the journey. Some mothers had given all the money in their possession to save their daughters from being violated. One said she had given 22 liras for a certain distance only. Poor women had to leave their babies and young children by the roadside; they were too exhausted to carry them any longer. The suffering of some in childbirth cannot be dwelt upon. One such, not of the poorest class, was thrust out of her house in —— when deportation began, and cruelly forced along the road. She died after two hours.

As long as I live I can never forget the camp I saw twice near Geulik station, not far from Tarsus. Here there were 10,000 to 15,000 Armenians awaiting further deportation towards the desert. They were in the broiling sun, with no shade or shelter save the rudest arrangements—anything that came to hand thrown over poles or sticks. There were all kinds of people and families of all ages, crowded together within a certain radius, beyond which they might not go. They looked scorched by the sun, their clothes were fast wearing out, and there were poor little children, boys and girls, taken from school, with simply nothing to do but await their fate, which mercifully they could not realise as the adults could. There was a stream of water a little distance off, and if only it had been clean it would have been a boon. It was used for rinsing clothes as well as drinking. There were no sanitary arrangements whatever, and the air was impregnated with foul odours. We witnessed all this from the train, which drew up at the station alongside the camp. The Government would not allow any help in money, food, or medicine to be given; if they knew of anyone so doing, they stopped it. In Tarsus, Mrs. X., who was working among the refugees all the time, trying to show sympathy and give help in any little way possible, was stopped at last. But I must go back to Adana.

As the Armenian men of Adana were drafted into the Army or Labour Battalions, and the Armenian shops were robbed at pleasure without payment, great numbers of families did not know where to look for food, and even the wealthier business men were beginning to see destitution looming ahead.

I think it was at the end of April (or May) that some thirty picked families (few of them particularly wealthy) were ordered to leave their homes for an unknown destination. This looked like the beginning of deportation; but owing, as we had reason to believe, to pressure being put on the Government at that time by the American Ambassador, who did his utmost to save Adana, Tarsus and Mersina from deportation, all these families save a few young men were allowed to return to their homes within three weeks. No one could understand this strange transaction, but fresh hope awoke in people's hearts. It was short lived.

Circumstantial stories of all kinds of oppression and cruelty in one place or another kept arriving day after day, but no one even then could foretell what exactly was coming or what special fate was in store for themselves. Gradually the people became hopeless. All hearts were sorely tested, but those that knew their God proved their strength and peace in Him. Some were enabled to go farther—to cast themselves upon God's will and accept this cup of suffering (so imminent) as from the Father's hand. Oh, those were terrible days of suspense and heart-strain. In my house, in a Greek quarter, I was able to give room to a family I had long known. The wife had been a Bible Woman in the city for twelve years; the son was a graduate of the college, and there were two daughters—one a teacher and the other just graduated from the American school. The husband had care of the Protestant church buildings, and he used to bring back the news daily from the market. Many were the prayers which went up to God from this dear woman and others who sought to comfort the people. Never before had so many meetings been held in the poor city homes among the women, who crowded outside the doors if there was no room inside. Fifty, sixty or eighty were quite usual numbers. The church services also were unusually crowded, and God granted new life to many hearts, especially among the young men remaining.

Then the orders for the deportation of Adana came. The people, of course, did not know what to do with their things, while those who lived from hand to mouth had not the wherewithal to get food even to start with, let alone other necessities. What could be sold was sold, but the things went for a mere nothing, except in a few cases, where goods were bought to befriend and help the sellers. The Missionaries had not money to spare to buy, with all the numbers beseeching help. Those who could sell nothing had to leave all their belongings and stores save what they could carry with them. One Armenian preacher who was constantly appealed to at this time, from morning until night, by the distracted multitude—asking whether their names were called yet, what was to be done, and so on—expressed the situation thus: "It is as if the people were drowning in a sea of trouble and each one were trying to catch at a straw to save himself."

To give an example of the stony-hearted attitude of the Government official in charge of this work of deportation, I may cite the case of a young man of good mental ability, who for many years had been teaching and helping the blind in many ways. Through spinal disease he had become very badly deformed and could not walk. He was taken down to the Sarai in a bath-chair, hoping to elicit pity and not be cast adrift with his deaf mother, whom he supported. The only answer he received was: "Get out with you and be gone; the sooner the better." Some money was given to this crippled young man, but long before reaching Aleppo he had spent all on conveyances.

Another instance of the inhumanity of man towards his fellows in suffering, of which we have since heard and read over and over again until our hearts can bear no more, was the treatment accorded to, and pity withheld from, the Armenian people from all regions who were being transported by railway during the great heat. They were packed like cattle, and as train after train passed through Adana station, the people cried out for water and thrust out their hands beseechingly, but to no avail, although water was actually at hand. No one must show them any mercy. This we heard from witnesses living near the station, who said that they could not endure the sight, and did not know how to remain where they were. When some of our special friends were starting, at the station, one of our party, Dr. Z., tried to give a basket of grapes to a family, but was not permitted. What happened to the crowds after they reached Aleppo we did not then know. From our deported Adana people there came piteous messages for money, as the little in hand was soon exhausted. Some short letters came through from the Aleppo centre. One wrote: "Better drown your girls than let them come here." Another, well known to me, wrote to his sisters, who were at the American school: "Be thankful you have such a place to be in as the place where you are, and that you are not here."

It is computed that 20,000 were deported from Adana alone. We can testify to the mercy which permitted our Cilician people to go *en masse*, *i.e.*, in families, save for those members already taken by the Government, ostensibly for the Army or the Labour Regiments. As far as we heard, those who were able to obtain means of transit and continued their journey from Osmania (whither they went by rail) to Aleppo, were not attacked or massacred on the way. How many were left behind sick or died in Osmania cannot be said.

Circumstances obliged me and some other members of the Missionary Circle to be away from the heat of the plain for part of July and August, and it was during these weeks that the great deportation *en masse* of the Armenian population took place from Adana. Though absent, one was straining for news all the time. When we were in the hills above Tarsus, details of the refugees and their plight were constantly being sent by Mrs. X. to her daughter and son-in-law, in whose company I was. One could only write "farewells" before the word to start was actually given, feeling sure that the order to depart would be extended to all our friends without exception. Our American friends said, in their kindness: "We are glad you were not here; it was too heart-breaking to bear." And, indeed, on our return the whole atmosphere of the place, the empty houses and streets of the city with scarcely an Armenian to be seen, spoke more of death than the burnt, empty city after the massacres of 1909.

I conclude with quotations from a letter written by a fellow-worker of many years standing. He and his wife and other members of his family left with the crowd of Protestants in August, 1915. The letter was given me about two weeks later by a relative. It reads thus:—

"God *can* shut again the mouths of lions. Do you know that God *has* shut the mouths of many lions for many years? We now understand that it is a great miracle that our nation (the Armenians) has lived so many years among such a nation (the Moslems). Oh, how can men become such devils in so short a time? May God restrain them. I am afraid they mean to kill some of us, cast some of us into most cruel starvation, and send the rest into the desert; so I have very little hope of seeing you again in this world. But be sure that, by God's special help, I will do my best to encourage others to die manfully. I will also await God's help for myself, to die as a Christian.

"May this country see that, if we cannot live here as men, we can die as men. May many die as men of God. May God forgive this nation (the Moslems) all their sin which they do without knowing.... May Jesus soon see many Mohammedan Christians as the fruit of His blood.

"May the war soon end, in order to save the Moslems from their cruelty and savagery, for they increase in devilry from day to day, and from their ingrained habit of torturing their fellow men. Therefore we are waiting on God, for the sake of the Moslems as well as the Armenians. May He soon appear."

XVI.
JIBAL MOUSA.

The villages on the southern and eastern slopes of Jibal Mousa are included administratively in the Vilayet of Aleppo, and, like other Armenian settlements in that province, were only given notice of deportation at a comparatively late date—in their case, the 13th July. Geographically and historically, however, they are intimately connected with the Cilician highlanders. Jibal Mousa is a direct southern continuation of Amanus, and Yoghan Oulouk and the other Jibal Mousa villages are kindred communities to Dört Yöl and Zeitoun. They are the southernmost outpost of the Armenian race towards the Arabic world.

By the time the summons was served on them, the Jibal Mousa villagers had been watching for four months the deportation of their Cilician kinsmen, and had realised to the full what this deportation meant. They resolved to resist, and retired into the fastnesses of their mountain, which rises north-west of the villages and on its further flank falls steeply into the sea. The documents in this section record their successful defence and dramatic rescue by a French squadron—the single happy incident in the national tragedy of the Armenians in the Ottoman Empire.

130. JIBAL MOUSA: THE DEFENCE OF THE MOUNTAIN AND THE RESCUE OF ITS DEFENDERS BY THE FRENCH FLEET; NARRATIVE OF AN EYE-WITNESS, THE REV. DIKRAN ANDREASIAN, PASTOR OF THE ARMENIAN PROTESTANT CHURCH AT ZEITOUN.

This narrative was written down after the arrival of the refugees in Egypt, translated into English by the Rev. Stephen Trowbridge, Secretary of the American Red Cross at Cairo, communicated by the translator to the Editor of the Armenian journal "Ararat," of London, and published by him in his issue of November, 1915.

From the day that Turkey entered the war there had been much anxiety among the people of Zeitoun as to whether the Turks would treat the Armenians of those mountain districts with some new form of cruelty and oppression. Zeitoun is—we must now say *was*—a city of seven thousand inhabitants, entirely Armenian, and surrounded by many villages also Christian, in the heart of the Taurus Mountains.

I have been serving for one year as the pastor of the Armenian Protestant Church in Zeitoun, and the narrative which follows is one of personal experience.

Early in the spring of this year (1915) the Government began to assume a threatening attitude towards Zeitoun, summoning the elders and notables of the city and commencing an inquisition with the punishment of the bastinado. Absurd and impossible charges were made against the Armenians for the purpose of extorting money. Meanwhile some 6,000 regular troops were quartered in the barracks above the city. An attempt to take the Armenian monastery by storm cost the Turks some casualties and failed of its object. The young men who were within stoutly defended themselves, and not until attacked by field artillery was the monastery taken.

Fifty of the leading men in Zeitoun were therefore summoned to the barracks "for a conference with the commander." They were at once imprisoned and their families were sent for. Everyone waited anxiously for these people to return, but after a while it was learned that they had been sent away to an unknown destination. A few days later another and larger group of families were ordered to the barracks, and were forthwith driven off with threats and curses to a distant banishment. In this way three or four hundred families at a time were sent off on foot, with no proper supply of food, by devious routes through the mountains, some north-west towards Konia, some south-east towards the hot and unhealthy plains of Mesopotamia.

Day by day we saw the various quarters of the city stripped of their inhabitants, until at last only a single neighbourhood remained. In addition to my duties as pastor I happened to be in charge of the Mission Orphanage. The commanding officer sent for me one morning and told me to make ready at once for departure. "Your wife is also to go," he said, "and the children in the Orphanage." We made our preparations hurriedly, for we were allowed to take but little with us. As we were leaving I looked back with an aching heart and saw our beloved church empty and lonely. The last company of our seven thousand people was streaming down the valley into banishment! We had seen massacres, but we had never seen this before! A massacre at least ends quickly, but this prolonged anguish of soul is almost beyond endurance.

The first day's march exhausted all of us. In the dark, as we lay down upon the open ground, Turkish muleteers came and robbed us of the few donkeys and mules that we had. Next day, in forlorn condition, the children with swollen and blistered feet, we reached Marash. Through the earnest request of the American missionaries, an order was secured from the governor for my wife and myself to return to my home town of Yoghanolouk, near the sea, twelve miles west of Antioch. The governor granted this permit on the ground that my wife and I were not natives of Zeitoun. My heart was torn between the desire to share banishment with some fragment of my congregation and the desire to take my wife to a place of comparative safety in my father's home. But the order having once been issued, I had no alternative but to obey.

At Aintab we found the large Armenian community in the utmost anxiety, but at that time the order to leave had not arrived. Rumours reached us that the villages by the sea were being threatened, but we thought best to continue southward, difficult though the journey was at such a time.

The last part of our way lay through a historic valley, the fertile plain of Antioch. It was here that Chrysostom preached in the fervour of his early ministry before he was called to Byzantium. And it was to a secluded chapel on our own mountain side that he used to withdraw for prayer and communion with God. As a boy I had often looked with wonder and reverence at the massive stones of the ruins of St. Chrysostom's Chapel. It was in this very Antioch that Barnabas and Paul laboured with such spiritual energy. And here they set forth upon their momentous task of spreading the Christian faith. The Roman road by which they walked from Antioch to Seleucia can still be traced in the valley below my native town, and the stone piers from which Roman ships set sail at Seleucia are not entirely demolished by the storms and earthquakes of the centuries.

The city of Antioch, once so gallantly defended by the Crusaders, has long been under the rule of the Turks, and the minarets of Islam are ten times more numerous than the church belfries. In April, 1909, the Protestant and Gregorian congregations suffered one of the most cruel persecutions in history.

The people of my own home town, Yoghanolouk, are simple, industrious folk. For years past their chief occupation has been the sawing and polishing by hand of combs from hard wood and bone. Many of our men are also expert wood-carvers. In the neighbouring villages the chief occupations are the culture of silk worms for producing raw silk, and the weaving of silk by hand looms into handkerchiefs and scarves. Our people are very fond of their churches, and since the opening of schools by the American missionaries most of our children have learned to read. Every home is surrounded by mulberry trees, and many beautiful orchards cover the terraced slopes towards the south and west. Travellers who have been to Southern Italy tell us that the villages near Naples very much resemble ours. The broad, rough back of Mousa Dagh (*i.e.*, Mount Moses), known in Arabic as Jibal-al-Ahmar, rises up eastward behind us. Every gorge and crag of our beloved mountain is known to our boys and men.

I mention these facts about my village home so that you may feel something of the quiet happy life which was so rudely and so completely broken up by this last attempt of the Turks to exterminate our race.

Twelve days after I had reached home an official order from the Turkish Government at Antioch was served upon the six villages of Mousa Dagh to prepare for banishment within eight days. You can scarcely imagine the consternation and the indignation which this order caused. We sat up all night debating what it would be best to do. To resist the forces of the Turkish Government seemed almost hopeless, and yet the scattering of families into a distant wilderness, raided by fanatical and lawless Arab tribes, seemed such an appalling prospect that the inclination of both men and women was to refuse the summons and withstand the anger of the Government. All, however, were not of this mind. The Rev. Haroutune Nokhoudian, the pastor of the Protestant Church in Beitias, for example, came to the conviction that it would be folly to resist, and that the severity of banishment might possibly be modified in some way. He was in favour of yielding. Sixty families from his own village and a considerable number from the next village, agreeing with him, separated themselves from us and went down to Antioch under Turkish guards. They were shortly expelled in the direction of the lower Euphrates. (We have lost all track of them now and may never hear of them again.)

Our firm friends, the American missionaries, were cut off from us 120 miles to the north at Aintab. Communications with the outside world being practically severed, we were thrown upon our own resources, and we realised that our one hope was in the mercy of God. Fervently we prayed that He would strengthen us to do our duty.

Knowing that it would be impossible to defend our villages in the foot-hills, it was resolved to withdraw to the heights of Mousa Dagh, taking with us as large a supply of food and implements as it was possible to carry. All the flocks of sheep and goats were also driven up the mountain side, and every available weapon of defence was brought out and furbished up. We found that we had a hundred and twenty modern rifles and shot-guns, with perhaps three times that number of old flint-locks and horse-pistols. That still left more than half our men without weapons.

It was very hard to leave our homes. My mother wept as if her heart would break. But we had hopes that possibly, while we were fighting off the Turks, the Dardanelles might be forced and deliverance come to the country.

By nightfall of the first day we had reached the upper crags of the mountain. As we were preparing to camp and to cook the evening meal, a pouring rain set in and continued all night. For this we were ill prepared. There had not been time to make huts of branches, nor had we any tents or waterproof clothing. Men, women and children, somewhat over five thousand in all, were soaked to the skin, and much of the bread we had brought with us was turned into a pulpy mass. We were especially solicitous to keep our powder and rifles dry. This the men managed to do very well.

At dawn next morning all hands went to work digging trenches at the most strategic points in the ascent of the mountain. Where there was no earth for trench-digging, rocks were rolled together, making strong barricades behind which groups of our sharp-shooters were stationed. The sun came out gloriously, and we were hard at it all day strengthening our position against the attack which we knew was certain to come.

Towards evening we held a mass meeting for the election of a Committee of Defence which should have supreme authority for our six communities. Some favoured an election by show of hands, but others argued that, as this was a matter of such vital importance, the regular Congregational method of choice by secret ballot should be followed, and they offered to get together enough bits of paper to carry out the ballot! Our people have become very much attached to these democratic methods taught by the missionaries. Without much delay scraps of paper, more or less torn and wet, were gathered and the ballot was cast. A governing council thus being established, plans were at once made for defending each pass in the mountain and each approach to the camp. Scouts, messengers, and a central reserve group of sharp-shooters were chosen and were assigned their duties.

The summons from the Government had been served on the 13th July. The eight days' grace had now almost elapsed, and we were aware that the Turks must have discovered our movements. The whole Antioch plain is peopled with Turks and Arabs, and there is always a strong military garrison in the Antioch barracks.

On the 21st July the attack began. The advance guard was two hundred regulars, and their captain insolently boasted that he would clear the mountain in one day. But the Turks suffered several casualties and were driven back to the base. When they advanced for a more general attack, they dragged up a field gun which, after some experimentation, secured the range and wrought havoc in our camp. One of our sharp-shooters, a lion-hearted young fellow, crept down through the brushwood and among the rocks until he was in very close range of the field gun, which was mounted on a flat rock. Having made himself an ambush of branches, he watched for a good opportunity. He was so near that he could hear the Turks talking to one another as they loaded the gun. Then as one gunner stepped out into view, the young man picked him off with the first shot. With five bullets he killed four gunners! The captain thereupon threw up his hands in dismay, and, not being able to discern our sharp-shooter, ordered the gun to be dragged to a place of shelter. Thus were we saved from a disastrous gun-fire for that day and several days to come.

But the Turks were gathering forces for a massed attack. They had sent word through many Moslem villages, calling the people to arms. Army rifles and plentiful ammunition were handed out from the Antioch arsenal, until the mob of four thousand Moslems thirsting for massacre became a formidable foe. But the chief strength of the Turks was in the three thousand regular troops accustomed to discipline and inured to hardship.

Suddenly one morning our scouts brought word to headquarters that the enemy was appearing at every pass in the mountain. Here and there the Turks had already gained the cliffs and shoulders of the crest. Our reserve body of defenders was—very unwisely, as we afterwards realised—sent in small groups to these various points. No sooner had our forces been thus divided than a massed attack in great force commenced through one ravine. All the other advances had been feints and were not followed up. By the time our men discovered the situation and rallied from distant points, the Turks had shot down our scouts and had poured through an important pass. To our dismay we saw them already in full occupation of high ground, threatening our camp. Reinforcements kept pushing up the mountain, and as the afternoon drew on we saw that we were completely outnumbered. We saw also that the range of the Turks' rifles was far superior to that of our old-fashioned firearms. By sundown the enemy had advanced three companies through the dense underbush and forest to within four hundred yards of our huts. A deep damp ravine lay between, and the Turks decided to bivouac rather than to push on in the darkness.

Our leaders hurriedly took counsel together, whispering very quietly and not allowing any fight in camp. Everyone knew that a crisis had been reached. Finally a venturesome plan was adopted: to creep round the Turkish positions in the dead of night and thus carry out an enveloping movement, closing in very suddenly with a fusillade and ending with a hand to hand encounter. If this plan should fail, we knew that everything was lost. Through the dark wet woods our men crept with extraordinary skill. It was here that our familiarity with those crags and thickets made it possible to do what invaders could not attempt. The circle was practically completed when, with a flash and a crash on all sides, our men delivered their attack, rushing forward with desperate courage.

In a very few moments it was evident that bewilderment and alarm had thrown the Turkish camp into the utmost confusion. Troops were rushing hither and thither in the black night, stumbling over rocks and logs, officers shouting contradictory commands and struggling vainly to rally their men. Evidently the impression was given of a very substantial Armenian attack, because in less than half-an-hour the Turkish colonel gave the order to retreat, and before dawn the woods were practically clear of the troops. More than two hundred Turks had been killed and some booty taken—seven Mauser rifles, 2,500 rounds of ammunition and one mule. There was no sign of any renewal of fighting. But we knew that our foes were not defeated; they were only driven off.

During the next few days they roused the whole Mohammedan population for many miles around—a horde of perhaps 15,000. With this larger number they were able to surround and lay siege to Mousa Dagh on the landward side. Their plan was to starve us out. On the seaward side there was no harbour nor any communication with a seaport; the mountain sloped directly into the sea. We were fully occupied in the care of our wounded and the reparation of the damage done in camp. Special meetings were held to thank God for deliverance thus far, and to intercede with him for our families and little ones. Gregorians and Protestants were fused into one faith and fellowship by this baptism of suffering. It was at this time that my wife was confined and gave birth to her first child, a son. She suffered much in the flight down the seaward trail some days later, but I carried her and helped her as much as possible. Thank God, she is in good health now and so is our little son.

When we discovered that our mountain was in a state of siege, we began to estimate our food resources. During the first week on the heights we had exhausted the bread, olives and cheese that we had brought from home. Very few had been able to bring flour or other cereals, so for a month past we had been living on our flocks, using the goats' milk for the little children and the sick, and slaughtering a number of sheep and goats every day. This constant meat diet was not good for us, but on the other hand we were profoundly thankful that we were spared the suffering of starvation. We made a careful count of the flocks, and found that even with a reduced ration of meat our supply would last not more than two weeks longer. Under the pressure of this anxiety we began to think of plans for escape by sea.

Before the siege had entirely closed in, we had sent a runner to make the dangerous journey of eighty-five miles through Turkish villages to Aleppo, the capital of the province, with an appeal to the American Consul, Mr. Jackson, to send us help by sea if possible. But it is not at all likely that our runner ever reached Aleppo. It occurred to us that possibly a battleship of the Allies might be in Alexandretta harbour, thirty-five miles to the north. So one of our young men who was a strong swimmer volunteered to creep through the Turkish lines and take a message in English strapped inside his belt. He succeeded in reaching the hills overlooking the harbour, but saw that there was no battleship and returned. His plan had been to swim out to sea, circling round to reach the battleship, thus avoiding the Turkish sentries on the roads leading in to Alexandretta.

We then prepared triplicate copies of the following appeal and appointed three swimmers to be constantly on the watch for any passing ship, to strike through the surf and swim out at an angle so as to meet the vessel:—

"To any English, American, French, Italian or Russian admiral, captain or authority whom this petition may find; we appeal in the name of God and human brotherhood.

"We, the people of six Armenian villages, about 5,000 souls in all, have withdrawn to that part of Mousa Dagh called Damladjik, which is three hours journey north-west from Souedia along the sea-coast.

"We have taken refuge here from Turkish barbarism and torture, and most of all from the outraging of the honour of our women.

"Sir, you must have heard about the policy of annihilation which the Turks are applying to our nation. Under cover of dispersing the Armenians as if to avoid rebellion, our people are expelled from their houses and deprived of their gardens, their vineyards, and all their possessions.

"This brutal programme has already been applied to the city of Zeitoun and its thirty-two villages, to Albustan, Göksoun, Yarpouz, Gurin, Diyarbekir, Adana, Tarsus, Mersina, Dört Yöl, Hadjin, etc. And the same policy is being extended to all the one-and-a-half million Armenians in different parts of Turkey.

"The present writer was the Protestant pastor in Zeitoun a few months ago and was an eye-witness of many unspeakable cruelties. I saw families of eight or ten members driven along the highway, barefooted children six and seven years old by the side of aged grandparents, hungry and thirsty, their feet swollen from the toilsome journey. Along the road one heard sobs and curses and prayers. Under the pressure of great fear, some mothers gave birth to children in the bushes by the side of the road. Immediately afterward they were compelled by the Turkish guards to continue their journey till kind death arrived to give an end to their torture.

"The remainder of the people who were strong enough to bear the hardships of the march were driven on under the whips of gendarmes to the plains of the south. Some died of hunger. Others were robbed along the way. Others were stricken by malaria and had to be left by the roadside. And, as a last act of this dark and foul tragedy, the Arabs and Turks massacred all the males and distributed the widows and girls among their tribes.

"The Government some forty days ago informed us that our six villages must go into exile. Rather than submit to this we withdrew to this mountain. We have now little food left, and the troops are besieging us. We have had five fierce battles. God has given us the victory, but the next time we shall have to withstand a much larger force.

"Sir, we appeal to you in the name of Christ!

"Transport us, we pray you, to Cyprus or any other free land. Our people are not indolent; we will earn our own bread if we are employed.

"If this is too much to grant, transport at least our women, old people and children, equip us with sufficient arms, ammunition and food, and we will work with you with all our might against the Turkish forces. Please, Sir, do not wait until it is too late!

"Respectfully your servant, for all the Christians here,

Dikran Andreasian."

September 2.

But days passed and not even a sail was seen. The war had reduced the coastwise shipping to a minimum. Meanwhile, at my suggestion, our women had been making two immense flags, on one of which I printed in large, clear English, "CHRISTIANS IN DISTRESS: RESCUE." This was a white flag with black lettering. The other was also white with a large red cross at the centre. We fastened these flags to tall saplings and set a watch at the foot to scan the horizon from dawn to dark. Some days we had rain and on others heavy mists and fogs, which are rather prevalent along our bit of coast.

The Turks again attacked us by several approaches, and we had some severe fighting, but never at such close quarters as during the first general engagement. From one point of vantage we were able to roll boulders down the precipitous mountain side with disastrous effects to the enemy. Our powder and cartridges were running low, and the Turks evidently had some idea of the straits we were in, for they began shouting insolent summons to surrender. Those were anxious days and long nights!

One Sunday morning, the fifty-third day of our defence, while I was occupied in preparing a brief sermon to encourage and strengthen our people, I was startled by hearing a man shouting at the top of his voice. He came racing through our encampment straight for my hut. "Pastor, pastor," he exclaimed, "a battleship is coming and has answered our waving!—Thank God!—Our prayers are heard. When we wave the Red Cross flag the battleship answers by waving signal flags. They see us and are coming in nearer shore!"

This proved to be the French *Guichen*, a four-funnel ship. While one of its boats was being lowered, some of our young men raced down to the shore and were soon swimming out to the stately vessel which seemed to have been sent to us from God! With beating hearts we hurried down to the beach, and soon an invitation came from the Captain for a delegation to come on board and explain the situation. He sent a wireless to the Admiral of the fleet, and before very long the flag-ship *Ste. Jeanne d'Arc* appeared on the horizon followed by other French battleships. The Admiral spoke words of comfort and cheer to us, and gave an order that every soul of our community should be taken on board the ships. The embarkation took some time, of course, and an English cruiser was invited to take part in the transportation to Port Said, Egypt. We were taken on board four French cruisers and one English, and were very kindly cared for. In two days we arrived at Port Said, and are now settled in a permanent camp which has been provided for us by the British authorities.

We are especially grateful to Mr. William C. Hornblower for the excellent organisation of this camp, and to Col. and Mrs. P.G. Elgood and Miss Russell for their untiring efforts on our behalf.

The Armenian Red Cross Society of Cairo, recently organised, of which the Gregorian Bishop is Honorary Chairman, Mr. Fermanian of the Kodak Company, Director, and Prof. Kayayan, Secretary, has sent us a staff of three doctors and three nurses.

An accurate census has been taken which shows that the survivors number:—

427	babies and children under four years of age,
508	girls from 4 to 14,
628	boys from 4 to 14,
1,441	women above 14 years of age,
1,054	men above 14.
4,058	total number of souls rescued.

After the Turks' first challenge, on the 13th July, we had eight days' parley and preparation; for fifty-three days we defended ourselves on Mousa Dagh; and a two days' voyage brought us to Port Said on the 14th September.

We do not forget that our Saviour was brought in His infancy to Egypt for safety and shelter. And the brethren of Joseph could not have been more grateful than we are for the corn and wheat provided.

131. JIBAL MOUSA: REPORT, DATED EGYPT, 28th SEPTEMBER, 1915, ON THE ARMENIAN REFUGEES RESCUED AND TRANSPORTED TO PORT SAID BY THE CRUISERS OF THE FRENCH FLEET; DRAWN UP BY MGR. THORGOM, BISHOP OF THE GREGORIAN COMMUNITY IN EGYPT.

(1.) *Number of the Refugees.*

Approximately accurate statistics have been made out here, which show that the refugees number 4,200, including:—

915	Men
1,408	Women
702	Boys
539	Girls
636	Infants
4,200	

(2.) *Origin of the Refugees.*

They all come from the villages of Selefka (Kaza of Leffia, Sandjak of Antakia, Vilayet of Aleppo), including:—

80	families from the village of	Makof
10	,, ,, ,,	Keboussia
160	,, ,, ,,	Kheder Bey
228	,, ,, ,,	Yoghanolouk
220	,, ,, ,,	Hadji-Habibli
170	,, ,, ,,	Beitias
868		

But these families do not represent the total number of families inhabiting each village, for

240	families in the village of	Keboussia
2	,, ,, ,,	Yoghanolouk

80	” ” ”	Hadji-Habibli
10	” ” ”	Beitias
332		

that is, 332 families in all, remained at home and were subsequently deported by the Turkish Government.

(3.) *Circumstances of the Insurrection and Exodus.*

The Turkish Government, in pursuance of its policy of clearing Armenia of the Armenians, had ordered, after the fall of Van, the deportation of all Armenian families. This order reached Selefka on the 30th July;[169] a week's grace was given for its execution. The villagers met together and, in spite of the advice of several of their leading members and of their priests, decided to revolt and die like brave men, rather than undergo the fate of the people of Zeitoun, Hadjin and Dört-Yöl.

These 868 families retired on to the mountain called Mousa Dagh, taking with them their cattle and supplies for several months.

Before leaving their villages, the insurgents invited the people of Kessab to join them. Kessab is separated from Selefka by a little stream, which was guarded by Turkish gendarmes. They were, therefore, unable to enter into direct communication with them, but they received a letter (we have seen this letter, and we have reason to believe that it was a fabrication of the Turkish Government's) in which the people of Kessab, who have a special reputation for bravery, purport to advise their neighbours of Selefka to submit to the Turkish authorities.

The period of grace expired on the 8th August, but they had already withdrawn into the mountains in the first days of August. On the 8th, the first collision took place between the Armenians and 200 regular troops; it lasted six hours.

The Armenians had barely 600 fighting men, armed with 150 Martini rifles and 450 shot guns. Four fighting men directed operations, eight guarded the non-combatants, and forty picketed the paths. The non-combatants dug out shelter trenches for the people and children, or made munitions, while the women looked after the food.

On one occasion a woman was bringing up water to the firing line; her jar was riddled by an enemy bullet, upon which the woman coolly put down the jar, plugged the hole and went to get fresh water, all under the enemy's fire. I cite this incident because I have been told that the rest took courage from the coolness of this woman to resist courageously to the end.

The insurgents had not forgotten to bring with them the sacred vessels from their churches, so that the five priests who were with them celebrated mass, and a pastor preached every evening.

On the 12th August, the second collision occurred with the Turks, who had 2,000 troops with two guns; it lasted twelve hours. On the 16th and 17th there were two violent encounters with regular troops, reinforced by Kurdish and Arab bashibazouks, 4,800 troops in all; during this encounter the Armenians captured from the enemy seven Mausers and 15,000 cartridges, as well as other munitions and equipment.

There followed an interval of twenty days; on the twenty-first, a serious battle with 7,000 soldiers, including 4,000 regulars.

From the very first days of the insurrection, the Armenians had sent down to the seashore a party of twenty people, who were relieved every 24 hours. They had with them a letter addressed to the Allied Powers, in which they prayed for help. They had hoisted a big flag—a red cross on a white ground—to attract the attention of the Allied fleet.

The Allied fleet was blockading the Turkish Mediterranean ports, and a French flotilla was on duty there. The armoured cruiser *Guichen* saw the flag, and the commander, Captain Joseph Brisson, put out a boat. A brave old Armenian threw himself into the water, and clambered on board the cruiser. The commander, moved by the heroism of this old man and by the details which he communicated to him, sent a wireless message to the commander of the cruiser *Jeanne d'Arc*, at Port Said. The *Jeanne d'Arc* arrived within 24 hours. The same day, the *Guichen* bombarded the neighbourhood of the church at Keboussia, which the Turks were attacking in order to massacre the Armenians who had taken refuge in the building. Meanwhile, a further wireless message from the Admiral on board the *Jeanne d'Arc* brought the armoured cruiser *Desaix* to the spot within another 24 hours, with an Armenian dragoman on board. The *Jeanne d'Arc* went off to Cyprus, and despatched three other armoured cruisers from there. The united squadron began to bombard the Turkish positions, to enable the 4,200 Armenians to come down to the water's edge, where they were embarked on board the cruisers. The embarkation took a day and a half.

The fighting had begun on the 8th August and ended on the 10th September. The Armenians had 20 killed and 16 wounded; the enemy had about 300 killed and more than 600 wounded.

We had already learnt these facts while the insurgents were still on their voyage, but we did not know where it was intended to land them. Cyprus, Algeria and Tunis were all suggested; then we heard that the French and British Governments were in consultation on the subject. On the 14th

September they arrived at Port Said. Sir Henry MacMahon, the High Commissioner, and General Maxwell gave immediate attention to the refugees. His Majesty the Sultan of Egypt sent a donation of £250.

The French Fleet entertained the refugees three days, and since then the British Government has taken charge of them. The first to be embarked on board the four cruisers were the old men, the women and the children; the fighting men remained two days longer on land. They asked for munitions to keep up the struggle, but the Admiral, acting on instructions received from his Government, refused their request, and so they arrived in Egypt two days later.

(4.) *The Situation of the Refugees at Port Said.*

They are installed in the Lazaretto, consisting of five or six stone buildings, and in 500 tents pitched round it. Everything has been organised by the military authorities. The tents are pitched in ranks divided into groups; each tent has its tent-commander, with a pennant and a number, and each group of tents has its group-commander, with a flag.

They have built them a large kitchen, conduits and baths. Two of the stone buildings are being used for office work, and the rest have been turned into hospitals.

The general state of health is good; there are about 80 sick, including the wounded.

The refugees have all the looks of a fighting race. They speak a dialect, but they are all orthodox members of the Armenian Church, except for an inconsiderable number of Catholics and Protestants.

At present the Government does not allow them to go outside the zone assigned to them.

The distribution of rations is punctually and methodically carried out.

(5.) *Maintenance of the Refugees.*

The Government has undertaken their maintenance, and it is believed that this arrangement will continue.

(*a*) *Hospital.*—Kept up by the Armenian Red Cross of Cairo. The Government, however, has also provided a head doctor and three assistants, two of them women. The Red Cross has contributed £120 for medical stores.

(*b*) *Clothes.*—The Armenian Red Cross of Cairo and Alexandria has made itself responsible for them.

(*c*) *Education.*—There are 1,000 children. The Government has placed a large tent at their disposal for use as a school. The General Armenian Union of Benevolence has undertaken the expense of their education.

(*d*) *Workshops.*—To give the refugees employment, work has been found for those who know how to make combs, wooden spoons, etc. The men will have money advanced to them as capital, and the women wool to knit stockings and socks, to give them an opportunity of setting to work and earning a living.

The approach of winter causes some anxiety, but we hope that the Government and the Armenian community in Egypt will take the necessary steps for securing them against the cold.

169. The dates given in this report do not tally with those in Mr. Andreasian's narrative, except that both accounts put the arrival of the refugees at Port Said on the 14th September. Mr. Andreasian puts the intervention of the *Guichen* on Sunday, the 12th September; but as he also states that the voyage took two days, while the present report makes the embarkation take a day and a half, the date given here for the appearance of the *Guichen* upon the scene, namely, the 10th September, is probably correct. On the other hand, Mr. Andreasian speaks from first-hand knowledge when he places the official summons to deportation on the 13th July (instead of the 30th July), the first fighting on the 21st July (instead of the 8th August) and the total length of the siege at 53 days; so that his statements on these points are likely to be more accurate.—EDITOR.

132. JIBAL MOUSA: ANOTHER REPORT ON THE REFUGEES AT PORT SAID, DRAWN UP BY MR. TOVMAS K. MUGGERDICHIAN, FORMERLY DRAGOMAN OF THE BRITISH CONSULATE AT DIYARBEKIR.

You must certainly have heard that, on the 14/27th September (1915), five armoured cruisers (four French and one English) brought to Port Said 4,200 Armenians from the six villages of the Selefka district, who have been given shelter in the Lazaretto, on the banks of the Suez Canal. I am happy to be able to tell you that the Anglo-Egyptian Government has kindly undertaken to house and feed these refugees until such time as they may be able to return to their country.

A little band of heroes from Selefka, hardly five to six hundred combatants, held out for fifty-five whole days against Captain Rifaat Bey and the force under his command—3,000 Nizam troops and more than 4,000 bashibazouks (Arabs and Turks), until the cruiser *Guichen* saw the flag in the form of a cross which these heroes had hoisted on the Mousa Mountain. This warship, with four others, went to their assistance and rescued them. These fine fellows had not more than 120 Gras rifles and about 400 flintlocks and shot guns. Sixty of them were good shots, and they picked off the Turkish artillerymen one by one, thus reducing their guns to silence—so much so that Rifaat Bey cried out: "These good Giaours sight through the needle's eye," and took to his heels. The Armenian fighting men of Selefka have had seventeen killed and twelve wounded, but they have killed fifty times as many of the enemy.

There are hardly 1,000 grown men among the refugees; the rest are women, girls, children and infants. The boys and girls less than fourteen years of age, who are by way of going to school, number about 800; there are also three men teachers and three women, five priests and the Pastor of Zeitoun, the Reverend Dikran Andreasian. Babies have been born on the Jibal Mousa, on board the warships and at Port Said. All these refugees are in need of clothes, for they have been able to rescue nothing, except their wives and children and their arms.

The "Armenian Red Cross," recently formed at Cairo, set itself to look after the wounded and the sick as early as the third day after the arrival of the refugees at Port Said. By General Maxwell's orders, the Director of the Intelligence Office gave the Armenian Red Cross official authorisation to work at Port Said in the Refugees' Camp. At present we have about seventy sick; all the wounded are on the road to recovery. The whole Armenian colony in Egypt has shown an exemplary diligence in collecting clothes, shoes, soap, combs, etc., in the name of the Armenian Red Cross, and in forwarding them to the refugees.

I have interviewed His Excellency Yakoub Artin Pasha to urge that the Armenian General Union should undertake to supply clothes to the refugees, and should occupy itself especially with the question of their education, which constitutes one of their most urgent requirements. His Excellency promised me to make all the necessary arrangements.

I am glad to be able to tell you that the refugees are happy to be at Port Said. At the same time, it is said that about 400 good fighting men proposed, and even begged, that they should be sent back to Turkey to bring aid to their compatriots who have taken refuge in the mountains.

It is regrettable that in such Armenian centres as Zeitoun, Hadjin and Kessab[170] the Armenians surrendered to the tyrannical Turkish Government by the urgent orders of His Grace the Katholikos of Sis. All these Armenians have been deported into the desert situated between Aleppo, Der-el-Zor and Mosul. These deported people have endured unheard of tortures and sufferings in the course of their journey; the women and girls have suffered savage outrages. It is said that the road is covered with unburied corpses of men, women and children; in fact, the refugees who have arrived at Port Said have seen these corpses with their own eyes, and it was the cumulative effect of all this that made the inhabitants of the six villages of Selefka decide to retire into the mountains and defend themselves.

Since the month of May, I have had no direct news from Harpout or Diyarbekir, but the news which I have gathered from other quarters is very disquieting.

The first news received from Marash, Aintab and Killis was good, but the last news, which comes from a trustworthy source, is equally disquieting. It is said that there have been massacres at Marash, and that the survivors, together with the Armenian inhabitants of Aintab and Killis, have been deported bodily to the deserts to the south of the province of Aleppo. We hear likewise that the Armenian population of Mersina and Adana and the neighbouring villages has been deported.

---

170. See Doc. 143 page 559.

XVII.
THE TOWNS OF OURFA AND AC.

The Armenian colony in Ourfa is the southernmost outpost of Armenia east of the Euphrates, as the Jibal Mousa villages are of Armenian Cilicia. Here, too, for many months, the Armenians had before their eyes the fate of their compatriots from the north, for Ourfa is the half-way house on the road from Diyarbekir to Aleppo, and the remnants of many convoys from Mamouret-ul-Aziz, Erzeroum and beyond passed this way on their journey to the Arabian desert. Thus, when the order for deportation came in due course to Ourfa, towards the end of September, 1915, they took the same action that the villagers of Jibal Mousa had taken two months before. They fortified themselves in their quarter of the town and resisted the order by force, for they knew that it was simply the first stage in their methodical extermination.

Unhappily, the result of the struggle here was not the same as at Jibal Mousa, and, indeed, the Armenians at Ourfa were in a hopeless position from the first. They were far away from the sea, and even in the town itself they were only a minority of the population. A fully equipped expeditionary force of Turkish regulars was immediately sent against them, and they succumbed, after resisting desperately for a month.

The town of AC. was another important Armenian outpost on the south-eastern fringe, which cannot be mentioned by its real name without compromising the persons referred to in the documents relating to it. The Armenians at AC. did not resist, and the process of deportation here followed its normal course.

133. OURFA: LETTER DATED OURFA, 14th JUNE, 1915, FROM MR. K.; COMMUNICATED BY THE AMERICAN COMMITTEE FOR ARMENIAN AND SYRIAN RELIEF.

I wish to inform you of conditions here. They are very bad, and daily getting worse. I suppose the U.'s told you of the horrible things taking place in Diyarbekir. Just such a reign of terror has begun in this city also. Daily the police are searching the houses of the Armenians for weapons, and, not finding any, they are taking the best and most honourable men and imprisoning them; some of them they are exiling, and others they are torturing with red-hot irons to make them reveal the supposedly concealed weapons. Four weeks ago they exiled fifteen men and their families, sending them to the desert city of Rakka, three days' journey south of here.

The Gendarmerie Department seems to have full control of affairs, and the Mutessarif upholds them. They are now holding about a hundred of the best citizens of the city in prison, and to-day the gendarmerie chief called the Armenian Bishop and told him that unless the Armenians deliver up their arms and denounce the revolutionists among them he has orders to exile the entire Armenian population of Ourfa, as they did the people of Zeitoun. We know how the latter were treated, for hundreds of them have been dragged through Ourfa on their way to the desert whither they have been exiled. These poor exiles were mostly women, children and old men, and they were clubbed and beaten and lashed along as though they had been wild animals. Their women and girls were daily criminally outraged, both by their guards and by the ruffians of every village through which they passed, as the former allowed the latter to enter the camp of the exiles at night, and even distributed the girls among the villagers for the night.

These poor victims of their oppressors' lust and hate might better have died by the bullet in their mountain home than be dragged about the country in this way. About two thousand of them have passed through Ourfa, all more dead than alive; many hundreds had died already from starvation and abuse along the roadside, and indeed nearly all are dying of starvation or thirst, or through being kidnapped by the Anaza Arabs in the desert where they have been taken. We know how they are being treated, because our Ourfa exiles are in the same place, and one young Armenian doctor, who was there making medical examinations of soldiers for the Government, has returned and told us[171].

Now this is the fate which is in store for the Ourfa Armenians also, unless someone delivers them. Having seen how the Zeitoun exiles have been treated, the Ourfa Armenians have said they will never submit to exile but will die in their homes instead, and who can blame them? We greatly fear that the cruel persecuting attitude of the gendarmerie in seizing, beating, and torturing the people will drive some of them to such desperation that they will resist, and that will surely provoke a general massacre. Up to date the Armenian Bishop and Protestant pastors have been most earnest and successful in keeping the young men, especially, under restraint, and this has prevented any outburst thus far, but as the Government is daily taking the wisest and best leaders of the people and imprisoning them, there are few left to restrain the others. The officers of the Government told the Armenian Bishop plainly that unless they delivered up their arms the Armenians here would be destroyed, but the people fear to deliver up their arms, for they remember that in 1895 the Government made all the Christians deliver up their arms and, as soon as they had done so, the Moslems fell upon the Christians and killed six thousand of them in two days. Now, if the Government would make the Moslems give up their weapons also, the Christians would cheerfully deliver up theirs, but the Government is not taking weapons from the Moslems. Ourfa is not a revolutionary centre and never has been. The people here have always been loyal to the Government and have never resisted, not even when they were butchered like sheep. Why the local Government persists in persecuting a population that has always had a good record for loyalty is very strange. There is no revolutionary organisation here; there may be thirty or forty men of revolutionary beliefs, but there has been no propaganda and no organisation.

134. OURFA: EXTRACT FROM A LETTER[172] BY MR. TOVMAS K. MUGGERDICHIAN; PUBLISHED IN THE ARMENIAN JOURNAL "GOTCHNAG," OF NEW YORK, 1st APRIL, 1916.

I had an interview with Mr. B. and Miss A. about the events in Turkey which they had witnessed before they escaped to Cairo.

Miss A. (an Englishwoman) was the principal of the orphanage at AC. for 18 years, and is acquainted with the Turkish language. She and Mr. B. passed through Aleppo, BF. and BJ., and have collected their information from trustworthy sources in these centres.

Two Armenians returned to Aleppo from Ourfa and reported that a Persian prince had arrived in Ourfa from Constantinople with the Ottoman deputy for Baghdad (probably Babanzadé Ismail Hakki Bey) and that they were the guests of Herr Jacob Künzler, a German-Swiss. Herr Künzler went with them to Severeg and on his return told some friends, among whom were the two Armenians aforementioned, that there was no more deliverance for the Armenians. The deputy for Baghdad had said to him: "It was decided in the Ottoman Parliament that we should massacre all the Armenians. We will not leave a single Armenian alive, and thus we will correct the old Sultan's mistake." At the same time he regretted that Herr Eckhard had betrayed the Armenians and excited the Turks against them. Herr Eckhard—the ex-president of the German Orphanage at Ourfa, and now the head of the shop and rug factory—is a German artillery captain, who came to Ourfa after the massacres of 1895-1896 as a missionary and a spy. In the autumn of 1915 he encouraged the Turkish, Kurdish and Arab mobs to attack the Armenians, and was responsible for a three-fold repetition of the massacres. The first massacre took place on the 19th August, 1915, in which 250 Armenians were killed; the second took place on the 23rd September, and lasted for a week, in which about 300 persons were killed and the city looted; the third took place about the 1st October. First, all the Armenians were ordered to get ready to go to Der-el-Zor. When they objected, saying that they had lost everything and had nothing left to take with them, Fakhri Pasha ordered them to be massacred. The massacre lasted 10 days. The German artillerymen destroyed the Armenian quarters, the church and everything, thus putting an end to the Armenian population of Ourfa.

It was then that the Rev. Apelian, the druggist Apraham Attarian, Solomon Effendi Knadjian, A. Abouhayatian and Hagopian were imprisoned on the demand of Herr Eckhard. The Rev. Apelian, Attarian and Hagopian were hanged, and Knadjian and Abouhayatian were shot.

---

171. See Doc. 144

172. Date unspecified; the place of writing was apparently Cairo.

135. OURFA: INTERVIEW WITH MRS. J. VANCE YOUNG, AN EYE-WITNESS OF THE EVENTS AT OURFA; PUBLISHED IN THE "EGYPTIAN GAZETTE," 28th SEPTEMBER/11th OCTOBER, AND REPRODUCED IN THE ARMENIAN JOURNAL "HOUSSAPER" OF CAIRO, 30th SEPTEMBER/13th OCTOBER, 1915.

Mrs. J. Vance Young is the wife of an English doctor at Beirout[173], and arrived in Egypt on board the American cruiser "Chester." She was among the last arrivals in this country from Alexandretta, and brought with her terrible details regarding the martyrdom of the Armenians at Ourfa. She was an eye-witness of the occurrences in this ill-famed town, which has been drenched so many times in Armenian blood.

An interview with Mrs. Young was published in the "Egyptian Gazette" of the 28th September, and we reproduce the following lines, which present the ghastly picture of the massacre:—

"On the 19th August the fusillade began, about five o'clock in the evening. We heard it during supper-time, and it lasted far into the night.

"Next morning Dr. J. Vance Young ventured to make his way into the town to see if he could be of any service. He saw all the streets littered with corpses. He got the impression that there was not a single Armenian left in Ourfa.

"It appeared that the massacres had been organised in advance, for a systematic domiciliary visit was made to every Armenian house; the men were shot or otherwise assassinated, while the women were driven from their houses with their children, to be marched away to the desert and perish there of hunger.

"All along the road from Ourfa to the coast Mrs. Young saw hundreds of putrified corpses, and also a few miserable survivors. The latter looked more like wild beasts than human creatures. She described this spectacle as being literally sufficient to unhinge one's reason.

"Almost all the business men at Ourfa were Armenians. Now they have all been massacred, including the sole chemist capable of mixing drugs."

173. One of the four hundred foreigners of Entente nationality in the Syrian provinces who were interned at Ourfa after the outbreak of war.

136. OURFA: POSTSCRIPT TO A MEMORANDUM (DOC. 141) BY A FOREIGN WITNESS FROM ALEPPO; COMMUNICATED BY THE AMERICAN COMMITTEE FOR ARMENIAN AND SYRIAN RELIEF.

Towards the end of September, the Armenians in Ourfa were ordered to leave the town and to be exiled as the Armenians in all the towns of this region have been. They refused to leave, however, and finally orders were given to expel them forcibly, and, if they offered any resistance, to take the necessary measures. They entrenched themselves strongly in their quarter, built barricades, made subterranean passages from one part of the quarter to another, and generally took every measure possible to defend themselves against attack. A force of about 6,000 soldiers, including artillery, under the command of Fakhri Pasha, commenced operations against them, and their quarter was bombarded during the first weeks of October. The Armenians were all supplied with rifles and ammunition, and had even managed to obtain mitrailleuses. They had apparently sufficient food to withstand a siege of some duration. We heard about the middle of October that seven officers and about 400 men had been killed on the Turkish side. By some means or other the Armenians managed to obtain possession of Mr. K. and seven belligerents who had been interned in Ourfa. These eight men were retained by them in their quarter as hostages. Mr. Jackson reported the detention of Mr. K. to the Embassy, which, of course, took the necessary steps in the matter, and about the 20th October a telegram was received in Aleppo from Mr. K. reporting that he was out of the Armenian quarter and safe. What happened to the seven belligerents could not be ascertained.

The position of the belligerents who are interned in Ourfa is naturally somewhat critical. It has caused considerable anxiety to the foreign consular officials in Aleppo, and they desire more urgently than ever that these belligerents should be removed to some place where they would be in greater safety.

137. AC.: STATEMENT BY MISS A., A FOREIGN RESIDENT AT AC., WRITTEN SUBSEQUENTLY TO HER DEPARTURE FROM TURKEY IN SEPTEMBER, 1915; COMMUNICATED BY THE REV. I.N. CAMP, OF CAIRO.

It was in March, 1915, that the first refugees began to pass through AC. After they had once begun to come, there was scarcely a day when one or more parties did not pass through. Some were large, and some consisted of only five or six hundred. With the exception of one party, they all had to stay out in an open field without any protection from the cold and rain, or later, when summer came, from the burning sun. The exception was a party from BM., who had paid £400 (Turkish) for the privilege of resting under some trees where there was water. This place was only five minutes' walk from the field where other parties were obliged to camp.

I myself one day saw an old woman beaten because, when opportunity came, she rushed off to get some water for a sick child. I do not want to give the impression that no one was allowed to get water, but I suppose the privilege was given according to the "bakshish" that had been paid. There were also some gendarmes who seemed to be thoroughly ashamed of their work, and who, so far as they dared, were merciful.

Each party had its own tale of horror. With few exceptions, they had been robbed; young wives and girls had been carried off; many had been dishonoured; many people had been brutally treated and had died on the road. One large party that had been on the march for four weeks were put into houses at Albustan, the occupants of which had been previously deported. They thought then that their journey was over, and held a praise-meeting after being comfortably settled. But they were at the mercy of the Turks, and all their young women and girls were carried off. Then they were sent on the march again; some of the girls were returned by the Turks, but most of them were kept.

The hard part for them was that they never got to the end of their journey. Just as soon as they thought they were at their destination and began to settle down and get a little work to do, they would at once be sent away from that place to another. We heard also that if money was given them they were obliged to move on. Any effort to give relief was looked upon as a defiance of the Government.

One Sunday afternoon a large party of refugees came to AC. just at sunset. We heard they were faint with hunger, but no one was allowed to give them any relief. We knew that there might be an opportunity to give some relief after dark, if any one ventured to go then. Feeling that I must do something, I took our matron and went to see what we could do. As we drew near the camp, we met some Armenians who were on the watch for a chance to give out some bread, and who told us that it would evidently be impossible for us to give any food that night, but that perhaps we could give some in the morning. The next morning, before dawn, we went again and found about four hundred Armenians of AC. along the road. As they saw us passing, some called out: "It is no use for you to go; no one is allowed near." However, we passed on, and when we got to where the gendarme was, he very crossly ordered us away. It was light by this time. Our matron appealed to him for a long time without avail. Finally, however, he said: "Well, give what you have quickly; but this (pointing to me) must not go any further than here." While we were distributing the food, the gendarme got angry and ordered me away. Then three horsemen appeared on the scene. They scolded the man in charge because he had not already got the refugees started on their march, and told him he was too lenient with them. One of them leaped from his horse, and with a whip in each hand went towards the AC. Armenians, who at once fled. He came to me and gave me a lash or two with the whip. I asked him what harm I was doing. He came again and shook me, saying: "You are from BN." (I had to dress as an Armenian in order to get to the refugees at all.) One of the two other officers came deliberately towards me with the intention of riding me down, but the horse turned his head after only bruising my arm. The matron, an Armenian woman, on seeing it, said: "She has done nothing wrong. She is no BN-li. Your horse is more merciful than you." We turned to go, and to my surprise the horsemen began speaking German with one another. So far as I was able to tell, they were not Turks but German officers. When we got on to higher ground, we saw these three men ride on in the direction of BM. The refugees were sent in the opposite direction, and all the time they were preparing to start they were being beaten. Other gendarmes arrived, and from every direction came the screams of the people as the whips touched them.

One evening, Dr. E. and Mr. F. went for a walk just at dusk. They saw along the road what they at first took to be a bundle of rags, about which scavenger dogs were circling, but on going nearer they found it to be a dying woman. After she had been refreshed by some warm milk which Dr. E. brought, she said: "Would that you had not brought me this, for I had longed to die." She soon did die. She was a rather young woman, and it was found out soon after her death that she was from a very good family.

Occasionally Dr. E. could get permission for a sick woman to stay until she was better; she would then be sent on with a later party. The first woman he helped in this way went on after a few weeks' rest with her new-born baby, but the second woman died[174]. On another occasion, the head Armenian nurse at the hospital had been sent down with some necessaries to help a party. When she first got to the place, the gendarme refused to let her pass. She begged him, as he hoped for mercy from Allah himself, to allow her to go to the woman in particular need. Finally, he gave permission, but, having already given the order for the party to move on, he said that little time was left. When they were ready to depart, the gendarme began to beat the father of the baby, and even gave the mother of a few hours a lash with his whip. The nurse protested, and said that, if the poor woman must go on, an animal must be given her; so the gendarme went forward a few steps, knocked an old man off his donkey, and told the husband of the woman to put her on. We heard later that the woman died before she got to the opposite end of the city.

Every party would bring with them either old people who had been left on the road or children whose mothers had died and who had been left behind. Whenever we went to see refugees, the piteous appeals we heard to save young women and girls from the Turks were heart-rending. And we were powerless to help them! Again and again we were threatened with what would be done to anyone who dared to help any of the refugees. But in spite of these threats several of the AC. people took babies who were left without any relatives. It was beautiful to see the love shown to these babies, many of whom were not at all attractive. The sad part of it was that, when the turn of the people of AC. came to go, some were too poor to take these adopted children along with them; but all did so who possibly could. One good man had adopted a sick baby and a lame girl. When he and his large family were deported, he came to ask me whether I could take or support his own three-months-old baby, in return for which he offered me two rings, all that he could spare.

As the refugees were driven from their mountain homes, the blind, lame, and invalids were at first left in BM. But after a time even they were driven forth. They left AC. one hot afternoon, about three hundred in number, under the care of a brave young widow, who had had charge of them all the time. There were only fourteen donkeys for the whole party.

When people left their homes, it was natural that they should want to take as much as possible along with them—mats, food, clothing, &c. Villagers who owned animals, especially muleteers, were the best off, because when others wanted animals the Turks asked such exorbitant prices that the poor people did not know what to do, especially if they had old people or young children in their families. So the owners of animals, not having to hire any of the Turks, were better off. The load-animal question became more and more difficult as the refugees got farther away from their homes, till some in desperation would leave their few possessions by the wayside. The gendarmes generally told them that their goods would be forwarded to them. But in the case of some goods that one party had left nine hours from AC., we know that a gendarme brought them on to the city and sold them by public auction.

Dr. L. asked whether he might go to the places where needy refugees were, and give them some help, if he could get any money from the United States. This request was most emphatically refused. He said: "Why, they will die." The answer of the Turkish official was: "What do you suppose they are sent there for?"

When the first parties came, the Government sometimes issued bread, but this policy did not last long. Sometimes the people of the city would be allowed to give bread, but this was rare. There were always people waiting for a chance to get near and give aid to the refugees. We were on the opposite side of the city, but our colleagues were nearer to the refugees. So the head of the institution gave permission for the food to be cooked there. Then it would be taken secretly by the students to the refugees. Usually only one guard was on duty at night, so the food was usually sent down at three or four in the morning, the best being given to the guard in order that he might allow it to pass in. Later on, the women of the city formed a committee and collected food from anyone able to give it. There was also a relief committee of four, who did a great deal towards alleviating the distress by giving bread and by furnishing native shoes to those who had none. Later, one of the lay members of this committee, the one who had been most active in the relief work, was the first among the people of AC., after the exemption of the Protestants, to be deported. When he asked why he had to go, he was told that it was because he had fed the enemies of the Government.

If I remember correctly, it was either on the 30th or the 31st July that the first people from AC. were deported. First the richest families of the Gregorians, and, later, the richest Protestants, were sent away. Just as the Protestants were leaving, we heard a rumour that they would not have to go, but they were hurried straight through to Hama, and other places, without the long delays on the road that others had had. We thought it was done purposely. The first party that went were attacked before they got to their first night's stopping-place, and had to protect their wives and daughters all night long. We heard later from Dr. L., who was then in Aleppo, that he had seen many of them and been told their story: how they had to be on the alert all night long; how one or two were killed and some wounded, and how one had gone mad. Before we got this news, the brother of one of our teachers, who had been sent into the city by the officer whose servant he was, told us that while nearing the city the previous evening he had seen the Mutessarif's son and four or five companions, all well armed, riding quickly out of the city in the direction in which the refugees had gone. We all thought that he had perhaps been sent to recall them, and were quite expecting to see them all come back again. Later, we understood that it was this party who had attacked and robbed them.

Soon after the first party of Protestants were sent away, Dr. E. received telegrams from the U.S. Ambassador, from the Consul in Aleppo, and from Mr. N. of Constantinople, saying that there would be no deportation of Protestants. Dr. E. took the three telegrams to the Mutessarif, who was not pleased and said that he had received no such news. Still, for a short time all was quiet, and it being time for College to open, the matter was talked over. Before any decision was reached, a student, a Turk, went to Dr. E. and asked when it would open, as if he were anxious to be back. Dr. E. took this as a sign that the Turks were not only willing but anxious for the College to begin; so, after conferring with the faculty, he told the enquiring Turk that they would open the following week. This, I think, was on Friday, and on Saturday all but two of the professors and teachers had notice that they must leave the city the following Monday morning. Dr. E. pleaded for time, but the Mutessarif was angry and asked him whether he did not know that he had power to send him away too if he wished to do so.

The professors were sent away the following Monday morning. A German lady, Mrs. C., formerly Miss D., who was the matron of the hospital at AC., was ordered to go along with her husband, an Armenian professor, into exile. When Dr. E. went to the Mutessarif about it, he answered: "Is she not his property, and is he not an Armenian?" The German Consul was not able to get permission for her to leave the country when her husband was anxious for her to get away. We heard later from Mrs. C. that they had only got just outside the city when a gendarme came round to each of them and said that, if they wanted to be guarded, they must give money. This they did. When they reached a little wayside station, they found many thousands of refugees waiting in an open field. On the fourth day of waiting, Mrs. C. saw some German officers on a train, and obtained from them a pass which enabled her to board the train for Aleppo. On the fifth day, she and her husband and baby were allowed to go by train to Aleppo, but his family had to wait and go on with the rest of the refugees. They, after many weeks of travel and after paying exorbitant sums of money, were sent to a fellahin village. Prof. C., according to the latest report, was teaching for nothing in a Moslem school in Aleppo.

Three of the pastors at AC. were imprisoned for months in dirty, dingy cells of the common prison. Three of the College professors had the same experience. Finally, permission was given for the gendarmes to take the pastors out long enough to preach, for it was feared they would otherwise go mad. The sermons they preached were said to be wonderful. These pastors were later released, but all the professors in the College were exiled except one, and another who had previously succeeded in getting away to Constantinople.

Soon after the crowds started, all kinds of sickness began and spread among the people, and later one of the two doctors left in AC. was sent to look after them. Sometimes they would wait for weeks, expecting to be taken by train to whatever place they were to be sent to. Then they would be told that each must hire an animal for himself. The hire would be put up so high that all their baggage would have to be left behind. The gendarmes told them that it would be forwarded to them, but a little later it was placed in a house from which some of the people had been deported, and sold at auction.

When the people were told that they must go, they at once tried to sell some of their goods, so that they might have a little money in hand. But it cannot be said that they really sold them, for one heard of good wool mattresses selling for one piastre; the highest I heard of was for twenty piastres, while in ordinary times they would sell for a hundred. Large copper pans and basins were sold for a mere song, until one day two Jews appeared on the scene and began paying much better prices. But in three days these men were imprisoned, so that the Turks could once more get things for as little as they pleased. Even goods that were being given to the poor by those having to leave were confiscated by the Government. Some antiquities and books that were being taken to the College shared the same fate. Anyone walking with a parcel was liable to be held up, searched, and robbed.

After the professors had been sent away, the pastors of the Protestant churches and the two remaining professors who had not been deported were put into prison. First, their homes were searched and all papers and any written matter were taken to the Sarai. The secretaries of the Christian societies were enquired about, and when it was found that some of them had been deported it was thought that they might be brought back; but they had not been brought back at the time of my leaving. While waiting in BJ., I heard that those who had been imprisoned had been released.

About the time deportations began in AC., all the non-Moslem schools were taken possession of by the Government, except those belonging to the American Board. At the same time, the large Armenian church and one of the Protestant churches were seized, but before I left AC. they were restored to their owners.

After the professors had been taken away, it was reported that no more Protestants, except those found at fault, would be sent away. But every day they kept sending a family or two away on the slightest pretexts. One of the relief committee workers was the first to be sent away. A letter said to have been sent to them, but which they never saw, was actually the alleged cause of deportation. The censor said that no mention of high prices, poverty, sickness, need of money, or slackness of work must be mentioned in letters.

So we prayed that any letters that might be sent to us should make no mention of relief money or of any other forbidden subject.

As soon as it was officially announced that the Protestants would not be deported, they held a thanksgiving service, at which the one in charge said: "Now that we are permitted to stay in our city, we must be very careful to give no occasion of complaint to the Government. If they ask for our sons as soldiers, we must give them up without murmuring; if for money, or goods, or clothing for the soldiers, let us give as if we appreciated the privilege of staying in our homes. Let us show them that we are loyal to the country. Let no one take into his home a child or anyone else who has been told to go, whether they be of those passing through the city as refugees or from among our own friends and relatives in the town. Let us show the Government that we will do all that is asked of us."

The goods in the drapers' shops all belonged to the Armenians; but during the deportations the Turks took whatever they wanted and paid nothing, so the owners in some cases sold their goods for almost nothing, or gave them away, or closed their shops. Soon after deportation, it was impossible to buy a button, though some native material could be secured in native houses where they had looms.

When the first lot of people from AC. were sent away, they were told that they were only going for a short time, and that they need not trouble about their homes and belongings, for the Government would carefully seal them and take care of their property. They had not been out of the city long when soldiers were quartered in the larger houses, some of which were rented for a trifle, the rent being paid to the Government. The poorer houses were given to the poorer Turks. Every evening all the possible exits from the city were carefully guarded; if we went from one building to another, we were held up and asked where we were going and for what. If our servant was found outside, he would always be searched and sometimes struck at, and told not to be out so late again. In the early days we were not allowed out after sunset, and later we were told the same, even if the sun were shining. This was said not only to me, the subject of a belligerent country, but also to neutrals as well.

An old college student, whose home was at E., managed, through the kindness of a friendly Turk, to escape to AC. He told us that the men of his town were all killed. We had previously heard that the men of that town and of the next village had been taken for military service, and set to making a road to BL. As soon as the road was finished, the men were taken to the side of the road they had made and were killed—chiefly by the knife, for the officer in command had told the soldiers he commanded not to waste powder on the Armenians.

An Englishman who had been given permission to leave the country (we wondered whether he ever got out) told one of our ladies of the sights he had seen while waiting for the train. He had seen feet swollen all out of shape lifted up and beaten with the heavy end of a gendarme's gun, just because people had said they could not walk any faster.

The steward of the College at AC. was sent away because his brother-in-law had sent his dentist's instruments to him with a letter, asking him to sell them and send the money on to him later, when he could tell him—the steward—where they were being deported to. But neither the instruments nor the letter ever reached the steward. He was merely told that they had been sent and that, because of it, he and his family of small children must go into exile. This was after the Protestants were told that they might stay.

Whenever the Turks thought that they had won any victory, they were almost unbearable, as, for instance, when word came that they had taken the Suez Canal. They then rejoiced both by day and by night, and were most insolent to Christians. An English flag was dragged through the filth of the streets, spat and trampled upon, &c. The noise continued all night long. At these times of supposed victories, they showed what they would do if ever they were really victorious.

It was beautiful to see the faith of some of the villagers. One evening a large party came in and very soon began singing hymns and holding a prayer-meeting. The following morning, when asked about it, they said that their pastor had been taken from them and killed, and that his last word to them was: "Keep up the prayer-meeting." And with kindling eyes they said: "We have never once missed it, though we have been seven weeks on the march."

Another party told how they had prayed that, if it were God's will, they might be spared the horrors of deportation, and said: "There must be some good in it for our nation, or God would not permit it. The only thing that troubles us is: Will our husbands ever be able to find us?" They little knew, poor women, that their husbands had already been killed, as we were told by others.

Just before the deportation began at AC., a high official, T. Pasha, came and called together the leading people, both Moslem and Christian. In a very kindly manner, he asked the Christians whether they were being kindly treated by the Moslems, &c., &c. He said that he had heard certain things, and that, if there was any truth in the statement that Armenians were being ill-treated, he himself would hang the Turk, were it his own brother, who should dare to treat a Christian unkindly; and he begged the Armenians to speak out without fear. He then went straight from AC. to BN., where he arranged for the deportation of all the BN. and BM. districts. Such plans were evidently intended to throw the Armenians off their guard.

In T. Pasha's party there were three German officers, but I could not say that German officers were supervising the deportations. The German Consul went through AC. to BM. and BN. before the deportation began. Though some people blamed him for it, we did not think he had so much power.

A great many of the Armenian doctors were taken for the Army. When there was any sickness among the service corps, one of the three Armenian doctors left in AC. was sure to be sent to attend the sick. In this way we lost a dear friend, who in the early days had been an assistant to Dr. L. He was sent to a camp where the soldiers, nearly all of them Armenians, were working on a section of a branch of the Baghdad Railway; typhus had broken out among them. Very soon a telegram came, saying that the old doctor was ill. Though he was the oldest doctor in AC. and had more Moslem patients than any other doctor in the city, no mercy was shown to him. Did he not belong to the accursed Armenian race? And was not his death of typhus, in the camp to which he had been obliged to go, a fate good enough for any such as he?

Early in March, 1915, the BM. Government took possession of Miss S.'s Orphanage and put Turks in charge of the girls and young women. Miss O., a Swiss lady in charge of a German Orphanage at BM., after all her charges[175] had been turned loose for deportation, as were the inmates of all the German orphanages early in the war, took under her care some of the old girls who were married and living in the districts in which the first deportations had taken place. After she had kept them for a short time, she was told by the German Consul that she must give them up. She thought that if she could get to someone in authority she could present the situation in its true light, so she went to Constantinople, but returned disappointed.

Early in the autumn we heard of a reign of terror at Ourfa, so that the very mention of the place seemed to alarm people. We heard that three men, one of them being H. Effendi, Miss J.'s faithful helper in charge of industrial work employing more than 2,000 persons, had been banished. Later, they were brought back to the city and tortured. Later still, in writing to his wife, Mr. K. said that H. Effendi's children were in the same case as some other children, whom we knew to be orphans; so we inferred that he had certainly been killed[176]. Still later, a driver told how he had been engaged to take three men to Diyarbekir for court-martial. They had gone but a short distance from Ourfa when the men were told to get out of the wagon. They were taken down a gully a short distance, and soon the driver heard shots. The four gendarmes came galloping up to the wagon and told the driver to drive on. One of them looked into the wagon and asked where the prisoners were. When the driver asked if they had not called them out of the wagon, he was told that he had allowed them to escape and that he himself must go before the court. So he had to drive back to Ourfa to the Sarai, where he was told to leave the things that belonged to the men he had started out with. Then he was allowed to go away free.

Q., Miss J.'s servant, had been killed, we heard, in a brutal way while he was going to Garmoush with some relief for a poor family. We also heard that there were two massacres at Ourfa, in the first of which only the men found in the streets were killed. The second time, homes were entered.

M., one of my orphan boys, had gone with Dr. P., and was working for him when he was told to leave the country. He was tortured to make him tell something incriminating about Dr. P. Later, when Dr. L. tried to get some news about the boy from the Diyarbekir refugees at Aleppo, their answer was: "Do not ask us about any male over twelve years old, for, as far as we know, they were every one of them killed."

The general impression was that Mr. K. was poisoned. We heard that he was in danger of a mental breakdown; but, on the evening previous to my leaving AC., Dr. E. was told by a Moslem muleteer who had come from Ourfa that Mr. K. had either died or been killed. I was told that I must acquaint the Consul with what Dr. E. had heard as soon as I reached Aleppo. On my telling the Consul, he showed me a telegram he had recently received from Mr. K. himself, which read: "Am safe and well in Government House." Later, in BJ., when we heard that he had poisoned himself, someone remarked that it would be easy for Mr. K. to be obliged to write and say that there was danger of a nervous breakdown, and then the way would be prepared for the news: "Poisoned himself." Someone else added: "Yes, just as was done when the prisoners were obliged to sign a letter, stating that they were all well, while at the very time there was an epidemic in their camp."

When we travelled ourselves from AC. to Aleppo, we saw a large camp of refugees, some distance from the road which we were on, but close to the small station of Kotmo, which connects with the Baghdad Railway. We had heard before leaving AC. that 37,000 were waiting for a train to take them on, but, judging from what we could see, there could not have been more than seven or eight thousand of them.

As we got near to Aleppo we passed a very long convoy of ox-wagons, mules, donkeys, and a few horses, carrying women, children, and some old men. Our driver got down and talked with a few. He was told that they were being sent from Adana and Mersina. They looked so much better off in every way than any refugees we had seen that they hardly seemed like refugees at all. There were many more men than usual among them.

Later, when we reached Aleppo, we were told that there were 20,000 refugees there, and that on some days the death-rate was as high as 400. A native doctor and his wife, wishing to give all their time to helping these poor people, had left their home and gone to the hotel in which we were staying. From them we got reports twice a day.

We heard of one party, who, when they left Harpout, numbered 5,000. Of this number, only 213 reached Aleppo. When they started, they were of all ages and both sexes. They went towards Aleppo down the Euphrates. When they came to cross the rivers that flow into the Euphrates, all the able-bodied men were drowned and their bodies left in the water. Farther on, all the survivors—now only old men, women and children—were entirely stripped of their clothing. Naked they waded through streams, slept in the chilly nights, and bore the heat of the sun. They were brought into Aleppo the last few miles in third-class railway carriages, herded together like so many animals. When the doors of the carriages were opened, they were jeered at by the populace for their nakedness. On their journey, they had come on a hot day in August to the banks of a river. There was a general rush to get water, but the gendarmes who were with them drew their revolvers and told them that anyone who got any water must pay a medjidia (about 3*s*. 2*d*.) for it. Some were able to give it, but the majority were not. After waiting there for some time, they were told that they must strip and get through the water as best they could. They had the right to the animals that carried their possessions, for they had paid for them for two days longer. They clasped hands and waded across, but waited in vain for the gendarmes to come across with their animals and provisions.[177] In this party were refined girls and young women from the best Armenian homes, who had been educated in the American colleges.

While waiting in BJ., the President of the College got a telegram from the U.S. Consul in Aleppo, asking him to send some doctors, as the death-rate was very high—as high as 400 a day, we heard. The President thought it best to ask Djemal Pasha before doing anything. When he did ask him, the answer came: "No, you must not send anyone. Let your Consul mind his own business!"

---

174. "Outside AC., a woman gave birth to a child in the refugee camp. She was taken to the College and put into a small room there. In spite of the best of care, she died in a few days and the child a little later. In her most delicate condition, she had been driven, cursed and beaten along the road from BM., some sixty miles away."—*Earlier and less detailed statement by the same witness.*

175. "More than a thousand."—*Earlier statement.*

176. "The Protestant pastor and a doctor were also killed."—*Earlier statement.*

177. "Later, another convoy of exiles came up, and took this party of forty women on with them."—*Earlier statement.*

138. AC.: LETTERS FROM AN ARMENIAN INHABITANT[178], DESCRIBING THE DEPORTATION OF ARMENIANS FROM CILICIA; COMMUNICATED BY THE AMERICAN COMMITTEE FOR ARMENIAN AND SYRIAN RELIEF.

Letter dated 6/19th April, 1915.

Every day two or three hundred people from Zeitoun are transferred to BM., under severe guard, and, after a short halt at night, are deported in unknown directions. The hotels and the two Armenian schools are full of these deported families from Zeitoun, Alabash and Furnus. The Government has decided to evacuate by force all the other Armenian regions. It is impossible to describe the misery which is resulting. Old men, invalids, and children four or five years old go in masses, barefooted.

Letter dated 17/30th May, 1915.

Since the first days of April, convoys have been coming from Zeitoun and the neighbourhood and passing southward towards the steppes of Mesopotamia. Reckoning only those that have crossed our city, the number of the deported rises to 6,700 persons. Furnus, Geben, Alabash, and the whole region of Zeitoun have been evacuated. Bosniak mouhadjirs replace the Armenians thus exiled. The Turks are in a perfect delirium. It is impossible to describe the horrors suffered by the deported Armenians. Violation, conversion and the rape of women and girls are ordinary and daily facts. The Armenian population of Zeitoun has been annihilated, one or two villages excepted. We are informed that 150 Armenians from Dört Yöl and 1,350 from Hassan-Beyli have been deported to Aleppo.

---

178. Name withheld.

XVIII.
VILAYET OF ALEPPO.

The Vilayet of Aleppo is not Armenian soil. It is the border province of the Arabic language and the Semitic race, and the only considerable Armenian communities it contains are the villages of Jibal Mousa (which have been dealt with already) and an urban colony in the town of Aintab. In the city of Aleppo itself the Armenian element is altogether insignificant, and it was not as a centre of population, but as a junction of routes, that Aleppo played an important and terrible part in the Armenian deportations of 1915.

Aleppo is the natural meeting-place of all the roads and railways in Asiatic Turkey. It lies immediately south of the great Taurus barrier, which divides the Turco-Armenian provinces of the north-west from the Arabian provinces of the south-east; and it also lies midway between the course of the Euphrates and the Mediterranean coast, at the point where the two approach most closely to one another. On the north-west, the railway leading to Aleppo from Constantinople and Konia over the Taurus and Amanus ranges has practically been completed; from the north a route comes down over the Cilician mountains through Marash and Aintab; from the north-east, through Ourfa, a carriage road converges on Aleppo from Diyarbekir, while southward and eastward the routes radiate out from Aleppo again—the Baghdad Railway, which proceeds due eastward across the Euphrates, and is already complete in this section as far as Ras-ul-Ain; the carriage road south-eastward down the Euphrates to Der-el-Zor; and, finally, the Syrian Railway, which runs due south from Aleppo to Damascus, Beirout and Medina.

All these routes were traversed by the convoys of Armenian exiles, and from the very beginning of the deportations they were continually arriving at Aleppo and leaving again, after a longer or shorter delay in the congested city, for their final destinations beyond.

Batches of Zeitounlis were already passing through Aleppo by the beginning of May, 1915, and the current of exiles from Cilicia went on flowing in a comparatively thin but steady stream during the next three months. At the beginning of August the volume was suddenly increased by the arrival of the first convoys, or remnants of convoys, from the north-east. These first arrivals were from Diyarbekir, and even they had been forty-five days on the road. They were followed in due course by all who survived the far longer journey from the Vilayets of Mamouret-ul-Aziz and Erzeroum. Meanwhile, an even greater mass of exiles had been converging on Aleppo along the Anatolian Railway from all the Armenian districts which its branches tap; but this stream was dammed up indefinitely by the mountain barriers where the railway was still incomplete, and even in December the convoys were still bivouacked on the slopes of Amanus. What was their subsequent fate—whether they died where they lay at Osmania and Islohia, or got through to Aleppo in any considerable numbers—there is little evidence to show. It is only known that 500,000 exiles altogether, out of those who converged upon Aleppo in 1915 from all the quarters above mentioned, were supposed to be still alive, in the spring of 1916, in the region between Aleppo, Damascus and Der-el-Zor.

139. ALEPPO: SERIES OF REPORTS FROM A FOREIGN RESIDENT AT ALEPPO; COMMUNICATED BY THE AMERICAN COMMITTEE FOR ARMENIAN AND SYRIAN RELIEF.

(a.) **Report dated 12th May, 1915.**

Between 4,300 and 4,500 families, that is, about 28,000 persons, are being removed by order of the Government from the districts of Zeitoun and Marash to distant places where they are unknown. Thousands have already been sent to the north-west into the provinces of Konia, Kaisaria, Kastamouni, &c., while others have been taken south-eastwards as far as Der-el-Zor, and report says to the vicinity of Baghdad. A traveller coming from Constantinople said that he met about 4,500 unfortunates on their way to Konia. The Armenians themselves say that they would by far have preferred a massacre.

(b.) **Report dated 3rd August, 1915.**

The idea of direct attack and massacre that was carried out in former times has been altered somewhat, in that the men and boys have been deported from their homes in great numbers and disappeared *en route*, and later on the women and children have been made to follow. For some time stories have been prevalent from travellers arriving from the interior of the killing of the males; of great numbers of bodies along the roadside or floating in the Euphrates River; of the delivery to the Kurds by the gendarmes accompanying the convoys of women and children and of all the younger members of the convoys; of unthinkable outrages committed by gendarmes and Kurds, and even of the killing of many of the victims.

At first these stories were not given much credence, but as many of the refugees are now arriving in Aleppo, no doubt any longer remains of the truth of the matter. On the 2nd August about 800 middle-aged and old women, and children under the age of ten years, arrived afoot from Diyarbekir, after forty-five days *en route*, in the most pitiable condition imaginable. They report the taking of all the young women and girls by the Kurds, the pillaging even of the last bit of money and other belongings, of starvation, of privation and hardship of every description. Their deplorable condition bears out their statements in every detail.

I am informed that 4,500 persons were sent from Sughurt[179] to Ras-ul-Ain, over 2,000 from Mezré to Diyarbekir, and that all the cities of Bitlis, Mardin, Mosul, Suverek[180], Malatia, Besné, &c., have been depopulated of Armenians, the men and boys and many of the women killed, and the balance scattered throughout the country. If this is true, of which there is little doubt, even the latter must naturally die of fatigue, hunger and disease. The Governor of Der-el-Zor, on the Euphrates River, who is now in Aleppo, says that there are 15,000 Armenian refugees in that city. Children are frequently sold to prevent starvation, as the Government furnishes practically no subsistence. The following statistics show the number of families and persons arriving in Aleppo, places whence deported, and number sent further on, up to and including the 30th July:—

WHERE FROM.	FAMILIES.	PERSONS.	SENT AWAY.
Tcheuk-Merzemen (Dört Yöl)	400	2,109	734
Odjakli	115	537	137
Euzerli	116	593	173
Hassan Beyli	187	1,118	514
Harni	84	528	34
Karspazar	51	340	—
Hadjin	592	3,988	1,025
Roumlou	51	388	296
Shar	150	1,112	357
Sis	231	1,317	—
Baghtché	13	68	—
Dengala	126	804	—
Drtadli	12	104	—
Zeitoun	5	8	—
Yarpouz	22	97	—
Albustan	10	44	—
Total	2,165	13,155	3,270

2,100 persons more arrived since the above figures were compiled.

Now all Armenians have been ordered to be deported from the cities of Aintab, Mardin, Bitlis, Antioch, Alexandretta, Kessab, and all the smaller towns in the Aleppo Province, estimated at 60,000 persons in all. It is natural to suppose that they will suffer the fate of those that have gone before, which is appalling to contemplate. The result is that, as 90 per cent. of the commerce of the interior is in the hands of the Armenians, the country is facing ruin. The great bulk of business being done on credit, hundreds of prominent business men other than Armenians face bankruptcy. There will not be left in the places evacuated a single tanner, moulder, blacksmith, tailor, carpenter, clay worker, weaver, shoemaker, jeweller, pharmacist, doctor, lawyer, or any of the professional people or tradesmen, with very few exceptions, and the country will be left in a practically helpless state.

The important American religious and educational institutions in this region are losing their professors, teachers, helpers and students, and even the orphanages are to be emptied of the hundreds of children therein, which ruins the fruits of fifty years of untiring effort in this field. The Government officials in a mocking way ask what the Americans are going to do with these establishments now that the Armenians are being done away with.

The situation is becoming more critical daily, as there is no telling where this thing will end. The Germans are being blamed on every hand, for if they have not directly ordered this wholesale slaughter (for it is nothing less than the extermination of the Armenian race), they at least condone it.

(c.) Report dated 19th August, 1915.

The city of Aintab is being rapidly depopulated of Armenians, several thousands having already passed through Aleppo on their way to the south. The accompanying gendarmes do nothing to protect their charges against attack by the way. The Armenian community of Aintab is the wealthiest of the kind in this part of the Empire. Their household belongings were left behind to be taken by the first plunderer to arrive. Most of the merchants of the city being Armenians, their stocks are likewise disappearing. It is a gigantic plundering scheme, as well as a final blow to extinguish the race.

Since the 1st August the German Baghdad Railway has brought nine trains of these unfortunate people to Aleppo, each of fifteen truck-loads and each truck containing from thirty-five to forty persons. All these in addition to many thousands that came on foot.

Since the 1st August 20,000 have so far arrived in Aleppo. The trains were mostly switched to the Damascus-Hama line, and run on south to disperse their contents among the Arabs and Druses, while a small proportion were permitted to remain in Aleppo for the time being. They all relate harrowing tales of hardships, abuse, robbery and atrocities committed *en route*, and, with the exception of those from Aintab, there were few if any men, girls over ten years or becoming young married women among them. Travellers from the interior have related to the writer that the beaten paths are lined with corpses of the victims. Between Ourfa and Arab-Pounar, a distance of about twenty-five miles, there were seen more than 500 unburied corpses along the highway.

On the 17th instant an order arrived from the Minister of the Interior to permit the Armenian Protestants to remain where they were. On the 19th another order came that all Armenians without distinction should be deported.

From Mardin the Government deported great numbers of Syrians, Catholics, Chaldeans and Protestants, and it is feared that all Christians may later be included in the order, and possibly even the Jews. The cry is "Turkey for the Moslems!" Judicious persons, well informed on the question, place the total loss of life up to the 15th August at over 500,000. The territory affected includes the provinces of Van, Erzeroum, Bitlis, Diyarbekir, Mamouret-ul-Aziz, Angora and Sivas; in these the Armenians have already been practically exterminated. This leaves Aleppo and Adana to be completed, and here the movement is in rapid progress.

(d.) Report dated 8th February, 1916.

I transmit herewith a copy of a report received from reliable sources in reference to the number of Armenian immigrants in this vicinity, between here and Damascus and in the surrounding country, and down the Euphrates River as far as Der-el-Zor, showing a total of about 500,000 persons. In connection with the relief sent by Mr. N. for these people, it would seem proper to state that the sum of £500 (Turkish) weekly is entirely inadequate to aid even a small part thereof. In fact, as a person cannot live on less than two gold piastres per day, it will require the sum of £10,000 (Turkish) (about £9,000 sterling) a day to keep those alive who are in good health, to say nothing of the sick.

The following are the statistics of Armenian immigrants according to the best information, up to the 3rd February, 1916:

Damascus as far as Ma'an, more than	100,000
Hama and surrounding villages	12,000
Homs and surrounding villages	20,000
Aleppo and surrounding villages	7,000
Ma'ara and surrounding villages	4,000

Bab and surrounding villages	8,000
Mumbidj and surrounding villages	5,000
Ras-ul-Ain and surrounding villages	20,000
Rakka and surrounding villages	10,000
Der-el-Zor and surrounding villages, more than	300,000
Total	486,000

140. ALEPPO: MEMORANDUM[181], DATED ALEPPO, 18th JUNE/1st JULY, 1915; COMMUNICATED BY THE AMERICAN COMMITTEE FOR ARMENIAN AND SYRIAN RELIEF.

The number of people from Zeitoun exiled to Konia is more than 6,000; they have been put in the Sandjak of Sultania or Kara-Pounar. More than 20,000 Armenians who have been forced to emigrate are being cast into the deserts amid nomadic tribes, leaving their houses, gardens and tilled lands to the Turkish mouhadjirs. Deprived of all that they possessed, the unfortunate people have not even any graves for their dead.

At Aleppo all the churches and schools are full of exiled Armenians. Rich and poor, teachers and pupils, all are brothers there, victims of the same blow. The inhabitants of the city do their utmost to alleviate the suffering. Those that are deported—women, old men, children—are obliged to cross the deserts on foot, under the burning sun, often deprived of food and water. The most modest complaint is stifled by the most barbarous threats. Overpowered by fatigue, exhausted by hunger, mothers in despair leave on the way their infant children, often only six months old, and continue their journey.... Even in this deplorable state, rapes and violent acts are everyday occurrences.... The Armenians deported from Hadjin could not be recognised as a result of their twelve days' journey.

---

179. Sairt (?).

180. Severeg.

181. Name of author withheld.

141. ALEPPO: MEMORANDUM[182] BY A FOREIGN WITNESS[183] FROM ALEPPO; COMMUNICATED BY THE AMERICAN COMMITTEE FOR ARMENIAN AND SYRIAN RELIEF.

Speaking generally on the question of the expulsion of the Armenians from their native places, you are perhaps not aware that they have all been exiled from the towns in Northern Armenia and Anatolia, such as Harpout, Diyarbekir, Bitlis, Moush, Marash, Zeitoun, Sivas, Erzeroum, etc. They are all being sent south and are gradually moved on from one place to another until they reach the borders of the Syrian Desert. They are met with as far south as Mayadin, an Arab village one day south of Der-el-Zor or seven days' carriage journey south of Aleppo. Practically all the towns in Syria (Aleppo, Damascus, etc.) are full of these exiles, whose condition is most pitiable, as may be imagined when one considers that some of them have been four or even six months on the road from their native places, passing through country which is practically barren and devoid of any means of obtaining proper sustenance. The Armenians are allowed to accumulate in a town until the numbers become so large that it is necessary to move them on to some other town further south, and the population commences to protest against their presence. One sees them in Aleppo on pieces of waste ground, in old buildings, courtyards and alleyways, and their condition is simply indescribable. They are totally without food and are dying of starvation. If one looks into these places where they are living one simply sees a huddled mass of dying and dead, all mixed up with discarded, ragged clothing, refuse and human excrement, and it is impossible to pick out any one portion and describe it as being a living person. A number of open carts used to parade the streets, looking out for corpses, and it was a common sight to see one of these carts pass containing anything up to ten or twelve human bodies, all terribly emaciated. These carts have since been provided with a lid and painted black, and one constantly sees bodies, mostly of women and children, being dragged out of courtyards and alleyways and thrown into them as one would throw a sack of coal. It is impossible to gauge the number of deaths per diem, but in the Armenian Cemetery trenches are dug and the bodies are simply brought there and thrown in indiscriminately. A number of priests remain at the cemetery all day, and perform some kind of funeral rite as the so-called interment is made. Every now and again an order is given for the town to be cleaned up, and the gendarmes and municipal guards go round and drive out the Armenians from their places of refuge, hustle them down to the railway station, pack them into the trucks like cattle and forward them to Damascus and different towns in the Hidjaz. Occasionally a large convoy is collected and put on the road to Der-el-Zor. Unnecessary brutality is shown in the expulsion of these people, the majority of whom are simply living skeletons, and one sees emaciated and hunger-stricken women and children beaten with whips like dogs in order to make them move.

If one walks round certain quarters of Aleppo at night, one sees an indescribable "something" lying on the ground; one hears a groan, and knows that it is one of these human wrecks who, the following morning, will be thrown into a cart and taken to the cemetery. Many of these people refuse to accept any help whatever, and say that they prefer to die and end their suffering rather than prolong it, since the future gives no hope of any alleviation. The stories they tell are beyond description. When they were expelled from any of the towns in Northern Asia Minor, all the men between the ages of fifteen and sixty were shot down before the eyes of the women and children, either before starting or some little way on the road. Some idea of the decimation of their numbers may be obtained when one learns that out of a convoy of 2,500, which left a village in the vicinity of Harpout, only 600 arrived in Der-el-Zor. One learns from their own stories that many of the women drowned their children in the river en route, since there was no visible means of nourishing them; and practically every family has been depleted through the men being killed, the children dying en route and many of the girls having been carried off by roving bands of Kurdish and Arab robbers on the way. One boy of fourteen years old, from Diyarbekir, described how his father and mother were shot and two of his sisters dragged away en route, so that there remained to him only two little sisters out of the whole family. English-speaking girl students of the American College in H. told stories of the torture of various priests and professors in H., in order to make them divulge the location of supposed arms and ammunition. One girl, who was a nurse in the Military Hospital, swore that one of their professors was attended to by her after having had the hair torn from his face and his finger and toe-nails pulled out[184]. One Armenian priest was said to have suffered the same torture, and finally to have been burned alive; the veracity of this, however, seems impossible in the Twentieth Century. It is no uncommon thing for women and girls who have any claim to good looks to be violated by the different Kurds and Arabs whom they meet on the way, and against whom it is impossible for them to defend themselves. Practically all these convoys are composed of women and children, and men between the ages of fifteen and sixty are rarely met with. Many of these people have been considerably well off, and brought away with them large sums of money secreted on their persons. This, of course, became known to the gendarmes and robbers en route, and they were despoiled of practically everything—not only their money, but their jewellery, clothing, bedding and everything else. Outside practically every town from Mayadin, on the Euphrates, up to Konia, one sees a camp containing anything from 2,000 up to 20,000 of these refugees, and one can imagine that such a large crowd of people, being thrown on to a population which already finds it difficult to obtain employment and food, would cause the position to become intolerable; they must naturally die of starvation, since food cannot be found for such extra numbers.

On all the main routes one finds a continual stream of refugees dragging themselves wearily along and going for ever southwards. Their ultimate destination is unknown to them, but apparently they have a dim hope of at last reaching some place where they will be able to live in comparative comfort and find nourishment. If they knew, however, what they would find and what would ultimately happen to them, they would no doubt prefer simply to sit down and wait for death without going any further.

One woman in Aleppo was raving mad, owing to having lost her child and being unable to ascertain his whereabouts.

Any attempts to help the refugees are immediately nipped in the bud by the authorities, and spies are continually watching the foreign consulates. Several Armenians who called at one of them were afterwards put in prison, and one woman was cruelly beaten by a gendarme, after being compelled to leave the consulate.

142. ALEPPO: MESSAGE DATED 17th FEBRUARY, 1916, FROM FRÄULEIN O.; PUBLISHED IN THE GERMAN JOURNAL "SONNENAUFGANG," APRIL, 1916.

I want to beg our friends at home not to grow weary of making intercession for the members of the Armenian nation who are in exile here. If there is no visible prospect of a change for the better, a few months more will see the end of them all. They are succumbing in thousands to famine, pestilence and the inclemency of the weather. The exiles at Hama, Homs and in the neighbourhood of Damascus are comparatively better of. They are left where they are, and can look about for means of subsistence. But further East, along the Euphrates, they are driven from place to place, plundered and maltreated. Many of our friends are dead.

XIX.
VILAYET OF DAMASCUS AND SANDJAK OF DER-EL-ZOR.

Aleppo was not intended to be the final destination of the Armenian exiles. A certain number of the earlier arrivals were sent to the swampy, malarious districts a short distance to the south and south-east of the city, but by far the greater number were forwarded at least several days' journey further afield.

Aleppo lies on the inner edge of a great desert amphitheatre, which is buttressed by the Lebanon, the Taurus and the mountains of Kurdistan, and slopes very gradually southeastward towards the alluvial lowlands at the head of the Persian Gulf, while southward it passes insensibly into the high desert lands of the Arabian Peninsula. This region presents a sharp climatic contrast to the tablelands of Anatolia and Armenia, which are the native country of the Armenian race. Climatically and geographically, Armenia and Anatolia are an integral part of Europe, while Syria and Mesopotamia are the outer fringe of Arabia, and akin, like it, to the Sahara region of North Africa. The frontier between the two climates is formed by the southward escarpment of the Taurus, and the transition between them is abrupt.

The ostensible motive for deporting the Armenians to this country was to remove them from the neighbourhood of the frontiers and from the coast and to plant them among a compact Moslem population of alien (Arabic) speech, where they would find themselves in political isolation as well as in a decisive numerical minority. The actual result was to subject people accustomed to a temperate climate to a climate of a Saharan character, and this under the worst conceivable conditions for such a change of environment—when the victims were destitute of food, clothing and shelter, and physically exhausted by months of travelling on foot over the roughest of roads.

The two chief places selected by the Ottoman Government as destinations for the exiles were Damascus, which lies due south of Aleppo, and is close, like Aleppo itself, to the inner rim of the amphitheatre, and Der-el-Zor, which lies considerably further inwards—six days' journey by carriage from Aleppo down the course of the Euphrates, where the river cuts through the desert between the mountains of Armenia and the alluvium of the Gulf. Some batches had been sent a further day's journey still, to Mayadin (Doc. 141, while there are even rumours of their presence (Docs. 11 and 121) within forty-eight hours' journey of Baghdad.

The condition of these exiles after their arrival is made sufficiently plain in the documents included in this section. Doc. 145 shows that by the 12th July there were already large numbers of Cilicians bivouacked at Der-el-Zor, while it appears from Doc. 143 that they did not begin to arrive at Damascus until the 12th August, 1915.

143. DAMASCUS: REPORT FROM A FOREIGN RESIDENT AT DAMASCUS, DATED 20th SEPTEMBER, BUT CONTAINING INFORMATION UP TO THE 3rd OCTOBER, 1915; COMMUNICATED BY THE AMERICAN COMMITTEE FOR ARMENIAN AND SYRIAN RELIEF.

Since the 12th August, 1915, convoys of Armenian exiles, consisting of from a few hundred to as many as two thousand individuals, have been marched through this city at varying intervals, averaging about two to three or more convoys per week.

On a sober estimate I should say that from 8,000 to 10,000 souls have already thus come through Damascus up to the present time. This has been going on since the 12th August, to my knowledge.

His Excellency the Governor-General of Syria informed me, upon my request, that these people are all Armenians who, because of uprisings and attempts to set up local revolutionary governments in the Vilayets of Van and Bitlis, are being exiled to the country round Damascus and will be distributed in groups of two, three and so on among the various more important towns and villages. His Excellency also informed me—upon my statement that, if the Government permitted, I believed that I could secure funds from the American Red Cross to aid these people, who undoubtedly would be very needy—that the Government would not sanction this, and that the Government was doing everything possible, furnishing food, tents, etc.

Numerous stories are current of hardship, want, suffering from hunger, forced marching when in no condition to walk, cruelty of guards, seizure of young women, giving away and selling of children that they might find homes, etc., etc., but I did not believe them, and even now I am sure that many of the worst stories that are circulating are much exaggerated. Still, there are some which I must credit.

One is that of a woman who, though six or seven months pregnant and naturally in no condition whatever to do the marches, was obliged to keep up with the procession until she dropped in her tracks and died. I have heard of several cases of young girls or boys being bought by people who wished to aid in some way and were importuned by parents to take their children as servants, that they might have homes. It was stated to me also that some soldier guards, in order to urge them on, whipped those who straggled on the march either from utter exhaustion or in quest of food or money from compassionate Christian inhabitants of the places through which they passed.

I have also heard of kindnesses extended by good Moslems who pitied these sufferers, and I overheard a common Moslem soldier—and it is known that such have hardly enough money for themselves—say that he had given two medjidias[185] to the Christian exiles.

Several times I went to the quarter through which the exiles were marched, to see them with my own eyes. Never, however, could I time my visit with their passage.

Kahdem, on the outskirts of the city, is a large piece of common ground where, after passing through Damascus, all the exiles are collected preparatory, it seems, to their being dispersed to the various towns where they are finally to stay.

Some days ago I visited this place to get some idea of conditions. It is a large open tract, practically devoid of grass and possessing but few trees. It was nearly covered with groups of ragged, road-stained, dejected, wholly dispirited individuals. There were only a very few tents or shelters of any kind, and these had the air of being mere improvisations. At the outer fringe of the people I was met by a policeman, who conducted me to the man in charge of the encampment. I saw practically nothing, and learned only what he told me. He was most courteous. According to him (and he said he kept count of it) there were that day something over 2,000 Armenians present on this field; up to that time about 20,000 had passed through Damascus for exile from practically all the vilayets inhabited by Armenians, except the region of Van. He thought they had not arrived from Van yet because it was so distant. A total of 100,000 Armenians were to be distributed among the towns surrounding Damascus before this deportation scheme would be complete, he said. A hospital for those who were ill had been instituted, and was then occupied by about fifty persons, I was informed. He further told me that there were practically no deaths, and that the Government furnished food for them, *i.e.*, for all the exiles. I left the Director of the Encampment's tent, and the only thing I saw while being conducted to the road was the wagon, outbound, that plies between camp and hospital. It appeared to be well filled. The Spanish Consul took the road to Kahdem the same day. He did not go as close as I, I believe.

One of the exiled Armenians who came to see me said he was a native of Kessab, near Aleppo. According to his statements, he had been on the march some ten days, and, upon being questioned, he told me that the suffering en route had been extreme for those who were not very strong. He said that along the road they had passed the bodies of those in the convoy ahead of theirs who had succumbed. This man declared that his wife and family were coming by train. He nearly broke down in the telling, and said he had no idea what would become of him and cared less.

On the 11th September, 1915, the Spanish Consul and myself happened to be in the Christian quarter, when we came upon a procession of the Armenian exiles on their way to Kahdem. One becomes accustomed to poorly dressed, ragged people in the interior whose faces never seem to have expressed joy, but in the faces of this band of silently trudging automatons one saw written a great weariness, despair and hopeless suffering stoically borne. There were men, women and children, only some of whom took heed of us when we offered them what change we happened to have. The greater part seemed interested only in doggedly pursuing their march until the night's halt might allow them to rest. It was then a little after six o'clock.

Old and young people were the chief components of the procession. Here there passed a boy hardly over ten years of age, overburdened by a smaller child upon his back; there a woman, with back bent by age, crawling painfully along by the aid of her staff; now a wee infant, crying for its mother lost on the march, on the heels of an old patriarch, dragging along his last possession, a little donkey; then a woman, evidently heavy with child, smothering a moan of pain at each forced step. Young women and men of middle age were noticeable by their absence. From various reports I have heard, it would appear that many exiles have been arriving by train, and that the total number that has passed this way now reaches 22,000.

From a person who has passed that way, I learn that, so far as he could judge, all Armenians south of Ismid were being exiled, and from the same informant, whose word cannot be questioned, I hear that thousands of Armenians were passed by him on the road. They were in the most horrible condition. At Osmania there were some 8,000 exiles quartered. He tells me that for some miles out from this place a most foul odour was noticeable, like that rising from a dirty chicken-run. Upon approaching the low ground on which the exiles were concentrated, the odour became sickening and noisome flies swarmed about him. Passing through the encampment, he saw many people ill, and the bodies of others half-submerged in the water that had collected in pools on the low-lying ground. Some told him they were only waiting for death to free them. On the road from there to Aleppo he passed thousands of exiles on the march, and at a small town near Aleppo he found about 100,000 Armenians encamped. He says that the mortality among these was very great. They had no food nor money to buy any, as it appeared that many convoys had been plundered on the road of what little they possessed by successive armed bands. The party of which my informant was a member had several times been accosted by armed persons in uniform, who thought they were Armenians.

I have heard from a source not quite so authentic, but in which a great deal of confidence may be placed, that the country lying north and north-east of Marash is being entirely denuded of Armenians; that at Homs there was a concentration camp of about 30,000, practically all without shelter; that there had been a massacre at Diyarbekir; that exiles from Kaisaria were allowed to sell their property (a small price only could be obtained in this forced sale) before being sent to Der-el-Zor. From this same source I was also informed that it was rumoured that many exiles had been drowned (by boats being overturned, and so on) in the Euphrates River, while making their crossing.

Just within the last few days—it is now the 3rd October—I was told by an eye-witness that a massacre took place on the 19th September at Ourfa, and that the Armenians were shot, stabbed, bayoneted or flayed by the population in general that day, but that afterwards the slaughter was still being continued by soldiers with bayonets and sharp sabres when this person left on the 22nd. It appears that the Armenian men were collected together, and that one by one they were led out to be slashed up and cut down by the long sabre-knives. In the first day's massacre three French and Russian civil prisoners were wounded by knife or flail; but I gathered that they soon recovered and that that was all that happened to these prisoners. The person who came from Ourfa told me that en route many women, children and old men were passed, and that soldiers were seen to strike some of these when they stopped to get a drink of water. Soldiers were overheard to say: "Wait until we get you to the Euphrates, and see what happens to you there!" or words to that effect. This information was given me by a person who, as stated above, was actually present at the massacre and who heard the remark above mentioned.

I do not know whether I shall be able to get this through or not. In every instance the faith that might be placed in statements has been indicated as precisely as the writer is able to judge; he can vouch absolutely, of course, only for the things seen or heard by himself as related above.

At Damascus everything appears to be very quiet. An egg was thrown into my carriage yesterday, the 2nd October, but that was by a small boy and indicated little. I do not believe that any trouble from the population is to be feared, unless incited by authority, and of this I have no apprehension.

144. EXILES ON THE EUPHRATES: RECORD, DATED ERZEROUM, JUNE, 1915, BY M. HENRY BARBY, OF AN INTERVIEW WITH DR. H. TOROYAN, AN ARMENIAN PHYSICIAN FORMERLY IN THE SERVICE OF THE OTTOMAN ARMY; PUBLISHED IN "LE JOURNAL," OF PARIS, 13th JULY, 1916.

Along the burning banks of the distant Euphrates, between sultry Mesopotamia and the Badiet-esh-Sham, the desolate desert of Syria, are encamped the several thousands of deported Armenians who have escaped the great massacre.

Their condition there is such that no words can express the horror of it. That is the unanimous testimony of the rare travellers who have succeeded in visiting the camps where the unhappy victims are dying off, between Aleppo and Baghdad. They are subjected to frightful sufferings—without shelter either against the deadly cold of last winter or against the terrific heat of the present summer, which grows more pitiless every day—and daily they are perishing in great numbers, though those struck down by death are the least to be pitied.

I am now in a position to cite unimpeachable testimony as to the facts of these unheard-of atrocities.

A Turkish army-physician, Dr. H. Toroyan—an Armenian by birth, as appears by his name—was commissioned by the Young Turkish Government to visit the exiles' camps. The horrors of which he was a helpless witness in the course of his mission, and the hideous scenes at which he was present, affected him so deeply that he determined to make his way out of Turkey, at the risk of his life, in order to reveal to the civilised world the barbarity and infamy of the guilty parties—that is, of the present rulers of Turkey and their accomplices.

Dr. Toroyan, in spite of the almost insurmountable difficulties with which he had to contend, succeeded in escaping and reaching Caucasia. There I met him and his first words with me were these:

"My unhappy countrymen deported to Mesopotamia have besought me to make an appeal on their behalf to the whole civilised world, to the Caucasian Armenians in particular, and above all to the Armenians in America, whose women and children are dying every day—decimated by suffering, hunger and disease and subjected to the devilish cruelty of the zaptiehs who are in charge of them in their place of exile."

He proceeded to show me the notes which he had taken day by day in the course of his tour of inspection down the Euphrates. It is a long series of awful pictures—stories of murders and tortures and revolting rapes. The bestial instincts of human nature are unleashed in the presence of tears and blood. The Turkish butchers amused themselves by massacring men "for pleasure" and hunting women like beasts of the field.

It was on the 25th November, 1915, that Dr. Toroyan left Djerablous and began to descend the Euphrates on a raft. At Djerablous he saw a convoy of Armenians from Syria and twenty-five Armenian families from Aintab, who were being driven along by gendarmes towards the military tribunal under blows of the lash. Other Armenian families were coming in from Kaisaria and Konia by railway. From the moment they left the train they became the victims of the most atrocious outrages. The Tchatchaus[186] carried off three hundred women and girls (the prettiest) in order to sell them as slaves. All these latter victims belonged to families from Diyarbekir, Mardin and Harpout.

But I will let Dr. Toroyan tell his own story:—

"This camp," he continued, "was still congested when I left it with Armenians from Adana and Cilicia. Most of them were women and girls. Two of them, whom I knew well but only recognised with difficulty, to so lamentable a condition were they reduced, cast themselves at my feet:

"'Tell the gallant soldiers (of the Allies) to come quickly to Mesopotamia,' they cried to me between their sobs; 'we are worse than dead.'"

The doctor went down on his raft with the current as far as Meskené. There he landed and, escorted by two Turkish gendarmes, paid a visit to the Armenian camp.

"The poor people were in rags which barely covered their bodies," he said, "and had nothing to shelter them against the weather. Some of them, crouched on the ground, were trying to protect themselves beneath tattered umbrellas, but most of them had nothing at all. I asked my gendarmes what all the strange little mounds of earth were which I saw everywhere, with thousands of dogs prowling round about them.

"'Those are the graves of the infidels!' they answered calmly.

"'Strange, so many graves for such a little village.'

"'Oh, you do not understand. Those are the graves of these dogs—those who were brought here first, last August. They all died of thirst.'

"'Of thirst? Was there no water left in the Euphrates?'

"'For whole weeks together we were forbidden to let them drink.'

"I arrived at last at the extremity of this vast field of graves. There were two old men there, crouched on the ground, sobbing. I questioned them: 'Where are you from?' They made no answer. They were stupefied by suffering. Perhaps they had lost the power of speech. Further on, however, another exile, prostrate on the ground, in the midst of other victims belonging to the same family, did give me an answer. I learnt that the camp contained 5,000 Armenians from Mersina and other Cilician towns.

"But now my two gendarmes came up to me. They pointed to a girl: 'Effendi, let us take her and carry her with us to Baghdad....'

"Without waiting for my answer they called the poor girl. She approached, shrieking with terror. She said several words to me in French. Before she was deported she had been a schoolmistress at Smyrna. She was dying of hunger. I tried to learn from her precise details about the martyrdom of the exiles, but she could answer nothing but: 'Bread! Bread!' Then she fainted and fell down unconscious.

"'She is dead! the schoolmistress, too, has died of hunger!' piteous voices cried around us. But the gendarmes were anxious to take advantage of their victim's unconsciousness to gain possession of her. Already they had seized her and were carrying her towards our raft. I stopped them. Then I poured several drops of brandy between the poor girl's lips and she came to herself again.

"A mother came to implore me. She offered her honour and her life if I would save her son, who was in agony, devoured by a fever. I gave her a little aspirine.

"And now they crowded round me in thousands—these poor emaciated beings with hollow cheeks and eyes, either dulled or unnaturally bright. From every side they flocked together with all the haste they could, and surrounded me with a tumult of despairing cries: 'Bread! Medicine!'

"The gendarmes rushed at them. Into this pitiful crowd they struck at random with kicks and blows as hard as they could. I left the scene, desperate at my powerlessness to alleviate this infinite suffering.

"I saw two women, one of them old, the other very young and very pretty, carrying the corpse of another young woman; I had scarcely passed them when cries of terror arose. The girl was struggling in the clutches of a brute who was trying to drag her away. The corpse had fallen to the ground, the girl, now half-unconscious, was writhing by the side of it, the old woman was sobbing and wringing her hands.

"I could not interfere. I had the strictest orders. Shaking with rage and indignation, I took refuge on my raft, which was moored to the river bank.

"In the middle of the night I was awakened by desperate shrieks. My two gendarmes, who had remained on shore, had seized some Armenian girls. It was their intention to violate them, and they were striking savagely at the exiles who were trying to interfere. The tumult, which I heard without seeing it, continued. At last the gendarmes returned, the boatman unmoored the raft and bent to his oars. We were starting. The great river boat glided slowly over the smooth water. Suddenly the gendarmes shouted and guffawed as if they were watching a fine farce: 'The girl! the girl we had to-night!' I looked, and saw floating on the surface a corpse which they had recognised and which I recognised too. It was the schoolmistress from Smyrna, the poor girl to whom I had spoken only a few hours before. It was she who, in the darkness, had been the victim of these two wild beasts."

145. DER-EL-ZOR: LETTER, DATED 12th JULY, 1915, FROM SCHWESTER L. MÖHRING, A GERMAN MISSIONARY, DESCRIBING HER JOURNEY FROM BAGHDAD TO THE PASSES OF AMANUS; PUBLISHED IN THE GERMAN JOURNAL "SONNENAUFGANG," SEPTEMBER, 1915.

At Der-el-Zor, a large town in the desert about six days' journey from Aleppo, we found the big han full to overflowing. All available rooms, roofs, and verandahs were occupied by Armenians. The majority were women and children, but there were also a certain number of men squatting on their quilts wherever they could find a spot of shade. As soon as I heard that they were Armenians, I started going round and talking to them. They were the people of Furnus (a village in the neighbourhood of Zeitoun and Marash); herded together here in these narrow quarters, they presented an extraordinarily melancholy appearance. When I enquired for children from our Orphanage at BM., they brought me a protégée of Sister O., Martha Karabashian. She gave me the following account of what had happened.

One day Turkish gendarmes had come to Furnus and arrested and carried off a large number of men, to turn them into soldiers. Neither they nor their families knew where they were being taken to. Those who remained were told that they would have to leave their houses within the space of four hours. They were allowed to take with them as much as they could carry; they might also take their beasts. After the lapse of the specified time the poor people had to march out of their village under the escort of soldiers (zaptiehs), without knowing where they were going or whether they would ever see their village again. To begin with, as long as they were still among the mountains and had some provisions left, things went well enough. They had been promised money and bread, and were actually given some in the early stages—as far as I can remember, it was 30 paras (1½d.) per head per day. But very soon these rations ceased, and there was nothing to be had but bulgur meal—50 drams (= 150 grammes) per head per day. In this fashion the Furnusli, after four weeks of extremely hard travelling via Marash and Aleppo, had arrived at Der-el-Zor. They had already been three weeks there in the han, and had no idea what was to happen to them. They had no more money left, and the provisions supplied by the Turks had also dwindled almost to nothing. It was days since they had had any bread. In the towns they had been barred in at night, and not allowed to speak to the inhabitants. Martha, for instance, had not been allowed at BM. to go to the Orphanage. She said to me sadly: "We had two houses and we had to leave everything;

now there are mouhadjirs[187] in them." There had been no massacres in Furnus and the zaptiehs, too, had treated the people well. They had suffered principally from lack of food and water on the march through the burning hot desert. These Yailadji or Mountaineers, as they called themselves, suffered twice as much from the heat as other people.

The zaptiehs escorting them told us then that, since the massacres, the Armenians had cherished such hatred against the Turks that the latter had always to go in fear of them. The intention now, they said, was to employ the Armenians in building roads, and in this way to move them on gradually to Baghdad. When asked the "wherefore" of this, the zaptiehs explained that the people had been in collusion with Russia. The Armenians themselves declared that they did not know the reason for their expulsion.

Next day, at the midday rest, we fell in with a whole convoy of Armenians. The poor people had made themselves primitive goat's hair tents after the manner of the Kurds, and were resting in them. But the majority lay on the burning sand without defence against the scorching sun. On account of the number of sick, the Turks had allowed them a day's rest. It is simply impossible to conceive anything more disconsolate than such a mass of people in the desert under the given circumstances. One could tell by their clothes that they had lived in considerable prosperity, and now misery was written on their faces. "Bread!" "Bread!" was the universal cry. They were the people of Geben, who had been driven out with their Pastor. The latter told me that every day there were five or six deaths among the children and the sick. This very day they had only just buried the mother of a girl about nine years old, who was now quite alone in the world. They besought me most urgently to take the child with me to our Orphanage. The Pastor gave precisely the same account of what had happened as the little girl at Der-el-Zor.

No one without personal experience of the desert can form anything approaching a conception of the misery and distress. The desert is mountainous, but almost entirely without shade. For days together the route leads over rocks and is extremely difficult going. On the left hand, as one comes from Aleppo, there is always the Euphrates, which trails along like a streak of clay, yet not near enough for one to be able to draw water from it. The poor people must suffer intolerable pangs of thirst; no wonder that so many sicken and die.

As it was the midday halt, we, too, unpacked our provisions and prepared to eat. That morning we had had bread and tea; our midday meal consisted once more of hard Arab bread, cheese and a tin of sardines. In addition we had a bottle of mineral water. It was not very sumptuous, and yet it was not an easy task to eat anything in face of that crowd of distressed and suffering humanity. We gave away as much as we possibly could, and each of my three companions silently pressed into my hand a medjidia (3s. 2d.) "for the poor people." A bag of bread from Baghdad, as hard as stone, was received with extraordinary gratitude. "We shall soak it in water and then the children will eat it," said the delighted mothers.

Another scene comes back to me, which will give an idea of their destitution. One of my companions threw away an empty glass bottle. An old man threw himself upon it, begged to be allowed to take it for himself, and gave profuse thanks for the boon. Then he went down to the river, washed it out, and brought it back filled with the thick clayey water, carrying it carefully in his arms like a treasure, to thank us for it once more. Now he had at least drinking water for his journey.

Followed by many good wishes we at last continued on our way, with the impression of this misery still weighing upon us. In the evening, when we reached the village, we met yet another Armenian convoy of the same kind. This time it was the people of Zeitoun. There was the same destitution and the same complaint about the heat, the lack of bread and the persecutions of the Arabs. A little girl who had been brought up by Kaiserswerth Deaconesses in the Orphanage at Beirout, told us of her experiences in good German:—

"Why does God allow it? Why must we suffer like this? Why did not they strike us dead at once?" were her complaints; "In the daytime we have no water for the children and they cry of thirst. At night the Arabs come to steal our bedding and clothes. They have taken girls from us and committed outrages against women. If we cannot drag ourselves further on the march, we are beaten by the zaptiehs."

They also told us that other women had thrown themselves into the water to escape their shame, and that mothers with their new-born children had done the same, because they saw no other way out of their misery. Along the whole desert route there was a dearth of food—even for us who had money to pay for it—on account of the number of Turkish soldiers passing through and resting at every han. In Zeitoun, too, no one had been killed; the people could mention no instance of it.

The Armenian is bound up with his native soil; every change of climate is extremely upsetting to him, and there is nothing he misses so much as clear, cold water. For this reason alone residence in the desert is intolerable for him. A speedy death for the whole family at once seems a better fate to the mothers than to watch death by starvation slowly approaching themselves and their children.

On my arrival at Aleppo I was at once asked about the Armenians, and how they were doing for supplies. Their case had been taken up in every possible way, and representations had been made to the Government on their behalf. All that could be obtained was permission for the formation of an Armenian League of Help, which the Government at Constantinople as well as the Vali of Aleppo had sanctioned. The Armenian community at Aleppo at once proceeded to raise a relief fund among themselves, and have been supporting their poor, homeless brethren with money, food and clothing.

In the Amanus mountains, on our second day's journey after leaving Aleppo, we met with Armenians again. This time it was the people of Hadjin and the neighbourhood. They explained to us that they were going to Aleppo, but they knew nothing beyond that. They had only been nine days on the road, and did not ask for any assistance. Compared with those in the desert, they were faring sumptuously; they had wagons with them carrying their household goods, horses with foals, oxen and cows, and even camels. The procession making its way up through the mountains seemed endless, and I could not help asking myself how long their prosperity would last. They were still in the mountains on their native soil, and had no suspicion of the terrors of the desert. That was the last I saw of the Armenians, but such experiences are unforgettable, and I publish them here with the most earnest appeal for help. Many of the Armenians may be guilty and may only be suffering what they have brought upon themselves, but the poor women and children need our help.

---

182. Undated.

183. Name withheld.

184. See Doc. 68, page 272, and Doc. 69, page 278.

185. 6s. 4d.

186. Tchetchens (?).

187. Moslem immigrants from Europe.

XX.
DOCUMENTS RECEIVED WHILE GOING TO PRESS.

146. DESPATCH FROM MR. HENRY WOOD (DOC. I.): FULLER VERSION, OBTAINED THROUGH THE COURTESY OF THE REPRESENTATIVE OF THE AMERICAN "UNITED PRESS" IN LONDON.

For nearly three months now the 2,000,000 Armenians of Turkey have been undergoing at the hands of the Young Turk Government a renewal of the atrocities of Abd-ul-Hamid, that so far has fallen short only of actual massacre.

So critical is the situation that Ambassador Morgenthau, who, alone, is fighting to prevent wholesale slaughter, has felt obliged to ask the co-operation of the Ambassadors of Turkey's two Allies. Baron von Wangenheim, the German Ambassador, and Margrave Pallavicini, the Austrian representative at Constantinople, have responded at least to the degree of joining with Ambassador Morgenthau in endeavouring to convince the Turkish Government what a serious mistake it would be for Turkey to permit again a renewal of all the atrocities of the old Turkish régime.

They have been successful to the extent of securing definite promises from the leading members of the Young Turk Government that no orders will be given for massacres. As long as these promises are maintained, no fear is felt, as the danger of a spontaneous uprising of the Moslem population against the Christians is now considered a thing of the past. The critical moment for the Armenians, however, will come, it is feared, when the Turks may meet with serious reverses in the defence now being made of the Dardanelles, or when the Armenians themselves, who not only are in open revolt but are actually in possession of Van and several other important towns, may meet with fresh successes. It is this uprising of the Armenians who are seeking to establish an independent government that the Turks declare is alone responsible for the terrible measures now being taken against them.

In the meantime, the position of the Armenians and the system of deportation, dispersion and extermination that is being carried out against them beggars all description.

Although the present renewal of the Armenian atrocities has been under way for three months, it is only just now that reports creeping into

Constantinople from the remotest points of the interior show that absolutely no portion of the Armenian population has been spared.

It now appears that the order for the present cruelties was issued in the early part of May, and was at once put into execution with all the extreme genius of the Turkish police system—the one department of government for which the Turks have ever shown the greatest aptitude both in organisation and administration. At that time sealed orders were sent to the police of the entire Empire. These were to be opened on a specified date that would ensure the orders being in the hands of every department at the moment they were to be opened. Once opened, they provided for a simultaneous descent at practically the same moment on the Armenian population of the entire Empire.

At Broussa, in Asiatic Turkey, the city which it is expected the Turks will select for their capital in the event of Constantinople falling, I investigated personally the manner in which these orders were carried out. From eye-witnesses in other towns from the interior I found that the execution of them was everywhere identical.

At midnight, the police authorities swooped down on the homes of all Armenians whose names had been put on the proscribed list sent out from Constantinople. The men were at once placed under arrest, and then the houses were searched for papers which might implicate them either in the present revolutionary movement of the Armenians on the frontier or in plots against the Government which the Turks declare exist. In this search, carpets were torn from the floors, draperies stripped from the walls, and even the children turned out of their beds and cradles in order that the mattresses and coverings might be searched.

Following this search, the men were then carried away, and at once there began the carrying out of the system of deportation and dispersion which has been the cruellest feature of the present anti-Armenian wave. The younger men, for the most part, were at once drafted into the Army. On the authority of men whose names would be known in both America and Europe if I dared mention them, I am told that hundreds if not thousands of these were sent at once to the front ranks at the Dardanelles, where death in a very short space of time is almost a certainty. The older men were then deported into the interior, while the women and children, when not carried off in an opposite direction, were left to shift for themselves as best they could.

The terrible feature of this deportation up to date is that it has been carried out on such a basis as to render practically impossible in thousands and thousands of cases that these families can ever again be reunited. Not only wives and husbands, brothers and sisters, but even mothers and their little children have been dispersed in such a manner as to preclude practically all hope that they will ever see each other again.

Simultaneously with these arrests of the population throughout the Empire, the police at Constantinople swooped down on the alleged leaders of an Armenian society that was declared to have for its object not only the wresting from the Turkish Empire of part of its territory for the establishment of an independent Armenia, but also the overthrow of the Turkish Government. These were tried by court martial, and on the 15th June nineteen of them were hanged in front of the Ministry of War at Constantinople. Among the number was one man who had been a cashier for the Singer Sewing Machine Company in one of its Turkish branches. As a result of vigorous protests which followed on the part of prominent people at Constantinople, the Turks at once promised that no more wholesale hangings should take place.

Of all the terrible vengeances so far meted out by the Turks in the present anti-Armenian crusade, none appear to have equalled that inflicted on the population of the city of Zeitoun. This was an Armenian town of 20,000 population which had never as a matter of fact been completely subjected by the Turks. Situated well up in almost inaccessible mountain fastnesses, it had even maintained a sort of independence.

With the participation of Turkey in the present war and the need of every possible man for military service, a detachment of Turkish soldiers was sent against the town, with orders to force the young Armenians to accept military service. The latter instead attacked the Turkish soldiers, killed some 300 of them and, with the additional arms thus secured, prepared for a determined resistance. An overwhelming Turkish force, however, was sent against the town; it fell, and then the Turks carried out in the extremest degree their newly devised system of deportation and dispersion.

Twenty thousand Turks from Thrace were taken to Zeitoun and established in the houses that for generations had belonged to the Armenian families. The latter were then scattered to the four winds of the Empire.

I talked with eye-witnesses who, coming to Constantinople from the interior, had seen this miserable population being dispersed and deported. They were being herded across the country by soldiers in groups ranging from 50 to several hundred. Old men who were unable to maintain the fast pace set by the mounted soldiers were beaten till they fell dead in their tracks. Children who were likewise too tender to stand the terrible strain dropped out by the wayside, while the mothers were driven relentlessly on with no hopes of ever again being able to find their little ones. Other mothers with babies in arms, unable to see the latter die under their very eyes, unable to give them the nourishment necessary to sustain life, and unable to bear the agony of leaving them by the wayside to an unknown fate, dropped them in wells as they passed, thus ending the sufferings of the little ones and having at least the consolation of knowing their fate.

The bulk of this miserable population from Zeitoun, that was able to withstand this herding across the desert interior of Asiatic Turkey, was planted largely in two places. One portion was established in a marshy region which, up to the present time, had never been habitable on account of the deadly malaria; the other portion was sent down in the direction of the Persian Gulf, to a locality so deadly that the poor victims prayed to be sent to the malarial marshes instead. Their prayers were in vain.

As in the system of deportation carried out in all other portions of the Empire, scores if not hundreds of these families from Zeitoun were separated and transplanted in such a manner as practically to preclude all possibility of their ever being reunited again.

In defence of these terrible measures which have been taken, the Turks at Constantinople declare that no one but the Armenians themselves is to blame. They state that when the present attack began on the Dardanelles, the Armenians were notified that if they took advantage of the moment when the Turks were concentrating every energy for the maintenance of the Empire, to rise in rebellion, they would be dealt with without quarter. This warning, however, the Armenians failed to heed. They not only rose in rebellion, occupying a number of important towns, including Van, but extended important help to the Russians in the latter's campaign in the Caucasus. As all these Armenians are Ottoman subjects, they have to be dealt with according to the stringent Turkish laws on such subjects.

While the Turks freely admit that this revolt of the Armenians was and is confined to those living near the Russian border, the authorities at Constantinople declare that at the present moment, when the very existence of the Empire is at stake from the attacks of outside enemies, it is quite out of the question for them to search out among the 2,000,000 Armenians of the Turkish Empire the comparatively few guilty ones and punish them alone. They declare that they have no choice except to ensure their safety against all the Armenians. By punishing all, they are certain to strike down the guilty ones and to prevent any more uprisings among the others.

While this is the Turkish side of the situation, there is also another side which I shall give on the authority of men who have passed practically their entire lives in Turkey and whose names, if I dared mention them, would be recognised in both Europe and America as competent authority. According to these men, the decision has gone out from the Young Turk Party that the Armenian population of Turkey must be set back fifty years. This has been decided upon as necessary in order to ensure the supremacy of the Turkish race in the Ottoman Empire, which is one of the basic principles of the Young Turk Party. The situation, I am told, is absolutely analogous to that which preceded the Armenian massacres under Abd-ul-Hamid. So far, however, the Young Turks have confined themselves to the new system of deportation, dispersion and separation of families.

To the Armenian population in general that is affected at the present moment by the carrying out of these orders, I have found but one exception. This is the Armenian population of Constantinople, which numbers about 70,000. There Ambassador Morgenthau assumed a sort of unofficial protectorate and guarantee for the Armenians, with the result that up to the present moment less than 300 of them have been molested.

So terrible have been the sufferings of the Armenians during the past three months that at the moment I left Constantinople, in order to be able to write this story, there had begun a reversal of feeling towards them even amongst the Turks themselves. The latter declared that the orders, which had been issued solely as a necessary safeguard for the Empire against the Armenians, had been carried out by the local authorities, especially in the districts far from Constantinople, with a degree of severity that had never been intended. Talaat Bey, Minister of the Interior, had even begun to permit a few dozen of the men, whose loyalty to the Turkish Government was beyond question, to return to their homes.

The condition of the Armenian population at the present moment, however, is pitiful beyond words. Practically all the families have been deprived of their means of support by the deportation of the husbands, fathers and sons. The women and children who have been left behind to shift for themselves are practically helpless, as at the present moment, when the entire Empire is being drained of every resource for the carrying on of the war, neither work nor food is to be had. In thousands of cases, too, the deported families have been planted among strong Musulman communities, where the Christian Armenians are despised and opposed at every turn.

In the midst of all this misery help is only being extended from two quarters. Ambassador Morgenthau, at Constantinople, is working day and night to induce the Turkish Government to relent from the severity of its measures, and the American missionaries throughout the Empire have also dropped all thought of religious propaganda in order to attend to the material needs of the victims. Their combined efforts, however, constitute hardly a drop of help in the whole sea of misery.

The situation is rendered especially difficult by the fact that nothing can be done in an official way even by governments like the United States. The Armenians are subjects of the Ottoman Empire, and the latter has the full right to deal with them as it thinks necessary in the interests of the Empire as a whole.

147. URMIA, SALMAS, AND HAKKIARI: FULLER STATEMENT BY MR. PAUL SHIMMON, EDITED, AS A PAMPHLET, BY THE REV. F.N. HEAZELL, ORGANISING SECRETARY OF THE ARCHBISHOP OF CANTERBURY'S ASSYRIAN MISSION.

The scene of the Assyrian massacres is the plain of Urmi (or Urmia) on the west side of the lake of that name in N.W. Persia. The city of Urmi is situated on the western side of the lake; further west are the mountains of Kurdistan, forming the frontier between Turkey and Persia. These mountains give shelter to the wild bands of Kurds (ever ready to descend on the plain of Urmi), who can easily retire to their inaccessible homes with their ill-gotten spoil. For some years past a Russian force has been stationed in the Urmi plain, with the object of keeping the Kurds under control. These troops were distributed between Khoi, Salmas, Urmi, and Soujboulak, at the extreme south of the lake. Urmi is an isolated spot, and, from a military point of view, ill-suited for defence against a strong attacking force. It is easily accessible to the Kurds from the west, while the two high passes on both north and south, and the lake on the east, seal up a besieged army in a very dangerous locality.

The plain of Urmi has a charm for all travellers; in the spring and early summer it is a veritable paradise. Its running waters, its gardens, its vineyards, orchards, and melon fields, its tobacco plantations and rice fields, give a variety of colour and a beauty of scene seldom met with in the East.

The plain of Urmi is the home of some thirty-five thousand of the Assyrian (or East Syrian) Christians, part of whom dwell in the city, the rest being distributed among seventy villages scattered over the plain. These people are cultivators of the soil and keepers of vineyards. Away to the west, united to them by religion and language, five the mountaineer Syrians. First, we have many villages in the districts of Tergawar and Mergawar, both in Persia; then comes Nochea, the seat of the Metropolitan Bishop, Mar Khananishu. Still further west, over the frontier into Turkey, in the very heart of the mountains, dwells the Patriarch, Mar Shimun, at once a civil and ecclesiastical ruler, who is responsible to the Turkish Government for the independent tribes of Baz, Djîlu, Tkhuma, and Tiari, who are spread over the tract of country which stretches from Djoulamerk to Amadia and then down towards Mosul.

The proverbial "calm before the storm" was literally true in the case of the massacre of the Syrian Christians. In the Urmi plain, the presence of Russian troops for many years past brought security and prosperity. Raiding on the part of the Kurds was stopped, and highway robbery was no longer heard of. It did not mean that the Moslems were any more friendly disposed towards the Christians; they feared them, that was all. The old hatred for the Christian race slumbered for a time, and dared not show itself, so long as the Russian troops were there to see that the peace was not disturbed.

Events began to take a different turn with the outbreak of war in Europe. The Kurds, always ready for a fight, began to plunder the rich districts of Tergawar and Mergawar; the Christian inhabitants fled to Urmi, and were distributed among the villages of the plain. In October, 1914, the Kurds made a determined effort to capture the city. A violent assault was made by them, and for a time they withstood the fire of the Russian artillery. They sacked and burned the villages of Anhar and Alwach, and advanced within gunshot of the city. Reinforcements arrived, and with the help of Syrians, armed by the Russians, the Kurds and Turks were driven back. Then it was that the Russian officers found that the Syrians could do great service in scouting, and they employed trained Syrians to keep open the lines of communication.

Such was the condition of affairs before the declaration of war between the Allied Powers and Turkey. After the declaration of war the curtain was withdrawn and the drama was played, the like of which has not yet been seen, even in this most cruel war.

The Turks had become aggressive on the Russian frontier near the Caucasus. In December they massed troops at Sari-Kamysh, near Kars, and sought to cut the railway to Tiflis. This created a scare in the Caucasus which was serious enough to cause a withdrawal of the Russian forces from N.W. Persia. Orders reached Urmi on the 30th December for the withdrawal of the Russian troops, but these were not made known to the European missionaries and Syrians until three days later. The news came like a thunderclap. The Christian inhabitants were entirely unprepared; when they awoke to the fact of the danger they were in, they found that the roads were all blocked, the Russian protectors had left, means of transport were wanting, the Kurdish and Turkish armies were almost at the city gates; they were caught in a trap. A large number of the Syrians outside the city and many Armenians were able to get away; most of these were from the Nazlu district, others were refugees from the Turkish frontier, some ten thousand in all. Two English missionaries then left, also the Belgian officials of the Persian Government and some prominent Syrians of Urmi. All the rest remained behind.

The Russian army left on Saturday, the 2nd January, and on the next day the Persian Moslems plundered the village of Tcharbash, and Dilgusha, the two districts which contained the houses of the well-to-do Christian population.

It was a painful sight to see the notable Moslems of the city taking part in this plunder. The whole city was out, "blessing each other's feast," as they termed it, and carrying off everything that came to hand. Houses were stripped of furniture, and even doors and windows carried away. There was also an attempt to plunder some of the houses within the city, but this was frustrated by the efforts of the French and American missionaries.

There is no doubt that the presence of the American missionaries, and of Mr. Nisan, who remained in the English Mission-house, prevented matters from taking a worse turn. The American flag, which was flying over the American and English houses, had some influence in restraining the brutal savagery of the mob.

In the villages, however, the reign of terror had begun. The Kurds had been informed of the Russian retirement, and were soon at work plundering and massacring the Christians in the Baranduz district (S. Urmi). Dizateka, Sâtloui, Aliabad, Shimshadjean, Babaroud, Darbaroud, Sardaroud, Teka, and Ardishai were already in their hands. Looting, plundering, massacre and rape were the order of the day. In one village, half Moslem and half Christian, the Syrians took shelter in the houses of their Moslem neighbours, and hid themselves under the heaps of snow in the yards. In Ardishai, Kasha Ablakhat, the Syrian priest, was escaping on horseback with his daughter; he was killed and the girl carried off to Kurdistan, where she was married by force to a Kurd. Four months later came the sad news that she had died. During her illness she had as companion another Syrian girl, also a captive. This other girl relates that the Moslem women came and turned the sick woman's bed towards the south, the direction to which all Moslems look on their deathbed. The invalid begged her companion to turn her face to the east, that she might die a Christian.

In another village all the male population but three were killed, or died of typhoid fever.

One young man had just arrived from the United States after an absence of nine years; he had come home to be married. The next morning, he, his mother, sister, and an uncle were all killed. Their property was carried off and 500 tomans in cash. Most of the people were killed in their flight; their bodies were not buried, for no one dared to go and perform this office. Many of the bodies were eaten by dogs.

There is one large village—Geogtapa—some five miles from the city of Urmi. To this place many people from the south of Urmi plain fled for safety, as they thought the inhabitants were well able to defend themselves. But on Monday night, the 4th January, a messenger from the Kurds came, saying that if the people surrendered and paid a large sum of money, their village would be spared. The villagers sent to Urmi to consult the village master, but long before the messengers returned the Kurds had commenced their attack on the place. The Christians put up a magnificent fight, but could not hold out long before overwhelming numbers. The Kurds were also assisted by the Persian Moslems, who were eager to pay off old scores against their Christian neighbours. As the day wore on the situation grew desperate. The cries of women and children, who had gathered in the churches, were heart-rending. The smoke of the burning buildings from four sides overcame the defenders. Finally all took refuge in the two churches on the brow of the hill, which dominates the village. Late in the afternoon, by God's providence, a rescue was made. Dr. Packard, the American missionary, with three Syrian attendants, came with the American flag and made terms of capitulation. The men, women, and children were to be allowed to go out alive, and the village and all the firearms were surrendered. Late that night, Dr. Packard, with some two thousand people, reached Urmi, where with difficulty shelter was found for them in quarters already crowded, in which they passed four months of untold horrors and suffering.

In Geogtapa, one elderly woman was left behind because she could not move on account of infirmity; her husband and daughter decided to stay with her. The Kurds killed the two old people, and on the daughter refusing to become Moslem, she also was killed.

Another pathetic case was that of an old priest and his wife, who thought if they gave up everything to the Kurds their lives would be spared. These people were visited by five different parties of Kurds in succession. They helped themselves to the property of the house, and took all the money they could find. Then came another party and asked for money; they were told there was nothing left. Then the old man, with the Bible in his hands, was murdered in the presence of his wife. They decided to kill the woman also, but in some mysterious way she avoided them and hid herself. After six days of hiding she crawled out and got to a neighbouring village, where she found shelter with some Moslems, who sent her to the city.

Nazlu District.

The Baranduz river villages and Geogtapa are south of the city of Urmi, and so were the first to fall a prey to the Kurds as they advanced from the south. The villages of the Nazlu district, such as Âda, Superghan, Mushawa, Sherabad, and Karadjalu, some of the wealthiest, not being in the line of advance, should have escaped the horrors of the other villages; but their turn came later, and their story of their woes is equally heartrending.

Âda, one of the largest villages, had been a place of refuge for many Syrians and Armenians late in the year 1914. Then when the Russian army passed that way many of the people followed them, to the number of sixty. The rest, however, all remained. Sunday, the 3rd January, passed off quietly, but the next day their troubles commenced. The Persian Moslems began to plunder the Syrian Christians. They broke open the houses, carried off the doors and windows, and emptied the buildings. No one was killed, however, although some shots were fired to intimidate the people. The Syrians exercised great restraint, as they feared a general massacre if they opposed the Moslems who came against them. The elders of the village, while this was going on, sent to the city to ask for protection. The messengers returned with a Turkish and Persian flag and a few soldiers, thinking this would be security for them; but they were deceived, for almost at once the Kurds attacked the village from all points. They stripped every man they found, took his money, and then killed him. As the others fled to the vineyards, they were followed by the Moslems, who killed them there. It is said that one Persian Moslem had killed twenty-five persons, and said: "I am not satisfied yet." Some eighty bodies lay about unburied; many who had been wounded were left to die of their wounds, as there was no one to tend them after they fell. The women and children, who had climbed to the roofs to avoid the fury of the Kurds, were afterwards brutally treated by their attackers, who behaved with the greatest barbarity. The churches were polluted, and the holy books destroyed. Many women were carried off and forced to become Moslems, and afterwards sold or married to their enemies.

A pathetic case is reported from Karadjalu. A woman, fleeing with her two children—her husband was abroad—met a Moslem mullah in her flight. He took the children, stripped them of their clothing, and threw them all into a stream, which was on the point of freezing. He then offered to marry the woman. On her refusal he left the woman on the road to her fate. She returned to the stream, and, taking her children from the water, carried them to a vineyard near by, where she placed them in a hollow place with some straw over them to try and warm them; both children died in the morning. Later the sorrowing woman found her way to Urmi, and five months afterwards the Russians caught this inhuman brute and made him suffer for his crime.

The flight to Urmi.

The city of Urmi became a veritable city of refuge for the Syrians and Armenians from the villages of the whole plain. By far the larger number found shelter in the American Mission premises, and some more in the compound of the English Mission, where Mr. Nisan was living. We have read of the flight from Antwerp in the *Times*, but it is a fairy tale compared with what happened in Urmi. Women arrived at the city in a bleeding condition. Some had been stripped of part of their clothes on the way, and arrived in one tunic shivering in the bitter cold of January; some told us how they had been stopped by four different bands of robbers; many were carried off, made captives, and forced to become Moslems.

The French Mission also afforded another place of refuge, where the French Lazarists, with Monseigneur Sontag and the Sisters of Charity, live. The crowded state of all the houses in the city quickly bred disease, which, combined with semi-starvation, made life unbearable. The Americans threw open their College and Hospital outside the city, and these were soon overcrowded. The Archbishop of Canterbury's Mission premises and the American yard close by formed one great quadrangle, and over this block the American flag was flying. In normal times these buildings could accommodate five hundred people; now there were some ten thousand crowded into this same area. After the first rush was over, the missionaries went to the villages, to search for this or that person who was missing. In this way many young women were restored to their families and delivered from Moslem captivity. But many of the less fortunate had to remain in the Moslem houses to which they had been carried. Many were ill and could not move; others were *enceintes*, and were ashamed to return to their homes. A young Moslem was carrying his Syrian "wife" to another village when he met Dr. Packard on the road. The girl threw herself at his feet and asked to be freed from her captor. She was taken to Urmi, only to die after a few weeks of typhoid fever.

The problem of feeding so large a number of people was a great one, and only half a pound of bread a day could be provided. But the worst suffering was caused by the overcrowding. Every available space was filled—rooms, churches, corridors, cellars, and stables, all alike were crowded with human beings.

Under these conditions, combined with the bad water supply and the lack of sanitary arrangements in an oriental city, it is not surprising that typhoid fever soon broke out and carried off thousands of people. More than four thousand lost their lives from this disease, while a thousand were killed by the Kurds in the villages. An accurate statement, prepared by the European missionaries, shows that 20 per cent. of the Urmi Christians perished in four months.

At the beginning of this reign of terror which we have described, the Kurds of Mamash, Mangur, Zarza, in the south, poured into the city. The Herki and the Begzadi from the west poured in at the same time. The son of one prominent sheikh from Shamsdinan came from Nochea and established himself in Dilgusha, just outside the city gates. On the arrival of the Turkish army, a few days later, order was for a time restored, and the Kurds and Moslems restrained from the bigger acts of violence. But as soon as the Turkish officers got hold of the reins of government the lives of the Christians became unbearable. For a time a Djihad—a Holy War—was spoken of on all sides, and the Christians gave up all hopes of being allowed to live. The Turks made it quite clear that they had come to serve Turkey, and did not conceal their desire to get rid of all Christians. They also set to work to fill their own pockets; 6,600 tomans were taken from the shop and store owners and other well-to-do people. They prepared a list of "suspected persons," who were to be put to death if not ransomed by the payment of a sum of money. In many cases the money was not forthcoming, and the prisoners were put to death.

It was in this way that Mar Dinkha, Bishop of Tergawar, met his death. Mar Elia, the Russian Bishop, was ransomed after a payment of 5,500 tomans had been made to the Turks.

The Tragedy of Gulpashan.

The case of the treatment of the village of Gulpashan is without parallel in the history of the Urmi massacres. It is the most wealthy and prosperous of all the villages of the plain, and its inhabitants are quiet and law-abiding people. When the sister village of Geogtapa was plundered and burnt, by an ominous fate Gulpashan was spared. Karani Agha, a Kurdish Chief, well spoken of as a man of high principle, had announced that the village was his property and that it was to be spared. For two months the people were left in peace. It was said to be due to a friendship which existed between the Christian village masters, one of whom was related to the German Consular Agent at Urmi, and the Moslems. A servant of the German Agent was there, and Turkish soldiers were placed to guard the village. On the 24th February, a band of Persian fedais, who had been unsuccessful in an attempt on Salmas, returned to Urmi and attacked the village. They feigned friendliness at first, until they had got the men of the place in their power. Then they tied them together with ropes and drove them to the cemetery, where they butchered them in a barbarous and cruel way. Then the men, still wild with blood, turned on the women, and, after treating them in an unseemly manner, put some of them to death. The American missionaries went afterwards and buried the dead, which they did in many other places also. This was the last of the massacres in the Urmi plain. The awful deeds that were perpetrated here were telegraphed to America, whereupon such strong representations were made by the United States Government that an order was given for their cessation.

The Massacre in Salmas.

In the plain of Salmas, to the west of Lake Urmi, there are many large and beautiful villages inhabited by Syrians and Armenians. For the most part these people had fled to Russia before the flight from Urmi took place; but their homes and fields shared the same fate as those in Urmi. The Turks found on their arrival there that a good number of Christians had hidden themselves in the houses of friendly Moslems. The Moslem Hadjis were ordered to prepare a letter, which every Christian must sign, stating that they had received kind consideration at the hands of their protectors. This was only a trick on the part of the Turks, for in this way they got to know the names and dwelling-places of about 725 Armenians and Syrians in Salmas. A few days later all these men, roped together in gangs, were marched to the fields at night between Haftevan and Khusrawa, and some were shot, while others were hacked to pieces, in one way and another, in the most horrible fashion. This happened in March, only three days before the return of the Russian troops. This timely arrival of help prevented the women of the place from sharing a like fate.

The Attack on the Syrians in the Turkish Mountains.

The rest of the awful story comes from the Turkish side, where the Patriarch and the larger number of the Syrians live in the mountains of Kurdistan. It was many months before news reached their brethren in Urmi as to what had been happening some hundred miles away. The Patriarch, Mar Shimun, was driven from his home in Quodshanis. He fled to Tiari with all the members of his household. The Patriarch's house was burnt, together with many other houses, including the house of the English Mission. Mar Shimun, writing to England a few days ago, tells us that for four months he has been a wanderer with his people, carrying on a war with the Turks and Kurds. They only gave up fighting when Turkish artillery was brought against them, which made it impossible for them to offer an effective resistance. Tiari and Tkhuma, both of which districts embrace many Christian villages, have been entirely destroyed. In August last 35,000 mountaineers fled to Salmas, Persia, but the larger part of the Syrians are still in the mountains wandering about from place to place, without food, and with no hope of anyone coming to their relief. The most pathetic part of the story is this. Surma, the Patriarch's sister, with Esther, her sister-in-law, and three small children, went down to Tchumbar in Tiari in June last for safety. With the approach of the Turkish army they soon had to flee to Dadoush, and from there to the great Church of Mar Audishu, in the Tâl country. They always had to travel on foot with just the clothes they could carry. "Often-times," Surma writes, "we were hungry, and the little children, who were with us, would fall asleep on the road, as we always had to travel at night." Surma spent three months in Mar Audishu, expecting to leave at any moment, when the enemy drew near. During that time there was food but almost no water, and none at all could be spared for washing or bathing. Occasionally they walked to a stream to bathe and wash their clothes.

The last day of their stay there was the saddest of all. On that day their brother Ishaya died of fever. Mar Shimun, hearing of his illness, had come over the day before. The enemy was then very near, and they could hear the sound of the guns in Tkhuma. Just when the funeral of their brother was to take place, Surma, Romi, and Esther with her children were compelled to leave the place, lest they should be caught by the enemy. Mar Shimun, two priests, and a few laymen remained behind at this time of danger to bury their brother. The burial service was quickly said and the body hastily interred, and Mar Shimun hastened after the fugitive women and children. They were only just in time, for, a few hours after their departure, the Turks arrived and made straight for the church, having heard that the Patriarch's household was there.

When writing to us on the 6th October, Mar Shimun says that he is in a village in Salmas, Persia, with his sisters and one or two members of his family. At the present moment there are with him 35,000 Syrians camped out in the plain of Salmas (4,000 feet above sea-level), sleeping in the fields with no clothes to cover them at night, clad in the rags which they have worn for many months, without food or shelter. The British Consul has telegraphed to England to say that unless these people are helped by charitable folk at home, two-thirds of them will die. No Christian nation has ever suffered for their religion as these people, and none has so great a claim on us as this unhappy Syrian remnant.

A List of the Ruined Nestorian Villages.

A. BARANDUZ DISTRICT:—

1. Darbaroud.
2. Sardaroud (Armenian).
3. Babaroud.
4. Ardishai.
5. Teka.
6. Alkian.
7. Kurtapa.
8. Shenabad.
9. Kosabad.
10. Mouradaloui.
11. Dizateka.
12. Shimshadjean.

13. Satloui.
14. Aliabad.
15. The Tazakands.
16. Diza of Baranduz.
17. Saralan.
18. Gulpashan.

B. URMI RIVER DISTRICT:—

1. Geogtapa[188] (partly destroyed).
2. Wazerabad.
3. Tcharbash.
4. Sangar—Burzukhan.
5. Sangar—Beglerbegi.
6. Alwaj.
7. Seir.
8. Haidarloui.
9. Mar Sargis.
10. Hasar and Kom.
11. Anhar.
12. Diza Agha Ali.[189]
13. Balaw.
14. Kizilashuk (chiefly Armenian).
15. Gerdabad (chiefly Armenian).
16. Mata d'Zaya and Karagöz.

C. Nazlu River District:—

    1. Ismael Agha's Kala.

    2. Armudagatch.

    3. Kosi.[190]

    4. Nazi.

    5. Karalari.

    6. Shumbulabad.

    7. Superghan.

    8. Ada.

    9. Mushabad.

    10. Yengidja.

    11. Khaneshan.

    12. Sherabad.

    13. Gavilan.

    14. Djemalabad.

D. Tergawar District:—

All villages, including—

    1. Queana.

    2. Mawana.

    3. Palulan.

E. Hakkiari District (Ottoman territory):—

All Tiari.

All Tkhoma, except Mazra'a.

All Barwar.

188. 400 families, the largest village in the district.
189. Nearest village to the city of Urmi.
190. Only one barn said to be left standing.

148. FIRST EXODUS FROM URMIA: NARRATIVE OF MR. J.D. BARNARD, OF THE ARCHBISHOP OF CANTERBURY'S ASSYRIAN MISSION; PUBLISHED IN THE "ASSYRIAN MISSION QUARTERLY PAPER," APRIL, 1915.

I have been asked to give a brief account of our journey home from Urmi. I will merely confine myself to the happenings on the road.

On the 3rd January we got upon our way, but we were in some doubt as to what course to pursue. The army, we were told, was taking the route northwards to Khoi, on the direct road to Russia. However, we did not like to quit the country altogether unless we were absolutely obliged, so we finally decided to make our way round the north of the Lake to Tabriz and there confer with our consul, if he were still present—reports varied on this point. An additional reason for the selection of this route was that M. Cordonnier was going in that direction, and his Customs officials who accompanied him were of incalculable assistance to us, as they knew the road, transacted all necessary business, and acted as an armed escort in case of an encounter with ugly customers by the way.

We had not gone far before we came up with a sight which we shall never forget to our dying day. As far as the eye could reach in either direction was a great river of fugitives, comprising very nearly the whole Christian population of the villages of the Urmi plain. They had had to flee at a moment's notice with such things as they could carry; a great number were absolutely without food; the nights were bitterly cold; and many old people and little children died by the way. Especially painful was the passage over the high pass leading into the plain of Salmas. It was covered with deep snow, which on the northern slope became ice, and the sight of these poor creatures slipping and stumbling down the steep descent, with the precious beasts of burden falling from fatigue and totally unable to rise again, was one that Belgium could hardly equal. Worst of all was the feeling that we were powerless to render any assistance. Many a mother cried for a lift for her little ones on our horses, but what could one do in the midst of thousands?

On the second day we parted from this sad procession, they going on towards Khoi, and we, as I said above, taking the road eastward round the Lake. We met with all manner of reports by the way; it was quite impossible to learn the truth of what had happened at Tabriz, and we never knew what the next bend in the road was to bring forth. At one halting-place we met with a striking instance of the ups and downs of an oriental career, being overtaken by an ex-official of some importance in the service of the Governor of Urmi, now humbly and shamelessly suing our companion, against whom he had so often worked, for a place in the douanes. As we rounded the end of the Lake we saw a great column of smoke rising up from Sherafkhané, the landing-stage for the boats on the eastern shore, and were informed that the supply of petroleum was being burnt to prevent its falling into the hands of the enemy, the boats having been previously sunk.

On reaching Sofian we found a considerable number of Russian troops in the village, and took courage. We tried to telephone through to Tabriz to enquire who was there, but without success, so left our tired animals to come on in the morning—we had been travelling most of the previous night—while we went on to Tabriz in a carriage which most opportunely happened to be obtainable. We arrived that evening, the fifth day of our wanderings, to find that all the English residents had left some days ago; so we proceeded to the American consulate to ask advice. This was concise and definite: "The Russian troops may leave any minute—the Turks are only nine miles away—you had better get on as fast as you can." Again fortune favoured us, and we managed to procure a carriage which had just returned from conveying our consul, Mr. Shipley, to the frontier, only waiting a few hours to refresh ourselves, while things were made ready....

149. ERZEROUM: LETTER, DATED 21st MARCH, 1916, FROM THE REV. ROBERT S. STAPLETON TO THE HON. F. WILLOUGHBY SMITH, U.S. CONSUL AT TIFLIS; COMMUNICATED BY THE AMERICAN COMMITTEE FOR ARMENIAN AND SYRIAN RELIEF.

I have just posted a letter to you in reply to yours of the 29th February. This letter comes in the form of a request from the Armenians here. Let me give a few details of happenings here this last year and a half as a preface to the request.

When the mobilisation began here in August, 1914, the Armenians responded to it in goodly numbers and were placed in the ranks as well as in the hospitals as nurses and attendants. During the first half of last year they were taken from the ranks and hospitals and placed in the road-gangs. The doctors and druggists were still retained as such, but pushed to the rear. The artisans of this land were mostly from this race, and many were retained here for such work, as there was need, even after the others were deported last June.

As the Turkish Army is retreating these bands are being massacred in cold blood. Here is an item that was brought to me by the brother of one of our school-girls. He had been in the road-gang and then was put in with a crowd of workers who were preparing a club-house here. In January they were sent to Erzindjan and there lodged in prison. When the Commander and Governor from here arrived there the first order was to take these fifty Armenians out and shoot them. Four escaped by falling and lying under the dead till evening, and then by hard travelling came here. It is said that other gangs are being treated in a similar way.

Now the request is to ask you if you have means to bring these facts to the attention of Mr. Morgenthau, that he might intercede in the name of humanity against this wholesale slaughter of these men who have been working for the Turkish Army. Not a few women and children are being rescued as this side advances, having been kept by the Kurds. We were able to keep about twenty girls, with two women and one of our men teachers, who is still with us as my interpreter.

The Armenians of Russia are spending a great deal of money and time in this rescue work, for which many have come here. They feel very deeply when they hear these reports from the other side of the fighting line. I sincerely hope that some pressure can be brought to bear to stop this cruelty.

A SUMMARY OF ARMENIAN HISTORY UP TO AND INCLUDING THE YEAR 1915.

I. THE EUROPEAN WAR AND ARMENIA.

The War has brought us into a new relation with Armenia and the Armenian people. We knew them before as the name of an ancient civilisation, a stubborn rearguard of Christendom in the East, a scene of mission work and massacres and international rivalry; but only a few of us—missionaries, geographers, travellers and an occasional newspaper correspondent—were personally acquainted with the country and its inhabitants. To most people they remained a name, and when we read of their sufferings or traditions or achievements they made little more impression than the doings of the Hittites and Assyrians, who moved across the same Near Eastern amphitheatre several millenniums ago. We had no living contact, no natural relation, with Armenia in our personal or even in our political life.

Such a relation has suddenly been created between us by the War, and it is one of the strangest ironies of war that it fuses together and illuminates the very fabric it destroys. The civilisation in which we lived was like a labyrinth, so huge and intricate that none of the dwellers in it could altogether grasp its structure, while most of them were barely conscious that it had any structural design at all. But now that the War has caught it and it is all aflame, the unity and symmetry of the building are revealed to the common eye. As the glare lights it up from end to end, it stands out in its glory, in matchless outline and perspective; for the first time (and possibly for the last) we see its parts simultaneously and in proper relation, and realise for one moment the marvel and mystery of this civilisation that is perishing—the subtle, immemorial, unrelaxing effort that raised it up and maintained it, and the impossibility of improvising any equivalent structure in its place. Then the fire masters its prey; the various parts of the labyrinth fall in one by one, the light goes out of them, and nothing is left but smoke and ashes. This is the catastrophe that we are witnessing now, and we do not yet know whether it will be possible to repair it. But if the future is not so dark as it appears, and what has perished can in some measure be restored, our best guide and inspiration in the task will be that momentary, tragic, unique vision snatched out of the catastrophe itself.

The Armenians are not protagonists in the War; they bear none of the guilt for its outbreak and can have little share in the responsibility of building up a better future. But they have been seared more cruelly than any of us by the flames, and, under this fiery ordeal, their individual character as a nation and their part in the community of the civilised world have been thrown into their true relief.

For the first time, England and the Armenians are genuinely in touch with one another. In this desperate struggle between freedom and reaction we are fighting on the same side, striving for the same end. Our lot in the struggle has not, indeed, been the same, for while England is able to act as well as to suffer, the Armenians have suffered with hardly the power to strike a blow. But this difference of external fortune only strengthens the inward moral bond; for we, who are strong, are fighting not merely for this or that political advantage, this or that territorial change, but for a principle. The Powers of the Entente have undertaken the championship of small nationalities that cannot champion themselves. We have solemnly acknowledged our obligation to fulfil our vow in the case of Belgium and Serbia, and now that the Armenians have been overtaken by a still worse fate than the Serbians and the Belgians, their cause, too, has been taken up into the general cause of the Allies. We cannot limit our field in doing battle for our ideal.

It is easier, of course, for the people of France, Great Britain and America to sympathise with Belgium than with a more unfamiliar nation in a distant zone of the War. It needs little imagination to realise acutely that the Belgians are "people like ourselves," suffering all that we should suffer if the same atrocities were committed upon us; and this realisation was made doubly easy by the speedy publication of minute, abundant, first-hand testimony. The Armenians have no such immediate access to our sympathies, and the initial unfamiliarity can only be overcome by a personal effort on the part of those who give ear to their case; but the evidence on which that case rests has been steadily accumulating, until now it is scarcely less complete or less authoritative than the evidence relating to Belgium. The object of the present volume has been to present the documents to English and American readers in as accurate and orderly a form as possible.

Armenia has not been without witness in her agony. Intense suffering means intense emotional experience, and this emotion has found relief in written records of the intolerable events which obsessed the witnesses' memories. Some of the writers are Armenians, a larger number are Americans and Europeans who were on the spot, and who were as poignantly affected as the victims themselves. There are a hundred and forty-nine of these documents, and many of them are of considerable length; but in their total effect they are something more than an exhaustive catalogue of the horrors they set out to describe. The flames of war illuminate the structure of the building as well as the destruction of it, and the testimony extorted under this fiery ordeal gives an extraordinarily vivid impression of Armenian life—the life of plain and mountain, town and village, intelligenzia and bourgeoisie and peasantry—at the moment when it was overwhelmed by the European catastrophe.

In Armenia, though not in Europe, the flames have almost burnt themselves out, and, for the moment, we can see nothing beyond smoke and ashes. Life will assuredly spring up again when the ashes are cleared away, for attempts to exterminate nations by atrocity, though certain of producing almost infinite human suffering, have seldom succeeded in their ulterior aim. But in whatever shape the new Armenia arises, it will be something utterly different from the old. The Armenians have been a very typical element in that group of humanity which Europeans call the "Near East," but which might equally well be called the "Near West" from the Indian or the Chinese point of view[191]. There has been something pathological about the history of this Near Eastern World. It has had an undue share of political misfortunes, and had lain for centuries in a kind of spiritual paralysis between East and West— belonging to neither, partaking paradoxically of both, and wholly unable to rally itself decidedly to one or the other—when it was involved with Europe in the European War. The shock of that crowning catastrophe seems to have brought the spiritual neutrality of the Near East to a violent end, and however dubious the future of Europe may be, it is almost certain that it will be shared henceforth by all that lies between the walls of Vienna and the walls of Aleppo and Tabriz[192]. This final gravitation towards Europe may be a benefit to the Near East or another chapter in its misfortunes—that depends on the condition in which Europe emerges from the War; but, in either case, it will be a new departure in its history. It has been drawn at last into a stronger orbit, and will travel on its own paralytic, paradoxical course no more. This gives a historical interest to any record of Near Eastern life in the last moments of the Ancient Régime, and these Armenian documents supply a record of a very intimate and characteristic kind. The Near East has never been more true to itself than in its lurid dissolution; past and present are fused together in the flare.

II. AN OUTLINE OF ARMENIAN HISTORY.

The documents in this volume tell their own story, and a reader might be ignorant of the places with which they deal and the points of history to which they refer, and yet learn from them more about human life in the Near East than from any study of text-books and atlases. At the same time a general acquaintance with the geographical setting and historical antecedents is clearly an assistance in understanding the full significance of the events recorded here, and as this information is not widely spread or very easily accessible, it has seemed well to publish an outline of it, for the reader's convenience, in the same volume as the documents themselves. As many as possible of the places referred to are marked on the map at the end of the book, while here, in this historical summary, a brief account may be given of who the Armenians are and where they live.

Like the English, the French and most other nations, the Armenians have developed a specific type of countenance, and yet it would not always be easy to tell them by sight, for they are as hybrid in their physical stock as every other European or Near Eastern people. There are marked differences of pigmentation, feature and build between the Armenians of the East, West and South, and between the mountaineers, plain-dwellers and people of the towns, and it would be rash to speculate when these various strains came in, or to lay it down that they were not all present already at the date at which we first begin to know something about the inhabitants of the country[193].

We hear of them first in the annals of Assyria, where the Armenian plateau appears as the land of Nairi—a no-man's-land, raided constantly but ineffectually by Assyrian armies from the lowlands of Mosul. But in the ninth century B.C. the petty cantons of Nairi coalesced into the Kingdom of Urartu[194], which fought Assyria on equal terms for more than two hundred years and has left a native record of its own. The Kings of Urartu made their dwelling on the citadel of Van[195]. The face of the rock is covered with their inscriptions, which are also found as far afield as the neighbourhood of Malatia, Erzeroum and Alexandropol. They borrowed from Assyria the cuneiform script, and the earliest inscriptions at Van are written in the Assyrian language; but they quickly adapted the foreign script to their native tongue, which has been deciphered by English and German scholars, and is considered by them to be neither Semitic nor Indo-European, nor yet to have any discernible affinity with the still obscurer language of the Hittites further west. We can only assume that the people who spoke it were indigenous in the land. Probably they were of one blood with their neighbours in the direction of the Caucasus and the Black Sea, Saspeires[196] and Chalybes and others; and if, as ethnology seems to show, an indigenous stock is practically ineradicable, these primitive peoples of the plateau are probably the chief ancestors, in the physical sense, of the present Armenian race[197].

The modern Armenian language, on the other hand, is not descended from the language of Urartu, but is an Indo-European tongue. There is a large non-Indo-European element in it—larger than in most known branches of the Indo-European family—and this has modified its syntax as well as its vocabulary. It has also borrowed freely and intimately from the Persian language in all its phases—a natural consequence of the political supremacy which Iran asserted over Armenia again and again, from the sixth century B.C. to the nineteenth century A.D. But when all these accretions have been analysed and discarded, the philologists pronounce the basis of modern Armenian to be a genuine Indo-European idiom—either a dialect of the

Iranian branch or an independent variant, holding an intermediate position between Iranian and Slavonic.

This language is a much more important factor in the national consciousness of the modern Armenians than their ultimate physical ancestry, but its origin is also more difficult to trace. Its Indo-European character proves that, at some date or other, it must have been introduced into the country from without[198], and the fact that a non-Indo-European language held the field under the Kings of Urartu suggests that it only established itself after the Kingdom of Urartu fell. But the earliest literary monuments of the modern tongue only date from the fifth century A.D., a thousand years later than the last inscription in the Urartian language, so that, as far as the linguistic evidence is concerned, the change may have occurred at any time within this period. One language, however, does not usually supplant another without considerable displacements of population, and the only historical event of this kind sufficient in scale to produce such a result seems to be the migration of the Cimmerians and Scythians in the seventh century B.C. These were nomadic tribes from the Russian steppes, who made their way round the eastern end of the Caucasus, burst through into the Moghan plains and the basin of Lake Urmia, and terrorised Western Asia for several generations, till they were broken by the power of the Medes and absorbed in the native population. It was they who made an end of the Kingdom of Urartu, and the language they brought with them was probably an Indo-European dialect answering to the basic element in modern Armenian. Probability thus points to these seventh century invaders as being the source of the present language, and perhaps also of the equally mysterious names of "Hai(k)" and "Haiasdan," by which the speakers of this language seem always to have called themselves and their country. But this is a conjecture, and nothing more[199], and we are left with the bare fact that Armenian[200] was the established language of the land by the fifth century A.D.

The Armenian language might easily have perished and left less record of its existence than the Urartian. It is a vigorous language enough, yet it would never have survived in virtue of its mere vitality. The native Anatolian dialects of Lydia and Cilicia, and the speech of the Cappadocians[201], the Armenians' immediate neighbours on the west, were extinguished one by one by the irresistible advance of Greek, and Armenian would assuredly have shared their fate if it had not become the canonical language of a national church before Greek had time to penetrate so far eastward. Armenia lay within the radius of Antioch and Edessa (Ourfa), two of the earliest and strongest centres of Christian propaganda. King Tiridates (Drdat) of Armenia was converted to Christianity some time during the latter half of the third century A.D.[202] and was the first ruler in the world to establish the Christian Faith as his State religion. Christianity in Armenia adopted a national garb from the first. In 410 A.D. the Bible was translated into the Armenian language, in a new native script specially invented for the purpose, and this achievement was followed by a great outburst of national literature during the course of the fifth century. These fifth century works are, as has been said, the earliest monuments of the Armenian language. Most of them, it is true, are simply rather painstaking translations of Greek and Syriac theology, and the bulk of the creative literature was theological too. But there was also a notable school of historical writers (Moses of Khorene is its most famous representative), and the really important result of the stimulus that Christianity brought was the permanent preservation of the language's existence and its development into a medium for a national literature of a varied kind.

Thus the conversion of Armenia to Christianity, which took place at a more or less ascertainable date, was an even more important factor in the evolution of Armenian nationality than the original introduction of the national language, and the Armenians have done well to make St. Gregory the Illuminator, the Cappadocian Missionary to whom the conversion was due, their supreme national hero[203]. Henceforth, church and language mutually sustained each other, to the great enhancement of the vital power of both. They were, in fact, merely complementary aspects of the same national consciousness, and the national character of the church was further emphasised when it diverged in doctrine from the main body of Christendom—not by the formulation of any new or heretical dogma, but by omission to ratify the modifications of the primitive creed which were introduced by the Œcumenical Councils of the fifth century A.D.[204]

This nationalisation of the church was the decisive process by which the Armenians became a nation, and it was also this that made them an integral part of the Near Eastern world. Christianity linked the country with the West as intimately as the cuneiform script of Urartu had linked it with the civilisation of Mesopotamia; and the Near Eastern phenomenon consists essentially in the paradox that a series of populations on the borderland of Europe and Asia developed a national life that was thoroughly European in its religion and culture, without ever succeeding in extricating themselves politically from that continual round of despotism and anarchy which seems to be the political dispensation of genuinely Oriental countries.

No communities in the world have had a more troubled political history than these Near Eastern nationalities, and none have known how to preserve their church and their language so doggedly through the most appalling vicissitudes of conquest and oppression. In this regard the history of Armenia is profoundly characteristic of the Near East as a whole.

The strong, compact Kingdom of Urartu lies at the dawn of Armenian history like a golden age. It had only existed two centuries when it was shattered by the invaders from the Russian steppes, and the anarchy into which they plunged the country had to be cured by the imposition of a foreign rule. In 585 B.C. the nomads were cowed and the plateau annexed by Cyaxares the Mede, and, after the Persians had taken over the Medes' inheritance, the great organiser Darius divided this portion of it into two governments or satrapies. One of these seems to have included the basins of Urmia and Van, and part of the valley of the Aras[205]; the other corresponded approximately to the modern Vilayets of Bitlis, Mamouret-ul-Aziz and Diyarbekir, and covered the upper valleys of the Tigris and Euphrates[206]. They were called respectively the satrapies of Eastern and Western Armenia, and this is the origin of the name by which the Haik and their Haiasdan are now almost universally known to their neighbours. The word "Armenia" (Armina)[207] first appears in Darius' inscriptions; the Greeks adopted it from the Persian official usage, and from the Greeks it has spread to the rest of the world, including the Osmanli Turks[208].

Under the Persian Dynasty of the Achæmenids and their Macedonian successors, the two Armenian satrapies remained mere administrative divisions. Subject to the payment of tribute, the satraps were practically independent and probably hereditary, but the rulers' autonomy did not enable their subjects to develop any distinctive national life. In religion and culture the country took on a strong Persian veneer; and the situation was not essentially changed when, early in the second century B.C., the two reigning satraps revolted simultaneously from their overlord, the Seleucid King of Western Asia[209], and each founded a royal dynasty of their own. The decisive change was accomplished by Tigranes (Dikran) the Great (94 to 56 B.C.), a scion of the Eastern Dynasty, who welded the two principalities into one kingdom, and so created the first strong native sovereignty that the country had known since the fall of Urartu five centuries before.

If Gregory the Illuminator is the ecclesiastical hero of Armenia, King Tigranes is his political forerunner and counterpart. He was connected by marriage with Mithradates, the still more famous King of Pontic Cappadocia, who may be taken as the first exponent of the Near Eastern idea. Mithradates attempted to build an empire that should be at once cosmopolitan and national, Hellenic and Iranian, of the West and of the East, and Tigranes was profoundly influenced by his brilliant neighbour and ally. He set himself the parallel ambition of reconstructing round his own person the kingdom of the Seleucids, which had been shaken a century before by a rude encounter with Rome, weakened still further by the defection of Tigranes' own predecessors, and was now in the actual throes of dissolution. He laid himself out a new capital on the northern rim of the Mesopotamian steppe, somewhere near the site of Ibrahim Pasha's Viran Shehr, and peopled it with masses of exiles deported from the Greek cities he devastated in Syria and Cilicia. It was to be the Hellenistic world-centre for an Oriental King of Kings; but all his dreams, like Mithradates', were shattered by the methodical progress of the Roman power. A Roman army ignominiously turned Tigranes out of Tigranokerta, and sent back his Greek exiles rejoicing to their homes. The new Armenian kingdom failed to establish its position as a great power, and had to accept the position of a buffer state between Rome on the west and the Parthian rulers of Iran. Nevertheless, Tigranes' work is of supreme political importance in Armenian history. He had consolidated the two satrapies of Darius into a united kingdom, powerful enough to preserve its unity and independence for nearly five hundred years. It was within this chrysalis that the interaction of religion and language produced the new germ of modern Armenian nationality; and when the chrysalis was rent at last, the nation emerged so strongly grown that it could brave the buffets of the outer world.

Before Tigranes, Armenia had belonged wholly to the East. Tigranes loosened these links and knit certain new links with the West. The period that followed was marked by a perpetual struggle between the Roman and Parthian Governments for political influence over the kingdom, which was really a battle over Armenia's soul. Was Armenia to be wrested away altogether from Oriental influences and rallied to the European world, or was it to sink back into being a spiritual and political appanage of Iran? It seemed a clear issue, but it was not destined to be decided in either sense. Armenia was to be caught for two millenniums in the uncertain eddy of the Nearer East.

In this opposition of forces, the political balance inclined from the first in favour of the Oriental Power. The Parthians succeeded in replacing the descendants of Tigranes by a junior branch of their own Arsacid Dynasty; and when, in 387 A.D., the rivals agreed to settle the Armenian question by the drastic expedient of partition, the Sassanid kings of Persia (who had superseded the Parthians in the Empire of Iran) secured the lion's share of the spoils, while the Romans only received a strip of country on the western border which gave them Erzeroum and Diyarbekir for their frontier fortresses. In the cultural sphere, on the other hand, the West was constantly increasing its ascendancy. King Tiridates was an Arsacid, but he accepted Christianity as the religion of the State he ruled; and when, less than a century after his death, his kingdom fell and the greater part of the country and the people came directly under Persian rule, the Persian propaganda failed to make any impression. No amount of preaching or persecution could persuade the Armenians to accept Zoroastrianism, which was the established religion of the Sassanian State. They clung to their national church in despite of their political annihilation, and showed thereby that their spiritual allegiance was given irrevocably to the West.

The partition of 387 A.D. produced as long a political interregnum in Armenian history as the fall of Urartu in the seventh century B.C. In the second quarter of the seventh century A.D., the mastery of Western Asia passed from the Persians to the Arabs, and the Armenian provinces changed masters with the rest. Persian governors appointed by the Sassanid King of Kings were superseded by Arab governors appointed by the Omayyad and Abbasid Caliphs, and the intolerance of Zoroastrianism was replaced by the far stronger and hardly less intolerant force of Islam. Then, in the ninth century, the political power of the Abbasid Caliphate at Baghdad began to decline, the outlying provinces were able to detach themselves, and three independent dynasties emerged on Armenian soil:—

(*a*) The *Bagratids* founded a Christian principality in the north. Their capital was at Ani, in the upper basin of the Aras, and their rule in this district lasted nearly two centuries, from 885 to 1079 A.D.

(*b*) The *Ardzrounids* founded a similar Christian principality in the basin of Van. They reigned here from 908 to 1021 A.D.

(*c*) The *Merwanids*, a Kurdish dynasty, founded a Moslem principality in the upper basin of the Tigris. Their capital was at Diyarbekir, but their power extended northward over the mountains into the valley of the Mourad Su (Eastern Euphrates), which they controlled as far upwards as Melazkerd. They maintained themselves for a century, from 984 to 1085 A.D.

The imposing remains of churches and palaces at Ani and elsewhere have cast an undue glamour over the Bagratid House, which has been extended, again, to all the independent principalities of early mediæval Armenia. In reality, this phase of Armenian history was hardly more happy than that which preceded it, and only appeared a Golden Age by comparison with the cataclysms that followed. From the national point of view it was almost as barren as the century of satrapial independence which preceded the reign of Tigranes, and in the politics of this period parochialism was never transcended. Bagratids and Ardzrounids were bitter rivals for the leadership of the nation, and did not scruple to call in Moslem allies against one another in their constant wars. The south-western part of the country remained under the rule of an alien Moslem dynasty, without any attempt being made to cast them out. Armenia had no second Tigranes in the Middle Ages, and the local renewals of political independence came and went without profit to the nation as a whole, which still depended for its unity upon the ecclesiastical tradition of the national Gregorian Church.

In the eleventh century A.D., a new power appeared in the East. The Arab Empire of the Caliphs had long been receiving an influx of Turks from Central Asia as slaves and professional soldiers, and the Turkish bodyguard had assumed control of politics at Baghdad. But this individual infiltration was now succeeded by the migration of whole tribes, and the tribes were organised into a political power by the clan of Seljuk. The new Turkish dynasty constituted itself the temporal representative of the Abbasid Caliphate, and the dominion of Mohammedan Asia was suddenly transferred from the devitalised Arabs to a vigorous barbaric horde of nomadic Turks.

These Turkish reinforcements brutalised and at the same time stimulated the Islamic world, and the result was a new impetus of conquest towards the borderlands. The brunt of this movement fell upon the unprepared and disunited Armenian principalities. In the first quarter of the eleventh century the Seljuks began their incursions on to the Armenian plateau. The Armenian princes turned for protection to the East Roman Empire, accepted its suzerainty, or even surrendered their territory directly into its hands. But the Imperial Government brought little comfort to the Armenian people. Centred at Constantinople and cut off from the Latin West, it had lost its Roman universality and become transformed into a Greek national state, while the established Orthodox Church had developed the specifically Near Eastern character of a nationalist ecclesiastical organisation. The Armenians found that incorporation in the Empire exposed them to temporal and spiritual Hellenisation, without protecting them against the common enemy on the east. The Seljuk invasions increased in intensity, and culminated, in 1071 A.D., in the decisive battle of Melazkerd, in which the Imperial Army was destroyed and the Emperor Romanos II. taken prisoner on the field. Melazkerd placed the whole of Armenia at the Seljuk's mercy—and not only Armenia, but the Anatolian provinces of the Empire that lay between Armenia and Europe. The Seljuks carried Islam into the heart of the Near East.

The next four-and-a-half centuries were the most disastrous period in the whole political history of Armenia. It is true that a vestige of independence was preserved, for Roupen the Bagratid conducted a portion of his people south-westward into the mountains of Cilicia, where they were out of the main current of Turkish invasion, and founded a new principality which survived nearly three hundred years (1080-1375). There is a certain romance about this Kingdom of Lesser Armenia. It threw in its lot with the Crusaders, and gave the Armenian nation its first direct contact with modern Western Europe. But the mass of the race remained in Armenia proper, and during these centuries the Armenian tableland suffered almost ceaseless devastation.

The Seljuk migration was only the first wave in a prolonged outbreak of Central Asiatic disturbance, and the Seljuks were civilised in comparison with the tribes that followed on their heels. Early in the thirteenth century came Karluks and Kharizmians, fleeing across Western Asia before the advance of the Mongols; and in 1235 came the first great raid of the Mongols themselves—savages who destroyed civilisation wherever they found it, and were impartial enemies of Christendom and Islam. All these waves of invasion took the same channel. They swept across the broad plateau of Persia, poured up the valleys of the Aras and the Tigris, burst in their full force upon the Armenian highlands and broke over them into Anatolia beyond. Armenia bore the brunt of them all, and the country was ravaged and the population reduced quite out of proportion to the sufferings of the neighbouring regions. The division of the Mongol conquests among the family of Djengis Khan established a Mongol dynasty in Western Asia which seated itself in Azerbaijan, accepted Islam and took over the tradition of the Seljuks, the Abbasids and the Sassanids. It was the old Asiatic Empire under a new name, but it had now incorporated Armenia and extended north-westwards to the Kizil Irmak (Halys). For the first time since Tigranes, the whole of Armenia was reabsorbed again in the East, and the situation grew still worse when the Empire of these "Ilkhans" fell to pieces and was succeeded in the fifteenth century by the petty lordship of Ak Koyunli, Kara Koyunli and other nomadic Turkish clans.

The progressive anarchy of four centuries was finally stilled by the rise of the Osmanli power. The seed of the Osmanlis was one of those Turkish clans which fled across Western Asia before the Mongols. They settled in the dominions of the Seljuk Sultans, who had established themselves at Konia, in Central Anatolia, and who allowed the refugees to carve out an obscure appanage on the marches of the Greek Empire, in the Asiatic hinterland of Constantinople. The son and successor of the founder was here converted from Paganism to Islam[210], towards the end of the thirteenth century A.D., and the name of Osman, which he adopted at his conversion, has been borne ever since by the subjects of his House.

The Osmanli State is the greatest and most characteristic Near Eastern Empire there has ever been. In its present decline it has become nothing but a blight to all the countries and peoples that remain under its sway; but at the outset it manifested a faculty for strong government which satisfied the supreme need of the distracted Near Eastern world. This was the secret of its amazing power of assimilation, and this quality in turn increased its power of organisation, for it enabled the Osmanlis to monopolise all the vestiges of political genius that survived in the Near East. The original Turkish germ was quickly absorbed in the mass of Osmanlicised native Greeks[211]. The first expansion of the State was westward, across the Dardanelles, and before the close of the fourteenth century the whole of South-Eastern Europe had become Osmanli territory, as far as the Danube and the Hungarian frontier. The seal was set on these European conquests when Sultan Mohammed II. entered Constantinople in 1453, and then the current of expansion veered towards the east. Mohammed himself absorbed the rival Turkish principalities in Anatolia, and annexed the Greek "Empire" of Trebizond. In the second decade of the sixteenth century, Sultan Selim I. followed this up with a sweeping series of campaigns, which carried him with hardly a pause from the Taurus barrier to the citadel of Cairo. Armenia was overrun in 1514; the petty Turkish chieftains were overthrown, the new Persian Empire was hurled back to the Caspian, and a frontier established between the Osmanli Sultans and the Shahs of Iran, which has endured, with a few fluctuations, until the present day.

In the sixteenth century the whole Near Eastern world, from the gates of Vienna[212] to the gates of Aleppo and Tabriz, found itself united under a single masterful Government, and once more Armenia was linked securely with the West. From 1514 onwards the great majority of the Armenian nation was subject to the Osmanli State. It is true that the province of Erivan (on the middle course of the Aras) was recovered by the Persians in the seventeenth century, and held by them till its cession to Russia in 1834. But, with this exception, the whole of Armenia remained under Osmanli rule until the Russians took Kars, in the war of 1878. These intervening centuries of union and pacification were, on the whole, beneficial to Armenia; but with the year 1878 there began a new and sinister epoch in the relations between the Osmanli State and the Armenian nation.

191. There seems to be no available name to convey the Janus-character of this region. "Balkan" has all the connotation, but the word is allocated already to a much too limited geographical area. "Levantine" covers a wider geographical field, but suggests merely the superficial characteristics which the Near Eastern peoples share with many others in a certain transient stage of development.

192. The limits of the Near East are not easy to define. On the north-west, Vienna is the most conspicuous boundary-mark, but one might almost equally well single out Trieste or Lvov or even Prag. Towards the south-east, the boundaries are even more shadowy. It is perhaps best to equate them with the frontiers of the Arabic language, yet the genius of the Near East overrides linguistic barriers, and encroaches on the Arabic-speaking world on the one side as well as on the German-speaking world on the other. Syria is essentially a Near Eastern country, and a physical geographer would undoubtedly carry the Near Eastern frontiers up to the desert belt of the Sahara, Nefud and Kevir.

193. There is one physical type, classified by ethnologists as "Armenoid" or "Anatolian," which seems to be both indigenous and persistent in the Anatolian Peninsula and in the triangle included between the Black Sea, the Mediterranean and the Caspian. Its characteristics are very individual—a "sugarloaf" skull, broad from side to side and sliced off at the back;

prominent cheek-bones; a fleshy, hooked nose; and a rather clumsy, thick-set body. These features are distinguishable in the ancient Hittites of Eastern Anatolia, as they are portrayed in the native and Egyptian monuments of the 14th and 13th centuries B.C.; in the modern Tchatchadzé nomads of Lycia (the extreme South-West of the Peninsula); and in a considerable percentage of the living Armenian people, scattered all over the Near East.

194. Called "Ararat" in the Bible and "Alarodioi" by Herodotus.

195. "The City of Dhuspas (Tosp) in the land of Biaina (Van)." In the course of history the names have been transposed; Van is now the town, and Tosp the district.

196. Round the present town of Isbir, in the Tchorok Valley.

197. The chief evidence for the racial unity of all these primitive populations is the survival of the name of Khaldis, the national god of Urartu, throughout the Armenian plateau. On the banks of the Aras we have the district of Khaldiran, and the northern affluents of the river are fed by Lake Khaldir. Further west, the modern Vilayet of Trebizond was called the Province of Khaldia under the late Roman Empire, and there is still a Diocese of Khaldia maintained by the Orthodox Greek Church in the immediate hinterland of Trebizond.

198. The original focus from which the Indo-European languages spread having been situated apparently in what is now Austria-Hungary and the Ukraine.

199. It is equally possible that the modern Armenian language was introduced into the country at an earlier date, and existed there side by side with the official language of the Urartu inscriptions. Egyptian records show that an Iranian people, the Mitanni (Matienoi), were established in Northern Mesopotamia as early as the 16th century B.C., and their name clung to the Urmia basin as late as Strabo's day. They were the western outposts of Indo-European settlement on the Iranian plateau. On the whole, however the Mitanni are more likely to have been the originators of the Kurdish language than of the Armenian.

200. In the classical form, of which the spoken language of to-day is a development.

201. Probably a synthesis of Hittite and Cimmerian, corresponding to the Urartu-Scythian blend which we have suggested as the origin of Armenian.

202. The traditional date varies from 261 to 301 A.D.

203. A suggestive parallel to the way in which another foreign missionary, St. Patrick, has become the national hero of Ireland.

204. In 553 A.D. the national individuality of the Gregorian (Armenian) Church was given formal expression by the foundation of a new ecclesiastical era.

205. Herodotus' "Province of the Matienoi, Alarodioi and Saspeires."

206. This is the probable extent of Herodotus' puzzling "Province of the Armenians and Paktyes," and the certain extent of the later Sophene.

207. The provenance of this name is as obscure as every other problem of Armenian origins. It may mean "the land of Erimenas," a king of Urartu, known from an inscription on a votive offering at Van, just as the neighbouring province of Azerbaijan derives its name from the satrap Atropates; or (as Lord Bryce suggests) it may be a "portmanteau word," perhaps compounded of Urartu and Minni, the Assyrian name for the upper basin of the Greater Zab. The name of Kat-Patuka (Cappadocia) is a possible analogy to this latter suggestion.

208. Turkish "Ermen-ler."

209. The Seleucid Dynasty had inherited most of the Asiatic dominions acquired by Alexander the Great when he conquered the Achæmenid (Persian) Empire.

210. This is the view of Mr. Herbert Adams Gibbons, the most recent historian of the early Ottoman Empire.

211. The people of the East Roman Empire in its latter days were Greeks in the sense that they spoke the "Romaic" modification of the Ancient Greek language; but most of them had only become Greeks by the loss of their native language at the date when the Armenians, unlike them, had successfully preserved theirs.

212. The Osmanlis besieged Vienna twice, and held a frontier within ninety miles of it for a century and a half.

III. DISPERSION AND DISTRIBUTION OF THE |ARMENIAN NATION.

We have now traced the political vicissitudes of Armenia down to its incorporation in the Ottoman Empire, and are in a position to survey the effects of this troubled political history on the social life and the geographical extension of the Armenian people.

At the present day the Armenians are, next to the Jews, the most scattered nation in the world, but this phenomenon does not begin to appear until a comparatively late stage in their history. At the time of the Partition of 387

A.D. they were still confined to a compact territory between the Euphrates, Lake Urmia and the River Kur. It was the annexation of the western marches to the Roman Empire that gave the first impetus to Armenian migration towards the west. After 387 A.D. the Roman frontier garrisons were moved forward into the new Armenian provinces, and these troops were probably recruited in the main, according to the general Roman custom, from the local population. But in the middle of the seventh century the Roman frontiers were shorn away by the advance of the new Arab power; the garrisons beyond the Euphrates were withdrawn towards the north-west, and, after a century of darkness and turmoil, during which all the old landmarks were effaced, we find that the "Armeniac Army Corps District" has shifted from the banks of the Euphrates to the banks of the Halys (Kizil Irmak) and become approximately coincident with the modern Vilayet of Sivas. This transference of the troops must have meant in itself a considerable transference of Armenians, and it can be taken for granted that the retiring armies were accompanied by a certain portion of the civilian population. We can thus date back to the seventh century the beginning of those flourishing Armenian colonies in the towns of north-eastern Anatolia which suffered so terribly in the ordeal of 1915.

The mountain zone between the Roman fortress of Sivas (Sebasteia) on the Halys and the Arab posts along the Euphrates, from Malatia to Erzeroum, was now debatable territory between the Moslem and the Christian Empires, and in the eighth century it was held by an independent community of Armenian heretics called Paulikians. These Paulikians led an untamed, Ishmaelitish existence. They were excommunicated for their tenets by the Gregorian Armenian Church, as well as by the Orthodox Patriarch at Constantinople, and they raided impartially in the territories of the Roman Empire and the Arab Caliphate. The Emperors waged against them a war of extermination, and anticipated the present Ottoman policy by deporting them from their mountain fastnesses to the opposite ends of the Imperial territory. In 752 A.D. a number of them were settled in Thrace, to exercise their military prowess in holding the frontier against the Bulgars; and, in 969 A.D., the Emperor John Tzimiskes (himself an Armenian) transplanted a further body of them to Philippopolis. It may be doubted whether there is any direct connexion between them and the present (Gregorian) Armenian colony in the latter city, but their numbers and influence must have been considerable, if one may judge by the vigorous spread of their tenets among the Bulgars and the Southern Slavs, and they are noteworthy as the forerunners of the Armenian Dispersion in Europe, as well as of the Protestant Reformation.[213]

Migrations on a larger scale were produced by the Turkish invasions of the eleventh century. In 1021 A.D., for instance, the Ardzrounian Dynasty of

Van surrendered its home territory to the Roman Empire in exchange for a more sheltered principality at Sivas. It only reigned sixty years in exile before it was overwhelmed there also by the advance of the Turkish tide; but the present Armenian villages in the Sivas Vilayet are doubtless derived from these Ardzrounian refugees. In the very year, again, in which the sovereignty of the Ardzrounids was extinguished at Sivas, the Bagratids of Ani founded themselves a second kingdom in Cilicia. We have spoken of this kingdom already; it is represented to-day by a chain of Armenian mountain towns and villages which stretches all the way from the headwaters of the Sihoun (Saros) and Djihoun (Pyramos) to the shores of the Gulf of Alexandretta.

The still more terrible invasions of the thirteenth century scattered the Armenians even further afield. The relations of Lesser Armenia with the Crusader Principalities opened for the Armenians a door into Western Europe. When the Roupenian Dynasty became extinct, it was succeeded by a branch of the French House of Lusignan summoned from Cyprus, and in 1335 there was the first secession from the national Gregorian Church to the Communion of Rome. These new adherents to the Papal allegiance spread far and wide over Latin Christendom. A strong colony of Armenian Catholics established itself at Lemberg, recently won by Polish conquest for the Catholic Church; and others settled at Venice, the European focus of the Levantine trade. In this Venetian settlement the tradition of Armenian culture was kept alive by the famous brotherhood of Mekhitarist Monks. They founded the first Armenian printing press here, in 1565, and maintained a constant issue of Armenian publications. Their greatest work was a magnificent thesaurus of the Armenian language, which appeared in 1836.

This Roman Catholic connexion has been of very great importance in preserving the link between Armenia and the west, and since the beginning of the nineteenth century the bonds have been strengthened by a Protestant strand. The American Missions in Turkey were founded in 1831. Debarred by the Ottoman Government from entering into relations with the Moslem population, they devoted themselves to the Christian elements, and the Armenians availed themselves more eagerly than any other Near Eastern nationality[214] of the gifts which the Americans offered. Four generations of mission work have produced a strong Protestant Armenian community, but proselytism has not been the deliberate object of the missionaries. They have set themselves to revive and not to convert the national Armenian Church, and their schools and hospitals have been open to all who would attend them, without distinction of creed. Their wide and well-planned educational activity has always been the distinctive feature of these American Missions in the Ottoman Empire. Besides the famous Robert College and the College for Women on the Bosphorus, they have established schools and other institutions in many of the chief provincial towns, with fine buildings and full staffs of well-trained American and Armenian teachers. Due acknowledgment must also be given to the educational work of the Swiss Protestants and of the Jesuits; but it can hardly compare with the work of the Americans in scale, and will scarcely play the same part in Armenian history. There is little need here to speak in praise of the American missionaries; their character will shine out to anyone who reads the documents in this volume. Their religion inspires their life and their work, and their utter sincerity has given them an extraordinary influence over all with whom they come in contact. The Ottoman Government has trusted and respected them, because they are the only foreign residents in Turkey who are entirely disinterested on political questions; the Gregorian Church cooperates with them and feels no jealousy, and all sections of the Armenian nation love them, because they come to give and not to get, and their gifts are without guile[215]. America is exercising an unobtrusive but incalculable influence over the Near East. In the nineteenth century the missionaries came to its rescue from America; in the twentieth century the return movement has set in, and the Near Eastern people are migrating in thousands across the Atlantic. The Armenians are participating in this movement at least as actively as the Greeks, the Roumans, the Serbs, the Montenegrins and the Slovaks, and one can already prophesy with assurance that their two-fold contact with America is the beginning of a new chapter in Armenian history.

Meanwhile the subjection of Armenia proper to the Mongol Ilkhans for nearly two centuries, and subsequently to the Shahs of modern Persia for certain transitory periods, produced a lesser, but not unimportant, dispersion towards the east. In the seventeenth century the skilled and cultured Armenian population of Djoulfa, on the River Aras, was carried away captive to the Persian capital of Ispahan, where the exiles started a printing press and established a centre of Armenian civilisation. Ever since then the Armenian element has been a factor in the politics and the social development of Iran, and from this new centre they have spread over the Indian Peninsula hand in hand with the extension of British rule.

Thus the Armenian nation has been scattered, in the course of the centuries, from Calcutta to New York, and has shown remarkable vitality in adapting itself to every kind of alien environment[216]. The reverse side of the picture is the uprooting of the nation from its native soil. The immigrant tribes from Central Asia did not make a permanent lodgment in the Armenian homelands. Some of them drifted back into Azerbaijan and the steppe country along the coast of the Caspian and the lower courses of the Aras and the Kur; others were carried on towards the north-west, along the ancient Royal Road, and imposed the Moslem faith and the Turkish language upon the population of Central Anatolia. The Armenian plateau, entrenched between Tigris, Euphrates and Aras, stood out like a rock, dividing these two

Turkish eddies. Nevertheless, the perpetual shock of the Seljuk and the Mongol raids relaxed the hold of the Armenians on the plateau. The people of the land were decimated by these invasions, and when the invaders had passed on beyond or vanished away, the terrible gaps in the ranks of the sedentary population of Armenia proper were filled by nomadic Kurdish shepherds from the south-east, who drifted into Old Armenia from the mountain girdle of Iran, just as the Albanians drifted into the Kossovo Plain from their own less desirable highlands, after the population of Old Serbia had been similarly decimated by the constant passage of the Ottoman armies.

This Kurdish penetration of Armenia had begun already by the tenth century A.D.; it was far advanced when the Osmanlis annexed the country in 1514, and it was confirmed by the policy of the Ottoman Government, which sought to secure its new territories by granting privileges to the Kurdish intruders and inviting their influx in greater numbers from their homelands in the sphere of influence of the rival Persian Empire. The juxtaposition of nomad and cultivator, dominant Moslem and subject Giaour, was henceforth an ever-present irritant in the social and political conditions of the land; but it did not assume a fatal and sinister importance until after the year 1878, when it was fiendishly exploited by the Sultan Abd-ul-Hamid.

But before we examine the relations between the Armenian nation and the Ottoman Government, it will be well to survey the distribution of the Armenian element in the Ottoman Empire, as it had developed during the four centuries of Ottoman rule that elapsed between the campaign of Selim I. and the intervention of Turkey in the present European War. The survey shall be brief, for it has been anticipated, sometimes in greater detail, in the separate notes prefixed to the different groups of documents in the volume.

A traveller entering Turkey by the Oriental Railway from Central Europe would have begun to encounter Armenians at Philippopolis in Bulgaria, and then at Adrianople, the first Ottoman city across the frontier. Had he visited any of the lesser towns of Thrace, he would have found much of the local trade and business in Armenian hands, and when he arrived at Constantinople he would have become aware that the Armenians were one of the most important elements in the Ottoman Empire. He would have seen them as financiers, as export and import merchants, as organisers of wholesale stores; and when he crossed the Bosphorus and explored the suburban districts on the Asiatic side, he might even have fancied that the Armenian population in the Empire was numerically equal to the Turkish. The coast of the Sea of Marmora was overlooked by flourishing Armenian villages; at Armasha, above Ismid, there was a large Theological Seminary of the Gregorian Church, and there were important Swiss and American institutions at Bardizag (Baghtchedjik) and Adapazar. At Adapazar alone the Armenian population numbered 25,000.

Beyond Adapazar, however, the Armenian element dwindled, and anyone who followed the Anatolian Railway across Asia Minor to the rail-head in the northern spurs of Taurus, would have felt that he was travelling through an essentially Turkish land. There were colonies of Armenian artisans and shopkeepers and business men in important places on the line, like Afiun Kara Hissar or Konia; but there were an equal number of Greeks, and both in town and country the Turks outnumbered them all. But once Taurus was crossed, the Armenians came again to the fore. They were as much at home in the Cilician plain and coastland as on the littoral of the Sea of Marmora and the Bosphorus. Adana, Tarsus and Mersina, with their Armenian churches and schools, had the same appearance of being Armenian cities as Adapazar or Ismid: and if at this point the traveller had left the beaten track and worked his way up north-eastward into the Cilician highlands, he would have found himself for the first time in an almost exclusively Armenian country, and would have remarked a higher percentage of Armenians in the population than in any other district of Turkey till he came to Van. But this belt of Armenian villages, though thickly set, was quickly passed, and when you emerged on the south-eastern side of it and stepped out on to the rim of the Mesopotamian amphitheatre, you had reached one of the boundaries of the Armenian Dispersion. There were Armenian outposts in the cities of the fringe—Marash, Aintab, Ourfa, Aleppo—but as soon as you plunged into the Mesopotamian steppe or the Syrian desert you were in the Arabic world, and had left Armenia behind[217].

The traveller would have seen more of the Armenians if he had turned off from the Anatolian Railway at Eski Shehr, a few hours' journey south of Adapazar, and taken the branch line eastward to Angora. At Angora the Armenians were again a conspicuous element, and the further east you went from Angora the more they increased in social and numerical importance. Beyond the Kizil Irmak (Halys), in the Sandjak of Kaisaria and the Vilayet of Sivas, they constituted the great majority of the urban middle class. The strongest centres of Armenian national life in Turkey were towns like Marsovan, Amasia, Zila, Tokat, Shabin Kara-Hissar or the City of Sivas itself, or such smaller places as Talas and Everek in the neighbourhood of Kaisaria. In all this region Turks and Armenians were about equally balanced, Turks in the country and Armenians in the town, and the proportions were the same in the riviera zone along the Black Sea coast—Samsoun and Kerasond and Trebizond—though here other racial elements were intermingled— Lazes and Greeks, and the advance guards of the Kurds.

Trebizond in ancient times was the last Greek colony towards the east, and it is always a place that beckons travellers forward, for it is the terminus of that ancient caravan route which stretches away across Persia into the far interior of the Asiatic continent. Anyone who started to follow this highway across the mountains, through Gumushkhané and Baibourt to Erzeroum, would have noticed little change in these first stages of his journey from what he had seen in the Vilayet of Sivas. There were the same Turkish countryside and the same Armenian towns, with, perhaps, an increasing Armenian element in the rural population, culminating in an actual preponderance of Armenian villages when you reached the plain of Erzeroum. With Erzeroum the second section of the caravan road begins; it crosses from valley to valley among the headwaters of the Aras and the Eastern Euphrates (Mourad Su), and winds away eastward at the foot of Ararat in the direction of Bayazid and Tabriz. But here the explorer of Armenia must turn his face to the south, and, as he does so, his eyes are met by a rampart of mountains more forbidding than those he has traversed on his journey from the coast, which stretch across the horizon both east and west.

This mountain barrier bears many names. It is called the Bingöl Dagh where it faces Erzeroum; further westward it merges into the ill-famed Dersim; but the whole range has a common character. Its steeper slope is towards the north, and this slope is washed by the waters of the Aras and the Kara Su (Western Euphrates), which flow east and west in diametrically opposite directions, flanking the foot of the mountain wall with a deep and continuous moat.

Whoever crosses this moat and penetrates the mountains passes at once into a different world. The western part of Turkey, which we have been describing so far, is a more or less orderly, settled country—as orderly and settled, on the whole, as any of the other Near Eastern countries that lie between the Euphrates and Vienna. The population is sedentary; it lives in agricultural villages and open country towns. But when you cross the Euphrates, you enter a land of insecurity and fear. The peasant and townsman live on sufferance; the mastery is with the nomad; you are setting foot on the domain of the Kurd.

This insecurity was the chronic condition of Armenia proper, and it was not merely due to the unfortunate political experiences of the land. In its geographical configuration, as well as in its history, the Armenian plateau is a country of more accentuated characteristics and violent contrasts than the Anatolian Peninsula which adjoins it on the west. It contains vast stretches of rolling, treeless down, where the climate is too bleak and the soil too thin for cultivation; and, again, there are sudden depressions where the soil is as rich and the climate as favourable as anywhere in the world. There are the deep ravines of rivers, like the Mourad Su, which carve their course haphazard across tableland and plain. There are volcanic cones, like the Sipan and the Nimroud Dagh, and lacustrine areas, like the basin of Lake Van. The geography of the country has partitioned it eternally between the shepherd and the cultivator—the comparatively dense and sedentary population of the plains and the scattered and wandering inhabitants of the highlands—between civilisation and development on the one hand and an arrested state of barbarism on the other. The Kurd and the Armenian are not merely different nationalities; they are also antagonistic economic classes, and this antagonism existed in the country before ever the Kurdish encroachments began. Most of the nomadic tribes that frequent the Armenian plateau now pass for Kurds, but many of them are only nominally so. In the Dersim country, for instance, which coincides roughly with the peninsula formed by the Western and Eastern branches of the Euphrates (Kara Su and Mourad Su), the Kurds are strongly diluted with the Zazas, whose language, as far as it has been investigated, bears at least as much resemblance to Armenian as to Kurdish, and whose primitive paganism, though it may have taken some colour from Christianity, is free to this day from the slightest veneer of Islam.[218] These Zazas represent an element which must have existed in the land from the beginning and have harassed the national rulers of Mediæval and Ancient Armenia as much as it harasses the modern Armenian townsman and peasant or the local Ottoman authorities.

On the eve of the catastrophe of 1915, this region beyond the Euphrates was a treasure-house of mingled populations and diversified forms of social life. Its north-western bastion is the Dersim, a no-man's-land of winding valleys and tiny upland plains, backing northwards on to the great mountain retaining-wall, with its sheer fall to the Euphratean moat. In the Dersim innumerable little clans of Zazas and Kurds lived, and continue to live, their pastoral, brigand life, secluded from the arm of Ottoman authority. A traveller proceeding south from Erzeroum would give the Dersim a wide berth on his right and cross the peninsula at its neck, by the headwaters of the Aras and the plain of Khnyss. He would strike the course of the Mourad Su where it cuts successively through the fertile, level plains of Melazkerd, Boulanik and Moush, and here he would find himself again for a moment (or would have done so two years ago) in peaceful, almost civilised surroundings—populous country towns, with a girdle of agricultural villages and a peasantry even more uniformly Armenian than the population of the plain of Erzeroum. The plain of Moush is the meeting-place of all the routes that traverse the plateau. If you ascend from its south-eastern corner and mount the southern spurs of the Nimroud volcano, you suddenly find yourself on the edge of the extensive basin of Lake Van, and can follow a mountain road along its precipitous southern shore; then you descend into the open valley of Hayotz-Tzor, cross a final ridge with the pleasant village of Artamid on its slopes, and arrive a few hours later in the city of Van itself.

Van, again, before April, 1915, was the populous, civilised capital of a province, with a picturesque citadel-rock overlooking the lake and open garden suburbs spreading east of it across the plain. The City of Van, with the surrounding lowlands that fringe the eastern and north-eastern shores of the lake, was more thoroughly Armenian than any part of the Ottoman Empire. In the Van Vilayet[219] alone the Armenians not merely outnumbered each other racial element singly, but were an absolute majority of the total population. These Armenians of Van played a leading and a valiant part in the events of 1915.

Yet Van, though a stronghold of Armenian nationality, was also the extremity, in this direction, of Armenian territory; south-east of Van the upper valley of the Zab and the basin of Lake Urmia were jointly inhabited by Christian Syrians and Moslem Kurds, until the Syrians, too, were involved in the Armenians' fate. To complete our survey, we have to retrace our steps round the northern shores of Lake Van till we arrive once more in the plain of Moush.

The plain of Moush is closed in on the south and south-west by another rampart of mountains, which forms the southern wall of the plateau and repeats with remarkable exactness the structure of that northern wall which the traveller encounters when he turns south from the plain of Erzeroum. This southern range, also, falls precipitously towards the north, first into the plain of Moush, and, further westward, into the waters of the Mourad Su, which wash it like a moat all the way to their junction with the Kara Su, below Harpout. And, like the northern range, again, the southern rampart unfolds itself to the south in a maze of high hills and tangled valleys, which only sink by degrees into the plains of Diyarbekir—a detached bay of the great Mesopotamian steppe. These southern highlands are known as the Sassoun; they are a physiographical counterpart to the highlands of Dersim, and are likewise the harbour of semi-independent mountaineers. But whereas the Dersimlis are pagan Zazas or Moslem Kurds, and were at constant feud with their Armenian neighbours, the Sassounlis were themselves Armenians, and were in the closest intercourse with their kinsmen in the valley of the Mourad Su and in the plains of Moush and Boulanik.

Sassoun was one of the most interesting Armenian communities in the Ottoman Empire. It was a federation of about forty mountain villages, which lived their own life in virtual independence of the Ottoman authorities at Bitlis or Diyarbekir, and held their own against the equally independent Kurdish tribes that ringed them round. They were prosperous shepherds and laborious cultivators of their mountain slopes—a perfect example of the cantonal phase of economic development, requiring nothing from outside and even manufacturing their own gunpowder. The Sassounli Armenians were in the same social stage as the Scottish Highlanders before 1745; the Armenians of Van, Sivas and Constantinople were people of the twentieth century, engaged in the same activities and living much the same life as the shopkeepers and business men of Vienna or London or New York.

Only an enterprising traveller would have struck up into Sassoun if he wished to make his way from Moush to Diyarbekir. The beaten track takes a longer course to the south-eastern corner of the plain, and then breasts the mountain wall to the south (where the branch-road turns eastward to Lake Van). From Norshen, the last village of the plain, an easy pass leads over a saddle and brings the traveller unexpectedly to the important city of Bitlis, which lies under the shadow of the ridge, immediately south of the watershed. Bitlis is the capital of a vilayet, and before Djevdet Bey retreated upon it in June, 1915, there was a numerous Armenian element in its population. But Bitlis, again, was one of the limits of the Armenian dispersion. The waters which rise round the city flow southward to the Tigris, and the highroad winds down with them towards the plains, which are inhabited by a confused population of Jacobites[220] and Arabs, Turks and Kurds. If you had followed the Tigris upstream across the levels to Diyarbekir, you would have passed few Armenian villages on the road, even before June, 1915; and at Diyarbekir itself, a considerable city, there was only a weak Armenian colony—a feeble link in the chain of Armenian outposts on the fringe of the Mesopotamian steppe. But Diyarbekir is on the line of that Royal Road by which men have gone up from time immemorial from Baghdad and beyond to the coasts of the Bosphorus and the Ægean. The highway runs on north-west across the flats, passes Arghana and Arghana Mines, climbs the southern escarpment of the Armenian plateau up the valley of the Arghana Su, skirts the Göldjik Lake on the watershed, and slopes down, still north-westwards, to Harpout, near the course of the Mourad Su. Many convoys of Armenian exiles traversed this road in the opposite direction during the summer months of 1915, on their way from their native plateau to the alien climate of the Arabian deserts. But our survey of the Armenians in Turkey is complete, and we can travel back in imagination from Harpout to Malatia, from Malatia to Sivas, and so on continually north-westward, till we return again to the point from which we started out.

This somewhat elaborate itinerary will have served its purpose if it has made clear the extraordinary vitality and versatility of the Armenian nation in the Ottoman Empire at the moment when its extermination was planned and attempted by the established Government of the country. The Government had been of little service to any of its subjects; it had never initiated any social or economic developments on its own part, and had invariably made itself a clog upon the private enterprises of native or foreign individuals. Yet, under this pall of stagnation and repression, there were manifold stirrings of a new life. Wherever an opportunity presented itself, wherever the Government omitted to intervene, the Armenians were making indefatigable progress towards a better civilization. They were raising the pastoral and agricultural prosperity of their barren highlands and harassed plains; they were deepening and extending their education at the American schools; they were laying the foundation of local industries in the Vilayet of Sivas; they were building up Ottoman banking and shipping and finance at Trebizond and Adana and Constantinople. They were kindling the essential spark of energy in the Ottoman Empire, and anyone acquainted with Near Eastern history will inevitably compare their promise with the promise of the Greeks a century before. The apologists of the Ottoman Government will seize with eagerness upon this comparison. "The Greeks," they will say, "revolted as soon as they had fallen into this state of fermentation. The Young Turks did more prudently than Sultan Mahmoud in forestalling future trouble." But if we examine the relations between the Ottoman Government and the Armenian people we shall find that this argument recoils upon its authors' heads.

IV. THE ARMENIAN PEOPLE AND THE OTTOMAN GOVERNMENT.

When the Ottoman Government entered the European War in 1914, it had ruled Armenia for just four hundred years, and still had for its subjects a majority of the Armenian people. Anyone who inquires into the relations between the Government and the governed during this period of Near Eastern history will find the most contradictory opinions expressed. On the one hand he will be told that the Armenians, like the rest of the Christians in Turkey, were classed as "Rayah" (cattle[221]) by the dominant race, and that this one word sums up their irremediable position; that they were not treated as citizens because they were not even treated as men. On the other hand, he will hear that the Ottoman Empire has been more liberal to its subject nationalities than many states in Western Europe; that the Armenians have been perfectly free to live their own life under a paternal government, and that the friction between the Government and its subjects has been due to the native perversity and instability of the Armenian character, or, worse still, to a revolutionary poison instilled by some common enemy from without. Both these extreme views are out of perspective, but each of them represents a part of the truth.

It is undoubtedly true (to take the Turkish case first) that the Armenians have derived certain benefits from the Ottoman dispensation. The caste division between Moslem and Rayah, for instance, may stamp the Ottoman "State Idea" as mediæval and incapable of progress; but this has injured the state as a whole more appreciably than the penalised section of it, for extreme penalisation works both ways. The Government ruled out the Christians so completely from the dominant Moslem commonwealth that it suffered and even encouraged them to form communities of their own. The "Rayah" became "Millets"—not yoke-oxen, but unshackled herds.

These Christian Millets were instituted by Sultan Mohammed II, after he had conquered Constantinople in 1453 and set himself to reorganise the Ottoman State as the conscious heir of the East Roman Empire. They are national corporations with written charters, often of an elaborate kind. Each of them is presided over by a Patriarch, who holds office at the discretion of the Government, but is elected by the community and is the recognised intermediary between the two, combining in his own person the headship of a voluntary "Rayah" association and the status of an Ottoman official. The special function thus assigned to the Patriarchates gives the Millets, as an institution, an ecclesiastical character[222]; but in the Near East a church is merely the foremost aspect of a nationality, and the authority of the Patriarchates extends to the control of schools, and even to the administration of certain branches of civil law. The Millets, in fact, are practically autonomous bodies in all that concerns religion, culture and social life; but it is a maimed autonomy, for it is jealously debarred from any political expression. The establishment of the Millets is a recognition, and a palliation, of the pathological anomaly of the Near East—the political disintegration of Near Eastern peoples and the tenacity with which they have clung, in spite of it, to their corporate spiritual life.

The organisation of the Millets was not a gain to all the Christian nations that had been subjected by the Ottoman power. Certain orthodox populations, like the Bulgars and the Serbs, actually lost an ecclesiastical autonomy which they had enjoyed before, and were merged in the Millet of the Greeks, under the Orthodox Patriarch at Constantinople. The Armenians, on the other hand, improved their position. As so-called schismatics, they had hitherto existed on sufferance under Orthodox and Catholic governments, but the Osmanlis viewed all varieties of Christian with an impartial eye. Mohammed II. summoned the Gregorian Bishop of the Armenian colony at Broussa, and raised him to the rank of an Armenian Patriarch at Constantinople. The Ottoman conquest thus left the Gregorian Armenians their religious individuality and put them on a legal equality with their neighbours of the Orthodox Faith, and the same privileges were extended in time to the Armenians in communion with other churches. The Gregorian Millet was chartered in 1462, the Millet of Armenian Catholics in 1830, and the Millet of Armenian Protestants in the 'forties of the nineteenth century, as a result of the foundation of the American Missions.

The Armenians of the Dispersion, therefore, profited, in that respect, by Ottoman rule, and even in the Armenian homeland the account stood, on the whole, in the Ottoman Government's favour. The Osmanlis are often blamed for having given the Kurds a footing in this region, as a political move in their struggle with Persia; but the Kurds were not, originally, such a scourge to the Armenians as the Seljuks, Mongols, or Kara Koyunli, who had harried the land before, or as the Persians themselves, whom the Osmanlis and the Kurds ejected from the country. The three centuries of Kurdish feudalism under Ottoman suzerainty that followed Sultan Selim's campaign of 1514 were a less unhappy period for the Armenians than the three centuries and more of anarchy that had preceded them. They were a time of torpor before recuperation, and it was the Ottoman Government again that, by a change in its Kurdish policy, enabled this recuperation to set in. In the early part of the nineteenth century a vigorous anti-feudal, centralising movement was initiated by Sultan Mahmoud, a reformer who has become notorious for his unsuccessful handling of the Greek and Serbian problems without receiving the proper credit for his successes further east. He turned his attention to the Kurdish chieftains in 1834, and by the middle of the century his efforts had practically broken their power. Petty feudalism was replaced by a bureaucracy centred in Constantinople. The new officialdom was not ideal; it had new vices of its own; but it was impartial, by comparison, towards the two races whom it had to govern, for the class prejudice of the Moslem against the well-behaved Rayah was balanced by the exasperation of the professional administrator with the unconscionable Kurd. In any case, this remodelling of the Ottoman State in the early decades of the nineteenth century introduced a new epoch in the history of the Armenian people. Coinciding, as it did, with the establishment of the American Missions and the chartering of the Catholic and Protestant Millets, it opened to the Armenians opportunities of which they availed themselves to the full. An intellectual and economic renaissance of Armenian life began, parallel in many respects to the Greek renaissance a century before.

This comparison brings us back to the question: Was the Armenian revival of the nineteenth century an inevitable menace to the sovereignty and integrity of the Ottoman State? Is the disastrous breach between Armenian and Turk, which has actually occurred, simply the fruit of wrong-headed Armenian ambitions? That is the Turkish contention; but here the Turkish case breaks down, and we shall find the truth on the Armenian side.

The parallel with the Greek renaissance is misleading, if it implies a parallel with the Greek revolution. The Greek movement towards political separatism was, in a sense, the outcome of the general spiritual movement that preceded it; but it was hardly an essential consequence, and certainly not a fortunate one. The Greek War of Independence liberated one fraction of the Greek race at the price of exterminating most of the others and sacrificing the favoured position which the Greek element had previously enjoyed throughout the Ottoman Empire. It was not an encouraging precedent for the Armenians, and the objections to following it in their own case were more formidable still. As we have seen, no portion of Ottoman territory was exclusively inhabited by them, and they were nowhere even in an absolute majority, except in certain parts of the Province of Van so that they had no natural rallying point for a national revolt, such as the Greeks had in the Islands and the Morea. They were scattered from one end to another of the Ottoman Empire; the whole Empire was their heritage, and it was a heritage that they must necessarily share with the Turks, who were in a numerical majority and held the reins of political power. The alternative to an Ottoman State was not an Armenian State, but a partition among the Powers, which would have ended the ambitions of Turk and Armenian alike. The Powers concerned were quite ready for a partition, if only they could agree upon a division of the spoils. This common inheritance of the Armenians and the Turks was potentially one of the richest countries in the Old World, and one of the few that had not yet been economically developed. Its native inhabitants, still scanty, backward and divided against themselves, were not yet capable of defending their title against spoilers from without; they only maintained it at present by a fortuitous combination in the balance of power, which might change at any moment. The problem for the Armenians was not how to overthrow the Ottoman Empire but how to preserve it, and their interest in its preservation was even greater than that of their Turkish neighbours and co-heirs. Our geographical survey has shown that talent and temperament had brought most of the industry, commerce, finance and skilled intellectual work of Turkey into, the Armenians' hands. The Greeks may still have competed with them on the Ægean fringe, and the Sephardi Jews in the Balkans, but they had the whole interior of the Empire to themselves, with no competition to fear from the agricultural Turks or the pastoral Kurds. And if the Empire were preserved by timely reforms from within, the position of the Armenians would become still more favourable, for they were the only native element capable of raising the Empire economically, intellectually and morally to a European standard, by which alone its existence could permanently be secured. The main effort must be theirs, and they would reap the richest reward.

Thus, from the Armenian point of view, a national entente with the Turks was an object of vital importance, to be pursued for its ultimate results in spite of present difficulties and drawbacks. About the middle of the nineteenth century there seemed every likelihood of its being attained. The labours of Sultan Mahmoud and the influence of Great Britain and France had begun to inoculate the Turkish ruling class with liberal ideas. An admirable "Law of Nationalities" was promulgated, and there was a project for a parliamentary constitution. It looked, to an optimist, as if the old mediæval caste-division of Moslem and Rayah might die away and allow Armenian, Turk and Kurd to find their true relation to one another—not as irreconcilable sects or races, but as different social elements in the same community, whose mutual interest was to co-operate for a common end.

This was the logical policy for the Armenians in the Ottoman Empire to pursue, and the logic of it was so clear that they have clung to it through difficulties and drawbacks sufficient to banish logic altogether—"difficulties" which amounted to a bankruptcy of political sense in the Imperial Government, and "drawbacks" which culminated in official massacres of the Armenian population. There were two causes of this sinister turn of events: the external crisis through which the Empire passed in the years 1875-8, and the impression this crisis made upon Sultan Abd-ul-Hamid, who came to the throne in 1876, when it was entering upon its gravest phase.

In these years the Empire had been brought to the verge of ruin by the revolt of a subject Christian population, the Bosniak Serbs, which spread to the other subject races in the Balkan provinces, and by a momentary breakdown in the diplomatic mechanism of the European balance of power, which enabled Russia to throw her military force into the scales on the Balkan rebels' behalf. The ruin was arrested and partially repaired, when Turkey lay prostrate under Russia's heel, by a reassertion of the balance of power, which deprived Russia of most of her gains and half the Balkan Christians of their new-won liberties. Abd-ul-Hamid was clever enough to learn from these experiences, but not, unfortunately, to learn aright, and he devoted all his astuteness to carrying out a policy far more injurious to the Empire than the troubles it was meant to avert. He seems to have inferred from the war with Russia that Turkey was not and never would be strong enough to hold its own against a first-class power; it was not her internal strength that had saved her, but the external readjustment of forces. Therefore, any attempt to strengthen the Empire from within, by reconciling its racial elements and developing its natural resources, was Utopian and irrelevant to the problem. The only object of importance was to insure against an attack by any single Power by keeping all the Great Powers in a state of jealous equilibrium. Now the breakdown of this equilibrium, in 1877, which had been so disastrous for Turkey, had been directly caused by an antecedent disturbance of equilibrium within the Empire itself. A subject Christian nationality had tried to break away violently from the Ottoman body-politic. Here was the root of the whole trouble, to Abd-ul-Hamid's mind, and the primary object of his policy must be to prevent such a thing from happening again. The subject nationalities of the Empire were not for him unrealised assets; they were potential destroyers of the State, more formidable even than the foreign Powers. Their potentialities must be neutralised, and the surest course, with them as with the Powers, was to play them off against one another. In fine, the policy of Abd-ul-Hamid was the exact antithesis of the instinctive Armenian policy which we have indicated above; it was not to strengthen the Empire by bringing the nationalities into harmony, but to weaken the nationalities, at whatever cost to the Empire, by setting them to cut each other's throats. Abd-ul-Hamid applied this policy for forty years. The

Macedonians and the Armenians were his special victims, but only the Armenians concern us here.

It was inevitable that the Armenians should be singled out by Abd-ul-Hamid for repression. When Turkey sued for peace in 1878, the Russian troops were in occupation of the greater part of the Armenian plateau, and the Russian plenipotentiaries inserted an Article (No. 16) in the Treaty of San Stefano making the evacuation of these provinces conditional upon the previous introduction of reforms in their administration by the Ottoman Government. A concrete scheme for the reorganisation of the six vilayets in question[223] had already been drawn up by a delegation of their Armenian inhabitants. It provided for the creation of an Armenian Governor-General, empowered to appoint and remove the officials subordinate to him; a mixed gendarmerie of Armenians and the sedentary elements in the Moslem population, to the exclusion of the nomadic Kurds; a general assembly, consisting of Moslem and Christian deputies in equal numbers; and equal rights for every creed. The Ottoman Government had approved and even encouraged this project of provincial autonomy when it feared that the alternative was the cession of the provinces to Russia. As soon as it had made certain of the Russian evacuation, its approval turned to indifference; and when the European Congress met at Berlin to revise the San Stefano Treaty, the Ottoman emissaries exerted themselves to quash the project altogether. In this they were practically successful, for the Treaty drawn up at Berlin by the Congress merely engaged the Ottoman Government, in general terms[224], to introduce "ameliorations" in the "provinces inhabited by Armenians," without demanding any guarantee at all[225]. The Russian troops were withdrawn and the ameliorations were a dead letter. The Ottoman Government was reminded of them, in 1880, by a collective Note from the six Powers. But it left the Note unanswered, and after the diplomatic démarches had dragged on for two years the question was shelved, on Bismarck's suggestion, because no Power except Great Britain would press it.

The seed of the "Armenian Reforms" had thus fallen upon stony ground, except in the mind of Abd-ul-Hamid, where it lodged and rankled till it bore the fruit of the "Armenian Massacres." The project had not really been a menace to Ottoman sovereignty and integrity. It was merely a proposal to apply in six vilayets that elementary measure of "amelioration" which was urgently needed by the Empire as a whole, and without which it could never begin to develop its internal strength. But to Abd-ul-Hamid it was unforgivable, for to him every concession to a subject Christian nationality was suspect. He had seen the Bulgars given ecclesiastical autonomy by the Ottoman Government in 1870 and then raised by Russia, within eight years, into a semi-independent political principality. Armenian autonomy had been averted for the moment, but the parallel might still hold good, for Russia's influence over the Armenians had been increasing.

Russia had conquered the Armenian provinces of Persia in 1828[226], and this had brought within her frontier the Monastery of Etchmiadzin, in the Khanate of Erivan, which was the seat of the Katholikos of All the Armenians. The power of this Katholikos was at that time very much in abeyance. He was an ecclesiastical relic of the ancient united Armenian Kingdom of Tigranes and Tiridates, which had been out of existence for fourteen hundred years. There was another Katholikos at Sis, a relic of the mediæval kingdom of Cilicia, who did not acknowledge his supremacy, and he was thrown into the shade altogether by the Armenian Patriarch at Constantinople, who was the official head of the Armenian Millet in the Ottoman Empire—at that time an overwhelming majority of the Armenian people. But Russian diplomacy succeeded in reviving the Katholikos of Etchmiadzin's authority. In the 'forties of the nineteenth century, when Russian influence at Constantinople was at its height and Russian protection seemed the only recourse for Turkey against the ambition of Mehemet Ali, the ecclesiastical supremacy of Etchmiadzin over Constantinople and Sis was definitely established, and the Katholikos of Etchmiadzin, a resident in Russian territory, became once more the actual as well as the titular head of the whole Gregorian Church. Russia had thus acquired an influence over the Armenians as a nation, and individual Armenians were acquiring a reciprocal influence in Russia. They had risen to eminence, not only in commerce, but in the public service and in the army. They had distinguished themselves particularly in the war of 1877. Loris Melikov, Lazarev and Tergoukasev, three of the most successful generals on the Russian side, were of Armenian nationality. Melikov had taken the fortress of Kars, and the Treaty of Berlin left his conquest in Russia's possession with a zone of territory that rounded off the districts ceded by Persia fifty years before. The Russian frontier was thus pushed forward on to the Armenian plateau, and now included an important Armenian population—important enough to make its mark on the general life of the Russian Empire[227] and to serve as a national rallying-point for the Armenians who still remained on the Ottoman side of the line.

Such considerations outweighed all others in Abd-ul-Hamid's mind. His Armenian subjects must be deprived of their formidable vitality, and he decided to crush them by resuscitating the Kurds. From 1878 onwards he encouraged their lawlessness, and in 1891 he deliberately undid the work of his predecessor, Mahmoud. The Kurdish chieftains were taken again into favour and decorated with Ottoman military rank; their tribes were enrolled as squadrons of territorial cavalry; regimental badges and modern rifles were served out to them from the Government stores, and their retaining fee was a free hand to use their official status and their official weapons as they pleased against their Armenian neighbours. At the same time the latter were systematically disarmed; the only retaliation open to them was the formation of secret revolutionary societies, and this fitted in entirely with Abd-ul-Hamid's plans, for it made a racial conflict inevitable. The disturbances began in 1893 with the posting up of revolutionary placards in Yozgad and Marsovan. This was soon followed by an open breach between Moslem and Christian in the districts of Moush and Sassoun, and there was a rapid concentration of troops—some of them Turkish regulars, but most of them Hamidié Kurds. Sassoun was besieged for several months, and fell in 1894. The Sassounlis—men, women and children—were savagely massacred by the Turks and Kurds, and the attention of Great Britain was aroused. In the winter of 1894-5 Great Britain persuaded France and Russia to join her in reminding the Ottoman Government of its pledge to introduce provincial reforms, and in the spring they presented a concrete programme for the administration of the Six Vilayets. In its final form it was a perfunctory project, and the counter-project which the Ottoman Government announced its intention of applying in its stead was more illusory still. It was promulgated in 1895, but the first of a new series of organised massacres had already taken place a few days earlier, at Trebizond, and in the following months the slaughter was extended to one after another of the principal towns of the Empire. These atrocities were nearly all committed against peaceful, unarmed urban populations. The only place that resisted was Zeitoun, which held out for six months against a Turkish army, and was finally amnestied by the mediation of the Powers. The anti-Armenian outbreaks were instigated and controlled by the Central Government, and were crowned, in August, 1896, by the great massacre at Constantinople, where for two days the Armenians, at the Government's bidding, were killed indiscriminately in the streets, until the death-roll amounted to many thousands. Then Abd-ul-Hamid held his hand. He had been feeling the pulse of public opinion, both abroad and at home, and he saw that he had gone far enough[228]. In all more than 100,000 men, women and children had perished, and for the moment he had sufficiently crippled the Armenian element in his Empire.

Yet this Macchiavellian policy was ultimately as futile as it was wicked. In the period after the massacres the Armenian population in Turkey was certainly reduced, partly by the actual slaughter and partly by emigration abroad. But this only weakened the Empire without permanently paralysing the Armenian race. The emigrants struck new roots in the United States and in the Russian Caucasus, acquired new resources, enlisted new sympathies; and Russia was the greatest gainer of all. The Armenians had little reason, at the time, to look towards Russia with special sympathy or hope. In Russia, as in Turkey, the war of 1877-8 had been followed by a political reaction, which was aggravated by the assassination of the Tsar, Alexander II., in 1881; and the Armenians, as an energetic, intellectual, progressive element in the Russian Empire, were classed by the police with the revolutionaries, and came under their heavy hand. Yet once an Armenian was on the Russian side of the frontier his life and property at least were safe. He could be sure of reaping the fruits of his labour, and had not to fear sudden death in the streets. During the quarter of a century that followed the Treaty of Berlin, the Armenian population of the Russian provinces increased remarkably in prosperity and numbers, and now, after the massacres, they were reinforced by a constant stream of Ottoman refugees. The centre of gravity of the Armenian race was shifting more and more from Ottoman to Russian territory. Russia has profited by the crimes of her neighbours. The Hamidian régime lasted from 1878 to 1908, and did all that any policy could do to widen the breach between the Ottoman State and the Armenian people. Yet the natural community of interest was so strong that even thirty years of repression did not make the Armenians despair of Ottoman regeneration.

Nothing is more significant than the conduct of the Armenians in 1908, when Abd-ul-Hamid was overthrown by the Young Turkish Revolution, and there was a momentary possibility that the Empire might be reformed and preserved by the initiative of the Turks themselves. At this crisis the real attitude of the different nationalities in the Empire was revealed. The Kurds put up a fight for Abd-ul-Hamid, because they rejoiced in the old dispensation. The Macedonians—Greek, Bulgar and Serb—who had been the Armenians' principal fellow-victims in the days of oppression, paid the Constitution lip-homage and secretly prepared to strike. They were irreconcilable irredentists, and saw in the reform of the Empire simply an obstacle to their secession from it. They took counsel with their kinsmen in the independent national States of Serbia, Bulgaria and Greece, and, four years later, the Balkan League attacked Turkey and tore away her Macedonian provinces by force.

The Armenians, on the other hand, threw themselves wholeheartedly into the service of the new régime. As soon as the Ottoman Constitution was restored, the Armenian political parties abandoned their revolutionary programme in favour of parliamentary action, and co-operated in Parliament with the Young Turkish bloc so long as Young Turkish policy remained in any degree liberal or democratic. The terrible Adana massacres, which occurred less than a year after the Constitution had been proclaimed, might have damped the Armenians' enthusiasm (though at first the proof that the Young Turks were implicated in them was not so clear as it has since become). Yet they showed their loyalty in 1912, when the Turks were fighting for their existence. It was only under the new laws that the privilege and duty of military service had been extended to the Christian as well as the Moslem citizens of the Empire, and the disastrous Balkan Campaign was the first opportunity that Armenian soldiers were given of doing battle for their common heritage. But they bore themselves so well in this ordeal that they were publicly commended by their Turkish commanders. Thus, in war and peace, in the Army and in Parliament, the Armenians worked for the salvation of the Ottoman Commonwealth, from the accession of the Young Turks in 1908 till their intervention in the European War in 1914. It is impossible to reconcile with this fact the Turkish contention that in 1914 they suddenly reversed their policy and began treacherously to plot for the Ottoman Empire's destruction.

V. THE DEPORTATIONS OF 1915: ANTECEDENTS.

There is no dispute as to what happened in 1915. The Armenian inhabitants of the Ottoman Empire were everywhere uprooted from their homes, and deported to the most remote and unhealthy districts that the Government could select for them. Some were murdered at the outset, some perished on the way, and some died after reaching their destination. The death-roll amounts to upwards of six hundred thousand; perhaps six hundred thousand more are still alive in their places of exile; and the remaining six hundred thousand or so have either been converted forcibly to Islam, gone into hiding in the mountains, or escaped beyond the Ottoman frontier. The Ottoman Government cannot deny these facts, and they cannot justify them. No provocation or misdemeanour on the part of individual Armenians could justify such a crime against the whole race. But it might be explained and palliated if the Armenians, or some of them, were originally in the wrong; and therefore the Ottoman Government and its German apologists have concentrated their efforts on proving that this was the case.[229] There are three main Turkish contentions, none of which will bear examination.

The first contention is that the Armenians took up arms and joined the Russians, as soon as the latter crossed the Ottoman frontier. The standard case its champions cite is the "Revolt of Van." The deportations, they maintain, were only ordered after this outbreak to forestall the danger of its repetition elsewhere. This contention is easily rebutted. In the first place, there was no Armenian revolt at Van. The Armenians merely defended the quarter of the city in which they lived, after it had been beleaguered and attacked by Turkish troops, and the outlying villages visited with massacre by Turkish patrols. The outbreak was on the Turkish side, and the responsibility lies with the Turkish governor, Djevdet Bey. The ferocious, uncontrollable character of this official was the true cause of the catastrophe. Anyone who reads the impartial American testimony on this point, in section II. of the present collection of documents, will see that this was so. And, in the second place, the deportations had already begun in Cilicia before the fighting at Van broke out. The Turks fired the first shot at Van on the 20th April, 1915; the first Armenians were deported from Zeitoun on the 8th April, and there is a record of their arrival in Syria as early as the 19th[230]. The case of Van, which the apologists have made so much of, simply falls to the ground[231], and they cannot rehabilitate themselves by adducing any previous revolt at Zeitoun. It is true that twenty-five fugitive conscripts defended themselves for a day in a monastery near Zeitoun against Turkish troops, and decamped into the mountains during the night. But this happened only one day before the deportation, and the deportation must have been decided upon far in advance, for it was preceded by a protracted inquisition for arms, and there were Moslem refugees from the Balkans concentrated on the spot, ready to occupy the Zeitounlis' houses the moment the rightful owners were carried off. During all these preliminary proceedings—most of which were violations of the charter of liberties held by Zeitoun from the Ottoman Government—the population as a whole (15,000 individuals as against the 25 who rebelled) very scrupulously kept the peace. This was the policy of the leaders, and they were obeyed by the people. Nothing happened at Zeitoun that can account for the Government's scheme of deportation.

There were several other instances in which the Armenians took up arms, but none of them are relevant to the case. They were all subsequent in date to these cardinal instances, and were simply attempts at self-defence by people who had seen their neighbours massacred or deported, and were threatened with the same fate themselves. The Armenians of Moush resisted when they were attacked by Djevdet Bey, who had already tried to massacre the Armenians of Van and had succeeded in massacring those of Sairt and Bitlis. The Armenians of Sassoun resisted when the Kurds had destroyed their kinsmen in the plain of Diyarbekir and were closing in upon themselves. This was in June, and the Nestorian Christians of Hakkiari resisted under the same circumstances and at the same date. Further west, a few villages took up arms in the Vilayet of Sivas, after the rest of the Sivas Armenians had been deported; and at Shabin Kara-Hissar the Armenians drove out their Turkish fellow-townsmen and stood for several weeks at bay, when they heard how the exiles from Trebizond and Kerasond had been murdered on the road. The defence of Djibal Mousa in August (the only story in this volume with a happy ending) was similarly inspired by the previous fate of Zeitoun. The resistance at Ourfa in September was another act of despair, provoked by the terrible procession of exiles from Harpout and the north-east, which had been filing for three months through Ourfa before the Armenian colony there was also summoned to take the road. These are all the instances of resistance that are reported, and they were all a consequence of the deportations, and not their cause. It may be added that, wherever resistance was offered, the Turks suppressed it with inconceivable brutality, not merely retaliating upon the fighting men, but, in most cases, massacring every Armenian man, woman and child in cold blood after the fighting was over. These cases were not palliations of the atrocities, but occasions of the worst excesses.

The second contention is that there was a general conspiracy of Armenians throughout the Empire to bring about an internal revolution at a moment when all the Ottoman military forces were engaged on the frontiers, and so deliver the country into the hands of the Allies. The prompt action of the Ottoman Government in disarming, imprisoning, executing and deporting the whole people—innocent and guilty alike—is alleged to have crushed this movement before it had time to declare itself. This is an insidious line of argument, because it refuses to be tested by the evidence of what actually occurred. If the actual outbreaks were isolated, inspired by panic, confined to self-defence, and posterior in date to the Government's own preventive measures, all that, on this hypothesis, is not a proof of the Armenians' innocence, but only of the Government's energy and foresight. Yet when this indictment is examined, it, too, is found to rest on the most frivolous grounds.

The revolution, it is alleged, was to break out when the Allies landed in Cilicia—but such a landing was never made; or it was arranged in conjunction with the landing at the Dardanelles—but the landing was made and the outbreak never happened. Indeed, it is hard to see what the Armenians could have done, for nearly all their able-bodied men between twenty and forty-five years of age were mobilised at the beginning of the war, and the age limit was soon extended in either direction to eighteen and fifty. The Turks make sweeping allegations about secret stores of bombs and arms, which prove to be false in every case where they can be checked. The Armenians certainly possessed a moderate number of rifles and revolvers, because, for the past six years, under the Young Turkish régime, they had been permitted to carry arms for their personal security, a privilege that had always been enjoyed, as a matter of course, by every Moslem in the Ottoman Empire. But evidently there were not enough arms in their possession to go round, even among the comparatively few men left behind after mobilisation; for when, in the winter of 1914-5, the Ottoman authorities made a house-to-house search for arms, and conducted their inquisition by atrocious physical tortures, the Armenians bought arms from each other and from their Moslem neighbours, in order to be able to deliver them up and suffer no worse punishment than mere imprisonment. This practice is recorded independently by several trustworthy witnesses from various localities[232].

The stories of bombs are more extravagant still. In the town of X., for instance, a bomb was unearthed in the Armenian cemetery, which was made the pretext for the most atrocious procedure against the Armenian inhabitants. Yet the bomb was rusty with age, and was believed to date from the days of Abd-ul-Hamid, when the Young Turks, as well as the Armenian political parties, were a secret revolutionary organisation and not averse to using bombs themselves. In the same town, a blacksmith in the employment of the American College was cruelly tortured for "constructing a bomb"; but the "bomb" turned out to be a solid iron shot which he had been commissioned to make for the competition of "putting the weight" in the College athletic sports.

It was also alleged that Armenians resident on the coast had been in treacherous communication with the Allied fleets. The Armenian boatmen of Silivri[233], for instance, on the Sea of Marmora, were deported on the ground that they had furnished supplies to British submarines; and before this, as early as April, 1915, half-a-dozen Armenians from Dört Yöl, a village on the Gulf of Alexandretta, were hanged at Adana on the charge of having signalled to the Franco-British cruiser squadron—a step which was followed up by the deportation of the whole population of Dört Yöl into the interior, to do navvy-work on the roads. This charge against Dört Yöl can be checked, for the witness of the hangings (a resident in Cilicia of neutral nationality and excellent standing)[234] states, from his personal knowledge, that only one Armenian from Dört Yöl had had any communication with the Allied warships. This evidence is authoritative, and it has probability on its side; for, if Dört Yöl was in regular communication with the Allied squadron, it is inconceivable that the Armenians of Djibal Mousa, a few miles further down the coast, should have taken 44 days to attract the same squadron's attention, when it was a question for them of life and death[235].

Thus the second contention breaks down, and we are left with the third, which lays little stress on justice or public safety and bases the case on revenge. The Armenian civil population in the Ottoman Empire, it is argued, owes its misfortunes to the Armenian volunteers in the Russian Army. "Our Armenians in Turkey," say the Turks in effect, "have certainly suffered terribly from the measures we have taken; they may even have suffered innocently; but can you blame us? Was it not human nature that we should revenge ourselves on the Armenians at home for the injury we had received from their compatriots fighting against us at the front in the Russian ranks— men who had actually volunteered to fight against us in the enemy's cause?"

This is almost the favourite argument of the apologists, and yet it is surely the most monstrous of any, for these Armenian volunteers owed no allegiance to the Turks at all, but were ordinary Russian subjects. Through territorial acquisitions and free immigration from across the frontier, the Russian Government had, by 1914, acquired the sovereignty over little less than half the Armenian race[236]. Russia was as much the lawful "fatherland" of this substantial minority as Turkey was of the remainder. It is a misfortune for any nation to be divided between two allegiances, especially when the states to which they owe them elect to go to war; but it is at least an alleviation of the difficulty, and one that does honour to both parties concerned, when either fraction of the divided nationality finds itself in sympathy, even under the test of war, with the particular state to which its allegiance is legally due. The loyalty of the Russian Armenians to Russia[237] cast no imputation upon the Ottoman Armenians, and was no concern of the Turks. The latter will probably explain that they had no objection to the Russian Armenians doing their duty, but resented their doing more: "The conscripts naturally answered the summons, but why did those who were exempt equip themselves so eagerly as volunteers? The Ottoman Armenians adopted a painfully different attitude. At the beginning of the war, the Young Turkish Party sent representatives to the Congress of the Armenian 'Dashnaktzoutioun' Party at Erzeroum, offered them concessions to their nationality, and called upon them to organise volunteers and join in the invasion of Russian territory[238]. Yet they decidedly refused—refused in this case when their kinsmen did not wait to be asked in the other. This reveals the real sympathies and aspirations of the Armenian people, not only the Armenians in Russia, but those in our country as well."

There is, of course, a crushing answer to these tirades. If the Armenians felt so differently towards the Turks and the Russians, then that was a serious reflection on their treatment by the Turks, and the logical way to change their feelings was to treat them better. Could the civilian Armenians who remembered the massacre of their innocent kinsfolk at Adana a few years before have been expected to volunteer in support of those who had commanded these massacres? Could their feelings have been other than they were? But so long as only their feelings were in question and their behaviour remained correct, the Turks had no right to proceed with them in any but a humane and constitutional manner. The argument can be driven home by a parallel. There are Polish volunteer legions in the Austro-Hungarian Army. What would the Turks' German apologists have said if the Russian Government had appeased its resentment against these Austrian-Polish volunteers by wiping out all the Russian-Polish civilians on their own side of the frontier?

It is a significant fact that all these Turkish complaints are directed against Russian Armenians in Russian service. There is no hint of treachery or malingering on the part of those Ottoman Armenians who had been drafted, many of them illegally, into the Turkish Army—no insinuation that their record was not as satisfactory in 1914 as in 1912[239]. To the editor's knowledge, the German apologists have only been able to fasten upon two "traitors" in the legal (though not in the moral) sense of the word. There have been refugees, of course, like Mourad of Sivas, who escaped into the Caucasus when the atrocities were in full course—men who had just been compelled to fight for their lives, and had seen their neighbours and kinsfolk massacred once more on all sides of them. Not even the German apologists would dare to censure these men under these circumstances for enrolling in the volunteers. But there are only two cases adduced of Ottoman subjects who went over to the Russians before the atrocities began—a certain Karakin Pasdermadjian, a deputy in the Ottoman Parliament, and another Armenian named Suren, stated to have been a delegate at the "Dashnaktzoutioun" Congress at Erzeroum. "In face of this," argues the German writer from whose pamphlet these instances are taken[240], "it was the Ottoman Government's duty to uphold public law and order. In wartime, measures of this kind assume an especially weighty and pressing character"—and with this generality he implicitly condones the atrocities of 1915. If this represents the official apologia of the Ottoman Government, the only answer is a *reductio ad absurdum*. On the same principle, when Sir Roger Casement landed from a German submarine on the Irish coast, it would have been the British Government's duty to deport all the Roman Catholic inhabitants of Ireland and maroon them, say, on the coast of Labrador or in the central desert of Australia. The parallel is exact, and leaves nothing more to be said, unless, indeed, what was said by Talaat Bey, the Young Turkish Minister of the Interior, in a recent interview with a correspondent of the *Berliner Tageblatt*[241]. "The sad events that have occurred in Armenia," he vouchsafed, "have prevented my sleeping well at night. We have been reproached for making no distinction between the innocent Armenians and the guilty; but that was utterly impossible, in view of the fact that *those who were innocent to-day might be guilty to-morrow.*" There is no need of further witnesses.

The various Turkish contentions thus fail, from first to last, to meet the point. They all attempt to trace the atrocities of 1915 to events arising out of the war; but they not only cannot justify them on this ground, they do not even suggest any adequate motive for their perpetration. It is evident that the war was merely an opportunity and not a cause—in fact, that the deportation scheme, and all that it involved, flowed inevitably from the general policy of the Young Turkish Government. This inference will be confirmed if we analyse the political tenets to which the Young Turks were committed.

The Young Turkish movement began as a reaction against the policy of Abd-ul-Hamid. Its founders repudiated his "neutralisation of forces"; they maintained that the Ottoman Empire must stand by its own strength, and that this strength must be developed by a radical internal reconstruction. From their asylum at Paris they preached the doctrines of the French Revolution—religious toleration, abolition of caste-privileges, equality of all citizens before the law, equality of obligation to perform military service, constitutional government through a representative parliament. And when they came into power, they made some attempt to put these doctrines into practice. In Turkey for a brief space of the year 1908, as in France twelve decades before, the vision of "Pure Reason" did bring peace and goodwill among men. Nearly all the foreign observers who were in the country when "Huriet" came, testify to this momentary, magic transfiguration of hatred into love; and the Armenians, who had desired more than any of their neighbours to see this day, might well believe that the Young Turks' ideal was identical with their own. Yet there were vital differences beneath the surface. The Young Turks realised that the Christian elements were an asset; they did not propose, at the outset, to destroy them, as Abd-ul-Hamid had done; but they wanted still less to co-operate with them as separate partners in the Ottoman State. The "Millets" were as abhorrent to them, as an institution, as the autocracy of Abd-ul-Hamid. They set up against the principle of the "Millet" the programme of "Ottomanisation." The Turkish leaven was to permeate the non-Turkish lump, until it had all become of one uniform Turkish substance. In Parliament this programme took such forms as a bill to make the Turkish language the universal and compulsory medium of secondary education[242], and the Armenian deputies found themselves opposing it in concert with the Liberal Party, which included the Arab bloc and stood for the toleration of national individualities. The Young Turks, in fact, had imbibed both the good currents and the bad in the modern political atmosphere of Western Europe—its democratic doctrines but its chauvinism as well. Most political theorists debarred from responsible practice give this same confused allegiance to incompatible ideals, and all, when they come into power, are compelled by circumstances to choose which master they will serve. In 1908, the choice of the Young Turks was not predestined; the "Committee of *Union* and *Progress*" might have set its face towards either of its divided goals; but disillusionment soon decided its orientation. The magic dawn of "Huriet" faded; the old, crushing burden of Ottoman Government descended upon shoulders not expert, like Abd-ul-Hamid's, at balancing the weight; the Austro-Bulgarian violation of the Treaty of Berlin and the subsequent territorial losses of the Balkan War shook the Young Turkish Party's prestige, aggravated the difficulty of their problem, and embittered their attitude towards its solution. The current of chauvinism gained upon them more and more, and their intervention in the European War demonstrated that its mastery was complete, for their calculations in intervening were of a thoroughly Prussian character. A military triumph was to restore them their prestige; it was to recover ancient territories of the Empire in Egypt, the Caucasus and the coveted Persian province of Azerbaijan; it was to shake off the trammels of international control, and solve the internal problem by cutting the Gordian Knot. But the hopes of conquest and prestige were early shattered by the strategical failures of the winter of 1914-5, which were almost as humiliating as those of 1912, and then the Young Turks concentrated savagely upon "Ottomanisation" at home.

Ottomanisation has become the Young Turks' obsession[243]. Their first act after declaring war was to repudiate the Capitulations; their latest stroke has been to declare the Turkish language the exclusive medium of official business in the Empire, with only a year's delay—a step which has caused consternation among their German allies. And in this mood they turned to the Armenian question, which happened at the moment to have reached an important phase.

In 1912-3 the diplomatists of Europe had once more met in consultation over the Ottoman Empire, and the Armenians had presented their case to the Conference at London, as they had presented it at Berlin thirty-five years before.[244] When the Conference proved unable to take cognizance of their petition, they applied to the individual governments of the Powers. The Russian Government took the initiative and drafted a new scheme for the administration of the Six Vilayets, which it submitted to the Signatories of the Treaty of Berlin. The German Government opposed, but was won over by the Russian diplomacy and by the representations of the Armenian delegates, who repaired to Berlin in person. Then, when the German opposition had been withdrawn, the Russian draft was revised by the Ambassadors of the Powers at Constantinople, accepted, with modifications, by the Young Turkish Government, and actually promulgated by them on the 8th February, 1914.

In its final shape, the scheme still embodied the main points of reform which had been regarded as cardinal ever since 1878. There was to be a mixed Gendarmerie, under a European chief, recruited from the Turks and Armenians, but closed to the Kurds; Moslem and Christian were to be equal before the law; the Armenian language was to be a recognised medium in the courts and public offices (a bitter clause for the Young Turkish nationalists); there were to be no restrictions on the multiplication of Armenian schools. Finally, the vilayets affected by the scheme[245] were to be divided into two groups, and each group was to be placed under a European Inspector-General. The two Inspector-Generals were authorised to appoint and dismiss all officials in their respective spheres, except those "of superior rank." They were themselves to be appointed by the Ottoman Government, on the recommendation of the Powers, for a term of ten years, and not to be removable within this period. The Government duly proceeded to select two candidates for these Inspectorates, a Dutchman and a Norwegian, but its treatment of these gentlemen soon showed that in diplomacy, at any rate, the Young Turks had adopted the methods of Abd-ul Hamid. A clause was inserted in the Inspectors' contract of engagement, empowering the Government to denounce it at any moment upon payment of an indemnity of one year's salary—a flat violation of the ten years' term provided for under the scheme; and the list of "superior officials" was inflated until the patronage of the Inspectors, which, next to their irremovability, would have been their most effective power, was reduced to an illusion. The unfortunate nominees were spared the farce of exercising their maimed authority. They had barely reached their provinces when the European War broke out, and the Government promptly denounced the contracts and suspended the Scheme of Reforms, as the first step towards its own intervention in the conflict.

Thus, at the close of 1914, the Armenians found themselves in the same position as in 1883. The measures designed for their security had fallen through, and left nothing behind but the resentment of the Government that still held them at its mercy. The deportations of 1915 followed as inexorably from the Balkan War and the Project of 1914 as the massacres of 1895-6 had followed from the Russian War and the Project of 1878. Only in the execution of their revenge the Young Turks revealed all the sinister features of their dissimilarity to Abd-ul-Hamid. The Sultan, so far as he differed from the familiar type of Oriental despot, had been an opportunist in the tradition of Metternich—a politician of mature experience and delicate touch, unencumbered by any constructive programme to disturb the artistry of his game of finesse. He repressed the Armenians to a nicety after preparing for it eighteen years. The Young Turks were adventurers who had caught the catchwords of another generation and another school—the apes of Danton and Robespierre, and doctrinaires to the core. For the old, anachronistic ascendency of Moslem over Rayah, to the maintenance of which Abd-ul-Hamid had cynically devoted his abilities, they substituted the idea of Turkish nationalism, which clothed the same evil in a more clearly-cut and infinitely more dynamic form. They were fanatics with an unreasoned creed, builders with a plan that they meant to carry through, and no half-measures would content them, no inhibitions of prudence or humanity deter them from the attempt to realise the whole. Hindrances only exasperated them to sweeping action, and a blind concentration on their programme shielded them from doubts. "Our acts," Talaat Bey is reported to have said, in the interview quoted above, "have been dictated to us by a national and historical necessity. The idea of guaranteeing the existence of Turkey must outweigh every other consideration." The first of these sentiments is the pure-milk of the eighteenth century ideologues; there is a Prussian adulteration in the second, which smacks of more recent times. It is the voice of the youngest, crudest, most ruthless national movement in Europe, and the acts which it excuses, and which the documents in this volume describe, were the barbarous initiation of the Near East into the European fraternity.

VI. THE DEPORTATIONS OF 1915: PROCEDURE.

The atrocities of 1915 are described in detail in the documents collected in this book, but it will be well to give in conclusion a bare summary of events, partly to make the detail less confusing to the reader, and partly to bring out the essential unity of design which underlay the procedure against the Armenians at the various dates and in the various provinces of the Empire to which the documents relate. This fundamental uniformity of procedure is more sinister than the incidental aggravations of the crime by Kurds, peasants, gendarmes or local authorities. It is damning evidence that the procedure itself, which set in motion all the other forces of evil, was conceived and organised by the Central Government at Constantinople.

The dismissal of the Inspectors-General and the abrogation of the reforms were followed immediately by the mobilisation of the Ottoman Army for eventual participation in the war, and with this the sufferings of the Armenians began. It has been mentioned already that the Young Turks had extended the duty of military service to their Christian fellow-citizens, and that the Armenian recruits had distinguished themselves in the Balkan War; but naturally the measure was not retrospective, and Armenians who were already past the statutory age of training when it was introduced, were allowed to pay the "Rayah" poll-tax as before, under the formula of an exemption-tax in lieu of military service. In the autumn of 1914, however, there was a general levy of all males in the Empire from twenty years of age to forty-five, and soon from eighteen to fifty, in which the Armenians, whether they had paid their annual exemption-tax or not, were included with the rest. There were also drastic requisitions of private supplies, by which the Armenians, again, were the principal sufferers, since they were the chief merchants and store-keepers of the country. These were considerable hardships and injustices, but they were not necessarily in themselves the result of a malevolent design. Apart from what actually followed, they might have been simply the inevitable penalties of a country which had been embarked by its Government on a struggle for existence.

In October, when mobilisation was completed, the Government had, in fact, declared war on the Allies, and in December its grandiose military operations began. Enver Pasha, with the main Ottoman forces, started an encircling movement against the Russian troops in Caucasia, along a front extending from Erzeroum to the Black Sea Coast; Halil Bey led a flying column across the frontier of Azerbaijan, and raised the Kurds; Djemal Pasha felt his way across the Sinai Peninsula towards the Suez Canal. For a week or two the invading armies met with success. They reached Ardahan, almost in the rear of Kars, they pushed the Russians back from their rail-head at Sari-Kamysh, and they occupied the capital of Azerbaijan, Tabriz. But then the campaign broke down in disaster. Two Turkish army corps were destroyed at Sari-

Kamysh in the first week of January, 1915, and the rest were driven out of Russian territory by the end of the month; on the 30th January, the Russians even re-occupied Tabriz. Djemal's Egyptian expedition was a month in arrear, but its fortunes were the same. He reached the Canal at the beginning of February, after a creditable desert march, only to return by the way he came, after an abortive night attack. There was no more question of the offensive for the Turks, but only of defending their own straggling frontiers; and this breakdown was a bitter blow to Young Turkish official circles, for it shattered half the hopes that had lured them into the war. The unmeasured optimism of the winter gave place to equally violent depression, and under the influence of this new atmosphere the persecution of the Armenians entered a second and more positive phase.

A decree went forth that all Armenians should be disarmed. The Armenians in the Army were drafted out of the fighting ranks, re-formed into special labour battalions, and set to work at throwing up fortifications and constructing roads. The disarming of the civil population was left to the local authorities, and in every administrative centre a reign of terror began. The authorities demanded the production of a definite number of arms. Those who could not produce them were tortured, often in fiendish ways; those who procured them for surrender, by purchase from their Moslem neighbours or by other means, were imprisoned for conspiracy against the Government. Few of these were young men, for most of the young had been called up to serve; they were elderly men, men of substance and the leaders of the Armenian community, and it became apparent that the inquisition for arms was being used as a cloak to deprive the community of its natural heads. Similar measures had preceded the massacres of 1895-6, and a sense of foreboding spread through the Armenian people. "One night in the winter," writes a foreign witness of these events[246], "the Government sent officers round the city to all Armenian houses, knocking up the families and demanding that all weapons should be given up. This action was the death-knell to many hearts."

The appalling inference was in fact correct, for the second phase of persecution passed over without a break into the third and final act, and it is evident that the whole train had been laid by the Ministry at Constantinople before the first arms were called in or the first Armenian thrown into prison. This carries the detailed organisation of the scheme at least as far back as February, 1915, and, indeed, the elaborate preparations that had already been made by the 8th April, the date of the first deportation at Zeitoun, presuppose at least as long a period. It is extremely important to emphasise these chronological facts, because they refute the attempt of the apologists to disconnect the last phase from the phases that preceded it, and to represent it as an emergency measure dictated by the military events of the spring.

In reality, the situation had been growing tenser before the spring began. In outlying villages, the inquisition for arms had been accompanied by open violence. Men had been massacred, women violated and houses burnt down by the gendarmerie patrols, and such outrages had been particularly frequent in the Vilayet of Van, where the soldiers seem to have been exasperated by their recent reverses and were certainly stimulated by the truculence of the Governor Djevdet Bey, who had returned to his administrative duties after his unsuccessful campaigning beyond the frontier. The crowning outrage was the murder of four Armenian leaders from the City, when they were on their way to an outlying district to keep the peace, at Djevdet's own request, between the local Armenians and their Moslem neighbours. The Armenian inhabitants of the City of Van took warning from the fate of the villagers and from this last and most sinister crime, and prepared themselves, in case of need, for self-defence. Their action was justified by Djevdet Bey himself, for he had been drawing a cordon round the garden suburbs of Van, where the majority of the Armenian population lived, and on the 20th April he unleashed his troops upon them without provocation. The Armenians of Van found themselves fighting for their lives against a murderous attack by what was supposed to be the lawful Government of their country. There had been the same sequence of events at Zeitoun. The search for arms had been accompanied by a formidable concentration of troops in the town, and the final phase had been opened, not indeed by a butchery, but by the deportation of the first batch of the inhabitants. This had occurred on the 8th April, twelve days before Djevdet Bey's outbreak at Van, and both events were previous to the new turn in the military situation. In fact, it was the distress of the Armenian civil population at Van that decided the Russian initiative. A Russian column, with a strong contingent of Russian-Armenian volunteers, forced its way towards the city from the direction of Bayazid, and relieved the defenders on the 19th May, after they had been besieged for a month. The strategy of encirclement was now retorted upon the Turks themselves, for on the 24th May another Russian column occupied Urmia, and drove the last of the Turco-Kurdish invaders out of Azerbaijan. A British expeditionary force was simultaneously pressing up the Tigris, and while events were taking this serious turn in the east, the heart of the Empire was threatened by the attack on the Dardanelles. By the end of May, 1915, the outlook was as desperate as in the bad days of 1912, but it must be emphasised again that the final phase in the procedure against the Armenians had already begun before these acute military dangers emerged above the horizon. The military straits in which the Young Turks found themselves in the spring of 1915 may have precipitated the execution of their Armenian scheme, but have no bearing whatever upon its origination.

On the 8th April, then, the final phase began, and the process carried out at Zeitoun was applied to one Armenian centre after another throughout the Ottoman Empire. On a certain date, in whatever town or village it might be (and the dates show a significant sequence), the public crier went through the streets announcing that every male Armenian must present himself forthwith at the Government Building. In some cases the warning was given by the soldiery or gendarmerie slaughtering every male Armenian they encountered in the streets, a reminiscence of the procedure in 1895-6; but usually a summons to the Government Building was the preliminary stage. The men presented themselves in their working clothes, leaving their shops and workrooms open, their ploughs in the field, their cattle on the mountain side. When they arrived, they were thrown without explanation into prison, kept there a day or two, and then marched out of the town in batches, roped man to man, along some southerly or south-easterly road. They were starting, they were told, on a long journey—to Mosul or perhaps to Baghdad. It was a dreadful prospect to men unequipped for travel, who had neither scrip nor staff, food nor clothes nor bedding. They had bidden no farewell to their families, they had not wound up their affairs. But they had not long to ponder over their plight, for they were halted and massacred at the first lonely place on the road. The same process was applied to those other Armenian men (and they numbered hundreds or even thousands in the larger centres) who had been imprisoned during the winter months on the charge of conspiracy or concealment of arms, though in some instances these prisoners are said to have been overlooked—an involuntary form of reprieve of which there were also examples during the French Reign of Terror in 1793. This was the civil authorities' part, but there was complete co-ordination between Talaat Bey's Ministry of the Interior and Enver Pasha's Ministry of War, for simultaneously the Armenian Labour Battalions, working behind the front, were surrounded by detachments of their combatant Moslem fellow-soldiers and butchered in cold blood.

The military authorities also made themselves responsible for the civil population of Bitlis, Moush and Sassoun, who were marked out for complete and immediate extermination on account of their proximity to Van and the advancing Russian forces. This task was carried out by military methods with the help of the local Kurds—another reversion to the tactics of Abd-ul-Hamid—but its application appears to have been limited to the aforementioned districts. In the rest of the Empire, where the work was left in the hands of the civil administration, the women and children were not disposed of by straightforward massacre like the men. Their destiny under the Government scheme was not massacre but slavery or deportation.

After the Armenian men had been summoned away to their death, there was usually a few days interval in whatever town it might be, and then the crier was heard again in the streets, bidding all Armenians who remained to prepare themselves for deportation, while placards to the same effect were posted on the walls.[247] This applied, in actual fact, to the women and children, and to a poor remnant of the men who, through sickness, infirmity or age, had escaped the fate marked out for their sex. A period of grace was in most cases accorded for the settlement of their affairs and the preparation of their journey; but here, again, there were cases in which the victims were taken without warning from the loom, the fountain or even from their beds, and the respite, where granted, was in great measure illusory. The ordinary term given was a bare week, and it was never more than a fortnight—a time utterly insufficient for all that had to be done. There were instances, moreover, in which the Government broke its promise, and carried away its victims before the stated day arrived.

For the women there was an alternative to deportation. They might escape it by conversion to Islam; but conversion for an Armenian woman in 1915 meant something more physical than a change of theology. It could only be ratified by immediate marriage with a Moslem man, and if the woman were already a wife (or, rather, a widow, for by this time few Armenian husbands remained alive), she must part with any children she had, and surrender them to be brought up as true Moslems in a "Government Orphanage"—a fate of uncertain meaning, for no such institutions were known to be in existence[248]. If the convert could find no Turk to take her, or shrank from the embraces of the bridegroom who offered himself, then she and her children must be deported with the rest, however fervently she had professed the creed of Islam. Deportation was the alternative adopted by, or imposed upon, the great majority.

The sentence of deportation was a paralysing blow, yet those condemned to it had to spend their week of grace in feverish activity, procuring themselves clothing, provisions and ready money for the road. The local authorities placed every possible obstacle in their way. There was an official fiction that their banishment was only temporary, and they were therefore prohibited from selling their real property or their stock. The Government set its seal upon the vacated houses, lands and merchandise, "to keep them safe against their owners' return;" yet before these rightful owners started on their march they often saw these very possessions, which they had not been allowed to realise, made over by the authorities as a free gift to Moslem immigrants, who had been concentrated in the neighbourhood, in readiness to step into the Armenians' place[249]. And even such household or personal chattels as they were permitted to dispose of were of little avail, for their Moslem neighbours took shameless advantage of their necessity, and beat them down to an almost nominal price, so that when the day of departure arrived they were often poorly equipped to meet it.

The Government charged itself with their transport, and indeed they were not in a position to arrange for it themselves, for their ultimate destination was seldom divulged. The exiles from each centre were broken up into several convoys, which varied in size from two or three hundred to three or four thousand members. A detachment of gendarmerie was assigned to every convoy, to guard them on the way, and the civil authorities hired or requisitioned a certain number of ox-carts (arabas), usually one to a family, which they placed at their disposal; and so the convoy started out. The mental misery of exile was sufficiently acute, but it was soon ousted by more material cares. A few days, or even a few hours, after the start, the carters would refuse to drive them further, and the gendarmes, as fellow-Moslems, would connive at their mutinousness. So the carts turned back, and the exiles had to go forward on foot. This was the beginning of their physical torments, for they were not travelling over soft country or graded roads, but by mule-tracks across some of the roughest country in the world. It was the hot season, the wells and springs were sometimes many hours' journey apart, and the gendarmes often amused themselves by forbidding their fainting victims to drink. It would have been an arduous march for soldiers on active service, but the members of these convoys were none of them fitted or trained for physical hardship. They were the women and children, the old and the sick. Some of the women had been delicately brought up and lived in comfort all their lives; some had to carry children in their arms too young to walk; others had been sent off with the convoy when they were far gone with child, and gave birth on the road. None of these latter survived, for they were forced to march on again after a few hours' respite; they died on the road, and the new-born babies perished with them. Many others died of hunger and thirst, sunstroke, apoplexy or sheer exhaustion. The hardships endured by the women who accompanied their husbands on Sir John Moore's retreat to Corunna bear no comparison with the hardships these Armenian women endured. The Government which condemned them to exile knew what the journey would mean, and the servants of the Government who conducted them did everything to aggravate their inevitable physical sufferings. Yet this was the least part of their torture; far worse were the atrocities of violence wantonly inflicted upon them by fellow human beings.

From the moment they left the outskirts of the towns they were never safe from outrage. The Moslem peasants mobbed and plundered them as they passed through the cultivated lands, and the gendarmes connived at the peasants' brutality, as they had connived at the desertion of the drivers with their carts. When they arrived at a village they were exhibited like slaves in a public place, often before the windows of the Government Building itself, and every Moslem inhabitant was allowed to view them and take his choice of them for his harem; the gendarmes themselves began to make free with the rest, and compelled them to sleep with them at night. There were still more horrible outrages when they came to the mountains, for here they were met by bands of "chettis" and Kurds. The "chettis" were brigands, recruited from the public prisons; they had been deliberately released by the authorities on a consideration which may have been tacit but which both parties clearly understood. As for the Kurds, they had not changed since 1896, for they had always retained their arms, which Abd-ul-Hamid had served out and the Young Turks could not or would not take away; and they had now been restored to official favour upon the proclamation of the Holy War, so that their position was as secure again as it had been before 1908. They knew well what they were allowed and what they were intended to do. When these Kurds and chettis waylaid the convoys, the gendarmes always fraternised with them and followed their lead, and it would be hard to say which took the most active part in the ensuing massacre—for this was the work which the brigands came to do. The first to be butchered were the old men and boys—all the males that were to be found in the convoy except the infants in arms—but the women were massacred also. It depended on the whim of the moment whether a Kurd cut a woman down or carried her away into the hills. When they were carried away their babies were left on the ground or dashed against the stones. But while the convoy dwindled, the remnant had always to march on. The cruelty of the gendarmes towards the victims grew greater as their physical sufferings grew more intense; the gendarmes seemed impatient to make a hasty end of their task. Women who lagged behind were bayoneted on the road, or pushed over precipices, or over bridges. The passage of rivers, and especially of the Euphrates, was always an occasion of wholesale murder. Women and children were driven into the water, and were shot as they struggled, if they seemed likely to reach the further bank. The lust and covetousness of their tormentors had no limit. The last survivors often staggered into Aleppo naked; every shred of their clothing had been torn from them on the way. Witnesses who saw their arrival remark that there was not one young or pretty face to be seen among them, and there was assuredly none surviving that was truly old—except in so far as it had been aged by suffering. The only chance to survive was to be plain enough to escape their torturers' lust, and vigorous enough to bear the fatigues of the road.

Those were the exiles that arrived on foot, but there were others, from the metropolitan districts and the north-west, who were transported to Aleppo by rail. These escaped the violence of the Kurds, but the sum of their suffering can hardly have been less. They were packed in cattle-trucks, often filthy and always overcrowded, and their journey was infinitely slow, for the line was congested by their multitude and by the passage of troops. At every stopping-place they were simply turned out into the open, without food or shelter, to wait for days, or even weeks, till the line was clear and rolling-stock available to carry them a further stage. The gendarmes in charge of them seem to have been as brutal as those with the convoys on foot, and when they came to the two breaks in the Baghdad Railway, where the route crosses the ranges of the Taurus and Amanus Mountains, they too had to traverse these, the most arduous stages of all, on foot. At Bozanti, the rail-head west of Taurus, and again at Osmania, Mamouret, Islohia and Kotmo, stations on either slope of the Amanus chain, vast and incredibly foul concentration camps grew up, where the exiles were delayed for months, and died literally by thousands of hunger, exposure, and epidemics. The portion of them that finally reached Aleppo were in as deplorable a condition as those that had made the journey on foot from beginning to end.

Aleppo was the focus upon which all the convoys converged. In April, it is true, half the Zeitounlis had been sent north-westward to Sultania, in the Konia district, one of the most unhealthy spots in the Anatolian Desert. But the authorities changed their mind, and despatched the exiles at Sultania south-east again, to join their fellow-townsmen in the Desert of Syria[250]. Thenceforward, the south-eastern desert was the destination of them all, and Aleppo, and in a secondary degree Ourfa and Ras-ul-Ain, were the natural centres of distribution.

Some of the exiles were planted in the immediate neighbourhood of Aleppo itself—at places like Moumbidj, Bab, Ma'ara, Idlib[251]—but these seem to have been comparatively few, and it is not certain whether their quarters there were intended to be permanent. Many more were deported southward from Aleppo along the Syrian Railway, and allowed to find a resting-place in the districts of Hama, Homs and Damascus. A still larger number were sent towards the east, and cantoned on the banks of the Euphrates, in the desert section of its course. There were some at Rakka; Der-el-Zor was the largest depôt of all, and is mentioned in this connection more frequently than any place after Aleppo itself; some were sent on to Mayadin[252], a day's journey further down the river, and Moslem travellers reported meeting others within forty-eight hours' journey of Baghdad[253]. No first-hand evidence has come in of their presence at or near Mosul, though they were frequently informed on their journey that their destination was to be there.

The dispersal of the exiles was thus extremely wide, as the authors of the scheme had intended that it should be, but certain features are common to all the places to which they were sent. They were all inhabited by Moslem populations alien to the Armenians in language and habits of life; they were all unhealthy—either malarious or sultry or in some other respect markedly unsuitable for the residence of people used to a temperate climate; and they were all remote from the exiles' original homes—the remotest places, in fact, which the Government could find within the Ottoman frontiers, since Christians were debarred from setting foot on the sacred deserts of the Hidjaz, and a British expeditionary force was occupying the marshes of Irak.

The Ottoman Government had to content itself with the worst districts at its disposal, and it did its utmost to heighten the climate's natural effect by marooning the exiles there, after an exhausting journey, with neither food, nor shelter, nor clothing, and with no able-bodied men among them to supply these deficiencies by their labour and resource.

The transmission of the exiles to these distant destinations was naturally slow—indeed, the slowness of the journey was one of the most effective of its torments. The first convoy started from Zeitoun on the 8th April, 1915; fresh convoys followed it during the seven ensuing months from the different Armenian centres in the Empire, and there is no record of any stoppage until the 6th November. On that date an order from Constantinople reached the local authorities, at any rate in the Cilician plain[254], directing them to refrain from further deportations; but this only applied to the remnant of the local Armenian residents, and the masses of exiles from the north and north-west who were still painfully struggling across the barriers of Taurus and Amanus, were driven on remorselessly to their journey's end, which cannot have been reached by them (or by such of them as survived) before the very close of the year. The congestion of the routes was partly responsible for this delay; but the congestion would have been still more pronounced if the scheme had not been carried out methodically, region by region, in an order which betrays more than anything else the directing hand of the Central Government. Cilicia was the first region to be cleared, just as it had been the principal region to suffer in the massacres of 1909. Strategically and economically, it was the most vital spot in Asiatic Turkey, and its large and increasing Armenian population must always have offended the sensibilities of the Young Turkish Nationalists. It was the natural starting-point for the execution of the Ottomanisation Scheme, and the deportations were in progress here fully six weeks before they were applied to the remainder of the Empire. Zeitoun was cleared on the 8th April; Geben, Furnus and Albustan within the next few days; Dört Yöl before the end of the month. At Hadjin, on the other hand, the clearance did not begin till the 3rd June, and dragged on into September; while at Adana, the city of the plain, there was only an abortive clearance in the third week of May, and the serious deportations were postponed till the first week in September.

The next region to be cleared was the zone bordering on Van and immediately threatened by the Russian advance, from the Black Sea to the Persian frontier. In the south-eastern districts of this zone—Bitlis, Moush, Sassoun and Hakkiari—the clearance, as has been remarked already, was not effected by deportation, but by wholesale massacre on the spot. Outlying villages of the Boulanik, Moush and Sassoun areas were destroyed in the latter part of May, and before the end of the same month Djevdet Bey retreated down the Bohtan Valley from Van, and massacred the Armenians of Saïrt. The Armenians of Bitlis were next massacred by Djevdet, on the 25th June; and, in the first week of July, 20,000 fresh troops arrived from Harpout and exterminated the Armenians of Moush—first the villagers and then the people of the town, which was bombarded by artillery on the 10th June. After making an end of Moush these troops joined the Kurdish irregulars operating against Sassoun, and on the 5th August, after bitter fighting, the surviving Sassounlis—man, woman and child—were annihilated in their last mountain stronghold. At the end of July the Ottoman forces temporarily re-entered Van, and slaughtered all the Armenian inhabitants who had not escaped in the wake of the Russian retreat. In June and July the Nestorian (Syrian) communities of the district of Hakkiari, in the upper basin of the Greater Zab, were also attacked by the Kurds and destroyed, except for a remnant which crossed the watershed into the Urmia basin and found safety within the Russian lines.

In the north-western districts of the frontier zone the semblance of deportation was preserved, but the exiles—women and children as well as men—were invariably massacred in cold blood after a few days on the road. Before the end of May there was a massacre at Khnyss, and on the 6th June the deportations began (with the same consummation) in the villages of the Erzeroum plain. At Erzeroum itself the first deportation took place on the 16th June, and the last on the 28th July (or on the 3rd August, according to other reports). The Armenian Bishop of the city was deported with this last convoy, and never heard of again. At Baibourt, the surrounding villages were similarly cleared before the town, and the townspeople were despatched in three convoys, the last of which started on the 14th June. From the town of Erzindjan four convoys started on successive days, from the 7th June to the 10th. Practically none of the exiles from Erzindjan, Baibourt or Erzeroum seem to have outlived the first stages of the journey.

At Harpout, the clearance began on the 1st June, and continued throughout the month. On the 2nd, 3rd and 4th July the adjoining town of Mezré was emptied as well. The convoys from these two places and the neighbouring villages were terribly thinned by atrocities on the road.

At Trebizond the deportations were carried out from the 1st to the 6th July, and seem to have been simultaneous in the various coast towns of the Vilayet. Here, too, deportation was merely a cloak for immediate massacre. The exiles were either drowned at sea or cut down at the first resting-place on the road.

In the Vilayet of Sivas, again, the villages were dealt with first, but the city itself was not cleared till the 5th July. At X. the men were deported on the 26th June, the women on the 5th July, and the last remnant, who had found protection with the American Missionaries, were carried away on the 10th August. All the men, and many of the women, were massacred on the road.

The Armenian population in the provinces west of Sivas, and in the metropolitan districts surrounding Constantinople, was removed by train along the Anatolian Railway to Konia, and thence towards Aleppo along the several sections of the Baghdad line. In all this region the scheme was put into execution distinctly later. At Angora the deportations began towards the end of July, at Adapazar about the 11th August; at Broussa there seems to have been no clearance till the first weeks of September, but this is stated to have been one of the last places touched[255]. At Adrianople, however, the Armenians were not deported till the middle of October; and at K., in the Sandjak of Kaisaria, not till the 12th/15th November.

The south-eastern outposts of the Armenian Dispersion were left to the last, although their immediate neighbours in the Cilician highlands had been taken at the very beginning. The villagers of Djibal Mousa were not summoned till the 13th July; Aintab was not touched till the 1st August, and then only cleared gradually during the course of the month. The summons to Ourfa, which was answered, as at Djibal Mousa, by defiance, was not delivered till the last week in September.

Glancing back over this survey, we can discern the Central Government's general plan. The months of April and May were assigned to the clearance of Cilicia; June and July were reserved for the east; the western centres along the Railway were given their turn in August and September; and at the same time the process was extended, for completeness' sake, to the outlying Armenian communities in the extreme south-east. It was a deliberate, systematic attempt to eradicate the Armenian population throughout the Ottoman Empire, and it has certainly met with a very large measure of success; but it is not easy to present the results, even approximately, in a statistical form. The only people in a position to keep an accurate account of the numbers affected were the Ottoman authorities themselves; but it is unlikely that they have done so, and still more unlikely that they would ever divulge such figures to the civilised world. We are compelled to base our estimates on the statements of private persons, who were excluded from detailed investigation by the jealous suspicion of the Government officials and were seldom able to observe events in more than a limited section of the field. We must make our computations by piecing together these isolated data from private sources, and since Oriental arithmetic is notoriously inexact (and this is scarcely less true of the Nearer than of the Further East), we shall only make use of testimony from foreign witnesses of neutral nationality. Such witnesses may be assumed to be comparatively free from unconscious exaggeration and completely innocent of purposeful misrepresentation, and we can accept their statements with considerable assurance.

The first step is to establish the number of Armenians living within the Ottoman frontiers at the moment the deportations began. All the other figures ultimately depend upon this, but it is harder than any to obtain, for there are no independent foreign estimates of this on record, and the discrepancy between the native estimates is extreme[256]. The Armenian Patriarchate, after an enquiry conducted in 1912, placed the number as high as 2,100,000[257]; the Ottoman Government, in its latest official returns, puts it at 1,100,000 and no more. Both parties have an equal political interest in forcing their figures, but the Armenians are likely to have had a greater respect for exactitude, or at any rate a stronger sense of the futility of falsification. The most "neutral" course under the circumstances is to halve the difference, and to take the number provisionally as being 1,600,000, with the qualification that the true figure certainly lies between this and 2,000,000, and probably approaches more closely to the latter. The rest of the necessary figures can fortunately be drawn from foreign neutral testimony, in which such baffling discrepancies are rarer.

The second step is to estimate the number of those who have escaped deportation. There are the refugees who have escaped it by crossing the frontier—182,000 into the Russian Caucasus and 4,200 into Egypt, according to detailed and trustworthy returns[258]. There are also two important Armenian communities in Turkey where practically all but the leaders have been left unmolested—those of Smyrna and Constantinople. At Constantinople about 150,000 Armenians must still remain. Then there are the Catholic and Protestant Millets, which were nominally exempted from deportation, and the exempted converts to Islam. It is impossible to estimate the numbers in these categories with any plausibility, for the conduct of the authorities in respect of them was quite erratic. Many of the converts to Islam[259], as well as Armenians of the other denominations, were given the same treatment as the Gregorians, and the actual percentage of conversions is unascertainable, for they were encouraged in some places and discouraged in others. We must also allow for those who managed to elude the Government's net. As a general rule, this category is more numerous in reality than it appears to be, and this is especially so in the Near East. But in the present case the Young Turks seem to have put a Prussian thoroughness into the execution of their scheme, and the margin of ineffectiveness was evidently narrow. In the towns, such as Zeitoun, Hadjin, Sivas, X., and Erzeroum, where we have sufficient testimony to cross-check the estimates presented, the clearance, by deportation or massacre, seems to have been practically complete. At Erzeroum, for instance, there were 20,000 Armenians before the clearance began, and when it was over there were not more than 100 left[260]. Concealment on any considerable scale can only have been practised in the villages, yet the number of those who have emerged from hiding since the Russian occupation is extraordinarily small. According to the investigations of the Patriarchate, there were 580,000 Armenians in 1912 in the Vilayets of Erzeroum, Bitlis and Van, which are now within the Russian lines[261]. The American Relief Committee has recently been informed by its agents on the spot that there are now only 12,100 left alive there[262]. Whatever arbitrary margin of reduction the absence of confirmatory statistics may make it necessary to subtract from the former figure, the proportion borne to it by the 12,100 survivors remains infinitesimal. Putting the communities at Constantinople and Smyrna and the refugees together at about 350,000, we shall certainly not be reckoning too low if we allow a quarter of a million for the Protestants, Catholics, converts and others who were spared, and estimate the total number of Armenians in Turkey who escaped deportation at not more than 600,000.

This leaves at least 1,000,000 to be accounted for by deportation and massacre, and probably 1,200.000 or more.

The third step is to estimate what proportion of these million Armenians has perished and what proportion survived, and here again our material is scanty and generalisation unsafe, the procedure of the authorities being erratic in this respect also. In certain vilayets, like Van and Bitlis, there was no deportation at all, but massacre outright; in others, like Erzeroum and Trebizond, and again at Angora, deportation and massacre were equivalent, the convoys being butchered systematically at an early stage on the road. In Cilicia, on the other hand, the men as well as the women seem to have been genuinely deported, and the convoys seem only to have been reduced by sickness and exhaustion. Yet even where there was no wholesale massacre on the journey, a convoy might practically be exterminated by degrees. A large combined convoy, for instance, of exiles from Mamouret-ul-Aziz and Sivas, set out from Malatia 18,000 strong and numbered 301 at Viran Shehr, 150 at Aleppo[263]. In this case, however, the wastage appears to have been exceptional. We have one similar instance of a convoy from Harpout which was reduced on the way to Aleppo from 5,000 to 213, a loss of 96 per cent.[264]; but in general the wastage seems to fluctuate, with a wide oscillation, on either side of 50 per cent.; 600 out of 2,500 (24 per cent.) reached Aleppo from a village in the Harpout district[265]; 60 per cent. arrived there out of the first convoy from the village of E. (near H.), and 46 per cent. out of the second; 25 per cent. arrived out of a convoy from the village of D. in the same neighbourhood[266]. We shall certainly be well within the mark if we estimate that at least half those condemned to massacre or deportation have actually perished.

We can check this estimate to some extent by the record of arrivals at certain important centres of traffic on the exile routes, or at the final destinations of the convoys. On the 16th August, 1915, for instance, an exceedingly competent neutral resident at Constantinople stated that, to his knowledge, there were then 50,000 exiles scattered along the route from Bozanti (the first break in the Baghdad line) to Aleppo; on the 5th November, another witness[267], who had just traversed this route, wrote back from Aleppo that he had passed 150,000 exiles between there and Konia. Again, 13,155 exiles had reached or passed through Aleppo by the 30th July, 1915, and 20,000 more arrived there between that date and the 19th August[268]. By the 3rd August 15,000 of these had been transmitted alive to Der-el-Zor, and this was only the beginning of the arrivals in the Zor district. No exiles reached Damascus before the 12th August, but between that date and the 3rd October, 1915, 22,000 of them had come through[269]. These are isolated data, and prove little in themselves, but in its Bulletin of the 5th April, 1916, the American Relief Committee has published a cable recently received in the United States from a competent source, in which the total number of Armenian exiles alive at that time in the regions of Der-el-Zor, Damascus and Aleppo is estimated roughly at 500,000[270]. This figure is possibly an exaggeration, but it is not incompatible with our two previous conclusions, that the total number of Armenians affected by the Young Turks' scheme was at least a million, and that at least 50 per cent. of these have perished. To the alleged 500,000 survivors in the three regions mentioned we must add an uncertain but inconsiderable margin for the exiles who may have been planted at Mosul or who may still, in March, 1916, have been held up on the road; and this will raise the original number affected to something approaching 1,200,000, which we considered, on other grounds, to be nearer the real figure than the bare million which we accepted.

We can sum up this statistical enquiry by saying that, as far as our defective information carries us, about an equal number of Armenians in Turkey seem to have escaped, to have perished, and to have survived deportation in 1915; and we shall not be far wrong if, in round numbers, we estimate each of these categories at 600,000.

The exact quantitative scale of the crime thus remains uncertain[271], but there is no uncertainty as to the responsibility for its perpetration. This immense infliction of suffering and destruction of life was not the work of religious fanaticism. Fanaticism played no more part here than it has played in the fighting at Gallipoli or Kut, and the "Holy War" which the Young Turks caused to be proclaimed in October, 1914, was merely a political move to embarrass the Moslem subjects of the Entente Powers. There was no fanaticism, for instance, in the conduct of the Kurds and chettis, who committed some of the most horrible acts of all, nor can the responsibility be fixed upon them. They were simply marauders and criminals who did after their kind, and the Government, which not only condoned, but instigated, their actions, must bear the guilt. The peasantry, again (own brothers though they were to the Ottoman soldiery whose apparent humanity at Gallipoli and

Kut has won their opponents' respect), behaved with astonishing brutality to the Armenians who were delivered into their hands; yet the responsibility does not lie with the Turkish peasantry. They are sluggish, docile people, unready to take violent action on their own initiative, but capable of perpetrating any enormity on the suggestion of those they are accustomed to obey. The peasantry would never have attacked the Armenians if their superiors had not given them the word. Nor are the Moslem townspeople primarily to blame; their record is not invariably black, and the evidence in this volume throws here and there a favourable light upon their character. Where Moslem and Christian lived together in the same town or village, led the same life, pursued the same vocation, there seems often to have been a strong human bond between them. The respectable Moslem townspeople seldom desired the extermination of their Armenian neighbours, sometimes openly deplored it, and in several instances even set themselves to hinder it from taking effect. We have evidence of this from various places—Adana[272], for instance, and AF.[273] in Cilicia, the villages of AJ. and AK.[273] in the AF. district, and the city of Angora. The authorities had indeed to decree severe penalties against any Moslem as well as any alien or Greek who might be convicted of sheltering their Armenian victims. The rabble naturally looted Armenian property when the police connived, as the rabble in European towns might do; the respectable majority of the Moslem townspeople can be accused of apathy at worst; the responsibility cannot rest with these.

The guilt must, therefore, fall upon the officials of the Ottoman Government, but it will not weigh equally upon all members of the official hierarchy. The behaviour of the gendarmerie, for example, was utterly atrocious; the subordinates were demoralised by the power for evil that was placed in their hands; they were egged on by their chiefs, who gave vent to a malevolence against the Armenians which they must have been harbouring for years; a very large proportion of the total misery inflicted was the gendarmerie's work; and yet the gendarmerie were not, or ought not to have been, independent agents. The responsibility for their misconduct must be referred to the local civil administrators, or to the Central Government, or to both.

The local administrators of provinces and sub-districts—Valis, Mutessarifs and Kaimakams—are certainly very deeply to blame. The latitude allowed them by the Central Government was wide, as is shown by the variations they practised, in different places, upon the common scheme. In this place the Armenian men were massacred; in that they were deported unscathed; in that other they were taken out to sea and drowned. Here the women were bullied into conversion; here conversion was disallowed; here they were massacred like the men. And in many other matters, such as the disposal of Armenian property or the use of torture, remarkable differences of practice can be observed, which are all ascribable to the good or bad will of the local officials. A serious part of the responsibility falls upon them—upon fire-eaters like Djevdet Bey or cruel natures like the Governor of Ourfa[274]; and yet their freedom of action was comparatively restricted. Where they were evilly-intentioned towards the Armenians they were able to go beyond the Central Government's instructions (though even in matters like the exemption of Catholics and Protestants, where their action was apparently most free, they and the Central Government were often merely in collusion)[275]; but they might never mitigate their instructions by one degree. Humane and honourable governors (and there were a certain number of these) were powerless to protect the Armenians in their province. The Central Government had its agents on the spot—the chairman of the local branch of the Committee of Union and Progress[276], the local Chief of Gendarmerie, or even some subordinate official[277] on the Governor's own administrative staff. If these merciful governors were merely remiss in executing the instructions, they were flouted and overruled; if they refused to obey them, they were dismissed and replaced by more pliant successors. In one way or another, the Central Government enforced and controlled the execution of the scheme, as it alone had originated the conception of it; and the Young Turkish Ministers and their associates at Constantinople are directly and personally responsible, from beginning to end, for the gigantic crime that devastated the Near East in 1915.

213. The Paulikian exiles inspired the South-Slavonic Bogomils; the Bogomils inspired the Albigenses of Languedoc, and possibly sowed some of the seeds of the Hussite movement among the Tchechs and Slovaks.

214. With the possible exception of the Bulgars.

215. The Armenian Protestants have even been admitted to the Gregorian National Assembly—a notable departure from Near Eastern tradition.

216. There is a flourishing colony of Armenian fruit-growers as far afield as Fresno, California.

217. Though even in Irak there were Armenian settlers, especially at Baghdad.

218. The nomadic Kurds, for that matter, are only skin-deep Mohammedans.

219. Excluding the district of Hakkiari.

220. A Syrian sect whose doctrines diverged, like those of the Nestorians, from the creed of the Catholic and Orthodox Churches, but in the contrary direction.

221. It appears to be uncertain whether this is really the literal meaning of the word, its current connotation being purely the political one.

222. The word "Millet" means simply "religious sect" in the Arabic language, from which it was borrowed by the Turks.

223. Erzeroum, Van, Bitlis, Diyarbekir, Mamouret-ul-Aziz, Sivas.

224. Article 61.

225. There was an equally vague clause to the same effect in the special "Cyprus Convention" between Turkey and Great Britain, but in neither treaty was there any guarantee of its observance. The Berlin Treaty merely provided that the Ottoman Government should communicate its measures of reform to the Powers, but, as they were never carried out they were never reported.

226. Russia began to acquire territory south of the Caucasus at the beginning of the nineteenth century, when the last King of Georgia ceded his Kingdom to the Tsar, to save it from the hands of the Turks and Persians.

227. Tiflis, the former capital of the Georgian Kingdom and now the administrative centre of the Russian Provinces of the Caucasus, has become practically an Armenian city in the course of the nineteenth century, and Armenian settlements have spread far further into the interior of Russia.

228. Though the British Government was the only Government that attempted to put pressure on the Turks to desist. In Germany it was the *mot d'ordre* that the massacres were a British invention with a political purpose, and the German Emperor shortly afterwards sent his portrait to Abd-ul-Hamid as a complimentary gift.

229. In such publications as *Vérité sur le mouvement révolutionnaire Arménien et les mesures gouvernementales* (Constantinople, 1916); or *Die Armenische Frage*, von C.A. Bratter (Berlin, Concordia-Deutsche Verlags-Anstalt, 1915).

230. Doc. 138.

231. In the pamphlet *Vérité sur le mouvement révolutionnaire Arménien et les mesures gouvernementales*, the following passages occur: "The Imperial (Ottoman) Government abstained from exercising any pressure or adopting any repressive measures against the Armenians until the day the revolt broke out at Van towards the middle of April, 1915" (page 10); "No coercive measure was decreed by the Imperial Government against the Armenians until the date of their armed revolt, which took place at Van and in the other military zones in the course of the month of *June*, of the year 1915, and until they had made common cause with the enemy forces" (page 15). These statements are direct falsehoods, as is also the statement (page 12) that—"After the

occupation of Van by the Russians and Armenians, the Moslem population of the town was pitilessly massacred." We have authoritative neutral testimony (*e.g.*, Docs. 120, 121, 122 and 15) on both these points, by which the Turkish statements are refuted. Yet these lying statements are the pivot of the whole apologia presented in this pamphlet.

232. See Docs. 68, 82, 94 and 122.

233. Doc. 98.

234. Doc. 123.

235. Docs. 130 and 131.

236. According to an official calendar, published at Alexandropol by authority of the Katholikos of Etchmiadzin, from which extracts have been communicated to the Editor by Mr. H.N. Mosditchian, the statistics of the Armenian population in Russia, up to date, are 1,636,486 for the Caucasus, and approximately two million for the Empire as a whole. For the Ottoman Empire, statistics compiled at the Armenian Patriarchate of Constantinople in 1912 estimate the Armenian population at 2,100,000; Turkish official statistics, on the other hand, admit no more than 1,100,000, which on their own showing would give Russia a majority.

237. For evidence of this loyalty, see Annexe B. to this summary.

238. Docs. 21 and 57.

239. The 25 recalcitrants at Zeitoun do not come into question, for the Zeitounlis were excepted from military service by special charter, and the attempt to conscribe them was a violation by the Ottoman authorities of Ottoman law.

240. *Die Armenische Frage*, von C.A. Bratter, Berlin, Concordia Deutsche Verlags-Anstalt, 1915. The reference is to pp. 9-10.

241. Reproduced in the Paris journal *Le Matin*, 6th May, 1916, in a special despatch dated Zürich, 5th May.

242. The vast majority of secondary schools in the Empire being, of course, American, Armenian or Greek, and practically none of them Turkish.

243. See Annexe A.

244. The Delegation of 1912 was nominated by His Holiness the Katholikos of Etchmiadzin. Its President was His Excellency Boghos Nubar Pasha.

245. The Ottoman Government, for statistical reasons, added the Vilayet of Trebizond to the original Six, the Moslem element being here in a sufficient majority to balance, to some extent, the Armenian majority in the rest.

246. Doc. 129.

247. Proclamations announcing and justifying the deportation of the Armenians are quoted in Docs. 83 and 120 of this volume, while the alleged text of one of them has been published complete in the Philadelphia *Saturday Evening Post* of the 5th February, 1915, and is reproduced here as Annexe C. to this summary. The latter document differs in its wording and in the order of its clauses from the versions quoted in the places mentioned above, but there is no reason to doubt its genuineness. Probably the Central Government communicated its instructions to the local authorities by telegraph or secret despatch, and the local authorities embodied these instructions, at their own discretion, in a printed proclamation to the inhabitants of their province.

248. See, however, Doc. 64.

249. These Moslem immigrants were particularly in evidence in Cilicia, and in the Vilayets of Erzeroum and Trebizond.

250. Docs. 114 and 123.

251. Docs. 4 and 139.

252. Doc. 141.

253. Docs. 11 and 121.

254. Doc. 115.

255. Doc. 101.

256. Though not more extreme than in other parts of the Near Eastern World, like Hungary, where statistics of nationality are a burning question of political controversy.

257. For Armenian statistical material see Annexes D. and E. to this summary.

258. The former figure is taken from the American Relief Committee's Fourth Bulletin, dated 5th April, 1916; the second from Doc. 131.

259. Doc. 88

260. Doc. 57 According to Doc. 53 the most authoritative of all those relating to Erzeroum, the number was actually 22.

261. The western districts of Erzeroum, which the Turks still hold, may be written off against Trebizond.

262. Bulletin of the 5th April, 1916.

263. Doc. 66

264. Doc. 137

265. Doc. 141

266. Doc. 70

267. Doc. 116

268. Doc. 139.

269. Doc. 143.

270. The items of this estimate are given in Doc. 139(d).

271. For further calculations see Annexe F.

272. Doc. 128

273. Doc. 126]

274. Doc. 119

275. See Doc. 87 relating to the town of X.

276. Docs. 72 and 128.

277. Doc. 70

ANNEXE A: "YESTERDAY A FIEF, TO-DAY OUR COUNTRY"; TRANSLATION OF AN EDITORIAL ARTICLE IN THE TURKISH JOURNAL "HILAL," 4th APRIL, 1916, COMMUNICATED BY THE AMERICAN COMMITTEE FOR ARMENIAN AND SYRIAN RELIEF.

The telegraphic agencies gave us the day before yesterday a summary of a lecture given in Vienna by the German deputy Traub, on his return from a journey to Turkey. After having paid tribute to the military qualities of the Turkish soldiers whom he had occasion to know closely during his stay on the Peninsula of Gallipoli, the eminent lecturer expressed the following opinion: "Turkey must not be considered by Europeans as a country to be exploited." Mr. Traub added that he was opposed to all missionary activities in the Turkish Empire.

These words are of the highest value to us, because in pronouncing them the Honourable German deputy expressed and recognised the profound change which has taken place in our country during these last years. In stating that foreigners must no longer consider Turkey as a vast field of exploitation, Mr. Traub has shown how the present situation of the Ottoman Empire differs from that of yesterday. At the same time he pointed out the necessity of abandoning the old ideas which had taken root with most Europeans as regards our country.

Turkey has always been considered by foreigners as a country where one could and should enrich himself by every possible means and without any charge or risk. For them it was a vast and magnificent fief which was to be exploited as a feudal lord managed his estate. Make as much money as possible, that was the motto of those who came to our country and who, actuated solely by the grasping desire for lucre, had no scruples or were untouched by the least noble or elevated considerations.

Whatever this conception may have been, and however reprehensible the conduct was of those to whom we refer, it would be unjust to consider them solely the result of the temperament of the Europeans living in Turkey. The regime of the Capitulations, odious for us, but full of delights for them, had contributed powerfully to form in our guests the strange ideas of which they were possessed. While the Sultan's own subjects had to submit to all kinds of charges and taxes, the foreigners residing in this Empire were not only entirely exempted, but also enjoyed privileges as numerous as they were important. This strange distinction justified the privileged ones in considering the others as creatures whose sole duty was to suffer everything and to assure the happiness of those to whom they had offered their hospitality.

The Hamidian administration also tended to support the point of view of the foreigners by encouraging them and permitting them all sorts of liberties.

The Sovereign, his ministers, and all officers of the administration had only one sure object in view, to assure for themselves a brilliant and easy life, without any anxiety. This confession alone profoundly wounds our national self-respect. We do not hesitate, out of respect for the truth, to call the old regime, which only yesterday was still in force, the shameless exploitation of the Turkish People. As regards the latter, it bore everything, it was incapable of reacting, because it had not yet become self-conscious.

On the eve of the proclamation of the Constitution, Turkey resembled rather closely Peru or Mexico, which, having been conquered by Pizarro and Cortes, respectively, were for many centuries under an administration totally devoid of all scruples.

This situation did not change immediately after the 23rd July, 1908; a new regime had been introduced in Turkey, but a new spirit had not yet entered the mind of the Turkish People. It required the great shocks of the Balkan War to revolutionise profoundly our souls and to give us self-consciousness. The day when under the influence of anxiety and suffering the Turkish

People asked themselves: "What am I? What have I done? What shall I do?"—that day was the real beginning of the new era for our country.

We need not dwell here at length on the changes which for nearly four years have taken place in all departments in Turkey. It is not our intention to write the history of the evolution of the soul of the Turkish People, and of the progress it has made. What we wish to speak of is the new situation which it has created for the foreigners.

The Turkish People, while it saw its own individuality develop, became conscious of its rights. It suddenly became evident to it that it was the only master in its own house and that nobody should exploit it or displace it in any field. The foreigners were in its eyes nothing but guests, who were entitled to its respect, but whose duty it was to become worthy of the hospitality they were enjoying.

The abolition of the Capitulations was the first manifestation of this new spirit we have just mentioned. Henceforth foreign subjects had to submit to the same burdens as the natives.

The suppression of the schools founded and directed by ecclesiastic missions or by individuals belonging to enemy nations, a measure which followed the abolition of the capitulary regime, was no less important. Thanks to their schools foreigners were able to exercise great moral influence over the young men of the country and they were virtually in charge of the spiritual and intellectual guidance of our country. By closing them the Government has put an end to a situation as humiliating as it was dangerous, a situation which, unfortunately, had already lasted too long. Other measures of a political and economic nature were taken to complete a work which might be called the taking possession of the country by its own sons, who had too long been deprived of their rights.

Thanks to this awakening, a little late but still in time, and thanks especially to this activity, Turkey has to-day become a "Fatherland," like Sweden, Spain, or Switzerland. Our country is no longer an estate or fief for anybody; it is the country of a people which has just been recalled to life, and which aspires, in its independence and liberty, to happiness and glory.

It is to this happy change that Mr. Traub referred in his lecture. The German deputy was one of the first to proclaim that henceforth the Turkish People will be the only masters in their own house and that nobody may any longer think of exploiting it or in any way tread their rights under foot. We are particularly pleased that an eminent representative of the noble nation which is our friend and ally speaks in this manner.

ANNEXE B: LETTER FROM MR. E. VARTANIAN, AN ARMENIAN-AMERICAN VOLUNTEER IN THE RUSSIAN SERVICE, TO HIS BROTHER-IN-LAW IN EGYPT; DATED 9th/22nd JULY, 1915, AND PUBLISHED IN THE ARMENIAN JOURNAL "HOUSSAPER," OF CAIRO.

We have been here three days. Some of us are going to be sent to Erivan; the rest of us are starting in two days for Van.

The enthusiasm here is very great. There are already 20,000 volunteers at the front, and they are trying to increase the number to 30,000. Each district we occupy is placed under Armenian administration, and an Armenian post is running from Igdir to Van. The Russian Government is showing great goodwill towards the Armenians and doing everything in its power for the liberation of Turkish Armenia.

When we disembarked at Archangel the Government gave us every possible assistance. It even undertook the transport of our baggage, and gave us free passes, second class, to Petrograd.

At Petrograd we received an equally hearty welcome, and the Governor of the city presented each of us with a medal in token of his sympathy. The Armenian colony put us up in the best hotels, entertained us at the best restaurants, and could not make enough of us. This lasted for five days, and then we continued our journey, again at the Government's expense, to Tiflis.

Everywhere on the way the population received us with cheers and offerings of flowers. Just as we were leaving Archangel, a young Russian lady came with flowers and offered one to each of us. I also saw a quite poor man who was so moved by the speech in Russian that one of our comrades had made, that he came and put his tobacco into the pipe of a comrade standing next to me, and kept nothing for himself but a bare half-pipeful. A third, an old man, was so moved by the speech that he began to cry and nearly made off, but a little while after I saw him standing in front of the carriage window and, with a shaking hand, holding out a hard-boiled egg to our comrade the chemist Roupen Stepanian. Probably it was his one meal for the day.

And so at every step we found ourselves in the midst of affecting scenes. At Petrograd Railway Station the crowd was enormous. There was an Armenian lady there who offered each of us a rose. There were boys and young men who wept because they could not come with us. At Rostov a young Russian joined our ranks. He was caught more than once by his parents at the stations further down the line, but he always succeeded in escaping them and rejoining us. We have christened him Stepan.

When we arrived at Tiflis, we marched singing to the offices of the Central Armenian Bureau, with our flag unfurled in front of us, and the people marched on either side of us in such a crowd that the trams were forced to stop running.

That is enough for to-day. My next letter shall be written from Armenia itself.

Please say nothing to my sister about this resolution that I have taken. I hope, of course, that she would know how to sacrifice her affection for her brother to her love for the nation and for liberty. I should curse any of my relations who lamented my resolution; they would have committed treason against the nation. There are five of us brothers; was it not imperative that at least one of us should devote himself to the cause of our national emancipation? Let us keep up our courage, realise the urgency of the moment and do our duty.

ANNEXE C: ALLEGED TEXT OF THE OTTOMAN GOVERNMENT'S PROCLAMATION ORDERING THE DEPORTATION OF THE ARMENIANS; REPRINTED FROM AN ARTICLE BY MISS ELEANOR FRANKLIN EGAN IN THE PHILADELPHIA "SATURDAY EVENING POST," 5th FEBRUARY, 1916[278].

Our fellow countrymen, the Armenians, who form one of the racial elements of the Ottoman Empire, having taken up, as a result of foreign instigation for many years past, with a lot of false ideas of a nature to disturb the public order; and because of the fact that they brought about bloody happenings and have attempted to destroy the peace and security of the Ottoman state, and the safety and interests of their fellow countrymen, as well as of themselves; and, moreover, as they have now dared to join themselves to the enemy of their existence[279] and to the enemies now at war with our state— our Government is compelled to adopt extraordinary measures and sacrifices, both for the preservation of the order and security of the country and for the welfare and the continuation of the existence of the Armenian community. Therefore, as a measure to be applied until the conclusion of the war, the Armenians have to be sent away to places which have been prepared in the interior vilayets; and a literal obedience to the following orders, in a categorical manner, is accordingly enjoined on all Ottomans:

First.—All Armenians, with the exception of the sick, are obliged to leave within five days from the date of this proclamation, by villages or quarters, and under the escort of the gendarmerie.

Second.—Though they are free to carry with them on their journey the articles of their movable property which they desire, they are forbidden to sell their lands and their extra effects, or to leave the latter here and there with other people, because their exile is only temporary and their landed property, and the effects they will be unable to take with them, will be taken care of under the supervision of the Government, and stored in closed and protected buildings. Anyone who sells or attempts to take care of his movable effects or landed property in a manner contrary to this order, shall be sent before the Court Martial. They are free to sell to the Government only the articles which may answer the needs of the Army.

Third.—Contains a promise of safe conduct.

Fourth.—A threat against anyone attempting to molest them on the way.

Fifth.—Since the Armenians are obliged to submit to this decision of the Government, if some of them attempt to use arms against the soldiers or gendarmes, arms shall be employed against them and they shall be taken, dead or alive. In like manner those who, in opposition to the Government's decision, refrain from leaving or seek to hide themselves—if they are sheltered or given food and assistance, the persons who thus shelter or aid them shall be sent before the Court Martial for execution.

---

278. Miss Egan writes that she managed to bring this document out of Turkey by copying it on the margins of the inner pages of a book, which she pretended to be reading when the Turkish officials searched her at the frontier. The book was examined, but the marginal pencilling passed undetected.

279. *i.e.*, Russia.

ANNEXE D: [280]: STATISTICAL ANALYSIS OF THE RACIAL ELEMENTS IN THE OTTOMAN VILAYETS OF ERZEROUM, VAN, BITLIS, MAMOURET-UL-AZIZ, DIYARBEKIR, AND SIVAS[281]; DRAWN UP IN 1912 BY THE ARMENIAN PATRIARCHATE AT CONSTANTINOPLE.

Nos.	Nations and Races.	Erzeroum.	Van.	Bitlis.	Mamouret-ul-Aziz.	Diyarbekir.	Sivas.	Total.	%	Total %	
1.	Turks	240,000	47,000	40,000	102,000	45,000	192,000	666,000	25.4		
2.	Circassians (immigrants)	7,000	—	10,000	—	—	45,000	62,000			
3.	Persians	13,000	—	—	—	—	—	13,000	3.4	Moslems, 45.1
4.	Lazes	10,000	—	—	—	—	—	10,000		
5.	Gipsies	—	3,000	—	—	—	3,000			
6.	Sedentary Kurds	35,000	32,000	35,000	75,000	30,000	35,000	242,000	9.2	16.3

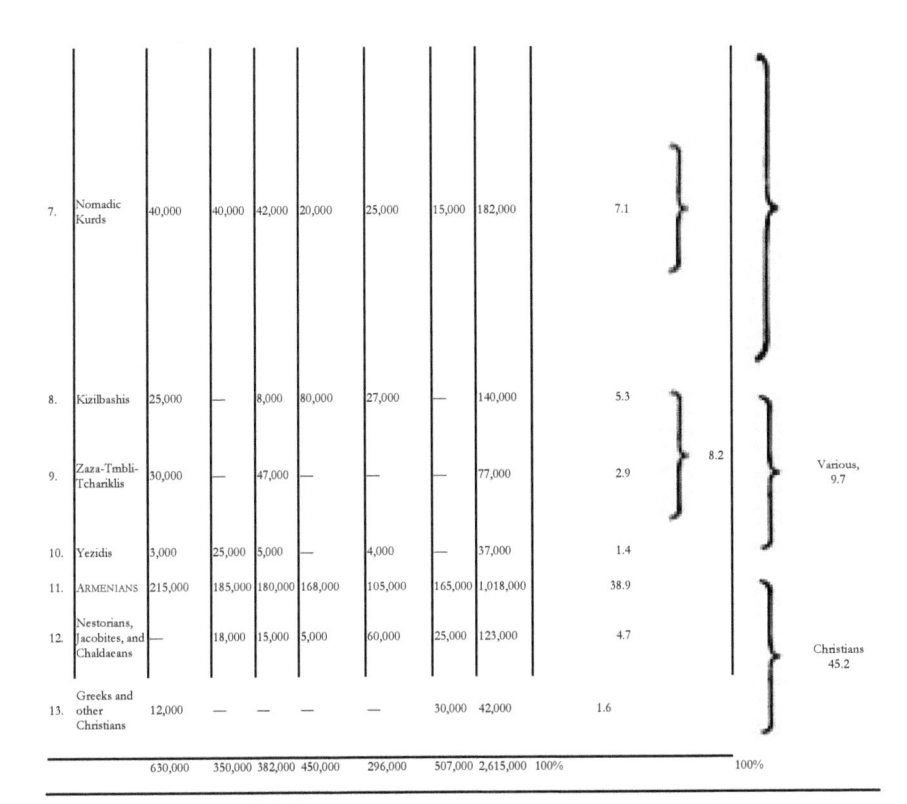

7.	Nomadic Kurds	40,000	40,000	42,000	20,000	25,000	15,000	182,000	7.1	
8.	Kizilbashis	25,000	—	8,000	80,000	27,000	—	140,000	5.3	} 8.2 } Various, 9.7
9.	Zaza-Tmbli-Tchariklis	30,000	—	47,000	—	—	—	77,000	2.9	
10.	Yezidis	3,000	25,000	5,000	—	4,000	—	37,000	1.4	
11.	ARMENIANS	215,000	185,000	180,000	168,000	105,000	165,000	1,018,000	38.9	} Christians 45.2
12.	Nestorians, Jacobites, and Chaldaeans	—	18,000	15,000	5,000	60,000	25,000	123,000	4.7	
13.	Greeks and other Christians	12,000	—	—	—	—	30,000	42,000	1.6	
		630,000	350,000	382,000	450,000	296,000	507,000	2,615,000	100%	100%

Moslems.

Turks	666,000		
Kurds	424,000	}	45.1%
Other Moslems	88,000		
TOTAL	1,178,000		

Various Religions.

Kizilbashis	140,000		
Zaza-Tmbli-Tchariklis	77,000	}	9.6%
Yezidis	37,000		
TOTAL	254,000		

Christians.

Armenians	1,018,000	}	45.2%
Nestorians	123,000		
Greeks	42,000		
TOTAL	1,183,000		

Summary of Totals.

Christians	1,183,000	=	45.2%
Moslems	1,178,000	=	45.1%
Various Religions	254,000	=	9.7%
GRAND TOTAL	2,615,000		

280. Reprinted from "La Question Arménienne à la Lumière des Documents," par "Marcel Léart" (Paris, 1913).

281. The analysis excludes certain portions of these provinces where the Armenians are only a minor element. These portions are as follows:— Hakkiari, in the Vilayet of Van; the south of Sairt, in the Vilayet of Bitlis; the south of the Vilayet of Diyarbekir; the south of Malatia, in the Vilayet of Mamouret-ul-Aziz; the north-west and west of the Vilayet of Sivas.

ANNEXE E: [282]: STATISTICAL SCHEDULE OF ARMENIAN SCHOOLS IN THE OTTOMAN EMPIRE, DRAWN UP IN 1901-2 BY THE ARMENIAN PATRIARCHATE AT CONSTANTINOPLE.

Geographical Districts	Schools.	Boy Pupils	Girl Pupils	Teachers.
THE SIX VILAYETS.				
Sairt	3	163	84	11

Amasia-Marsovan	9	1,524	814	54
Shabin Kara-Hissar	27	2,040	105	42
Erzeroum	27	1,956	,178	85
Kighi	27	1,336	367	43
Baïbourt	9	645	199	32
Diyarbekir	4	690	324	27
Harpout	27	2,058	496	58
Eghin	4	541	215	22
Tchemesh-Getzak	12	456	272	15
Arabkir	18	713	223	25
Tcharsandjak	12	617	189	18
Etesia	8	1,091	571	26
Gurin	12	736	78	20
Darandé	2	260	70	5
Divrig	10	757	100	20
Sivas	46	4,072	549	73
Bitlis	12	571	63	20
Erzindjan	22	1,389	475	63
Kamakh	13	646	28	16
Bayazid	6	338	54	13
Moush	23	1,034	284	35
Van	21	1,323	554	59
Lim and Gedoutz	3	203	56	6
Akhtamar	32	1,106	132	36
Derdjan	12	485	10	12

Isbir-Kiskim	3	80	—	3
Passin	7	315	—	7
Khnyss	8	352	15	12
Dikranakerd	2	180	—	5
Palou	8	505	50	15
Malatia	9	872	230	19
	438	29,054	7,785	897

CILICIA.

Aïntab	9	898	708	58
Antioch	10	440	47	10
Aleppo	2	438	249	18
Hadjin	4	508	69	12
Zeïtoun	10	605	85	15
Sis and the Neighbourhood	7	476	165	19
Adana	25	1,947	808	69
Marash	23	1,361	378	44
	90	6,673	2,509	245

THE REST OF THE EMPIRE.

Adrianople	6	314	251	22
Rodosto	9	1,017	856	48
Ismid	38	5,404	3,103	212

Biledjik	10	1,120	143	21
Kutahia	5	825	349	23
Smyrna	27	1,640	1,295	109
Angora	7	895	395	29
Kaisaria	42	3,795	1,140	125
Samsoun	27	1,361	344	59
Trebizond	47	2,184	718	85
Baghdad	2	68	46	11
Yozgad	12	1,197	557	43
Broussa	16	1,345	733	54
Balikesri-Panderma	8	700	634	35
Tokat	11	1,408	558	50
Kastamouni	3	110	50	2
Konia	3	213	137	12
Armasha	2	190	110	6
	275	23,786	11,419	946
GRAND TOTAL	803	59,513	21,713	2,088

282. Reprinted from "La Question Arménienne à la Lumière des Documents," par "Marcel Léart" (Paris, 1913). These statistics appear to be the most recent available, but it must be noted that they are fourteen years out of date, and that the figures must have risen considerably by April, 1915.

ANNEXE F: STATISTICAL ESTIMATE INCLUDED IN THE FIFTH BULLETIN OF THE AMERICAN COMMITTEE FOR ARMENIAN AND SYRIAN RELIEF, DATED NEW YORK, 24th MAY, 1916.

1. *The Extent of the Catastrophe.*

The most extensive and most difficult work carried on by the American Committee for Armenian and Syrian Relief lies within the borders of the Turkish Empire. Here, in January, 1915, the Armenians numbered between sixteen hundred thousand and two million. Precise statistics do not exist. The estimates of the Turkish Government are usually considered to be too low and those of the Armenian Patriarchate sometimes too high, suggesting a tendency in the one case to minimize and in the other to exaggerate the size and consequent importance of the Armenian population.

Twelve months later, in January, 1916, from one-third to one-half of the Armenians in Turkey had fallen victims of deportation, disease, starvation or massacre.

As we note from a letter of Dr. Wilson's, dated Erivan, Russian Caucasus, 4th February, 1916, there were then 182,800 Armenian refugees in the Caucasus and 12,100 in the districts of Turkey at that time conquered by the Russians. The subsequent extensions of the Russian conquests towards the west and south have brought to light numbers of Armenians who were in hiding. At the end of 1915, there were also 9,000 Armenian refugees in Salmas, Persia.

All these statistics are subject to fluctuation, due to the removal of the refugees from one region to another and also to the varying dates on which the enumerations or estimates were made. Bearing these critical considerations in mind we may tabulate the best figures as follows:—

Aleppo, Damascus, Zor	486,000
Refugees in other parts of Turkey	300,000
Russian Caucasus	182,800
Armenians in districts of Turkey conquered by Russia	12,100
Armenians in Salmas, Persia	9,000
	989,900

If we may add to these numbers the undeported Armenian populations in Constantinople and Smyrna, perhaps 150,000 in all, we can perhaps estimate the total number of survivors at under 1,150,000. If we accept the estimate that the Armenian population of Turkey at the beginning of 1915 was between 1,600,000 and 2,000,000, we should compute the number of deaths at between 450,000 and 850,000. We shall probably be safe in saying that the Armenian dead number at least 600,000.

Six hundred thousand men, women and children died within a year. There was recently held in New York City a Preparedness Parade, which marched up Fifth Avenue twenty abreast and took about thirteen hours to pass a given point. From 10 a.m. till well into the evening, this great army of over 125,000 continued to tramp up the street. If the Armenian men, women and children who died in Turkey within a twelvemonth should rise again and march in solemn procession to beg the assistance of the American people for their surviving brothers, the procession would not be 125,000, but 600,000, four times as long. Marching twenty abreast it would take two days and two nights to pass Great Reviewing Stand.

The mortality was higher in some regions than in others. From certain Armenian villages in the neighbourhood of Harpout, whose population was about two thousand, only 15·2 per cent. reached the goal of their deportation. Even if we make generous allowance for the number of men from these villages who may be still alive in the Army, and for the women and children who may have saved their lives by becoming Moslems, the mortality is unspeakably high. From other regions perhaps 25 per cent. have reached their goal, after marching hundreds of miles across the mountains down into the hot plains. From those portions of Asia Minor which are so situated that the Railway could assist in the deportation, the percentage of loss of life was far smaller, though here insufficient food and insanitary concentration camps have swollen the tolls of death. Especially from the cities on or near the coast of Cilicia, namely, Mersina, Tarsus and Adana, the deportation did not involve great loss of life. The Armenian inhabitants of Constantinople and of Smyrna, who really live in those cities and had not recently moved thither from the country, have not been deported.

Consequently the total number of surviving Armenians in Turkey is greater than our Committee had feared. The fact that there are more survivors than we at first believed obliges us to enlarge our relief work till it becomes adequate to the crisis.

2. *The Needs of the Survivors.*

Mr. W.W. Peet, Business Agent and Treasurer of the four Turkish Missions of the American Board of Commissioners for Foreign Missions with headquarters at Constantinople, has sent information, received by the State Department on the 17th March, to the effect that there are at least eight hundred thousand refugees in Turkey who need help. One-half or more of these are reported by the American Consul at Aleppo to be in the districts of Damascus, Zor and Aleppo.

The general direction of deportation has been to force the exiles to go by train or on foot to the neighbourhood of Aleppo, whence they have been distributed in two directions. One of these is the region served by the Hidjaz Railway, built a few years ago to meet the needs of the Moslem pilgrims to Mecca. The station of Ma'an, near the ruins of the ancient city of Petra, the point beyond which the Hidjaz Railway has always declined to transport Christians, is the southernmost point where Armenian exiles are to be found.

The other territory to which large numbers of exiles have been deported is the region of Der-el-Zor on the Euphrates, six days' journey east-south-east of Aleppo. The Armenians have had to walk thither from Aleppo, though some of them struck across by a more direct route from the Armenian cities on the north.

(Here follow, in the original, Documents 139(d) and 14 of this volume.)

Fortunately, the American Consul at Aleppo, Mr. Jackson, has the co-operation of the German Consul, Mr. Roessler in the work of relief.

Certain members of the American Committee have for months felt great anxiety as to the condition of the nearly 500,000 exiles distributed to the region east and south of Aleppo. Details as to their condition have been hard to secure. Now we know what we had suspected before—that many exiles have only grass to eat and that hundreds are dying daily of starvation.

3. *The Way for Relief is Now Open.*

In 1915, the Turkish Government declined to give cordial co-operation in the work of relieving the necessities of the Armenians. The authorities at Constantinople did not wish to have the Armenians helped by foreigners, because they thought it might encourage some of them in treasonable hopes. Constantinople therefore favoured having the relief money distributed through Turkish officials.

According to the New York *Times* of the 19th October, 1915, the Turkish Government informed the State Department at Washington that the American Red Cross would not be permitted to send surgeons and nurses to the aid of the Armenians in the Turkish Empire. The Turks barred not merely American Red Cross surgeons, nurses and relief agents, but also all other neutral foreigners.

Early in 1916 some obstacles have fallen. On the 23rd March, 1916, Mr. Phillips, the American Chargé d'Affaires at Constantinople, sent, on behalf of the Constantinople Chapter of the Red Cross, the following significant cablegram to the Secretary of State:—

"Turkish Government now welcomes help, and through Minister of Interior authorizes American Red Cross, co-operating with Red Crescent, to conduct relief work for civilians of all races. Great suffering throughout country, particularly at Constantinople and suburbs along the shores of Marmora, at Adrianople, Broussa and Smyrna. In these regions five hundred thousand, not comprising Armenian refugees, need help for bread. Hundreds dying of starvation. No relief in sight. Sugar and petroleum oil at famine prices. Typhus is spreading, high mortality. For immediate relief ten thousand pounds sterling estimated required for Constantinople Chapter administration before 1st May to procure foodstuffs. For more permanent relief, suggest importation supplies by sea from Roumania and America. Neutrality guaranteed by American Red Cross to Entente Powers. Distribution controlled by Constantinople Chapter through agencies, soup kitchens and dispensary. Some can pay cost price and industrial work proposed for others."

In answer to this appeal, certain friends of our Committee raised £12,000 sterling and transmitted it to Constantinople, to be distributed by the Turkish Red Crescent for sufferers in Turkey, regardless of religious barriers.[283]

INDEX OF PLACES REFERRED TO IN THE DOCUMENTS IN THIS VOLUME.

The figures placed against the names in this index denote the number of independent witnesses who mention the places in question, in the various connexions specified in the headings to each column. Two or more documents emanating from the same source cannot be regarded as independent testimony and are, therefore, not separately enumerated.

The index includes references to names which have been withheld by the editor himself and are represented in the text by arbitrary signs, but not, of course, references to names which have been withheld from the editor and are represented in the text by blanks. The names of places beyond the Ottoman frontier where refugees have passed or stayed have been placed between brackets, to distinguish them from places in Ottoman territory through or to which exiles have been forcibly conducted by the Ottoman Government.

NAME OF PLACE.	Massacre, Forcible Conversion, or Deportation, of Armenian Inhabitants. Armenians Replacement by Moslem Mouhadjirs (immigrants).	No Mention of Mouhadjirs.	Arrival, Passage of Armenians Deported or taking Flight from Elsewhere.
A.			
Abijalu	—	1	—
Ada	—	1	—
Adana	1	11	3
Adana, vilayet	—	1	—
Adapazar	1	5	—
Adiaman—Hussi Mansour	—	3	—
Adiljevas	—	1	—
Adranos	—	—	1
Adrianople	—	2	—
Afiun Kara-Hissar	—	1	3
Aghja Daghi	—	—	1

(Aghtalia)	—	—	1
Agno	—	1	—
(Ailar)	—	—	1
Aintab	—	10	4
Ak Shehr	—	2	—
Alabash	—	3	—
Alashkerd	—	3	—
Alashkerd District	—	1	—
Alayund	—	—	1
Albek	—	1	—
Albustan	—	5	1
Aleppo	—	2	32
Aleppo, vilayet	—	2	—
Alexandretta	—	1	—
(Alexandropol)	—	—	2
(Alexandropol Town and District)	—	—	1
Alidjan—Aladin	—	2	—
Amasia	—	7	2
Angegh	—	1	—
Angora	—	10	2
Angora, vilayet	—	2	—
(Annenfeld)	—	—	1
Antioch	—	1	1
Antok	—	1	—
Arabia	—	—	2
Arabkir	—	4	1

Arab-Pounar	—	—	1
Ardishai	—	1	—
Ardjish—Akantz	—	5	—
Arghana	—	—	2
Arghana Maden	—	—	1
Armasha	—	1	—
Armasha Convent	—	1	—
Arslanbeg	—	1	—
Artamid	—	1	—
Artananz	—	1	—
(Arzap)	—	—	1
(Ashtarak)	—	—	2
Asia Minor	—	—	1
Asi Yozgad	—	—	1
Atabey	—	1	—
Attil	—	1	—
Avazaghpur	—	1	—
Ayash	—	1	1
Azizia	—	1	—
B			
Bab	—	—	2
Babylonia	—	—	1
Baghdad	—	—	5
Baghlou	—	1	—
Baghtché	—	1	1
Baghtchédjik—Bardezag	—	10	—

Baibourt	—	8	1
Bairak	—	2	—
Bairamoglu	—	—	1
Bakir Maden	—	—	1
(Bakou)	—	—	2
Balikesri	—	1	—
(Bambak)	—	—	1
Baranduz	—	1	—
Barbaroud	—	1	—
(Barsoun)	—	—	1
Bashkala	—	6	1
Batoum	—	—	1
Bayazid District	—	1	—
Baz	—	1	—
Beinam Boghazi	—	—	1
Beirout	—	1	1
Beitias	—	2	—
Beniani	—	1	—
Benli	—	1	—
Bergri-Kala	—	—	2
Berwar	—	1	—
Besné	—	1	—
Biredjik	—	—	1
Bisherig	—	1	—
Bitlis	—	13	—
Bitlis, vilayet	—	4	—
Black Sea Littoral	—	1	1

Boghaz Kessen	—	2	—
Bohtan District	—	1	—
Bor	—	1	—
Bosphorus, Villages on the Upper	—	1	—
Boulanik	—	3	—
Bozanti	—	1	5
Broussa	—	7	—
Broussa, vilayet	—	1	—
C (Caucasia, Cis—Northern Caucasia)	—	—	1
Cilicia	—	5	—
Constantinople	—	6	3
Constantinople, American School at	—	1	—
Cosi	—	1	—
D			
Dadush	—	1	—
Damascus	—	—	8
Darawar	—	1	—
(Delidjan)	—	—	3
Degala	—	1	—
Dengala	—	2	—
Derdjan	—	—	1
Deré Keui	—	1	—

Der-el-Zor	—	—	19
Derenda	—	2	—
Dersim	—	1	1
Develou	—	1	—
Deyirmeni River	—	—	2
Dhimotika	—	1	—
Dilgusha	—	1	—
Diliman	—	3	2
Divrig	—	3	—
Diyarbekir	—	15	2
Diyarbekir, vilayet	—	3	—
Djabaghtchour	—	1	—
Djera	—	1	—
Djerablous	—	1	—
(Djevanshir District)	—	—	1
Djevizlik	—	—	1
Djeziré	—	1	—
Djibal Mousa—Mousa Dagh—			
Djibal-al-Ahmar	—	3	—
Djoulamerk	—	1	—
(Djoulfa)	—	—	5
Dom	—	1	—
Döngöl	—	1	—
Dört Yöl	1	11	—
Doudjik—Tcharuk Dersim—Tcharik	—	1	1

Drtadli	—	1	—
Duzasar	—	1	—
E			
Egin	—	3	—
(Elenovka)	—	—	1
(Elizavetpol)	—	—	1
(Elizavetpol Government)	—	—	3
Enderessi	—	1	1
Entilli	—	—	3
Eregli	—	1	5
Eremer	—	1	—
Erendjik	—	1	—
Erer	—	1	—
(Erivan)	—	—	2
(Erivan Government)	—	—	5
Erzeroum	1	17	—
Erzeroum, vilayet	—	6	—
Erzindjan	1	8	5
Eski Shehr	—	2	2
Etchangeri—Kiangri—Kingri	—	1	1
(Etchmiadzin)	—	—	2
Euphrates District	—	—	1
Euphrates River	—	—	5
Euphrates River, Tributaries of	—	—	1

Euzerli	—	1	—
Everek	—	2	—
(Evlakh)	—	—	1
Ezli	—	1	—
F			
Fekké	—	—	1
Frank-norshen	—	1	—
Fundadjak_	—	3	—
Furnus	1	4	—
G			
Gargar District	—	2	—
Garjgan	—	1	—
Gawar	—	4	—
Geben	—	6	—
Gegvé	—	1	—
Gemerek	—	4	—
Gemleyik	—	1	—
Geogtapa—Göktepé	—	3	1
Gereg	—	—	1
Geulik Station	—	—	3
Gheizin Han	—	—	1
Ginj District—Gendjé	—	1	1
Gishgishla	—	—	1
Göksoun—Gourksoun	—	2	—
Gotni	—	1	—

Govdoun	—	1	—
Gulpashan	—	6	—
Gumushkhana	—	—	2
Gurin	—	2	—
Gurla	—	1	—
Gvars	—	2	—
H			
Habesh	—	1	—
Habousi	—	1	—
Hadji-Habibli	—	1	—
Hadjin	2	12	—
Haftevan	—	2	—
Haiatzor—Hayotz-Tzor—(?)			
Haig Valley	—	2	—
Hai Keui	—	1	—
Hama	—	—	4
Hankeui	—	—	1
Harni	—	2	—
Harounia	—	—	1
Harpout—Kharput	—	21	3
Hassan	—	1	—
Hassan-Beyli	—	6	2
Hassan-Tchelebi	—	—	1
Hassanova	—	1	—
Hauran	—	—	3
Hazaren	—	2	—

Herag—Erba'a	—	2	—
Hergerd	—	1	—
Hirj	—	—	1
Homs	—	—	3
Husseinig	—	1	—
Hussi Mansour	—	1	—
I			
Idlib	—	—	2
(Igdir)	—	—	6
Ilidja	—	—	1
Ineboli	—	1	—
Iriawa	—	2	—
Islohia	—	—	2
Ismayil	—	—	1
Ismayil Agha's Kala	—	1	—
Ismid	—	6	—
Ismid, sandjak	—	1	—
Isnik—Nicomedia	—	1	—
Istanos	—	2	—
Itchmé	—	1	1
Izoli Hadji	—	—	2
K			
Kachin Han	—	—	1
Kahdem	—	—	1
Kaisaria	—	13	2
Kaisaria, Villages in the District of	—	2	—

Kamakh	—	2	3
Kamakh Boghaz	—	—	2
Kangal	—	2	—
Kapou Kays	—	1	—
(Karabagh District)	—	—	1
Karadjalou-Garadjalu	—	2	—
Karagatch	—	1	—
Karagöz	—	1	—
(Karakeliss)	—	—	2
Karaman	—	—	1
Kara-Pounar	—	—	3
Karasu	—	2	—
Karer	—	—	1
Karmad	—	—	1
(Kars)	—	—	1
(Kars, Town and District)	—	—	1
Karsakh	—	1	—
Karspazar	—	2	—
Karsz	—	1	—
Kartzor	—	1	—
Kasha	—	1	—
Kassaba	—	1	—
Kavash District	—	2	—
(Kazakh)	—	—	1
Kazi Mahara	—	—	1

Keban	—	1	—
Keboussia	—	1	—
(Kedabek)	—	—	1
Keghi-Kighi	—	4	—
Keghvank	—	—	2
Keklik Tepé	—	—	1
Kelidj	—	2	—
Kerasond-Kiresoun	1	1	—
Keremet	—	1	—
Keshan	—	1	—
Kesirig	—	1	—
Kessab	—	4	—
Ketcheurd-Katchayourt	—	1	—
Ketch-Magara	—	1	—
Keumer Han	—	—	2
Khanishan	—	1	—
Khantzart District	—	—	1
Khantzod	—	1	—
Khashkhaldoukh	—	1	—
Khaskegh	—	1	—
Kheder-Bey	—	1	—
Kheiban	—	1	—
Khlat	—	1	—
Khnyss	—	5	—
Khoi	—	1	4
Khoronk	—	1	—

Khorsan	—	1	—
Khourakhon	—	1	—
Khozmo Pass	—	—	1
Kiakhta—Kyakta	—	—	2
Kilidjlar	—	—	1
Killis	—	1	1
Kirk Göz	—	—	1
Kizil Agatch	—	1	—
Komer	—	1	—
Koms-Goms	—	3	—
Konia	—	6	17
Konia, vilayet	—	1	2
Kotchan	—	1	—
Kotchesur-Kotch Hissar	—	1	—
Kotmo	—	—	3
(Kourpalou)	—	—	1
Kozolouk	—	1	—
Kudchi	—	—	1
Kurdistan	—	2	—
Kurdmeidan	—	1	—
Kurk	—	1	—
Kurtapa	—	1	—
Kurt-Belené	—	1	—
L			
Lappashli	—	1	—
Lebanon	1	—	—

Lsounk	—	1	—
M			
Ma'an	—	—	1
Ma'ara	—	—	2
Makof	—	1	—
Malatia	—	4	4
Malgara	1	1	—
Maltepé	—	1	—
Mama Hatoun-Derdjan	—	1	2
Mamouret	—	—	1
Mamouret-ul-Aziz, vilayet	—	5	—
Mandjaluk	—	2	—
Mansouria—Monsoria	—	1	—
Maragha	—	1	—
Marash	—	13	3
Mar Audishu	—	2	—
Mardin	—	6	1
(Markar)	—	—	1
Marmardjik	—	1	—
Marmora, Coasts of	—	1	—
Marsovan	—	15	—
Marsovan District	—	1	—
Mayadin	—	—	1
Mediterranean, Coasts of	—	1	—
Meghd	—	1	—
Mekragom	—	1	—
Melashkerd-Melazkerd	—	2	—

Mergavar	—	1	—
Mersina	—	5	—
Meskené	—	—	1
Mesopotamia	—	—	11
Mess Nor Keui	—	1	—
Messoudia	—	1	—
Mezré	—	6	—
Miandoab	—	1	—
Mikhalidj	—	—	1
Mirkedjia	—	—	1
Moks, kaza	—	1	—
Morinig	—	1	—
Mosul	—	—	11
Mosul, Region of	—	—	1
(Mouandjik)	—	—	1
Moumbidj	—	—	2
Mourad Su—Eastern Euphrates	—	—	2
Moush	—	12	—
N			
(Nahichevan)	—	—	2
(Nahichevan, Town and District)	—	—	1
Nazi	—	1	—
Nazlu District	—	1	—
Nigdé	—	1	—
(Nijni-Akhti)	—	—	1
Niksar	—	2	—
Norag	—	1	—

Nordoz	2	—
(Novo-Bayazid)	—	1
(Novo-Bayazid, Town and District)	—	1
(Novo-Nikolaievka)	—	1
O		
Odjakli	1	—
Olti	—	1
Ordou	2	—
Ortakeui	2	—
Osmania	—	9
Oulash	1	—
Ourbadji Oglou Deré (near Baibourt)	—	1
Ourfa	14	4
Ourough	1	—
Ovadjik	1	—
P		
Palu	—	1
Panderma	2	—
(Parakar)	—	1
Passin District	3	1
Pazou	2	—
Pelou	2	—
Pera	1	—
Perkenik	1	—
Perkhous	1	—

Perri	1	—
Pertchendji	—	1
Plel	1	—
(Plour)	—	1
Polatlu	1	—
(Port Said)	—	3
Q		
Quodshanis	5	—
R		
Radjou	—	2
Rahva	1	—
Rakka	—	5
Ras-ul-Ain	—	3
Rodosto	1	—
Roumlou	2	—
S		
Sabandja	2	—
Sahajian District	1	—
Sairt	3	—
Salekan	1	—
Salmas	4	4
Salmas District	3	—
Salt Desert of Anatolia	—	1
(Samaghar)	—	1
Samsoun	10	3
Sarai	2	—
Sassoun	3	—

Scutari	—	1	—
Selefka	—	2	—
Severeg	—	—	1
Shabin Kara-Hissar	—	6	—
Shadakh	—	1	—
Shadakh Region—Shatakh Kaza	—	3	—
Shahbagh	—	1	—
Shakh	—	1	—
Shaklak	—	1	—
Shar Kishla—Sari-Kishila	—	3	4
(Sharori)	—	—	1
Sheer—Shar	—	3	—
Sheitan Dere <ssi>	—	—	2
Shekhlan	—	1	—
Shivilgi	—	1	—
(Shousha District)	—	—	1
Shushantz	—	2	—
Silivri	—	1	—
Sis	—	5	1
Sivas	—	17	4
Sivas District—Sivas vilayet	—	10	—
Slivan	—	1	—
Smyrna	—	1	—
Sordar	—	1	—
Sortra	—	1	—
Soudjboulak	—	1	—
Soulouk	—	1	—

Sourp Garabed Monastery	1	—
Soushehri	2	—
Sughurt—Sairt (?)	2	—
(Suhoi Fontan)	—	1
Sultania	—	6
Süngürlü—Soungourlou	2	—
(Surmalin)	—	1
Surudj	—	1
Suverek	1	—
Syria	—	4
T		
Tabriz	3	—
Tal	3	—
Talas	5	1
Talas, Villages in the District of	1	—
Tamar	1	—
(Tarsa-Tchai)	—	1
Tarsus	3	8
Tasholouk	1	—
Tchai	—	1
(Tchaikent)	—	1
Tchalgara	—	1
Tchamli-Bel	—	2
Tchamulan	—	1
Tcharbash	1	—
(Tchardahli)	—	1

Tchargousha	1	—
Tchar-Sandjak	1	—
Tchar-Shamba	2	—
Tchemesh-Getzak	2	—
(Tchibouhli)	—	1
Tchiftlik, near Tokat	—	2
Tchingiler	2	—
Tchomakli	1	—
Tchorlu	1	—
Tchoroum—Chorun	4	—
Tchoukour	1	—
Tchumbar	1	—
Tchunkoush	1	—
Tchutlug—Khoutlig	1	1
Tedjir	—	1
Teheran	—	1
Tel-Armen	1	—
Telouk-Khaina	—	1
Ten	1	—
Tergawar	1	—
Tiari	5	—
(Tiflis)	—	1
(Tiflis, Town and District)	—	1
Tigris River	—	2
Tireboli	1	—
Tkhouma—Tkhoma	5	—
Tokat	6	—

Totz	1	—
Toutlikeui	—	1
Trebizond	10	—
Trebizond, vilayet	3	—
Turchal	—	2
Tzeronk	1	—
U		
Urmia—Urmi	12	1
Urmia District	3	—
Ushnuk	—	1
V		
(Vaharshapat, Town and District)	—	1
Van	14	1
Van, vilayet	3	2
Van-Dosp District—Timar	1	—
Varak Monastery	2	—
(Veri Ailaulou)	—	1
Vezir Köprü	3	—
Viran Shehr	—	2
Vostan	2	—
Y		
Yalova	1	—
Yarpouz	2	—
Yeghek	—	1
Yenidjé	1	—
Yeni Han (near Tokat)	—	1
Yeni-Shehr	—	1

Yerebakan	—	1	—
Yermag	—	—	1
Yoghanolouk	—	2	—
Yozgad	—	2	—
Yulduz Han (near Sivas)	—	—	1
Z			
Zara	—	1	—
Zeitoun	4	19	—
Ziaret	—	1	—
Zila	—	1	2
Zindjirderé	—	1	—

150. MESSAGE, DATED 22nd JULY, 1916, FROM MR. N., OF CONSTANTINOPLE; COMMUNICATED BY THE AMERICAN COMMITTEE FOR ARMENIAN AND SYRIAN RELIEF.

N. desires his correspondents beyond the borders of Turkey to be confidentially informed:—

"That he has word from German Relief Agents at Aleppo, sent through German Embassy, who report visits of their helpers to wide district, including Der-el-Zor and other places on Euphrates and in desert. They have seen thousands of deported Armenians under tents in the open, in convoys on the march, descending River in boats and in all phases of their miserable life. Only in few places does Government issue any rations, and those quite insufficient. People therefore themselves forced to satisfy their hunger with food begged in that scanty land or found in the parched fields. Agents found them eating grass, herbs, and locusts, and in desperate cases dead animals and human bodies are reported to have been eaten. Naturally, death-rate from starvation and sickness very high, and increased by brutal treatment of the authorities, whose bearing toward exiles as they are being driven back and forth over desert is not unlike that of slave-drivers. With few exceptions no shelter of any kind is provided, and the people coming from cold climate are left under scorching desert sun without food or water. Temporary amelioration can only be obtained by the few able to pay officials.

"Misery and hopelessness of the situation is such that many are reported to resort to suicide. Illustrating methods employed, agents report gathering group of one hundred children whom they placed in care of educated young widow from Hadjin. Two weeks later these children were deported, and from two survivors found further down convoy route it was learned that the rest had perished. House mother, crazed by treatment of her charges, was among deported moving on. Boat-loads sent from Zor down the River arrived at Ana, one hundred and thirty miles away, with three-fifths of passengers missing. There appears, in short, to be steady policy to exterminate these people, but to deny charge of massacre. Their destruction from so-called natural causes seems decided upon."

283. The Ottoman Government appears to have placed new difficulties in the way of this relief, before it could be brought into practical operation.— EDITOR.